THE WAR

Being
the part played in the Great War
by the Royal Air Force

VOL. VI

by
H. A. JONES

The Naval & Military Press Ltd
in association with
The Imperial War Museum
Department of Printed Books

HISTORY OF THE GREAT WAR

BASED ON OFFICIAL DOCUMENTS

BY DIRECTION OF THE HISTORICAL SECTION OF
THE COMMITTEE OF IMPERIAL DEFENCE

Printed and bound by Antony Rowe Ltd, Eastbourne

PREFACE

IN this final volume the story of the war operations and developments of the air services is brought to a conclusion by narratives dealing with the events leading to the creation of the Royal Air Force; with supply and man-power problems; the genesis and work of the Independent Force; the campaigns in 1918 in Palestine, Trans-Jordan, and Syria, in Mesopotamia, Persia, and Russian Azerbaijan, in Macedonia, and in Italy; with air action throughout the war in India; with naval aircraft co-operation in 1918 in home waters and in the Mediterranean; and with the Allied offensives on the Western front. In the appendix volume, which accompanies the text, papers of value to the student of air power have been assembled, together with a number of specially prepared statistical compilations.

Of particular interest is the account of war-time problems of supply and of man-power, circulated departmentally in 1934, in which the difficulties, delays, and high costs associated with the improvisation on a large scale of a technical service are revealed. Of the same degree of interest are the results, now set out for the first time in the section dealing with German night bombing in the eleventh chapter, of the more important air attacks made on depots, &c., on the Western front in 1918.

The author offers his thanks to the President of the *Reichsarchiv*, renamed the *Forschungsanstalt für Kriegs- und Heeresgeschichte*, for placing certain of the German official records at his disposal during a visit to Berlin in 1934. These documents, among which there were some important gaps, had reference to the damage inflicted by Allied bombing attacks on targets in German territory during the war, and the results of the research are incorporated in the narrative dealing with the operations of the Independent Force. The information obtained from the German official records was amplified and supplemented from a series of reports made by officers of the

PREFACE

staff of the Independent Force who visited many bombing targets and examined witnesses as soon as hostilities had ceased.

The author would like to take this last opportunity to make some acknowledgements. He thanks the official military historian and his staff, and the secretary and staff of the Historical Section of the Committee of Imperial Defence, for the advice and help they have always placed so freely at his disposal. He is also in the debt of the Military Branch of the Historical Section with regard to maps 2 to 9, 11 to 14, and 16, which have been taken, sometimes with adaptation, from the official military histories. In the absence of Professor D. Nichol Smith in America the proofs were read by Dr. W. P. Barrett, who made many valuable suggestions. Finally the author pays tribute once again to the splendid assistance he has received, from beginning to end of the work, from the staff of the former Air Historical Branch.

H. A. JONES.

TABLE OF CONTENTS

CHAPTER I. The Creation of the Royal Air Force . . . . . pp. 1–27

Strength of Western front. Other fields of victory? Lessons of the daylight attacks on England. Decision to double the air services. Forty long-range bombing squadrons. Views of Sir Douglas Haig.

Summary of attempts to co-ordinate matters affecting the naval and military air services. Weaknesses of the Air Boards. Lieutenant-General J. C. Smuts recommends formation of an Air Ministry and amalgamation of the two air services. Government accept in principle.

Air Organization Committee. Work of Sir David Henderson. Sir Douglas Haig critical of the Smuts Report.

German night-bombing campaign against England. Urge for retaliation. Lieutenant-General Smuts asked to investigate. 'Backward in all our preparations.' War Cabinet decisions about priorities. Importance of the War Priorities Committee.

Doubts whether a separate Air Force would be formed. Announcement in the Commons. Lord Cowdray resigns. Air Force (Constitution) Act. The First Air Council. Housing the Air Ministry. *Ardians* and *Bannerets*.

CHAPTER II. Problems of Supply and of Man-Power . . . . . pp. 28–100

Engines and men, limiting factors of air expansion. Aircraft industry late in the field. Inexpert labour. December 1916 engine output 600 per month. Requirements 2,000 per month. New production programmes.

Standardization of Engines . . . . p. 32
Engine chosen for mass production. Guidance of Advisory Committee for Aeronautics. Misgivings.

The Sunbeam 'Arab' Failure . . . p. 34
Reasons and effect.

The Hispano-Suiza . . . . . p. 35
Modifications of design retard output. Defects of some engines made in France. Engines and morale. Reward of Admiralty foresight.

Failure of the B.H.P. Engine . . . p. 37
Changes in design. The aluminium cylinder. Difficulties of casting. Effect on output.

A War Cabinet Investigation . . . p. 39
Government (July 1917) decision to double the air services increased the engine requirements to 4,500 monthly. German night-bombing

campaign, September 1917, reopens question of air expansion. A shock for the Cabinet. The priority problem.

The Bentley Rotary . . . . . p. 43
Large orders. A new engine, the *Dragonfly*, arouses enthusiasm. And misgivings. *Bentley* or *Dragonfly*?

Rolls-Royce Output . . . . . p. 45
Importance of Rolls-Royce engines in 1918 programme. Foresight of the Rolls-Royce Company. Advocacy of the Central Factory idea in 1916. Air Board reluctance. Lost opportunities. Repairs problems. Making Rolls-Royce parts in America for assembly in England. Delays.

The Liberty Engine . . . . . p. 51
A successful design. Production difficulties in America. How the British air programmes were affected.

National Aircraft Factories . . . . p. 53
The Ministry of Munitions and problems of air expansion. The Government as aircraft manufacturers. Costs and output of the National Factories.

Man-Power . . . . . . p. 57
Unemployment fears in 1914. Skilled workers enlist. Lost to the engineering firms. Mr. Balfour surveys the man-power problem. A statesmanlike paper. Lord Kitchener objects to control.

Industrial unrest. Mr. Lloyd George and the Ministry of Munitions. Equipment for seventy divisions. 'Dilution' of labour.

Man-power difficulties. Shortage of army recruits. Too many exemption badges. Attempts to take men from protected industries. Strikes.

Unrestricted U-boat warfare, 1917, imposes new claims on man-power.

Air Expansion programmes affected by man-power difficulties. War Office set up a Dilution Board. Expansion dependent upon the recruitment of women.

Women in the Services . . . . . p. 70
Brief account of the recruitment of women to the armed forces. Women in the air services. The Women's Royal Air Force. Women overseas. Royal Air Force Nursing Service.

Man-Power Committee . . . . p. 74
Man-power crisis. Man-power Committee formed. Their draft report, December 1917. Main recommendation. Order of priority for personnel. A comb-out in the army. Help from the American army. American mechanics with Royal Flying Corps units.

TABLE OF CONTENTS

America and the Air War . . . . p. 78
The American air programme. A telegram from the French premier changes the outlook. A British Aviation Mission to the U.S.A. General aspects of the entry of America into the war. Some effects on the British aircraft industry. The silver spruce shortage.

Effect of the German 1918 Offensive . . p. 82
Increasing the army's man-power. Taking men from protected industries. Reasoned protest of Mr. Winston Churchill, Minister of Munitions. Effect on engine output.
Training factories of the Ministry of Munitions.
Statistics of men, women, and boys in the aircraft industry.

Propaganda among the Workers . . . p. 85
Outlook of early war days. The worker as a man apart. Muddling through. The time element in war. Proposals of the managing-director of the Rolls-Royce Company. Propaganda efforts of the Ministry of Munitions. 'Boyd Cable'. His writings and lectures. *Lecture Branch* of the Aircraft Production Department. Artists at work.

Air Expansion Programmes . . . . p. 89
Details of the various programmes.

Importance of Reserves . . . . p. 91
Statistics of aircraft wastage. What they show. Need for large reserves. Some reflections.

A Summary . . . . . . p. 95
Praise for the departments responsible for aircraft supplies. Some of the difficulties overcome. Control of linen. Developing the cultivation of flax. Dopes. The manufacture of cellulose acetate. The magneto industry. Bowden tubes. Value of aircraft contracts outstanding at end of the war.
Summary of the main reasons why the air expansion programmes were not fulfilled.
General comments.

CHAPTER III. The Independent Bombing Force. Matters of Policy . . pp. 101–117
A communication from His Majesty the King of Spain. The bombing of undefended towns. An arrangement with Germany? A statement in the Bavarian Chamber. The legal question. Views of the British General Staff. The Government retain freedom of action. Sir William Weir succeeds Lord Rothermere as Air Minister. His

TABLE OF CONTENTS

memorandum to the Cabinet on Air Ministry policy. Decision of the Air Policy Committee of the War Cabinet.
A strategic bombing force. Its control. The Supreme War Council. Versailles discussions. General Duval is puzzled. The French view that the bombing force should be placed under Foch. What constitutes a balance of aircraft resources? *Joint Note No. 35*. An Inter-Allied Bombing Force. M. Clemenceau refers to Marshal Foch. Views of Foch. Removing the Independent Force to England? Lord Weir writes to M. Clemenceau. A memorandum of Marshal Foch in reply. Impasse.
A change in the outlook on the Western front. The War Cabinet consider the new conditions. British Government agree to place the Independent Force under the Generalissimo. Major-General Trenchard as Commander-in-Chief of the Inter-Allied Independent Air Force. Heads of the Agreement.
Comments on the appointment.
Additional facts for the student. Military theory. Other considerations.

CHAPTER IV. Operations of the Independent Force 1917–18 . . . . pp. 118–174

The Luxeuil naval bombing wing, 1916. German evidence of bombing results. Air defences of Germany reorganized. Balloon aprons. Bombing operations in early months of 1917. The naval bombers disband. Comments.

The Forty-first Wing . . . . p. 122

German night bombing of England, September 1917. Counter-offensive. A new wing formed. Bombing plans. The French plan. Attacks on the aerodrome of the bombers at Ochey. Typical raids on German industrial and other targets, October 1917 to June 1918. No. 55 Squadron. The day attack on Cologne of 18th May. The night bombers. Helping the French.

The Independent Force . . . . p. 135

Major-General Trenchard's views about the employment of the Force. Comments. Day and night attacks.
No. 99 Squadron. A raid on Thionville station. The D.H.9 aeroplane. New squadrons arrive. Many attacks on Rhineland towns. Handley Pages of No. 215 Squadron low down over Mannheim. German opposition in the air increases. The Burbach works damaged.
Helping the French and American armies.
Arrival of No. 45 Fighter Squadron.
A 1,650-lb. bomb on Kaiserslautern. Small arms factory destroyed. Heavy casualties in Bonn. A Metz powder magazine blows up.

TABLE OF CONTENTS

General Observations . . . . . p. 152
German statistics of bombing attacks. The major effects of the raids. Air raid alarms. What German records show. The Volklingen works. Alarms and loss of output. The morale of the workers. The Badische chemical works.
 The German balloon barrage.
 A survey of the results of railway bombing. Buildings of solid construction. Tribute to the German railway staffs.

Aerodrome Bombing . . . . . p. 158
Reasons for attacks on German aerodromes. Results achieved. Particulars of German attacks on British aerodromes analysed. Lessons and comments. Orders of Marshal Foch.

Independent Force Expansion Programmes . p. 164
The Independent Bombing Force never existed. Paper squadrons. Makeshift bombers.
 Bombing from England. No. 27 Group. The Super-Handley Page. Berlin within reach.
 Proposal to move the Independent Force to Prague.

CHAPTER V. Air Operations in Palestine in 1918 . . . . . pp. 175–238

After the capture of Jerusalem. The Palestine Brigade, Royal Flying Corps. Work of the squadrons.

The Jordan Valley . . . . . p. 177
Driving the Turks across the Jordan.
 A Dead Sea adventure.
 A change in the enemy supreme command. The character of General Liman von Sanders. Changes in the enemy dispositions.
 Securing the line of the Wadi el 'Auja.

The Arab Campaign . . . . . p. 183
The Arab Northern Army. Colonel T. E. Lawrence. 'X' Flight of No. 14 Squadron with the Arabs. Reconnaissances and bombing.

The 'Amman Raid . . . . . p. 185
Forcing the passage of the Jordan. Rain and sleet. Australians in Es Salt. Air Reconnaissances. Failure.
 The German offensive in France. Palestine plans shelved. Divisions move to France.

The Hejaz Railway . . . . . p. 193
Operations by the Arab armies. Work of 'X' Flight.
 In the Jordan valley. What air reconnaissance revealed.

TABLE OF CONTENTS

The Es Salt Raid . . . . . p. 194
Harvest time east of the Jordan. Advance into Moab. Envoys from the Beni Sakr tribe. Why the raid failed. Surprise intervention of Turkish reinforcements. Why they were not discovered from the air. Credit for the Turkish commander.

Summer Operations . . . . . p. 200
Work of the squadrons during minor operations. Air reinforcements.

Balloon Observation . . . . . p. 202
Work of the Balloon Sections.

'X' Flight with the Arabs . . . . p. 204
Operations at Mudauwara.

The Final Offensive . . . . . p. 205
The plan. Value of air superiority.
Plight of the German air service. Order of battle of the Palestine Brigade. Part played by the Royal Air Force in the preliminary operations. Deceiving the enemy. Liman von Sanders inflexible.
    The offensive opens. Air bombing. Communications shattered. The fog of war. Keeping the German aeroplanes out of the air.
    Surveying the ways of retreat. Laying smoke screens from the air. What the air reports revealed. Bombing the Turks. Panic flight. A pilot's adventure. Bringing in the German mail. Using the El 'Affule aerodrome. Into Nazareth. Liman von Sanders escapes.
    The position on the evening of the 20th September. Ways of escape across the Jordan.
    The 21st September. Intensive air attacks on the Turkish columns. The Wadi el Far'a bombing. Valley of death.
    Closing a gap across the Jordan. End of Turkish Seventh Army.

Chaytor's Force . . . . . . p. 228
The Turkish Fourth Army moves late. Colonel Lawrence confers with General Allenby. Air reinforcements for the Arab army. Air fighting over the Arabs.
    Chaytor's Force in the Jordan valley. In pursuit of the Turks. Air bombing. 'Amman captured.
    The Turkish force in Ziza station. Message dropped from the air for Turkish commander. Surrender demanded. Threat of air bombing. Loot-seeking Bedouin. The Turks surrender.
    The general advance. The move to Damascus. Aircraft co-operation. Damascus entered. Burned aeroplanes on Riyaq aerodrome. The advance to Aleppo. Air adventures.

TABLE OF CONTENTS xiii

CHAPTER VI. Mesopotamia, Persia, and India . . . . . . pp. 239–272

A War Office telegram summarizes position in the Near East. Role of the army in Mesopotamia.

Tribal conflict on the Persian border. Aeroplanes in action. Driving the Turks from the Tuz Khurmatli–Qara Tepe area. Aircraft co-operation. Kirkuk entered. Withdrawal. Disposition of the air units, May 1918.

Persia and the Caspian Sea . . . . p. 248

Colonel Bicharakoff's Russian detachment. British take over in Kazvin. Russians move to Enzeli with a British detachment. The action at Manjil. Two aeroplanes help. Holding the Jangalis in check. A tribute to the work of the aeroplanes. The action at Resht. Aeroplane bombing. Air base at Enzeli. The Jangalis submit.

The Christians of Urmia . . . . p. 251

The Christians of Urmia withstand Turkish attacks. They ask for British help. A message to Urmia by air. An ammunition convoy sets out. Delay. The Turks enter Urmia. Massacre. Encampments for the refugees.

The Caspian . . . . . . p. 252

Colonel Bicharakoff joins the Bolshevik revolutionaries. New governors of Baku ask for British aid. British mission to Baku. Reinforcements with aeroplanes go to Baku. They help to defend the town against Turkish attacks. Work of the aeroplanes. Withdrawal.

A threat to the lines of communications. Large bodies of Turks at Tabriz and Urmia. The hills of Kuflan Kuh. Air reconnaissances reveal attack impending. The attack opens. Fierce fighting. Timely arrival of British troops withdrawn from Baku. Air bombing attacks. Propaganda from the air. A pilot on foot in Persia. A modest report. Final operations in Persia.

The Autumn Campaign in Mesopotamia . . p. 262

The military situation in the Middle East summarized in a War Office telegram, 25th September. Final offensive in Mesopotamia. The air units. Survey work of the squadrons. On the move. Turks abandon the Fat-ha positions. Air bombing. The stand at Sharqat. Final battle. The Turks surrender. Mosul vilayet occupied.

War Operations in India . . . . p. 268

The central flying school at Sitapur, 1914. No. 31 Squadron from England. Air operations on the Mohmand border, 1916. The aerodrome at Risalpur.

Unrest in North Waziristan and in Khost. 'Flying chariots.' A Mahsud lashkar. Aeroplanes overawe the tribesmen. A Peace Jirga.

TABLE OF CONTENTS

No. 114 Squadron formed at Lahore. The Marri tribes astir, February 1918. The Khetran tribes join in. Punitive measures. Bombing villages and camps. Unconditional submission. Peace.

CHAPTER VII. The Italian Front . pp. 273–292

The break-through at Caporetto. Role of the German air service. British and French reinforcements for Italy. Air squadrons. The air situation on the front when the British arrive.

Trench warfare. Reconnaissances and bombing. Attack on Istrana aerodrome. Bombing and counter-bombing.

Reduction of the British force, March 1918. Signs of an impending enemy offensive. The Austrian attack, 15th June. Across the Piave. British aeroplanes concentrated to help the Italians. Bombing the Piave bridges. The Austrian advance checked. The Piave in spate. Bridges washed away. Italian counter-attacks. The Austrians withdraw. Bombing the retreating troops. An Austrian account of the bombing of the bridges.

Air help for the Italians in a minor offensive. Air fighting. Attack on Austrian flying training schools.

The Battle of Vittorio Veneto . . . p. 288

The Italian Commander-in-Chief opens a final offensive. The plan. Royal Air Force concentration in the Asiago area. Air photography. The offensive opens, 27th October. Contact patrols. Reporting the advance. 'Situation' flights. Final bombing operations.

CHAPTER VIII. Macedonia. Final Air Operations, 1918 . . . . pp. 293–313

General Milne's request for an increase of air strength. Inadequate response. An Allied military operation. The Greek Army in action. Royal Air Force co-operation. News of an impending Bulgar attack. Why the attack did not take place.

General Franchet d'Espérey as Allied Commander-in-Chief. Planning a general offensive. Air bombing attacks.

Requirements of General Milne for the offensive. A shortage of tyres and spare parts for transport. Effect of destruction by German bombers of tyres and spare parts in Western front depot.

The plan for the offensive. The British sector. A preliminary action. Air combats. Observing for the artillery.

The attack opens, 15th September. British attack two days later. Order of battle of the Royal Air Force units. Air work during the battle. Enemy pilots inactive.

Landing agents behind the enemy lines.

Air reconnaissances tell of the Bulgar retreat. Bombing troops and transport. The Kosturino defile. Long-distance reconnaissances.

TABLE OF CONTENTS

Bulgars demoralized. Tribute to the Bulgarian First Army. Bombing in the Kryesna pass. 'Choked with transport.' Attacking the columns. Reports of officers who examined the routes. Collapse of Bulgaria.
    British army to move against Turkey. Royal Air Force movements. Armistice.

CHAPTER IX. The Mediterranean in 1918 . . . . . . pp. 314–328

Reorganization of air units in the Mediterranean. Dispositions and duties of the air groups.

Kite Balloons with Convoys . . . . p. 316

Increased employment of kite balloons. Where should the balloon ship be stationed? Divided opinion. Examples of balloon work.

The Otranto Barrage . . . . p. 318

Importance of the Straits of Otranto. Activities of U-boats. Constitution of the Otranto barrage. Aircraft versus U-boats. Bombing attacks on U-boat bases in the Adriatic.

The Aegean Group . . . . . p. 323

Duties of the Group. Bombing and counter-bombing.

The Egypt Group . . . . . p. 325

Seaplanes and kite balloons at Alexandria and Port Said. Escorting convoys.
    Duties of Mediterranean aircraft in connexion with military operations. Italian offensive in Albania. Aircraft co-operation. A combined action against Durazzo. Bombing in Macedonia.

CHAPTER X. Naval Air Developments and Operations, 1918. Home Waters . pp. 329–96

General influence of the U-boat campaign.

Aeroplane versus *U-boat* . . . . p. 329

Change in U-boat tactics. Activity close to the coasts. Suitability of aeroplanes for patrols. The D.H.6. 'A reasonable measure of bluff.' Disadvantages of the D.H.6. Fine work of the patrol personnel. An Admiralty tribute.

Admiralty Air Requirements . . . p. 334

A statement of Admiralty policy for the employment of aircraft. Establishments. Supply difficulties. Reductions in the programme. The position at the end of the war.

TABLE OF CONTENTS

Hydrophone Experiments . . . . p. 341
Various types of hydrophones. Their use in seaplanes and airships.

Anti-Submarine Aircraft Patrols . . . p. 343
Mileage flown in 1917 and 1918. Comparisons. Value of the patrols.

U-boats Destroyed . . . . . p. 345
An account of some of the attacks by aircraft on U-boats.

Submarine Attacks on Convoys . . . p. 348
Air Escort work. Statistics for 1918.

Mine-fields in the Heligoland Bight . . p. 350
Hampering the passage of U-boats. Air reconnaissances of the mine-fields.
  Lighters built to carry flying-boats. Making use of the lighters to convey fighter aeroplanes. Two schemes for reconnaissance. Operations under Scheme 'B'.

Destruction of a Zeppelin . . . . p. 355
The Zeppelin *L.62* makes a routine patrol. Plotting her course in London. A flying-boat goes out to attack her. Air report. The *L.62* blows up.
  Vulnerability of the airships increases the importance of the German seaplane service. Expansion of the seaplane bases. Types of seaplanes employed. Air fights. Periodical sweeps by the Harwich Force. Flying-boats in action. The report of the leader. The aircraft carrier *Furious* in a Bight operation.
  Attacking Zeppelins in their sheds. The great raid on Tondern. The *L.54* and *L.60* destroyed.

Coastal Motor-boat Operations . . . p. 367
Plans for a motor-boat dash across the mine-fields. A kite balloon and flying-boats play a part. Disappointments.
  Flying off a lighter. Colonel C. R. Samson nearly drowned.
  The Harwich Force sets out for the Bight. German seaplanes in view. A Zeppelin sighted. An abortive search by flying-boats. Lieutenant S. D. Culley flies off the lighter. He destroys the *L.53* in flames. The missing motor-boats. How disaster overcame them. A strange fight.
  An attempt to bring the German seaplanes to action. Why it failed.
  Air warfare in the southern part of the North Sea. *Flanders I.* Many encounters. 'Unwarlike' operations.

The Belgian Coast and Flanders . . . p. 380
Changes in the Dover–Dunkirk air command. Policy of the Air Council. Proposal to organize a northern bombing force to attack German naval targets. Why it did not come into being.

TABLE OF CONTENTS xvii

The German offensive in March and April 1918 entails a drain on Dunkirk aircraft. Help expected from the United States naval authorities. Delays. The American Northern Bombing Group begins operations, 14th October 1918.

Dunkirk squadrons under naval control, April 1918. Naval attempts to block the entrance to the canal at Zeebrugge and to Ostend harbour. Work of aircraft in co-operation. Dunkirk air strength reduced. Need for concentrated bombing attacks on shipping crowded at Bruges. An opportunity missed. Admiral Keyes complains. Comment.

The bombing of Varssenaere aerodrome. Great damage inflicted.

CHAPTER XI. Prelude to Victory . pp. 397–436

The Battle of the Aisne, 1918 . . . p. 397

Exhausted British divisions moved to quiet sector of French line, May 1918. They are involved in the German Aisne offensive. Why the enemy attack achieved surprise. Work of No. 52 Squadron. Tell-tale dust-clouds. Complacency and detection.

The Battle of the Matz . . . . p. 400

General Foch expects new German attack on Montdidier-Noyon front. He asks for British squadrons. The IX Brigade moves south. The French *Air Division*. A true strategic reserve. French orders for the employment of the IX Brigade squadrons. The German offensive, 9th June. Work of the British squadrons. End of the battle.

A memorandum by Major-General J. M. Salmond. An appreciation of the military situation by General Foch. Plans for air reconnaissances. The IX Brigade squadrons return to the British area.

The bombing of railway communications. Memoranda of the Inter-Allied Transportation Council. The proposals of General Plumer. A scheme for bombing to hinder an enemy concentration on the line La Bassée–Ypres. Bombing results.

The Second Battle of the Marne . . . p. 412

Foch expects a German attack in Champagne. The squadrons of the IX Brigade move back to the French front. Movements of British divisions. No. 82 Squadron accompanies them. The German attack, 14th July. The IX Brigade and the French *Air Division* in action.

General Foch launches a counter-offensive. The turn of the tide.

Minor Operations . . . . . p. 415

General Foch suggests minor British attacks to pin down German reserves. The Hamel attack by the Fourth Army. Night-flying to overpower the noise of assembling tanks.

xviii   TABLE OF CONTENTS

Work of the squadrons in the attack. No. 9 Squadron and the dropping of ammunition.

Plans for resuming the offensive. Freeing Amiens and the Paris-Amiens railway. General Rawlinson told to go ahead. General Foch asks Sir Douglas Haig to take control of the battle.

German Night Bombing . . . . p. 419

The German advance in March and April 1918 compresses the British lines of communications areas. One lateral railway line.

Importance of the railway bridge over the Canche estuary at Etaples. Other important bridges. British action to strengthen the bridges and to provide alternative arrangements.

Bombing attacks on the Étaples bridge. Severe casualties in hospital camps.

Warning arrangements on the *Nord* railway system. Importance of warning system in general.

Bombing attacks on Ordnance Depots. No. 12 (Blarges) and No. 20 (Saigneville) severely damaged. 69 million rounds of S.A.A. destroyed. Total destruction 12,500 tons of ammunition.

Comments on bombing policy.

A night-fighter squadron for France. Searchlights, guns, and aeroplanes in co-ordination. Record of No. 151 Squadron.

A German bombing success of major military importance. No. 2 Base Mechanical Transport Depot in flames. 'All our eggs in one basket.' Monetary damage nearly as great as caused by all the aeroplane raids on Great Britain. Effect on transport position on Western front. And on Macedonian front.

The vulnerability of targets.

Death of Major J. T. B. McCudden and of Major Edward Mannock.

Air Preparations for the Battle of Amiens . p. 433

Methods to obtain surprise. Proposals for the employment of the Royal Air Force. British, French, and German air strengths for the opening of the battle.

CHAPTER XII. The Amiens Offensive . pp. 437-68

The 8th of August. Mist. Exceptional targets for low-flying attack. Samples of the air work. Laying smoke screens from the air.

Roads crowded with transport and troops. Importance of the Somme bridges. Bombing concentrated against the bridges. German fighters protect the bridges. A tense conflict. 'Terrible losses' of the Richthofen squadron. The squadron withdrawn from the battle.

The offensive and the defensive policies in the air. The *B.M.W.* engine. Importance of technical superiority.

Air attacks on the bridges continue by night and day. What happened.

TABLE OF CONTENTS xix

A change in bombing tactics. End of the attacks. Bombing railway communications. The D.H.4 and D.H.9, a comparison.

The Bombing of the Somme Bridges: a Commentary . . . . . p. 454

A summary of the battle. The arrival of German reinforcing divisions. Was the bombing policy well founded?

Some Lessons of the Battle . . . . p. 463

A memorandum by the Fourth Army Commander. When low-flying attacks were of value. Lessons of air co-operation with tank units. And of Contact Patrol work.

The French Air Service . . . . p. 467

Bombing targets allotted to the French *Air Division*.

CHAPTER XIII. The Battle of Bapaume pp. 469–509

Sir Douglas Haig's plans for a continuation of the offensive between the Somme and the Scarpe. Marshal Foch defers to the views of Sir Douglas Haig.

A preliminary operation. Squadron movements for the attack. III Brigade operation orders.

The preliminary battle opens, 21st August. Mist and rain. Air co-operation being late. Work of No. 73 Squadron against anti-tank guns.

Night bombing.

Day bombing attacks on railways, 22nd August.

The main offensive, 23rd August.

Sir Douglas Haig's telegram revealing a new outlook on the war in the west.

A new organization in connexion with low-flying attacks. Wireless Central Information Bureau.

The bombing of railway junctions. Helping the tanks.

Night bombing by German pilots. Destruction on the aerodrome at Bertangles. No. 48 Squadron withdrawn from the line to be re-equipped.

German aerodromes bombed. Adventures of corps squadron pilots and observers. No. 17 American Squadron.

The Battle of the Scarpe . . . . p. 484

An extension of the general battle. Movements of air squadrons. Air Plans. Co-ordinating the activities of the low-flying squadrons. Bad weather. Air work in the battle.

Statistics for British and French air services, March to October.

TABLE OF CONTENTS

The Drocourt–Quéant Switch . . . p. 492
First and Third Armies attack astride the Arras–Cambrai road. Duties of the air squadrons.

The Attack . . . . . . p. 495
5 a.m. 2nd September. Success. Work of the corps squadrons. Valuable air reports. Combats. The German infantry fall back.
   A slackening of activity. General comments on the air work in the battle.

The Battle of Havrincourt and Epéhy . . p. 504
Preliminary operations. Destroying kite balloons. The attack succeeds. Night bombing. No. 151 Squadron. A memorandum on the tactical employment of fighter aeroplanes. German plan for incendiary bomb attacks on Paris and London. Marshal Foch asks for counter-bombing help from the Royal Air Force. Attacks on German aerodromes.

CHAPTER XIV. Victory . . . pp. 510–58

Breaking the Hindenburg Line . . . p. 510
The general position. A final effort to end the war. Plans of Marshal Foch. The Hindenburg defence system.
   Air plans and concentration.

Low-flying Attacks . . . . . p. 516
Schemes for the employment of low-flying aircraft.

Offensive Patrols . . . . . p. 517
Patrol orders.

The Head-quarters IX Brigade . . . p. 518
Bombing and reconnaissance orders.

The Battle of the Canal du Nord . . . p. 518
The attack opens, 27th September. Success. Reporting the advance from the air. The low-flying attacks. Putting a gun out of action. A trophy for Cranwell.

The Capture of the Hindenburg Line . . p. 523
The corps engaged. Detailed knowledge of the enemy defence system.

Scheme of Air Co-operation . . . . p. 524
Air Plans.

The Attack . . . . . . p. 526
Key of the enemy positions. Brilliant action of the 46th (North

TABLE OF CONTENTS

Midland) Division. American troops advance too far. Many cut off. Confusion. Need for air reconnaissances. Mist and the fog of war. Laying smoke screens from the air. Attacking kite balloons.

The Battle in Flanders . . . . p. 531
His Majesty the King of the Belgians. Towards Ghent. Naval air help for the Belgians. The II Brigade. Low-flying casualties. Delivering rations by air. Bombing. Damage at Lichtervelde sidings.

The Second Battle of Le Cateau . . . p. 535
250 miles of battle on Western front. Climax approaching. Remainder of Hindenburg system captured. Along the Selle river.

Flanders . . . . p. 539
Offensive in Flanders resumed, 14th October. Advance to the Dutch frontier. Low-flying attacks. The weather helps the retreating Germans. A tribute to the Royal Air Force by H.M. the King of the Belgians.

The Selle River . . . . . . p. 541
Selle positions captured. Air attacks. Two V.C. awards. Attacking the lines of communication. The bottle-neck through Namur and Liége. German pilots fight hard to hinder the bombing attacks.

Comparisons between the D.H.9 and the D.H.9a as bombers. Inferior equipment expensive and dependent upon chance. Intense air fighting, 30th October. Eightieth Wing and attacks on German aerodromes.

The final phase.

A summary and comment. The offensive and defensive policies in the air.

Envoi.

INDEX . . . . . . pp. 559–83

LIST OF APPENDICES
[IN SEPARATE VOLUME]

I. Memorandum on the organization of the Air Services, by Lieutenant-General Sir David Henderson, July 1917 1

II. Air Organization. Second Report of the Prime Minister's Committee on Air Organization and Home Defence against Air Raids, dated 17th August 1917 (Smuts's Report) 8

III. Sir Douglas Haig's views on a separate Air Service, 15th September 1917 14

IV. 'Munitions Possibilities of 1918.' Extract from a paper dated 21st October 1917 by Mr. Winston Churchill, Minister of Munitions 18

V. The Bombing of Germany. Copy of a memorandum handed by Major-General H. M. Trenchard to the Prime Minister, Mr. Lloyd George, January 1918 . 22

VI. Memorandum on Bombing Operations. Forwarded by C.I.G.S., War Office, to General Sir Henry Wilson, British Military Representative, Supreme War Council, 17th January 1918 . . . 24

VII. Memorandum by Sir William Weir, Secretary of State for the Royal Air Force, on the responsibility and conduct of the Air Ministry, May 1918 . . 26

VIII. Memorandum by Marshal Foch on the subject of an Independent Air Force, 14th September 1918 . 29

IX. Joint Note No. 35. 'Bombing Air Force.' Addressed to the Supreme War Council by the Military Representatives 30

X. The Bombardment of the Interior of Germany. Memorandum by Marshal Foch, based on Joint Note No. 35 31

XI. Heads of Agreement as to the constitution of the Inter-Allied Independent Air Force. An agreement reached between the British and French Governments and transmitted, through the Supreme War Council, to the American and Italian Governments for approval 41

XII. Statistics of work of squadrons of the Independent Force, including wastage. June–November 1918
Facing p. 42

XIII. Industrial Targets bombed by squadrons of the 41st Wing and the Independent Force. October 1917–November 1918 42

xxiv APPENDICES IN SEPARATE VOLUME

XIV. Volklingen Steel Works. Analysis of Damage caused by Air Raids in 1916, 1917, and 1918 . . . 85

XV. State of Independent Force, Royal Air Force . . 87

XVI. Organization of Royal Air Force, Middle East, 30th September 1918 . . . . *Facing p.* 88

XVII. Summary of Anti-Submarine Air Patrols from 1st May to 12th November 1918. (Home Waters) . *Facing p.* 88

XVIII. Comparison of Anti-Submarine Flying Operations between Groups Nos. 9, 10, and 18. From 1st July to 30th September 1918 88

XIX. A short review of the situation in the air on the Western front and a consideration of the part to be played by the American aviation. Memorandum by Headquarters, R.F.C., France, December 1917 . . 89

XX. Fighting in the Air: Memorandum issued by British G.H.Q., France, February 1918 . . . 92

XXI. Bombing Operations. Memorandum submitted to G.H.Q., by Major-General J. M. Salmond, G.O.C., Royal Air Force, France: June 1918 . . 110

XXII. Protection against Enemy Aeroplanes. Translation from a German document, July 1918 . . 113

XXIII. Methods of Bombing. Report from the Experimental Station, Orfordness: October 1918 . . . 114

XXIV. Order of Battle of the Royal Air Force, France, on 8th August 1918 116

XXV. The Battle of Amiens. Memorandum by G.O.C. V. Brigade, Royal Air Force. 14th August 1918 . 123

XXVI. Strength of the Royal Air Force, Western front, including Independent Force and 5th Group. 11th November 1918 125

XXVII. Types of Aircraft, 1914–18: Technical Data; Table A, Aeroplanes. Table B, Seaplanes and Ship Aeroplanes *Facing p.* 130

XXVIII. List of Squadrons, Royal Flying Corps and Royal Air Force, which served on the Western front, 1914–18. 130

XXIX. List of Naval Squadrons which served with the Royal Flying Corps and Royal Air Force on the Western front, 1914–18 142

XXX. Location of R.A.F. units, Western front, 11th November 1918 144

APPENDICES IN SEPARATE VOLUME

STATISTICAL SECTION

XXXI. British Aircraft produced and Labour employed, August 1914 to November 1918. (Figures for Germany, France, Italy, and America given, where available, for comparison) 154

XXXII. Price list of various British war-time airframes and engines 155

XXXIII. Firms and Labour employed on British aircraft production (excluding airships). Comparative detailed statement for the years 1916, 1917, and 1918 . . 158

XXXIV. British naval airships built 1914–18 . . . 159

XXXV. Strength of British air personnel August 1914 and November 1918 160

XXXVI. Total casualties, all causes, to air service personnel, British and German, 1914–18 . . . 160

XXXVII. Comparison, by months, of British flying casualties (killed and missing) and hours flown on the Western front, July 1916 to July 1918 . . . 161

XXXVIII. Deliveries of anti-aircraft guns and ammunition (excluding naval) 1916 to 1918 . *Facing p.* 162

XXXIX. Number of British anti-aircraft guns on the Western front, including Independent Force, July and November 1918 162

XL. Strength of Allied Aircraft on all fronts: June 1918
Facing p. 162

XLI. Disposition of aircraft and engines on charge of the Royal Air Force at 31st October 1918. Table A, Aeroplanes and Seaplanes (Airframes). Table B, Engines . . . . . *Facing p.* 162

XLII. Length of front held by British in France, various dates, 1917 and 1918 162

XLIII. Hostile Bombing Activity on British front in France, May to October 1918 163

XLIV. Summary Statistics of German air raids on Great Britain, 1914–18 164

XLV. Anti-Aircraft Defences in Great Britain. Schedule of types, disposition, and strengths of aircraft, guns, height-finders, searchlights, and sound-locators, and strength of personnel, 10th June 1918 . . 165

XLVI. Strength in personnel of Royal Air Force in various theatres of war at 31st October 1918 . . 172

LIST OF MAPS

1. Area of Operations of the Independent Force, 1918 . *Facing p.* 152
2. Palestine 175
3. Palestine and Syria 183
4. The envelopment of the Turkish Seventh and Eighth Armies 205
5. Megiddo, 1918. Situation at Zero Hour, 19th Sept. 1918 217
6. Megiddo, 1918. Situation at 12 m.n. 19th/20th Sept. 1918 219
7. Theatre of Operations in Trans-Jordan . . . 234
8. The Operations of 'Dunsterforce', 1918 . . 249
9. Mesopotamia 264
10. Italian Front, 1918 273
11. Macedonia 293
12. Situation, Sea to Vardar, 15th July 1918 . . 296
13. Allied Offensive of September 1918: Plan of Breakthrough (Macedonia) 299
14. The Battle of Dojran. 18th September 1918 . . 304
15. Mediterranean Sea 315
16. Italian Operations in Albania, 1918 . . . 326
17. Sphere of Naval Air Operations in Home Waters, 1918 380
18. The German Offensive in Champagne, 1918 . . 414
19. British Offensive, South of Lens, August–November, 1918 437
20. Battle of the Canal du Nord, 1918 . . . 511
21. Battles of the Hindenburg Line, 1918 . . . 530
22. British battles during 1918 (8th August to 11th November) 550
23. Railway Map of Western theatre of War . . *at end (after index)*

The following maps were
not reproduced in this edition:
1, 3, 4, 9, 10, 11, 15, 17, 18,
19, 20, 21, 22, 23.

CHAPTER I
THE CREATION OF THE ROYAL AIR FORCE

THE year 1917 was a year of sombre texture. The collapse of the Nivelle campaign, so hopefully planned, which led to mutinies in the French army, the costly British offensives on the Western front which brought no adequate compensating victories, the overrunning of Romania soon after she had come into the war, the defection of Russia, the depredations of the U-boats, and the aeroplane attacks, by day and by night, on London and the southern counties, all helped towards a feeling of depression. It is true that the entry of America into the war meant that the background was shot through with hope, and it is true, also, that there was evidence that Austria was weakening, but America seemed a long way away and was wholly unprepared, while there was small chance that Germany would allow Austria, even if she so wished, to make a separate peace.

There were members of the British Government who found it difficult to believe, especially after the Allied Somme offensive in 1916, that victory could be achieved through battering at the immensely strong trench systems on the Western front. They were troubled also by the carnage which attacks on these systems entailed. They turned their eyes away from France and searched the battle-fields of the world, seeking to find some place where defence was not predominant, some theatre of war where there were weaknesses through which the structure of the central powers might be shattered.

It was perhaps natural that as air warfare developed, and particularly after the entry of the United States into the war—a happening which bred visions of fleets of aeroplanes rising from the American factories—some people should turn to the skies and wonder whether a large-scale and sustained air offensive might force the enemy to sue for peace. The German aeroplane attacks on southern England, more especially the first daylight attack on London on the 13th of June 1917, seemed to confirm that this was the way. The casualties resulting from the daylight raid on the capital exceeded those inflicted in the County of London area by all of the Zeppelin attacks which had been made up to that time. This was due in part to chance, as well as to the fact that people had been taken by surprise in the streets at a busy hour of the day; but when all allowances had been made it still seemed that aeroplane bombing, on a large scale, was a menace of indefinite possibilities. At a Cabinet meeting, held a few hours after the raid, Sir William Robertson, the Chief of the Imperial General Staff, had urged that the numbers of British aeroplanes should be greatly increased, even though this could be done only at the expense of other weapons. The Cabinet came to the same conclusion and requested the Air Board to consult with the Ministry of Munitions, the War Office, and with other Departments concerned, and to submit a scheme for expansion.

After various memoranda had been prepared, a meeting took place at the War Office on the 21st of June 1917, and it was decided to recommend an increase in the service squadrons of the Royal Flying Corps from 108 to 200. The proposal received Cabinet approval on the 2nd of July, when it was also decided that there should be a corresponding increase in the strength of the Royal Naval Air Service.

The intention was that the majority of the additional squadrons should be equipped for bombing.[1] Sir Douglas Haig was informed of the War Cabinet decision on the 13th of July in order that he might keep in mind the question of aerodrome accommodation. The British Commander-in-Chief in France found it difficult to understand the policy of the Government. In his reply to the War Office he pointed out that he had been given no reasons why it had been found necessary to increase the Royal Flying Corps, and he said that it did not appear that the decision had been based upon the requirements of the British armies in France. In his view the proposed additional bombing squadrons were of secondary importance, and their organization should not be allowed to prejudice the

[1] The proposed distribution was: France and Italy, 86 squadrons; other theatres of war, 40; long-distance bombing squadrons, 40; reserve, 34.

maintenance in France of the seventy-six fighting, reconnaissance, and night flying, squadrons which had been sanctioned for service on the Western front. A War Office letter on the 2nd of August assured Sir Douglas Haig that these squadrons would be given precedence, and he was asked, at the same time, to say what he thought about the further development of offensive tactics, such as attacks against troops on the ground by large numbers of aeroplanes.

Sir Douglas Haig replied that he did not consider anything was to be gained by diverting resources to build aeroplanes for low-flying attacks, which could be classified as of secondary importance. After provision had been made for the seventy-six squadrons already sanctioned, the requirement next in urgency was the provision of ten bombing squadrons for offensive operations against German aerodromes. 'In this way alone', he said, 'it is 'possible to compel the enemy to fight on his side of the 'line at a distance from the battle front.' He asked to be informed of the exact nature of the bombing operations which it was proposed that the new striking force should undertake.

He was again reassured that the ten bombing squadrons would be given precedence together with the seventy-six squadrons of the existing programme. He was told, however, that no detailed plans had been prepared for the employment of the bombing squadrons in excess of the requirements of the armies, 'firstly because such plans 'will be dependent to some extent on the military situation 'at the time when the squadrons become available, and 'secondly because the War Cabinet are now considering 'the establishment of a separate Department of State to 'control and administer the Air Services, and in the event 'of such a Department being formed, the strategical 'disposition and the employment of such surplus force 'may be among its functions.' Finally, the War Office requested Sir Douglas Haig to take measures to provide for the eventual accommodation of forty squadrons, additional to the eighty-six already agreed to, and suggested that these squadrons should be arranged in groups of from ten to fifteen, in areas from twenty to forty miles behind the trench lines.

Meanwhile, as indicated in the above reply to Sir Douglas Haig, there had been happenings at home which had profoundly affected air policy. On the 7th of July, five days after the Government had decided upon the large-scale expansion of the air services, the German bombing squadron had made its second daylight attack on London, and the problems of air defence in particular, and of the organization of the air services in general, had formed a subject for anxious discussion at War Cabinet meetings held on days subsequent to the raid.[1]

We may leave the War Cabinet to their discussions, for the moment, and briefly recapitulate the attempts which had been made, up to that time, to establish some body which would be able to co-ordinate matters affecting the naval and military air services. It will be recalled that the first effort of the kind in the war, the establishment of a Joint War Air Committee in February 1916, under the chairmanship of Lord Derby, had proved a failure.[2] The committee had been set up as permanent, but it had lasted no longer than two months, chiefly because it had lacked executive authority. In his letter of resignation to the Prime Minister, Lord Derby had said that the two air services could not be brought closer together unless they were amalgamated, but although he believed that this was the inevitable solution he thought the change too difficult to make in time of war. 'A step towards amalgamation', he had concluded, 'might be made by giving wider powers 'to a reconstituted committee presided over by a chairman 'having direct access to the War Committee.[3] But the 'subject is so complex that I hesitate to make any recom-'mendations as to what these wider powers should be, in 'so much as every proposal which would take control of 'the Wings from the Admiralty and War Office respec-'tively, would inevitably bring in its train objections to 'which I cannot suggest answers.'

---

[1] See Vol. V, pp. 38–45.
[2] See Vol. III, Chapter IV.
[3] Predecessor of the War Cabinet.

BOARD OR MINISTRY?

The wider powers given to the Air Board, the body which succeeded Lord Derby's committee, have already been set out.[1] Once again, however, executive authority was withheld from the Board. It was 'free to discuss matters of general policy in relation to the air', and, if the Admiralty or the War Office declined to act upon its recommendations, the President of the Board might 'refer the question to the War Committee'. The expert members of the Board, however, were representatives of the Admiralty and of the War Office, and mere freedom to discuss tended to aggravate rather than eliminate differences of view between the two departments. Lord Curzon, the President of the Board, in a report to the Government, dated August 1916, stated that the definition of the powers of the Board would have been more precise had it not been for objections raised by the Admiralty, but he pointed out that statements had been made in Parliament, when the Air Board was formed, which left no doubt that the Board was not to be so restricted as the somewhat vague outline of its duties might imply. Mr. H. J. Tennant, Under Secretary of State for War, had said in the House of Commons in May 1916: 'It will charge itself with the larger and wider 'questions of thinking out the possibility of developing its 'own body possibly with a regular Department under it— 'what is called an Air Ministry.' Mr. Bonar Law, speaking for the Government, had been more specific, and had stated that the new body would grow until it had allocated to it all the duties of an Air Ministry.

The first Air Board, however, never grew up, whatever may have been the original intentions of the Government. Because it possessed no executive functions it was powerless to resolve difficulties as and when they arose. Indeed, the troubles which continued to hamper the administration and growth of the air services may be largely ascribed to the unwillingness of the Government to pay attention to the reasons which caused the failure of Lord Derby's committee. That such a body of experienced administrators, appointed to a so-called permanent committee, should have concluded within a few weeks that their task was a

[1] Vol. III, pp. 271-2.

hopeless one might have been expected to lead to drastic action. Although the announcements made in the House of Commons seemed to imply that such action had been, or would be, taken, the first Air Board was little more effective than the short-lived Joint War Air Committee. It did useful work, in minor ways, but it could initiate little, and precious months were wasted during which plans, backed by adequate authority, might have been laid far ahead.

The second, or Cowdray, Air Board had been made definitely responsible for the design of aeroplanes and seaplanes, for the numbers to be ordered, and for their allocation to the two air services.[1] The Board worked with great energy, took measures which led to an encouraging expansion in production, and was able to frame schedules of output which, on paper, exceeded anticipation. By the early summer of 1917 Lord Cowdray, the President, looking at his paper schedules, could see a surplus of aircraft above what would be required to meet the essential needs of the navy and of the army. He took the view that this *Surplus Aircraft Fleet*, as he called it, should constitute a bombing force which might be put to effective use only if the Air Board possessed a war staff. Sections 2 and 3 of the New Ministries and Secretaries Act, 1916, under which the Board had been constituted, read:

'2. The Board shall be free to discuss matters of policy 'in relation to the air and to make recommendations to 'the Admiralty and War Office thereon.

'3. The Admiralty and War Office will concert their 'respective aerial policies in consultation with the Air 'Board.'

So far, then, as policy was concerned, the second Air Board was in no stronger position than the first. It was charged with a vague responsibility, but it could do no more than talk or recommend. At a meeting of the Board held on the 11th of July 1917 Lord Cowdray referred to the daylight raid on London on the previous Saturday, and

[1] The Ministry of Munitions was responsible for production, for inspection during manufacture, and for handing the aircraft to the services in accordance with the allotments made by the Air Board.

said there was no doubt that the popular outcry about the air policy of the Government would become acute. Air policy was not a question that could be settled at occasional conferences, and the Board could not discharge the duties laid upon it under Sections 2 and 3 of its charter unless it was given a special staff. The discussion which followed the President's opening remarks illuminated the delicate position of the Board in this matter. It was bluntly stated by some of the members that if the Board took upon itself to say what were the uses to which aeroplanes or seaplanes should be put, the War Office and the Admiralty would resent and resist such intervention. It was decided that the members of the Board should think the question over with a view to a special discussion at an early date.

Unknown to the Board, however, the matter was, at that moment, being taken out of its hands. The War Cabinet, meeting elsewhere on the same day, decided to set up a committee, consisting of the Prime Minister and Lieutenant-General J. C. Smuts, to examine:

(i) the defence arrangements for Home Defence against air raids[1] and

(ii) the air organization generally and the direction of aerial operations.

Lord Cowdray, unaware of this action of the Government, proceeded with his plans for making the Air Board effective to formulate policy. He appeared at a meeting of the Board on the 16th of July with a memorandum, the main point in which was a plea for the allocation to the Board of an air staff. He told the members, however, that after he had written the memorandum he had received an extract from the minutes of the War Cabinet for the 11th of July informing him, for the first time, of the decision to set up a special committee. He had seen the Prime Minister that morning and had been told that Mr. Lloyd George had only lent his name to the Committee, and that the whole matter would be dealt with by Lieutenant-General Smuts. It was clear that the General was dealing with a subject which fell within the

[1] The report and the decisions upon the subject of home defence have been dealt with in Vol. V, pp. 41–4.

province of the Board, and the President said he had arranged to see him for a discussion that afternoon. At a meeting of the Board next day Lord Cowdray told the members about the interview. The War Cabinet, he had been given to understand, was of the opinion that the powers of the Air Board must be extended to cover matters of air policy. He had explained that this was a view held by his colleagues on the Board, but that he himself had, hitherto, contended that the existing powers of the Board were sufficient. Lord Cowdray stated that his views had changed after talking the subject over with General Smuts, and that he had come to the conclusion that the Board should be permanently established with enlarged powers.

In a memorandum to Lieutenant-General Smuts on the 28th of July he set out his considered views. After giving the duties of the Air Board, as outlined in its charter, he proceeded: 'It is, I believe I may say, almost 'universally and fully recognized that an independent air 'service will unquestionably be demanded as soon as ever 'it is possible for one to be formed. But when drawing up 'the draft charter, for the approval of the Cabinet . . . I 'considered that during the war the Board should confine 'itself to supplying the Navy and the Army with aircraft 'and to controlling the distribution between the two ser- 'vices of the aircraft manufactured. I felt that during the 'war to attempt to create an independent aerial service 'controlled by the Air Board was not wise or practical and 'especially so owing to the opposition of the Admiralty 'to any such scheme. The many problems which will have 'to be thrashed out and settled between the Services con- 'cerned, before the Independent Air Service can become 'effective, point to the necessity of their discussion being 'begun forthwith, so that the Air Board may be fully 'prepared to take over the administration of the Indepen- 'dent Air Service immediately the war is finished. . . . I am 'driven to request that the Air Board should now be turned 'into a permanent Ministry, presumably by Act of Parlia- 'ment, so as to place it into a position to secure a war staff 'of recognized experts. This staff would recommend to

'the Board the Policy that ought to be followed. It would
'also be studying and preparing the King's Regulations,
'Pay Warrant, etc., so that the machinery required to
'constitute the Air Service could be set in motion on
'receipt of instructions to do so. . . . It appears to me be-
'yond question that during the war the administration
'of the Naval and Military Air Services as they at present
'exist, or will exist when their imperative needs are satis-
'fied, should not be changed. . . .'

It is clear that Lord Cowdray had in mind a body little different from the existing Air Board. He wanted a permanent staff, but chiefly to work out the details for a possible change *after* the war. Although such a staff might guide the Board on matters of policy, it is difficult to see how that would have improved the position so long as the navy and the army were free to follow their own air policies. There would have been three policies instead of one. Lord Cowdray recognized this difficulty when he wrote, in his memorandum, about the Surplus Aircraft Fleet. 'Which Ministry should administer it', he said, 'should be determined by the Cabinet after hearing the 'views of the War Staffs of the Army and Navy and Air 'Board. The policy advocated by the Air Board would 'be the result of special study by air experts free from 'distractions arising from administrative work and, there-'fore, it should be worthy of serious consideration. Whilst 'it appears to me, but I have not discussed the subject with 'the two services, that by agreement with them it should 'be possible for the Surplus Aircraft Fleet to be placed 'directly under the Air Board without any serious disloca-'tion of existing arrangements, I cannot, with my present 'knowledge, recommend this. . . .'

It cannot be said that action based on Lord Cowdray's memorandum would have gone much of the way to settle the existing difficulties. Lieutenant-General Sir David Henderson, the military member of the Air Board, went much farther. In a memorandum,[1] submitted to Lieutenant-General Smuts on the 19th of July, he surveyed the whole problem with some detachment before

[1] Appendix I.

giving his personal views. He made it clear that he thought the two services should be combined 'under the control 'of a Ministry with full administrative and executive 'powers'. He believed that there would be temporary loss of efficiency, but that if the Government estimated that the war would last until June 1918 the change should be made. 'To minimize this loss of efficiency', he said, 'it 'would be advisable to draw up a complete scheme for the 'Air organization, and to take advice on the legal and ad-'ministrative questions . . . before announcing any change 'of policy, and after the announcement of the policy it 'would be necessary to disregard entirely amateur advice 'and suggestions, and to leave the Air Board and the 'Services to work out their own salvation as best they may.'

Lieutenant-General Jan Christian Smuts gave a ready ear and an impartial study to all aspects of the problem. His record and personality were factors of importance. He had come to England from German East Africa, where he had directed the campaign against Lettow-Vorbeck's forces, in March 1917 to attend an Imperial Conference, and he had subsequently been invited by Mr. Lloyd George to join the War Cabinet. This invitation he had accepted on the understanding that he would be concerned with military matters and would not be called upon to take any part in political questions. When the first daylight attack on London began Lieutenant-General Smuts was in his rooms at the Savoy Hotel, and he was a spectator of the subsequent happenings in the air on that Wednesday morning. When the attack had ended he made a tour of the places where bombs had fallen, and although he found that the damage was comparatively small, he was impressed by the obvious effect of the raid on the morale of the people. At War Cabinet meetings held after the attack Sir William Robertson, speaking for the General Staff, was a little impatient about the attention given to the feelings of the population of London. Lieutenant-General Smuts respected the views of the Chief of the Imperial General Staff, which were natural from the soldier's point of view, but he had himself seen enough to realize that the population had been shaken, and this psychological factor was of a kind which a commander must take into account.

Lieutenant-General Smuts knew that there had been controversy about the air services, some of it bitter, and that most of those who were prominent in political or service life had taken sides, or had adopted a definite attitude. When he was asked by Mr. Lloyd George to report upon the whole air problem he had been reluctant to do so because of its political aspects, but he was overborne when the Prime Minister said he would cover the political side of the matter by calling himself chairman of the committee. Mr. Lloyd George, no doubt, realized that the reluctance of Lieutenant-General Smuts, and the reasons upon which it was founded, were assets of value in the discharge of a delicate task. Gifted with a searching and analytical mind, General Smuts stood detached from British internal affairs, political or service, and what he said and did commanded a wide respect. Those who came to confer with him were convinced that his one concern was to find an unprejudiced solution of the problem, and they believed that he would not make up his mind until after he had heard, and carefully weighed, every aspect.

General Smuts presented his first report, on the subject of the air defence of the London area, on the 19th of July. This report, which was approved, has been dealt with.[1] His second report, with which we are here concerned, was placed before the War Cabinet on the 17th of August. It is the most important paper in the history of the creation of the Royal Air Force and is reprinted in full as Appendix II, but its main points may be summarized. The view was expressed that air developments had been such that the time was approaching when aircraft would cease to be merely ancillary to naval and military operations, and would be used for independent operations. 'Nobody that witnessed the attack on London 'on the 7th July could have any doubt on that point. . . . 'As far as can at present be foreseen there is absolutely 'no limit to the scale of its future independent war use.

[1] Vol. V, pp. 41–4.

'And the day may not be far off when aerial operations
'with their devastation of enemy lands and destruction
'of industrial and populous centres on a vast scale may
'become the principal operations of war, to which the
'older forms of military and naval operations may become
'secondary and subordinate. . . .' The programmes of
aircraft production, sanctioned by the War Cabinet,
would, he said, result in a future surplus of aeroplanes
after the requirements of the army and of the navy had
been met, and the creation of an Air Staff to plan and
direct independent operations was a matter of some
urgency. Furthermore, the design of aircraft and engines
for such operations must be settled in accordance with
the policy which would direct their future strategic employment, a fact which made urgent the need to form an
Air Ministry. The report had something to say on the
subject of man-power. The progressive exhaustion, which
afflicted all the combatants, would, it was stated, determine more and more the character of the war as one of
arms and machinery rather than of men. 'The side that
'commands industrial superiority and exploits its advan-
'tages in that respect to the utmost ought in the long run
'to win. Man-power in its war use will more and more
'tend to become subsidiary and auxiliary to the full
'development and use of mechanical power. . . .' The
submarine had already shown what startling developments
were possible in naval warfare. 'Aircraft is destined to
'work an even more far-reaching change in land warfare.
'But to secure the advantages of this new factor . . . we
'must create a new directing organization, a new Ministry
'and Air Staff which could properly handle the instru-
'ment of offence and equip it with the best brains at our
'disposal.'

The report recommended, therefore, that an Air Ministry should be formed as soon as possible to control and
administer all matters in connexion with air warfare of
every kind, and that the new Ministry should proceed
to work out the arrangements for the amalgamation of
the two air services, and for the legal constitution and
discipline of the new service. Meanwhile it was desirable

that the change should not be publicly announced in advance in order to avoid offering the enemy any stimulus to corresponding efforts.

On the 24th of August the War Cabinet met and decided to accept, in principle, the recommendation that a separate service for the air be formed. It was further decided that a committee, under Lieutenant-General Smuts, should be appointed to investigate the details of amalgamation, and to prepare the necessary draft legislation for submission to Parliament.[1]

This body was known as the Air Organization Committee, and on its work much of the shape and general architecture of the Royal Air Force depended. The moving spirit behind the activities of the committee was Sir David Henderson. Sub-committees, under his general supervision, settled questions of the composition of the Air Council and of the distribution of duties among its members, drafted a Bill for the constitution of the new Ministry, explored the multitudinous details connected with the amalgamation of the two services and with Discipline, the Pay Warrant, and King's Regulations. This was work for which the logical mind of Sir David Henderson and his practical experience well fitted him. Every member of the committee toiled at high pressure, but none more than Lieutenant-General Henderson, who held nothing back and whose energy burned like a flame when, as here, his heart and mind were engaged.

While the air organization committee was dealing with the office work of amalgamation, there were misgivings about the whole policy, particularly at General Headquarters in France. A copy of the report of Lieutenant-General Smuts had been forwarded by the War Office to Sir Douglas Haig for comment.[2] In the General Head-

[1] The members, additional to the Chairman, were Lord Cowdray, Major J. L. Baird, M.P., Lieutenant-General Sir David Henderson, Commodore G. M. Paine, and Lord Hugh Cecil. Major C. L. Storr and Sir Paul Harvey were joint secretaries.

[2] The Commander-in-Chief pencilled notes, on the copy which he used, as follows: He underlined, in the recommendation numbered (6), the words *from time to time* (l. 1), and *during the period of such attachment* (l. 3), and added the comment, 'All boats are not under the Admiralty! We

quarters' file in which the matter was discussed there are memoranda, unsigned, which set out reasons against the formation, at that time, of an Air Ministry. The contention on which the whole argument for a separate air service was based, it was said, was that the war could be won in the air as against on the ground, which was a mere assertion unsupported by facts. 'An Air Ministry 'with civilian head', it was stated, 'uncontrolled by any 'outside naval and military opinion, exposed as it would 'inevitably be to popular and factional clamour, would be 'very liable to lose its sense of proportion and be drawn 'towards the spectacular, such as bombing reprisals and 'home defence, at the expense of providing the essential 'means of co-operation with our naval and military forces.'

In his reply[1] to the War Office, however, sent on the 15th of September 1917, Sir Douglas Haig confined his examination of the subject to what was necessary to ensure the efficiency of the air service under the new organization, 'the principle of the formation of a separate Air ser-'vice having already been approved by the War Cabinet.' He also remarked dryly that he had further limited his consideration of the matter 'to our requirements in this 'war, the winning of which demands the concentration of 'all our energies . . .' He had, he said, carefully studied the report, and he found that some of the views put forward about future possibilities went beyond anything justified by his experience. He thought that a full examination of the problems associated with long-distance bombing would show that the views expressed by the committee required considerable modification, and he desired to point out the 'grave danger of an Air Ministry, charged with such 'powers as the Committee recommends, assuming control 'with a belief in theories which are not in accordance with 'practical experience'. After reviewing the difficulties

have pontoons and Inland Water Transport barges, steamers, etc.' Against the statement about the necessity for securing air predominance on a large scale, in paragraph 11, he underlined the words, *having secured it in this war we should make every effort and sacrifice to maintain it for the future*, and added, 'I agree'.

[1] Reprinted as Appendix III.

associated with long-distance bombing from aerodromes in French territory, Sir Douglas Haig had much to say about the supply of aeroplanes and trained personnel. 'After more than three years of war', he said, 'our 'armies are still very far short of their requirements, and 'my experience of repeated failure to fulfil promises as 'regards provision makes me somewhat sceptical as to the 'large surplus of machines and personnel on which the 'Committee counts in . . . its report. . . . Nor is it clear 'that the large provision necessary to replace wastage has 'been taken into account. . . .'

This letter from Sir Douglas Haig reached home at a time when the German air service had caused Whitehall to probe once again into air problems. At the beginning of September 1917 the German bombing squadron had begun an intensive night-bombing campaign. After the attack on London of the 4th/5th of September the War Cabinet met and their discussion revealed a strong feeling for carrying the air war into Germany. Lieutenant-General Smuts was requested to investigate the recent German attacks, to report his views about the provision of protection for the civil population, and to submit proposals for bombing operations against Germany. His memorandum on the question of the German air raids was circulated to the Cabinet on the 6th of September.[1] He proceeded, with characteristic thoroughness, to explore the various aspects of the larger question of bombing Germany, and he soon came to the conclusion that we were backward in all our preparations. On the 18th of September he circulated a memorandum, to which he attached important statements by Sir William Weir on the supply position, by Sir David Henderson on the scale of the contemplated bombing offensive in the spring and summer of 1918, and notes on Sir William Weir's memorandum by Sir David Henderson, Commodore Godfrey Paine, and by Major-General W. S. Brancker.[2]

Sir William Weir, who was at the time the Controller of Aeronautical Supplies in the Ministry of Munitions, made it clear that the programme of aircraft expansion

---

[1] See Vol. V, pp. 64–5.   [2] See also pp. 39–42.

could not be realized unless the whole industrial organization was reviewed and the necessary priorities given to aircraft supplies. He pointed out that the problem could only be decided 'by a consideration of true war policy, the 'influence of aerial strategy, and a definite aerial plan of 'campaign. It is necessary to insist on this point as even 'now the aeronautical programme may be suffering in its 'character from an indefinite knowledge of actual aerial 'policy for next year. It is necessary also to reiterate the 'extreme urgency of an immediate settlement of this ques-'tion, as any change in the existing programme for the 'spring of 1918 can only be brought about with ample 'notice so that the manufacturing arrangements can be 'adjusted. . . .' Major-General Brancker stated that it was useless to accelerate the supply programme if other limiting factors were not similarly dealt with. There was a shortage of training-type aeroplanes, there was delay in providing aerodromes and buildings, and the recruitment of mechanics was proceeding at a slow pace. The Board of Agriculture was reluctant to allow arable land to be taken over for new aerodromes, but all suitable non-arable land had already been taken up. Major-General Brancker urged that the War Cabinet should say definitely that the Board of Agriculture must release 4,000 acres of arable land urgently required by the air services. Commodore Godfrey Paine added representations about an imperative need to increase the supply of pilots and mechanics. In his covering memorandum, Lieutenant-General Smuts pointed out that the whole question of air expansion was really one of fundamental war policy to be decided by the Cabinet after hearing the advice of their military experts.[1]

The various memoranda, together with Sir Douglas Haig's letter, were fully considered by the War Cabinet at a meeting on the 21st of September. It was decided that Sir John Hunter should be appointed to supervise the construction of new aerodromes and that 4,000 acres of arable land should be taken over for this purpose. On the broader questions it was clear, as Sir William Weir had said in his memorandum, that air expansion

[1] See pp. 40–1.

depended upon priorities, a matter which intimately concerned the Admiralty and War Office. The Cabinet decided, therefore, that the subject must be considered further, and a strong committee, under Lieutenant-General Smuts, was appointed to report upon the whole situation, to make recommendations about priority, and to say fully what effects any priorities which might be granted would have upon the army and the navy.

This committee, called the *Aerial Operations Committee*, began work immediately[1]. At their first meeting the members decided that they could do what they had been instructed to do only if they were constituted a standing committee with authority to settle all questions of priority, not alone for the air programme, but for all munitions programmes. A memorandum was accordingly drawn up by the chairman and was considered by the War Cabinet on the 8th of October. The proposals put forward were adopted, and the name of the committee was changed to *War Priorities Committee*, which was given powers to settle questions of priority in connexion with the production of all munitions of war.

This was a revolutionary step, and it was a direct result of the difficulties associated with the problem of aircraft expansion. It may be noted that thereafter Lieutenant-General J. C. Smuts, in his capacity of chairman of the War Priorities Committee, was called upon to discharge some of the more important duties allocated by theorists to a Minister of Defence. Once again there was the asset of the prestige and authority which he enjoyed because of his aloofness from British internal service and political affairs. He sat in judgement on the claims for material which were put forward, and he made his allocations in accordance with his interpretation of the whole war policy of the Government. If the programmes submitted by the service departments were cut down there were seldom any murmurings. It was accepted that the demands

[1] Its members, additional to the Chairman, were: Sir Eric Geddes, First Lord of the Admiralty; Lord Derby, Secretary of State for War; Lord Cowdray, President of the Air Board; and Mr. Winston Churchill, Minister of Munitions. Major C. L. Storr was secretary.

received an impartial scrutiny, and that when modifications were made it was because the industrial resources of the country, as conditioned by the war policy of the Government, did not permit of strict fulfilment.

Meanwhile no public announcement had been made of the intention to form a separate air service, and because of the general ignorance of the Government's actions on the subject of air policy and expansion, there was considerable public criticism. At its meeting on the 21st of September the War Cabinet had considered announcing to the Press the decision to form a separate air service, but had deferred the question. There were some, in close touch with the Government, who were beginning to despair about the formation of a unified air service. The question was again raised by Lieutenant-General Smuts at a Cabinet meeting on the 8th of October, at which Mr. Lloyd George said he had consulted Mr. Holt Thomas, who had had considerable experience in aeronautical matters, and his opinion was that the time was not yet ripe for the formation of an Air Ministry, and that an announcement in the Press would therefore be premature. After much discussion the Cabinet decided to adjourn the debate to give opportunity for Lieutenant-General Smuts to look further into the matter. On the 10th of October Admiral Mark Kerr[1] was told by Lord Cowdray that it was almost certain no independent bombing force to attack Germany would be formed. The admiral had, after making a close study of the German air position, reached the conclusion that the Germans were giving priority to the building of aeroplanes, and that a large-scale bombing campaign against England must be anticipated. He therefore addressed to Lord Cowdray a forceful memorandum pointing out 'the extraordinary danger of delay in forming 'the Air Ministry and commencing on a proper Air 'Policy'. The memorandum was circulated among the members of the War Cabinet.

[1] Admiral Mark Kerr had returned to England from commanding the British Adriatic Squadron in August 1917, and the Admiralty had placed his services at the disposal of the Air Board to assist in forming the new Air Ministry.

At their meeting on the 15th of October the War Cabinet once more reviewed the position. The discussion revealed misgivings whether it would be possible to form an Air Ministry during the war without causing serious dislocation, and the War Cabinet decided to make a somewhat cautious announcement in Parliament that a Bill would be introduced to co-ordinate the air services 'and provide for the eventual setting up of an Air Ministry'. It was further decided that an Air Policy Committee of the War Cabinet should be formed, under the chairmanship of Lieutenant-General Smuts, to advise the Cabinet pending the establishment of an Air Ministry. The members were the First Lord of the Admiralty, the Secretary of State for War, and the President of the Air Board. Various officers, including Major-General Trenchard from France, were called into consultation by the committee from time to time.

It will be observed that the War Cabinet decision referred to the 'eventual' formation of an Air Ministry, and it seems clear that the Air Policy Committee was set up for the reason that the Government were undecided whether the separate Ministry would be created during the war. Parliament, however, met on October the 16th, after the summer recess, and there seems little doubt that the Government were made aware of a determined feeling among the members of the House of Commons that no further procrastination would be tolerated. However that may be, when Mr. Bonar Law stood in the Commons on the 16th to make his eagerly awaited statement he irrevocably committed the Government. 'A Bill', he said, 'to constitute an Air Ministry has been prepared and will 'shortly be introduced'. Disquiet, however, was not wholly dissipated as is clear from the contents of a memorandum circulated to the members of the War Cabinet by Lord Milner[1] on the 26th of October. He opened by saying that he thought the position with regard to future air policy was a long way from satisfactory, and he pointed to the need for an early discussion by the War Cabinet of the whole question. Such discussions as had taken place

[1] A member of the War Cabinet without portfolio.

in the past had usually arisen out of the results of German air raids, and he was not happy that the various decisions reached were consistent with each other or were being put into effect. 'I thought', he went on, 'that, if there was 'one point on which everybody at all conversant with the 'subject was agreed, it was the necessity of an Air Staff 'constantly reviewing the whole field of Air Policy, co-'ordinating the requirements of Army and Navy, and 'devising the best methods of offence and defence in the 'new art of independent aerial warfare. Without such a 'body I cannot imagine how we are to know either how 'to make the best use of the machines we have got or what 'types of machines we should build in the future, and what 'should be the relative numbers of the various types. 'Ministry or no Ministry therefore—and I gather that 'a full-fledged Ministry will take some time to construct '—an Air Staff "composed on the lines of the Imperial 'General Staff" is an urgent necessity. . . . Who is in 'the meantime doing the work of that Air Staff which, 'by common consent, is so urgently required? Is it the 'Committee which has been appointed to advise the 'Cabinet on all matters of Air Policy? If that is to be 'our only Air Staff during the critical time ahead of us, 'I venture to say that the arrangement is quite inadequate. 'It is not clear from the minutes of its first meeting whether 'the Committee is intended to discharge executive func-'tions, or merely to give advice. Even if the wider view 'of its functions is taken, how is it possible for a Committee 'meeting once or twice a week, however able its members, 'to think out the increasingly numerous and difficult 'problems of aerial warfare and to control our operations 'in the air. . . . I feel that we cannot accept with a light 'heart the responsibility of continuing with the ill-defined 'organization, which is all that we at present appear to 'possess.'

This letter was discussed by the War Cabinet, but no decisions were reached, presumably because the work of the air organization committee had proceeded so far that the draft Bill, it was expected, would be ready for the House of Commons within two or three weeks. Finally, at a meeting on the 6th of November, the War Cabinet approved the Bill and decided that it should be laid before Parliament.

The next step was a curious one. On the 16th of November 1917 a letter appeared in *The Times* over the signature of Lord Northcliffe. It was addressed to the Prime Minister and gave, in some detail, the reasons which moved Lord Northcliffe to refuse an invitation to take charge of the new Air Ministry. The letter was read by Lord Cowdray with something of a shock, for it seems fairly clear, from the discussions of the Air Board, that as President he had assumed that he would continue to be the responsible Minister when the Air Board had been enlarged as the Air Ministry. The revelation made by Lord Northcliffe rendered the position of Lord Cowdray difficult and he therefore resigned. At a War Cabinet meeting held on the same day as the letter appeared in *The Times*, Mr. Lloyd George gave a personal explanation to the members. He had, he said, approached Lord Northcliffe with a view to his acceptance of the post of Secretary of State for Air, but there was no justification for the published letter, which had naturally placed Lord Cowdray in a difficult position. The Prime Minister read to the War Cabinet a letter, explaining the circumstances, which he proposed to send to Lord Cowdray. It was agreed, after discussion, that some such step was necessary.

So it was that Lord Cowdray went. He did not, we have seen, believe in the beginning that the creation of a separate service for the air, however desirable, was possible in time of war, but those who were in close touch with him have testified that his views underwent a change. It seems obvious, however, that the Government would wish to appoint, as first Minister for the Air, one who believed whole-heartedly in the unification of the two air services, and there was excuse for doubting whether Lord Cowdray fully met that desire. The manner of his departure was, all the same, unfortunate, for he had deserved well of the air service to which, indeed, he showed many marks of his devotion up to the time of his death. His work is written clear in the minutes of the discussions of the

Air Board.[1] He had to guide men of conflicting interests equipped with inadequate powers. The agenda for each meeting of the Board was usually a crowded one, made up of items of great diversity, but the discussions, under Lord Cowdray's direction, were business-like, and decisions were, for the most part, prompt and clear-cut.

Lord Cowdray was succeeded as President of the Air Board by Lord Rothermere on the 23rd of November 1917. Meanwhile, the Air Force Bill[2] had been introduced in Parliament, and it received Royal assent on the 29th of November. On the 21st of December 1917 and on the 2nd of January 1918 Orders in Council were issued defining the composition and duties of the members of the Air Council. The second of these Orders stated that the Air Council would come into being on the 3rd of January 1918. Lord Rothermere was on the same day appointed first Secretary of State for the Air Force,[3] and the other members of the Air Council, appointed at the same time, were:

Lieutenant-General Sir David Henderson, K.C.B.
  (Additional Member and Vice-President).
Major-General Sir Hugh Trenchard, K.C.B.
  (Chief of the Air Staff).
Rear-Admiral Mark Kerr, C.B.
  (Deputy Chief of the Air Staff).
Commodore Godfrey M. Paine, C.B.
  (Master-General of Personnel).
Major-General W. S. Brancker
  (Controller-General of Equipment).
Sir William Weir
  (Director-General of Aircraft Production in the Ministry of Munitions).

---

[1] The Second Air Board held 150 meetings in all between the 3rd of January 1917 and the 28th of December 1917.

[2] The Bill became law as the 'Air Force Act', but the title was later changed to the 'Air Force (Constitution) Act'.

[3] The Secretary of State was variously referred to as 'of the Air Force', 'for the Air Force', 'for the Air Forces', and 'for Air'. In March 1918 it was announced officially that His Majesty had approved the designation of 'Secretary of State for the Royal Air Force'. When the Air Council, after the war, became responsible for civil aviation, the title was altered (March 1919) to 'Secretary of State for Air'.

Sir John Hunter, K.B.E.
    (Administrator of Works and Buildings).
Major J. L. Baird, C.M.G., D.S.O., M.P.
    (Parliamentary Under-Secretary of State).

The acting Secretary to the Council was Mr. W. A. Robinson, C.B., C.B.E., and the Assistant-Secretary Mr. H. W. W. McAnally.

It will be seen that Major-General Trenchard had been relieved of his command in France to take up the appointment of the first Chief of the Air Staff. He brought to the new Ministry his unrivalled knowledge of war in the air, and, reluctant as they were to take him from his command in France, the Government believed that his presence in Whitehall was essential during a critical period. What his departure from France meant may be told in the words of Sir Douglas Haig, written in a letter to Lord Derby during the battle of Cambrai in October 1917. 'I am convinced', he said, 'that the proper place
'for Trenchard is in actual command of the Flying Corps
'in the field in France. It is out of the question he can be
'spared now whilst the battle is continuing. As regards
'the future it is quite evident that the Germans will make
'a serious and sustained effort before long to gain the
'mastery of the air. In addition we are, as you know, about
'to undertake bombing operations on a scale and in a
'manner which in my opinion should be controlled by
'Trenchard himself. The importance of Trenchard's per-
'sonality with the Flying units in the Field and its direct
'effect in maintaining the offensive spirit in the air so vital
'to the success of our Armies in the Field is not, I think,
'fully realized at home. You asked me to write my views
'absolutely frankly and I have no hesitation in saying that
'it is more than probable that the removal of Trenchard
'from active command in the Field would, in a short time,
'directly impair the offensive fighting efficiency of the
'Royal Flying Corps. The effect of this would not only
'be very quickly felt in France but in England also, quite
'possibly with serious results. To repeat, Trenchard's
'proper sphere is in the Field, but he must be placed in a

'position so that he can get his requirements met from 'home.'

That Major-General Trenchard was brought home in spite of these representations shows how important the Government considered it was that his experience should be made available to guide the newly formed Air Ministry. It may also be said that the fears expressed by the Commander-in-Chief were unfounded. The work of Major-General Trenchard during the two and a half years in which he commanded the Royal Flying Corps in France was not lost. The spirit which he had done much to create lived on, as it still lives on, with an independent life of its own.

There was a long search to find a suitable building to house the new Air Ministry. An endeavour was made to acquire the County Hall, Westminster, and when this attempt was coldly repelled, eyes were cast on the building of the Metropolitan Water Board, also in vain. Attention was next turned to museums, and the Victoria and Albert and British Museums were considered, without, however, any encouragement from the Trustees. Eventually the proposal that the Air Ministry should be housed in the British Museum, leaving the Hotel Cecil to the Ministry of Munitions, reached the point (the Trustees still protesting) when submission was made to the War Cabinet for approval. Happily for all concerned, the proposal was not sanctioned, and the Air Ministry eventually took up its abode in the Hotel Cecil, where it remained until after the war.[1]

The new Ministry had a difficult and complex task. It had to assemble and organize the necessary administrative and technical staffs, to take over the duties which had been the concern of the War Cabinet committee on air policy presided over by Lieutenant-General Smuts, and to take all the essential steps for the amalgamation of the two flying services into the Air Force.[2] And it had to

[1] The Department gave up the Hotel Cecil in July 1919 and moved to Kingsway, to buildings subsequently renamed Adastral House.

[2] At an Air Council meeting on the 19th of February 1918 it was stated that His Majesty had approved the title 'Royal Air Force'. A Royal proclamation, announcing this fact, was published on the 7th of March 1918.

work against time. Enough had been done within a few weeks to make it possible for the announcement to be made that the Royal Air Force would come into being, as a separate service, on the 1st of April 1918.[1]

Among the many questions which had to be dealt with was that of naming the officers of the new service. The air organization committee had approved suggested titles, prepared by Sir David Henderson, mostly taken from the navy or the army. The War Office, however, expressed the view that the new service should have distinctive titles of its own, and also drew attention to the point that, in the suggested list, naval titles were given to senior officers and military titles to junior officers, a subtlety of distinction which might cause some resentment. The Admiralty stated simply that the use of naval titles, especially those of the higher ranks, was objectionable, even if given a prefix such as 'Air', and suggested that military titles should be adopted exclusively, or else others, suggestive of the air, fabricated. A list of new titles was manufactured as follows: *Ensign, Lieutenant, Flight-Leader, Squadron-Leader, Reeve, Banneret, Fourth-Ardian, Third-Ardian, Second-Ardian, Ardian, Air Marshal.* An alternative list slightly varied the ranks above *Squadron-Leader*. The suggestions were: *Wing Leader, Leader, Flight Ardian, Squadron Ardian, Wing Ardian,* and so on. Members of the service will read these titles with interest, the more so because the only two which are in use are Squadron Leader and Air Marshal. 'Reeve', perhaps, savoured a little too much of legal authority, but one may regret 'Banneret', which has a flavour and associations, more especially as the leader of a formation in the air went into battle flying a streamer which formed a rallying mark as did the banner of the knight for his vassals. 'Ardian' comes from the Gaelic 'Ard', meaning 'chief', and 'Ian' or 'Eun', a 'bird'. The translation, perhaps, detracts something from its dignity. Names have a fantasy of their own. Strange sounding as they may appear, at first hearing, they soon come to be accepted and pass

[1] The lighter-than-air service was not taken over from the Admiralty until October 1919.

quietly into the language. There was no reason why a unit of the air service should be called a 'squadron', any more than a 'company' or a 'group', which were the original suggestions, but so much tradition has become attached to the word that it would be difficult to imagine a squadron being called anything different. No 'Ardian' will ever grace a Lord Mayor's banquet, nor 'Banneret' pass on his way, evoking memories of another age, because a much over-worked committee considered the proposed new titles as the last item of a long and tiring agenda, and they took the line of least resistance and decided to keep to the list which they had approved at their previous meeting. This list, with the Admiralty and War Office objections, was placed before the War Cabinet, who decided to adopt the Admiralty view that the officers of the Air Force should be given military titles. So it was that on the 1st of April 1918 all those naval officers who transferred to the Royal Air Force signified their attachment to the air by changing their naval titles for military ones.[1]

The unity which, at long last, had been achieved in the service, was not, unhappily, a feature of the first Air Council. There appeared grave differences of view between the Chief of the Air Staff and the Secretary of State. There would be no profit in traversing the story of these differences. It will be enough to say that Major-General Trenchard took a much wider view of the responsibilities of the Chief of the Air Staff than it appeared to him the Secretary of State was willing to accord, but it is clear, also, that there were differences of temperament. On the 18th of March Major-General Trenchard submitted his views in a memorandum to Lord Rothermere and, on receipt of a reply next day, tendered his resignation. Because he held that an announcement, at that time, might jeopardize the scheme of amalgamation, the Secretary of State deferred bringing the matter before the War Cabinet until the 10th of April, and, on the 13th, he informed the Chief of the Air Staff that his resignation was accepted.

[1] New titles for the commissioned ranks of the Royal Air Force, as they exist to-day, were announced in orders promulgated by the Air Council on the 27th of August 1919.

Major-General F. H. Sykes was appointed in his place, and then Sir David Henderson, the Vice-President of the Air Council, resigned on the grounds that he could not work with the new Chief of the Air Staff. On the 25th of April it was announced that Lord Rothermere had resigned his appointment as Secretary of State[1] and, a few days later, Sir Henry Norman, who had been appointed by Lord Rothermere as an 'additional member' of the Air Council, followed suit. That was the end of the disintegration. Lord Rothermere was succeeded as Secretary of State, on the 27th of April, by Sir William Weir, the Director-General of Aircraft Production. There were other minor changes subsequently and, when the war ended, the composition of the Air Council was as follows:

The Rt. Hon. Lord Weir of Eastwood, P.C.
    (Secretary of State for the Royal Air Force).
Major J. L. Baird, C.M.G., D.S.O., M.P.
    (Parliamentary Under-Secretary of State).
Major-General F. H. Sykes, C.M.G.
    (Chief of the Air Staff).
Major-General W. S. Brancker, A.F.C.
    (Master-General of Personnel).
Major-General E. L. Ellington, C.M.G.
    (Controller-General of Equipment).
Major-General Sir G. M. Paine, K.C.B., M.V.O.
    (Inspector-General of the Royal Air Force).
Sir Arthur Duckham, K.C.B.
    (Director-General of Aircraft Production,
      Ministry of Munitions).
Sir John Hunter, K.B.E.
    (Administrator of Works and Buildings).
        Secretary:
W. A. Robinson, Esq., C.B., C.B.E.

---

[1] Lord Rothermere had intimated at the beginning of March that ill health might prevent him continuing in his appointment, but he stated that he would not go until after the amalgamation had become an accomplished fact. He had suffered much distress through the death a few weeks before, from wounds received in action, of his eldest son, Captain the Hon. H. A. V. St. G. Harmsworth, M.C.

CHAPTER II
PROBLEMS OF SUPPLY AND OF MAN POWER

THE two limiting factors in the war-time expansion of the air services were engine-supply and man-power. Aeroplanes, or, as they would now be called, airframes, could be produced by unskilled labour with expert supervision, but the making of engines called for highly skilled attention. Because it was late in the field the aeronautical industry was compelled to make use of an undue amount of inexpert labour, and one result was that there was much waste due to the rejection of defective work.[1] There was the complication that the air services were ever searching for mechanics in order to satisfy expansion demands. The total number of men required to maintain one front-line aeroplane serviceable was high,[2] and every increase in the number of squadrons created important new claims for trained mechanics. It was difficult to assess, economically, the allowance for spare parts, whether for engines, aeroplanes, or accessories, because the demand for spares depended upon such things as battle losses and salvage and repair facilities, which could not be closely estimated.

Statistics compiled in the spring of 1917 revealed that a period of thirty-four weeks elapsed from the time an aeroplane design was approved and the time when the type was produced in bulk, and that the corresponding period for an engine was sixty-four weeks. Most of what was produced throughout 1917, therefore, had been initiated in 1916 by the air departments of the Admiralty and of the War Office. By the end of 1916, however, the two service departments had fulfilled their part. The Ministry of Munitions alone had the comprehensive organization and the experience to adapt and to expand the existing

[1] The dilution of labour in twenty-one representative aircraft firms in October 1917 was 37·5 per cent. (compared with 32·7 per cent. in April 1917).

[2] A calculation made in the autumn of 1917 showed that it was necessary to reckon a total of 47 men as required for each aeroplane kept serviceable at the front. (A year later this figure had been reduced to 40.) The total number of workers, skilled and unskilled, required to *produce one aeroplane a month* in 1917 was shown to be 120.

AIR PROGRAMMES

resources for large-scale production. Competition, tolerable so long as there was a margin of effort still not absorbed in war work, was no longer acceptable in 1917, when the allotment of man-power and of material was raising many anxious problems. To obtain priorities for aircraft production a strong and authoritative voice was necessary, and this could best be supplied at the time by the Minister of Munitions, who controlled all except naval war material.[1]

To understand the position, so far as it concerned demand, when the Ministry of Munitions became responsible for aircraft supply in January 1917, it will be necessary to go back a little. In June 1916 Sir Douglas Haig had submitted his expansion programme which increased the total number of squadrons for service on the Western front to fifty-six by the spring of 1917 (excluding ten long-range bombing squadrons). The programme, which was approved, raised the aggregate number of service squadrons from seventy, already sanctioned by the Government, to eighty-six,[2] and required a corresponding increase in training squadrons from thirty-two to sixty (including the Central Flying School, calculated at four squadrons). In September 1916, however, the character of the air war in France had changed. The Germans brought into action against the Royal Flying Corps the newly formed *Jagdstaffeln*, equipped with Albatros and Halberstadt fighters mounting twin machine-guns synchronized to fire through the propeller. These German aeroplanes were better fighting weapons than anything possessed by the Allied air services at the time and they soon exerted an influence. At the end of September 1916 Sir Douglas Haig had warned the Army Council that he would require more and better fighting aeroplanes and, on the 16th of November, he had recommended the

---

[1] At a meeting of the Air Board in November 1916 Sir David Henderson, the director-general of military aeronautics, speaking of the provision of raw material for the building of Hispano-Suiza engines in France, had said that his department was constantly fighting to get more labour and material, but that it was not strong enough to obtain what was needed.

[2] 56 squadrons in France, 10 in other theatres of war, 10 additional long-range bombing squadrons previously asked for by Sir Douglas Haig, and 10 Home Defence squadrons.

provision of twenty additional fighting squadrons, which would give him two fighting squadrons for each artillery squadron.

This demand increased the total number of service squadrons to be provided to 106.[1] Furthermore, it had by this time become clear that the estimate that sixty training squadrons would suffice to maintain eighty-six service squadrons was too low, mainly because not enough allowance had been made for pilot casualties overseas, and the new estimate was that ninety-five training squadrons would be necessary to maintain 106 service squadrons. The Army Council duly sanctioned these expanded demands and added two night-flying squadrons to the number of training units. Thus in December 1916 the total of approved squadrons for the Royal Flying Corps was 203 (106 service and 97 training), as compared with 102 (70 service and 32 training squadrons) in June. That is to say, within about six months in 1916 the establishment for the Royal Flying Corps had been doubled.

It was calculated that, reckoning a total of eighty engines for each service squadron,[2] about 8,000 up-to-date engines would be required. The training squadrons, it was stated, must make do with engines which had become obsolete, or with those which had been sent back from the front. At the end of 1916, when this calculation was made, the Royal Flying Corps possessed about 5,200 engines, of which 3,300 were classified as up-to-date. Wastage was estimated to work out at 100 per cent. per annum, and the total output requirements, based upon a decision to make the expansion to a total of 8,000 engines effective within six months, were set down as 2,000 engines per month, including 300 a month for naval aircraft and 200 for contingencies.

The output of engines in December 1916 was at the rate of about 600 per month, and Lord Curzon, the President of the first Air Board, was of the opinion that no expansion of output was possible without reorganization and some form of centralized control. It was mainly for

[1] Two squadrons were subsequently added for night flying.
[2] In June 1916 the basic figure of engines per squadron was forty-six.

this reason that the Air Board had been reorganized in January 1917 and that the responsibility for aircraft supplies had been transferred to the Ministry of Munitions. The Aeronautical Department in the Ministry was formed by a staff of about 1,200 officers and officials from the Admiralty and War Office,[1] and was placed under the charge of Mr. William Weir who, on the 24th of January 1917, was appointed Controller of Aeronautical Equipment. He was also given a seat on the reorganized Air Board (the second, or Cowdray, Air Board) together with Mr. Percy Martin who, with the title of Controller of Petrol Engine Supply, was responsible, in the Ministry of Munitions, for the allotment of contracts for all engines, whether for tanks, mechanical transport, or aircraft.

A programme to produce 2,000 engines each month was at once laid down (in January 1917), but it could not be realized before, at the earliest, the autumn of 1917. The problem was how to tide over the opening months of the year when the Germans, it was anticipated, would make their strongest efforts to gain air superiority. Help was sought from the Admiralty, and naval aircraft, fighting squadrons, and aircraft engines, were placed at the disposal of the Royal Flying Corps, but they did not suffice. In April 1917, when the situation was at its worst, the number of flying hours for each officer killed or missing on the Western front dropped to ninety-two as compared with 295 for August, 1916, and with a monthly average of about 190 for the whole war period.

That the supply situation was grave for part of 1917 may have owed a little to the outlook of Lord Curzon, the President of the first Air Board. In November 1916, when consideration was being given by the Air Board to an Admiralty proposal to order 8,000 Hispano-Suiza aircraft engines in France,[2] Lord Curzon had said that 'the increasing exhaustion of the belligerents rendered it 'doubtful whether a supply in the latter half of 1917 'or early 1918 would be of any service for the purposes of

---

[1] By the Armistice the staff had increased to 17,250.

[2] 3,500 were to be allotted to Britain, 3,000 to France, and 1,500 to Russia. Britain was to provide all raw material.

'the war. . . . We were every month coming nearer to the 'point of general exhaustion beyond which the war could 'not go on. . . . An analogy of ships[1] was not a perfect one, 'for ships would be of use even after the war, but to be 'left with a very large number of aeroplanes might be 'highly inconvenient.' In spite of Lord Curzon's objections the Air Board confirmed the Admiralty order of 8,000 Hispano-Suiza engines in France, and in the first quarter of 1918, when they were delivered in great quantities, these engines saved the supply situation.[2]

Standardization of Engines

When, in January 1917, the Ministry of Munitions came to place orders in accordance with the output programme of 2,000 engines per month many difficulties had to be faced. At the time the programme was put forward there were engines of forty different designs under construction, and it was realized that if mass production was to be achieved there must be some standardization of types of engine. Unhappily a grave mistake was made in the beginning—a mistake which was destined to upset the whole engine production programme for the remainder of the war. One of the more important types which came under consideration was the 200 horse-power water-cooled engine, and in this class there were four engines of comparable qualities. They were the B.H.P. (Beardmore-Halford-Pullinger) and a Sunbeam, both of six cylinders, and the Hispano-Suiza and another Sunbeam of eight cylinders. At the beginning of January 1917 the internal combustion engine sub-committee of the Advisory Committee for Aeronautics[3] had been asked by the Air Board to consider these four engines and to say which was

---

[1] It had been pointed out that the Admiralty followed a definite routine of ordering for a period of eighteen months ahead.

[2] The Hispano was mainly ordered from the Mayen Company in France. The firm built a large factory for which money was advanced by the British Government (approximately £2 million). Output, however, did not begin until late in 1917.

[3] The Advisory Committee for Aeronautics had been appointed by Mr. Asquith, Prime Minister, in 1909, to 'secure the co-operation of the laboratory with the services' (See Vol. I, pp. 158-9).

most suitable for mass production. The members of the sub-committee made a very thorough examination and, at the end of January, they recommended the adoption of the eight-cylinder Sunbeam. Although the engine had not yet developed 200 horse-power the sub-committee expressed the opinion that it would produce this power without any danger of a break-down. They also recommended the B.H.P. engine as being superior to the six-cylinder Sunbeam. Acting on these expert recommendations, the Air Board requested the Ministry of Munitions to place contracts for the eight-cylinder Sunbeam, later known as the Sunbeam Arab. The Austin company received orders for 1,000 of these engines, a number which was doubled by new contracts placed in July 1917.[1] An order for 1,000 Arabs was also given to the firm of Willys Overland in America instead of orders for a similar number of Hispano-Suiza engines, as had been intended before the sub-committee reported in favour of the Sunbeam Arab.

At the time when these large orders were placed with different manufacturers, the Sunbeam Arab was an untried engine and there was at least one officer who questioned the wisdom of placing so much reliance upon an engine which had yet to be proved. This was Captain R. H. Verney, of the Aeronautical Inspection Directorate, and he wrote a letter to the internal-combustion engine sub-committee pointing out many details of the Sunbeam engine which were still experimental as compared with the Hispano-Suiza. The members of the sub-committee thereupon reconsidered the matter, but they decided that there was no reason to modify their original findings. In particular, they pointed out that they had kept in mind the difficulties, referred to by Captain Verney, connected with the production of aluminium castings, but it was their conviction that the troubles were not insuperable. The whole matter was reviewed by the Air Board at their meeting on the 21st of March, and the statement was then

[1] Orders for the Arab were also placed with the Lanchester, Napier, and Sunbeam firms. The total orders, 4,400 engines, exceeded those for any other type of engine in the 1917–18 programme. It was anticipated that 1,800 would be delivered by the end of 1917.

made that the B.H.P. and R.A.F. 4a engines were in the same category, and that there were, in fact, no fewer than 4,000 engines due for delivery between June and December 1917 which depended upon the success of the aluminium cylinder.

The B.H.P. type was put into production about the same time as the Sunbeam Arab. An order for 2,000 B.H.P. engines was placed with the Siddeley Deasy Company. The firm of Wolseley were given the task of producing the Hispano-Suiza engine in England. So far as rotary engines were concerned, attention was mainly centred on the 130 horse-power Clerget, which was being manufactured in England and in France, but an engine designed by Lieutenant W. O. Bentley, first known as the A.R.1., and later as the B.R.1., or Bentley Rotary, was being favourably considered for future development.

The position, about March 1917, may be thus summarized. The engines on which production was mainly concentrated were the Sunbeam Arab, the B.H.P., the Hispano-Suiza, Rolls-Royce, and R.A.F. 4a, the 130 horse-power Clerget, the 110 horse-power Le Rhone, and the Bentley Rotary. On the 1st of March a total of 19,709 engines were on order.

The Sunbeam Arab Failure

By May 1917 it was becoming apparent that the engine programme was in jeopardy. The Sunbeam Arab, on test, had revealed weaknesses of cylinder and crank chamber, and many modifications had had to be introduced. The engine was so unsatisfactory that at an Air Board meeting on the 2nd of May Lord Cowdray said that it was desirable, if it were possible, that the Hispano-Suiza engine should be manufactured in place of the Arab, but Mr. Martin pointed out that the differences between the two engines were such that the firms which were making the Sunbeam Arabs could not be switched over to the manufacture of the Hispano-Suiza. A fortnight later the outlook appeared less menacing. The Sunbeam Arab, after modifications in the design had been incorporated, had satisfactorily completed a run of 100 hours on the test bench.

Subsequently, however, it was found necessary to introduce further modifications. There were also many changes in the specifications for material, mainly for gearwheels, propeller shafts, pump spindle, cylinder blocks, &c., and it was not until the end of the year that the design of the Sunbeam Arab had been finally settled. The original calculations, on which the expanded programme for the Royal Flying Corps had been partly based, had allowed for an output of 1,800 Arab engines before the end of 1917: the number delivered was eighty-one.

The failure of the Sunbeam Arab engine, a failure which entailed much waste of effort and money, and limited the expansion of the air services, should not be lightly passed over. In war, risks must be run, but there are some risks which are only rarely justifiable. It was a gamble to choose an untried engine with many experimental features for mass production, more especially because grave misgivings had been expressed by at least one officer of practical experience. Whether the members of the subcommittee, upon whose advice the engine was chosen for production, were adequately apprised of the important part which the Sunbeam Arab was scheduled to play in the whole aircraft production programme it is impossible to say. The assumption is that they were, but, in any event, their responsibility was a grave one and they cannot be absolved from some blame for an error of judgement of which the consequences were serious.

The Hispano-Suiza

There was trouble also with the 200 horse-power Hispano-Suiza under manufacture by the Wolseley Company. On the 7th of May 1917 Sir William Weir had to report that the engine, on test, had broken four successive crankshafts after an average run of no more than four hours. After further trials and conferences, eleven modifications were made in the design, with the result that the rate of output had to be considerably revised. Meanwhile, in an attempt to safeguard the position, the Wolseley Company had been asked to make 400 Hispano engines of the existing 150 horse-power type, but even this order did not go smoothly.[1] It was, apparently, not made sufficiently clear to the Wolseley firm that it was the existing type which they were required to reproduce, and they therefore set about the design of a new high-compression engine which would develop 150 horse-power. Much time was wasted before the mistake was rectified, and whereas it had been expected that, by the end of August 1917, 140 of these engines would have been delivered, the number produced was ten.

There was trouble, too, with the early 200 horse-power Hispano engines delivered in England from the French firm of Brasier. Many of these engines would not stand up to their work and they had to be sent to the Clement Talbot factory for overhaul. One serious defect which was disclosed was a faulty hardening of the gearwheels and propeller shaft, and these parts had to be replaced by spares of British manufacture. In October 1917, however, the general engine position had become so critical that some of the French Hispanos were passed with soft gears, on the plea that engines of incomplete efficiency were better than none at all. It may be that there was adequate justification for such a step. If so, it is difficult to discover. The engines were faulty and therefore dangerous in the air, and to order a pilot to fly an aeroplane in which he must, to his normal risks, add the risk of death or injury because of known defective material, is a way to undermine morale. A soldier who has no confidence in his weapons is already half-way to defeat. A pilot who knows that he must mistrust his engine is in equally bad plight because he is aware that when the engine fails, all his qualities, no matter how brilliant, will avail him little.[2]

[1] The order was subsequently increased to 1,100. The type became known as the Wolseley Viper.

[2] Entries were made in the log-books issued with these engines which said that their running should be carefully watched. It was also stated that the gearwheels on the airscrew shaft were unevenly case-hardened, and had been fitted, on instructions, because no others were available.

The engines were only accepted by the Aeronautical Inspection Directorate (which looked upon them as unsatisfactory) on direct written instructions.

Commanders of units complained that the entry in the log-book had a very adverse effect on the morale of pilots called upon to fly aeroplanes fitted with these engines.

One important result of the production failures of the Sunbeam Arab and of the Hispano-Suiza engines was to postpone the re-equipment of the R.E.8 squadrons in France with Bristol Fighters. At an Air Board meeting in the middle of August 1917 Sir William Weir said that the change was due to begin about April 1918, and he asked whether it was desirable to substitute the Bristol Fighter for the R.E.8 during the fighting season. If the change was deferred until September 1918, the result would be that 1,360 Hispano engines would be made available for other purposes. The discussion was a lively one, during which it was said that there could be no justification for giving pilots an inferior aeroplane if it was possible, with extra energy, to provide a better one. It was ultimately agreed that the original programme for the substitution of Bristol Fighters for the R.E.8 aeroplane should stand. At a meeting a fortnight later, however, Sir William Weir returned to the argument. A result of the replacement programme would be a shortage of Hispano and Sunbeam Arab engines. After some discussion the Board agreed to postpone the change over from the R.E.8 to the Bristol Fighter until September 1918.

Another result of the production failures of these two engines was that, in January 1918, there were about 400 new S.E.5 aeroplanes lying in store because there were no engines for them. Aeroplanes would, as delivered, have continued to accumulate in the acceptance parks, and the position in the early months of 1918 would have been serious indeed if it had not been that the French Hispano-Suiza engines, particularly those made by the Mayen Company in their specially built factories, were delivered in large quantities in fulfilment of the orders for 8,000 placed as a result of British Admiralty insistence at the end of 1916. The fighting personnel of the Royal Air Force in 1918 had every reason to applaud the foresight and tenacity of the naval staff in Whitehall.

Failure of the B.H.P. Engine

The story of the B.H.P. engine is no more exhilarating. When the engine was made in small numbers it proved to be satisfactory, but before it could be produced in mass the Siddeley Deasy Company, who held orders for 2,000, had to introduce changes in design of a kind necessary for bulk production. There was delay before these changes could be brought into operation, and further modifications were subsequently judged necessary after trial of the engine in the air. One result was that when, in July 1917, the first batch of engines was delivered to the Aircraft Manufacturing Company to be fitted in D.H.4 aeroplanes, it was found that the engines were very different from the drawings around which the aeroplanes had been built. The engines, as delivered, would not fit the aeroplanes made to receive them, and the latter had to go back into the shops for important alterations.

This, however, was a minor happening. The worst failure was in the production of the aluminium cylinder blocks. By July 1917 enough had been made to enable the Siddeley Deasy Company to reckon upon a production of 100 engines a month, but it was soon discovered that more than 90 per cent. of the cylinder blocks were defective. A statement submitted to the Air Board in July showed that 20 per cent. of the rejections were due to defective castings, and 35 per cent. each to porousness and to damage sustained in machining. In addition, a few which had no obvious faults failed on test. The difficulties associated with the production of an efficient aluminium cylinder persisted throughout most of the summer of 1917, and the output programme, for this reason alone, was put back six months. Finally, when the engines began to be produced in reasonable quantities there was trouble with the exhaust valves, which burnt out. More time was expended while this defect was remedied, and thus it was that the full output of B.H.P. engines was not achieved until the spring of 1918. By that time general progress in air warfare had reached a stage when the power developed by the B.H.P. engine was insufficient to enable the aeroplanes in which it was fitted to do the work expected of them. In other words, the engine had become obsolete before the mass production stage had been reached.

A War Cabinet Investigation

We have so far discussed developments in the light of the January 1917 programme for an output of 2,000 engines per month. It will now be necessary to consider matters arising out of the Government decision, following the German daylight bombing attack on London in June 1917, to double the air services, that is, to increase the number of military service squadrons from 108 to 200, with a corresponding increase in the Royal Naval Air Service. As a result, the Government sanctioned an extended engine output which would ultimately reach 4,500 each month, including supplies from overseas.[1] The limit of 4,500 per month was fixed for Treasury purposes, and there was an understanding that when this figure was being approached the matter was again to be brought before the War Cabinet for further expansion if judged desirable. It is of interest that a twelve months' supply of complete aeroplanes and seaplanes, with their spares, on the basis of an output of engines of 4,500 per month, was estimated to cost a little over £200 million sterling, that is to say, about £20 million more than the total budget of Great Britain for 1913.[2]

The Government had registered their decision about air expansion and did not again consider the matter in detail until September 1917, when the Germans began their night-bombing campaign against England. The War Cabinet asked Lieutenant-General J. C. Smuts to formulate proposals for carrying the air war into Germany at the earliest possible moment and, on the 18th of September, he placed before the members of the Cabinet an illuminating memorandum which was read by them with

---

[1] 3,500 each month from British sources, 500 from America, and 500 from France. The figures do not include spare parts which were estimated as an additional 75 per cent.

[2] The actual value of the contracts placed for *all* aircraft, spares, and accessories, for the year 1918 was £157,753,583. The corresponding amount for 1917 was £48,714,642. For *military* aircraft and supplies, the contracts placed in 1914 were valued at £1,568,882; for 1915 at £8,215,165; and for 1916, £21,963,083: the corresponding figures for naval aircraft and supplies for these years are not available.

a sense of shock. 'I am', he said, 'somewhat alarmed by 'the backwardness of our preparations, and would ask the 'War Cabinet to give the matter their most earnest atten-'tion. Both from an offensive and defensive point of view 'our air preparations and operations deserve the closest 'attention. That the enemy is making a very special effort 'in the air is undoubted. General Trenchard is quite clear 'that the enemy has never been stronger in the air than he 'is to-day, and that relatively we are not so strong as we 'were some months ago. . . . General Trenchard, there-'fore, presses most strongly for an acceleration of our air-'craft programme so that this position may be improved 'instead of worsened before the winter. . . . As regards the 'campaign of next spring and summer, the fear amongst 'officers is chiefly that the enemy is making very great 'preparations to recover ascendency in the air, and that 'success for him in that respect may have very far-reaching 'consequences on the course of the war. Even from a purely 'defensive point of view, therefore, we are called upon to 'make a very great effort in the air. But our preparations 'should be on such a scale as not only to make our defen-'sive position secure, but to enable us to gain a decisive 'superiority on the battle fronts so that the road may be 'clear for our offensive bombing policy against the in-'dustrial and munition centres of Germany.'

The aircraft programme which General Trenchard wanted accelerated was not, as might readily be assumed, the one which increased the total number of Royal Flying Corps service squadrons to 200, but the earlier one, approved in December 1916, under which the total of service squadrons was 106. It was clear from the papers placed before the Cabinet by Lieutenant-General Smuts that not only was there no hope whatsoever, with the existing organization of resources, of fulfilment for the larger programme, but that the earlier and much more modest programme was in jeopardy. 'I consider', said Lieutenant-General Smuts, 'that the Cabinet have really no option, 'but must give the fullest and most complete priorities 'necessary not only to carry it into effect but even to 'accelerate it. If this is not done, we shall run risks which

'may well prove disastrous. . . . The more limited air pro-
'gramme should be carried out at all costs, and with the
'same priorities which were accorded to the shell pro-
'gramme in 1915. . . . There remains the more difficult
'question of the more extended air programme of 200
'service squadrons, which will give far greater scope to an
'air offensive next year. The question is really one of
'fundamental war policy to be decided by the Cabinet
'after hearing the advice of their military experts. From
'a merely military point of view how do we propose to
'win the war? Can the Navy win it, and if not, should we
'expend our resources on additions to the Navy which
'cannot affect the course of events, at any rate during the
'present war? Is there a reasonable prospect of the Army
'winning a decisive victory, on the Western or any other
'of our fronts? And if, with the sobering experience which
'we have had for the last three years, we do not expect
'any decisive military victory, but only such success as
'will effectively undermine the enemy morale and dispose
'him to a reasonable peace, then it is to be considered
'whether an extended air offensive will not conduce more
'powerfully to that result than almost any other form of
'military operations. I am disposed to think so, although
'the subject is not one on which one would choose to be
'dogmatic. I hope it may be possible, not only to give
'the necessary priorities for the more limited programme,
'but for any reasonable additions which might conduce to
'a more effective air offensive next spring and summer. . . .'

This memorandum of Lieutenant-General Smuts had something of an explosive effect. The members of the War Cabinet had been led to believe that there would be a substantial surplus of aircraft production available in 1918, after the requirements of the army and of the navy had been met, and it was, indeed, mainly to direct this surplus that a separate Air Ministry had been proposed. Now they were being informed by Lieutenant-General Smuts that even the much smaller earlier programme of expansion, sanctioned for work with the armies, was not being fulfilled, and that the resources were not available to double the air services as the Government had decided to do in July 1917. The main result of the discussions which centred round the memorandum was the setting up of the War Priorities Committee.[1]

Although General Smuts had become alarmed at the backwardness of the preparations for air warfare, it is clear that he would have been still more perturbed if he had not been in an atmosphere which, judged by the results, was one of optimism. A statement was placed before the Air Board on the 6th of September 1917 which set out what the position would be in June 1918 so far as concerned aeroplanes and engines. It was shown that the output of training aeroplanes would suffice, as from January 1918, to train pilots for 200 service squadrons. Furthermore, there would be a substantial surplus of engines, after the requirements for 132 service squadrons had been met, and the question the Air Board was asked to consider was how this surplus might best be used towards the completion of the programme for 200 service squadrons. The engines would be of a kind which would produce fifteen additional bombing squadrons and eighteen fighting squadrons, or a total of thirty-three squadrons towards the sixty-eight. The bombing squadrons would be equipped with B.H.P. or Fiat[2] engines, and the fighting squadrons with Hispano-Suiza, Sunbeam Arab, Clerget, or Bentley rotary engines. How much these estimates were coloured by hope is seen from the following table:

As at June 1918

Types	Estimated Total	Estimated Surplus	Actual Deliveries	Deficit
B.H.P. and Fiat	4,115	1,183	2,374	558
Hispano-Suiza and Sunbeam Arab	7,219	1,055	3,711	2,453
Clerget and B.R.1	4,580	1,064	2,486	1,030

[1] See Chapter I, pp. 15–17.
[2] On the initiative of Sir William Weir, 2,000 Fiat engines (250 horse-power) had been ordered in Paris at the end of August 1917. They were contracted for delivery between January 1918 and June 1918, and 1,000 were for America and 1,000 for ourselves for employment in D.H.9 aeroplanes.

The Bentley Rotary

Meanwhile, in the autumn of 1917, great hopes had been placed on the new Bentley rotary engine, of similar design to the B.R.1, but of a nominal 200 instead of 150 horse-power. In April 1917 the Air Board had ordered three B.R.2 experimental engines, and when the first was tested at the beginning of October it gave 234 horse-power and ran in a way which made the experts enthusiastic. A programme was thereupon drawn up which contemplated a monthly output of 1,500 Bentley engines by July 1918. At an Air Board meeting at which this programme was discussed, Major-General Brancker said that the new Bentley could be employed in every aeroplane in France, except bombers, and Sir William Weir called attention to the importance of this statement, which meant that a great move in the direction of standardization could be achieved. By the middle of October orders for the B.R.2 had already been placed for deliveries which would ultimately reach 900 engines per month.

Unhappily the ill luck which dogged those responsible for engine supply again supervened. The placing of large orders for the Bentley meant that rotary-type engines were being adopted on a scale incomparably larger than anything that had before been contemplated. As a fact, the B.R.2 duly fulfilled every expectation, and if a few weeks had passed without another design appearing on the test bench there is no doubt that the Air Board would have gone ahead with their Bentley programme with no effective misgivings. Two days after the Air Board had made their decision, however, the attention of the members was called to a new engine. This was the A.B.C. *Dragonfly* fixed radial,[1] and it was described as an extremely simple engine, both in design and for production purposes. It would be cheap to make, and it was considered that production could begin within three or four months. It was revealed

---

[1] A.B.C. Motors, Limited, of Walton-on-Thames, had been invited, in April 1917, to submit designs for an engine for the 1918 programme. They had, in August 1917, been given an order for three experimental engines to be called the *Dragonfly*.

in discussion that the *Dragonfly*, in a suitably designed aeroplane, would give 300 horse-power and a speed of 156 miles per hour at 15,000 feet, and that it was expected to reach this height in eight and a half minutes. The task of the Air Board was a difficult one. The members were rather in the position of a punter confronted with impressive news from different stables. They had backed the wrong engines before, and the consequences had been grave. There was a feeling that it was not right to concentrate great resources on the production of the Bentley if the A.B.C. *Dragonfly* was likely to prove a better engine. There were, however, differences of opinion about the possibilities of the *Dragonfly*. It was argued that the engine was an unknown quantity, and it was said that manufacturers had expressed doubts about its efficiency, and that some of them were of the opinion that the engine had been cut down too finely in the matter of weight.[1] The choice was between the B.R.2, which was not very different in design from its predecessor, the well-tried and successful B.R.1, and an untried engine, with novel experimental features. The members of the Board, mindful, no doubt, of the unhappy results of past orders on a large scale for untried engines, began cautiously. They decided not to disturb their contracts for the B.R.2, and to ask the Vickers Company, of Crayford, to produce the *Dragonfly* as a speculative measure. As time went on, however, faith in the *Dragonfly* grew apace, and large contracts for the engine were placed during 1918. Not only did the *Dragonfly* prove to be a failure from the production point of view, but it was also dangerous in the air. Output had barely begun at the time of the Armistice so that the failure had no effect on the war, but manufacture did absorb labour which might have been employed in making the Bentley or other tried engines, and, certainly, had the war continued into 1919, the failure of the A.B.C. *Dragonfly* would have put an effective brake, once again, upon the expansion of the air service.[2]

---

[1] 380 lb. for 300 horse-power.
[2] Orders for some 12,000 *Dragonfly* engines were placed. Experiments to make the engine a success were not abandoned as useless until 1921.

Rolls-Royce Output

In the 1918 air expansion programme Rolls-Royce engines were given a predominating place. The Rolls-Royce Company, in the early days of the war, made engines of Renault and Royal Aircraft Factory design, but the firm were encouraged by the Admiralty to develop a high-powered engine of their own, the contract which was given to them being of an indefinite kind, framed to avoid putting any unnecessary restriction in their way. The first experimental Rolls-Royce 250 horse-power 12-cylinder engine, afterwards called the *Eagle*, ran on the test bench in March 1915, and the first batch was delivered to the services in October of the same year. Meanwhile two other designs, for a 75 horse-power 6-cylinder engine (the *Hawk*) and for a 190 horse-power 12-cylinder (the *Falcon*), had been put in hand. The Rolls-Royce engines were a success from the beginning, and it was soon apparent that the air services would want all they could get. Output, however, could not easily be expanded because manufacture required much handwork of a highly skilled kind. Rolls-Royce were reluctant to hand over their designs to other makers, particularly to manufacturers in America, because they were jealous of their good name and they did not believe that other makers, without the Rolls-Royce experience, could produce an engine of the required standard.

In June 1916 the President of the Air Board had invited representatives of engine firms to a conference to discuss the possibilities of accelerating engine output by March 1917. Mr. Claud Johnson, who spoke for Rolls-Royce, put forward a lengthy memorandum which he had prepared in consultation with Mr. Royce. 'Although it is probable', he wrote, 'that for military reasons the urgent problem is 'the provision of the greatest number of aircraft by a certain

The engine gave great power for its weight, for a short time, and there are those who believe that it would have justified itself on the basis of a change of engine after each patrol. 'They did get it to the stage 'in which it was reliable for two and a half hours', says Mr. C. G. Grey, 'and it gave such colossal power for its weight . . ., that if we had got those 'engines through in quantities and had equipped a number of squadrons 'with them they would have paid for themselves on their results.'

'date, it is suggested that the greater task, namely, the 'attainment and retention for this Empire of the dominion 'of the air should not be interfered with.' He pointed out that forty-nine days after the opening of the war, his company had written a letter to a high official at the War Office suggesting that the war would be largely an affair of machine-guns, and expressing the willingness of the Rolls-Royce firm to make them. A reply had been received which said that 'only one firm makes these, viz. Vickers, 'and I am told here that their output, which is of course 'very large, is amply sufficient for all Army and Navy 'requirements.' Eight months later Rolls-Royce had been begged to start at once the manufacture of machine-guns. He quoted this instance as an example of a lack of vision which was, he suggested, affecting the air expansion programme. There was a new factory nearing completion at Derby, but because it could not be fitted out in time for production to be taken into account in the March 1917 programme, the authorities refused to allow Rolls-Royce to proceed with its equipment. He was himself firmly convinced that the air services would require not only the additional 500 engines per year which could be produced at the factory, but many more for 'building and keeping 'up-to-date an air fleet of a magnitude which it is difficult 'to conceive at present'.

The output of engines, Mr. Claud Johnson explained, was conditioned by (i) the number of workmen, (ii) the quantity of machine tools, and (iii) the supply of material, all of which were controlled by the Government. He went on to specify the extent to which the output of Rolls-Royce engines could be increased according to how much additional labour, &c., was allotted to his firm. He also pointed out difficulties he had had with sub-contractors. After they had entered into agreements with him they sometimes received orders for other work, to which they gave preference, from the Admiralty or the War Office, and the result was that the output of parts upon which Rolls-Royce depended was subject to incalculable delays. This state of affairs could be remedied, he said, only by an effective control over the sub-contractors. His practical suggestion was that the Air Board should select a number of big manufacturers who had produced successful aircraft engines of a desired type. These firms, say half a dozen, would constitute central factories for the manufacture and improvement of various types of engine. The remaining firms could then be told by the Air Board that they would be required to devote themselves to making parts for one of the selected engines. The sub-contractors could be allotted to the central factories according to geographical position, fitness, and to the output desired for the various types. Each central factory should be made responsible for the design and manufacture of jigs and tools required by the sub-contractors, and should also be responsible for ordering the material, including what was required by the sub-contractors. All engine-testing should be done at the central factory. The central factory idea thus advocated was adopted, but not until nearly two years had elapsed.[1]

Some of the points made by Mr. Claud Johnson may be quoted for their general interest:

'Most designers regard their production with the same 'pride as good mothers have for their babies. A depart-'ment which is engaged in design of a certain article 'cannot be fair critics of similar articles created by other 'designers.'

'So far as the present war is concerned, it would perhaps 'be unwise to rely on newly invented engines and wiser 'to choose the best existing engines, and concentrate on 'manufacturing them in the largest possible numbers.'

'Aero engines comprise such a large number of different 'parts that, instead of multiplying the number of establish-'ments producing completed engines (each of which would 'have to overcome the difficulties of learning the secrets 'of the manufacture of each part), it would be better that 'each sub-contractor should make a few parts in large 'numbers.'

'Existing contracts departments under the Treasury 'are controlled by men who have been reared in red tape, 'and by systems which make rapid achievement impossible.

[1] See p. 51.

'They have been surrounded by regulations until many
'of them have become as timid as chickens and as obstinate
'as mules.'

By February 1917 the position as it concerned the Rolls-
Royce output had become serious, and a minute signed by
Major-General Brancker stated that unless the shortage
of Rolls-Royce engines could be remedied it would become necessary to abandon the equipment of several
D.H.4 squadrons: it was indeed already difficult to maintain the three F.E.2d and D.H.4 Rolls-Royce squadrons
in the field. Of forty-two 250 horse-power Rolls-Royce
engines promised for January 1917, only sixteen had been
delivered, and no more than ten 190-horse-power engines
had come from the same makers in fulfilment of a promise
of thirty-two. There was some strong talk at an Air Board
meeting on the 12th of February and Lord Cowdray, the
President, said that if it was judged necessary the Ministry
of Munitions would not hesitate to put their own manager
into the firm.

One of the reasons why the production of Rolls-Royce
engines was delayed was an accumulation of repair work.
The parts were not interchangeable, so that spare gear
could not be supplied, and all disabled engines had to be
sent to the makers. The Rolls-Royce Company had been
alive to the possibilities of congestion which this necessity
brought in its train, and they had proposed to the Air
Board in the autumn of 1916 that they should be allowed
to build a special repair shop. The Board, however, had
withheld consent. In June 1917 Sir William Weir once
again brought the matter to the notice of the Board and
pressed for a favourable decision, but Mr. Martin pointed
out that an alternative scheme was under consideration
whereby the naval and military air services would become
responsible for their own repairs to Rolls-Royce engines,
and after listening to Mr. Martin it was decided not to
sanction the special repair factory which the firm was
anxious to construct. Within a short time, however, the
Board changed its mind. In July 1917 the members of the
Board, disquieted because of the serious delays in the repair of Rolls-Royce engines, and mindful that the sum of

money involved was small, at long last agreed to allow the firm to go ahead with the building of a special repair factory which would, it was estimated, be working within six months.

In the same month, however, the Board put a brake upon another ambition of the firm. A telegram was received from Mr. Claud Johnson in which it was stated that Rolls-Royce had the opportunity to acquire a factory capable of producing, between June 1918 and February 1919, 2,000 *Eagle* engines at a price of £2,400 per engine, and he asked whether the Air Board was interested. The Board decided that a reply should be sent thanking Mr. Johnson, but declining the proposal.

In August the accumulation of repair work at the Rolls-Royce factories was such that new production was falling alarmingly behind schedule. The Air Board decided that the only thing to be done was for the Government to take over the works of the Clement Talbot Company to help the Rolls-Royce Company with repairs. The scheme which finally emerged was one whereby the Clement Talbot firm were made responsible not only for the repair of Rolls-Royce engines, but also for manufacture of the *Falcon* type engine at the rate of twenty engines per week.[1] Some members of the Rolls-Royce staff were immediately transferred to Clement Talbot's, but many months elapsed before the scheme was working satisfactorily. By February 1919 the firm had repaired about 600 engines, but they had not been able to produce any, mainly because of delays in the acquisition of the necessary machine tools.

Negotiations for the establishment of a Rolls-Royce factory in America had been opened in the middle of 1916, but they had come to nothing chiefly because the British firm were unwilling to enter into any arrangement which gave them no more than a money interest in the American company. The Air Board, in June 1917, discussed the question of coercing the Rolls-Royce Company to come to a reasonable arrangement, but, happily, after some heated discussion, the idea of compulsion was

[1] The factory was made a national one under the management of the Clement Talbot Company, see pp. 53–7.

abandoned. In August 1917 Lord Northcliffe[1] sent a telegram from America urging that orders should be placed in that country for 2,000 or more Rolls-Royce engines, and as a result of this telegram negotiations were begun with the object of making the Pierce Arrow factory in America available for the manufacture of the engines. No agreement, however, could be reached, and as an alternative it was suggested that America might make finished parts which could be assembled by the Rolls-Royce Company in England. This proposal received the approval of the firm and of the Air Board in October 1917, and it was eventually agreed that the British Government should order in America, and pay for, 1,500 sets of *Eagle* engine parts for delivery before the end of 1918. As a result, contracts were placed in America for Rolls-Royce parts to a total amount of about $11 million,[2] and new buildings, for assembly of the parts, were added to the Rolls-Royce works at Derby.

Before, however, the final order to go ahead could be given the approval of the British Treasury had to be signified, but so many questions were raised that there ensued appreciable delay. One important result was that machine tools which had been earmarked for this work had to be released for other manufacturers, and when eventually the Treasury did approve the scheme no machine tools were immediately available, and there was more delay while they were being accumulated. Because of these avoidable setbacks, and because, also, of subsequent manufacturing disappointments in America, no Rolls-Royce engines made from American parts had been assembled at the time of the Armistice.

Meanwhile, in the middle of December 1917, when a programme for an increase of the Royal Flying Corps to

[1] In June 1917 a British War Mission under Lord Northcliffe was sent to the United States to co-ordinate and supervise the work of all British war missions. Lord Northcliffe remained in charge until November 1917. When, in February 1918, Lord Reading arrived in America as Ambassador Extraordinary, the British War Mission was subordinated to him.

[2] A large number of American firms undertook the work, notable among them being F. B. Stearns & Co., of Cleveland, Ohio; the Taft-Pierce Manufacturing Co., of Woonsocket; and the H. H. Franklin Manufacturing Co., of Syracuse.

a total of 240 service squadrons was drawn up, it was specified that approximately one-third of these squadrons would be equipped with Rolls-Royce or Liberty engines, one-third with the B.R.2, and the remainder with Hispano-Suiza, Sunbeam, or B.H.P. engines. Because of the great importance of the Rolls-Royce engine in the new programme, it was decided to form a separate section of the Engine Supply Branch to deal exclusively with Rolls-Royce production and, at the same time, a number of Government-controlled firms were placed at the disposal of the section to be used to assist the Rolls-Royce company. Among them were the Clement Talbot works, the National Shell Factory at Derby, and a part of the Dudley National Projectile Factory. The arrangement was that Rolls-Royce should be looked upon as the principal contractors with full responsibility for the placing of subcontracts. Thus the suggestions for a central factory put forward by Mr. Claud Johnson in June 1916 were belatedly adopted.

Although the production output necessary for the fulfilment of the final air expansion programme of the war had not by a long way been approached before the armistice, it should be set on record that 6,554[1] splendid engines manufactured by the Rolls-Royce Company were delivered to the services during the war, a greater number than was produced by any other British firm. In addition there was all the business of repair, including the supply of great quantities of spare parts. The works complement of the Rolls-Royce factories in October 1918 was 8,342 hands, with a dilution ratio of 39 per cent.[2]

The Liberty Engine

When America entered the war she was in a state of unreadiness and had to face and overcome many of the same sort of difficulties as Britain had had: furthermore, much of the supply of essential raw material was already

---

[1] 4,080 *Eagles* (250–375 h.p.); 1,969 *Falcons* (190–250 h.p.); 205 *Hawks* (75–90 h.p.); 200 Renault; and 100 R.A.F.

[2] This may be compared with the Siddeley Deasy Company, who were producing the B.H.P. with a dilution ratio of 28 per cent.

taken up by the Allies. We are here concerned with the Liberty engine, on the supply of which Britain came to place great reliance for her programme of bombing squadrons for the offensive against German industrial centres. The design of the Liberty engine was begun at the end of May 1917, and the first standardized eight-cylinder model was run on a bench test on the 23rd of July, and flown in an aeroplane on the 20th of August 1917. Representations by General Pershing on the 13th of July, and demands for increased horse-power, led to the abandonment, in December 1917, of the eight-cylinder type in favour of a twelve-cylinder model which had been designed about the same time. The first experimental twelve-cylinder Liberty had passed a fifty-hour bench test on the 25th of August 1917, and had been flown in a D.H.4 in October.[1] Then the trouble began. The schedules of production had continuously to be scaled down. On the 1st of November 1917, for example, it was estimated that fifty-five engines would be delivered in that month, that 280 would be forthcoming in December, and that the rate of output would expand rapidly until, in May 1918, a monthly figure of 4,800 would be reached. Total deliveries of Liberty engines were, according to the November 1917 schedule, to reach a figure of 9,420 by the end of May 1918. In fact, up to the 25th of May 1918, no more than 1,100 of the engines had been produced.

The causes of the disappointment were various, but they were not dissimilar from what we had ourselves experienced. A major difficulty was a lack of tools, jigs, gauges, &c., while another was the amount of modification made in the design. One manufacturer, for instance, reported that 1,022 changes had been made in the design between September 1917 and February 1918. Nevertheless, if one discounts the optimistic forecasts, tribute must be paid to the achievement which produced 1,100 complete engines in a little less than twelve months from the time the original was designed. The production of the

[1] Rated at 314 horse-power on the original bench test, the twelve-cylinder Liberty was raised to 395 horse-power in October, and to 450 horse-power in May 1918. This represented a weight of 1·8 lb. per horse-power.

Liberty may be compared with that of the British Sunbeam Arab which was subject to comparable modifications. This engine was designed in 1916, but by the end of 1918, after two years, only 1,195 had been delivered.

Before the end of 1917 the Allied Governments were asking for Liberty engines in large numbers. The United States Navy Department also wanted Libertys, as did the American Army Ordnance Bureau for installation in tanks. That is to say the demands were widespread. By January 1918 the number of Libertys asked for by Britain had reached a total of 3,000. According to the original arrangements these were to be delivered at the rate of 500 per month, beginning in January 1918. The first shipment of Liberty engines, however, was not made until March and they numbered ten. Twenty came in April, 175 in May, 225 in June, and 620 in July, and then deliveries stopped.

Meanwhile, the British department of aeronautical supplies was sending representations to America, urging the completion of the contracts for 3,000, and seeking acceptance for new contracts for an additional 2,500. In anticipation that America would be able to make deliveries more or less in accordance with the schedules, arrangements had been made in Britain for the construction of large numbers of D.H.9 bomber aeroplanes which were specially suitable for the Liberty. The failure to meet British requirements caused great anxiety, and many appeals were addressed to America, but it was as much as the Americans could do to meet their own clamant demands. The promise was made, however, that 750 Liberty engines would be delivered each month in the first half of 1919.[1]

National Aircraft Factories

When, in July 1917, the Government decided to double the air services, it seemed to the Ministry of Munitions

[1] In a memorandum on man-power dated the 25th of September 1918, Mr. Winston Churchill said that Mr. Ryan, the U.S. Under-Secretary for Aviation, had informed him that the American Admiralty claimed absolute priority for Liberty engines. 'A great part of these precious engines', he said, 'on which the whole of our air offensive bombing programme depends has, up to date, been swallowed up by American aviation.'

that, because the productive capacity of the existing manufacturing concerns had reached something like a limit, developments of a new kind must be initiated. Experience in other branches of the Ministry showed that the most satisfactory producers of munitions of war were those who worked on a large scale, and it was eventually decided, therefore, not to pursue further the policy by which aircraft contracts were distributed among a very large number of small producers, involving some tuition and much inspection for which not enough expert staff was available, but to concentrate instead on a few large units; in other words, to build and equip some National Aircraft Factories.

Something of the kind had already been started for aero engines. In January 1917 an arrangement had been made with the firm of Mitchell, Shaw & Company, Government contractors, by which Mr. Mitchell bought the works of the Goss Printing Company at Hayes in order that his firm might undertake a large contract for engine parts. The purchase and equipment money was provided by the Government, but a clause in the agreement stated that the factory would become the property of Mr. Mitchell at the end of the war on payment of a nominal sum of £100. The Mitchell, Shaw Company were to supply the engine parts at cost, and it was calculated that this arrangement would ensure a total saving of some £200,000, that is to say, about double the original cost of the factory to the Government. The arrangements entered into with Mr. Mitchell, however, were terminated in October 1917 when full control of the Hayes Factory passed to the Ministry of Munitions.

At the same time the Ministry decided to proceed with its intention to construct and equip other factories. Sanction was obtained to spend £1,500,000 on three factories, each of which was to have a productive capacity of 200 medium-sized aeroplanes each month. Sites were chosen at Waddon (Croydon), Aintree (Liverpool), and Richmond (London). The factories were to be managed by Holland, Hannen, & Cubitt, Ltd., by the Cunard Steam Ship Company, Ltd., and by the Sopwith Aviation Company respectively, but the last-named firm eventually decided to remain independent and the Richmond project was therefore abandoned and, instead, a partly built factory at Heaton Chapel (Manchester) was taken over for management by Crossley Motors, Ltd.

In November 1917 the policy was extended. The motor works of Clement Talbot, Ltd., were fully acquired for the repair of Rolls-Royce engines, those of the Motor Radiator Manufacturing Company at Greet and Sudbury for the manufacture and repair of radiators,[1] and the premises of a cinema firm (Bohemia, Limited) at Finchley for the production of balloons. In the summer of 1918 kiln works at Lancing and at Swindon were taken over for drying aeroplane timbers. Thus the Government during the war became directly responsible for a number of national aircraft undertakings which, for convenience, may be tabulated as shown on the following page.

The excursion of the Government into the aircraft industry must, so far as it concerns the manufacture of aeroplanes, be written down as a failure. Expenditure was often lavish, and the control exercised was lax, confused, and confusing. The figures for production expenditure which are given in the table err on the side of modesty. Materials were mostly supplied by or through the Ministry of Munitions. There were many difficulties about ascertaining, for accounting purposes, the prices of such materials and of services rendered. When the accounts came to be closed it was decided to enter all unpriced items as free issues, and in consequence the true expenditure, and the cost, therefore, of the aircraft produced at the national factories, can never be known. The reasons for the failure were many, a notable one being the inexperience of the factory managers in aircraft work. Other causes derived from the precipitate way in which the initial arrangements were made. A Ministry of Munitions document dealing with the national

[1] The National Radiator Factories, Greet and Sudbury, proved highly successful. They were already well established when taken over, and the factory management was allowed to recruit and train its own employees. The management also kept accounts in the same way as a private company and continued to tender for Government radiator contracts.

NATIONAL FACTORIES
(*Aeroplanes, Engines, Balloons, &c.*)
COSTS AND OUTPUT

Factory.	Production.	Expenditure to March 1919. (a) Capital Expenditure. (b) Production Expenditure.	Labour Strength (Nov. 1918) (a) Men (b) Women.	When Production began.	Total Output to March 1919.
National Aircraft Factory, Waddon. (N.A.F. 1.)	D.H.9 Airframes and spares. Interruptor gears	(a) £778,300 (b) £1,102,612	(a) 1,959 (b) 1,638	March 1918	241 Airframes. 3,000 Interruptor Gears.
National Aircraft Factory, Heaton Chapel. (N.A.F. 2.)	D.H.9 and D.H.10 Airframes.	(a) £544,500 (b) £1,198,512	(a) 1,600 (b) 940	January 1918	326 Airframes.
National Aircraft Factory, Aintree. (N.A.F. 3.)	Bristol Fighter Airframes.	(a) £692,900 (b) £627,697	(a) 1,580 (b) 1,054	March 1918	126 Airframes of which 36 had been delivered up to 1st October, 1918.
National Balloon Factory, Finchley	Cacquot and 'Nurse' balloons	(a) £35,000 (b) £36,075	(a) 27 (b) 270	April 1918	118 balloons.
National Aircraft-engine Factory, Ladbroke Grove, Kensington. (Clement Talbot, Ltd.)	Repair of Rolls-Royce engines.	(a) £141,700 (b) £535,415	(a) 1,623 (b) 371	January 1918	608 engines repaired (Approximate value, £723,520).
National Aircraft-engine Factory, Hayes.	Construction of parts for Clerget, Hispano, B.R.1. and B.R.2, &c., engines.	(a) £211,346 (b) £534,106	(a) 548 (b) 213	January 1917	Various engine parts and spares to the estimated value of £348,992.
National Radiator Factories, Greet and Sudbury.	Construction, salvage, and repair of aircraft radiators	(a) £64,600 (b) £30,760	(a) 366 (b) 314	January 1918	6,297 Radiators. 15,889 lb. Tubes. 384 Shutters.
National Timber-Drying Kilns, Swindon.	Drying Timber	(a) £6,510 (b) (Managed by G.W.R. Co.)		July 1918	9,800 cubic feet of timber.
Lancing.		(a) £6,500 (b) (Managed by L.B. and S.C. Rly. Co.).		July 1918	5,000 cubic feet of timber.

aircraft factories says that 'the clamour for increased out-'put made it impossible to wait for more economical 'methods'. The Ministry cut red tape to the minimum and made flexible arrangements with its agents with the sole object of hastening production. Unfortunately, the Ministry had no effective check upon what was being done, and the confused direction continued until July 1918, when a new branch, the National Aircraft Factories Department, was established in the Ministry, under Mr. Alexander Duckham, responsible for the discharge of all administrative duties connected with output, efficiency, finance, labour, &c.

Production at the factories began much later than had been anticipated, and once the production stage had been reached the rate of progress fell far short of what had been allowed for. It is possible that had the war continued into late 1919 or 1920 the national aircraft factories would have justified themselves in the matter of output, costs of production, and general efficiency. That is as may be. What is certain is that the factories were slow and costly to get started, and what is more than probable is that the same amount of money and energy expended upon the extension of existing private concerns would have brought quicker and larger returns. It would be unwise to make too much play with figures, which can be dangerous symbols, but it may be said that each aeroplane made by the Government in its own factories cost an unreasonably higher sum than similar aircraft bought from private manufacturers. Each Bristol Fighter produced at Aintree, for example, would appear to have cost at least £5,000, whereas the contemporary contract price, with private makers, was about £1,350. If, in addition, the amount expended on Aintree on capital account was apportioned between the aeroplanes produced in the factory the figure of £5,000 would be doubled.[1]

Man-power

The outbreak of war in 1914 had an immediate disturbing effect on industry. Enterprise gave way to

---

[1] The Controller of the National Aircraft Factories Department stated in May 1919: 'It is regretted it has been found impossible to supply a 'schedule showing the capital expenditure of the Factories. It does not 'appear to have been the business of any one Ministry Department or 'authority to keep complete records of the amounts so expended, and all 'efforts to obtain reliable figures have so far failed. . . .' Apparently it was possible, later, to arrive at figures for capital expenditure, and the figures, as finally decided, are incorporated in the table.

caution, many men lost their employment, and there was a widespread feeling that the working classes would suffer much distress. Local authorities were urged by Whitehall to expedite plans for public works, and patriotic organizations were formed to give assistance to the unemployed, but it came to be realized after a few months that the need for labour for munitions of war, and to replace men volunteering for service with the armed forces, would more than offset the displacement of workers in discontinued industries.

In the beginning it was not difficult for the armament firms to obtain such additional labour as they needed, but by the end of 1914 they were complaining that the supply of trained workers was nearing exhaustion. The main cause was the free enlistment of skilled men in the services. By the end of October 1914 the engineering trades, for example, had lost 12·2 per cent. of all pre-war workers: this figure had increased to 15·4 per cent. by February 1915, and to 19·5 per cent. by July of the same year.

Some attempt to control the recruitment of expert labour was made in December 1914, when the War Office instructed recruiting officers to reject men from armament and other specified trades. About the same time the problem was considered by the Committee of Imperial Defence, and early in January 1915 Mr. A. J. Balfour, one of the members of the committee, wrote a paper entitled the *Limits of Enlistment* in which he pointed out that the success of the appeal made by Lord Kitchener, the Secretary of State for War, for military recruits had raised the question whether there was 'any limit beyond which, *in* 'the interests of a country as a fighting power*, enlistment 'might not have to be carried'. Apart from the production of war materials, he said, no man essential for the railways, the mercantile marine, for collieries, or for the civil service, could be spared. In other words, there were many citizens physically fit to fight, and no doubt willing to fight, who must not be allowed to do so. So much was obvious, but were there other classes to which the same remarks might apply? For convenience he would omit all reference to anything outside immediate material

LORD KITCHENER OPPOSES

requirements, for example, to public order or to national credit. It was certain that we must make enormous imports of food and raw materials, and probably of munitions of war, and we must, therefore, make immense foreign payments, which could be done by borrowing abroad, by selling securities, or by exporting goods. The last named, he held, was the one practicable and desirable way, and it followed that all enlistments which would cripple industries producing for export, or for that part of the home market in which any diminution of output would have to be made good by importation, would weaken the general fighting efficiency of the nation.

It is probable that serious attention would have been given to the statesmanlike memorandum of Mr. Balfour, and that the Government would have set up some committee to deal with questions concerning the allocation of man-power, had it not been for the powerful opposition of Lord Kitchener, the Secretary of State for War. When the subject was debated by the Committee of Imperial Defence on the 27th of January 1915 Lord Kitchener said that the demands for labour to satisfy Mr. Balfour's propositions, or others like them, might prejudice recruiting more than at first sight seemed likely. He was opposed to any system which meant the rejection of a willing recruit. What Lord Kitchener said at this stage of the war carried so much weight that argument was apt to be dulled, and the result was that the meeting contented itself with passing a 'conclusion' as follows: 'Employers of labour 'and trade unions should be appealed to to co-operate as 'far as possible, having regard to the special conditions of 'particular trades, to secure the employment of men in-'eligible through age or other reasons to become recruits, 'and of women in place of eligible men who may be taken 'as recruits.'

The view of Lord Kitchener, that workers who volunteered should be helped to enlist, made it impossible for effective restrictions to be placed upon recruiting officers. Nor was any check supplied by outside influences. On the contrary, skilled workers who remained at their posts, especially those who appeared young and physically fit, were often insulted in the streets and they were also taunted in some sections of the press. The necessity for an enormous expansion in munitions production did not become known to the general public until long after it had been appreciated by the Government, and it was the responsibility of the Government, therefore, to give a lead.

In the early part of 1915 there was industrial unrest, mainly because an increase in the cost of living had not been balanced by higher wages. By this time the demand for many kinds of labour had outstripped the supply, and the workers were well aware of the strength of their bargaining position, but they were also responsive to the appeal to patriotism. It seemed, however, that employers and merchants were not being discouraged in any effective way from exploiting the needs of the nation, and as the workers became convinced that no real attempts would be made to curb employers generally, they apparently saw no reason why they themselves should not join in the scramble for a bigger share of the increasing national expenditure.

The problem of unrest was discussed, in March 1915, at a conference between representatives of the workers, led by Mr. Arthur Henderson, and members of the Government and of the service departments. An agreement was ultimately reached by which those who spoke for the trade unions undertook to advise their members against any stoppages of work in factories producing war materials, while those who spoke officially pledged the Government to limit the profits of all important firms engaged on war work. It was, however, one thing to draw up paper conclusions and another and different thing to make them effective. Three months passed before the pledge to limit profits was given legislative sanction and in the time of waiting many labour disputes arose.

In May 1915 came the revelation in *The Times* about the shortage of shells at the front which led to the reconstruction of the Government and to the setting up of the Ministry of Munitions, with Mr. Lloyd George as first minister: the Act creating the ministry received Royal assent on the 9th of June 1915. The Minister of Munitions enjoyed wide powers, defined, so far as they affected labour, by the statutes known collectively as the Munitions of War Acts, 1915–17. The main Act, which gave the Minister comprehensive powers to organize the skilled labour of the country for war production, became law on the 2nd of July 1915.

At a conference held at Boulogne in June 1915 the French military representatives had talked to Mr. Lloyd George of the need for heavy guns and howitzers. In the conditions of trench warfare, they had said, heavy pieces, of six-inch calibre or upwards, firing high explosive shells, were as necessary as field guns. To equal the combined German and Austrian output of ammunition the French calculated that the Allies would have to produce a total of $1\frac{3}{4}$ million shells per week.[1] British General Head-quarters in France endorsed the conclusions reached as a result of the Boulogne conference, and Sir John French, the commander-in-chief, accordingly submitted a statement showing what his requirements would be for heavy guns in support of a British force calculated to reach an ultimate strength of fifty divisions. When the statement was forwarded by the War Office to the Ministry of Munitions a request was appended that enough heavy guns should be included to equip an additional twenty divisions, and that an adequate allowance should be made also for wastage and for reserves. This decision to raise, equip, and maintain a total force of seventy divisions placed all problems of industrial organization and of man-power on an entirely new plane. The expanded programme for munitions output required the immediate release from military service of 100,000 skilled workers who must be replaced, and the creation of new divisions would call for a total recruitment of $1\frac{1}{2}$ million men.

It was the conviction of Mr. Lloyd George that compulsory military service had become necessary, but his Government colleagues were not ready to go so far. Their view was that compulsion must be deferred until the volunteer

[1] At this time the British weekly output of shells was at the rate of 125,000.

system should have been given a final trial. Accordingly, on the 11th of October 1915, Lord Derby was appointed Director of Recruiting, and he launched what was called the 'Derby scheme', by which voluntary recruitment entered upon its last phase. In a report to the Government in January 1916 Lord Derby revealed that 651,660 single men, not starred as essential war workers, had failed to attest a willingness to serve. The Prime Minister therefore took steps to redeem a pledge he had made on behalf of the Government that single men would be called to the colours before the married, and he introduced a Military Service Bill which came into force on the 11th of February 1916.

Meanwhile Mr. Lloyd George, having failed for the time being to carry his wider policy of compulsory national service, had directed his great energy towards making better use of the labour available under the existing system. This, in effect, meant an organized 'dilution' in face of strenuous opposition from the craft unions. For years the unions had been influenced by fears of a glut of goods which, in their view, must lead to unemployment and to a general lowering of the standard of living of the workers. As a result they had spun a web of rules and customs to restrict output. The number of apprentices was strictly limited, there was an insistence that only skilled men might work certain machines, overtime was regulated, the lines of demarcation between processes were sharply defined, and men or women who had not entered in the prescribed way for progressive initiation through the mysteries of a craft were shunned. These conventions and others like them were based upon the principle that demand could not be sustained if supply was allowed to expand without let. In other words, the so-called 'ca'canny' policy of the trade unions derived from a wish to secure for the workers some benefit from the increasing efficiency of the machine. The policy, however, whether or not it might be well conceived for times of peace, was one which put many brakes upon the national effort in time of war, more especially in a war of attrition which had to be prosecuted with every resource of the country. We cannot here follow the various measures taken by the Minister of Munitions, but it may be noted that, as was perhaps inevitable, resistance to the dilution of labour was protracted and sometimes bitter.

By the autumn of 1916 Britain had reached a serious stage in the development of her fighting strength. Each department of State had been concerned with its own special problems without much thought for the needs of other departments. The manufacture of munitions and military equipment, naval and mercantile construction, the output of coal, the working of docks and railways, the supply of gas and electricity, the various branches of the export trade, the production and distribution of food and other necessaries, competed, together with the services, for the manhood of the country. Grave difficulties had arisen between the Ministry of Munitions and the War Office about the exemption of munition workers from military service. The Government had been compelled in August 1916 to set up a Man-Power Distribution Board, with Mr. Austen Chamberlain as chairman, charged with the duty of settling questions which might arise between Government departments about the allocation or economic employment of man-power. In a report put forward by the Board in November 1916 it was stated that the army required an additional 314,000 men for general service by March 1917, of whom no more than 114,000 were likely to be obtained by medical re-examination, through expiry of temporary exemptions, or by attainment of military age. It would be necessary, therefore, to withdraw 200,000 exempted men from industry. The Board recommended that the Ministry of Munitions and the Admiralty[1] should cancel the protection badges issued to able-bodied workers of military age under twenty-six years old, but there were also a number of provisions in accordance with which no fully skilled man would be called to the colours, and by which no one firm could lose more than a proportion of its operatives.

---

[1] The Admiralty from the beginning had resisted interference with the labour at their disposal. It had been agreed, in October 1916, that inspection and dilution in shipyards, and in the shops of firms engaged on marine engine work, should be the entire responsibility of the Admiralty.

The recommendations of the Man-Power Board, which were strenuously opposed by the Ministry of Munitions, came at a moment when there was grave industrial unrest, fostered by a belief that the arrangements for allocating man-power were neither fair nor efficient. The centre of disquiet was Sheffield, where men in the engineering trades resented the way in which skilled workers were being drafted into the army at the same time as dilution by semi-skilled or unskilled men of apparently the same physical categories was in progress. The storm broke when a certain fitter had his badge taken away and had to join the army. The particular engineer shop stewards' committee, without the authority of its union, organized a strike which was to become effective if the fitter was not sent back. The strike was begun, in Sheffield and Rotherham, on the 16th of November, and it involved tens of thousands of skilled workers who were joined, in sympathy, by men at Barrow on the 18th. On that morning, however, the fitter, who had been released hurriedly from military service, showed himself in Sheffield at a meeting of the strikers and they thereupon decided to return to work.

The strike trained a searchlight on the proposal put forward by the Man-Power Board that workers under the age of twenty-six should have their exemption badges withdrawn. In the end the Government refused to approve the recommendation and accepted instead a suggestion made by the Minister of Munitions that his department should seek, by direct negotiation, a working agreement with the War Office. An agreement was arranged, but it had not long been in operation before the military authorities came to the conclusion that the army had no prospect of obtaining the men it required. On the 28th of November 1916 the military members of the Army Council were moved to address a memorandum to the Secretary of State for War with a request that it be laid before the Government. In the memorandum it was stated that it would be impossible, after April 1917, to keep the armies in the field up to strength unless immediate steps were taken to introduce some system by which recruitment ceased to be hedged about with over-riding conditions and restrictions. It was recommended that the military age should be raised to fifty-five years, and that all men up to that age should be employed on whatever services the Government deemed to be essential for the winning of the war. When the memorandum was considered by the War Committee, on the 20th of November, the adoption of compulsory national service was approved in principle for all men up to the age of sixty years, and a committee was appointed to work out the details. By the time, however, that the committee had completed its report, Mr. Asquith's Government had fallen. The new Coalition Ministry, under Mr. Lloyd George, decided not to proceed with the scheme, but to appoint instead a Director-General of National Service (Mr. Neville Chamberlain) and a Minister of Labour (Mr. John Hodge) to take over between them all the duties hitherto discharged by the Man-Power Board.

Mr. Neville Chamberlain soon found himself entangled in the same mesh of restrictions as had imprisoned those who had handled the problem before him. He formed the opinion that the only way to maintain the strength of the army was to take men from exempted industries, and when he presented his first report, in January 1917, he bluntly recommended that all men between the ages of eighteen and twenty-two should be made available for military service. This, the so-called 'clean-cut' proposal, was accepted by the Government, but they laid down a number of conditions which had the effect of making the cut anything but clean. So many types of workers were exempted as a result of the added conditions that Mr. Neville Chamberlain had to report, a fortnight later, that the number of men it would be possible to recruit outside the exempted classes would be negligible.

Meanwhile the Government had recorded a general decision that men fit for military service should be released for the army by the end of January as follows: 30,000 from agriculture, 20,000 from mining, 50,000 from munitions, and an unspecified number from the railways. On the 13th of February 1917 Dr. Addison, who had succeeded Mr. Montagu as Minister of Munitions in the new

Government, warned the War Cabinet that if the decision to take 50,000 men from work on munitions was made effective the fall in output would be serious. As a result, yet another Government committee was appointed to investigate the probable effect on industry if men should be taken for the army in accordance with the general decision set out above. The members of the committee were also instructed to confer with Sir Douglas Haig. In their report, presented at the end of March 1917, it was stated that to meet the full needs of the army it would be necessary to take 330,000 men from protected industries between April and July 1917. It was clear to the committee, however, that if this number was in fact withdrawn the supply of essential war material would be endangered. The committee therefore recommended that a reduced number of 250,000 should be released during the four months, that they should be obtained by quotas from various specified sources (not including shipbuilding), and that a general schedule of protected occupations should be drawn up to supersede all the existing arrangements covering exemption from military service.

The new scheme, which was approved by the War Cabinet, was launched on a troubled sea. An attempt was in progress at the time to dilute labour in commercial firms not specifically engaged on war work, an extension of the dilution of labour which skilled workers resented. The unrest reached a climax at the beginning of May 1917, when 200,000 workers came out on strike, mainly in Lancashire, and before the strike had been settled one and a half million working days had been lost. The general feeling among the workers might be described as one of watchful suspicion, and it is perhaps no matter for surprise that the task of drawing up acceptable schedules of protected occupations proved impossible. The trade unions, with which protracted negotiations were conducted, imposed a condition in accordance with which all diluted labour in any given area must be taken for military service before apprentices or skilled men engaged on munitions work could be recruited. As a result of this, and of other restrictions, no more than 18,000 men had been released from munitions industries by the end of July 1917, instead of 124,000 which the committee had estimated would represent the contribution of these industries towards the reduced number of 250,000 allotted to the army by the War Cabinet.[1]

Meanwhile the German campaign of unrestricted U-boat warfare, which had opened in February 1917, had introduced new claims on the country's man-power. In April Britain lost half a million tons of merchant shipping, and the outlook had become so clouded that energetic action was essential wherever it might be expected to help defeat the U-boat. A great programme of rapid mercantile construction was set on foot, and at the same time, in order to economize shipping space, timber felling on a large scale was undertaken throughout Britain, and an agricultural programme was adopted which aimed to make the nation and the army less dependent upon imported food supplies. There were various other measures, and all of them together were responsible for large and imperative drains on man-power.

At the beginning of August 1917 the Government were impelled to set up a new Man-Power Committee, consisting of Lord Milner, Lieutenant-General J. C. Smuts, and Mr. G. N. Barnes, with full authority to settle, on behalf of the War Cabinet, in consultation with the departments concerned, all questions of recruitment and of man-power. The committee quickly decided that the recruiting organization should be embodied as part of the National Service Department, which, in consequence, was raised to the status of a Ministry. The new Ministry was to review the whole field of man-power; to arrange for the transfer of workers from less important to more urgent national work; to propose lists of reserved occupations; to obtain men for the armed forces within the limits laid down by the Government and to determine their physical fitness; and was to arrange for the provision

---

[1] A report made to the War Cabinet in August 1917 stated that recruits coming forward during the year had been far below the estimated numbers and were insufficient to replace the wastage involved in offensive operations.

of labour, male and female, to take the place, wherever necessary, of men recruited for the services.

In August 1917, also, a committee of the Munitions Council[1] considered the munitions programme for 1918. It was estimated that this would absorb the services of about 25,000 additional skilled men, of 58,000 unskilled men, and of 70,000 women. The greatest new demand would be for the aircraft industry, which would want 10,000 of the skilled men, 40,000 of the unskilled, and 50,000 of the women. It might have been possible for the Ministry of Munitions to make arrangements to supply the desired number of skilled workers without serious dislocation if there had not existed priority claims for labour by the two service departments. The new ship-building programme brought into being by the unrestricted U-boat campaign required an additional 12,500 skilled and 67,500 unskilled hands, and the Board of Admiralty stood firm on the position that they could supply none of this labour by way of transfers from other Admiralty work. The Government had consequently instructed the Ministry of Munitions to release men of experience in marine engineering, and this ruling meant in effect that the Ministry would be responsible for supplying all the skilled men required by the Admiralty. The Ministry was also under an obligation to supply experienced workers to the War Office for service as artificers in technical units. The arrangement was that 6,000 of these men should be released by the end of November 1917, and it seemed certain that the demand for artificers would be of an expanding kind. The Ministry of Munitions could see no way to obtain the men, especially the skilled workers, for the 1918 munitions production programme unless it was relieved of its obligations towards the Admiralty and the War Office. In the result the obligations of the Ministry remained, and the tussle for man-power con-

---

[1] When Mr. Winston Churchill succeeded Dr. Addison as Minister of Munitions one of his first acts was to reorganize the administration into ten large units, each in charge of a head directly responsible to the Minister. Each head was a member of a standing Munitions Council, organized on the lines of the Board of Admiralty or Army Council.

tinued through the winter until, in March 1918, as shall be told, the whole problem was changed as a result of the German military offensive on the Western front.

Enough has been said to show that by the middle of 1917 the depletion of British man-power had reached a point when it had become difficult to find the labour for the existing programme of aircraft expansion. The reader is now in a position to appreciate the major implications of the Government decision of July 1917 to double the air services. In particular, the low general priorities accorded the aircraft industries had a repeatedly hampering effect. For example, dilution of labour led to an expanding demand for jigs and gauges, but in June 1917 the Ministry of Munitions was unable to produce a mere ninety-two tool makers urgently required for aircraft work. This scarcity of all-important tool makers continued, and in September, to meet outstanding demands for 203 such workers, the best endeavours of the Ministry could provide only the odd three.

It was calculated by the Royal Flying Corps that the July programme which doubled the air services would require, apart altogether from the industrial side of the problem, about 17,000 pilots and 5,500 observers, who must be trained before the end of 1918, and an additional 61,000 mechanics. Furthermore, it was imperative that work on thirty-five new aerodromes, each to accommodate three or four squadrons, should be started without delay. 'I feel quite reasonably confident', wrote the Director of Recruiting in the middle of July 1917, 'that we will be 'able to find all the men required for the Royal Flying 'Corps, but it is quite certain that this large expansion 'of the Flying Corps personnel will affect infantry drafts, 'and further it will only be possible to meet the R.F.C. 'requirements for skilled men if all other demands for men 'of the same trades are kept within the lowest possible 'limits, and if steps are taken to see that the men of these 'trades who go to other Corps are really required at their 'trade and are really employed in such a way that their full 'skill is utilized.'

One method adopted to obtain some of the men required was the appointment by the War Office in July of a Dilution Officer whose duty was to examine the air service stations at home and to report upon possible savings of skilled labour. It was soon apparent, however, that an investigation of the kind needed was too much for the judgement and responsibility of one officer, and in the following month he was replaced by a board consisting of a president, an assistant, a medical officer, and a trade dilution officer. The Board, which visited seventy air stations, submitted three interim reports, and a final report dated the 16th of November. In the squadrons at home the Board found that the engine fitters were already diluted to a point which was dangerous. 'The fact must 'be remembered', the final report said, 'that the mistakes 'made by these men through lack of skill result in the 'destruction of valuable machines, and probably also the 'loss of pilot and observer. From the dilution point of 'view it should be realized that the work carried out by 'the Royal Flying Corps cannot be compared with any 'other technical branch of the army, as in the latter cases 'it is almost always possible to retrieve the work of bad 'workmanship as the material is on the ground. In the 'case of an aeroplane in nearly every instance failure 'means destruction.' The members of the Board were impressed by the degree in which the expansion of the air services depended upon the recruitment of women. They calculated that about 30,000 women must be provided at home, and they said that the sooner the women were recruited and trained the better because the demand for men would thereby be lessened. The Board had been made aware that lack of suitable accommodation was retarding the employment of women, and they urged that this matter should receive immediate attention.

Women in the Services

In view of the importance attached to the recruitment of women it will be of interest to review briefly the story of their association with the armed forces. In the first year of the war women were mainly employed as nurses,

WOMEN IN THE SERVICES

although there were also a number of female shorthand typists. In 1915, owing to the inexperience of recruits and to a shortage of trained cooks, food, though good and plentiful, was often badly prepared and served, and this led the Marchioness of Londonderry to suggest in July that a Women's Legion should be created to help the army with its cooking and cleaning. The War Office agreed, as an experiment, to substitute women for men in convalescent camps, where cooking and similar domestic services were provided by soldiers. The first party of women recruits was taken by Miss L. C. Barker to the Dartford convalescent camp in August 1915, and their value was proved in a way which led to an early extension of the arrangement, first to other convalescent camps and then, in the spring of 1916, to general military camps at home. In 1916 women were also employed to drive service motor transport, and in February 1917 this activity received formal sanction when the War Office laid down the conditions of service for women drivers in the Royal Flying Corps and in the Army Service Corps.

In January 1917 a report was submitted to the War Office by an officer who had examined the possibilities of economizing man-power with the armies in France, urging that women should be substituted for men in every suitable occupation outside the front-line fighting area. Those soldiers released who were not of first-class physical fitness might be sent back to England to take the place of men of a higher physical category who would thereby be made available for front-line service. The report stated in particular that in the aircraft depots in France there appeared to be great scope for the replacement of category 'A' men by women. After much discussion an Army Council Instruction was signed in March 1917 setting out the terms and conditions of service for women, in substitution for men, in specified occupations along the lines of communication, and at the bases, in France.[1]

---

[1] The classes of employment specified were: (*a*) clerical, typist, shorthand typist; (*b*) cooks, waitresses, and domestic staff; (*c*) motor transport service; (*d*) store-keepers, checkers, and unskilled labour; (*e*) telephone and postal service, and (*f*) miscellaneous services.

The next step was taken on the 7th of July 1917, when an Army Council Instruction expounded a scheme for the organization of a Women's Army Auxiliary Corps (W.A.A.C.). Enrolment was to be for one year, or for the duration of the war, whichever proved the longer period, and recruits were required to say whether they would be willing to serve overseas. Women candidates for employment in the Royal Flying Corps, except photographers, were called upon to produce certificates of efficiency in their class. If they could not produce certificates, but were otherwise considered to be generally suitable, they were invited to undergo a course of instruction, at their own expense, with a firm approved by the War Office. The officer class in the corps was divided into controllers, who corresponded to staff officers, and into administrators, who might be likened to regimental officers. Forewomen and assistant forewomen approximated to non-commissioned officers.[1]

The process of absorbing women into the Royal Flying Corps proved to be slow, partly because there was a dearth of acceptable recruits, and partly because little of the existing accommodation was considered suitable. The latter difficulty, which was general, led, in December 1917, to a reorganization of the W.A.A.C. into two branches, (*a*) mobile and (*b*) immobile. The former included all women who were liable to be moved as required for service anywhere at home or overseas, while the latter was made up of women locally employed who could continue to live at home. Further regulations signed in June 1918 changed the name of the corps to that of Queen Mary's Army Auxiliary Corps (Q.M.A.A.C.).

Meanwhile, in September 1917, on account of the critical nature of the man-power situation, it had been judged necessary to extend the employment of women, wherever possible, to the navy. Reports from home stations, including those of the Royal Naval Air Service, were called for, and towards the end of the year Dame Katherine Furse, the commandant of the Voluntary Aid Detachment

---

[1] Mrs. Chalmers Watson, M.D., was appointed Chief Controller, and Mrs. H. C. I. Gwynne-Vaughan, Chief Controller in France.

(V.A.D.) Corps, was appointed to organize a corps of women for naval work. On the 4th of February 1918 Admiralty Weekly Orders were issued giving the regulations for the formation of a service to be known as the Women's Royal Naval Service (W.R.N.S., or, colloquially, 'Wrens'): Dame Katherine Furse was appointed director. Like its sister military service the W.R.N.S. was organized as two branches, mobile and immobile.

When the Royal Air Force was formed on the 1st of April 1918 it became necessary to constitute a separate corps for women—the Women's Royal Air Force—to which those already employed with the air arm in the W.A.A.C., the W.R.N.S., or the Women's Legion,[1] might transfer at their will. The new service began with 67 officers and 6,738 other ranks transferred from the W.A.A.C., with 46 officers and 2,821 ratings from the W.R.N.S., and with 496 drivers from the Women's Legion. Lady Gertrude Crawford was appointed first Chief Superintendent of the Women's Royal Air Force, and was succeeded in May by the Honourable Violet Douglas-Pennant with the title of Commandant. This officer had to deal with the multitudinous difficulties, many of them of a novel kind, attending the rapid organization of a new service. She was succeeded, in September 1918, by Mrs. H. C. I. Gwynne-Vaughan who, at the time of the Armistice, had under her control about 25,000 women. No members of the Women's Royal Air Force served overseas while the war was still in progress. A number of women saw service, towards the end of the war, in the aircraft engine repair shops at Rouen, but they had been posted as members of the Women's Army Auxiliary Corps and they were allowed to continue without transfer to the new service. In October 1918 arrangements were made for a contingent of the Women's Royal Air Force to join the Independent Force in France for clerical, domestic, and stores duties, but hostilities ended before the women could leave. Their chance came, however, in the spring of 1919 when they were called upon to take the place of men anxious to be

---

[1] Women transport drivers attached to home Royal Flying Corps units were enrolled as members of the Women's Legion.

demobilized. The first draft went overseas, to France, in March 1919, and a second contingent joined the army of occupation at Cologne in the following month. Their arrival in Germany caused interest and speculation. Under the leadership of Mrs. Gwynne-Vaughan, however, the women had acquired a high sense of discipline and a pride of service, and their presence and efficiency soon came to be taken for granted. Many of the women took so kindly to service life that they hoped a place might be found for them in the permanent establishment in the Royal Air Force. The drastic reduction of the force after the war, however, left no room for them, and the disbandment of the Women's Royal Air Force had been completed by the end of 1920.[1]

Royal Air Force Nursing Service

It will be appropriate to make brief reference here to the Royal Air Force Nursing Service which was formed in June 1918. The staff served at first in the sick quarters at various stations in England and Scotland and at convalescent centres. Towards the end of 1918 Royal Air Force nurses replaced Army nurses in the hospitals at Blandford and at Hampstead. In 1919 and again in 1920 the question of amalgamating the Royal Air Force Nursing Service with the Army Nursing Service was considered as an economy measure, but the decision was that no saving would result, and the service therefore retained its identity. In January 1921 it was established as a permanent branch of the Royal Air Force, and in June 1923 became Princess Mary's Royal Air Force Nursing Service.

Man-Power Committee

It has been told how a committee, afterwards called the War Priorities Committee, was set up in September 1917, when investigations by Lieutenant-General J. C. Smuts

---

[1] An account of the Women's Royal Air Force, and of the life of those who served in it, is contained in *Women of the Royal Air Force*, by A. Chauncey. Life in the Immobile Branch is recounted in *Eight Months with the Women's Royal Air Force*, by Gertrude A. George. See also an appendix—'The Women's Royal Air Force'—contributed by Dame Helen Gwynne-Vaughan to *Sir Sefton Brancker*, by Norman Macmillan.

revealed that the approved expansion of the air services could not be fulfilled.[1] At its second meeting, held on the 28th of September 1917, the committee approved the following recommendations:
  (i) that the reduced airship programme, and the aeroplane programme of 200 squadrons to be completed by the end of 1918, should have priority after the shipbuilding,[2] and
  (ii) that the completion of the two aircraft programmes was sufficiently important to justify a reduction in the production of other munitions, e.g. shells and rails.

The committee proceeded to act in accordance with these recommendations, but as the year neared its end and the casualties in the heavy fighting on the Western front continued to mount, it was clear to the Government that the man-power question had reached a state of crisis, and that a final careful stock must be taken of the human resources of the country and of their economic employment. Accordingly a new Man-Power Committee was appointed with the Prime Minister as chairman. The committee worked rapidly and a draft report was ready by the middle of December, 1917. The report was amended in minor particulars from time to time until the German offensive in France in the spring of 1918 brought about such a drastic change in the whole position that the report was shelved. Meanwhile, however, many of its recommendations had been put into force. The view taken by the members of the committee was that 'the enemy 'in 1918 will be so strong on the Western and Italian 'fronts as to preclude any reasonable probability of a 'decision on those fronts in favour of the Allies. The 'military advisers of the Allied Governments have recom- 'mended a defensive policy on the Western front, at any 'rate for the first half of 1918. In these circumstances it is

---

[1] See Chapter I, p. 17.
[2] It is of interest that the German authorities, to ensure fulfilment of their air expansion programme drawn up in June 1917 (called the *American Programme*), gave priority to aircraft after the submarine service. (See Vol. IV, pp. 273–5.)

'evident that the staying power of the Allies must be safe-
'guarded until such a time as the increase in the American
'forces restores the balance of superiority decisively in their
'favour. The safeguarding of staying power involves not
'only the maintenance of the armies, but of the nations,
'and in both respects our Allies are becoming increasingly
'dependent upon ourselves. This country has to bear the
'principal burden of maintaining the sea-power of the
'Allies; for dealing with the enemy's submarines; for ship-
'building; for transport of food and supplies of all kinds for
'the peoples, armies, and munition factories; for the supply
'of coal and many kinds of ordnance and munitions; and in
'a great degree for the financial support of all our Allies.
'Even the transport of American troops depends ultimately
'to a considerable extent on maintenance of our ship-
'ping. . . .'

The main recommendation of the committee stated:

'The following principles should be adopted in the
'distribution of our man-power, whatever the number
'of men available may be:
 '(a) the fighting personnel requirements of the Royal
    'Navy and of the Air Services should have absolute
    'priority over all other services;
 '(b) after the fighting personnel requirements of the
    'Royal Navy and Air Services, shipbuilding should
    'have priority over all other demands, and, after
    'shipbuilding, the construction of aeroplanes and
    'tanks;
 '(c) food production, timber felling, and the provision
    'of food storage accommodation, since their object
    'is to set free shipping, must be regarded in the
    'same category as shipbuilding;
 '(d) the priority accorded to shipbuilding, food produc-
    'tion, and timber felling is subject to the general
    'supervision of the Minister of National Service for
    'the prevention of the waste of labour.'

The committee also made twenty-seven other recommendations which need not be considered here.

The priorities accorded to aircraft and personnel from
the end of 1917 made easier the way of expansion.

In November 1917 Major-General J. M. Salmond, the director-general of military aeronautics, estimated the number of other ranks still required to complete the sanctioned programme for 200 service squadrons. His table showed:

	Men.	Women.
Total establishment	158,250	20,900
Existing strength	90,250	3,045
Deficiency	68,000	17,855

About the same time, Sir Douglas Haig, in order that timely provision might be made for future developments in the air, put forward his programme of requirements up to the summer of 1919. For France (and Italy) he recommended the provision of a total of 113 squadrons, exclusive of the sixty-six squadrons which it was proposed should be employed for long-distance bombing operations. The War Office suggested that the total number of service squadrons, including twenty-one shown as to 'meet eventualities', should be raised to 240. The approximate increase in personnel for the additional forty squadrons, maintenance, and training equivalents, was 2,360 officers, 14,000 men, and 4,500 women, excluding allowance for wastage.

There followed a vigorous comb-out in the army, but because the numbers of men of technical bent or training so obtainable were few, help was sought from General J. J. Pershing, the American Commander-in-Chief. It was arranged that some 15,000 American mechanics should be sent direct from the United States to England for service with Royal Flying Corps units. The trained British personnel thus released would be made available for service squadrons, whether formed or forming. While this arrangement was of immense help to the British, it also worked to the advantage of America, whose mechanics were enabled to complete their training under the most favourable conditions and with service-type aircraft. America agreed to maintain the strength of the attached mechanics, passing those who had gained full training to American air units in France, and replacing them by mechanics untrained in aeronautics.¹ This American help reduced the estimated requirements for British mechanics to 67,000 to be spread over fourteen months. Of this number 18,400 were wanted by the end of February 1918, and so well did the endeavours to procure the men succeed with the advantage of priority that the number was actually exceeded by nearly 6,000.

America and the Air War

When America entered the war in April 1917 a three-year air programme was drawn up which was considered at the time to be ambitious. In the programme, allowance was made for a total production of 3,700 aircraft in 1918, a number thought to be the maximum attainable. The whole American outlook, however, was changed as a result of a telegram received in Washington on the 26th of May 1917 from M. Ribot, the French Premier, as follows:

'It is desired that in order to co-operate with the French 'Aeronautics, the American Government should adopt the 'following programme: the formation of a flying corps of '4,500 airplanes—personnel and material included—to be 'sent to the French front during the campaign of 1918. 'The total number of pilots, including reserve, should be 'of 5,000 and 50,000 mechanicians. Two thousand planes 'should be constructed each month, as well as 4,000 engines, 'by the American factories. That is to say, that during the 'six first months of 1918, 16,500 planes (of the last type) 'and 30,000 engines will have to be built. The French 'Government is anxious to know if the American Government 'ment accepts this proposition, which would allow the 'Allies to win the supremacy of the air.'²

The American authorities, with characteristic generosity of outlook, translated the telegram into a detailed programme of air development for which an appropriation of 640 million dollars was taken. By the end of 1917, however, the Americans had become anxious about the progress

---

[1] There was some delay in carrying out the arrangements. The 15,000 should have been supplied by the 1st of March 1918, but on that date no more than 3,931 had arrived. Within a month, however, the number had grown to 10,819 and to 16,224 by the 1st of September 1918. America also supplied military labour for work on aerodromes and buildings.

[2] See *The American Air Service*, p. 66, by Captain Arthur Sweetser.

being made, and it even appeared doubtful whether they would be in a position to provide the squadrons required to ensure aircraft co-operation with the estimated number of American troops which would be at the front in the summer of 1918. The British authorities were willing at all times to place at the free disposal of America such lessons as they had themselves learned as a result of their long and sometimes painful experience in connexion with the development of their own air-expansion programmes. They were glad, therefore, to have an opportunity, in the spring of 1918, to send to America a British aviation mission headed by Major-General W. S. Brancker. As a result of the mission it was arranged that a number of British flying and technical officers should be placed at the disposal of the American authorities in connexion with the fulfilment of their aviation programme. Another result was that the Production Department in America sent two representatives to Europe to confer with General Pershing. These contacts with realities led to a modified air programme, which was duly approved. Whereas the original programme allowed for 266 service squadrons, exclusive of long-range bombers, the new one, which it was hoped would be completed by June 1919, aimed at an inclusive total of 202 service squadrons.

The story of the intervention of America in the war contains some lessons of interest. We are not here concerned with the moral influence of her entry, admittedly incalculable, nor with the naval and military aspects of the help she gave, which were of very great importance, but only with a strictly limited effect, that upon the British air services. The Central Powers, owing to the blockade, had been unable to look upon America as a source of supply, whereas the Allies, because of their command of the sea, had been able to buy freely. So far as concerns supply, therefore, it may be said that America was on the side of the Allies from the beginning. When, however, she began to organize forces of her own, subsequent to her declaration of war, she could do so only at the expense of the Allies in the early stages, even though great general benefits would ultimately accrue from American organization on a national scale.

What America did, in effect, was to step suddenly into all markets equipped with absolute priorities. The supply of timber for British aeroplanes was immediately affected. The woods used were silver spruce, and what might be called spruce substitutes, namely, walnut, ash, poplar, mahogany, and other hardwoods: except ash and poplar, all this timber was imported. When war broke out in 1914 there were good supplies of suitable timber in store in this country, but by October 1916 a shortage was foreseen. It had then been agreed that the Admiralty should assume responsibility for buying all the timber required by Great Britain from abroad and for inspecting and shipping it, an arrangement which endured until October 1917.

Of all the woods, silver spruce, light, strong, and resilient, which grew abundantly in the forests of Oregon and Washington, proved the most suitable for aircraft. The Allied Governments, competing against one another in the American market, through lumber brokers, had sent the price of spruce soaring, but their demands had led to the establishment of an industry of a kind, and supplies had been forthcoming in gradually expanding quantities. As soon as America entered the war she realized that, with the added competition for silver spruce necessary for the satisfaction of her own vast air programme, the industry could not be expected to develop at the speed and on the scale required without State help. The measures taken to control and to increase production were many,[1] but the difficulties which had to be overcome were formidable, and, as demand kept expanding, supplies were always lagging behind, with the result that not much could be spared for the Allies.

By October 1917 the position had become critical so far as the British aeronautical industry was concerned. Nothing crossed the Atlantic in this month in satisfaction of outstanding Admiralty contracts and nothing again in November. The first shipment of general timber allocated to Britain by the American Aircraft Construction Board arrived in December, but it contained only ten standards

[1] See *The American Air Service* (Sweetser), ch. ix.

of silver spruce. During the four months ending the 5th of January 1918 no more than 150 standards of silver spruce and substitutes had arrived against British contracts for more than 40,000 standards.

The existing stocks of suitable timber in Britain had to be allocated with the most scrupulous attention, and wood which was below specification had sometimes to be used. The position continued to be serious through the early months of 1918, and it was aggravated by the German offensive on the Western front. This led to an acceleration in the rate of flow of American troops across the Atlantic, with the result that no shipping could be spared for the transport of timber supplies. When timber shipments on a modest scale were resumed in May 1918 it was found that some of the wood was unsuitable for aircraft construction. It was not until the autumn of 1918 that the American authorities were being fully rewarded for the energy they had expended in the organization of the timber industry, and it then became possible to allot adequate shipments to Europe, but by that time Britain, which had evolved a suitable built-up spar and had also satisfactorily developed other sources of supply, had become less dependent upon American timber. The silver spruce failure was certainly serious, but the effect upon the output of British aircraft was less than might have been because that output, as we have seen, was mainly limited by the set-back in the production of engines.

In a report which he submitted to the War Cabinet in September 1918 Lord Weir pointed out that America could not be expected to provide any early help with regard to long-distance bombing. He explained that the Americans had only twenty-four mixed squadrons, for which the aeroplanes had mostly been supplied from European sources.[1] If the American army engaged in an offensive on the Western front it must be expected that the American air service, which would be called upon to make good inevitable casualties, would continue to be weak for some time.

[1] The American Expeditionary Force was supplied with about 320 British aeroplanes.

Effect of the German 1918 Offensive

On the 23rd of March 1918, two days after the German attack was launched against the British Third and Fifth Armies in France, the War Cabinet instructed the Minister of National Service to put forward immediate proposals for an increase of man-power for military purposes, and, as a result, a military service bill was prepared and introduced in Parliament by the Prime Minister on the 9th of April. It fixed the age limits for military service between 18 and 50, and empowered the Government to cancel, by proclamation, certificates of exemption other than those granted on occupational grounds. The Bill was passed through Parliament in seven days and received Royal Assent on the 18th of April. Two days later the Government issued a proclamation which said that, except certain special classes, no Grade I men aged 19 and 20 were to be retained after the 17th of May, and aged 21 to 23 after the 17th of June, by firms working for the Admiralty, Ministry of Munitions, or for the War Office. On the other hand, discretionary powers about the retention of men was to remain with the Admiralty and the Ministry of Munitions subject to review by a committee, on which the department interested in a particular case was to be represented. The firms were notified of the new procedure on the 25th of April and were told that every effort must be made to avoid loss of output, by rearrangement of works, by substitution, or by such other methods as were open to them. If certain men were considered indispensable claims could be submitted for their retention.

The Ministry of Munitions, as a result, was called upon to release men for the army, but it had also, at the same time, to maintain military supplies, or even in some instances to increase them. That this could not be done was soon apparent. On the 12th of July Mr. Winston Churchill laid a memorandum before the War Cabinet in which he directed attention to the serious consequences which must result from the continued drain of skilled men from munitions production. He pointed out that since the beginning

THE GERMAN OFFENSIVE

of the year 100,000 men, nearly all of them skilled, had had to be released by the Ministry of Munitions, and he pleaded that, with the changed conditions on the Western front, the time had come when the whole policy should be reconsidered. The American forces in Europe had expanded to a total of one million men, and it was clear that the real solution of the man-power problem lay in the speedy transportation to France of the great numbers which had been recruited in America, in their training and organization on the battle front, and in their equipment and supply. The first million who had come over, he said, had been equipped almost entirely by Britain and France. 'But for the fact', he said, 'that we had been able to supply 'them with artillery, machine-guns, rifles, trench mortars, '&c., and feed them with munitions of all kinds, no use in 'the present crisis could have been made of this first 'million'. The reports which he had received from America indicated that the American Army in France would be almost wholly dependent during 1918 on British and French artillery production. In addition to what was needed for the Americans, and to meet requests for increased munitions for the British Expeditionary Force, there were, said Mr. Churchill, immense demands connected with the expansion of the Air Force. 'The aero- 'plane engine programme had in the last two months fallen 'off very seriously indeed, and the extremely good situation 'which I was able to report to the Cabinet at the beginning 'of the year no longer holds good.[1] Last week the produc- 'tion was only 688 against an estimate of 1,132. In one 'firm making crankshafts for an urgently needed type of 'aeroplane engine, they have already lost seven out of eight 'highly skilled mechanics on one essential stage of manu- 'facture. The consequent loss of crankshafts involved the 'loss of twenty-five aeroplanes per week. . . . Once the 'emergency of this summer has been surmounted, we

---

[1] Mr. Churchill had told the War Cabinet at the beginning of March that deliveries, as promised, led him to the conclusion that by the end of June 1918 there would be a large stock of aeronautical material without the requisite man-power to handle it. The deliveries, however, as we know, fell far short of expectations.

'ought not to rupture our munitions supply, particularly
'our supply of modern vital appliances, for the sake of
'adding 20,000 men or less to our army of over three
million....'

A month later Lord Weir stated in a memorandum:
'The engine position during the last three months has
'been bad, and I am informed by Mr. Churchill, and I
'fully believe it myself, that the "comb-out" in March is
'largely responsible for disarranging the growth of out-
'put which was proceeding fairly satisfactorily.' At the
time this memorandum was written there were 4,200
aeroplanes in store with no engines to go into them.

The Ministry of Munitions did much in the way of
training workers. An instruction scheme had been started
at technical schools at the end of 1915, but in September
1916 the need for something more was felt and factories
were acquired to serve as schools where men could be
given training, on modern machines, in the particular
operations they would be required to do. To meet the
heavy demands for semi-skilled operatives in 1917 for
aeronautical work the Ministry of Munitions greatly extended its training facilities. Additional factories, with
their full complement of tools, were acquired, and where
no suitable factories could be had new buildings were
erected and equipped. The output of semi-skilled workers
from the Ministry's training factories increased as the war
progressed and was of some help in reconciling contractors
to dilution of labour within their works.[1]

In January 1917, in twenty-eight representative aircraft
firms, there was a 19·6 percentage of dilution by women.
By the middle of June the percentage, for women and
boys, was 37·5, and by December 1917, 44 per cent. It
would seem that this figure more or less marked a limit
for the time being because the comparable dilution figure
at the time of the Armistice was 46 per cent.

The following table sets out particulars of the total

---

[1] Up to the end of the war the training sections of the Ministry of Munitions had supplied 14,834 hands for the aircraft industry.

labour employed in the aircraft industry in Britain in 1916, 1917, and 1918:

	Date.	No. of firms.	Per cent. of dilution.	Men.	Women.	Boys.	Total.
Aug.	1916	491	31·7	40,974	12,615	6,484	60,073
Nov.	1917	771	40·1	104,102	52,734	17,133	173,969
Oct.	1918	1,529	46·1	187,526	126,544	33,042	347,112

Propaganda among the Workers

There were attempts during the war, which deserve mention for their general interest, to associate the workers with the operations at the front. The idea that men in protected industries were by way of being parasites, exorbitantly rewarded, was one which some people of limited vision stubbornly maintained. The cleavage between the lowly paid soldier in the line, enduring unimaginable hardships and constant risks, and the able-bodied worker enjoying home comforts, was, in any event, well marked, and was one which might easily be made dangerously wide.

Unhappily, in the early months of the war, the idea was officially encouraged, rather than discouraged, that it was the duty of the able-bodied skilled worker, as of any other, to get out of his workshop and into uniform. As a corollary, those who stayed at their posts were apt to be looked upon as shirkers, a fact to which their attention was drawn in various ways, subtle and blunt. One result was that the worker tended to dissociate himself from the war. He was outside the pale, and there was not released in him any exaltation of spirit, a matter to which a psychologist would pay attention. The workers as a whole, he might point out, suffered in some degree from a sense of frustration.

We are a sentimental people and we are perhaps inclined, at any rate in the beginning, to conduct the ruthlessly realistic business of war in a sentimental way. It was sentiment, for instance, which led Lord Kitchener, whose vision was often remarkably clear, and who foresaw a long war, to kill Mr. Balfour's first attempt at a scientific evaluation of the country's man-power by his declaration that he was opposed to any system which rejected a willing recruit. We talk, with a feeling almost of pride rather than of shame, about 'muddling through', but we might be less complacent if we stopped to count the avoidable additional cost in lives and in wealth. As a nation we have moral courage, organizing ability, and great tenacity of purpose, but we are apt to be intellectually lazy, being content to wait upon facts from which, it must be admitted, we are usually quick and shrewd to draw inferences. Thus, in war, we have always required time in which to develop our resources, and by good fortune and policy we have usually been able to obtain, at a cost, whatever time was necessary. It may be noted, in passing, that the development of air warfare has made it doubtful whether time will ever again be purchasable to retrieve unpreparedness.

One result, then, of our characteristic method of making war was for a long time to divorce the worker from the soldier, and it may be that much of the unrest which threatened and disturbed war industries was fostered by the worker's feeling that he was a man apart.

In any event, owing to the development of the machine, and to the growing division of labour, the processes performed by an individual workman tended to become drab and monotonous. In June 1916 Mr. Claud Johnson, the general managing-director of the Rolls-Royce Company, placed before the Air Board some suggestions for, as he called it, 'the encouragement of labour'. He referred to the colourless existence of a man always employed in making some small part of an aero engine, and said: 'He may never 'see the complete engine, a part of which he makes. He may 'never hear the roar of the exhaust of the engine during 'its bench tests, and, much less, see it propelling a war-'plane upwards. His imagination is not great, and it is 'difficult for him to realize that he is taking a part in the 'winning of the war. I suggest that he should be told that 'every 20th (or some such number) engine shall be fitted 'to an aeroplane which shall be called after his works, such 'as "Wolverhampton No. I", "Wolverhampton No. II". 'In reports of war planes the name and number of the

'planes should be quoted. Cinema views of aeroplanes
'fitted with engines in the manufacture of which a sub-
'contractor has taken part should be exhibited in the local
'cinemas (films supplied by Air Board). And, lastly, men
'employed on making air engines who keep a certain per-
'centage of good time and do a certain percentage of over-
'time should have presented to them badges which they
'can wear as an indication that they have worked well
'voluntarily towards the winning of the war. The badges
'might take the form of stripes or wings on the arm so that
'a man might gain and wear a number of them.'

We need not concern ourselves with the details of Mr. Johnson's suggestions. All we need to note is that, speaking from great experience, he emphasized that it was desirable to give the worker a personal interest in the war.

It happened that, in June 1915, Lieutenant E. A. Ewart, an officer serving with the Royal Field Artillery in France, had published a book called *Between the Lines*, over the name 'Boyd Cable'. The Ministry of Munitions, with the permission of the author, printed and distributed copies of the book to munition workers (an ultimate total of 100,000 was so disposed of), and the considered opinion of Ministry officials was that the book helped to create in the mind of the worker understanding and sympathy which made for a greater output.

In February 1917 Captain Ewart was invited to study the conditions of air fighting with a view to spreading propaganda among the workers in the aircraft industry. His 'terms of reference' were that what he wrote should be interesting and impressive of the fact that every aeroplane was wanted in the field. He spent some time with squadrons in the line, flying as he thought necessary, and then returned to England, where he toured the aircraft factories and gave lectures to the workers. Reports from manufacturers indicated that the talks had been of value, and many requests were made that similar ones should be given. Accordingly Captain Ewart spent alternate periods on the Western front and in England, where he talked to the workers of what he had seen, illustrating his lectures with lantern slides made from air photographs.

A subsequent development was a series of letters written from the front to give information to factories about the operations of their products. There was, for example, the 'Handley Page' letter, which told of some stirring incident in which this type of aeroplane was concerned, said a word or two about the importance of night-bombing, and concluded with a neatly expressed hope that the Handley Page workers were doing their utmost to increase output. The factory serial numbers of the particular aeroplanes were quoted, and the workers could therefore identify their product, a fact which gave all operatives something of a sporting interest in the arrival of the letters from the front. They were circulated in various ways. In many factories a roneo copy was given to the men because it was found that some of them liked to read the letter at home as evidence that they were doing important work. The more firmly the idea of importance became rooted, the more difficult it would be for the men to justify strikes or other interruptions of output.

In the early part of 1918 the propaganda activities were extended. A scheme was put forward which involved offices in London, and a panel of lecturers, and approval took the form of the establishment of a *Lecture Branch* of the Aircraft Production Department. A suggestion was made that authentic pictures of air fighting should be published, and Mr. Joseph Simpson, the artist, offered his services without fee. He went to France in May 1918 and made his head-quarters at the Aeroplane Supply Depot at Bergues where he had a varied stock of aircraft to serve as models. He was given details of incidents considered suitable for painting, and when he had made his rough drawings he took them to the squadron to submit them to the criticism of the flying personnel who had taken part in the action depicted. On the finished picture the squadron markings and the factory serial numbers were inserted on the aeroplanes. The artist was at liberty to sell the first serial rights to an illustrated paper, but the copyright rested with the Aircraft Production Department which could, at its discretion, give prints away or sell them. What usually happened was that a brief story of the episode was added and that prints, bought by arrangement with the illustrated paper in which the picture had appeared, were sent to the factories where the particular types of aeroplane were built, and to makers of the engines, magnetos, plugs, &c. Some firms bought many thousands of copies of those pictures which were of special interest to them and made their own arrangements about distribution. Incidents of naval air warfare were similarly painted by Mr. Charles Dixon, the marine artist. The pay envelopes of the workers in the various aircraft factories also came to be used to carry small propaganda pictures with a line or two of appropriate text.

These belated war-time efforts to give the worker some appreciation of the importance of his personal contribution towards winning the war were good so far as they went, and tribute must be paid to the foresight of the Ministry of Munitions, and to the practical imagination of Colonel E. A. Ewart. Those who love truth do not care for propaganda because they are suspicious of its tendentious qualities. It may be that the propagandist can never tell the whole truth, but it is clear that, in the long run, the closer he gets to what is true the more successful he will be. The examples of which we have written have the merit that they told of actual happenings and that care was taken to ensure accuracy of detail. A nation goes to war to impose its will upon another nation. In this conflict of wills, propaganda, whether or not we approve of this method of making war, is certain to become a major weapon.

Air Expansion Programmes

During 1918 various air programmes were put forward by the Air Council. The biggest was that for which the sanction of the War Cabinet was sought in July 1918. It made up a total of 340 service squadrons of an average establishment of 20 aeroplanes.[1] Government approval was never given because it was considered improbable that the requisite man-power could be made available. The programme was amended to make the total 328 squadrons,

[1] The existing programme was for a total of 292 service squadrons for which the War Cabinet had given approval in March 1918.

but the Air Council was warned by Lieutenant-General J. C. Smuts, the chairman of the Air Policy Committee of the War Cabinet, that the men to maintain 328 service squadrons could not be supplied. This programme, however, held the field, unofficially, until towards the end of October 1918, when, as a result of the changed conditions on the Western front, the Air Council was of the opinion that every possible squadron should be put into the field by June 1919, even at the expense of subsequent developments. The expansion programme was therefore reduced to a total of 275 service squadrons to be in the field by June 1919. The war ended before this modified programme could be discussed by the War Cabinet.

The position at the Armistice was as follows: there were on the Western front 86 squadrons,[1] plus 10 with the Independent Force, and, in addition, 6 Independent Flights; in Italy, 4 squadrons; in the Middle East, 14, plus 1 Flight; on Home Defence in England and Ireland, 18 squadrons; on anti-submarine work in home waters, 37; in the Mediterranean, 15; and 1 squadron and 7 Flights with the Grand Fleet. That is to say, the Royal Air Force disposed of a total of 132 service squadrons plus 8 Flights with the armies and Independent Force, 3 squadrons and 1 Flight at Dunkirk, and 53 squadrons plus 7 Flights with the navy. Thus the programme of July 1917, which sanctioned a total of 200 military service squadrons, and allowed for doubling the strength of the Royal Naval Air Service, had not been approached by the Armistice.

It is of interest to compare what Sir Douglas Haig had on the Western front at the end of the war, with the requirements as stated by him in June 1916. On the 15th of that month he had put forward a programme for a total of fifty-six squadrons to be in France by the early spring of 1917 'at the latest, and sooner, if possible'. At the same time he had asked for ten bombing squadrons for expeditions 'on 'a large scale against objectives situated at a great distance. 'So far as land operations are concerned it is possible that 'such expeditions might give useful results if the time and

---

[1] This figure does not include three squadrons and one Flight, formerly naval, working in the area of the Belgian coast.

'place for them be selected carefully in connexion with 'special military requirements. Otherwise they might do 'harm rather than good, and in any case they will always 'be attended by considerable risk of loss in personnel and 'machines.' As a result of the new situation created by the reorganization of the German air service and of the introduction of enemy new type fighting aeroplanes in the autumn of 1916, Sir Douglas Haig had, in November 1916, added a request for twenty additional fighting squadrons. They were not to interfere with his June programme, except that they were to take precedence over the ten long-distance bombing squadrons. This brought the total of service squadrons required for employment with the armies in France to eighty-six[1]. If the former naval squadrons engaged on military duties are deducted, there were in France, at the Armistice, eighty-five military and independent bombing squadrons and a few independent Flights. That is to say, that the comparatively modest programme of 1916 had just about been fulfilled by November 1918.

Importance of Reserves

An analysis of some of the statistics for aircraft wastage during the war shows the importance of adequate reserves. To start a new squadron 100 per cent. of aircraft (that is, complete with engines) additional to establishment had to be provided in the first place. For example, a squadron of eighteen aeroplanes required six extra to cover wastage during mobilization and transit to France, six to go overseas as Expeditionary Force reserve at the same time as the squadron, and six more for allotment to training units to

[1] The total number of service squadrons for all theatres was 108, but excluding the ten bombing squadrons. These were not definitely included in the War Office approved programmes presumably because, as stated in a minute by Sir David Henderson, 'No decision has yet been arrived at 'as to whether the army or the navy is to be responsible for such operations, 'and in view of the difficulties which confront us, it seems inadvisable to 'expend energy on a project which the navy appear to be undertaking 'with the assent of Government.' It was not until the June 1917 decision to expand the total Royal Flying Corps service squadrons to 200 that long-distance bombing was included.

produce pilots for the squadron. Subsequently, to replace wastage and to build up a reserve, nine aeroplanes had to be provided each month, representing fifty per cent. of the squadron's strength. In general, the rates of wastage allowed for were approximately as follows:

Type and establishment.	Monthly wastage percentage.
Single-seater fighter (24)	66
Two-seater ,, (18)	50
Corps squadrons (18)	50
Bombers (18 or 10)	33⅓
Home Defence squadrons (24)	20
Middle East squadrons (18)	20
Training squadrons (18)	20

The wastage rates for engines were calculated on a different basis. Engines were allotted to overseas squadrons as follows: air-cooled, 80; water-cooled, 75; and rotary, 100. For home defence the allotment was 40 per squadron, while for training units two additional engines were allowed for each aeroplane. The wastage figures were estimated on this large-scale allotment to each squadron and worked out at about seven per cent. per month for squadrons in France, and at four per cent. for those squadrons working in the Middle East, and on home defence duties, or engaged in training. It may be remarked, incidentally, that it was bad accounting to make the calculation for engine wastage on a basis different from that for aeroplanes (or airframes). It was bad because it might be made to appear that the rate of engine wastage for each squadron was very much smaller than that for aeroplanes. There was at least one occasion when the Government appear to have been misled into a belief that this was so. The aeroplane figures, however, had reference to the number of front-line aeroplanes with each squadron, whereas the engine figure included heavy reserves carried in each squadron, and presumably also took no notice of the large number of spares for each engine which represented an additional reserve.

In July 1917 Sir William Weir gave various figures to the Air Board which support the above calculations. To

WASTAGE FIGURES

maintain 100 squadrons of eighteen aeroplanes in the Field, he said, required the production of 1,000 aeroplanes each month, while for home defence and for training the rate was about half. Thus 1,500 aeroplanes would have to be provided each month to maintain 1,800 in the Field.[1]

It may be useful to consider some general implications of the above figures. During the war, with an aircraft industry in being, and organized for large-scale output, about eight months elapsed before an aeroplane of new design reached the production stage, while the comparable figure for an engine was something over a year. Any nation which wishes to keep its air service in an adequate state of readiness would require to possess reserves sufficient to maintain its front-line squadrons at full strength during the period necessary for industry to get under way for large-scale production. Prudence, mindful of the unforeseen difficulties which attended war-time production, especially of engines, might suggest that a delay of twelve months should be taken into account. If, however, allowance is made for post-war industrial improvements, and the interim period is cut down by, say, one-half, the position is that six months' supplies should be held to provide for a monthly wastage at the rate of about eighty per cent. In other words, the minimum reserves, cautiously reckoned, which an Air Force should hold, in readiness at any time, ought, according to the above calculations, to be about 500 per cent. in excess of its first-line air strength. The figure can only be indicative, not exact, for it makes no allowance for expansion, nor, on the other hand, for output from the time of the opening of hostilities.

So long as aircraft design is subject to rapid change, the holding of enormous reserves, which can only have a short and useless life before they are passed to the scrap-heap, must constitute a burden which statesmen will wish to avoid. What is clear is that the air weapon has conferred

---

[1] It is of interest that French calculations supplied to the Air Board in October 1917 showed that to maintain 4,000 aeroplanes ready at the front with necessary reserves, a monthly output of 2,400 aeroplanes and 4,000 engines was required.

an advantage upon any nation which may be tempted by the possibility of an aggressive war. Such a country might build up reserves, against an approximate date, in the firm belief that the war might be won in the air before the opposing nation had time to organize its aircraft industry for production on a war scale. Provided the defending country began with inadequate reserves, the aggressor nation should find itself, after a short period of intensive fighting, with a mastery of the air which could not be effectively challenged for some time, perhaps for months. If such conditions came about, the defending nation would be unable to take action against air attacks aimed at the destruction of its aircraft industrial centres, and so might never be enabled to develop its air strength at all. If these observations be well founded, and they appear to be indisputable, it is clear that adequate, even generous, reserves, whether of aircraft or pilots, or of industrial organization for immediate and sustained output, are indispensable if a nation is to be in a position to maintain air warfare. Some words of Mahan, written with no thought of the air weapon, illuminate and fortify the abiding importance of what has been said above. 'If time be,' he says, 'as is every-'where admitted, a supreme factor in war, it behooves 'countries whose genius is essentially not military, whose 'people, like all free people, object to pay for large military 'establishments, to see to it that they are at least strong 'enough to gain the time necessary to turn the spirit and 'capacity of their subjects into the new activities which 'war calls for. If the existing force by land or sea is strong 'enough so to hold out, even though at a disadvantage, the 'country may rely upon its natural resources and strength 'coming into play for whatever they are worth,—its 'numbers, its wealth, its capacities of every kind. If, on 'the other hand, what force it has can be overthrown 'and crushed quickly, the most magnificent possibilities of 'natural power will not save it from humiliating conditions, 'nor, if its foe be wise, from guarantees which will post-'pone revenge to a distant future.'[1]

[1] *The Influence of Sea Power upon History*, by Captain A. T. Mahan, pp. 48–9.

A Summary

This survey of the organization of the country's manpower, and of the supply difficulties which prevented fulfilment of the air programmes, has been no more than cursory. It has been mainly concerned with failures, and with the causes for them, and not enough has been said about the positive achievements of the departments responsible for aircraft supplies. It would be possible to write, in sober truth, a glowing volume about the difficulties overcome, about the ingenuity and adaptability of the contracting and experimental departments and of the manufacturers, about the bold, even romantic way in which, upon necessity, whole industries were taken over and organized.

To obtain the fabric to cover the aircraft the Ministry of Munitions had to control the whole linen output of the country, and when Russia, a main source of supply for flax, went out of the war the cultivation of flax seed within the Empire was intensively developed. The production of a suitable 'dope' for the treatment of the fabric presented a whole series of problems. It was essential, if the lifting power of the wings was to be retained, to prevent any passage of air through the fabric. Some kind of paste such as tapioca, and also beeswax and glue, were tried, but it was found that the moisture in the air created a sagging tendency in fabric so treated, and although a slackness thus produced was of no great importance so long as it was insufficient to affect the aerodynamic qualities of the wings, pilots did not like to fly aeroplanes on which the wings were not taut. The word 'dope' is of American slang origin, meaning a stupefying drink or a drug, and the name was adopted because the application of the liquid added tonic qualities which the fabric did not in its untreated state possess. The word, however, came in the first place from the Dutch *doop*, sauce (*doopen*, to dip), so that it was well applied. The basis of the earlier dopes was a low nitrated cellulose, formed by the action of nitric and sulphuric acids on cotton, and because it was highly inflammable a fire-proofing substance, triphenyl phosphate, was added, but the drawback of inflammability, which could not be entirely eliminated, led to the supersession of nitro-cellulose dopes by others of acetate kind.

It was found that dopes formed from cellulose acetate were not only non-inflammable, but also tough, pliable, clear, and durable. The manufacture of cellulose acetate originated in Germany, and when war broke out the only sources of supply open to Britain were two foreign firms, one in Switzerland and the other in France. The British dope manufacturers made their own arrangements about buying raw materials, and there was no official attempt to see that an economical use of the materials was made. By the middle of 1915 it was becoming difficult to obtain cellulose acetate, and the War Department thereupon assumed responsibility for making purchases in bulk, not only for the Royal Aircraft Factory and for War Office aircraft contractors, but also for some Admiralty contractors. In July 1915 tenders were issued by the directorate of military aeronautics for 100 tons of cellulose acetate to be made in England, but there was only one response, from Dr. Dreyfus of the Cellonite Company, Basle, who reserved the right to deliver half of the total quantity from Switzerland. As Dr. Dreyfus was the only tenderer his offer and conditions were accepted, but there ensued difficulties, mainly having reference to the financial arrangements, and he eventually returned to Switzerland. He was subsequently approached by financiers who had already tried, without success, to manufacture cellulose acetate in this country, and, in March 1916, the British Cellulose and Chemical Manufacturing Company was formed to produce, by the Dreyfus process, acetate of cellulose, methyl acetate, and other chemicals. A site for a factory was bought at Spondon, near Derby, and building began in August 1916. After much negotiation the Government agreed, on conditions, to refund to the company the capital expenditure incurred during the war upon plant up to a maximum equal to the excess profits duty actually charged in respect of each year's working during five years from the formation of the company.[1]

---

[1] New terms were agreed, under changed conditions, in June 1918. Up

In January 1917, after samples of its products had been passed by Ministry of Munitions inspectors, the company was given its first direct contract for forty tons of acetate of cellulose, and because the aircraft programme was expanding rapidly and no other British source of supply appeared to offer prospects of early production, the company was accorded priorities for labour and material in order that the factory might be completed in the shortest possible time. The first ton of cellulose acetate from Spondon passed inspection in April 1917. The new company got going just in time because, in July, the French authorities commandeered the whole output of the French factory (the Usines du Rhône Company) which had been an important source of supply. By the spring of 1918, in spite of many difficulties, the home production of cellulose acetate was such that Britain had become independent of France and Switzerland for supplies, and it was found possible, in July, to arrange a supply to the Americans of twenty-five tons of cellulose acetate per month, although the demand for dope on British account had, in the meantime, increased by more than twenty-five per cent. above what had been allowed for in the production programme.

The development of the magneto industry may also be noted. In 1914 there was only one British firm producing magnetos, with a yearly output of 1,140, but at the end of the war fourteen firms were employed in this branch of the aircraft business with an output, for 1918, of 128,637. Bowdon tubes for pressure gauges were unobtainable in this country until a firm of gold refiners successfully took up their manufacture. Nor, before the war, had such instruments as revolution indicators been made in Britain.

In general, the supply of material and the rate of output had to be so controlled that the rhythm of production over the whole industrial field was maintained with the greatest possible smoothness: a break-down in the supply of any one component had effects which were far-reaching. The value of contracts for aeronautical material outstanding at the end of the war totalled £165 millions, a sum which

to that time the company had made no profit so that the duty concession was of no value.

represented more than one-half of all the commitments of the Ministry of Munitions.

It will perhaps help the reader if we here summarize the main reasons why the July 1917 programme, which allowed for the air service to be doubled, was not fulfilled, and why the projected large-scale air offensive against German industrial and military targets was never realized. The main reasons may be set out as follows:

(i) The selection of untried engines for mass production.

(ii) Failure to encourage to the utmost an expansion of output of Rolls-Royce engines. It was said that the Rolls-Royce was the only engine which did not have 'teething troubles', but partly through difficulties associated with producing the engine in bulk, and partly because it required specialist skilled labour for repair, it was not until 1918, when other engine supply failures had brought about a grave situation, that whole-hearted efforts were made to expand the production of Rolls-Royce (*Eagle* and *Falcon*) engines.

(iii) The reliance placed upon the *Liberty* engine. An important part of the bombing programme was made to depend upon the timely supply of these engines, but although the output estimates which came from America were conservatively discounted before the *Liberty* was taken into British official programmes, we were not sufficiently guided by our own experience with new engine designs. In October 1917 Lord Northcliffe, cabling to the Cabinet and to the President of the Air Board, set out what American manufacturers hoped they would be able to achieve, but he pointed out the limiting factors, and said he thought it was unlikely that more than 5,000 fighting aeroplanes, fitted with *Liberty* engines, would be on the Western front in July 1918. When July came there was not one such aeroplane in France. Yet the story of the design and production of the *Liberty* engine compares favourably with that of any similar British engine. It would have been wise to measure the production of *Liberty* engines in strict accordance with our own experience. We were in a position, as American manufacturers were not in the early stages, to realize, and to make some allowance for, all the inevitable difficulties and disappointments which lay between the design of an engine and its production in mass.

(iv) The lack of priority for aircraft production, particularly for skilled labour, until the end of 1917. The limiting effect was accentuated because the aircraft industry came late into the field.

(v) The comb-out of munition workers in order that more soldiers might be put into the field after the German offensive opened on the Western front in March 1918. The effect on output, of aircraft and its accessories, as of other weapons and munitions of war, was immediate.

(vi) The need to make good abnormal losses of aeroplanes and material as a result of the German 1918 offensive.

(vii) The failure of the engine repair organization to keep pace with the accumulation of damaged engines. As a result, the establishment of engines per squadron had to be increased, and additional engines were sent to France, to be held in reserve, which would otherwise have been employed to equip new aircraft.[1]

There were other obstacles and difficulties, such as a shortage of ball-bearings, of magnetos, and of silver spruce, but these and similar ones were of secondary importance because the air-expansion programme was always limited by the output of engines.

It is clear, from what has been said, that in a war of attrition, such as that waged between 1914 and 1918, the

[1] Repairs were made by service units and, from the end of 1917, by civilian contractors. During the year ended the 30th of June 1918 more than 14,000 engines came in for repair. It was expected that 30,000 would require repair for the year ending 30th of June 1919. It was suggested that the number to be repaired should be fixed at 3,000 per month, 2,200 to be dealt with by the service and the remainder by civilian contractors. The main object of making the service responsible for the major repair work was that service discipline eliminated the possibility of labour troubles. There was also the advantage that it provided good opportunities for technical training. In fact, the civilian contractors could not keep pace with repair requirements. In June 1918, for example, there was a total outstanding deficiency of 1,491 repaired engines from civilian firms as compared with the scheduled output.

State which is empowered to override private rights and contracts, and to coerce each individual to take his or her appointed place in accordance with the national policy and organization for prosecuting the war, has important advantages. Such a State, in the ordinary way of preparation, would, in addition to its armed forces, have ready comprehensive plans for organizing the whole production of the country in order that, if and when the need arose, the maximum military strength and endurance of the nation might be developed with rapidity, efficiency, and economy. Preparation of this kind would require the listing of the adult population according to age, occupation, physical fitness, and so forth. Priorities, immediately enforceable, would have to be devised, according to the nature of the war, for the production of munitions, military equipment, medical supplies, necessary food and clothing, and the maintenance of exports so far as they were required to obtain essential imports. Indeed the whole field of national economy would have to be planned in order that those activities which did not contribute to military efficiency might be determined and, wherever possible, eliminated. At the same time nothing must be done to undermine the maintenance of civilian morale.

The idea that the State should exercise unlimited dictatorial powers, even in war, is one which is repugnant to many minds. War, however, is a devastating, inexorable business, and whatever impedes a nation from developing its war effort has to be bitterly paid for in human suffering. In organizing the State for war, compulsion alone is of small value. Compulsion must rest upon the will of the people, and sacrifices may be demanded only in the degree in which a majority of the people believe them to be unavoidable.

CHAPTER III
THE INDEPENDENT BOMBING FORCE
Matters of Policy

IN February 1918 the Spanish Ambassador in London orally informed the Secretary of State for Foreign Affairs that His Majesty the King of Spain had been in communication with the German Government with the object of getting some check placed upon the bombing of undefended towns. The matter was subsequently discussed at a War Cabinet meeting and it was agreed that a courteous reply should be sent to the Ambassador informing him that the British had always objected to the bombardment of undefended towns and would consider any proposals on the subject which the Germans had to put forward.

The sequel was a statement, made in the Bavarian Chamber, which appeared to signify an offer on behalf of Germany to abandon air attacks on open towns if the Allies agreed to do the same. Meanwhile, various memoranda on the legal and historical aspects of air bombing had been prepared. In one of these, drawn up by the General Staff at the War Office, it was pointed out that the German General Staff had always argued that the 'sole 'criterion as to the legality of a bombardment is whether 'the place possesses military value to the enemy at the time', a view with which the British General Staff expressed agreement. It had been found impossible to define, with any chance of general acceptance, what constituted an undefended town, and, in any case, when the matter had been debated internationally in the past no one had foreseen a cordon of troops extending from the sea to Switzerland. This was a new feature which modified all existing theories. As warfare developed so the defence of a town had had to be undertaken at increasing distances from its centre. The original defence walls of Paris, for example, were now well within the city, but although the trench lines defending Paris were, at their nearest, many dozens of miles distant from the capital they no longer afforded protection against long-range bombardment. In other words, a town might be rendered immune from bombardment, under modern conditions, only by lines drawn, or by operations conducted, at an appreciable distance. It would, therefore, be difficult to rebut the argument that the entire areas protected by the existing Allied lines, or by the corresponding cordon of ships in the North Sea, were 'defended'. Once this was admitted it followed that the bombardment of these areas by any means whatever, whether by land, sea, or air, was legitimate, 'since no legal 'duty has been imposed on attacking forces to restrict 'bombardment to actual fortifications, and the destruction 'of its public and private buildings has always been regarded 'as a legitimate means of inducing a town to surrender. . . . 'The fundamental criterion of the legitimacy of belligerent 'operations is—Do they manifestly subserve military in-'terests and are they justifiable on the grounds of military 'necessity?'

When the statement made in the Bavarian Chamber was considered by the Cabinet, together with the memoranda prepared by the experts, the opinion was expressed that the enemy offer was influenced by the knowledge that Germany must expect to suffer more damage from air bombing than she could hope to inflict, and that if it was agreed, for example, that bombing should be confined to an area within twelve to twenty miles from the front line, the effect on the Western front would be that the bombing by both sides would be concentrated against French and Belgian towns. In other words, to abandon the bombing of distant objectives would be to profit the enemy.[1] Furthermore, in the interest of future peace, it was undesirable that the civil population of Germany

[1] That the War Cabinet rightly interpreted the German attitude is confirmed by an authoritative article in *Die Luftwacht* in October 1928. This article, on the subject of Home Defence in Germany, by Major Grosskreutz, says: 'On March 31st 1918 the German Higher Command 'was invited to put forward measures with respect to a question then 'before the Reichstag, namely, the possibility of coming to an arrangement 'with regard to air raids. The reason was that the severe moral shock to 'the population of the towns in western and south-western Germany sub-'jected to enemy air raids called for effective and speedy measures.'

should be the one population among the belligerents to enjoy immunity from the worst sufferings of war. It was concluded that Mr. Bonar Law should not make a statement in the House of Commons unless questioned, and that he should then base his reply on the propositions:
  (i) That we had not bombed open towns, except in rare cases, as direct reprisals.
  (ii) That we were most desirous of diminishing the sufferings of non-combatants, especially women and children.
  (iii) That we could not give up the right to bomb genuine military objectives.

Thus the Government retained freedom of action for the development of long-distance bombing operations. Although the decision to form an Air Ministry, however, had been based on the need for an Air Staff to study the problems associated with such strategic bombing, the Government had not, in fact, laid down any definite policy by which the Air Ministry might formulate its proposals.

At the beginning of May Sir William Weir succeeded Lord Rothermere as Air Minister and, on the 23rd, he circulated to the War Cabinet a memorandum in which he set out the considerations which should, he thought, regulate the policy of the Air Ministry. After making the assumption that the Air Ministry had been constituted because of a conviction that 'a rapid development of aerial 'forces devoted to the interruption of German industrial 'effort and kindred objects', might make a substantial contribution towards bringing about a demand for peace, he stated that the Air Ministry should be recognized as 'the 'authority on air policy, and the Air Staff must command 'the fullest knowledge of all methods of the utilization of 'aircraft and their effectiveness in practice'. Bombing operations against long-distance targets would require a large measure of freedom and independence from other military schemes.

The memorandum was referred by the War Cabinet to its Air Policy Committee for final decision. This body made a few minor emendations and then circulated the memorandum, as its decision, on the 10th of July. It stated: 'The Air Ministry is responsible to the War Cabinet 'for securing that utilization of the available aerial forces of 'the country which will prove most effective in its results 'against the enemy, with the limitation that the operational 'control of the forces allocated to the Navy or the Army 'rests with those Departments respectively.' It also stated that 'the continuous bombing of German industrial 'centres presents very important possibilities and valuable 'results may be achieved by the use of even a small force 'commencing to operate now, and by its rapid progressive 'development'.[1]

Meanwhile arrangements had been put in hand for the organization of a strategic bombing force. On the 13th of May the Air Council informed the War Cabinet that, in their opinion, the time had arrived to constitute an Independent Force for large-scale bombing attacks on Germany. They proposed, therefore, to organize the existing Brigade as a separate command under Major-General H. M. Trenchard who would work directly under the Air Ministry. Because long-distance bombing operations would, in the future, partake of an international character, the Air Ministry further proposed that the broad lines of action should be laid down by the Supreme War Council at Versailles on the advice of its military representatives.

In a supplementary memorandum, a few days later, Sir William Weir stated that the French would probably object to the independent command of the bombing force and would put forward strong claims that it should operate under the Generalissimo, General Foch. 'I would repre-'sent most strongly', he proceeded, 'the possible dangers of 'such an arrangement, and would point out the necessity 'of supporting the independence of this command to a 'similar degree as a naval command.' In conclusion, he asked the War Cabinet to place before the Supreme War Council, at the earliest possible date, the following propositions:

(i) Confirmation of the Independent Long-Range Bombing Command.

[1] The full terms of the decision, as set out in the modified memorandum, are given as Appendix VII.

(ii) Its ultimate development into an Inter-Allied command under a British General Officer Commanding, so long as the British portion of the command is the larger.

(iii) M. Clemenceau to obtain the support of the French army authorities to this scheme.

The War Cabinet duly adopted the Air Minister's memorandum, and a telegram was sent to M. Clemenceau, the French Prime Minister and Minister for War, informing him of the institution of an Independent Force and asking that Major-General Trenchard be given all the necessary facilities. M. Clemenceau replied that he had issued instructions to General Duval[1] to make the necessary arrangements with Major-General Trenchard.

When, however, the subject came up for discussion at Versailles, it soon became clear that the way of the Independent Force would not be smooth. At the beginning of May a committee consisting of five members each from Great Britain, France, America, and Italy had been set up by the Supreme War Council to deal with questions of air policy. This body had held its first meeting on the 9th of May and had discussed, among other subjects, the question of long-distance bombing operations. The debate was on general lines and ended on the note that the various representatives should give consideration to the details of available means, of objectives, of the types of aeroplanes to be employed, and of the zones in France from which operations might be conducted. It was agreed that the matter could then be debated more fully at the next meeting. Before the next meeting took place, the British Government had informed M. Clemenceau of their decision to set up an Independent Force, and General Duval came to the second Versailles meeting on the 31st of May with M. Clemenceau's telegram, announcing this decision, in his pocket. He opened the discussion with a puzzled reference to the word 'independent'. The Allies, he said, had been consistently seeking for co-operation and co-ordination and he failed to understand how an independent command

[1] Deputy Chief of the French General Staff in charge of the Air Service at French General Head-quarters.

could be reconciled with this search. Major-General Sykes, the Chief of the Air Staff, explained that the first duty of the force would be long-distance bombing outside the army zone, but that its second duty would be to assist the armies and that, if necessary, the Generalissimo could request the help of Major-General Trenchard in an emergency. General Duval objected that the matter was very serious: the committee was asked to say that the primary object was to bomb Germany and the secondary one to beat the Germans in the field. This, he contended, was a mistake. What was needed was the unification, under one commander, of all the forces, not their dissemination. There was limited space in France for the construction of aerodromes, and the French Government wished to allot ground only if it was to be utilized for the defeat of the enemy in the field. He took exception to the proposal that the Generalissimo might only request the help of the commander of the Independent Force. 'From a military 'point of view', he said, 'orders are better than requests.'

Major-General Sykes pointed out that it was the considered policy of the British Government that once the necessities of the army had been determined and allowed for, the balance of aircraft resources was to be devoted to bombing squadrons, a statement which prompted General Duval to retort with Gallic irony that he would be grateful to any authority who could establish the limit of what was necessary to a battle. The greatest commanders, he said, had always solved this problem by putting into the battle every resource they had.

We need not further pursue the discussion. In the end the members of the committee could come to no agreement, and it was decided that the question should be referred to the Supreme War Council. Whether because of pressure of other work, or from reluctance to grasp the thorns of the problem, the Supreme War Council allowed the weeks to pass without giving its attention to the matter and then, on the 21st of July, the Inter-Allied Aviation Committee made another attempt to reach agreement, again entirely without success.

On the 24th of July Major-General Sykes reported the

discussions and difficulties to the War Cabinet. At this meeting Sir Henry Wilson, the Chief of the General Staff, said that he had had a conversation with General Foch who had told him that when the fighting season was over he would raise the question of the Independent Force. The opinion of General Foch was that Major-General Trenchard should come under his command or else the Independent Force should move out of France.

The War Cabinet decided to bring forward the whole question at the next meeting of the Versailles Council. French action, however, forestalled this intention. On the 27th of July the French military representative on the Council circulated a note and draft resolution, on the subject of an Inter-Allied Bombing Force, for the approval of the other military members of the Council, and on the 3rd of August this note, after minor amendment, was signed by the military representatives of France, Britain, America, and Italy, for presentation to the Supreme War Council. It was known as *Joint Note No. 35* (Appendix IX) and recorded the opinion of the military representatives that, as soon as Allied resources in men and material allowed, an Inter-Allied Bombing Air Force should be constituted on the Western front. The force should be equipped with weight-carrying aircraft with a wide radius of action and should be at the disposal of the Generalissimo in France who would nominate its commander after consultation with the Commanders-in-Chief of the various Allied armies under his orders. It was expedient, said the note, in anticipation of the constitution of this force, and without waiting for the Allied Governments to decide whether the enemy should first be summoned to stop bombing Allied towns under penalty of reprisals, to begin to elaborate a plan for methodical attacks on enemy towns and industrial centres.[1] Finally it was suggested that any similar bombing force which might be set up in a theatre of operations outside France, should be placed under the control of the commander-in-chief of the armies in the theatre. This suggestion arose out of an emendation made by the British military representative,

---

[1] The Inter-Allied Aviation Committee was requested to go ahead with these plans.

who possibly had in mind independent bombing operations conducted from British soil. Whether this was so or not, the fact remains that, as nothing was specifically said to the contrary, an Independent Bombing Force, operating from England, would, in accordance with the terms of the note, be placed under the Commander-in-Chief, Home Forces. There is no need to lay stress on this point, but it may be remarked that the arguments for placing the bombing force under the operational control of the Commander-in-Chief in a theatre of war overseas did not apply at home. The Secretary of State for Air, advised by his Air Staff, was indubitably in a better position to direct, in accordance with the policy of the War Cabinet, independent operations from British soil. If the Government had accepted the *Joint Note* in its entirety the separate existence of the Air Ministry would have been immediately threatened.

The *Joint Note*, in fact, never came before the Supreme War Council because there was no meeting of that body between July and October. The note did, however, form the basis of important discussions between the French and the British Governments. On the 13th of August M. Clemenceau sent the note to Marshal Foch and asked him to draw up a general programme for the air bombardment of the interior of Germany, and to examine the conditions under which it would be possible to give effect to the programme. Basing his study of the question on the *Joint Note*, Marshal Foch, who replied on the 13th of September, proposed that an Inter-Allied Bombing Force should be formed under the command of Major-General Trenchard to operate, under the Generalissimo, in accordance with a bombing programme accepted by the Supreme War Council. He reserved the right, during military operations, to use the whole, or part, of the bombing force in battle. He concluded by urging M. Clemenceau to obtain the approval of the French Government to the *Joint Note* and to use 'his high authority to hasten the consent of the other Allied Governments'.

Before this reply had been dispatched, the Air Ministry had reason to anticipate its tenor. They knew from Sir

Henry Wilson, the Chief of the Imperial General Staff and a personal friend of Marshal Foch, that the French Generalissimo would insist on controlling any part of the Independent Force on French soil. The Air Ministry feared that if this happened the squadrons of the Independent Force would be lost to the British Army, which might, in emergency, find itself starved for the benefit of our Allies. In a memorandum drafted by the Air Staff it was stated: 'The Air Staff are so firmly convinced of 'the absolute necessity for the creation of an independent 'striking force and its employment in accordance with the 'declared policy of the Air Staff, that they are prepared, in 'the event of the control of the Independent Force in France 'being vested in the Generalissimo on the Western front, 'to recommend the removal of the entire force, as it stands, 'to England. The Independent Force would then be based 'in Norfolk, and only emergency landing grounds main- 'tained in France.' This memorandum, which was written for submission to the War Cabinet, was never placed before that body. Instead, Lord Weir, the Air Minister, with the concurrence of Mr. Lloyd George, wrote to M. Clemenceau on the 26th of August. In this letter he set out very fully the motives which had moved the British Government to form an independent bombing force, and he submitted that he was justified in demanding the same measure of autonomy as would be granted to a naval force, and that the Independent Force should be treated as ready to act in co-operation with the army, but not as auxiliary or subordinate to it.[1] M. Clemenceau again referred the matter to Marshal Foch who replied to Lord Weir's letter in a separate memorandum on the 14th of September. This is reprinted as Appendix VIII, and the attitude of Marshal Foch will be sufficiently indicated here if we quote an early paragraph. 'Since the military power 'of the enemy is represented by his army,' he wrote, 'and since the sole means we have for destroying his army 'is our own army, it is on our army that we must con- 'centrate all our efforts in order to render it as strong and

[1] Lord Weir had had a talk with M. Clemenceau on the 19th of August and had spoken to him on the lines of his letter.

'well armed as possible. In consequence, any combination 'tending to diminish the army or hinder its development 'on the plea of organizing a new force capable of reducing 'the enemy, must be rejected.' He concluded by repeating that the bombing force could not be exempted from the authority of the command responsible for the united action of all the combatant forces.

M. Clemenceau replied to Lord Weir on the 24th of September by repeating the arguments and intentions of Marshal Foch. By this time, however, the conditions on the Western front had changed. When the War Cabinet came to consider M. Clemenceau's memorandum a victorious end to the war was at last in sight. In their note, by way of reply, which was sent on the 3rd of October, it was stated that the British Government were strongly of the opinion that an even greater effect than had hitherto been achieved would result from a direct air offensive against Germany in the event of a later stabilization of the line nearer the frontier. On the other hand, the potential disintegration of the enemy's battle front represented a new condition which justified a reconsideration of the method for the employment of the force. When the scheme had been formed the British Government had, according to the opinion of their military advisers, to contemplate the prospect of defensive warfare, throughout 1918 and possibly 1919, on the front then existing. It had been important, therefore, to develop to the utmost the arm which alone offered the opportunity of carrying the offensive into the heart of Germany. Under the changed conditions on the Western front it was possible to contemplate a fluid and progressive line of battle which might take the Allied armies into Germany itself. In such an emergency, said the note, it was recognized that difficulties of transport and administration, &c., were such that a long-range bombing force might most effectively operate under the immediate command of the Commander-in-Chief of the Allied Armies, and it was for these reasons that the British Government were prepared to accede to the request of the French Government that Major-General Trenchard's force should be placed under the supreme command of

Marshal Foch. An agreement, accordingly, was drawn up for the approval of M. Clemenceau, on behalf of the French Government, and it was suggested that the agreement might be ratified by the Allied Governments at the next meeting of the Supreme War Council. The French Government notified their acceptance of the draft proposals on the 17th of October and, in anticipation of acceptance by the Italian and American Governments, Major-General Trenchard was informed officially, on the 26th of October, of his appointment as Commander-in-Chief, under the supreme control of Marshal Foch, of the Inter-Allied Independent Air Force. The heads of the agreement about the constitution of the force were set out as follows:

1. *The object of the Force.*
To carry war into Germany by attacking her industry, commerce, and population.

2. *The Plan of Campaign.*
Air raids must be on a large scale and repeated, forming part of a methodical plan and carried on with tenacity.

3. *Execution of the Plan.*
The complete realization of this scheme is not to be undertaken until the imperative requirements of the fighting have been satisfied or during the intervals of the fighting.

It will therefore be possible to carry out this plan in two ways according to circumstances.

(*a*) *During periods of active operations.* The requirements of battle will have to be met first, thus reducing in varying proportions the strength of forces available for raids on the interior of Germany. The bombing action being begun will, however, have to be pursued *even with a reduced strength.*

(*b*) *During steady or quiet periods.* Bombing raids on the interior of Germany become the chief work of our bombing squadrons. Having satisfied the Air Service requirements of the Army, all available long-range aeroplanes will be free to take part in the raids.

4. *The establishment of the Inter-Allied Independent Air Force.*

This establishment will include Allied Flights of heavy weight-carrying aeroplanes with a wide radius of action, and will probably be reinforced later by further available Allied Flights of the same type.[1]

The Force will be placed under the command of General Trenchard, as Commander-in-Chief, assisted by a staff including, besides the present staff, an officer of each of the nations represented in the Bombing Force.

General Trenchard will be under the supreme command of Marshal Foch for operations.

5. *The name of the Force shall be the Inter-Allied Independent Air Force.*

The appointment of Major-General Trenchard was one of great interest and of even greater possibilities. Marshal Foch, in his various memoranda on the subject, made clear his view that the squadrons of the bombing force should be available for direct co-operation with the armies during battle. In an earlier volume,[2] when comment was made on the Generalissimo's orders, issued soon after his appointment, which had reference to the concentration and effective employment of Allied aircraft, it was suggested that the orders could not be fulfilled, in the spirit or the letter, because no air officer was appointed to command, under the Generalissimo, all Allied offensive aircraft, that is, fighters and bombers. This suggestion was made with strict reference to the bombing and fighting aircraft definitely allotted for work with the armies in the field, and did not take into account a strategic bombing force such as that to which Major-General Trenchard was appointed. Had the war endured into 1919 it is possible that there would have been changes of importance in the

---

[1] *Author's note.* The Allied bombers which it was intended to place under Major-General Trenchard were stated to be: French Bomber Group No. 2 and Italian Bomber Group No. 18. American squadrons were to be added later. Major-General Trenchard, as commander-in-chief, was given full control of the tactical employment of his Force.

[2] Vol. IV, p. 349.

direction of the air services on the Western front. Marshal Foch consistently stated his opinion that the effective concentration of aircraft was essential to success and that he must, as Generalissimo, be given full powers to effect this concentration, irrespective of national susceptibilities or of national army boundaries. His firm desire to obtain control of the bombing force was in strict accordance with this outlook. Just as he reserved the right to divert, according to his judgement, the bombing squadrons from attacks on German industrial centres to attacks on selected military objectives when battles were in progress, so, when the battle-front was quiet, it is logical to assume he would have been prepared to divert some of the bombing strength allotted to the armies in order to augment the striking-power of the strategic bombing force. Major-General Trenchard had been General Officer Commanding the Royal Flying Corps in France from the middle of 1915 until January 1918. Under his direction the air service and its activities had expanded enormously. From a knowledge of his record while commanding the Royal Flying Corps in the field, one may hazard the statement that he would possibly have concluded that the Allied air services could not have developed their full effectiveness in 1919 unless his command was extended to include all Allied aircraft on the Western front except the necessary minimum, consisting mainly of reconnaissance and artillery observation units, definitely allotted for co-operation with the armies in the field. It may be that Marshal Foch would have built up a reserve force from the Allied air services. It is clear from his memorandum (Appendix X) that his conception of the right employment of the Independent Force could have differed in no great degree from what he might have laid down as the guiding principles for the employment of a strategic air reserve. In other words, it seems logical to suggest that Major-General Trenchard's command might have been extended to include such a reserve. The speculation, although academic, is worth making because the Allied armies on the Western front did not at any time throughout the war obtain the advantages which their combined superiority in aircraft should have given them.

The conditions in 1919 would have been such that, for the first time in the war, the striking formations of the Allied air services might have enjoyed a single direction.

On the other hand, it must be pointed out that, had it appeared likely the war would continue well into 1919, the British Government would most probably not have given way on the question of subordinating the Independent Bombing Force to the French Generalissimo. The arguments put forward by the French were no different in kind from those which had been advanced, with force and conviction, by Sir Douglas Haig and by other military and naval authorities. After exhaustive debate, and after full consideration of all aspects of what might without disrespect be called the military point of view, the Government had decided to conduct a campaign of independent air warfare against the heart of Germany. The possibility is that had the outlook on the Western front in October remained unaltered, and had the French Government persisted in its opposition to the presence of an independent bombing force on French soil, then the British Government would have considered moving that force, in its entirety, to Britain.

The student has had the various arguments on this important subject set before him and he will, no doubt, according to his general views, form his own conclusions. There are, however, a few additional considerations which are relevant to the problem. The word 'independent' was, perhaps, ill chosen. The realistic French military mind at once conjured up a vision of an alien force conducting, from the French battle area, a private war of its own according to the strange doctrines of black-coated gentlemen across the Channel. The word independent, indeed, introduced so soon after dire necessity had compelled a form of unity of command for the Western front, in itself constituted something of a challenge. There was one French General who, when he heard the name of the force, exclaimed: 'Independent of whom, of God?' It may be that some such title as 'British Bombing Force' would have made for quieter discussion. Whether that would have been so or not, it is a fact that until the Independent Force was placed under the supreme control of Marshal Foch, that is to say, during most of the time of its existence, it was, so far as possible, disregarded by the French high military authorities. Had it not been for Major-General Trenchard's determination, helped by his own personal relations and those of Major Maurice Baring with some of the French authorities, more particularly with General de Castelnau, commanding the French Eastern Group of Armies, and with his staff, the Independent Force might never have been enabled to operate. French head-quarters were mindful of difficulties about allotting ground for aerodromes and camps, and all the business of communications and of ground organization had to be arranged in an atmosphere that, outside General de Castelnau's sphere of influence, was seldom helpful.

This is no matter for hard words. The French were frank and logical from the beginning. The statement of General Duval, already given, may be repeated, namely, that there was a limited space in France for the construction of aerodromes, and that the French Government wished to allot ground only if it was to be utilized for the defeat of the enemy in the field. It should be remembered, also, that when the discussions were taking place, it was not simply a question of a few squadrons. A programme was, in fact, prepared which gave the Independent Force more squadrons than existed with the British Armies in France when the war ended.[1] There is no evidence that the details of this programme, which was never formally approved by the War Cabinet, were communicated to the French Government, but one may assume that the French authorities were well aware that the British Government intended and hoped to make the Independent Force a formidable command. And from the French point of view the objections to a large organization, over which they could exercise no effective control, cumbering their lines of communication, in an area where military concentrations for offence or for defence might at any time become necessary, were, perhaps, unanswerable.

With the French views about the operational control of

[1] See p. 171.

the Independent Force, every serious student of warfare must feel some sympathy. In a land campaign, such as that of 1918, the Generalissimo alone could judge what was the decisive time and place for operations. What would have been the military use, for instance, of the spasmodic bombing of German industrial centres at a time when the Allied armies were threatened with disaster by a German offensive? If the Generalissimo decided—as he alone could—that it was imperative to direct the full weight of his bombing offensive towards the interruption of traffic on the lines of communication leading to the decisive battle-front, imagine his position if he had to go cap in hand to enlist the goodwill of an independent air commander who was subject to the control of a body remote from the stresses and rapidly changing conditions of the battle. It does not really affect the argument that Major-General Trenchard would, in the circumstances envisaged, have placed his force without doubt at the disposal of Marshal Foch. There is another general point to be considered which has no particular reference to times of crises. It should be remembered that the independent bombing squadrons, to reach their objectives, had to fly over the battle area where the fight for air superiority was continuous. The activities of the bombing formations were partly dependent on the effectiveness of the air offensive waged by those squadrons which were under the ultimate control of the Generalissimo. On the other hand, it should be borne in mind that the bombing operations against distant objectives caused a number of fighting aircraft to be diverted for defence and to that extent influenced the air situation at the front.

So much, then, for pure military theory. There were, however, factors which came into play, as they would again in comparable circumstances, which had nothing to do with theory. Marshal Foch had no security of tenure. Changes in the French political atmosphere might lead, at any time, to a change of generalissimo. The grave uncertainty on the Western front, arising from the pressure exerted by the German offensives, might bring about swift alterations in French military strategy of a kind which might not, at least to British minds, give sufficient weight to the position of the British armies. The idea, under these conditions, that the control of a number of British squadrons should pass inevitably to the French was one which the Air Ministry was naturally reluctant to accept. Chiefly, however, there was conflict about how the war should be waged. Was the air weapon merely an auxiliary, with no independent functions of its own, as some strategists trained and practised in an older school of warfare insisted, or could it, if properly employed, go a long way towards forcing the enemy to sue for peace, as the air staff believed? Had the Air Council felt assured that the generalissimo, no matter who he might be, would share its own views about the efficacy of what may be termed strategic bombing, it is unlikely that there would have been any tenacious opposition to his being given control of the British bombing squadrons. It was precisely because the Air Council felt, not assurance, but misgiving, that it fought, as it must, for the independence of the force. Finally it must be pointed out that there were some who objected to the independence of the force, not because they held narrow views about the military employment of the air weapon, but because they believed that to break up the air service into independent detachments was a backward step. The air is one element, and to create, voluntarily, a distinct force for bombing, and to adhere with gritty tenacity to the idea of its independence, was to make a case for further disintegration. What the Air Council claimed for its bombing units, it was argued, the army might similarly claim for its attached air squadrons, or the navy for, say, its anti-submarine aircraft detachments. In other words, to separate a particular bombing force from the main body, which also undertook bombing operations, was an act calculated to divide and not to unify the air services.

CHAPTER IV
OPERATIONS OF THE INDEPENDENT FORCE
1917–18
[Map, p. 152]

The Luxeuil Bombing Wing

THE study of the independent bombing operations against German industrial targets should rightly begin with No. 3 Naval Wing which was formed in France, at Luxeuil, near Belfort, in the summer of 1916.[1] The main object of the British Admiralty was to inflict damage on the German works in the Saar industrial area where, there was reason to believe, steel for U-boats was being manufactured in large quantities. The naval bombers began to co-operate with French pilots in a series of organized attacks early in October. Evidence made available after the war leaves no doubt that the combined bombing offensive had some of the results anticipated by the British Admiralty. On the 18th of November 1916 the president of the powerful steel works union of Düsseldorf telegraphed to the German high command: 'At a meeting of the Board of Administration 'held to-day, reference was made by the steel works on the 'Western front to the serious dislocation of work caused by 'air raids. The perpetually increasing curtailment of night 'work due to these raids not only results in an average de-'crease of thirty per cent. of the steel works' output, but it 'is feared that night work may soon have to be entirely sus-'pended. Since, in order to carry out the vast programme, 'we are instructed to increase production at these very 'works on the Western front, we consider that better pro-'tection is absolutely necessary. All the works managers 'agree that the present military protection is entirely 'inadequate. We should be deeply grateful to the army 'administration if opportunity could be given as soon as 'possible for a representative to explain this serious posi-'tion.'[2]

At the time this telegram was received the German high

[1] See Vol. II, pp. 451–3.
[2] Major Grosskreutz in *Die Luftwacht*, June 1928.

command was already giving careful attention to the problems of air defence. Germany had been particularly shocked by a raid on Karlsruhe made by French aeroplanes on the 22nd of June 1916, the day of Corpus Christi, when 120 civilians had been killed and 146 injured. There had followed a public outcry for protection and, by the early autumn, some Flights of single-seater fighters had already been distributed over the industrial area on the Western front from Cologne to Freiburg. There was, however, little co-ordination between these scattered Flights and the anti-aircraft gunners or the warning posts, an unsatisfactory state of affairs which had been remedied on the 8th of October 1916, when the Kaiser, by Order in Council, amalgamated 'all means of air combat and air defence with 'the army, in the field and in the home areas, into one 'unit'.[1]

The result of this order was the appointment of a commander-in-chief of the air forces with, under him, a commander of the home air defences who was given control of the warning system, the gun and searchlight units, and the aeroplane defence Flights. One of the first actions of the new air command was to appoint officers who had already distinguished themselves on the battle-front to important posts in the home air defence organization. At the same time anti-aircraft units were withdrawn from the battle front and allocated to positions in back areas, and searchlights were allotted to obvious industrial targets. The number of lights was consistently increased until, by the middle of 1917, all important objectives were protected by inner and outer rings of lights. Machine-guns were also diverted to the main industrial works because it was judged that there was no other way to combat low-flying bombers. At first the guns were manned by selected workers, but during the summer of 1917 military machine-gun sections were established for this form of home defence.

Some additional single-seater fighter Flights were formed for home defence at the beginning of 1917 and, with the existing Flights, were employed to give, so far as possible, an interconnected line of fighters from the

[1] Major Grosskreutz in *Die Luftwacht*, June 1928.

Rhenish–Westphalia industrial area to the Swiss frontier, with advanced detachments which had orders to attack and turn back the bombers. Another effect of the Allied bombing campaign was a demand from many German factories for balloon and kite barrages, but it was not until March 1917 that balloon detachments for industrial protection were formed. Barrage detachments were allocated to the Saar, to the Lorraine–Luxembourg, and to the Rhineland industrial areas. Although they were said to have entailed an excessive expenditure of time, labour, and equipment, and were, in consequence, disliked by the German military authorities, the effect on the morale of the workers was reckoned to be so great that additional barrage detachments were subsequently formed. 'Those 'in fear of a raid', wrote Major Grosskreutz, 'had the 'feeling that they were surrounded by a protective wire 'barrage, which constituted a soothing influence not to 'be under-estimated. It was highly important that the 'psychological effect of the enemy air raids, so harmful to 'the morale in Germany, and to the work in the areas in 'which armaments were produced, should be countered as 'far as possible.'[1]

In the opening months of 1917 the Luxeuil naval bombers were handicapped by the weather. Even when conditions were otherwise favourable, the valleys in which the German industrial works were situated were often shrouded in mist. Furthermore, when the cold was severe, as it was during most of February 1917, there was trouble due to freezing oil because the hangars on the advanced aerodrome at Ochey were not heated. What was possible was done to keep the aeroplanes warm enough for flying, but a few only could normally be kept serviceable. There was a raid, on the 23rd of January, by ten escorted bombers on the blast furnaces at Burbach, another on the same objective by thirteen bombers on the 25th of February, by ten again on the 4th of March, and by six on the 22nd of March. There were attacks also, by six bombers, on the aerodrome at Morchingen (Morhange), on the 16th, and, during the ensuing night, by one Handley Page on

[1] *Die Luftwacht*, August 1928.

the railway station at Moulin-les-Metz. In April, with two exceptions, the bombing was confined to single Handley Pages. On the 5th the railway junction at Arnaville was attacked; on the 14th blast furnaces at Hagendingen; and, during the same night, the depot and aerodrome at Chambley. The only organized daylight attacks in April were made on the 14th on Freiburg in Breisgau when, in two raids, a total of twenty-three British aeroplanes (fifteen bombers), and fifteen French (six bombers), dropped two and a half tons of bombs, together with leaflets which said that the raid was a reprisal for the sinking of the hospital ship *Asturias* by a German submarine.[1] Three British two-seater aeroplanes failed to return from the raids, but all the French pilots reached home safely: it was afterwards known that four of the six missing British flying personnel had been killed. According to German information the bombs fell in the most thickly populated quarter of the city, and in any event the raid seems to have been a true 'reprisal' because there is no record that a military objective was given to the pilots: their reports make note of 'a reprisal raid on the centre of the town'.

The Luxeuil bombing wing was broken up in the spring of 1917 in order that help might be given to the Royal Flying Corps. What remained of the wing was withdrawn, in May 1917, to complete the equipment of No. 10 (Naval) Squadron for service with the armies on the Western front. The Admiralty were influenced, when they agreed to disband the wing, by what Sir Douglas Haig had to say about the results of the raids made by the naval bombers. The main concern of the Board, as has been stated, was to reduce the output from such German steel works as were within striking distance, and Commodore Godfrey Paine, the Fifth Sea Lord, asked Sir Douglas Haig if he had any information to show whether the bombing of blast furnaces had restricted the output of steel as much as had been

---

[1] The *Asturias*, showing full regulation lights, had been torpedoed off Start Point at midnight on the 20th of March 1917 with a loss of 50 lives. The raid was also a reprisal for a torpedo attack on the hospital ship *Gloucester Castle*, on the 30th of March, when 3 lives were lost. Both ships were towed into port.

claimed, to which Sir Douglas Haig replied: 'No such in-
'formation has reached me, and it would, therefore, appear
'highly improbable that the output has been seriously
'affected.' The Fifth Sea Lord then asked if the naval
bombing operations had drawn German aeroplanes away
from the British front, to which the answer was a definite
'No'. Although the number of German squadrons opposite
No. 3 Wing might have increased, said Sir Douglas Haig,
the explanation would be that there had been a general
expansion all along the front, and particularly opposite the
British.

There is not much doubt that Sir Douglas Haig objected
to an independent naval air detachment operating from
French soil against what he considered to be military
targets. Writing to the War Office in November 1916, he
had pointed out that the imperative need was for squadrons
in the battle line where they could affect the issue of the
battle. 'Long-distance bombing', he had said, 'as a means
'of defeating the enemy is entirely secondary to the above
'requirements. Its success is far more doubtful, and even
'when successful both theory and practice go to show that
'usually its results are comparatively unimportant.'

With our fuller knowledge it is clear that the effect produced by the naval bombing wing was disproportionate
to the number of raids, which were comparatively infrequent and are not to be judged by the material results.
The British and French bombing attacks went some way
to shake the morale of the industrial population and had
an adverse effect on the output of munitions of war, but
chiefly they compelled the Germans to divert aeroplanes,
labour, and material to the beginnings of widespread
schemes of home defence.

The Forty-first Wing

The next step in the bombing of Germany by British
aircraft was taken in consequence of the night aeroplane
attacks on London which began in September 1917. It
has been recounted in an earlier volume[1] how the War
Cabinet decided, in consequence, to wage a counter-

[1] Vol. V, pp. 88, 90–1.

offensive against targets in Germany. It happened that at the beginning of September a hundred Russian pilots were under training in England and that fifty D.H.4 aeroplanes for these pilots were being built to the order of the Russian Government. Because the winter season was approaching, when operations would be at a standstill on the Russian front, and because the D.H.4's would be a welcome addition to our own strength, the British Government asked Russia to forgo delivery of these fifty aeroplanes on condition that seventy-five in their place would be supplied in the spring of 1918. With this proposal the Russian Government agreed, and it was partly because of the Russian 'windfall', as it was called, that the British War Cabinet considered that it was in a position to initiate long-range bombing operations against Germany.[1]

Major-General Trenchard was instructed, at the beginning of October, to take immediate action against German objectives which could be reached from the neighbourhood of Nancy, and he at once formed a special unit, the Forty-first Wing, under the command of Lieutenant-Colonel C. L. N. Newall. The squadrons which made up the Wing were Nos. 55 (D.H.4) for day-bombing, and 100 (F.E.2b) for night bombing, both withdrawn from the British front, and No. 16 Naval Squadron, of night-bombing Handley Pages, which represented the Admiralty contribution to the long-range bombing operations.[2] A normal load of bombs was twelve of 112-lb. weight carried by each Handley Page, and two of the same weight by the D.H.4's and the F.E.2b's.[3] The head-quarters of the wing were

[1] The engines for the Russian D.H.4's were Fiats, bought by Russia in Italy. The Fiat D.H.4's were not employed for the independent bombing operations into Germany, but their employment elsewhere on the Western front released Rolls-Royce D.H.4's.

[2] No. 16 (Naval) Squadron, originally called 'A' Squadron and, afterwards (from the 1st of April 1918), No. 216 Squadron, was specially formed at Manston: the Handley Pages with which the squadron was originally equipped were taken off anti-submarine patrol duties. They were flown to Ochey, under the leadership of Squadron Commander K. S. Savory, in the middle of October.

[3] Bombs of 230-lb. weight were often carried and, sometimes, of 25-lb. or 40-lb. weight. The last named were phosphorous bombs.

established at Bainville-sur-Madon on the 11th of October, and the aerodrome for the three squadrons was situated at Ochey where also two French squadrons were housed.

Plans for the employment of the bombers had to be carefully considered. The easterly limit of the area which might come under attack was roughly the line Cologne–Frankfurt–Stuttgart, about 125 miles distant from the existing trench line in the neighbourhood of Ochey. Within this area lay many vital industries. There were the coal and iron fields of Lorraine and the Saar, the great chemical works of the *Badische Anilin- und Soda- Fabrik* at Mannheim and Oppau, and many miscellaneous factories engaged on war production, such as aircraft engines, locomotives and rolling stock, submarine parts, and magnetos. The targets offered by the coal industry were difficult ones, but the iron works, more especially those with blast furnaces, stood out with some prominence and were, moreover, sensitive to bombing because damage to vital parts, say to the blast furnaces or the power stations, would mean that the works would be put out of action for an appreciable time. Germany had to rely upon the Lorraine and Luxembourg areas for nearly eighty per cent. of her supplies of iron ore, much of which, variously estimated between 20 and 50 per cent., was smelted locally. The view of the French general staff was that the iron industry, on which the German war effort largely depended, was the most important target open to the bombers, and that it could best be attacked by blocking the railways by which the iron ore was transported. In this way the whole output, including that which passed eastwards into Germany for treatment, might come under attack. The French plan, therefore, which had been officially adopted in the summer of 1917, aimed at the systematic bombing of the stations on the periphery of the iron basins, namely, Metz-Sablons, Metz-Woippy, Conflans-Longuyon, Athus-Pettingen, and, above all, Thionville and Bettembourg. It was calculated that some 10,600 trucks, of fifteen tons, were transported through these junctions daily, about half taking the ore to the works on the right bank of the Moselle, to Westphalia, and to the Rhine, and the other half returning to the

Lorraine and Luxembourg mines to be loaded. If the eight key junctions could be blocked the isolation of the iron deposits would be attained.

As soon as the Forty-first Wing arrived at Ochey, the commander-in-chief of the French armies of the north and north-east wrote to Sir Douglas Haig outlining the French bombing plan and asking whether the British bombing squadrons could be instructed to co-operate as occasion offered. Sir Douglas Haig replied that the British aeroplanes at Ochey had for their principal mission 'long-range 'attacks on German commercial towns as reprisals for enemy 'air raids on Allied towns'. He went on to say: 'While the 'British pilots are learning the country they will be able to 'carry out attacks on targets in the Sarrebruck area, but 'not in the Briey–Longwy area which lies outside the line 'of approach to their main objectives. As soon as the 'British pilots have learned the country sufficiently to find 'their way to the Rhine by night, they will be able to co-'operate in attacks on targets in the Briey–Longwy area as 'well, whenever the weather is not settled enough for long-'distance raids into Germany. The officer commanding 'the Forty-first Wing, Royal Flying Corps, who commands 'the British air forces at Ochey, is being instructed to place 'himself in communication with the general officer com-'manding the French Group of Armies of the East and to 'carry out the latter's instructions as regards co-operation 'within the limits stated above.'

Comment must be made about the word 'reprisals' employed by Sir Douglas Haig. It is obvious that he was using the term in a popular and not a legal sense. A reprisal strictly means that a violation of the laws of warfare is answered by a similar violation. So long as the German bombers attacked definite military targets, such as, for instance, Woolwich Arsenal or other munition factories, or naval dockyards, it could not be seriously adduced that they were violating the rules of warfare. Reprisals were popularly called for because, whatever may have been the intent, the German bombs dropped on England seldom found military targets, but exploded instead among the civilian population. The British counter-bombing offensive cannot properly be associated with the word 'reprisals' because the bombing was not directed against the German people. The objectives, as will be made clear in this narrative, were chosen for their importance in the system of German war production and military transport.

The bombing campaign of the Forty-first Wing was opened on the 17th of October 1917 by eight D.H.4's of No. 55 Squadron which attacked the Burbach works near Saarbrücken, an objective which had often been visited by the naval bombers of the Luxeuil Wing. A German official report of the attack reads: 'Three bombs fell on the rail-'way behind the eastern coke ovens, near a condensing 'tower, and in front of the foundry casino. Damage resulted 'to the railway lines, the walls of the condensing tower, and 'especially to the casino buildings and to neighbouring 'houses belonging to officials of the company: damage '17,000 marks.' The night raids began, in bad weather, on the evening of the 24th of October when nine Handley Pages of 'A' Naval Squadron, and fourteen F.E.2b's of No. 100 Squadron, again attacked the Burbach works, as well as targets along the railway line between Falkenburg and Saarbrücken. Pilots, some of whom dropped their bombs from a few hundred feet, reported that the town of Saarbrücken was well illuminated. Two of the Handley Pages and two F.E.2b's failed to return from this first raid. On the night of the 30th/31st of October twelve F.E.2b's attacked the steel works and the station at Volklingen. A number of hits were made on the sheds, and the damage was estimated by the Germans at 47,646 marks.

The weather in November was unfavourable for long-distance operations and, except for a raid made on the 1st by No. 55 Squadron on Kaiserslautern, no bombing attacks were undertaken. The Germans, however, twice bombed the aerodrome at Ochey during the month. The first time, in a mist, on the 15th/16th, and again on the 22nd/23rd. On the second occasion three small bombs hit an aeroplane shed and damaged three aeroplanes.

The most notable raid in December, when the weather was again generally unfavourable, took place on Christmas Eve when ten D.H.4's of No 55 Squadron, in two formations,[1] made a first attack by British pilots on Mannheim at midday (objectives: factories and railways); one of the D.H.4's was forced to land and the occupants were made prisoners. According to German official reports no military damage was inflicted by this attack, but two civilians were killed and twelve wounded.

The aerodrome at Ochey was twice bombed during December, on the evening of the 4th and once more on the 5th. The first of these attacks caused much damage, both on the British and French sections of the aerodrome. Two heavy bombs hit the French sheds, with the result that ten French aeroplanes were destroyed and seventeen damaged. In his report about the German bombing attack, the officer commanding No. 100 Squadron wrote: 'The con-'tents of one large French hangar were well ablaze, and 'we sent over as many fire extinguishers as we could spare 'with a voluntary fire picquet under some officers and the 'sergeant-major who managed finally to extinguish the 'fire, but not until several machines had been burnt out.' The main damage in the British section of the aerodrome was the demolition of part of No. 100 Squadron's workshops.

The attacks on the aerodrome of the British and French bombers seemed to presage an intensive campaign to hamper the bombing offensive against Germany, but they proved to be isolated occurrences and the bombing squadrons were subsequently little worried in this way. The French had requested that the British bombing squadrons should refrain from attacking German aerodromes, but after the Germans had bombed Ochey for the third time the French outlook changed. At first, however, the French stipulated that the bombing should be confined to the aerodromes from which the enemy set out to attack Ochey, but this proved an impossible condition because it could never be said with certainty which enemy aerodrome was being used for any particular raid.

[1] No. 55 Squadron normally adopted a Flight formation of six aeroplanes in a triangle: two such Flights formed a squadron formation and they worked in close touch under one leader. On this occasion two pilots had had to return with engine trouble.

On the 1st of February 1918 the bombing force was raised to the status of a brigade under the command of Brigadier-General C. L. N. Newall. This Brigade—the VIII—had been formed on the 28th of December 1917, but it did not begin work as such until the 1st of February 1918 when an independent head-quarters was opened in the Chateau de Froville, near Bayon.

A detailed account of the bombing operations by the various squadrons would make tedious reading, and for a full list of the attacks on industrial and railway targets the student may refer to Appendix XIII. Until May 1918 the one day squadron, No. 55, and the two night squadrons, Nos. 16 (Naval) and 100, continued to be responsible for all the long-distance attacks, but in that month they were reinforced by two squadrons equipped with D.H.9 aeroplanes. One of these was No. 99 Squadron,[1] which was taken on the strength of the Forty-first Wing on the 27th of April, but did not arrive from England until the 3rd of May after being delayed on the way by bad weather. The squadron made its first raid on the 21st of May when six pilots bombed the Metz-Sablon railway triangle, an objective frequently visited by the independent bombing squadrons. The railway at Metz was an important key point in the German lines of communication. There were great stores sheds adjacent to the railway and, furthermore, there was always an appreciable collection of locomotives and rolling-stock in the sidings of the Metz-Sablon triangle. On the 9th of June twelve pilots of No. 99 Squadron bombed steel works and blast furnaces at Dillingen. The other D.H.9 squadron was No. 104, which arrived from England on the 19th of May and made its first attack on the 8th of June on the Metz–Sablon triangle.

In all, between the 17th of October 1917, when the first raid was made, and the 5th of June, that is, the day before the formation of the Independent Force proper, the British bombing squadrons made fifty-seven raids, and the objectives included specified targets in Karlsruhe, Mannheim,

[1] An authentic account of the activities of this squadron is contained in the *History of 99 Squadron*, by Squadron Leader L. A. Pattinson, D.S.O., M.C., D.F.C.

Cologne, Mainz, Stuttgart, Coblenz, Thionville, and Saarbrücken.

The activities and the spirit of No. 55 Squadron may well be illustrated by a brief account of operations during some days of fair weather in March 1918. After being held down on its aerodrome by snow and rain for a fortnight, the squadron made a first visit to Mainz—116 miles beyond the lines—on the 9th of March. The objectives were factories, barracks, and railways, which were attacked at 12.25 p.m. from 13,000 feet, by ten D.H.4's in two formations, and photographs taken by the bombers showed bursts and fires among warehouses near the river and in and near the central railway station. A subsequent notice issued by the Cologne police, advising the inhabitants of the town to take cover when air raid alarms were given, instanced the attack on Mainz which, it was stated, had resulted in many deaths.

The pilots were out again next day on their way to Stuttgart, which lay 104 miles beyond the lines. Eleven D.H.4's crossed the trenches, in two formations, at 10,000 feet, their main objective being the Daimler motor works outside the town. All pilots reached and bombed their target, and although air photographs showed no direct hits, it was reliably reported that the works, together with some aero-engines, had been damaged.[1] Immediately after the bombs had been dropped, three German aeroplanes appeared, and their pilots kept up a long-range attack for some time. One D.H.4, which was forced by engine trouble to break formation, was repeatedly assailed by the enemy aeroplanes, but the pilot reached his aerodrome with a wounded observer and a petrol tank holed by bullets. Another D.H.4 was forced down in enemy territory and its two occupants were made prisoners.

On the 12th of March the squadron made a first raid on Coblenz, 130 miles over the lines. The town (objectives: factories, barracks, and railway) was reached at midday by nine pilots, and bombs were released from 13,500 feet, but there was a haze and the bursts were not clearly seen. It

---

[1] The German records show that the bombs fell close to the works and caused damage valued at 80,000 marks: five civilians were wounded.

was reported at the time that the bombs fell in the town and caused fires and casualties. German records show that one bomb exploded in the barracks among a company of soldiers lined up to receive their midday meal and that four of the soldiers were killed and twelve wounded. The total casualties, including civilians, were nine killed and sixty-one wounded, but the damage was not great. Attacks by five German fighters immediately after the raid were repulsed by the bombers. A letter written by an eye-witness, and later found on the body of a dead soldier on the Western front, referred to the great havoc caused in the town and concluded: 'We have lived through terrible 'hours in the last day. Oh, my God, if only this misery was 'at an end, this useless murder of men.' Great numbers of letters, written in a similar strain, fell into the hands of the British infantry. It would be unwise to lay undue stress upon them, but there is little doubt that they had some influence on the morale of the German troops, who were thus made aware of the extent of the British bombing offensive, and who received exaggerated accounts of its results. That the air war was being carried increasingly into Germany, and that the German air service was, apparently, powerless to prevent this, was not calculated to improve the spirit of the soldiers at the front.

The target next day, the 13th of March, was Freiburg in Breisgau, which was attacked by eight D.H.4's. The objectives were munition works, barracks, and railways, but the accuracy of the attack was affected by a fierce onslaught which was made by about fifteen German fighters over the town, as a result of which three of the D.H.4's were shot down. The majority of the bombs fell in the neighbourhood of the railway station and they caused appreciable damage, and injury to five persons: among the buildings hit by stray bombs were a church and a hospital.

On the 16th of March twelve D.H.4's of No. 55 Squadron were ordered to bomb the Badische chemical works at Mannheim, but four pilots turned back with engine trouble, and another because of damage by enemy aircraft which attacked the formation on its outward journey. As heavy cloud banks lay along the route the bombs were dropped on Zweibrücken. Another attempt to reach Mannheim was made next morning by ten pilots who found the Rhine valley obscured by fog and therefore bombed the alternative targets, factories and railway at Kaiserslautern, instead: thirteen of the eighteen bombs dropped fell in the town and it is known that the damage, to factories and houses, was considerable (estimated by the Germans at 123,666 marks) and that there were numerous casualties. Next day, the 18th, Mannheim was reached and bombed by nine pilots, and photographs showed bursts near the buildings of the Badische works which were the main objective. It was afterwards known that one bomb fell on a machine shop and caused slight damage, and that another, a phosphorous bomb, hit a building in which cotton waste was stored: the store burned for several hours and was destroyed. The civilian casualties were four killed and ten wounded.

We may conclude this brief notice of the operations of No. 55 Squadron with a further reference to their work on three days in May. On the 16th twelve pilots bombed Saarbrücken and had a running fight with double their number during which one D.H.4 fell in flames and observers in three others were wounded, while three German fighters fell out of control. In spite of the intense opposition of the German fighters this attack was one of the most successful made on the railway system at Saarbrücken, where all traffic was brought to a standstill for eight hours. One bomb wrecked a shunting engine in which the driver was killed, rails were torn up on three tracks, the main workshops received two direct hits and suffered much damage, a water-main was broken, a footbridge destroyed, two stationary trains were damaged, twelve soldiers were killed and forty-nine injured, and signals, telegraph, and telephone installations were destroyed.

On the following afternoon twelve pilots of the squadron attacked the railway at Metz-Sablon. The bombs fell chiefly in the station and in the station square. At the time the attack was made a visit was expected from high military officers, and a guard of honour, mounted and dismounted, was in waiting. In the station square thirty soldiers and civilians were killed and wounded and several horses were killed, and in the station itself a bomb which exploded alongside a standing train was responsible for the death of eleven officers and for injury to forty-six soldiers.

Next day, the 18th of May, No. 55 Squadron made a long-distance raid on Cologne. The town had not been attacked by British aeroplanes by day since October 1914, when a naval pilot had dropped small bombs from a single-seater aeroplane. It had, however, suffered a night attack on the 24th/25th of March by a Handley Page from No. 16 (Naval) Squadron. The attack of No. 55 Squadron on the 18th of May, made by six D.H.4's, was led by Captain F. Williams. The pilots left their aerodrome at Tantonville[1] at 6.35 a.m., and two and a half hours later reached Cologne, which was bombed from 14,500 feet (objectives: railways and factories). The town was taken by surprise because the observation service had broken down, with the result that the inhabitants had received no sort of air raid warning. In consequence, the casualties were high, some forty persons being killed and about one hundred injured. Serious damage was done to thirty-eight buildings to a total value of 340,000 marks. The D.H.4's were three times attacked, and one observer, after shooting down an enemy aeroplane, was mortally wounded. There were reactions to this raid similar to those which had followed the more important German attacks on England. Questions were asked in the Reichstag, and anxiety spread to all the Rhineland towns. It is significant also that after this first daylight attack in force on Cologne, it was urged in many responsible quarters in Germany that steps should be taken by the German Government to agree with the Allies to abandon or limit bombing attacks from the air.[2]

The night-bombing squadrons, although their attacks were less spectacular than those of the day bombers, exerted a greater general moral effect. In the daytime the people

[1] No. 55 Squadron had moved to Tantonville on the 7th of November 1917.
[2] The German official records confirm that this attack made a deep impression. They also give varying numbers for the casualties, the highest figures being 41 killed, 83 severely wounded, and 40 lightly wounded.

on the ground could see the worst. The raiders came in formation, dropped their bombs and went, or else were merely on passage to some other objective. In any event, the danger period was set between limits which were fairly clearly defined. At night, however, there was no definition. The bombers did not attack in formation, but moved about singly, at irregular intervals of time, and they usually flew at low heights, making a noise that was full of menace. All over the area within range of the British bombers, people received the air raid warning and had to take whatever precautionary measures had been ordered, perhaps dozens of times for every attack their particular town or works suffered. It was the 'alarms', more than the specific attacks, which led to idleness, temporary or prolonged, and therefore lowered output, and it was at night that it was difficult to keep the alarms within a reasonable relation to the possible danger.

The two-seater F.E.2b night bombers of No. 100 Squadron attacked medium-distance targets, mostly up to about seventy miles distant on the enemy side of the trenches, while the three-seater Handley Pages of No. 16 (Naval) Squadron had the endurance to reach the important towns in the Rhineland area.

On the night of the 24th/25th of March No. 100 Squadron made one of the more successful of its many attacks on the German railway communications. The objective was Metz-Sablon, on which bombs were dropped intermittently by twelve F.E.2b's. A German report on the results of the attack reads as follows: 'Last night from '8.55 p.m. onwards hostile aircraft appeared over Metz. 'The fall of bombs, so far confirmed, was as follows: Several '(incendiary) fell on a goods train standing on the main 'track No. 6 (eastern arm of the Metz-Sablon triangle) in 'the station. Fifteen trucks caught fire and seven munition 'wagons among them exploded. Tracks Nos. 6 and 16 were 'very extensively damaged and others suffered in addition '(in all twenty lines). Two wagons were hurled to the 'right and left by the force of the explosion, one striking 'a corner house near the railway, the other landing near the 'Metz–Frescaty road and destroying a small house. Seven

'houses in all were seriously damaged. Portions of the
'debris struck the most northerly gasometer at the apex
'of the triangle and damaged it very extensively. The
'force of the explosion was so great that the building south
'of the gasometer had its roof blown off, while exploding
'shells damaged the machinery. As a result of this explosion,
'traffic was held up on the main Bensdorf–Courcelles–
'Metz–Thionville line for several hours. The moral effect
'of this raid was very great. Nothing approaching this had
'happened before and as a result all the houses bordering
'the railway were evacuated by order.'

Towards the end of March 1918 General de Castelnau, commanding the French Eastern Group of Armies, asked that the two British night-bombing squadrons should be placed temporarily at his disposal in order that he might employ them to attack the railway communications in the Châlons-sur-Marne sector where it appeared that the Germans were concentrating for an offensive. British headquarters agreed, and on the 1st of April Nos. 100 and 216 Squadrons, together with the Forty-first Wing headquarters, moved to Villeseneux, near Rheims, where they came under the orders of the Commandant, French Aviation. The squadrons, however, were not favoured with fair weather, and bombing attacks could be made only on six nights up to the 9th of May when the period of attachment to the French ended.[1]

On the night of the 17th/18th of May Nos. 100 and 216 Squadrons, returned from the French area, attacked Thionville where appreciable damage was caused and twenty-five soldiers and ten civilians were killed. In an attack by three Handley Pages of No. 216 Squadron on the chemical works at Mannheim on the night of the 21st/22nd of May, a bomb broke a gas main in the Oppau section of the works, and as a result the factory had to close for two days. This was the only occasion in the war when the Oppau section of the Badische chemical works had to cease activity as a result of air raid damage.

On the morning of the 31st of May there was a successful attack by No. 55 Squadron on the railway station, and

[1] See Vol. IV, pp. 283–4.

on a munition factory, in the town of Karlsruhe. Eleven D.H.4's, led by Captain F. Williams, flew towards Mannheim, with the intention to bomb the Badische works, but as heavy cloud banks were encountered over the Vosges the leader decided to make his attack on Karlsruhe. The town was reached about 8.0 a.m. and twenty-two bombs of 112-lb. weight were dropped on the station and on factories. Photographs which were taken at the time showed one bomb bursting in a known munitions factory. German official documents reveal that the factory was blown up, that the station was hit, and that the total damage was valued at 700,000 marks: the casualties were four people killed, and seventy-four injured. About fourteen German aeroplanes were encountered by the bombers near Karlsruhe and one of the enemy pilots, with fine daring, dived through the formation and shot down a D.H.4 in flames.

The Independent Force

The Independent Force, under the command of Major-General Sir H. M. Trenchard, came into being officially on the 6th of June 1918,[1] and comprised the two wings which made up the VIII Brigade, namely, the Forty-first (day squadrons Nos. 55, 99, and 104) and the Eighty-third (night squadrons Nos. 100 and 216). 'Preparatory work on 'the construction of aerodromes,' says Major-General Trenchard, 'with a view to accommodating a larger force, 'had been undertaken before my arrival, and had been 'handled with zeal and tact by the General Officer Com- 'manding the VIII Brigade. The work accomplished by 'General Newall formed a foundation upon which I was 'at once able to build in making arrangements to accom- 'modate an increased number of squadrons. . . . My first 'work was to at once push on and arrange for the accom- 'modation of a force of sixty squadrons. . . . This work was 'practically completed by the 1st November, 1918.'

Major-General Trenchard's ideas for the employment of the Independent Force are well summarized in the

---

[1] Major-General Trenchard had arrived in the Nancy area on the 20th of May. He took over the tactical command of the Force on the 5th of June, and the administrative and complete control on the 15th of June.

dispatch from which the above quotation is taken.[1] 'The 'question I had to decide', he says, 'was how to use this 'Force in order to achieve the object, i.e. the break-down of 'the German Army in Germany, its Government, and the 'crippling of its sources of supply.

'The two main alternative schemes were:

'1. A sustained and continuous attack on one large 'centre after another until each centre was destroyed, 'and the industrial population largely dispersed to 'other towns; or

'2. To attack as many of the large industrial centres as 'it was possible to reach with the machines at my 'disposal.

'I decided on the latter plan, for the following reasons:

'(i) It was not possible with the forces at my disposal to 'do sufficient material damage so as to completely 'destroy the industrial centres in question.

'(ii) It must be remembered that, even had the Force 'been still larger, it would not have been practical 'to carry this out unless the war had lasted for at 'least another four or five years, owing to the limita-'tions imposed on long-range bombing by the 'weather. . . .

'By attacking as many centres as could be reached, the 'moral effect was first of all very much greater, as no town 'felt safe, and it necessitated continued and thorough 'defensive measures on the part of the enemy to protect 'the many different localities over which my force was 'operating. At present the moral effect of bombing stands 'undoubtedly to the material effect in a proportion of '20 to 1, and therefore it was necessary to create the greatest 'moral effect possible. . . .

'My Intelligence Department provided me with the 'most thorough information on all targets such as gas 'factories, aeroplane factories, engine factories, poison-gas 'factories, &c., each target having a complete detailed and 'illustrated plan, and maps were prepared of every target 'that was within reach. These were supplemented in a

[1] Dispatch of Major-General Sir H. M. Trenchard, dated 1st January, 1919.

'large way by the aerial photographs taken by reconnais-
'sance machines.

'Before it was possible to attack Germany successfully
'it was necessary to attack the enemy's aerodromes heavily
'in order to prevent his attacking our aerodromes by night,
'and by destroying his machines to render his attacks by
'day less efficacious. I considered that it was probable
'during the spring and early summer of 1919 that at least
'half my force would be attacking the enemy's aerodromes,
'whilst the other half carried out attacks on long-distance
'targets in Germany. . . .

'I also had to decide, when it was impossible for squadrons
'to reach their objectives well in the interior of Germany,
'what alternative objective should be attacked, and which
'attacks would have the greatest effect in hastening the end
'of hostilities. I decided that railways were first in order of
'importance, and next in importance the blast furnaces.

'The reason of my decision was that the Germans were
'extremely short of rolling stock, and also some of the main
'railways feeding the German Army in the West passed
'close to our front, and it was hoped that these com-
'munications could be seriously interfered with, and the
'rolling stock and trains carrying reinforcements or reliefs
'or munitions destroyed. They were also fairly easy to find
'at night.

'I chose blast furnaces for the second alternative targets,
'as they were also easy to find at night, although it was
'difficult to do any really serious damage to them owing to
'the smallness of the vital part of the works. . . .'

With one possible exception,[1] the results justified Major-General Trenchard's policy. In the light of our later knowledge it would be difficult to suggest how the few independent bombing squadrons might have been more effectively employed. The German people in 1918 were suffering from war weariness, fostered, among other things, by short rations and by Allied propaganda. It is true that the Germans were stimulated by the offensive which began on the Somme on the 21st of March, but when that offensive came to its indecisive end, and when

[1] See the section on aerodrome bombing, pp. 158–64.

the subsequent onslaughts in Flanders, and against the French armies, were seen to follow a similar course, the war weariness returned, and it increased sharply after the defeat inflicted on the enemy as a result of the British Amiens attack on the 8th of August. That is to say, the nerves of the German people, during the time the Independent Force was operating, were at a tension which ensured a maximum moral effect from bombing attacks.[1] The more these were spread, therefore, the greater that effect must be.

If it be suggested that better results might have been obtained had the bombing been directed more against German industrial targets, the answer is that what could be done was limited by technical equipment, and by the capacity of the flying personnel. The makeshift bombers with which the operations had to be conducted were of limited range, and they could not be sent out to the limit without account being taken of the weather and general conditions. Nor could a bombing squadron be sent into action immediately it arrived at the front from England. It was desirable that three or four weeks should be allotted for final training, and when the squadron was judged to be ready for service flying, it was still necessary, as a beginning, to restrict the attacks to targets at short and medium distances. After weighing all the contemporary factors Major-General Trenchard had to be sure that what he asked of his pilots and observers was something they could do and keep doing. His aim was to avoid spectacular attacks with the danger or certainty that periods of inactivity during recovery would follow. His belief, firmly rooted, was that the most consistent military effect would come from a high level of general achievement. In this he was surely right, and his policy, judged by results, was well suited to his belief.

The D.H.9's of No. 104 Squadron made their first attack

---

[1] In a conversation with the author, *Archivrat* Dr. Klemp, a war-time pilot subsequently responsible for research at the *Reichsarchiv* into military air operations, was emphatic in support of this view. Had the same attacks been made earlier in the war, he suggested, their moral effect would have been much less.

in the early morning of the 8th of June when twelve pilots set out for the Metz-Sablon railway station. As soon as the bombing formation appeared over Metz it was attacked by three German fighters which continued to follow the bombers back to the lines. An observer in one of the D.H.9's was wounded, and one of the three German aeroplanes went down, apparently in trouble. Nos. 99 and 104 Squadrons attacked Metz again on the 12th of June when some of the bombs hit the artillery barracks and caused great damage as well as some casualties among soldiers. In a raid on Saarbrücken on the 24th of June, nine aeroplanes of No. 104 Squadron were attacked by four German fighters, one of which fell in flames through the British formation, narrowly missing one of the bombers: among the D.H.9's one pilot and two observers were wounded, but all returned safely. Saarbrücken was once more attacked, by No. 99 Squadron, a little later in the morning without opposition in the air.

On the 25th of June all three day-bombing squadrons had hard fighting, but the objectives, at Saarbrücken, Offenburg, and Karlsruhe, were attacked, although one aeroplane from each squadron fell in Germany: a pilot of No. 104 Squadron, badly wounded in the right arm over Karlsruhe, brought his D.H.9 home and landed it safely. Karlsruhe was again attacked next day by all three squadrons, but of the three formations of twelve aeroplanes each which set out, only twenty pilots reached the objective. German records show that damage was caused to buildings to the estimated value of 250,000 marks, and that a man was killed. During the night of the 26th/27th of June, damage was done to the Badische chemical works at Mannheim by a Handley Page of No. 216 Squadron. On the 29th, when ten D.H.4's of No. 55 Squadron attacked Mannheim again, five people were killed and sixteen wounded, and damage to buildings estimated at 151,000 marks was caused.

Throughout the month of July the independent squadrons attempted to reach Cologne, Stuttgart, and other distant industrial and military targets, but during half the month clouds lay thick over the Rhine valley and no attacks were possible. All efforts to reach Cologne failed, but Coblenz was bombed three times by day and Stuttgart once by night. During a night attack on Mannheim, where the chemical works continued to be a favourite target, four bombs failed to release from their rack: they were eventually dislodged by the observer when the Handley Page was passing over the town of Heidelberg.

On the morning of the 16th of July twelve pilots of No. 99 Squadron, in two formations, followed at a few minutes' interval by two similar formations of No. 55 Squadron, set out to bomb the Bosche and Daimler works at Stuttgart, but thunderstorms encountered on the way led to the attack being made on Thionville station instead. All the pilots of No. 99 Squadron reached the objective, but some of No. 55 lost direction and six only attacked the target. This raid proved to be one of the most successful of its kind made by British aeroplanes in the war. It was known at the time, chiefly from the evidence of air photographs, that great damage was inflicted. It is now possible to give, from German reports, details of the destruction. The German authorities estimated that about twenty bombs fell in the station (the total of bombs dropped were seven 230-lb., twenty 112-lb., eight 25-lb., and two 40-lb. phosphorous). A munition train received two hits and, as a result, fifteen trucks began to explode and some of them caught fire. Bursting shells fell upon six stationary ammunition trucks and these also began to explode. Shells were soon flying in all directions and they set fire to goods sheds and to the many loaded trucks standing in the sidings. In one of a number of sheds on a road opposite the railway station loose shells were stacked. It was not long before these also started to explode, with the further result that two nearby buildings, which housed small arms ammunition and hand grenades, caught fire and were destroyed with their contents. Not far from the munitions train which had been hit at the beginning of the attack, a horse transport train, containing forage and other stores as well as horses, was standing: the train was wrecked and most of the horses were killed or wounded. Apart from the destruction of the goods sheds and station offices, five locomotives were damaged beyond repair, fifty trucks were destroyed and fifty more seriously damaged, and water mains, water towers, and rails were wrecked. The casualties were eighty-three military killed and wounded, and ten civilians killed. The public went to earth in cellars and dug-outs at 2.0 p.m. and did not dare, because of the exploding ammunition, to come out in the open again until after dark.

On the night of the 16th/17th of July nine F.E.2b's of No. 100 Squadron bombed blast furnaces at Hagendingen. One bomb pierced a tunnel, in use as an air raid shelter, leading from the offices to the railway. Nine workmen in the tunnel were killed and fourteen seriously injured, and a subsequent result was that the construction of elaborate dug-outs at various parts of the works was undertaken.

There was a noticeable increase, during the month of July, in the opposition from German fighting formations, and fifteen bombers were lost in air combat. The biggest fight took place on the 31st of July and involved D.H.9's of No. 99 Squadron, twelve of which had set out at 5.30 a.m. for Mainz. Three of the pilots turned back with engine trouble before the trenches were reached, but the remainder went on their way until they came near Saarbrücken when they were attacked from above and below by about forty German fighters. The leader of the bombing formation believed that it would be impossible, in face of the enemy opposition, to reach Mainz, and he decided to attack Saarbrücken instead. Four of the bombers were shot down before Saarbrücken was reached, but the five remaining pilots dropped their bombs on the railway. The German fighters continued to attack and two only of the D.H.9's recrossed the lines. The loss of fourteen experienced officers (five killed and nine prisoners) was a severe blow, and the squadron could not resume bombing raids until reinforcements had been given adequate training in formation flying. The squadron records show that most of the pilots who had newly joined the squadron from England had arrived with little experience of flying in formation, and the success of day raiding depended on the efficacy with which formation could be kept.

Nor was the D.H.9, with its 200 horse-power B.H.P. engine, a satisfactory aeroplane to fly. The engine, about which there had been trouble in the production stage,[1] was not reliable, and bombing formations of D.H.9's were apt to be very much reduced in strength before the lines were crossed, for the simple reason that the engines would not develop enough power to enable pilots to keep their station. Nor when flying at its best can it be said that the D.H.9, fitted with the B.H.P. engine, was good enough for really effective long-distance attacks by daylight, more particularly because its 'ceiling' was comparatively low. Major-General Trenchard had been opposed to the employment of this aeroplane from the beginning, and even before the first of the type had been received in France he had spoken strong words on the matter to the members of the Air Board. He had warned them, in November 1917, that the D.H.9 with the B.H.P. engine would be out-of-date as a day bomber by June 1918, and his prophecy was duly fulfilled.[2]

In August the Independent Force was increased by four squadrons. On the 9th, No. 97 (Handley Page) Squadron arrived from England, on the 19th, No. 215 (Handley Page) Squadron joined from the Expeditionary Force, and on the 31st, Nos. 115 (Handley Page) and 110 (D.H.9a) Squadrons arrived from England. No. 97 Squadron began active service operations on the 19th, and No. 215 on the 22nd. During the month, also, the F.E.2b's of No. 100 Squadron were gradually replaced by Handley Pages, the re-equipment of the squadron being completed early in September. By the end of August Major-General Trenchard decided that the D.H.9's with B.H.P. engines could no longer be considered service type bombers, and that the losses which it must be expected they would suffer did not justify again sending them over the lines.[3]

[1] See pp. 37–8.
[2] Writing from France in June 1918, Major-General Trenchard said it was imperative to make every effort to replace the D.H.9's with D.H.9a's, fitted with Liberty engines.
[3] It is of interest that in his report for October 1918 dealing with the work of the Royal Air Force on the Western front, Major-General J. M. Salmond, pointing out that air operations depended upon the degree of

FRANKFURT ATTACKED

Raids into Germany were made during August against Düren, Frankfurt, Darmstadt, Coblenz, Karlsruhe, and Mannheim, by day, and against Cologne and Frankfurt by night. Frankfurt (objectives: factories and railway) was bombed, for the first time, by twelve D.H.4's of No. 55 Squadron on the 12th of August from a height of 14,000 feet. On the outward journey the formation was attacked over Mannheim by about forty fighters, and the attacks were maintained all the way to the objective and throughout the return journey. In spite of the hostile fighters, the bombers reached the town and returned safely with the loss of one observer killed by machine-gun fire: two enemy fighters were destroyed. According to German official reports the bombs fell in the centre of Frankfurt and caused damage valued at 500,000 marks. The casualties were sixteen killed and twenty-two wounded, and there were official complaints that the inhabitants did not take precautions as ordered: it was said that there was too much standing about in the streets, or rushing to door or window to see what was happening. Frankfurt was subsequently twice attacked during August by No. 216 Squadron, at night, but no casualties were inflicted and the damage was not heavy.

Darmstadt, another new objective, was bombed by ten pilots of No. 55 Squadron on the morning of the 16th of August. They had set out to attack munition works and the railway station at Cologne, with the Benz aircraft engine works at Mannheim as an alternative target if the weather proved unsuitable for the longer journey. Owing to massed clouds, visible in the direction of Cologne, the leader of the bombing formation decided to attack the alternative target, but on the way he became satisfied that he could get farther, and he therefore went on to

air superiority attained, said: 'This is demonstrably true, at the present 'time, of D.H.9 Squadrons with 200 B.H.P. engines, for although this 'type of aeroplane has sufficient petrol, and oil, to enable it to reach objec- 'tives 100 miles from the lines, its low ceiling, and inferior performance, 'oblige it to accept battle when, and where, the defending forces choose, 'with the practical result that raids tend to become restricted to those 'areas within which protection can be afforded by the daily offensive 'patrols of scout squadrons. . . .'

Darmstadt where his target was the railway. The bombers were attacked on the homeward journey by twenty German fighters, and three of the D.H.4's were shot down. German records show that the inhabitants of the town, who were warned in good time, were quick and orderly in taking precautions, and that the casualties were few, namely, four killed and four wounded (damage 88,000 marks).

A less ambitious raid by No. 55 Squadron on the 8th of August calls for mention. Twelve D.H.4's set out in the afternoon to attack the factories at Rombach, and although along much of the route cloud banks extended from 2,000 to 14,000 feet, the formations, led by Captain B. J. Silly, reached and attacked their objectives. It is known that the twenty-four bombs dropped fell on or close to the works: two blast furnaces were damaged, and there were hits on the rolling-mills, with the result that the works had to be shut down for eight hours.

A raid on Cologne had been attempted by twelve pilots of No. 55 Squadron on the 1st of August, but when they arrived over their objective they had found the whole area obscured by clouds, and the leader of the formation had therefore continued to Düren where all the bombs were dropped. The police at Düren had received an air-raid warning, and they caused fire bells and church bells to be sounded, but the first bombs began to fall as the bells started to ring. The streets were consequently crowded with people who had rushed from house and factory to discover what was wrong, and as they had had no experience of bomb attacks there was consternation and panic. The reason they had not been drilled to take air-raid precautions was because the German authorities had not thought that Düren, an unfortified city, was subject to danger. One bomb exploded near a municipal milk supply office where many people were waiting. Ten persons were killed outright, six others mortally injured, and eighteen seriously injured. After this experience of a bomb attack arrangements were made to warn the inhabitants by means of electric sirens and other devices, and dug-outs were built in many parts of Düren. There was, however, no second attack on the town, although the inhabitants were subsequently given the alarm many times when British aeroplanes were in the neighbourhood. Cologne (objective: railway station) was reached on the night of the 21st/22nd of August by two Handley Pages of No. 216 Squadron. Six persons in the city were killed and ten injured, and damage was caused to twenty-two buildings to a total value estimated at about half a million marks.

It may be remarked that the D.H.4's of No. 55 Squadron carried fuel sufficient for a journey of about five and a half hours, and that the raids made by the squadron in August to Düren, Frankfurt, and Darmstadt, lasted between five and five and a half hours so that the bombers operated with little or no margin of safety.

Six attacks were made during August on chemical works, notably those of the Badische firm at Mannheim. One of these attacks deserves special mention. Two Handley Pages of No. 215 Squadron (pilots, Captain W. B. Lawson and Lieutenant M. C. Purvis) left their aerodrome at 8.0 p.m. on the 25th of August on the first attempt to be made by the squadron to attack the Badische works. One pilot approached the target from the north-west, through a searchlight barrage and under gun-fire, and, gliding down from 5,000 feet, made his attack from a height of 200 feet. The lights in the works had been put out, but the searchlights, in their attempts to find the bomber, were trained almost horizontally, and they clearly illuminated the works for the bombing crew. Many of the bombs (sixteen 112-lb. and ten 25-lb.) were seen to explode among the buildings, and when they had been released the pilot continued to fly low for some minutes while the machine-guns from the Handley Page traversed the area. The second pilot came in close behind the first and made a somewhat similar attack from 500 feet. Both aeroplanes returned safely to their aerodrome after a difficult journey through thunderstorms. The Germans in and near the works looked upon this attack as particularly daring, and their evidence was that the bombers only narrowly missed the tall factory chimneys. Many of the bombs, possibly as a result of the low height from which they were dropped, failed to explode, but four which penetrated one of the buildings burst among a freezing-plant which could not be brought into action again for twelve days. In all, seventeen bombs fell in the Mannheim works and eighteen in the sister factory at Oppau, but the latter bombs did not, according to German information, cause serious damage.

There was a steady increase during August in the amount of opposition encountered by the bombing formations, and, in combat, twenty-one British aeroplanes were lost. Six more failed to return from raids for reasons not due to fighting, and fifty-four were wrecked from various causes on the British side of the lines. No. 104 Squadron, on the way to Mannheim on the 22nd of August, was attacked by about forty enemy fighters, and two of the D.H.9's were shot down before the town was reached: fighting continued over the target, but the bombers attacked their objectives, without inflicting serious damage. On the return journey, in further fierce fighting, five more D.H.9's were shot down.

In September the weather conditions continued to be unsuitable for long-distance bombing, particularly when the phases of the moon would have favoured night flying. There were strong winds, low clouds, and much rain, and on nineteen days and eighteen nights no raids were attempted. The two squadrons which had joined the Independent Force at the end of August made their first attacks in September. No. 110 (D.H.9a) Squadron[1] bombed Boulay aerodrome on the 14th, and No. 115 (Handley Page) Squadron made its first attack during the night of the 16th/17th. During the month Stuttgart was bombed by day, Frankfurt and Mannheim were attacked by day and by night, and Karlsruhe, Kaiserslautern,[2] Cologne, Bonn, and Mainz were bombed by night.

An attack by five Handley Pages of No. 216 Squadron on the Burbach works during the night of the 2nd/3rd

[1] No. 110 was the first squadron to be equipped with the D.H.9a, fitted with the 400 horse-power Liberty engine (normal bomb load: three of 112-lb. weight). The aeroplanes were the gift of His Serene Highness the Nizam of Hyderabad.

[2] German figures are available which show that in seven raids during the war property in Kaiserslautern was damaged to the total value of 2,700,000 marks.

of September may be mentioned because of the known damage inflicted. One bomb, of 550-lb. weight, and some of 112-lb. weight, were seen from the aeroplane to make hits on buildings. German records show that eight bombs exploded in the works. Seven caused only minor damage to buildings and to railway trucks, but the eighth, possibly the heavy bomb, burst in a machinery and carpentry shop, which was destroyed. The damage was estimated at 400,000 marks, greater than was caused by any other bomb which fell on the Burbach works during the war.

On the morning of the 7th of September there was an attack on the Badische works at Mannheim by ten aeroplanes of No. 104 Squadron and by eleven of No. 99 Squadron. The formations from the two squadrons, led by Major L. A. Pattinson of No. 99 Squadron, were assailed throughout the journey. Soon after crossing the lines on the way out six or more enemy fighters attacked the rearmost aeroplanes, three of which were shot down. When the target was reached some fifteen enemy fighters attacked, but they did not prevent the bombers from flying across their objective and releasing their bombs, almost together, from a height of 10,000 feet. One of the bombers was shot down in the fighting over Mannheim, but the remainder flew safely home.[1] Mannheim was bombed again, by day, by Nos. 55 and 110 Squadrons on the 16th, and, by night, by Nos. 100 and 216 Squadrons on the 20th/21st, but in neither instance was the damage important. The German casualties as a result of the two attacks were two killed and eleven wounded. In the day raid on the 16th, three of the bombers were shot down by German home defence pilots.

On the night of the 16th/17th of September seven Handley Pages from the various squadrons were lost. Five of these, of No. 215 Squadron, set out for Cologne and Mannheim, and one of them, after dropping bombs on a town which the pilot thought was Bonn, but which more likely was Cologne and its neighbourhood, landed in Holland with engine trouble. According to German official records

---

[1] German official records show that no casualties were caused by the bombing and that the damage was not great.

the others were shot down by anti-aircraft gun-fire after various places had been bombed. The towns which suffered most were Saarbrücken and Treves, where damage to buildings totalled a value of 100,000 marks. In Treves three people were killed, but the only other casualties of the night were brought about by a Handley Page which was forced down near Dillingen. Careless handling, by a too curious spectator, of one of the bombs carried on the Handley Page led to an explosion which killed eight onlookers, severely wounded nineteen, and lightly wounded twenty more. The number of rounds fired against the Handley Pages by the various German anti-aircraft guns during this night are listed in the German records: it is revealed that a total of 16,063 shells were expended over a wide area, and that 173 searchlights were in action.

In the afternoon of the 25th of September eleven aeroplanes of No. 110 Squadron bombed Frankfurt from 17,000 feet. Some damage was caused to buildings (estimated at 146,000 marks) and the casualties were one killed and seven wounded. There was fierce fighting over the town, during which two German aeroplanes were destroyed: four of the D.H.9a's failed to return, and in those which reached home one observer was dead and a pilot and an observer were wounded.

At the request of Marshal Foch, many bomb attacks were made during September on railways in co-operation with attacks by the French and American armies. The plans to help the American attack on the St. Mihiel Salient on the 12th of September were:
    (i) Before the American offensive was timed to begin, the railways at Metz-Sablon, Thionville, Bettembourg, Ehrang, and Tetershen, and the aerodromes at Frescaty, Boulay, Montoy, and Buhl, were to be bombed by night and day.
    (ii) In the period of the artillery preparation, the bombing was to be concentrated on the railway systems at Metz-Sablon, Thionville, and Courcelles, and on the aerodromes at Frescaty, Boulay, and Montoy.

(iii) During the actual attack, the bombing was to be narrowed down to the railways at Metz-Sablon and Courcelles.

The plans could not be executed because of bad weather. Before the American offensive began, and on the opening day—the 12th of September—little bombing was possible. During the night of the 12th/13th, however, Metz-Sablon and Courcelles were heavily attacked, and the bombing continued, against the railway and the aerodrome objectives, until the night of the 16th/17th. In this period sixty-one tons of bombs were dropped, about half of them on the Metz-Sablon railway triangle.

On the 23rd of September Major-General Trenchard received a letter from Marshal Foch in which particulars were given of an offensive to be made by French and American troops from Verdun to the river Suippes. The Generalissimo requested the Independent Force to co-operate by bombing railway junctions, particularly Mézières. The Allied offensive began at 5.0 a.m. on the 26th, and during this day and the following night fourteen tons of bombs were dropped by the Independent squadrons on the railways at Mézières, Thionville, Ars, Audun-le-Roman, and Metz-Sablon, and also on Frescaty aerodrome. The day bombers had hard fighting over Metz and six of them failed to return. No bombing was possible during the remaining nights of the month because of adverse weather.

A fighting squadron—No. 45—equipped with Sopwith 'Camels', joined the Independent Force from Italy on the 22nd of September, but Major-General Trenchard decided not to send the squadron on escort duties until it should be re-equipped with special Sopwith 'Snipes' having an endurance of four and a half hours. The squadron had not been so re-equipped when hostilities ceased, and in the meanwhile its activities had been confined to patrols in the front-line area.

In October fog, mist, and low clouds often made raiding impossible. No new squadrons joined the Independent Force during the month, but there was some reorganization as a result of the arrival of two wing head-quarters. The head-quarters of the Eighty-fifth Wing arrived on the 5th of October, and of the Eighty-eighth Wing on the 19th. The latter Wing took over Nos. 45 and 110 Squadrons.

There was a notable raid on Kaiserslautern during the month. On the night of the 21st/22nd orders were issued for four Handley Pages, each carrying one 1,650-lb. bomb, to attack this objective, and for four others to drop a full load of small incendiary bombs. Three of the Handley Pages carrying the heavy bombs, and two with the incendiary bombs, reached and attacked Kaiserslautern. One of the heavy bombs fell in the court-yard of a small arms factory, a building of three stories, 100 metres square, which was almost entirely demolished. In the cellars under the building about forty people from the neighbourhood were sheltering: except a child, killed outright, they were all eventually rescued unhurt. The factory, American-owned, had made sewing-machine parts before the war, but during the war it had been compulsorily placed under German control and had been reorganized to manufacture cartridge clips. In addition to the factory, where the damage was estimated at 500,000 marks, houses over a wide area were affected. The other bombs on Kaiserslautern on this night mostly fell on waste ground, but the blasting effect of the heavy bombs caused severe damage to houses. Another 1,650-lb. bomb was dropped on Kaiserslautern on the night of the 23rd/24th, and other objectives attacked on the same night were Coblenz, Mannheim, and Wiesbaden.

The last-named town was bombed by a Handley Page of No. 97 Squadron which had set out to attack Coblenz,[1] but the visibility was bad and the 1,650-lb. bomb was dropped on an unidentified but fairly well lighted town lower down the Rhine which, as it proved, was Wiesbaden. The bomb caused so much destruction that the inhabi-

[1] The operation orders gave the Badische works at Mannheim and the Krupp works at Essen as objectives on this night. The pilot's report shows Coblenz as his objective, presumably given to him in person. The alternative targets, as quoted officially, were Kaiserslautern or Saarbrücken.

tants were convinced that a group of bombs, chained together, had been dropped. The Wiesbaden fire brigade was compelled to call in military assistance, and the rescue work continued for three days. Twelve bodies were recovered from the debris of the houses and, in addition, thirty-six people were treated for severe injuries. This attack on a town mainly concerned with the care of the sick and wounded aroused strong feeling throughout Germany, which, as was not always the case, was told the full and gruesome details. It has already been said that Wiesbaden was not an allotted objective and that it was by chance, and regrettably, that the town was bombed.

On the 31st of October the railway station at Bonn was attacked by six pilots of No. 55 Squadron, led by Captain D. R. G. Mackay: the bombs burst in the centre of the town, with the result that twenty-nine people were killed and about sixty wounded. The inhabitants had received no warning until just before the attack had begun and they had seemed at a loss to know what to do or where to go: many of the casualties were caused among people who were jostling to get into a tram. After the attack posters were displayed about the town urging the people of Bonn to seek cover immediately an air-raid warning was given, and to stay under cover for the duration of an alarm.

The Independent Force squadrons once again co-operated in October, at the request of Marshal Foch, with the French and American armies in their offensive between Rheims and Verdun. Forty tons of bombs were dropped on the railways at Metz-Sablon and twenty tons were distributed over the railway centres at Mézières and Thionville, and the aerodrome at Frescaty. In an attack on the Sablon station on the morning of the 5th of October, made by twelve pilots of No. 104 Squadron, a bomb destroyed a cellar which had been converted to serve as an air-raid shelter and was, at the time of the raid, occupied by about one hundred railway workers: twelve of them were killed and twenty-three were injured. On the night of the 9th/10th of October, when Metz was bombed by Nos. 97, 215, and 216 Squadrons, one or more bombs fell on the powder magazine on the Metz Weise island. The ensuing explosion shook the town, and the powder magazine was still smouldering four days later: a German estimate put the monetary value of the damage caused at one million marks.[1]

In the final days of the war, before the declaration of the Armistice on the 11th of November, unfavourable weather prevented long-distance raids. The railways at Ehrang were attacked by No. 55 Squadron on the 10th of November, under conditions of haze and heavy clouds. The main targets in November were German aerodromes, notably that at Morhange, on which a total weight of eight tons of bombs was dropped.

General Observations

The reader has been given a brief account of some of the more important raids on German industrial and other centres, and he also has, for reference, a full list of British attacks set out in Appendix XIII. It will help further to elucidate the efficacy of the attacks if the information already given is supplemented by some observations of a more general character. German official figures show that the total attacks, British and French, on German territory, were as follows:

Year.	By day.	By night.	Estimated number of bombs.
1915	44	7	940
1916	21	75	917
1917	45	130	5,234
1918	119	234	7,117
Total	229	446	14,208

The total German casualties, civilian and military, were 746 killed and 1,843 injured, and the damage was estimated at 24 million marks, say, £1,200,000. These were the direct destructive effects of the bombing attacks, but

---

[1] The casualties, military and civil, as a result of all the air attacks, British and French, on Metz throughout the war, were 132 killed and 300 injured. The barracks south of the railway triangle were many times hit and damaged.

they may be set down among the less important results. The major effects, in order of importance, may be listed as (i) a weakening of the national will, particularly in 1918 when the nerves of the people, through hunger and general war weariness, were acutely sensitive; (ii) a falling off in the production of essential war materials, partly because the morale of the workers was lowered by the attacks, but chiefly through loss of time as a result of air-raid alarms, and (iii) a diversion of fighting squadrons, anti-aircraft guns and searchlights, and of a great amount of material and labour, to active and passive schemes of defence.

A German authority has summed up as follows: 'The 'direct destructive effect of the enemy air raids did not 'correspond with the resources expended for this purpose. 'On the other hand, the indirect effect, namely, *falling off* '*in production of war industries*, and also the *breaking down* '*of the moral resistance of the nation*, cannot be too seriously 'estimated.'[1]

It is not perhaps sufficiently realized that air-raid alarms were given over the whole area covered by the passage of bombing aircraft (and often in adjacent areas also), and that it was the time lost in taking shelter as a result of the alarms which was mainly responsible for the reduction of output. A diary kept by the Roechling iron works at Volklingen in the Saar district revealed that during the month of September 1918, when only one attack was made, the operatives were given the air-raid alarm on forty-four occasions. Two or three alarms were sometimes given in the same night, and the disturbance to sleep and nerves was intensified. The Mannesmann works at Bous were bombed eight times between September 1916 and November 1918, and the damage was said to have been very small, estimated at a total of about £400. In the same period, however, the Mannesmann works received 301 air-raid alarms, as a result of which 454 working hours were lost, with a consequent drop in output, estimated by the managers at 9,440 tons. At the Volklingen works, in the same years, there were 327 alarms and a loss of output of 30,680 tons

[1] Major Grosskreutz in *Die Luftwacht*, October, 1928.

of steel.[1] The full results of the air attacks and alarms were analysed by the directing staff of the Volklingen works during the war, and the table, which is reprinted as Appendix XIV, may be read as typical of what happened in other industrial concerns subjected to similar attacks and warnings.

There is evidence to show that the effect of the air raids on the morale of the workers was uneven. Where attacks were not only infrequent, but also comparatively harmless, air-raid alarms did not cause undue worry. In such places the workers sought the shelter of dug-outs, or other protection, and they stayed until the 'all-clear' signal was given, but although their enforced herding might be looked upon as inconvenient or annoying, there was seldom a feeling of tension. There were occasions when impromptu dances were held in shelters for the duration of an alarm. Where, however, severe damage had once been inflicted, and the attack in general had been of a terrifying nature, subsequent alarms worked upon raw nerves and there was no inclination to dance. At the Volklingen, Burbach, and Hagendingen steel works, all of which suffered severe damage at times, the frequency of air-raid warnings during the summer and autumn of 1918 so affected the weary and undernourished operatives that their efficiency diminished sharply. There were German authorities who believed that a stage had been reached in the autumn of 1918 when intensification of the bombing attacks must have caused a break-down of labour in those steel works which had suffered most.

The Badische works at Mannheim, and the sister works at Oppau, which employed about 14,000 hands, were bombed on fifteen occasions during the war, thirteen times by the British and twice by the French, and were given the alarm 256 times. The damage was estimated at a total of about

---

[1] The most devastating attack on the Volklingen works was one made by French aeroplanes in March 1917, when a bomb hit the benzol installation and the resultant damage exceeded one million marks. To deceive the bombing pilots dummy buildings were erected on slag-heaps near the works at Volklingen, as they were at some other places, notably at Bous. It is of interest that the workers expected, and received, increases in wages because of the strain of the air-raid alarms.

520,000 marks and was therefore of no outstanding importance, but the effect of the raids and of the alarms on the morale of the workers, especially in 1918, was appreciable. The number of bombs which fell in or close to the works was 230, but the buildings, like many similar ones in industrial Germany, were of massive construction, some having outer walls three feet in thickness. The bombing crews did their part. They navigated their aeroplanes to the allotted targets, but the bombs dropped, mostly of the 112-lb. type, were not heavy enough to cause the desired destruction. A few bombs of 1,650-lb. weight were being carried by the Handley Pages to enemy objectives towards the end of the war and it may be assumed that not many hits from bombs of this type would have been required to put the Mannheim chemical works out of action.

Officials of the Badische works who were interviewed by an officer of the Independent Force soon after the armistice, used the word 'annoying' when speaking in general terms of the British bombing attacks. The daylight alarms, they said, caused limited inconvenience, but the night alarms affected morale as well as output. It was notable in 1918, after an epidemic of influenza had lowered the physical resistance of many of the workers, that the moral effect of the air-raid alarms was greatly increased. The attack on the night of the 25th/26th of August 1918, when the two Handley Pages of No. 215 Squadron bombed the works from a low height, made a deep impression. It was true that many of the bombs dropped by the two aeroplanes failed to detonate,[1] and that those which hit and exploded were of the 112-lb. or smaller kind and did not cause great damage, but the daring of the bombers, who seemed to fly nonchalantly round the chimney-tops and to make unhurried use of their machine-guns, depressed the spirits of the workers. The balloon, searchlight, and anti-aircraft gun barrages, which had been placed round the factories, had been looked upon as affording a fair measure of protection, certainly against low-flying attacks, but the raid revealed to the workers that their feeling of moderate

[1] That a number of bombs (sometimes 25 per cent. or more) failed to explode was a common feature of the attacks.

security was falsely based, and seemed also to register the indifference, even the contempt, of the British bombers for the defence arrangements. Had the two Handley Pages each carried on this night a 1,650-lb. bomb, fitted with delay-action fuses, the German war chemical industry might have suffered a major disaster. The point is hypothetical, but it is worth making by way of comment on the statement that the air attacks on the Mannheim works were no more than 'annoying'.

There were two occasions when the German balloon barrage was responsible for bringing an aeroplane to ground, once, in 1916, when a French aeroplane crashed after fouling a balloon, and again in January 1918, when a British F.E.2b, of No. 100 Squadron (pilot, Second Lieutenant L. G. Taylor; observer, Second Lieutenant F. E. Le Fevre), on the way back from Treves, ran into trouble.[1] The pilot, who, with his observer, was taken prisoner, reported after the war as follows: 'Ahead of us I saw the 'town of Esch in Luxembourg, and hearing a shout from 'my observer, I followed his pointing arm and saw that the 'town was defended by a balloon barrage, which is a steel 'net held up by balloons at intervals of about fifty yards. 'The balloons were at a height of about 4,000 feet, and it 'was impossible to get over them in our crippled condition, 'so I kept straight on, hoping to pass through the barrage 'without hitting a wire. My observer immediately opened 'fire on the balloon above in the vain hope of setting it on 'fire and dropping the net, but nothing happened. We 'were now passing under the balloon and for a moment I 'had the feeling that we must have missed the wires, but 'suddenly the machine gave a violent lurch, and was thrown 'backwards: I immediately put the nose down, but the 'speed indicator dial only registered 30 m.p.h. I wondered 'why the machine did not stall and plunge to the ground. 'The aileron controls went out of order immediately we 'struck the net. We went down to the ground, dragging

[1] Kite and balloon barrages were also employed at night in the defence schemes of Bruges docks, Zeebrugge, and possibly other targets. It is believed that a Handley Page was destroyed in May 1918 as a result of fouling the wires at Bruges.

THROUGH A BALLOON NET

'the balloon and net. We finally got close to the ground, 'which was heavily wooded. The planes and nacelle were 'riddled with shrapnel holes, and one of the tail booms was 'nearly cut in two near the main planes. The nose was 'driven into the ground and one wing was crumpled up 'underneath the engine. The other wing was sticking 'straight up into the air, and I saw the balloon wire which 'had been our final undoing. It had just missed the nacelle 'by about two feet, and had entered both top and bottom 'planes just in front of the bomb rack. It had sawed its 'way anglewise towards the propeller from this point, and 'had cut the aileron balance wires through, passed through 'the steel bomb rack and was finally held up by the Michelin 'flare rack which was of fairly heavy steel, but it had com-'pletely worked its way through about three-quarters of 'the distance from leading to trailing edges of both top and 'bottom planes, and the first long front landing and flying 'wires were hanging as they had been sawn through.'

The results of the bombing operations against railway stations and rail communications generally may be summed up as, on the whole, disappointing. Some striking instances of destruction have been given, of added importance because Germany was short of rolling stock, and there was, also, much dislocation of traffic. The damage and interruption, however, were less than might have been because of the German quality of thoroughness. The railway buildings were of solid construction, the tracks were well laid with brick foundations at important junctions, and many of the store sheds had concrete roofs which often proved thick enough to detonate the smaller bombs. In the main stations machine-guns were placed on bridges, in signal boxes, on the roofs of offices, and at other vantage points, and substantial dug-outs and shelters were built. To mitigate the effect of a possible break-down at important points alternative lines were built, and comprehensive schemes were worked out for emergency diversions of traffic. The schemes came under frequent review and there seems little doubt that the system was made as flexible as was possible in the circumstances. Tribute must be paid to the German railway staff who played their part in a grim struggle. The aim of the bombers was to dislocate the traffic system, especially in battle periods when movements were above the normal. The railway officials had to be alert, by swift decision, to counter, so far as lay in their power, every attempt at interruption. It is certain that the frequent air-raid alarms caused much dislocation, although such evidence as exists does not suggest that the disturbances were ever serious or prolonged enough to exert a vital influence on the progress of military operations.

Aerodrome Bombing

Of the 543 tons of bombs dropped by the squadrons of the Independent Force, 220 tons were aimed at German aerodromes. One modern view is that such attacks represent a diversion of force justified only if adequate results can be expected, and when it is not practicable to direct the air bombing offensive against more vital centres of the enemy. Some of those who hold this view have said that the bombing of German aerodromes by the independent squadrons went far beyond what was necessary. A majority of the bombs aimed at aerodromes should, they contend, have had industrial works for objective.

The reader will be given such available facts as have a bearing on the subject and he must form his own judgement. No more than one fighter squadron was allotted to the Independent Force, but because it had not been suitably equipped before the end of the war it never came into effective action. Aerodrome bombing, therefore, was the only means by which the Force could wage an air offensive against the enemy squadrons on its front. It must be remembered that the night-flying F.E.2b's did not have the endurance to reach the Rhineland industrial area, and that the German aerodromes were suitable targets, among others, within their range. Furthermore, enemy aerodromes also formed useful alternative targets for the longer range bombers on occasions when the weather conditions were unfavourable for distant operations.

Aerodrome bombing by the Independent Force had two objects:

(i) to inflict damage on the German night-bombing squadrons and generally to subdue them in order to make them unable, or unwilling, to attack the aerodromes of the Independent Force, and

(ii) similarly to damage and subdue the German fighter squadrons so as to make the way of the British day bombers easier.

The aerodromes most frequently attacked were situated at Boulay, Buhl, Morhange, and Frescaty, but about twenty others were also bombed, some of them once only. Unfortunately, not many German official records have been preserved which contain information about the results of the bombing, and those which have survived give only summary particulars. At Boulay, for example, a report for the week ending the 20th of August 1918 shows that bombing attacks during the week destroyed five aeroplanes and damaged ten. In the following week, when a dummy aerodrome set up nearby diverted many bombs, the losses on the real aerodrome were two aeroplanes destroyed and five damaged. On the night of the 3rd/4th of September two large hangars on the aerodrome received direct hits during an attack, and both were wrecked, one of them by fire, but the German records appear to indicate that on this night the hangars were empty of aeroplanes.

It is known that an attack on the aerodrome at Morhange on the night of the 16th/17th of August had important results. Three hangars, one large and two small, were hit and destroyed by fire with their contents. In each of the smaller hangars two fighter type aeroplanes were housed, but although it was believed at the time that the large hangar also contained aeroplanes, there is some evidence that it housed transport. A third small hangar in the same attack was riddled with bomb splinters and its two aeroplanes rendered unserviceable, while a bomb struck the corner of yet another hangar and destroyed one aeroplane. On the night of the 21st/22nd of August, when Morhange was once more attacked, four of seven aeroplanes which were hit by splinters were rendered useless.

On the 22nd/23rd of August there was a notable attack on Volpersweiler, the aerodrome of the German 19th Army

Aircraft Park. A fire was caused which lighted the night for miles around, and it can now be stated that one of the bombs set fire to a large petrol dump. Another hit a railway-siding platform on which munitions, presumably aeroplane bombs, were stacked: they exploded and helped to spread destruction. There were also direct hits by bombs on aerodrome buildings which contained about one hundred aeroplanes, and it may be assumed that the number of aeroplanes destroyed and damaged was formidable. A brief entry in a German official document reads: 'The 'enemy caused considerable damage by concentrated 'attacks on the aerodromes of Morhange and Volper-'sweiler.'

There is little that can be said with certainty about the results of the attacks on the aerodrome at Frescaty. It is known that in a raid on the night of the 26th/27th of February 1918 the largest hangar on the aerodrome, a building about 100 yards long and 20 yards wide, was set on fire and destroyed with all its aeroplanes, the number of which cannot be stated.

Such are the available particulars, and, although they are admittedly meagre, they indicate that the total material damage inflicted was important. What is also certain is that on those aerodromes which were frequently attacked the morale of the personnel was affected. The Germans took such steps as they could to mitigate the results of the bombing. Dummy aerodromes were established in some places, aeroplanes were dispersed as deemed necessary to temporary landing-grounds, and personnel were given quarters in villages away from the aerodromes. On the main aerodromes dug-outs were constructed as air-raid shelters and special protection was provided for important stores such as bombs and petrol.

Although the information from the German side is too scanty for judgement to be formed upon this important subject, we are not wholly dependent upon the German records. The results of the organized bombing attacks on British aerodromes in France can be tabulated, and they throw further light on the question. The main enemy attacks were as follows:

Date.	Aerodrome.	No. of bombers.	British aeroplanes. (a) Destroyed. (b) Damaged.	Remarks.
1917 July 6/7	Bray Dunes	6	(a) Nil (b) 12	
Oct. 1/2	St. Pol (depot)	24	(a) 29 (b) Nil.	Great damage to sheds, &c. 7 aeroplanes also destroyed on French aerodrome.
1918 June 5/6	Coudekerque, &c.	24	(a) 5 (b) 37	5 hangars destroyed.
,, 6/7	Coudekerque and Teteghem	30	(a) 1 (b) 9	4 hangars destroyed, 6 damaged: aeroplanes were out when attack took place.
Aug. 24/5	Bertangles	5	(a) 11 (b) 3	Transport and buildings destroyed.
Sept. 23/4	Marquise (depot)	13	(a) 26 (b) 73	48 killed and 124 injured; transport, engines, and buildings damaged.
6 raids		102	(a) 72 (b) 134	

The table, so far as it goes, is striking. It will be observed that, apart from other results, sometimes considerable, two British aeroplanes were destroyed or damaged for each German bombing aeroplane engaged. The total enemy losses were six aeroplanes, which were wrecked through forced landings before reaching their aerodromes on the homeward journeys: in only one instance were the crew injured. In other words, the table would appear to show, at a superficial glance, that with negligible risk and reasonable luck, an air force might quickly disable an opposing air force by means of a sustained bombing offensive waged against its aerodromes. The matter, however, is not quite so simple. It must be borne in mind that although the table takes note of the chief concentrated attacks by regular German bombing squadrons on British Western front aerodromes, it can still be said that the figures are selective. For a comprehensive picture it would be necessary to take into account all the spasmodic bombing of aerodromes on the Western front, and if this were done the results would be shown to be far less favourable to the bombing aircraft. It will be noted that of the total damage most was inflicted at the two aircraft depots at St. Pol and at Marquise. All that need be said by way of comment is that if ever again similar targets should be offered to a nearby enemy (Gothas could reload with bombs and return to their targets three or four times during one night) they would be crying to the skies for early destruction: nor would they cry in vain.

There was an occasion when the French suffered even more heavily than the British air service. In September 1917, during a period of air concentration behind Verdun, a series of attacks during two successive nights resulted in the destruction of eighty-five French aeroplanes, and in damage to many more.

The truth is that whether or not aerodrome bombing is worth while is a matter of common sense, not of hard and fast rules. The answer will depend upon all the attendant circumstances, general, strategical, tactical, and technical. An air force will aim at the dispersion and concealment of its aircraft, but there may be times, perhaps because of a restriction of land suitable for aerodromes, when a dangerous degree of concentration may be unavoidable. If for this or any other reason a truly vulnerable target is offered it will surely not be missed. Although dispersion may not be difficult for operating squadrons, it will be less easy for the aircraft parks and depots in which the reserve aeroplanes and stores must be housed. Towards the end of the war the Germans found it essential to build massive concrete shelters in the North Darse at Bruges to protect submarines from air bombing.[1] Had the war continued it might have become necessary to provide

[1] See Vol. IV, pp. 104–5.

comparable protection, whether above or below ground, for the main aircraft reserves.

Many of the German aerodromes during the war, like many of the British, offered vulnerable targets, and they were therefore suitable objectives for the Independent Force squadrons. It may be that too great a proportion of the activities of the bombing squadrons was directed against aerodrome targets. That is a matter of opinion. Perhaps, in the circumstances of 1918, when the Germans were finding it difficult to maintain supplies to meet the expanded demands for aircraft, it might have sufficed had Major-General Trenchard held his hand and ordered intensive attacks on the enemy aerodromes only if and when German aeroplanes became active in bombing the aerodromes of the Independent Force. It was never his way, however, to let the enemy dictate his policy, and, in any event, he had no other means of subduing the German fighting formations in the path of the independent squadrons. Furthermore, the fact that the Germans had supply difficulties in 1918 made the destruction of aeroplanes and technical stores additionally valuable because their replacement was, at best, delayed and, at worst, impossible. When all is said, what remains true is that Major-General Trenchard's object was achieved. The aerodromes of the Independent Force day and night bombers were not seriously molested—of moral as well as of material importance—and the German defensive fighters, with some exceptions, were unable to prevent the day bombers from attacking their distant objectives.[1]

---

[1] Statistics have been compiled relative to the attacks on industrial and railway objectives (that is, excluding aerodromes). These show that, between October 1917 and November 1918, 76 per cent. of aeroplanes which set out bombed some objective. 14 per cent. did not bomb because they had to return owing to engine trouble, and 10 per cent. because of unfavourable weather conditions. Of the 76 per cent. which dropped bombs, 55·5 per cent. attacked their allotted targets, that is, targets given as primary or alternative objectives for the specific raid. 20·5 per cent. attacked targets of their own choosing, but more often than not such targets were those known to the pilots to be on the approved list of military objectives. Of all aeroplanes which set out 3·9 per cent. never returned to their aerodromes.

We may appropriately conclude this summary with an instruction of Marshal Foch, made when the composition and duties of an Inter-Allied bombing force were under discussion. 'The commander of the Inter-Allied Force', he said, 'in order to maintain aerial supremacy must by 'stern fighting oppose any enemy air forces who will 'attempt to hinder the action of his units, especially his 'day bombers. To this end he should attack enemy aero-'dromes and destroy them—an essential condition to the 'success of his operations. This destruction of aerodromes '—for the same reason—must be undertaken by the 'Eastern Army Group according to the means at its dis-'posal. In order that these raids be conducted methodically, 'a common plan for the two aviation forces is necessary. 'This plan will be drawn up by General Trenchard.'

Independent Force Expansion Programmes

The operations of the independent bombing squadrons have been reviewed. It will now be revealed that the Independent Bombing Force never came into existence. At the signing of the armistice Major-General Trenchard had under his command nine long-distance bombing squadrons, that is to say, just one squadron short of the number he had asked for in his expansion programme submitted in June 1916, long before an independent force was thought about. It should also be pointed out that the aeroplanes which bombed by day had been designed for reconnaissance, and that the F.E.2b, with which No. 100 Squadron had to make do for night bombing for so long, had become obsolete on the Western front as a fighter-reconnaissance aeroplane in the autumn of 1916. In other words, the independent operations were for the most part made by makeshift bombers.

It will be recalled that when the Government decided, after the June daylight raid on London in 1917, to double the air services, Sir Douglas Haig had been told by the War Office that the additional squadrons to be provided would be mainly equipped for bombing.[1] It was suggested that he should make arrangements for the accommodation and

[1] See p. 2.

maintenance of forty bombing squadrons on the assumption that the last of them would have arrived in France by the end of August 1918. These squadrons were to be extra to the eighty-six (including the ten long-distance bombing squadrons referred to above) already approved for service with the armies in the field. The War Office had something to say about the type of aeroplane with which the bombing squadrons would be equipped. Because it was immediately available for production on a large scale, orders had been given, it was said, for the fighter-reconnaissance aeroplane, the D.H.4, but with such minor modifications as might appear necessary, subject to the overriding condition that production was not to be delayed. Sir Douglas Haig was also told that efforts would be made, meanwhile, to evolve a type of aeroplane which would have a longer radius of action than the D.H.4 in order that the area of bombing operations might be extended.

It is clear that Sir Douglas Haig was thus led to believe, in the summer of 1917, that by the end of August 1918 he would have at his disposal fifty squadrons for long-distance bombing operations, and he therefore at once began the necessary arrangements for the accommodation of forty squadrons within the British zone, and for ten squadrons within the French zone near Nancy, which was nearest to the Rhine industrial areas.[1] In a letter to the War Office on the 24th of August 1917, the Commander-in-Chief pointed out that it must be expected that the Germans would oppose the raids with their best fighters, and it would therefore be necessary, he considered, that about twenty-five per cent. of the aeroplanes should fly without bombs in order that they might be able to act as escort. These escorting aeroplanes should, he suggested, be armed with at least four guns, two firing forwards and two to the rear.

The number of D.H.4's, with such minor modifications as appeared necessary, specially ordered in June 1917 for

[1] For supply, &c., purposes it was deemed advisable that the squadrons should be within the British zone, but owing to the restricted range of the bombing aircraft it was necessary that they should begin operations from the French zone.

the bombing programme was seven hundred. At a meeting of the Air Board on the 23rd of July the controller of technical design produced plans involving modifications to the D.H.4 on such a scale that what resulted could be looked upon as a new type, which had been given the identity D.H.9. Whereas the D.H.4 lost seventeen miles an hour when flying fully loaded at 10,000 feet, the new type would retain its speed (112 miles per hour) at this height and would, in addition, give a rather longer radius of action. The Air Board did not at once decide to vary the order for seven hundred D.H.4's, but at their next meeting, three days later, when the subject was again discussed and an assurance was given that a change in the design would mean no more than an initial delay in production of from three to four weeks, the Board adopted the D.H.9 in place of the D.H.4.

It will be observed that the members of the Air Board were thinking only of day bombing. There had been some discussion about night bombing, and the Admiralty representative on the Board had made a favourable report about the Handley Page, but the military members had pointed out that the Royal Flying Corps had no use for the Handley Page because the army preferred extra speed to extra weight-carrying capacity, and the military view was that night bombing was unsatisfactory because it was less accurate than day bombing. At their meeting on the 23rd of July the members of the Board had made a decision which, in effect, registered their disbelief in the value of night bombing: they decided that all orders for experimental heavy bombing aeroplanes should be postponed.

The decision was not long allowed to stand. The controller of the technical department expressed his disapproval in forcible language and then, at a meeting of the Board on the 30th of July, Sir William Weir reopened the question. In the result the Air Board decided to give orders for 100 Handley Pages for night bombing, and to place orders, also, with the Handley Page and with the Vickers companies, for three experimental heavy bombers.[1]

[1] From this order resulted the super Handley Page (type V.1500) and the Vickers Vimy bomber. It is of interest that at the meeting Lord

DAY OR NIGHT BOMBING?

In spite of this decision, however, some members of the Board continued to be uneasy. At a meeting on the 3rd of August Major-General Henderson told the members that Major-General Trenchard did not recommend the construction of a large number of twin-engined bombers because of their vulnerability in the air. He preferred the D.H.4 for day raiding, the moral effect of which was considered to be greater than that of night raiding. No action was taken at the meeting, but the Admiralty representative, Captain V. Vyvyan, R.N., mindful that the navy had had experience with day and night bombers, that is, with the D.H.4 and with the Handley Page, whereas the army had knowledge only of the D.H.4, thought it would be useful if he obtained reports from the naval air commander at Dunkirk.

At a meeting on the 10th of August he told the members of the Board that he had received reports from Dunkirk which showed that the night-flying Handley Page suffered fewer casualties than the D.H.4, and also showed that, in the opinion of the naval air commander, night bombing was more accurate than day bombing. These views, which differed from those held at the time by the Royal Flying Corps, occasioned some surprise, and the Board decided that the Dunkirk reports should be immediately circulated among the members. The reports made the following points:

   (i) There are more clear and calm nights than days during the year, therefore night operations can be more regular.

  (ii) Owing to the inaccuracy of anti-aircraft fire at night a high performance is not required, and about four times the weight per horse-power of bombs can be carried in a night bomber as can be carried by day.

 (iii) The aeroplane can descend lower over a target at night, which makes for increased accuracy.

 (iv) When attacks are made on aerodromes enemy

Cowdray, the President, gave as an additional reason for providing heavy bombers the possibility that German aircraft might become so negligible that slow bombers would be able to fly by day with a small escort.

fighting aeroplanes will be in their sheds at night, whereas in the day empty sheds may be bombed.
(v) A night-bombing aeroplane can operate night after night, but as day bombers are nearly always hit over well-protected areas by A.A. and machine-gun fire, it is found that only about one-half of them can be kept in commission.
(vi) No difficulty is found on clear nights, even when there is no moon, in locating an objective.
(vii) Train activity, movements of convoys and movements of men, nearly always take place at night.

It was also said that 'one very important item in the 'use of heavy bombing machines operating at night is that 'they can proceed to their various destinations unescorted, 'and the danger from enemy aircraft and anti-aircraft 'guns is exceedingly slight when compared to day-bombing 'machines, which, in this area, are nearly always shot about 'by one or the other'.

After the members had had time to consider the reports the Board decided to refer the whole matter, for comment, to Major-General Trenchard. His reply, dated the 7th of September, expressed general agreement with the Dunkirk reports, but laid stress upon the point that success in night bombing was chiefly a matter of careful training. Three days later, on the 10th, Sir Douglas Haig sent a letter to the War Office in which he asked that at least twenty-five per cent. of any additional bombing squadrons provided for France should be equipped as night bombers: speed and climbing capabilities could be sacrificed, he said, to bomb-carrying capacity.

Meanwhile the German night-bombing campaign against England had begun, by moonlight, on the 2nd of September, a fact which robbed the discussion about the merits or otherwise of night bombing of any meaning. On the 6th the Air Board had decided to order an additional two hundred Handley Pages, and they increased the number by another hundred, making four hundred in all, as soon as they received Sir Douglas Haig's letter of the 10th of September.

In November 1917 Major-General Trenchard in France

received information which made him immediately uneasy about the type of aeroplane to be provided for his long-distance bombing programme in 1918. He wrote to Major-General J. M. Salmond, at that time director-general of military aeronautics, on the 16th to say he had heard unofficially from Mr. Geoffrey de Havilland that the D.H.9 would be inferior in performance to the D.H.4 equipped with the 275 horse-power Rolls-Royce engine, and would be unable to fly in formation at 15,000–16,000 feet fully loaded with bombs. 'I do not know', said Major-General Trenchard, 'who is responsible for deciding upon 'the D.H.9, but I should have thought that no-one would 'imagine we should be able to carry out long-distance 'bombing raids by day next year with machines inferior in 'performance to those we use for this purpose at present. 'I consider the situation critical and I think every en-'deavour should be made at once to produce a machine 'with a performance equal at least to the existing D.H.4 '(275 Rolls-Royce) and to press on with the output with 'the utmost energy.... I am strongly of opinion that un-'less something is done at once we shall be in a very serious 'situation next year with regard to this long-distance day 'bombing....' Major-General Salmond brought the matter as one of urgency to the notice of the Air Board, but Sir William Weir made it clear that it was a choice of having the D.H.9 with the B.H.P. engine, or of having nothing at all. Major-General Trenchard attended a meeting of the Board on the 28th November and repeated his objections.

Meanwhile, on the 14th of November 1917, Sir Douglas Haig, voicing the views of Major-General Trenchard, had asked that the outstanding orders for D.H.9's should be reduced to what was necessary to produce and maintain fifteen squadrons because, with increasing opposition to be expected from German fighters, the D.H.9 with the B.H.P. engine would be outclassed as a day bomber about June 1918.[1] It might be employed as a night bomber after that date, and it might also continue to be useful for day bombing provided it was fitted with Rolls-Royce or 'Liberty'

[1] See also p. 142.

engines. In his letter the Commander-in-Chief stated that it might become necessary to concentrate on night bombing as time went on, and he asked therefore that four of the ten Handley Page squadrons allotted should be sent out, if possible, before any of the fifteen D.H.9 squadrons. There was thus, between July and November 1917, an entire change in the military view about the relative importance and value of night and day bombing.

We have considered some of the technical considerations which affected the bombing programmes. It will be of interest now to see how the programmes themselves developed and changed. The June 1917 general expansion programme allowed, we have seen, for fifty bombing squadrons, of which ten were to be allotted for work with the armies. When, in November 1917, Sir Douglas Haig put forward his expansion programme up to the summer of 1919, he recommended that for long-distance raids against targets in Germany provision should be made as follows:

Type	Squadrons
Day Bombers	25
Night Bombers	20
Long-distance fighters (2- or 3-seater)	20
Long-distance squadron of aeroplanes carrying a moderately heavy Q.F. gun	1
	66[1]

Sir Douglas Haig's programme was considered by the War Office and, after its formation in January 1918, by the Air Council. To avoid delay the Air Council presented to the War Cabinet, for approval, what was called the 'Rothermere' programme, which referred only to military air requirements: it increased the total of military service squadrons from 200 to 240. It was said that the Air Council would submit a later programme to include all the requirements of the unified air service in all theatres of war to the end of 1919. Meanwhile, preliminary sanction was urgently needed for the extra forty squadrons asked for by the Army Council. It is of interest that figures

[1] The ten squadrons hitherto shown separately for work with the armies were incorporated in this figure.

quoted in the 'Rothermere' programme showed that the recommendations would entail 3,428 aeroplanes in constant commission on the Western front, of which 1,028 would be long-distance bombing aeroplanes. The programme was considered by the War Cabinet on the 7th of March 1918, and general approval was given for 240 military air squadrons. At the same time a doubling of the naval air squadrons was sanctioned.

The next step was a submission by the Admiralty and War Office of their detailed requirements to the end of September 1919. The Air Ministry embodied these requirements, with amendments, in a provisional programme, totalling 340 service squadrons, which was forwarded to the other two service departments on the 20th of June. In this programme the allowance for the Independent Force was forty squadrons in France (twenty-five day and fifteen night) and twenty in England (Handley Page night bombers). There was no mention in the programme of fighting squadrons as asked for by Sir Douglas Haig in connexion with his long-distance bombing operations. In forwarding the provisional programme to the Admiralty and to the War Office, the Air Ministry pointed out that the allocations did not fully represent the views of the Air Council who were strongly of opinion that a greater proportion of the total available resources should be devoted to long-range bombing operations. The provisional programme was amended in minor particulars early in July, mainly because of supply considerations, and the total became 328 service squadrons, those allocated to the Independent Force being reduced from sixty to fifty-four. Meanwhile the Air Ministry, while awaiting the reactions of the other service departments, was working on a new programme which would be more representative of the Air Council views. In the new programme, the squadrons allotted to the army and to the navy were appreciably reduced. The navy lost thirty-three of its 'paper' squadrons and the army lost seventeen, all of which were given to the Independent Force to make its total 104 squadrons (of which twenty were to be fighting squadrons).[1] According

[1] Sixteen squadrons of single-seaters and four of two-seaters.

to this programme the percentages were: Army 36 per cent.; Navy 25·8 per cent.; Independent Force 32 per cent.; and Home Defence 6·2 per cent.

One member of the Air Council, however, was persistent in his doubts about the wisdom of depleting the air strengths allotted to the other services, and also whether it was practicable for the Independent Force to accommodate so many squadrons. Because of his insistence, members of the Air Council visited Major-General Trenchard at Independent Force head-quarters in France. There they learned that there were grave difficulties in the way of obtaining aerodrome accommodation, and that Major-General Trenchard did not require any fighting squadrons for the time being. It was impossible, he said, to define the type of fighting aeroplane which would be needed and he would prefer that the fighting squadrons should be allotted to the Expeditionary Force on condition that if and when the need arose the Independent Force would have a call on them.

After the visit to Independent Force head-quarters, the general programme was amended to give the Independent Force sixty-eight squadrons, and it was then forwarded to the Admiralty and to the War Office for comment. This was not long in forthcoming, and both departments submitted their views to the War Cabinet which, in turn, referred the whole matter to its Air Policy Committee. This committee met on the 5th of September and cut down and readjusted the programme. Lord Weir, the new Air Minister, mindful that, by June 1919, aeroplanes for the bombing of Germany would also be supplied by France, Italy, and America, agreed to reduce the number of squadrons allotted to the Independent Force to forty-two in France and fourteen in England. The final step in the war programmes of air expansion was taken in October 1918, when the disintegration of the German armies had brought about a new situation. The Air Council decided that the time had come when it was desirable to take a short view, and that the air expansion programme could be reviewed on the basis that every possible squadron should be placed in the field within about six months. A new programme, therefore, which did not go beyond June 1919, was submitted to the War Cabinet at the end of October. In this, the total of service squadrons was reduced from 328 to 275, and the allotment to the Independent Force was cut down to forty squadrons in France and to eight in England.

This brief outline of the expansion programmes tells a story of changing hopes and of disappointments. A beginning was made with forty bombing squadrons which were to be in the field by August 1918,[1] and the peak point was reached in the programme which allotted the Independent Force 104 squadrons, which were to be on service by September 1919. At the end the number had been changed to forty once more, to be in the field by June 1919. Against this background of chastened ambition must be set the fact that when the war ended Major-General Trenchard had, on independent service in France, no more than nine bombing squadrons and one fighting squadron.

The independent Bombing Force which was to work from England was also under the command, for operations, of Major-General Trenchard. This Group, No. 27, began to organize early in September 1918, under Lieutenant-Colonel. R. H. Mulock, at Bircham Newton, Norfolk. It was to include two wings, the Eighty-sixth and Eighty-seventh, and the intention was that the former should operate from England and that the latter should, after formation, go overseas. The first squadron to be mobilized for this Group was No. 166. The head-quarters and squadron personnel were carefully selected and the pilots and observers, many of them from night-flying F.E.2b squadrons in France, were given a special course of navigation at the school at Andover.

The aeroplane with which the force was to begin operations was sometimes known as the super-Handley Page, but officially called the V/1500 type. It had four engines, and could carry thirty 250-lb. bombs, and a crew of six.

[1] A War Office letter to Sir Douglas Haig, dated October the 8th 1917, brought the date forward. It was anticipated, said the letter, that all forty bombing squadrons would be dispatched by the end of June 1918.

The components of the first of the super-Handleys were made under pledges of secrecy by Harland & Wolff at Belfast. The first flight took place in May 1918, but the aeroplane was destroyed in a crash in the following month and this caused delay in production. The second aeroplane of the type was not ready until the middle of October when it was tested and was said to be very comfortable to fly. A total of 255 super-Handley Pages were ordered from various firms, including the Handley Page company. At the signing of the armistice there were three ready, and Berlin had been brought within bombing range of England, although it is unlikely that anything of real military value could have been achieved before the spring of 1919.

It is of interest that when, towards the close of the war, the nationalities which made up the empire of Austria-Hungary declared their independence, it was intended to bomb Berlin and other German cities from the north of Bohemia. Major-General Trenchard organized a small reconnaissance party to report on the aerodrome facilities at Prague and on the general state of the country, and he made arrangements to send forward a train loaded with stores and supplies sufficient to maintain six Handley Pages for one month. It was arranged that the bombers should fly by way of southern Germany as soon as the reconnaissance party had reported, and that if all went well other squadrons of the Independent Force should follow. Marshal Foch proposed that for local protection two Czecho-Slovak divisions should be placed at the disposal of Major-General Trenchard, who objected, however, that the responsibility for the security of the air contingent should not rest with him, but with an Allied army commander: the signing of the armistice put an end to the scheme.

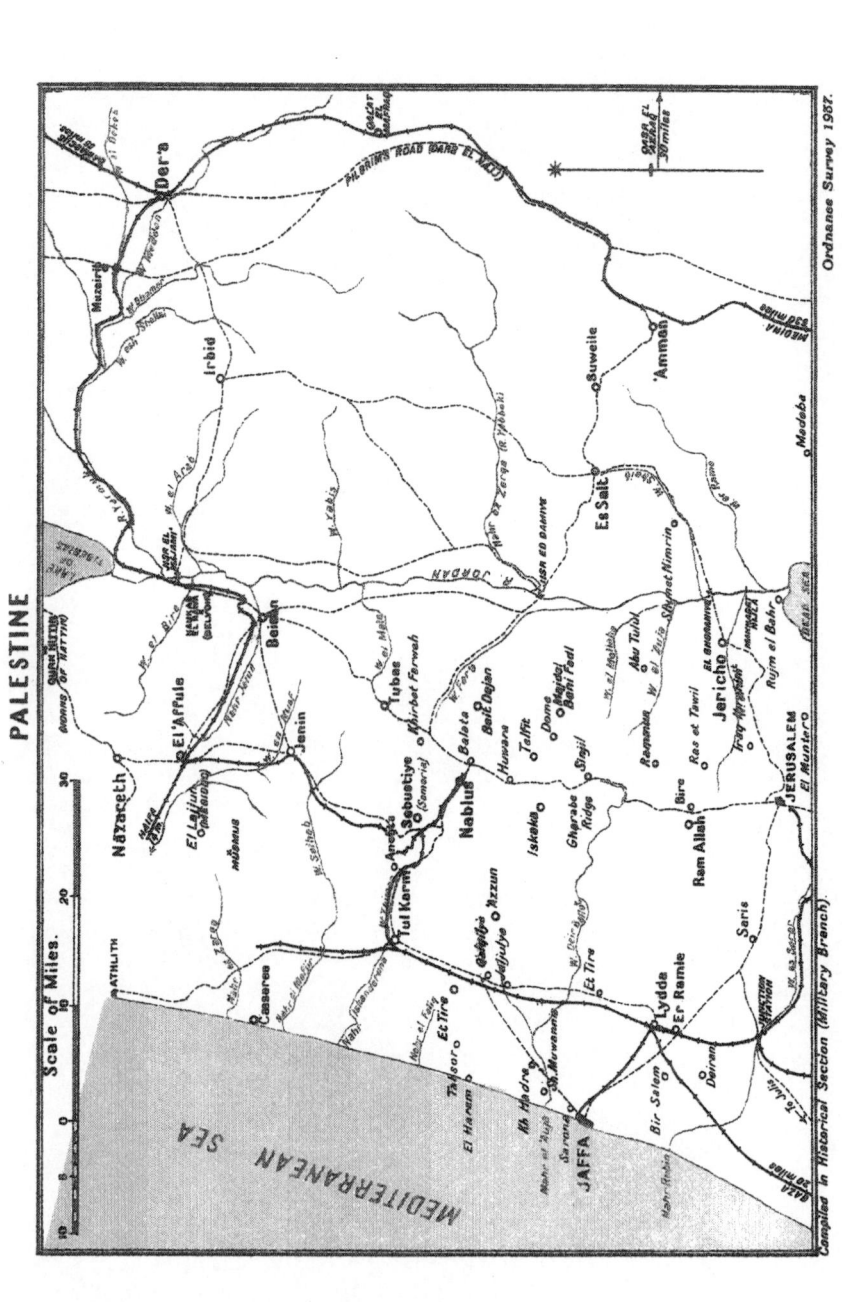

CHAPTER V

AIR OPERATIONS IN PALESTINE IN 1918

[Maps, facing, and p. 183]

AFTER the capture of Jerusalem on the 9th of December 1917 it was impossible for General Allenby to halt. Jerusalem and Jaffa were still within range of Turkish artillery, and it was necessary that the Turks should be pushed back as soon as possible, on either flank of the British front, far enough to ensure the security of these two towns. On the night of the 20th of December the XXI Corps, on the British left, began to move. The 52nd Division, by a fine feat of arms, crossed the Nahr el 'Auja, swollen with rains, and established itself on the right bank. The successful passage of this river made possible a general advance by the XXI Corps. The further forward movement began at 8.0 a.m. on the 22nd and met with no serious resistance, with the result that at small cost the Turks were driven to a line about eight miles distant from Jaffa, and the town was placed beyond the range of normal enemy artillery fire.

On the British right some days of intense preparation on roads and water supply were necessary before an advance could be made to free Jerusalem from pressure. All was ready by the 24th of December, but a downpour of rain on that day and the next delayed the operation, and then the situation was suddenly changed when the British intelligence service discovered, from decoded wireless messages and other sources, that the Turks were about to make an attempt to recover the town: their attack began, astride the Nablus road, at 1.30 a.m. on the 27th. Not only did it fail, but, because it exhausted the enemy troops, it also facilitated the success of the British counter-attack which was made in accordance with the original plans for the advance. By the night of the 30th of December the XX Corps had progressed on a twelve-mile front to a depth of from two to three miles, and Jerusalem together with the line of lateral communications along the Jerusalem–Jaffa road had been freed from danger.

While these operations were in progress the Palestine Brigade, Royal Flying Corps, was disposed as follows: No. 113 Squadron, working with the XXI Corps on the left, was at Deiran, and No. 14 Squadron, with the XX Corps on the right, was at Junction Station, which was also the head-quarters of the Fifth (Corps) Wing. The army wing—the Fortieth—made up of No. 67 (Australian) Squadron and of No. 111 Squadron, was at Julis. The 21st Balloon Company had one section, No. 50, at Sarona with the XXI Corps, and the other, No. 49, at Saris with the XX Corps.

The main work of the squadrons subsequent to the fall of Jerusalem was reconnaissance, but there was also some co-operation with the artillery and desultory bombing of enemy camps. On the 22nd of December, when the XXI Corps had advanced north of Jaffa, the weather was fine and contact patrol observers had reported the main British and enemy movements. As soon as it was seen that the Turks were retiring, the squadrons of both wings had been ordered to bomb the enemy. The main attacks were made on infantry and transport in the neighbourhood of Qalqilye and Jaljulye where air reconnaissances had reported some crowding. About three hundred light-weight bombs were dropped during the day by thirty-six aeroplanes, and about 7,000 rounds of ammunition were fired on the Turkish troops from low heights: the retreating Turks were also shelled from the sea by destroyers and monitors. The fire of one of the monitors, the *M. 31*, against Turkish infantry in Tabsor, was observed for by an aeroplane of No. 113 Squadron, and two hits among the soldiers were signalled.

On the 23rd of December bad weather set in and there was little flying until the 27th. In the afternoon of the 26th, when the weather began to improve, an air observer who made a strategical reconnaissance reported a slight increase of Turkish activity in the Jericho area; but the visibility was still poor and nothing was seen which gave indication of the impending enemy attack on Jerusalem. The Turkish intentions were, however, as has been told, known from other sources and the Royal Flying Corps was instructed to keep watch for enemy movements from dawn on the 27th, and to pay attention, in particular, to possible reinforcements on the march southwards from Nablus. Aided by the return of clear weather, the squadrons flew over the battle area on the 27th, but no important movements of Turkish troops were seen. Next day, however, the air observers reported enemy columns in retreat along the road from Jerusalem to Birè and along the further section from Birè to Nablus, and attacks on the columns were made throughout the day, with bombs and machine-guns, by a total of seventeen pilots. On the 29th the main air work was reconnaissance to report the British advance and the further Turkish movements and dispositions, but 26 bombs were dropped by No. 14 Squadron on infantry and on camps north of Birè. By the 30th of December the XX Corps had taken up its new positions north of Birè and the action ended.

The next immediate task for the Royal Flying Corps was photography of the enemy area, more particularly in order to correct the numerous inaccuracies in the existing maps. This work was done with fine efficiency by the Australian squadron which, during the last fortnight in January 1918, photographed 624 square miles of territory.

The Jordan Valley
[Maps, pp. 175, 234]

No further northward advance could be undertaken until the floods caused by the winter rains subsided, and improvements in the road and railway communications made it possible for supplies to be accumulated forward. Meanwhile, in order to make his right flank safe, General Allenby decided to drive the Turks across the river Jordan. Such an operation, successfully concluded, would prevent enemy raids into the country west of the Dead Sea, and would also bring about conditions favourable for a subsequent attack against the Hejaz railway. Early in February 1918 the communications had been improved sufficiently to make the Jordan attack possible, and it was duly begun on the 19th.

During the time of preparation, two strategical and two tactical air reconnaissances were made on each fine day to keep watch on the Turkish camps and defences. The squadrons also fulfilled a heavy programme of photographic work for the making of maps. German pilots, operating from aerodromes at El 'Affule and Jenin, were active, particularly throughout January, but the Bristol Fighters and S.E.5's of the Royal Flying Corps maintained air superiority, and the work of reconnaissance and photography proceeded without appreciable hindrance. The aerodrome and railway station at El 'Affule were attacked (one hundred and two 20-lb. bombs) on the 3rd of January, and the aerodrome at Jenin (ninety-two 20-lb. bombs) next day. On the 25th of the month six pilots who had set out to attack the camps at Huwara, on the Birè–Nablus road, found a long column of troops on the move north of that place and dropped many bombs among them.

On the 13th of February the head-quarters and a nucleus Flight of a new squadron—No. 142—were taken on the strength of the Fortieth (Army) Wing at Julis. The Flight was provisionally equipped with B.E.12a aeroplanes allotted from No. 1 Squadron, Australian Flying Corps.[1]

The fighting which began on the 19th of February took place in a wilderness of deep-cut gorges and barren hills, almost devoid of communications. The XX Corps, on the opening day, captured Rammun, 'Iraq Ibrahim, El Muntar, and Ras et Tawil. While the infantry were moving forward the observers of No. 14 Squadron reconnoitred the whole tactical area and they reported that there were no concentrations of Turkish troops. In the afternoon an air observer called for artillery fire against a formed party of about 300 enemy infantry seen marching along the Birè–Nablus road: the guns opened fire without delay, and the Turks were scattered after suffering casualties. Strategic reconnaissances by the squadrons of the Fortieth (Army) Wing kept watch on the country east of the Jordan and north of the Wadi el 'Auja. No important Turkish movements were reported, but a decrease in the camps at

---

[1] On the 6th of February No. 67 (Australian) Squadron, Royal Flying Corps, had officially become No. 1 Squadron, Australian Flying Corps.

Jericho and Rujm el Bahr was noted, and a new pontoon bridge near El Ghoraniye was discovered across the Jordan.

On the morning of the 20th, when the British advance was resumed, it was seen from the air that enemy columns were retreating on Jericho in disorder, and that the camps at Rujm el Bahr had been abandoned and were burning: there were movements also of troops and transport eastwards from Jericho towards the Jordan.

For the next four days flying was impossible owing to a gale. The indications in the air reports of the 20th of February that the Turks were evacuating the area were shown to be correct. On the morning of the 21st British cavalry entered Jericho, which they found cleared of military stores. Troopers who rode out to Rujm el Bahr, on the Dead Sea, discovered that the grain stores had been removed. West of the Jordan, between the Dead Sea and the Wadi el 'Auja, there appeared to be no Turkish soldiers except at the El Ghoraniye bridgehead on the Jericho–Es Salt road, and covering the ford across the Jordan at Makhadet Hijla. Although there was some cause for disappointment because the Turks had not been cut off, the main object of the operations had been attained and the right flank of the British forces in Palestine had been made secure. It was the opinion of those who took part in the Jericho advance that the country across which the movements were made was the most difficult which had been encountered during the campaign up to that time. The tangled nature of the ground increased the value of the mapping and reconnaissance work of the air squadrons: there were instances during the advance on the 20th when cavalry, with whom touch had been lost, were found by air observers specially sent to search for them.

An attempt, of some interest although unsuccessful, was made by the Royal Flying Corps to rob the Turks of their boat transport on the Dead Sea. At the suggestion of Lieutenant-Colonel R. Williams the fuselage and engine of a Martinsyde aeroplane were placed on twin floats to form a so-called hydroplane (known as *Mimi*) which was taken by lorry to a point near Jericho, and was thereafter carried to the shores of the Dead Sea by men of the Egyptian army escorted by a platoon of the 2/20th London Regiment. The hydroplane was erected during the day and night of the 28th of February and, before dawn on the 1st of March, a start was made for a group of boats on the eastern shore of the Dead Sea. Captain J. A. D. Dempsey was the pilot and with him were Captain P. D. Drury and 1st Air Mechanic Doig, Australian Flying Corps. The idea was that Captain Drury and Air Mechanic Doig should, under cover of fire from two Lewis guns fitted in the hydroplane, go overboard, swim to the boats, cut them adrift, and then hitch them to the hydroplane which would endeavour to tow them to the western shore. The plan, however, miscarried. On the outward journey the rudder-yoke on the hydroplane broke, and the machine drifted southwards out of control and was eventually beached. The hydroplane could not be repaired on the spot, but Captain Dempsey thought he saw a chance of making the attempt in a different way. He took the floats off the machine and converted them into boats, each to carry four men. With the help of paddles made from petrol boxes and other wood the two crews set out on the evening of the 2nd of March, but once more luck was not with them. A strong current carried the boats away from their objective, and after paddling hard for more than seven hours the crews fetched up on the eastern shore of the Dead Sea, five miles south of where the Turkish boats were lying. While the men were taking a rest, the Royal Flying Corps officers (Captains J. A. D. Dempsey, P. D. Drury, and Lieutenant E. Bell), helped by the light of the moon, made a local reconnaissance, and at dawn the return journey was accomplished.

Although the advance to Jericho had made the British right flank secure, it had not won a frontage wide enough, clear of the Dead Sea, for operations to be undertaken east of the Jordan. General Allenby planned, therefore, to push forward to the line of the Wadi el 'Auja on his right, and he hoped that he would later be able to force the passage of the Jordan, capture Es Salt, and destroy the

Hejaz railway at 'Amman. If the operations succeeded he would leave a detachment at Es Salt in order to prevent repairs to the railway, while he prepared for a general advance west of the Jordan, to take place about the middle of April.

While General Allenby was making his plans there was a change in the enemy supreme command which was destined to lead to a change also in the defensive tactics of the Turkish armies. On the 1st of March the German General der Kavallerie Liman von Sanders, who had commanded the Turkish Fifth Army, succeeded General von Falkenhayn. Whereas Falkenhayn was a man of flexible temper who had a lively belief in the value of manœuvre for defence as well as for offence, Liman von Sanders had more rigid qualities which induced him to pay a strict attention to the value of ground. His outlook was embodied in plans which aimed at keeping a firm grip on the front. To do this he was compelled to employ his reserves well forward, and the resources at his disposal were such that he could not, at the same time, assemble any useful reserve of manœuvre. It will be shown that there was a notable stiffening in the quality of the Turkish defence from March 1918 onwards, but when, later in the year, General Allenby attacked in strength and ruptured the front, the inflexibility of the strategy of Liman von Sanders contributed to the disaster which overtook the Turkish armies.

The movement to secure the line of the Wadi el 'Auja started during the night of the 8th of March. Before the advance began air reconnaissances had revealed significant changes in the Turkish dispositions. On the 5th of March a new pontoon bridge had been reported across the Jordan at Jisr ed Damiye, and two days later it was noticed that the bridge at El Ghoraniye had disappeared. At the same time it was seen that the Turkish camps east of the Jordan, between Es Salt and Shunet Nimrin, had been very much reduced. The changes which were taking place were rapid and puzzling, but it was inferred from the air reports that the main movement was in a north-westerly direction, from Es Salt towards Nablus. It can now be stated that this conclusion was well founded. Liman von Sanders, the new German commander, had taken energetic action. He had issued orders to the Turkish *XX Corps*, which had retreated across the Jordan after the British occupation of Jericho, to recross the river and take up a position on the left of the Turkish *III Corps* which was astride the Nablus road: the movement began on the night of the 4th/5th of March.

By the 11th of March the British XX Corps had gained its allotted objectives about the line of the Wadi el 'Auja, but the cost had been comparatively high owing to the resistance offered by well-placed machine-gunners. On the most important day of the action, the 9th, the Royal Flying Corps had not been able to give much help on account of fog and cloud, but the observers reported movements from the camps east of the Jordan, and also new camps along the Jisr ed Damiye–Nablus road. On the same day a camp near Sinjil, on the Birè–Nablus road, was attacked by No. 1 Squadron, Australian Flying Corps, and bombs were seen to burst among tents and troops and to set fire to a petrol dump: transport and men on the Birè–Nablus road were bombed by three pilots of No. 142 Squadron. On the 10th of March, in improved weather, the air observers reported the British and Turkish dispositions, and there was some bombing of enemy troops and camps along the Birè–Nablus road, but on the 11th, the final day of the action, mist and rain again prevented useful flying.

In order to bring its right into conformity with the advance made by the XX Corps, the XXI Corps attacked on the 12th of March. The attack succeeded at small cost, mainly because of the British preponderance in artillery, heavy and light. No. 113 Squadron had worked methodically with the artillery from the time when the XXI Corps crossed the El 'Auja at the end of December: all the important Turkish positions had been registered, with the result that the British guns so dominated the battle area when the infantry made their attack on the 12th of March that a weak force (three Brigades on a front of seven miles) sufficed to bring success.

There was intermittent activity by the enemy air service, and occasional attempts were made by German two-seaters, protected by fighters, to register the Turkish artillery. During one of the combats to which this led, Captain R. M. Drummond of No. 111 Squadron, after shooting down one of six enemy fighters, was himself forced down with engine trouble. With spluttering engine, and under persistent attack by the German fighters, Captain Drummond journeyed home at a low height, being compelled on four occasions to taxi along the ground: during one such landing in enemy territory he carried away on his undercarriage a clothes-line stretched between two tents, the occupants of which were breakfasting nearby.

As a result of the operations which had begun on the 8th of March, the general line had been advanced along a front of about twenty-six miles to a maximum depth of seven miles, and a strong defensive position had been won which would ensure safety on the flank while the action was fought east of the Jordan.

The Arab Campaign
[Map, facing]

The main reason why General Allenby wished to cross the Jordan and destroy the Hejaz railway at 'Amman was a desire to help the Arabs. To make the part played by the Arabs intelligible, and because aeroplanes assisted the forces of the Emir Feisal, it will be necessary to take note of the happenings in the desert after the capture of 'Aqaba in July 1917. Major T. E. Lawrence had been told by head-quarters in Egypt that he could count upon adequate British support for the Arab Northern Army, based on 'Aqaba, and he had asked for an air detachment to be employed for the bombing of stations on the Hejaz railway, and particularly Ma'an, where the Turks had an aerodrome. On the 9th of September 1917 a detachment from No. 14 Squadron, under Captain F. W. Stent,[1] had been

---

[1] Captain Stent was succeeded in command of the Flight by Captain F. H. Furness-Williams on the 17th of January 1918. On the 16th of May the command was taken over by Captain V. D. Siddons who retained it to the end of the campaign.

sent to 'Aqaba from Palestine, but bombing attacks on Ma'an station had already begun in August. From an advanced landing ground at Quntilla, seventy miles from El Arish in the direction of 'Aqaba, 'C' Flight of No. 14 Squadron (four B.E.'s) had attacked Ma'an station and camps on the 28th of August, and on the following day had twice bombed camps at El Fuweile and at Abu el Lasan. Colonel T. E. Lawrence tells what happened, beginning with the attack on Ma'an: 'Two bombs into the barracks 'killed thirty-five men and wounded fifty. Eight struck 'the engine-shed, heavily damaging the plant and stock. A 'bomb in the General's kitchen finished his cook and his 'breakfast. Four fell on the aerodrome. . . . In the follow- 'ing dawn they were off once more, three of them this time 'to Abu el Lissan, where the sight of the great camp had 'made Stent's mouth water. They bombed the horse lines 'and stampeded the animals, visited the tents and scattered 'the Turks. As on the day before, they flew low and were 'much hit, but not fatally. . . .'[1] The pilots, who had flown their B.E.'s to Quntilla on the 26th, carrying four days' supplies, returned to their aerodrome on the Palestine front on the 30th.

When the special detachment arrived at 'Aqaba in September for permanent attachment to the Arab forces it became known as 'X' Flight, which formed an independent and self-contained unit under the administrative orders of air head-quarters in Egypt. For operations the Flight worked under Lieutenant-Colonel P. C. Joyce in command of the British section of the Arab Northern Army. The Flight began with three B.E.12's, but it received, in October, two B.E.2e's and one D.H.2. Working from a landing-ground at 'Aqaba the Flight began a routine of reconnaissances of the Turkish camps along the Hejaz railway, notably those at Ma'an. The reconnaissances were usually made by pilots of the single-seater B.E.12's who carried twelve or sixteen 16-lb. bombs to drop on Ma'an station and similar targets.

While the aeroplanes were co-operating with the Arabs in the Ma'an area, other Arab forces, pushing forward west

[1] *Seven Pillars of Wisdom*, p. 342.

of the railway, had, by the end of 1917, taken Esh Shobek and Et Tafila, the latter place forty-five miles north of Ma'an and only some fifteen miles from the south-east corner of the Dead Sea. A Turkish detachment sent to recover Tafila in January 1918 had been annihilated, and Falkenhayn had then decided to concentrate a force, stiffened by German troops, at El Qatrani, on the railway between Ma'an and 'Amman. This force, drawn from the 'Amman area, drove the Arabs back to Shobek at the beginning of March.

Meanwhile, farther south, the Arab campaign had also suffered a check. On the 22nd of January 1918 the Arabs had attacked Mudauwara station with the help of aeroplanes. Three pilots, working from an advanced landing-ground at Abu Suwana, had three times attacked the station and gun-positions with bombs of 100-lb. and 20-lb. weight, but the Arabs had been unable to overcome the resistance of the Turks. A pilot who flew over the Mudauwara station on the following morning, ready to bomb the Turks, discovered that the Arabs were in full retreat. He saw a German aeroplane on the ground near the station and attacked it with bomb and machine-gun fire, with the result that the aeroplane was damaged and had to be dismantled and sent back to the base for repair.

The position in the middle of March, as it affected the operations about to be made east of the Jordan, may be thus summarized. East of the river towards 'Amman the Turks had been greatly reduced in strength, first, by the withdrawal which had taken place from the Es Salt–Shunet Nimrin area towards Nablus, and, secondly, by the southward diversion of a force to Qatrani to meet the Arab threat. If the impending British attack on 'Amman induced the enemy to recall the Qatrani force the Emir Feisal might be enabled to advance and capture Ma'an.

The 'Amman Raid
[Maps, pp. 183, 234]

The expedition to 'Amman set out on the night of the 21st of March. Strategic air reconnaissances had, for some days, watched the area between the Birè–Nablus road and the Hejaz railway, the latter being reconnoitred from Qal'at el Mafraq in the north to Qatrani in the south. Early in February the beginnings of an aerodrome had been discovered at Qatrani, and by the end of the month the aerodrome had grown to an appreciable size. Small cavalry and infantry camps were also found in the neighbourhood of the aerodrome, and similar camps were located at El Kerak to the west, all of which were bombed from time to time. On the 19th of March, two days before the advance was planned to begin, a mixed enemy force of about 1,000 cavalry and infantry was seen from the air to be moving on Qatrani from Kerak, and an increase in the encampments at the latter place was noted. One 230-lb. and twenty-two 20-lb. bombs were dropped on Qatrani station and camps by four pilots, and there is some evidence that as a result a few trucks were set on fire, but it appears that otherwise little damage was caused. Attempts were made to destroy the Turkish pontoon bridge across the river Jordan at Jisr ed Damiye, which was five times bombed, but although some of the bombs were released from 200 feet the nearest exploded ten yards from the bridge and no damage was caused.

To make co-operation with the advancing troops easier an aerodrome was established by No. 14 Squadron at Jericho, and 'A' Flight of the squadron moved there from Junction Station. Visibility throughout the 21st of March was good and air reconnaissances reported the Turkish dispositions between the Jordan and 'Amman in some detail. No important movements were seen until about 3.0 p.m. when a large body of Turkish infantry was observed approaching the Jordan at Ghoraniye, and cavalry were seen moving towards Makhadet Hijla. As a result of the air report the 2/18th London Regiment was ordered to Makhadet Hijla to reinforce the 2/19th which had been ordered to make the passage at that place.

Throughout the night of the 21st/22nd the British attempt to force the passage of the river, which was swollen with rains, proceeded. At Ghoraniye the boats were swept away by the swift current, but at Makhadet Hijla the attempt was eventually successful, and, by daybreak on the

22nd, the 2/19th London Regiment had crossed, although the troops found it impossible to make further progress through the rain-sodden country before nightfall. Air reconnaissances on the 22nd disclosed no unusual enemy movements, but told of activity in the camps at Es Salt and of an increase in the rolling-stock in 'Amman station. The additional rolling-stock indicated an arrival of reinforcements for which there was confirmation in an expansion of the camps in the neighbourhood: an aeroplane hangar was seen in position east of the station. On the morning of the 23rd the Auckland Mounted Rifles crossed at Makhadet Hijla and cleared the left bank of the Jordan to Ghoraniye, where a foot-bridge had been established by 4.30 p.m. By the end of the day there were five bridges across the river, at Makhadet Hijla and Ghoraniye, and the 60th Division and most of the cavalry had crossed. The British plans had allowed for a swift passage of the Jordan both at Ghoraniye and Makhadet Hijla, and for an immediate subsequent advance to the foot-hills astride the 'Amman road. It was not, however, until the morning of the 24th of March that a general advance eastwards from the river could be made, and the delay prejudiced the success of the operation.

The advance on the 24th began at 8.30 a.m. in stormy weather. Pilots who flew ahead of the 60th Division attacked Turkish troops and transport at Shunet Nimrin with sixty-seven 20-lb. bombs, a few of which made direct hits. The 60th Division captured Shunet Nimrin and advanced four miles along the 'Amman road, while the mounted troops followed the tracks towards 'Ain es Sir and Na'ur. The 1st Australian Light Horse Brigade took up a position about Umm esh Shert to cover the left flank and dispatched a regiment up the track to Es Salt.

Rain and sleet, which set in about 2.0 a.m. on the 25th, made the tracks difficult for infantry and cavalry movements, and particularly for the camels, and kept the Royal Flying Corps on the ground. The 181st Brigade reached a point about one mile short of Es Salt, where it halted at 4.15 p.m. The 179th Brigade advanced slowly along the Wadi Abu Turra track, picqueting the heights as it went, but the Brigade was instructed later in the day that this was an unnecessary precaution because there was no indication in the air reports that opposition was to be expected along this route. The Brigade thereupon pushed straight ahead and, four miles from Es Salt, met the Australian regiment which had moved up from Umm esh Shert. Orders were given to take Es Salt that evening and, at 6.0 p.m., the Australians rode into the town without opposition. To the south, the cavalry, through rain, mist, mud, and bitter cold, reached Na'ur on the evening of the 25th and Ain es Sir on the morning of the 26th.

The sun broke through the clouds on the 26th of March, but the men and horses were tired out after their continuous day and night marches in the rain, and it was judged impossible to advance on 'Amman until the next morning. Two raiding expeditions against the railway, north and south of 'Amman, were, however, ordered to take place during the night of the 26th/27th. That to the south was successful and a section of the line seven miles south of 'Amman station was blown up by a party of the New Zealand Brigade. The northern detachment, however, encountered a superior cavalry force and was driven off without fulfilling its mission. Air reconnaissances on the 26th were made difficult by intermittent cloud banks, but the tactical and strategical areas were surveyed and no important enemy movements were revealed. The bridge across the Jordan at Jisr ed Damiye was attacked by five pilots with four 112-lb. and twelve 20-lb. bombs, but no direct hits were made. Next morning pilots who again set out to bomb the bridge found that it had been removed, and they therefore dropped their bombs on camps in the neighbourhood.

An attack on 'Amman on the morning of the 27th by mounted troops alone—the infantry had not yet come up —could make little progress, although raiding parties cut the railway north and south of the town which was, as a result, temporarily isolated. 'Amman and its neighbourhood was kept under observation from the air throughout the day and much enemy activity was discovered. Four pilots from each of the two corps squadrons (Nos. 14 and 113) attacked 'Amman with fifty-five 20–lb. bombs.

The attack on the town was resumed at 1.0 p.m. on the 28th, but, though strengthened by the arrival of two battalions of infantry and of mountain artillery, once again made little progress. Air observers followed the movements of the British troops and examined the Turkish dispositions, which were shown to be little changed. On the 29th enemy movements were revealed which made for uneasiness. From the air reports it appeared that reinforcements had approached 'Amman from the north, having detrained near the bridge destroyed by the Australians. It was apparent, also, that troops had been brought across the Jordan from Jisr ed Damiye to positions north of Es Salt where they threatened from the flank the British line of communications. In consequence the 1st Australian Light Horse pushed farther up the ridge in the Jordan valley known as Red Hill in order that they might more effectively cover the Umm es Shert crossing. Another disquieting feature was the sudden appearance over Shunet Nimrin of thirteen German aeroplanes which dropped bombs that killed and wounded 175 camels and caused 36 casualties to troops and to Egyptians of the Camel Transport Corps. Special air reconnaissances were ordered to ascertain whether the enemy activity presaged a general attack. The air observers failed to discover any appreciable Turkish movements in the Es Salt–Shunet Nimrin area, but the possibility that trouble might be brewing remained.

At 2 a.m. on the 20th of March, in heavy rain, the attack on 'Amman was resumed in greater strength, but although it was gallantly pressed by the tired troops success could not be achieved, chiefly because of a lack of artillery support. As soon as it appeared that failure was certain, the action was broken off and orders were given for a withdrawal across the Jordan. By the 2nd of April the whole force, except for a garrison left on the east bank to hold a bridgehead, had crossed the river.

The 'Amman failure, which came at a time when matters were going ill in France, was the first set-back which the British forces in Palestine had experienced since the second battle of Gaza a year before, and it did much to restore the confidence of the Turkish troops and to give them faith in Liman von Sanders, their new commander-in-chief. The causes of the failure are obvious enough. The delay in crossing the swollen waters of the Jordan was serious, but what chiefly affected the operation was the wet weather which hampered progress, exhausted the men, and prevented artillery from being moved forward.

A minor feature of the operations was a method by which aeroplanes picked up messages from the ground. They were taken by a weighted hook at the end of a line from a cord stretched between two poles held by two officers about 25 yards apart. In this way pilots in the air received instructions to make special reconnaissances urgently required, or to convey important information to other British formations. For example, on the morning of the 29th of March, Captain H. I. Hanmer (observer, Lieutenant J. B. Carr), of No. 14 Squadron, picked up a message from the head-quarters of the Australian and New Zealand Mounted Division asking that a reconnaissance be made of the roads and railways north and south of 'Amman. When the aeroplane returned to drop the observer's report, which was apparently not retrieved, the pilot picked up another message in which the dispositions of the Anzac Division were outlined for the information of the 60th Division: this message was dropped on the 60th Division advanced head-quarters within about twenty minutes.

A weakness in the British line of communications calls for comment. At one time during the advance there was only one bridge across the Jordan open for traffic. Owing to a rise in the river the approaches to the other bridges had been rendered so boggy that they had become impassable, even for camels. The bridge which remained open had long causeways at each end, and had the enemy, through air bombing, made this bridge unserviceable, a position of some gravity would have been created. Happily no attempts to destroy the bridge were made. It may be argued that the failure of the Royal Flying Corps to shatter the bridge used by the enemy at Jisr ed Damiye had demonstrated how difficult it was to achieve success, but it must be pointed out that the Jisr ed Damiye bridge did not

PLANS SHELVED

possess the same importance as the bridges which formed the sole means of communication between the British troops operating east of the Jordan and their bases. The mere threat that the line of communications might be ruptured by air attack would have created a feeling of anxiety that must have influenced General Allenby's plans.

The grave situation in France resulting from the German offensive had an immediate effect on the campaign in Palestine. After the capture of Jerusalem the British Government had asked General Allenby to outline plans for the exploitation of his successes, and they had at the same time informed him that he would be reinforced by the 7th Indian Division from Mesopotamia. He had replied that his next step would be an advance to the Wadi el 'Auja, after which he would operate against the Hejaz railway on his right, and also push his left forward gradually to Tul Karm. At the same time that these minor movements were being made preparations for a large-scale offensive would be under way. It had appeared to the British Government that General Allenby's plans were not bold enough. The desire of the Government was that Turkey should be eliminated from the war at a blow, and they had invited General Allenby to state what forces he considered would be necessary for an advance to Aleppo, which would result in the cutting of Turkish communications with Mesopotamia: as an alternative he was asked to say what forces he would require to enable him to occupy the whole of Palestine. General Allenby had submitted plans in conformity with the alternative proposals put to him, and the Government had thereupon sent Lieutenant-General J. C. Smuts to Egypt, early in February 1918, to confer, on behalf of the War Cabinet, with the military and naval commanders, including the Chief of Staff of the Mesopotamian Expeditionary Force, about the best way of co-ordinating all measures in the Middle East with a view to knocking Turkey out of the war. Lieutenant-General Smuts had summarized his conclusions in a telegram sent to England on the 15th of February 1918. He had stated, in effect, that the force in Mesopotamia should stand on the defensive and transfer reinforcements to Palestine for a major offensive in that theatre of war. It will not be necessary to consider the detailed strategic scheme because, although it received the approval of the British Government, it had to be shelved almost at once as a result of the German threat on the Western front. Even before the storm broke the War Office had decided to transfer white troops to France from Palestine and to replace them by Indian regiments. General Allenby was informed that each Yeomanry Brigade in his force would consist, in the future, of one British and two Indian regiments, and that nineteen Indian battalions would replace the same number of British in the infantry divisions. Subsequently, when the magnitude of the German offensive on the Somme was fully revealed, still more drastic changes in Palestine were ordered.

The 52nd Division was relieved in the coastal sector by the 7th Indian Division and left for France early in April. The 74th Division followed at the end of the month, and there was a further drain of Yeomanry regiments, infantry battalions, machine-gun companies, and siege batteries, which necessitated a complete reorganization of the Palestine force to incorporate replacements from India, and precluded any possibility of a major offensive being undertaken before the end of the summer.

In spite of the loss of experienced divisions, General Allenby decided, before calling a halt to the operations, to attempt the capture of Tul Karm. The attack began on the 9th of April, but the Turks were found to be alert and well prepared, and when it became clear that success could be achieved only at heavy cost the action was broken off, with some slight gains on the right flank. The Turkish positions before and during the attack were reconnoitred by No. 113 Squadron, whose reports contained many references to new entrenchments and battery positions, and to work on the conditioning of roads along the lines of communication. The squadron also followed a daily programme of co-operation with the artillery, chiefly to observe for counter-battery fire.

The Hejaz Railway

[Map, p. 183]

The centre of activity now shifted to the eastern area where, early on the 11th of April, the enemy made an abortive and costly attack on the Ghoraniye bridge-head. On the same day the Arab forces under the Emir Feisal cut the railway north and south of Ma'an station. On the 13th of April the Arabs captured Jebel Semna, a Turkish post south-west of Ma'an, and on the following day they made an entry into the station itself, but as they could make no impression on the strong Turkish positions which covered the station from the north they withdrew to Semna once more. Aeroplanes of 'X' Flight, using an advanced landing-ground, bombed Ma'an while the Arabs were attacking. Pilots who arrived over the station on the 17th, ready to drop bombs, were made aware by ground signals that the Arabs were in possession: next day, when the Arabs had gone back to Semna, Ma'an was bombed again.

Meanwhile a mixed force, under the general command of Lieutenant-Colonel A. G. C. Dawnay, of the Hejaz Operations Staff, was attacking the line south of Ma'an. In the afternoon of the 19th of April two Martinsyde aeroplanes co-operated in a successful dash made by this force against Tell esh Shahin station. As soon as the pilots appeared over the area strips were laid out on the ground asking them to bomb at once, and as the aeroplanes dived to attack, Bedouin, supported by armoured cars, delivered their assault and took the station by storm with fifty-four prisoners.

As a result of the various operations against the railway, long sections of line had been destroyed between Ma'an and Mudauwara, and they remained derelict until the end of the war. The pilots of 'X' Flight dropped a total of two and a quarter tons of bombs and took fifty photographs during their special reconnaissances of the line.

While the Arabs were raiding the Hejaz railway, General Allenby, by way of help, made a demonstration in force in the Jordan Valley. He wanted the enemy to believe that a new advance was about to take place against 'Amman, a possibility which would keep reinforcements from being sent towards Ma'an. The action took place on the 18th of April, when mounted troops were sent forward to feel their way in the direction of Shunet Nimrin, but the Turks covering the place opened such a stinging fire that progress became impossible and a withdrawal was ordered at 6.30 p.m.: the main result of the skirmish was that the Turks were made alert against any similar attempt.

Air reconnaissances throughout April had supplied many indications that the Turks were working hard to strengthen their defences. In the early part of the month it was seen that the damage done to the line at 'Amman as a result of the raid made at the end of March was being rapidly repaired, and it was reported from the air on the 10th that the line had been restored. Activity in the Jordan Valley was also disclosed, none of it considerable, but sufficiently widespread to leave no doubt that Liman von Sanders intended to strengthen his grip on the whole of his eastern area. During the week beginning the 12th of April an exceptional number of new trenches and breastworks, particularly near Shunet Nimrin, were reported by No. 14 Squadron.[1] After the demonstration made east of the Jordan on the 18th of April the squadron was ordered to keep special watch for movements towards Shunet Nimrin, particularly from the neighbourhood of Es Salt. The reconnaissance reports revealed that important changes of disposition were proceeding: the camps in the area of Shunet Nimrin were shown to be expanding, entrenchments were being multiplied, and new positions for guns were seen in preparation.

The Es Salt Raid
[Maps, pp. 175, 234]

General Allenby decided to make another, and stronger, raid east of the Jordan. Harvest time was approaching, and a successful advance into Moab, after the wheat and barley had been reaped and gathered, would prevent

---

[1] The detached Flight of No. 14 Squadron returned to Junction Station from Jericho on the 4th of April. The Flight moved out again to Jerusalem on the 27th of April.

valuable supplies from reaching the Turkish troops. The Commander-in-Chief, therefore, planned to 'seize the 'first opportunity to cut off and destroy the enemy's force 'at Shunet Nimrin, and, if successful, to hold Es Salt till 'the Arabs could advance and relieve my troops'.[1] He would have preferred to make the attack in mid-May, when the reorganization consequent upon the transfer to France of a part of his force could be expected to be well advanced, but envoys from the Beni Sakr tribe, encamped at Madeba, reached General Allenby with an offer of co-operation, in an attack east of the Jordan, on condition that it was made before the 4th of May. After that date they would be compelled, they said, to disperse to distant camps on account of a lack of supplies.

The operation was therefore timed to begin on the 30th of April. It failed, partly because the Beni Sakr tribe did not give their promised help, but chiefly owing to the surprise intervention of favourably placed Turkish reinforcements. Liman von Sanders, confident that he must expect a repetition of the British attack on 'Amman, had ordered the battalions which had defended the town at the end of March to take up positions at Shunet Nimrin to cover the main road to Es Salt. The air reconnaissance reports had given a fairly clear indication of the ensuing movements. Not only, as has been told, did they disclose a growth in the camps and entrenchments at Shunet Nimrin, but they also revealed decreases in the camps in the neighbourhood of 'Amman. Liman von Sanders further concentrated, during April, a cavalry division and the Caucasus Cavalry Brigade, with other miscellaneous units, under the general command of Colonel Essad Bey, on the west bank of the Jordan near Mafid Jozele, in an area which was reconnoitred from the air almost daily before the British advance began. Yet this enemy concentration—of great importance because of its position on the flank of the advance—escaped detection. The wadis and nullahs were of a kind to aid concealment, but unusual precautions must be looked for to explain why the force was not reported. It is of interest, therefore, to read an account of a visit to the

[1] Dispatch, 18th of September 1918.

camps made by Liman von Sanders. 'When first I searched 'for Essad Bey's camp in the Jordan Valley on the Roman 'road', he says, 'I had great difficulty in finding it. It was 'extremely cleverly hidden. There was visible no collec- 'tion of buildings that looked like a camp. Isolated tents 'or huts made of branches such as are constructed by the 'Bedouin were scattered about in an irregular fashion, and 'not a horse was to be seen. On closer inspection it was 'discovered that where no nullahs could be found for them 'the stables had been sunk below ground-level. Each stable 'was surrounded by a sloping hedge of branches, which 'also afforded protection from the sun. No aviator could 'recognize a cavalry camp or even suspect its existence.'[1] The Turkish commander must be given credit for the painstaking way in which his efforts to hide his force were conceived and put into effect.

Another enemy force which was destined to make an important intervention was the Turkish *24th Division*, encamped at Telfit and Dome, east of the Nablus road. During the night of the 28th/29th of April that part of the division which was at Telfit moved to Dome. The concentration of the *24th Division* at Dome had nothing to do with the impending British advance east of the Jordan. It was made in conformity with enemy plans for a projected attack at Musallabe, but the result was that the division was well placed, on the morning of the 30th, for rapid movement to the Jordan. As soon as the British intentions became apparent Liman von Sanders ordered the division to cross the river, either at Mafid Jozele or Jisr ed Damiye, and attack.

The camps at Telfit and Dome had been reported from the air. On the 29th, when the concentration of the *24th Division* at Dome had already been made, the main attention of the air observers had been directed to the country between the Jordan and the Hejaz railway, but one observer had flown over the Telfit–Dome area about 6.45 a.m. and had reported minor movements with no change in the camps at Dome. Exactly when the Telfit part of the Turkish division reached Dome cannot be stated, but

[1] *Fünf Jahre Türkei*, p. 272.

whether on the march, or in its new camp, it escaped detection, and this must be written down as a failure on the part of the air service.

The operation orders issued to the Fortieth Wing by Lieutenant-Colonel A. Shekleton for the 30th required reconnaissances to be made at noon, and also as late as possible in the afternoon, to search as follows:

(i) for any indication of enemy movement in the area between Nablus and the Jordan towards Jisr ed Damiye;
(ii) for any movement towards Es Salt from north, north-east, or from 'Amman, and
(iii) for any movement of Arabs co-operating in the area between Madeba and Ziza.

For some reason not apparent in the official records the reconnaissances were not made at the times ordered and they did not follow the exact routes laid down. The movements of the Turkish *24th Division* towards the Jordan were not seen. About 11 a.m. it was reported that there was a notable increase of activity in the Lower Wadi el Far'a area, and that there were bodies of enemy cavalry east of the ford at Jisr ed Damiye. A reconnaissance made between 3 p.m. and 5.45 p.m. again noted much cavalry and transport in the Lower Wadi el Far'a area, and also told of activity on the roads between Es Salt and 'Amman. At the latter place it was seen that the encampments in and near the town had decreased since the morning, and it seemed clear that the Turks had set their faces westwards to meet the British advance. No movements of friendly Arabs in the neighbourhood of Madeba were observed from the air.

The British advance had begun on the 30th of April. Troops of the 60th Division captured the outpost positions at Shunet Nimrin, but could make no further progress throughout the day against the main defences. The Australian Mounted Division made a remarkable dash for Es Salt, which was entered at 6.30 p.m. A brigade had been left to cover the Jisr ed Damiye track, but Turkish cavalry and infantry, who had crossed the Jordan at a place which was out of view from the ground, attacked the Australian screen, causing the men to fall back, with the result that the Jisr ed Damiye route was never endangered and the Turks were able to move across the river without fear of interference.

On the 1st of May things went badly. The 60th Division resumed its attack on the main Turkish position in the morning, but could make no impression. Meanwhile, on the flank, it had become clear at daylight that formidable numbers of Turks had passed over the Jordan at Jisr ed Damiye. It was not long before they attacked strongly, and the British were pressed back, with a loss of nine guns. By noon, a line had been taken up to cover the Umm esh Shert track, the sole remaining way of escape open to the cavalry who had entered Es Salt the previous evening.

The sky was clouded over in the forenoon of the 1st of May and the visibility was poor. In the afternoon there was some improvement in the weather, and air reconnaissances confirmed that enemy troops were east of the Jordan at Jisr ed Damiye in considerable numbers, and disclosed also that important movements of Turkish cavalry were being made towards 'Amman from the south. Two aeroplanes of No. 1 Squadron, A.F.C., which had set out to make the dawn strategical reconnaissance on the 1st of May, failed to return. It was learned later that one of them had been damaged by fire from the ground near 'Amman and forced to land. While the pilot and his observer were setting fire to their aeroplane the second pilot (Lieutenant F. W. Haig) had landed alongside and picked up the two officers, but when he was moving over the ground to take off again, one of the undercarriage wheels collapsed and the aeroplane pitched forward and was rendered unserviceable. It was set on fire, and the four officers were eventually made prisoners.

On the 2nd of May things went a little better on the ground, but the air observers flew home with disquieting news. They had to tell of Turkish reinforcements arriving from various directions. In the morning a large increase in the rolling-stock in 'Amman station was noted with a troop train steaming into the station from the north, there were formed bodies of cavalry and infantry moving along the 'Amman–'Ain es Sir track, and abnormal movements of cavalry, guns, and infantry in the Lower Wadi el Far'a in the direction of the Jordan, and there was much coming and going along the Jisr ed Damiye–Es Salt track. In the afternoon pack animals and troops were seen moving from 'Ain es Sir towards Shunet Nimrin, and in the Jordan area a barge was found making repeated journeys ferrying troops across the river at Jisr ed Damiye.

Fighting began on the 3rd of May before dawn and the enemy pressure was everywhere strengthened. In the afternoon General Allenby decided that there was nothing to be gained and much to be risked by a continuance of the operation, and he therefore empowered Lieutenant-General Sir H. G. Chauvel to order a withdrawal: this was completed by midnight on the 4th. German aeroplanes made a brief attack, with machine-guns, on a retreating column on the morning of the 4th, but otherwise enemy aircraft did not intervene during the retreat. No. 14 Squadron did good work throughout the 4th when they reported the British and Turkish movements, dropping their messages at corps and divisional head-quarters, and sometimes also on columns of cavalry. Pilots of the Fortieth (Army) Wing carried bombs during their offensive patrols and strategical reconnaissances and dropped them on targets offered by the Turks as they followed up the British.

From the air point of view the feature of interest in this minor operation was the failure to discover the Turkish concentrations on the west bank of the Jordan before the action began. Had General Allenby suspected the presence of the Turkish *3rd Cavalry Division* and the *Caucasus Cavalry Brigade* near Mafid Jozele, and had he known of of the concentration of the Turkish *24th Division* at Dome, or of its subsequent movement to the Jordan, he would no doubt have strengthened his dispositions on the flank in order to deny the Turks the free use of the Jisr ed Damiye and Mafid Jozele crossings. The fact that the Beni Sakr Arabs did not fulfil their undertaking to close the 'Ain es Sir track and so cut off Turkish reinforcements from Shunet Nimrin also contributed something to the failure. While the action was being fought the air squadrons did all that could be expected of them, in view of the difficult nature of some of the country in which movements took place. The observers gave valuable indication of the arrival of enemy reinforcements, and the messages dropped from the air kept the British commanders informed of the main movements of their columns. When reconnaissance had been fully provided for, attempts, necessarily intermittent, were made to harass the Turks with bomb and machine-gun, and on two occasions medical supplies, urgently needed, were dropped for the cavalry in Es Salt.

The two raids across the Jordan failed to achieve their immediate object, but the raids should not be judged in isolation. General Allenby hoped and believed that he would have the means, later in the year, to undertake a decisive offensive, and he was impressed with the advantages which might be obtained if he struck in the Plain of Sharon. The raids east of the Jordan would, he anticipated, make the enemy command uneasy about the opposite flank, especially about the safety of the railway at the important focal point of Der'a. In this the 'Amman and Es Salt raids succeeded. The Turkish troops in the Jordan valley, and eastwards, were greatly strengthened at the expense of the coastal and central areas, a diversion of forces that affected the progress of the operations which, later in the year, ended the Palestine campaign.

Summer Operations

Owing to the torrid conditions during the summer months, and to reorganization made necessary by the continued transfer of troops to France, there were few actions of importance in the period between the Es Salt raid across the Jordan and the final offensive in September. On the 8th of June the 7th Division, in order to improve its front in the area of the coast, captured two low hills which had formed observation posts for the enemy: No. 113 Squadron helped by observing for the fire of the British guns.

On the 1st of June No. 142 Squadron had been transferred from the Fortieth (Army) Wing to the Fifth (Corps)

Wing. The pilots and observers of the squadron had been attached to No. 14 Squadron to gain experience in the work of co-operation with the army and, on the 6th of June, No. 142 Squadron became responsible for the enemy area in front of the Desert Mounted Corps in the Jordan valley, relieving No. 14 Squadron. On the 27th of June the contact patrol Flight ('C') of No. 142 Squadron moved to Jerusalem from Er Ramle. Turkish prisoners taken early in July spoke of an impending attack in the Jordan valley, and No. 142 Squadron was asked to keep a special watch for enemy movements. The reports of the observers indicated considerable minor activity, but did not disclose any exceptional concentrations of troops. The minor movements behind the Turkish lines were at their maximum on the 12th of July, and it was reported from the air on the following day that they had almost ceased. The front was quiet on the 13th, but about 1 a.m. on the 14th sentries in the British forward trenches could hear unusual noise in the Turkish lines at Abu Tulul, and at 3.30 a.m. German and Turkish troops attacked. The attack, boldly made by the Germans, who complained that they were ill supported by their Allies, failed entirely at a cost of 448 prisoners, of whom 377 were German. While the action was being fought the Jodhpore Lancers made a charge in the Jordan valley and frustrated an attack which was about to be made on the Jordan bridge-head. The main fighting had already ended when the first reconnaissance aeroplane of No. 142 Squadron appeared over the front at 4.50 a.m. The observer reported the movements of several small bodies of enemy infantry and cavalry, but he saw no concentrations of troops, and subsequent air reconnaissances confirmed that no enemy reinforcements were marching to the area, and left no doubt that the attack was of a local nature.

The only additional operations before the September offensive began which need be mentioned were two British raids. On the night of the 27th of July the 53rd Sikhs entered the Turkish advanced trenches near the coast at El Haram and brought back thirty-three prisoners with a loss to themselves of four men. A mosaic of the Turkish positions was compiled for the use of the Sikhs by No. 113 Squadron and the air observers also made special detailed reports, before the action, about the nature of the entrenchments. The second raid, on a larger scale, was made by the 10th Division on the night of the 12th of August against positions on the steep Gharabe ridge, west of the Nablus road. The Turkish area was reconnoitred and photographed, chiefly by No. 14 Squadron, and a mosaic of the enemy entrenchments was made. Furthermore, a replica of the enemy defences, as pictured by the information obtained from the air, was built in the training area, and the 29th Brigade of the 10th Division, which had been withdrawn from the line on the 10th of July for special training, was able to rehearse the details of the attack. The result was that the raid was perfectly executed and the Turks, taken by surprise, lost 14 machine-guns and 239 prisoners.

In August 1918 the Palestine Brigade, Royal Air Force, was reinforced. On the 14th No. 144 Squadron came under the orders of the Brigade, and by the end of the month it had been fully equipped with D.H.9 aeroplanes at Junction Station, the aerodrome of No. 14 Squadron. On the 14th, also, one Flight of a single-seater fighter squadron, No. 145, equipped with S.E.5a's, was incorporated in the Brigade. The other Flights of the squadron remained with the Training Brigade in Egypt until the 14th of September. When the September offensive began the Palestine Brigade included the three corps squadrons of the Fifth Wing: Nos. 14, 113, and 142; and four squadrons of the Fortieth (Army) Wing: No. 1 A.F.C., and Nos. 111, 144, and 145. There were also three balloon sections making up the 21st Balloon Company (Nos. 49, 50, and 57), and the Aircraft Park at Qantara with its advanced stores depot at Er Ramle.

Balloon Observation

The work of observation, particularly for the fire of the artillery, had been greatly helped by the balloon sections. In January 1918 there were two sections in Palestine, Nos. 49 and 50, the former with the XX Corps in the hilly country on the right, and the latter with the XXI Corps in the coastal area. In the middle of March a new section, No. 54, arrived on the front and relieved No. 49 Section, which was transferred to the coast to reinforce No. 50 Section. No. 54 Section had little luck. The country which the observers saw from their basket was very broken and it was not easy for them to obtain useful information. Furthermore, the balloon was frequently attacked by German aeroplanes. On the 8th of May it had reached a height of 5,300 feet—a record at that time for a balloon in Palestine—and was about to be hauled down when it was set on fire by an enemy pilot. The observer, Lieutenant W. H. Hargreaves, jumped, but some of the bridles of his parachute had been cut by bullets and it failed to open. On the following day the balloons of the two sections in the western area were likewise destroyed by enemy aeroplanes, but the observers reached ground safely with their parachutes.

Owing to the disappointing results obtained by No. 54 Section on the hills, the balloon was withdrawn in May and the section was disbanded. In July a new section, No. 57, was added to the strength of the 21st Balloon Company and began work in the coastal area early in August. During this month the three sections provided observation for 316 'shoots' with the artillery, a majority of the targets being enemy batteries. As an example of the amount of work which could be done by one balloon observer it may be mentioned that on a day in August Lieutenant L. W. Baker helped to register gun-fire on thirty-two enemy targets, a feat which kept him in the air for five and a half hours. The methodical work of the balloon observers may not appear exciting, but it contributed a not unimportant share to the final victory. In the neighbourhood of the coast in particular the country was well suited to balloon observation and the visibility was usually good, especially in the mornings and in the evenings when the enemy area was given a sharp definition by the slanting rays of the sun. The balloon observers had completed their best work on the day when the September offensive opened. On the first day of the attack they added some useful information about Turkish movements and they received, by heliograph, a few important messages from the advancing British infantry, but the rate of progress became so rapid that this form of observation could no longer be employed and the balloons were deflated.

'X' Flight with the Arabs
[Map, p. 183]

Throughout the summer 'X' Flight, still based on 'Aqaba, continued to give the Arabs a helping hand. On the 12th of May 1918 three pilots, making use of an advanced landing-ground, had co-operated with a Sherifian detachment during an attack on Jerdun station. The aeroplanes appeared in the early morning at the moment when the Arab attack was beginning, and although the pilots could drop only a few light-weight bombs on the Turkish positions, the timeliness of the bombing made it easier for the Arabs to capture their objective, together with 140 prisoners. The Arabs stayed long enough to destroy the station, which was too distant from their base to be permanently held, and then withdrew.[1]

In June 'X' Flight moved from 'Aqaba to El Gueira, and it was subsequently kept occupied by photographic and general reconnaissances, and by occasional bombing attacks, particularly on Ma'an and Mudauwara stations.

In July the large Arab camp at Tahonie, about five miles west of Ma'an, was bombed by enemy aeroplanes. 'X' Flight had in its possession no more than two fighting aeroplanes, Nieuport Scouts, and these were sent to a landing-ground at Tahonie from which patrols were made from time to time over the enemy aerodrome at Ma'an. On the 9th of August one of the Nieuport pilots shot down an enemy aeroplane which crashed near Jerdun

---

[1] A message conveying the thanks of the Sherif Feisal said: 'The attack-'ing infantry were advancing and close to the position. The bombing was 'most excellent and accurate; nearly all the bombs fell inside the fortifica-'tions and the slight casualties sustained by the Sherifian troops is attributed 'to the skill of your pilots.'

station. About this time a Bristol Fighter was received by the Flight and it joined in the patrols made over the aerodrome at Ma'an. Enemy aeroplanes, however, were seldom seen, but occasional 'tip-and-run' bombing raids continued to be made on Tahonie.

Meanwhile there had been successful operations at Mudauwara. General Allenby had agreed that two companies of the Camel Brigade should be sent to capture the station, a feat which had up to that time seemed beyond the strength of the Arabs. The two companies had marched out from the Suez Canal on the 24th of July and they reached 'Aqaba on the 30th. On the 7th of August Mudauwara station was reconnoitred and bombed from the air and, next morning, the attack was made, the officers who took part making use of copies of a photographic mosaic specially compiled for them by 'X' Flight. When the first pilot appeared over the enemy positions on the 8th he found that one of the three Turkish redoubts, the southern, had already been captured, and an agreed signal laid out on the ground informed him that a bombing attack on the northern redoubt was desired. Soon after he had dropped his bombs three more pilots arrived and they also attacked the redoubt, which was quickly captured. The camel force subsequently pushed forward from Mudauwara to blow up the main bridge at 'Amman, a movement planned with reference to the September offensive in Palestine, but when, on the 20th of August, the column arrived at a point about fifteen miles south-east of 'Amman its presence was discovered by an enemy aeroplane observer, and because a surprise raid was no longer possible the column was withdrawn to Bayir, sixty miles north-east of Ma'an, and ultimately to Beersheba.

The Final Offensive
[Maps, pp. 175, 183, facing]

During the summer months General Allenby turned over in his mind plans for the renewal of the offensive in Palestine on a decisive scale. He came to his final plan, of great boldness and simplicity, by stages. He had to take into account early rains, due at the beginning of November, and although he need not anticipate that they would be severe he must reckon that they might make the Plains of Sharon and Esdraelon impassable for transport except along one or two roads. He decided, therefore, to begin his campaign about the middle of September.

Broadly summarized, his plan was to mass the greater part of his infantry and cavalry along the eight miles of front in the plain between the railway and the sea, and, by an overwhelming attack north-eastward, to break the Turkish defence system and clear a way for the cavalry to pass through to cut the Turkish rail and road communications. The most important of the enemy centres was Der'a, the junction of the Palestine and Hejaz railways, but this objective was out of reach of General Allenby's armies and it was allotted to the Arabs under Sherif Feisal.

General Allenby outlined his general intentions in personal instructions issued to his corps commanders on the 1st of August. On the 22nd, however, he expanded his scheme of operations and it may be said that his amended plan had for ultimate object nothing less than the annihilation of the Turkish armies in Palestine. The main attack was to be made on the left by the XXI Corps (Lieutenant-General Sir E. S. Bulfin) and by the Desert Mounted Corps (Lieutenant-General Sir H. G. Chauvel), while the XX Corps (Lieutenant-General Sir Philip W. Chetwode) was to advance astride the Nablus road. In the Jordan valley demonstrations to induce the enemy to expect an attack east of the river were to be made by Chaytor's Force (Major-General Sir E. W. C. Chaytor). At Qasr el Azraq, fifty miles east of 'Amman, the advanced column of the Arabs was to concentrate for raids against the railway north, south, and west of Der'a.

After gaining a line from Qalqilye, on the railway nine miles south-south-west of Tul Karm, to the mouth of the Nahr el Faliq, the XXI Corps was to swing its left forward and advance in the direction of Nablus and Samaria. The Desert Mounted Corps was to push rapidly through to El 'Affule, forty miles distant from the British trenches on the coast and six and a half miles south of Nazareth. At Nazareth was the head-quarters of Liman von Sanders, and it was directed that a detachment should ride forward from El 'Affule to attempt the capture of the enemy Commander-in-Chief and his staff. The plans contemplated that El 'Affule would be reached on the second day of the attack, and if this happened the line of retreat of the enemy troops west of the Jordan by way of the Plain of Esdraelon would be cut. At El 'Affule the cavalry would also find themselves within a march of Beisan in the Jordan valley, and timely occupation of Beisan would cut the alternative road from Nablus to Damascus by way of Samakh on the southern shore of the Sea of Galilee.

The offensive began on the 19th of September. By this time the Royal Air Force in Palestine dominated the air, a fact which was to have a powerful influence on the battle. This dominance had not been brought about by a preliminary air offensive, but was the result of pressure exerted without intermission throughout the summer. It is beyond dispute that during the hot months the German pilots and observers had had a sorry time. Ill-equipped, remote from their sources of supply, attached to a neglected Turkish army whose morale was weakening, they had to meet aeroplanes superior in performance and number, piloted by officers imbued almost to the point of recklessness with the offensive spirit. The German pilots could seldom take to the air without being fiercely attacked. Time after time they were compelled to return to their aerodromes without being able to fulfil the missions which they had set out to attempt. They suffered steady casualties, and because they never knew when replacements would arrive, if at all, they must have realized that they were a force dying through slow attrition, impotent to do the work which waited and accumulated. All the British squadrons took part in the fighting by which the enemy pilots were subdued, but the employment of No. 1 Squadron Australian Flying Corps brought it most opportunities for combat and it would hardly be an exaggeration to say that the Bristol Fighters of the Australians kept the sky clear.

Whether they were engaged on strategical reconnaissance, bombing attacks, or offensive patrols, the Australian flying officers never let pass an opportunity to seek out and fight enemy aircraft, usually pursuing their quarry to the ground where the destruction was often completed. During one week in June enemy pilots crossed the British lines one hundred times. In the last week of August the visits had dropped to eighteen, and during the three following weeks were further reduced to a total of four. General Liman von Sanders has summed up the position as follows: 'The 'German air personnel on the Palestine front had, through-'out the summer, experienced a very difficult time against 'the British. The German aeroplanes were greatly inferior 'in climbing capabilities and in speed to the modern British 'types. Two consignments of aircraft sent out as replace-'ments proved, almost without exception, to be useless. 'Owing to the urgent needs of the German Western front 'further replacements were out of the question. Between 'the spring and the autumn the excellent air service lost 59 'pilots and observers. In September air reconnaissances of 'the British positions had almost ceased. Immediately a 'German aeroplane put in an appearance it would be 'attacked by such superior British formations that air 'reconnaissance was impossible.'[1]

Before we pass from this question of air superiority the part played by the air organization in Egypt must be noticed. The Training Brigade (Brigadier-General P. L. W. Herbert) of the Middle East command constituted, in effect, a reserve of pilots and observers for the Palestine Brigade, and no shortage in personnel had to be feared. For the September offensive moreover officers of experience and proved worth were provided by the Training Brigade for special duties not normally required under conditions of static warfare. In particular, air service officers were attached, for liaison, to the staffs of the military commanders, and they were able, as the operations progressed, to make many suggestions for aeroplane co-operation.

On the morning of the 19th of September, when the

[1] *Fünf Jahre Türkei*, p. 343.

THE PALESTINE BRIGADE

offensive opened, the Order of Battle of the Palestine Brigade, Royal Air Force, was as follows:[1]

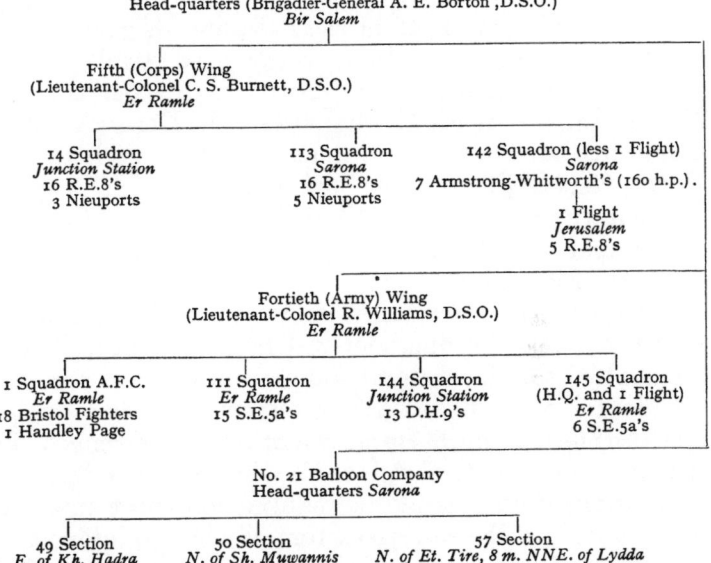

The Aircraft Park known as 'X' remained at Qantara, but an advanced stores and motor transport pool had been established at Er Ramle. It will be noticed that two of the corps squadrons had some Nieuport single-seaters in their possession, the reason being that it was considered desirable to give them fighters which would be at hand to help the corps aeroplanes if they should be attacked. The Nieuports had, in other words, been specially provided for local protection, but it happened that they proved of value in a way which had not been foreseen. Once the battle began the single-seater fighter pilots often flew home with early news of important events. It may be said that they constituted an express reconnaissance service for reporting the major happenings in a battle situation which underwent rapid changes. A word must be said also about the Handley Page with No. 1 Squadron, A.F.C., the only aeroplane of its type in the Middle East. It had been

[1] The figures quoted for the various squadrons are for aeroplanes serviceable.

flown out from England at the end of July by Brigadier-General A. E. Borton, accompanied by Major A. S. C. Maclaren, and it was to prove a powerful reinforcement of the bombing strength of the Palestine Brigade.

The three corps squadrons co-operated as follows: No. 113 Squadron with the XXI Corps in the coastal sector, No. 142 Squadron (less 'C' Flight) with the Desert Mounted Corps in the same area, No. 14 Squadron with the XX Corps, and 'C' Flight of No. 142 Squadron with Chaytor's Force in the Jordan valley. This left three squadrons and one Flight for strategical reconnaissance work and for offensive operations.

No special instructions were issued to the Royal Air Force by the Commander-in-Chief. Instead, Major-General W. G. H. Salmond and his senior air officers were called into conference, and they were encouraged to suggest plans for the maximum employment of the air strength. For the success of General Allenby's scheme it was desirable: (i) that the Turks should be induced to expect an attack, if anywhere, in the eastern sector; (ii) that no information should be allowed to reach the enemy command of the movements behind the British lines from east to west, nor of the eventual concentration behind the XXI Corps front; and (iii) that, once the battle began, knowledge of the early forward movements of the British cavalry in the coastal plain should remain hidden from the enemy higher command. The air officers contributed their ideas for effective concealment. In the eastern sector camps were left standing, horses moved about dragging brushwood to raise dust, and dummies were placed in the horse-lines. It could be assumed that if enemy aeroplanes attempted to make a reconnaissance of the area they would fly at great heights, certainly above 14,000 feet, and the suggestions put forward by the air commanders were of a kind to deceive observers looking down from such heights. The intention was not to provide special air patrols of the eastern sector, but to allow enemy observers to make fleeting reconnaissances if they attempted to do so. On the other hand, strong and continuous patrols by fighting aircraft in the coastal area, especially between 12.30 p.m. and 2.30 p.m. when the horses would be watered, were planned. Movements were made by night, and if a movement had not been completed by 2.30 a.m. the troops had orders to halt and conceal themselves. Military police were posted by day to see that the orders were understood, and their instructions were to signal, by whistle, the approach of enemy aeroplanes in order that troops might be warned to stay under cover. Those who were on the move when the warning whistle blew were to halt immediately and they were forbidden to fire on the enemy aeroplane. All cooking was to be done by means of solidified alcohol instead of smoke-betraying fire, and no lights were to be shown at night. As a result of these and similar arrangements aimed at concealment, the enemy saw nothing of General Allenby's concentration for the battle. Surprise was achieved, but it was a near thing because the enemy obtained a warning of the attack from an unexpected quarter. On the 17th of September an Indian deserter crossed to the Turkish lines and he prattled about a British attack to be made in the coastal sector in two days' time. The news was given to Liman von Sanders, but he would not believe it, thinking that the Indian had been specially sent across by the British Intelligence service with the object of misleading him. An enemy intelligence map which was subsequently found among the papers at Liman von Sanders's head-quarters in Nazareth made it clear that the enemy command entertained no sort of suspicion about the magnitude of the blow which the British had prepared. There is no evidence that the German Commander-in-Chief ordered a special air reconnaissance to test the truth of the deserter's statement. This would have been the part of wisdom, even though the information appeared to be tainted, and the loss of many aeroplanes would have been a light price to pay for such vital knowledge. The commander of the Turkish Eighth Army, who was more reluctant to discredit the deserter's story, pleaded to be allowed to withdraw to the Et Tire line, a movement which would assuredly have prejudiced the full success of the British offensive, but Liman von Sanders resolutely refused to allow any ground to be abandoned. It is possible that had a reconnaissance been attempted by a fast single-seater, making an approach from the sea in rear of the British lines at a low height, in conjunction perhaps with a feint reconnaissance from the direction of the Turkish lines, the effort would have succeeded. It is not to be doubted that had the need and urgency been made clear to the German air service, whatever risks were necessary would have been taken to obtain the information which meant so much to the safety of the Palestine front. The enemy high command cannot be absolved from blame for its apparent indifference.

Apart from the maintenance of patrols over the western area, the Royal Air Force put forward no special activity before the battle began. It had been suggested that a preliminary bombing offensive against enemy aerodromes, artillery dumps, and certain communication centres, should be made, but, after full consideration, the air command reported strongly against this suggestion on the grounds that a bombing offensive of the kind was certain to make the German command alert, and with this view the military staff ultimately concurred.

An exception was made in the eastern area in conjunction with operations by the Arabs under Sherif Feisal and Colonel T. E. Lawrence. The Arabs had moved northward to 'Azraq, fifty miles east of 'Amman, and a detachment of two aeroplanes of 'X' Flight (one Bristol Fighter and a B.E.) had flown to 'Azraq for reconnaissance of the three railways which centred on Der'a, objectives for the raiding activities of the Sherifian forces. A direct attack on Der'a was also contemplated, but the Arabs could undertake this operation only if the Royal Air Force promised 'so heavy a daylight bombing of Der'a station 'that the effect would be tantamount to artillery bombard-'ment, enabling us to risk an assault against it with our few 'men.'[1] On the 11th of September a Bristol Fighter from Palestine landed at 'Azraq with dispatches, and Colonel Lawrence learned from the pilot that an air bombardment of the intensity he desired was out of the question. He decided, therefore, to give up all idea of a direct attack,

[1] *Seven Pillars of Wisdom*, p. 585.

and to concentrate instead on cutting the railway communications on all sides of Der'a.

On the 15th of September the Bristol Fighter with 'X' Flight, after reconnoitring the railway north of Der'a, met and fought an enemy two-seater which was destroyed in flames, but the Bristol Fighter was itself so damaged by bullets that it had to be sent to Palestine for repair.

While the Arabs were making one of their demolition raids on the 16th, six D.H.9's of No. 144 Squadron dropped five 112-lb. and forty-eight 20-lb. bombs on Der'a junction from 1,000 feet. 'About two in the afternoon as we 'drove towards the railway', wrote Colonel Lawrence, 'we 'had the great sight of a swarm of our bombing planes 'droning steadily up towards Der'a on their first raid. The 'place had hitherto been carefully reserved from air attack, 'so the damage among the unaccustomed, unprotected, 'unarmed garrison was heavy. The morale of the men 'suffered as much as the railway traffic: and till our on- 'slaught from the north forced them to see us, all their 'efforts went into digging bomb-proof shelters.'[1] Der'a was bombed again on the 17th by a similar number of D.H.9's. The attacks inflicted damage on the station buildings and neighbouring camps, depressed the occupants of the town, and encouraged the Arabs, but what was of chief importance was that the air activity in the eastern sector, at a time when there was comparative quiet in the western area, helped further to deceive the enemy into the belief that the eastern sector remained the vital one.

There is evidence that German aeroplanes were transferred from the Jenin aerodrome to Der'a on the 17th of September. On this day, when an Arab force was blowing up a part of the line, eight aeroplanes from Der'a attacked them with bombs and machine-guns. Lieutenant H. R. Junor, in a B.E.12 from 'X' Flight detachment at 'Azraq, had left on his own initiative to make a reconnaissance of the Der'a aerodrome, and he appeared just when the Arabs were being bombed. 'We watched with mixed feel- 'ings, for his hopelessly old-fashioned machine made him 'cold meat for any one of the enemy scouts or two-seaters:

[1] *Seven Pillars of Wisdom*, p. 590.

'but at first he astonished them, as he rattled in with his 'two guns. They scattered for a careful look at this un- 'expected opponent. He flew westward across the line, 'and they went after in pursuit, with that amiable weak- 'ness of aircraft for a hostile machine, however important 'the ground target. We were left in perfect peace'.[1] Lieutenant Junor, when his petrol was nearly finished, was eventually forced to land near the Arabs he had helped. His aeroplane was damaged on landing and was afterwards hit by a bomb from one of the pursuing aeroplanes. There was no reserve aeroplane at 'Azraq, so the pilot asked for temporary employment with the Arabs and he was put in command of a Ford car in which he ran along the railway towards Der'a and blew up a stretch of the track.

The employment of the squadrons of the Palestine Brigade, once the battle began, reveals how carefully the staff had planned. An initial bombing offensive was directed against the main Turkish telegraphic and telephonic centres, whose positions were known from intelligence sources and from air photographs. The bombing was begun by the Handley Page piloted by Captain Ross M. Smith who set out at 1.15 a.m. on the 19th of September, with sixteen 112-lb. bombs, to attack the central telephone exchange of the Army Group, at El 'Affule. At 6.30 a.m. five D.H.9's of No. 144 Squadron attacked the same objective with four 112-lb. and thirty-two 20-lb. bombs, and eight pilots of the squadron attacked it again at 11.25 a.m. (eight 112-lb., sixty-four 20-lb. bombs). An examination of the target after the British advance revealed the majority of the telephone wires lying tangled in bomb craters.

The objectives next in importance were the head-quarters and telephone exchanges of the Turkish Eighth Army at Tul Karm, and of the Turkish Seventh Army at Nablus. No. 144 Squadron attacked the Nablus targets at 5.20 a.m. and, a little later, the head-quarters at Tul Karm were bombed by No. 142 Squadron. No. 14 Squadron also co-operated with dawn attacks on three minor Turkish

[1] *Seven Pillars of Wisdom*, p. 596.

head-quarters. Some hits on the various head-quarters were reported by the bombing pilots, but no details of the damage inflicted can be given. General Liman von Sanders, however, throws light upon the general military results of the bombing. 'Shortly after daybreak', he says, 'British air squadrons appeared over the head-quarters of 'the Seventh and Eighth Armies, over the camps of the 'various corps head-quarters, and over the central tele-'phone offices of the Army Group at 'Affule. From low 'heights they attacked with bombs and destroyed part of 'the telephone line. . . . Telephonic and telegraphic com-'munication between Tul Karm and Nazareth ceased 'about 7 a.m. The wireless station of the head-quarters of 'the Eighth Army also failed to reply when called.'[1]

It appears that communication between Nablus and Nazareth was restored about noon, and Liman von Sanders then learned the surprising news that the British had broken through the Turkish Seventh Army in the coast sector. Nablus also reported that it had been impossible to establish communication with the Seventh Army head-quarters at Tul Karm. Thereafter, only meagre and con-flicting reports reached Liman von Sanders. Nor could he look to his air service to dissipate the fog of war. 'Since 'early morning', he says, 'head-quarters had felt the great 'drawback that the German air service had been unable to 'observe and report what was happening on the battle 'front and along the lines of retreat.'[2]

The arrangements made to keep the German aeroplanes on the ground on the 19th of September were specially suited to the conditions on the Palestine front, where the morale of the enemy pilots and observers had suffered as a result of the aggressive tactics of the Royal Air Force throughout the summer. The chief enemy aerodrome was at Jenin, and patrols by pairs of S.E.5a's of Nos. 111 and 145 Squadrons were maintained over this aerodrome from dawn to dusk. Each pilot carried four 20-lb. bombs which were to be released when any sign of activity was seen. As each relieving pair of S.E.5a's arrived over Jenin, the

[1] *Fünf Jahre Türkei*, p. 346.
[2] Ibid., p. 352.

departing pilots were to drop what bombs remained, either on the aerodrome or on the station. Twelve pairs of S.E.'5s were so engaged during the day and 104 bombs were dropped: no German pilot left the ground.

To sum up, the Royal Air Force, by early bombing on the 19th, severed an important part of the telephonic and telegraphic communications and so prevented the enemy commands from acquiring more than a fragmentary knowledge of what was happening, and by continuous patrol overawed the German air service and rendered it impotent.

Before the progress of the offensive can be considered, some additional preliminary arrangements for aircraft co-operation must be noted. Owing to the difficult nature of the country the lines of retreat open to the Turks were defined. Every possible route was photographed from the air, and those defiles in which bombing attacks upon moving columns would exert a maximum effect were methodically noted. If guns or transport could be caught and bombed in the defiles it was almost certain that the way of escape of the enemy would be blocked. The main lines of retreat were (*a*) Tul Karm to Samaria; (*b*) Samaria to Jenin; (*c*) 'Anebta, on the Tul Karm road, to Jenin; (*d*) Nablus–Wadi el Far'a–Jisr ed Damiye, and (*e*) Balata–Wadi el Far'a–Khirbet Ferweh–Beisan. The arrangement was that when the battle began the routes were to be kept under observation by Bristol Fighters of No. 1 Squadron (Australian Flying Corps), fitted with long-range wireless sets. Royal Air Force head-quarters would thus be enabled to receive immediate information about retreating Turkish columns and would be in a position to judge the times and places best suited for a concentrated bombing offensive. In addition to this special watch over the important routes, general strategical reconnaissances were to be made during the operations.

The tactical duties of the corps squadrons were pre-arranged with similar attention to detail. No. 142 Squadron, attached to the Cavalry Corps, was charged with the duty of keeping Cavalry head-quarters, and General Head-quarters, informed of the progress of the leading cavalry divisions, and was also required to maintain liaison between

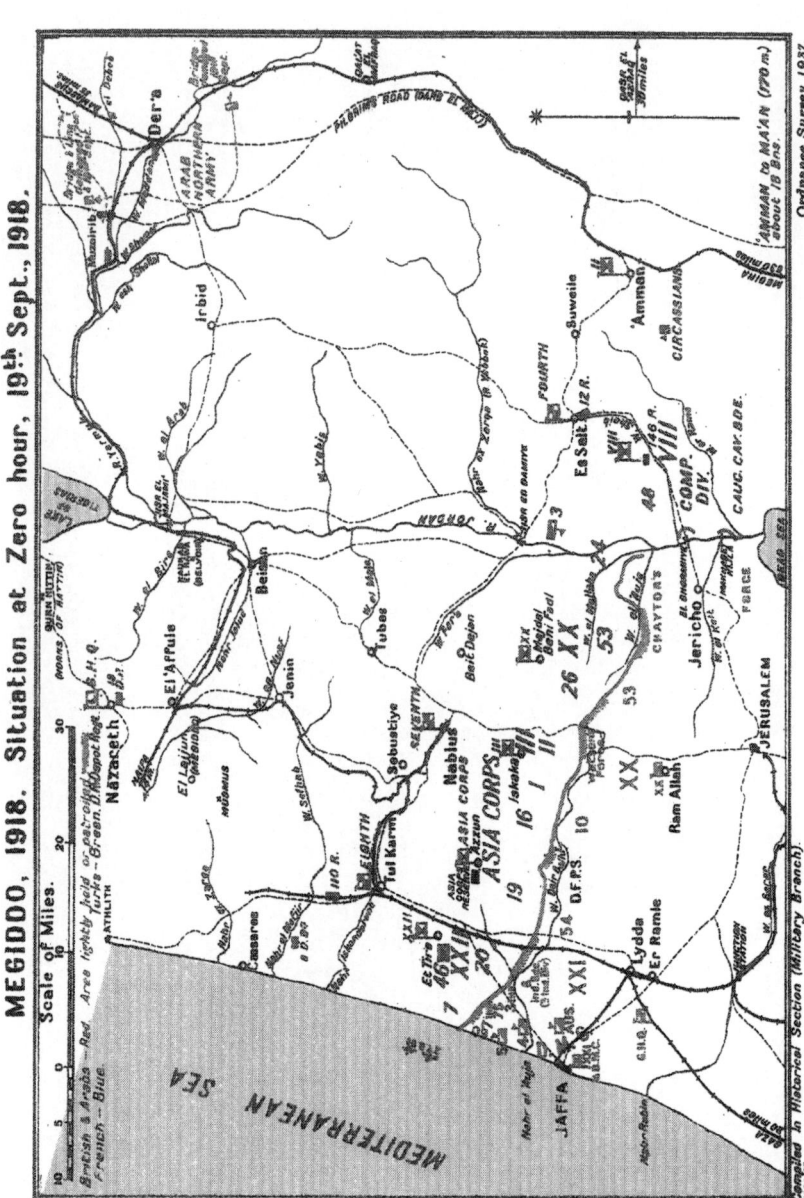

these head-quarters. A liaison officer, Lieutenant-Colonel W. H. Primrose, with equipment by which pilots could, if the occasion arose, pick up messages without the need to land, was attached to cavalry head-quarters. Observers of No. 113 Squadron, working with the XXI Corps, were to drop their messages at divisional and brigade head-quarters, and were to receive messages as necessary by way of a Popham signalling panel. When the forward movement began, the head-quarters of the XXI Corps were to keep the squadron fully informed of the successive new centres upon which messages for subordinate commanders were to be dropped. The infantry carried disks and flares and had orders to display them when called upon to do so by a Klaxon horn signal from a contact-patrol aeroplane. The infantry were also instructed to light flares if in the early stages of the advance British shells were found to be falling short; by a special urgent wireless call the air observers could convey an immediate warning to the corps artillery head-quarters.

The attack by the XXI Corps began at 4.45 a.m. on the 19th of September and the Turks were quickly overwhelmed. A novel attempt to help the infantry was made by No. 113 Squadron. An apparatus had been invented by the Royal Air Force in the Middle East by means of which sixty candles could be dropped successively to create a smoke screen about 400 yards long. Twice on the 19th of September screens were put down on the front of the XXI Corps by two pilots. The places where the screens were to be made were chosen before the attack began; the first was laid according to plan, but on the second occasion the pilots found that the infantry had already advanced far beyond the appointed line, and they therefore reconnoitred the front and eventually dropped their smoke candles to screen a Turkish position which was seen to be holding up the British advance. No further opportunities to exploit this form of aircraft co-operation occurred because, although the infantry could call by ground signal for a screen if required, the Turks were entirely overrun.

About 7 a.m. the Desert Mounted Corps began to tread a way along the beach, and through flagged paths in the

Turkish wire, and half an hour later were moving against the enemy rear communications. Soon after they started off a pilot and observer of No. 113 Squadron, who were engaged on artillery patrol on the front of the XXI Corps, saw the leading regiment (Hodson's Horse) of the 13th Cavalry Brigade, the head of the advanced guard, trotting along the beach. They watched the horsemen cross the Nahr el Faliq and move towards the coast road. A little distance off the road was a house and an orchard, a likely point of resistance, and the pilot therefore flew over it and discovered that the orchard was crowded with Turkish troops and transport. The air observer scribbled this information, and dropped the message on the leading squadron of Hodson's Horse which galloped forward and attacked at once. The Turks, who were taken by surprise, could open only a wild fire, and the dashing action of the troopers led to the quick capture of the orchard with sixty prisoners, two guns, and twelve wagons, at a cost of one man killed and two men wounded.

At noon on the 19th an air report was brought in which illuminated, as in a flash, the nature of the British success, and made it clear that an opportunity had come for the Royal Air Force to strike. It was revealed that masses of Turkish troops, cumbered with mixed transport, were retreating along the road running east from Tul Karm through 'Anebta towards Nablus. Air photographs, previously obtained, had indicated that the route traversed a defile along which it would be impossible for transport to leave the road. All available aircraft were immediately ordered to bomb the column in the defile, and the unhappy Turks were given their first real experience of concentrated aircraft attacks. Bristol Fighters, D.H.9's, and S.E.5a's of the army wing, together with the squadrons of the corps wing, took part in the attacks which continued throughout the afternoon. Six 112-lb. and more than three hundred 20-lb. or 25-lb. bombs were dropped, and many thousands of rounds of machine-gun ammunition were fired from low heights. As was afterwards discovered, the material damage was high and the retreating Turks were disorganized and delayed. 'The British air squadrons', writes Liman von

Sanders, 'relieved every half hour, flew very low and con-
'tinuously bombed, and they covered the roads with dead
'men and horses and shattered transport. The repeated
'attempts of officers to rally at least some of the demora-
'lized troops were made in vain as the men were entirely
'indifferent and were concerned only for their own sal-
'vation!'[1] It is known that the enemy twice contrived to
clear a way through the road after some of the early bombing, but that they subsequently abandoned the attempt:
the road was left blocked with tangled bodies and
transport.

By nightfall on the 19th of September the British left
had swung forward to Tul Karm and some 7,000 prisoners
with 100 guns had been captured. The two Turkish
divisions in the Plain of Sharon had ceased to exist as effective military formations, and the men who had escaped
capture were in panic flight, mindful only of their safety.
What they did not know was that British cavalry were
already moving through the Samarian hills to bar the way
of escape.

As it was anticipated that the cavalry might reach El
'Affule before dawn on the 20th, the night attacks by the
Handley Page were directed against Jenin station and
aerodrome on which two tons of bombs were dropped
during two visits. When later the Jenin aerodrome came
to be captured it was revealed that three aeroplanes had
been destroyed by the night bombing and it appeared
that others had received sufficient damage to make them
unfit to fly.[2]

The first news from the air on the morning of the 20th
was awaited with impatience. The pilots and observers
of No. 1 Squadron, Australian Flying Corps, who made
the early strategical reconnaissances, had the best general
view of the Turkish plight. Four Bristol Fighters of the
squadron left at 5 a.m., two for the western area of opera-

[1] *Fünf Jahre Türkei*, p. 352.
[2] When Jenin aerodrome was captured three two-seaters and eight
Pfalz single-seater scouts were found burned. There were also eight
damaged engines, a quantity of damaged stores, and about thirty un-
damaged aircraft machine-guns.

tions and two for the eastern. They were back again soon after 8 a.m., having dropped messages telling of what they had seen on the advanced head-quarters of the XXI Corps and on the head-quarters of the XX Corps.

The pilots and observers had looked down in the western area upon the camps between 'Anebta and Deir Sheraf and had seen that most of them had been burnt or abandoned. In El Masudiye station Turkish infantry were engaged in the hurried loading of trains. Most significant of all were scattered movements of cavalry, camelry, and transport, all along the road from Burqa towards Jenin. At Jenin itself the dumps appeared normal, but two fires were seen burning near the station, and a partial dismantling of the hangars on the aerodrome left no doubt that the evacuation of the area was under way. At El 'Affule there was rolling stock in the station, but no engines, and although four aeroplanes were standing on the aerodrome the hangars and marquees had gone. Just after making their flight over El 'Affule the Bristol Fighters had come upon advancing British cavalry, and they had looked back to watch the troopers moving rapidly towards El 'Affule. The Australian pilots and observers who reconnoitred the eastern area had less that was abnormal to report. They had seen that the aerodrome at Balata had been abandoned, as had some of the camps in the neighbourhood of Nablus, and they had noticed transport in rapid movement towards Beisan on the road through Tubas, but it was clear that the Turkish Seventh Army had not as yet been generally alarmed.

The reports brought in by the Bristol Fighters, which were confirmed and amplified by reports from other pilots and observers, led to intensive bombing attacks on the columns retreating along the road to Jenin and the road to Beisan. As the day wore on the Turkish movements increased, and in the afternoon it was seen that all the dumps at Jenin were ablaze. By the time that darkness wrapped the Judean hills the Royal Air Force had dropped ten tons of bombs upon the retreating Turks and their transport and had fired 40,000 rounds of machine-gun ammunition into them. An idea of the confusion within the enemy lines may be obtained from the adventures which befell an S.E.5a pilot, Second Lieutenant E. R. Stafford, of No. 145 Squadron. He had left his aerodrome at Er Ramle at 11.30 a.m. on the 20th to patrol over the road from Jenin to El 'Affule, with orders to attack any suitable targets which presented themselves. When he was flying above Jenin at noon he saw about 500 Turkish soldiers assembled in the main street and he dived upon them and scattered them with fire from his twin machine-guns. He then continued along the road to El 'Affule and attacked motor-cars and a small column of mechanical transport. Shortly afterwards, at the moment when he was diving upon a party of soldiers, the engine in the S.E.5a failed and a forced landing had to be made west of the Jenin–El 'Affule road. The pilot set fire to his aeroplane and moved off on foot to make his escape, but he was pursued and captured by mounted Turkish officers who had galloped forward from the party he had been in the act of attacking when the engine failed. The Turks took the pilot back to the road and told him as they went that he would be handed over to the local commander when the party reached El 'Affule. Before Second Lieutenant Stafford had left his aerodrome at Er Ramle he had been told that air reports had revealed British cavalry in El 'Affule, but he kept a discreet silence and awaited the shock which he knew the Turks would duly receive. The Turkish officers, however, as they approached El 'Affule, were apparently made uneasy, and after examining the place through their field-glasses they turned their party about, but they had not gone far before what were unmistakably Indian cavalry appeared ahead of them. Accepting what seemed inevitable they hoisted white handkerchiefs and bits of garment on sticks and rifles and turned to march into El 'Affule where their surrender was accepted.

The pilot, free once more, went to the former German aerodrome at El 'Affule where Royal Air Force aeroplanes were already in possession. When he arrived he found that one of the British pilots was about to leave for Er Ramle with German mail which had been flown down from Riyaq a few hours earlier. What had happened was that soon after the advanced cavalry had entered El 'Affule, at about 8 a.m., a Bristol Fighter pilot, engaged on a strategical reconnaissance, was making to land on the aerodrome to report to the cavalry when he noticed a German two-seater aeroplane which was approaching with the obvious intention of landing also. The Bristol Fighter pilot courteously gave way, keeping watch as the German descended. When the two-seater came to rest it was captured by a waiting armoured car, and it was revealed that the pilot had flown from Riyaq with two bags of German mail consigned to head-quarters at El 'Affule.

From the afternoon of the 20th of September the El 'Affule aerodrome was used as an advanced landing-ground for reconnaissance aeroplanes. That is to say, about thirty hours after the British offensive had been launched, aircraft of the Royal Air Force were operating from an aerodrome which was forty miles inside the Turkish lines when the attack had begun. Supplies of petrol, oil, and spares were flown to El 'Affule from Er Ramle and from Sarona.

After entering El 'Affule at 8 a.m. on the 20th the advanced cavalry of the 4th Cavalry Division had turned eastwards towards Beisan, which was reached at 4.35 p.m. A reference to the map will show how the main ways of escape to the north had thus been cut. The 5th Cavalry Division, meanwhile, had made a brilliant dash for Nazareth. The 13th Brigade of this division had ridden into Nazareth soon after dawn on the 20th, had captured the head-quarters of the Army Group with members of the staff and important documents, and had only just missed taking General Liman von Sanders himself. In the late afternoon the 3rd Australian Light Horse, which had swung south-east from El Lajjun, galloped into burning Jenin where they made prisoners of the rabble of soldiers still in the town, many of whom had been subjected to aircraft bombing as they had pursued their escape along the Burqa–Jenin road.

The position on the evening of the 20th of September, as the air reports revealed, was one of absorbing interest. In the west the Turkish Eighth Army had been shattered. In the centre the Turkish Seventh Army, slow to take alarm, was stirring, but its lines of retreat to the north were already in British hands and the only way to safety lay in an easterly direction across the river Jordan. To the east the Turkish Fourth Army had quietly maintained its positions throughout the day in ignorance of the drama being played out west of the Jordan.

The routes to the Jordan which lay open to the remnants of the Turkish Eighth Army, and to the Turkish Seventh Army, on the evening of the 20th were:
  (i) Nablus–Ain es Subian–Tubas, and thence to the river at Makhadet el Mas 'Udi or the more northerly crossing at Makhadet Abu Naji.
  (ii) Nablus–Ain es Subian–down the Wadi el Far'a to 'Ain Shible, and thence in a north-easterly direction to the crossing at Makhadet el Mas 'Udi.
  (iii) By way of the old Roman road through Beit Furik.
  (iv) through Majdal Beni Fadl.
  (v) and, most important of the routes south of Nablus, but also the most difficult to reach, down the Wadi el Far'a to the crossing at Jisr ed Damiye.

The XX Corps on the 20th of September had made some progress in difficult country, but the resistance of the Turkish Seventh Army had remained unbroken. It seemed clear, however, that when it came to be fully realized that British cavalry lay across the lines of communication at El 'Affule and Beisan, the Turkish Seventh Army would break up and its one concern would be escape. Lieutenant-General Sir P. W. Chetwode, commanding the XX Corps, gave orders to the 53rd Division to push forward during the night, regardless of fatigue and distance, in an attempt to reach and secure the Wadi el Far'a road and thus cut all the lines of retreat to the Jordan except those leading in a north-easterly direction through Tubas and through 'Ain Shible.

The 158th Brigade of the 53rd Division had, by the evening of the 21st, cut the two southerly routes to the Jordan through Majdal Beni Fadl and through Beit Furik. The division was then ordered to stand fast because there was no longer any need to intercept the columns pouring down the Wadi el Far'a road to the safety of the river. The way had been blocked by the Royal Air Force. The 10th

Division, which had brought the section of the road between Nablus and Ain es Subian under fire at noon on the 21st, had by the evening reached the road north-east of Nablus. There was no need for the division, fatigued after two days of strenuous marching and fighting in the rough ground of Mount Ephraim, to push forward to secure the guns and transport on the Wadi el Far'a road because the air bombing had been so effective that there was no chance of anything being moved.

The story of the 21st of September, the outstanding day in the history of the Palestine Brigade, begins with the dawn reconnaissance patrol sent out by No. 1 Squadron, Australian Flying Corps. Two Bristol Fighters (pilots, Captain A. R. Brown and Lieutenant S. A. Nunan; observers, Lieutenants G. Finlay and F. C. Conrick) left at 5 a.m. and found that Turkish guns and transport were pouring into Balata, east of Nablus, and moving on to Ferweh and the Wadi el Far'a road. No activity was seen along the Beisan road through Tubas, all the movement being down the Wadi el Far'a. A message was sent back by wireless just before 6 a.m. and general bombing of the Turks was ordered at once. The two reconnoitring Bristol Fighters dropped 16 bombs and fired 600 rounds of machine-gun ammunition on transport on the section of road between Balata and Ferweh. Except from the air the ways of retreat across the Jordan, whether through Tubas or through 'Ain Shibli, could not be blocked in time to prevent a great part of these retreating columns from escaping. At 6.30 a.m. three Bristol Fighters from No. 1 Squadron, Australian Flying Corps, the first to be sent out in response to the wireless message, attacked the column. At 9 a.m. a reconnaissance by No. 113 Squadron reported scattered movements on the Beisan road through Tubas, and considerable movements on the roads and wadis east of Tubas leading to the Jordan. By 11 a.m., by which time the pressure exerted by the advancing 10th Division was leading to chaotic movements, the air observers had a view of a continuous stream of transport and troops crowding and jostling along the Wadi el Far'a to 'Ain Shible. It was arranged that two bombing aeroplanes should arrive over the Balata-

Ferweh–'Ain Shible road every three minutes, with, in addition, a bombing formation of six every half hour. The attacks were not made precisely as intended, but they were maintained fairly continuously until about noon, when intensive bombing of the Upper Wadi el Far'a ceased to be necessary, and full attention could be turned to the Tubas road area.

The chief attacks fell to the Bristol Fighters of No. 1 Squadron, Australian Flying Corps, each carrying eight 20-lb. bombs, to the D.H.9's of No. 144 Squadron, each carrying one 112-lb. and eight 20-lb. bombs, and to the S.E.5a's of Nos. 111 and 145 Squadrons (four 20-lb. bombs), but the three corps squadrons (14, 113, and 142) also took a part in the attacks. Throughout the day $9\frac{1}{4}$ tons of bombs were dropped and 56,000 rounds of machine-gun ammunition were fired amongst the retreating Turks. In the official war diaries for this day there are eighty-eight reports of bombing by individual pilots, and eighty-four reports of machine-gun attacks. Laconic as the reports are, they yet convey a terrible picture of maddened Turkish soldiers among heights and precipices from which there was no easy way of escape. Drivers were seen to jump from their lorries, which crashed out of control into the transport in front and often carried a piled-up mass into the ravines below. Horses were seen to stampede and men to rush anywhere in panic, many of them waving signals of surrender to the pilots, some of them prostrating themselves, as it were in supplication to these new mechanical furies from out of the heavens. Once the bombing of the head of the transport columns in the Wadi el Far'a had caused an effective dam, the attacks degenerated into a slaughter which made many pilots sick who took part. Few Turks had the courage to fire back at their darting enemy, but there was some rifle fire from men who had escaped to the hills overlooking the wadi, and two of the aeroplanes fell in the passes and their occupants were killed.

'I dived', says a typical report of a machine-gun attack, 'and fired continually on the thickest part of column. They 'were literally sprayed and I succeeded in inflicting heavy 'casualties'. As an example of the bombing, we may quote from a report: '4 direct hits, one in a body of cavalry 'roughly 50 strong: the bomb appeared to have practically 'demolished them as less than 6 got up and ran away. All 'the rest fell and remained stationary. 3 bombs direct hits 'on large lorries. One lorry blown off road into valley by 'direct hit; the other two bombs fell among transport on 'road causing wreckage. The road must be impassable for 'transport.'

The road was indeed impassable for transport, but it was not until army officers rode forward next day that the completeness of the blockage was revealed. The damage as a direct result of hits by bombs was not unduly great. It was evident that the blind panic induced by the air attacks had done much to create the chaos. At one part of the road lorries, abandoned in motion, had crashed forward into guns which had been carried with their teams into other transport wagons, and the accumulation had gone tearing on, shedding lorries and guns over the precipice on the way, until at last it had been brought to a standstill by its own weight. Along the length of the defile lay the torn bodies of men and of animals. It took many days before some sort of order and sanitation could be restored to the road. There were found in all about 100 guns, 55 motor lorries, 4 motor-cars, 837 four-wheeled wagons, 75 two-wheeled wagons, and 20 water-carts and field kitchens: a great part of the transport had to be burnt on the spot.

Some of the Turkish troops who had endeavoured to escape along the Tubas–Beisan road had continued to Beisan without knowing that it was in British hands and had been made prisoners as they arrived. Others, more suspicious or more alert to the possibilities of the situation, had left the main road and had made for the Jordan crossings. It will be recalled that air observers had seen such movements towards the Jordan on the morning of the 21st, but it would appear that Lieutenant-General Sir H. G. Chauvel, commanding the Desert Mounted Column, did not receive information that the crossings at Makhadet Abu Naji and Makhudet el Mas 'Udi were being used until the evening of the 22nd, too late for action to be taken that night. It had not been possible for the 4th Cavalry Division, which had reached Beisan on the afternoon of the 20th, and had secured the crossings immediately east and south-east of that place, to move south down the Jordan valley. In the words of the military historian: 'From Beisan to Jisr ed Damiye was a 'distance of 25 miles, and it was suddenly realized on the 'afternoon of the 22nd that this constituted a serious hole 'in the net. The failure to close it by a movement south-'ward along the Jordan on the part of the 4th Cavalry 'Division simultaneous with the approach of Chaytor's 'Force to Jisr ed Damiye[1] was, in fact, the sole blot on an 'operation the main line of which had hitherto been per-'fection itself. It must be remembered, however, that the 'Division had had to piquet the road from Beisan half-way 'to El 'Affule, that it had been encumbered with prisoners, 'and that rations had not been delivered at Beisan until the 21st.'[2]

When Lieutenant-General Chauvel heard that the Jordan gap was being exploited he ordered the 4th Cavalry Division to move south along both banks of the river on the morning of the 23rd to intercept the retreating Turks. Meanwhile, on the 22nd, the enemy troops had been attacked from the air, particularly along the 'Ain Shible–Beisan road. Nearly four tons of bombs had been dropped upon them and 30,000 rounds of machine-gun ammunition fired and there had, as a result, been many signs of panic with a noticeable waving to the pilots of white flags.

A part of the 4th Cavalry Division moved down the Jordan valley as ordered on the morning of the 23rd and surprised the rear-guard of the Asia Corps in the act of crossing at Makhadet Abu Naji. After a brief action 800 prisoners were taken, including a divisional commander. Meanwhile another action had developed at a ford a mile or so farther south which, after a fierce fight, resulted in the capture of an additional 4,000 Turks. After their strenuous day the cavalry went into bivouac for the night about four miles south-west of Makhadet Abu Naji. The southward

[1] Chaytor's Force secured the crossing at Jisr ed Damiye on the 22nd.
[2] *Military Operations: Egypt and Palestine*, by Captain Cyril Falls, Vol. II, Pt. II, p. 538.

sweep was resumed next morning, the 24th, as soon as rations had been received. Captain H. I. Hanmer (observer, Second Lieutenant F. E. Thomson) of No. 142 Squadron left the advanced aerodrome at El 'Affule at 8 a.m. on the 24th to make a reconnaissance. At about 10 a.m., when flying over the area east of Tubas, large numbers of Turkish infantry and cavalry were seen making their way down the bed of the Wadi Marma Fiad towards the crossing at Makhadet El Mas 'Udi. Messages giving this information were scribbled and dropped on the 11th Cavalry Brigade as well as on the head-quarters of the 4th Cavalry Division: it happened that about the same time reports of the Turkish movement were received from an advanced observation post of the Middlesex Yeomanry. An exciting race for the Jordan crossings[1] ensued. A few Turks succeeded in escaping in disorder over the river, but the main body was headed off, and after a fierce engagement on both sides of the river, in which the Turks suffered heavy casualties, the enemy troops, to the number of 5,000, were rounded up as prisoners. The Turkish Seventh Army had ceased to exist.

Chaytor's Force

[Maps, pp. 183, 234]

While the débâcle west of the Jordan had been taking place the Turkish Fourth Army, east of the river, had been inactive. Even as late as the evening of the 21st of September, when the two Turkish Armies west of the river had already ceased to possess fighting value, air reconnaissance reports showed the Turkish camps between 'Amman and Shunet Nimrin to be normal. In the afternoon of the 22nd, however, the air observers had found that the whole area of the Fourth Army was astir.

Before the operations of Chaytor's Force can be considered it will be necessary to refer to the progress of the Arab campaign. When the offensive in Palestine opened the advanced Arab force was at El Umtaiye, south-east of Der'a, where it was strategically well placed for operations

---

[1] There was also a ford about a mile south of the Makhadet El Mas 'Udi crossing.

against the three railways, important sections of which the Arabs had already cut. On the 21st of September a Bristol Fighter had landed at El Umtaiye with dispatches, and Colonel T. E. Lawrence then learned for the first time of the break through on the coast, news which changed the whole outlook for the Arabs. Colonel Lawrence decided to pay an immediate visit in the Bristol Fighter to headquarters in Palestine, and a few hours later he was conferring with General Allenby. He learned that the next main advance would be a march on Damascus in which the Arabs would be able to co-operate. Colonel Lawrence pointed out that the German pilots were very active in the neighbourhood of Der'a and that the Arabs were much handicapped by their impotence in the air. Major-General W. G. H. Salmond and Brigadier-General A. E. Borton were asked by General Allenby what could be done to help. The difficulty was one of supply, but Major-General Salmond said that this difficulty might be overcome by using the Handley Page as a sort of air tender. He asked whether this bomber, which was heavy and also required a long run, would find ground suitable for landing east of the Hejaz railway, and the reply of Colonel Lawrence was that he thought there would be no difficulty, but he preferred that an expert should go back with him to see for himself. Next morning two Bristol Fighters and one D.H.9 set out for El Umtaiye, but when the aeroplanes arrived the Arabs were no longer there. They were duly traced to Umm es Surab and it was learned that they had retreated in order to escape from the attention of German aircraft. The noise of the approaching British aeroplanes had sent the Arabs scattering to cover, but they came running forward in jubilation after the pilots had landed.

The party had not long been seated at breakfast when the cry of 'aeroplanes' was raised by the Arabs, and an enemy two-seater, with three single-seater fighters in company, quickly came into view. The Bristol Fighter pilots and their observers rushed to their aeroplanes and within a short time the German two-seater had been destroyed by Captain Ross M. Smith and his observer, Lieutenant E. A. Mustard: some bombs exploded when the enemy aeroplane was burning on the ground. The single-seaters had meanwhile disappeared and the two Bristol Fighter pilots therefore returned, but they had not long landed when a warning of hostile aeroplanes was again given. The Bristol Fighters went away once more and found three Pfalz scouts, presumably the same as had escorted the destroyed two-seater. They were flying low over the burning wreckage of the German aeroplane, and when they were attacked, two of them at once landed: the third was pursued by the Bristol Fighters until it went down on the Der'a aerodrome. In the afternoon an enemy two-seater appeared over the Umm es Surab camp and dropped bombs from 10,000 feet. Lieutenant G. C. Peters, in one of the Bristol Fighters (observer, Lieutenant J. H. Traill), took off immediately and caught up with the enemy north of Der'a. After a brief attack at close range, the enemy aeroplane went down in smoke and seemed to be destroyed when it hit the ground. Later, when the Arabs advanced, they found the wreckage of the German aeroplane with two charred bodies.

Next day Captain Ross Smith, accompanied by Brigadier-General Borton, landed the Handley Page safely at Umm es Surab. Its arrival created excitement, and news of the resources at the disposal of the Arabs was soon carried far and wide. On the landing-ground the Handley Page stood with the Bristol Fighters near, and the Arabs grouped themselves around in wonder, saying: 'Indeed and at last they 'have sent us THE aeroplane, of which these things were 'foals.'[1] The Handley Page carried in its fuselage, and on its bomb racks, about a ton of petrol for the use of the Bristol Fighters, together with spares and oil and a miscellaneous assortment of supplies which included tea, sugar, medical stores, and also mail. The Handley Page returned to Er Ramle after Brigadier-General Borton had arranged that it should be employed to make night attacks on Mafraq and Der'a.

The force in the valley of the Jordan commanded by Major-General Chaytor was responsible for the defence

[1] *Seven Pillars of Wisdom*, p. 619.

of the British right flank during the early part of General Allenby's offensive. So long as the Turkish Fourth Army remained intact Major-General Chaytor could do little more than demonstrate, but as soon as withdrawal began, as a consequence of the Turkish disaster west of the river, his force was in a position to harass the retreating troops and, of particular importance, to capture the crossing at Jisr ed Damiye and so close a main way of escape for Turks fleeing from the area west of the Jordan. The task allotted to the Arab army was to contain the Turkish Fourth Army until such time as Chaytor's Force had driven the enemy out of 'Amman, and subsequently to cut the Turkish way of retreat.

Liman von Sanders, after he had been put to flight from Nazareth on the morning of the 20th, had made his way to Samakh on the southern shore of the Sea of Galilee and then, when he learned that Beisan was in British hands, had moved on to Der'a where he had arrived on the 21st. After issuing orders to the Turkish Fourth Army to retire to the Yarmuk valley he himself had proceeded to Damascus.

It was realized from the air reports on the 22nd of September that the Turks east of the Jordan were withdrawing and orders for the pursuit were issued at 11.35 p.m. Contact patrol observers of No. 142 Squadron on the 23rd reported the British and Turkish movements. The Turkish camps at Shunet Nimrin were seen from the air in the morning to be deserted, and the place was later occupied by the British: by the evening Es Salt had been captured. The operation orders issued to the Royal Air Force squadrons for the 23rd had stated that aeroplanes were to stand by for the bombing of enemy forces in retreat in the Es Salt–'Amman area. The dawn reconnaissance of No. 1 Squadron, Australian Flying Corps, on the 23rd had reported a column of all arms moving down the road from Es Salt to 'Amman and various bodies of troops making for 'Amman from the south-west. This news was the signal for concentrated bombing. It was now the turn of the Fourth Army to suffer as the two armies west of the Jordan had suffered. There were no defiles in which the transport could be bombed to cause a blockage, but there was, on the other hand, little cover. Furthermore, 'Amman was the central point upon which bodies of troops converged, the only gateway through which to escape, and 'Amman, with its increasing congestion, lay wide open to attack from the air, as did the route and stations northwards to Der'a. The bombing was begun by a formation of six Bristol Fighters of No. 1 Squadron, Australian Flying Corps, which attacked the columns on the Es Salt–'Amman road: each Bristol Fighter dropped six 20-lb. bombs and the pilot and observer fired all their machine-gun ammunition into the terrified Turks. Throughout the rest of the day this squadron concentrated its attacks on 'Amman and its neighbourhood. In the morning seven D.H.9's of No. 144 Squadron, each carrying one 112-lb. and eight 20-lb. bombs, attacked Mafraq station, in accordance with the arrangements made to help the Arabs, and three D.H.9's attacked Der'a. In the afternoon the D.H.9's turned their attention to the streaming columns on the Es Salt–'Amman road, as did the S.E.5 pilots of No. 111 Squadron. Nineteen such attacks are recorded in the records of this squadron and there were many hits on troops, with panic all along the route. An impressive raid was also made by No. 113 Squadron under the leadership of the squadron commander. This squadron had little corps work to do, owing to the disappearance of the Turks on its front, and it was able to send its full strength of eighteeen R.E.8's on the 23rd to bomb the Es Salt–'Amman columns. Two old R.E.8's could not climb high enough to surmount the hills, but sixteen got through and dropped a hundred and twenty-two 20-lb. bombs with devastating effect. About 10 p.m. the Handley Page dropped sixteen 112-lb. and ten 15-lb. incendiary bombs in Der'a railway station. In all, during the day, $6\frac{1}{4}$ tons of bombs were dropped and more than 33,000 rounds of ammunition were fired, almost exclusively in the area east of the Jordan.

There was a lull in the air attacks on the 24th, and, on the ground, Chaytor's Force was mainly engaged with overcoming the supply difficulties caused by damage done to the roads by explosives laid by the Turks. Next day, the 25th, the intensive bombing was resumed. The main target was a mixed column at Mafraq station which was first reported by the dawn reconnaissance. Twenty-three flights were made during the day by pilots of No. 1 Squadron, Australian Flying Corps, and sixteen by pilots of No. 144 D.H.9 Squadron, and a total weight of $3\frac{1}{3}$ tons of bombs were dropped and 19,000 rounds fired. The material damage inflicted was great, and many explosions occurred in Mafraq station.

On the 25th the British mounted troops had advanced early on 'Amman. An air observer over the town co-operating with the attacking troops reported by message dropped at 10.40 a.m. that 'Amman was being evacuated. This information was true, but the Turks held a series of strong posts covering the railway station, in which they put up a stout resistance with the object, no doubt, of protecting the arrival of the evacuating trains of the Turkish troops from the direction of Ma'an. In this they were unsuccessful. At 2 p.m. the defence was overcome and 'Amman was captured with about 2,500 prisoners. Major-General Chaytor's task now was not to pursue the Turks escaping from 'Amman, but to bar the road to the troops from Ma'an.[1]

Air reports showed that these were moving along the railway. In order to hold them up, the line was cut north of Ziza and the 5th Australian Light Horse Regiment was stationed to watch the gap. Early on the 28th the Australians reported that the Turks were in Ziza station with three trains, and the report was passed to General Headquarters with a request that a message should be dropped by aeroplane to inform the Turkish commander that all water which he could reach was in British hands, and that, if he did not surrender, his troops would be bombed from the air on the following day. The message was duly dropped

[1] Air reconnaissances by 'X' Flight from Gueira had reported Ma'an being evacuated by the Turks on the 22nd of September with the Arab troops advancing into the town. 'X' Flight, including the detachment which had operated from Azraq, now began to pack up. It left Gueira for 'Aqaba on the 26th of September, and, early in October, went to Suez where the Flight was disbanded.

on the 28th and, next morning, at 10.30 a.m., a trolley, flying a white flag, moved up the line with a message that the Turks would surrender, but asked for protection from the hordes of mounted Bedouin who stood against the sky-line ready to fall upon the Turks for loot, particularly of arms and ammunition.

The Turkish commander had delayed sending the news of his intention to surrender and it was doubtful whether there was time to prevent the Royal Air Force from making its concentrated bombing attacks. Lieutenant-Colonel D. C. Cameron, the Australian officer commanding the British regiment in touch with the Turks, therefore sent into the Turkish lines the sign which, when displayed on the ground, would indicate the position of his own regimental head-quarters to any British air observer who saw it. The sign was laid out behind the Turkish trenches to convey the impression to the Royal Air Force bombers, if they appeared, that he had transferred his head-quarters to the Turkish lines. As it happened, the precaution proved unnecessary because the message cancelling the bombing attack was received in time to stop the aeroplanes from starting.

Under instructions given to them by Major-General Chaytor the Turks stood to arms throughout the night, with Australian troopers at their side, and they resisted a number of attempts made by the loot-seeking Bedouin to rush the corner of the position where the trains and hospitals were situated. When the sun came up on the 30th the Bedouin, who would not face machine-gun fire, were no longer to be feared, and the full surrender of the Turks was accepted.

The total captures of Chaytor's Force for the period of the operations were 10,322 prisoners, 57 guns, 132 machine-guns, rolling stock, and stores. The figures might have been a little higher because patrols of the 1st Australian Light Horse Brigade which had ridden out to Mafraq on the 27th had reported several trains in the station filled with sick and wounded and stores of ammunition. When it became possible to run a motor engine with a few trucks to Mafraq with the object of putting the place in order it was found that the sick and the wounded had died or had

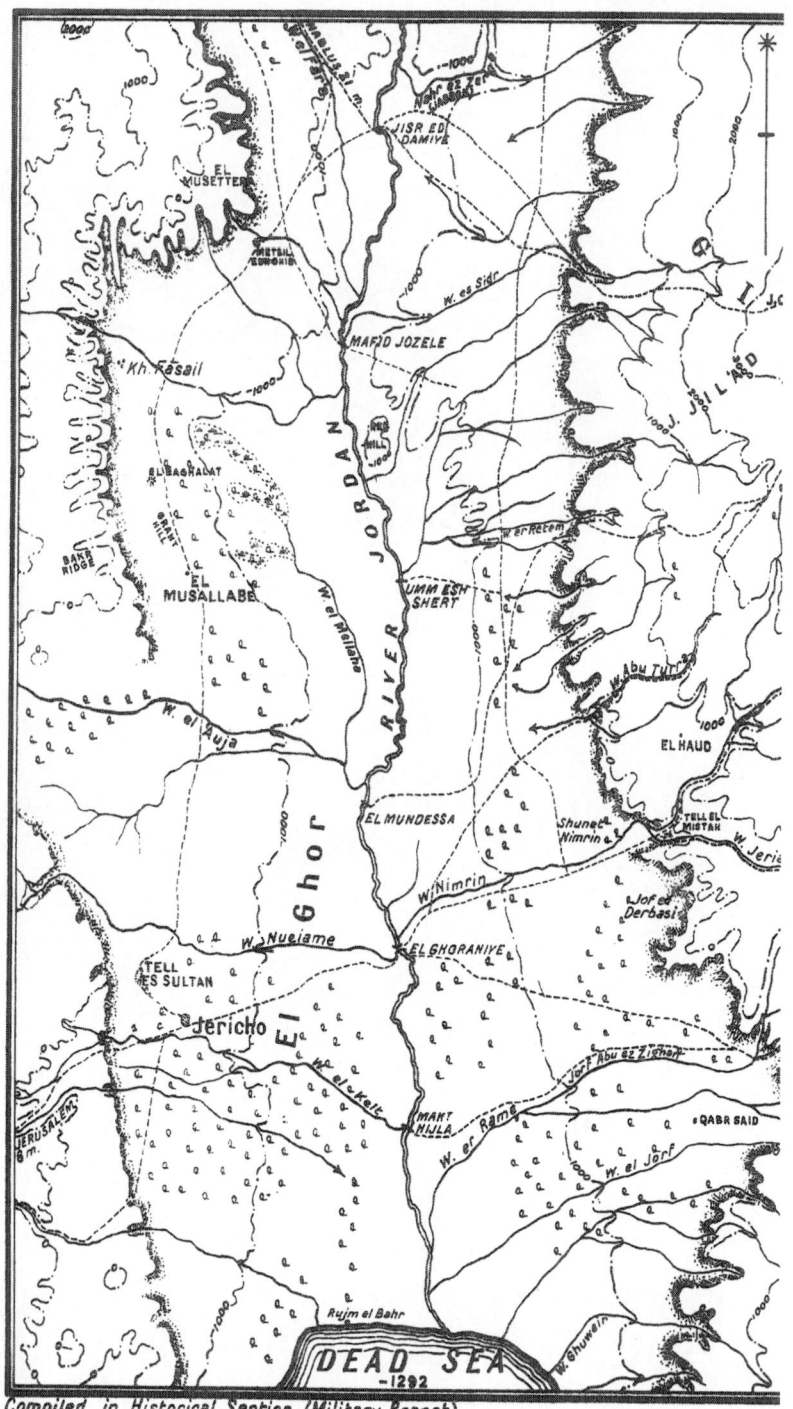

Compiled in Historical Section (Military Branch).

Theatre of Operations in TRANS-JORDAN.

First Trans-Jordan Raid, 21st March – 2nd April; Second Trans-Jordan Raid, 30th April – 4th May; & Operations of Chaytor's Force 20th–29th September, 1918.).

Scale of Miles.

Heights in Feet.

Ordnance Survey 1937.

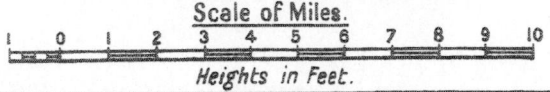

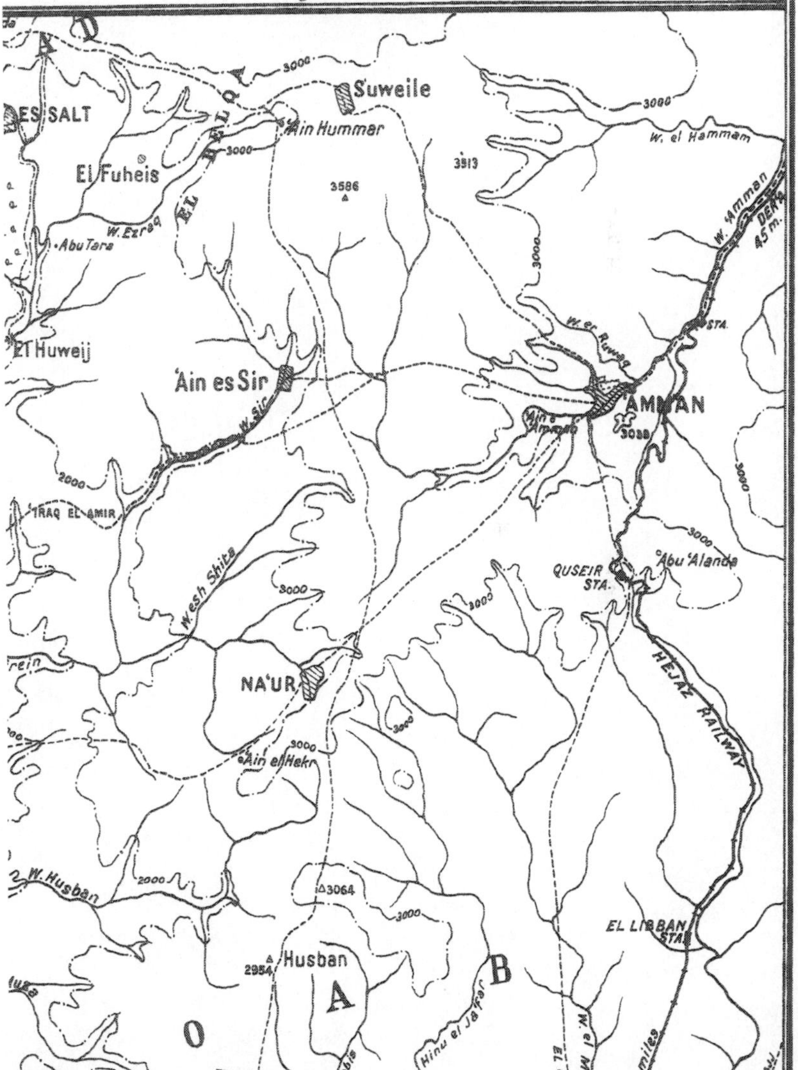

been killed by the Arabs who had also carried away everything portable.

Meanwhile on the 26th of September Sir Edmund Allenby had issued orders for a general advance by the Desert Mounted Corps to Damascus, and by the XXI Corps to Beirut. The cavalry was to start immediately, two divisions (Australian Mounted and 5th Cavalry) moving west of the Sea of Galilee direct, and the other (4th Cavalry) by way of Der'a in order to co-operate with the Arab forces which were in pursuit of the demoralized remnants of the Turkish Fourth Army. On the 27th of September, the day after the 4th Cavalry Division had set out to help them, the Arabs placed themselves astride the Turkish line of retreat at Sheikh Sa'd, seventeen miles north of Der'a, and in the terrible fighting which followed settlement was enacted for many accounts of long standing. On the 28th the 4th Cavalry Division joined hands with the Arabs near Er Remta and the combined advance on Damascus proceeded.

On the 26th, the day the move on Damascus had begun, there were about 45,000 Turks and Germans in the city or in retreat towards it, and although they were disorganized they could have been given, if the requisite time had been allowed, a measure of fighting cohesion. So rapid, however, was the pursuit that 20,000 of the enemy troops making for the safety of Damascus were overtaken and killed or captured before they could reach the city. Damascus was entered by the Arab Army and by the Desert Mounted Corps on the morning of the 1st of October, and all that then remained of the Turkish Palestine armies was a rabble of about 17,000 men in flight towards the north. Beirut was reached by the 7th (Meerut) Division, which had marched by way of Tyre and Sidon, on the 8th of October.

While these rapid movements in pursuit of the Turkish remnants were being made the Royal Air Force had continued to play a part, although with diminishing opportunities. For co-operation with the XXI Corps in its advance on Beirut a Flight of No. 113 Squadron had moved from El 'Affule at the end of September to Haifa, where one Flight from No. 1 Australian Squadron and another from No. 144 Squadron were also stationed. Damascus was reconnoitred from the air on the 27th of September and, next day, a forward landing-ground was opened at Quneitra, immediately after the Australian Mounted Division had reached that place. From Quneitra, on the 28th, the enemy aerodrome at Damascus was bombed, and air reconnaissances next day reported that the aerodrome buildings had been gutted by fire. Petrol and oil for the Quneitra landing-ground were carried from El 'Affule by air. It was not long before the supplies at El 'Affule became exhausted, and because road transport was subject to considerable delays Nos. 14 and 113 Squadrons were organized as a temporary supply service on the 30th of September, on which day the squadrons carried 928 gallons of petrol and 156 gallons of oil from Junction station aerodrome and from Sarona to 'Affule. On the morning of the 1st of October, following close upon the heels of the Arabs and of the cavalry, Royal Air Force aeroplanes landed at Damascus.

With the fall of Damascus, General Allenby decided to advance to the line Riyaq–Beirut. The Desert Mounted Corps moved on Riyaq on the 5th of October and, finding no opposition, occupied the place next day. On the aerodrome at Riyaq were discovered the remains of thirty aeroplanes recently burned by the enemy. One Flight of No. 1 Squadron, Australian Flying Corps, kept specially mobile for co-operation with the cavalry, had moved from Haifa on the 4th of October to Damascus and, as soon as Riyaq had been entered, made use of the former enemy aerodrome there as an advanced landing-ground.

An important feature of the air work in the final phases of the operations was the distribution of maps to the Desert Mounted Corps and to the XXI Corps. The air observers also dropped many messages to tell of the condition of the roads ahead of the advancing troops, and of the whereabouts of the retreating Turks. There were many bombing attacks by the squadrons of the Fortieth Army Wing.

On October the 9th General Allenby ordered the Desert

Mounted Corps to occupy Homs and the XXI Corps to continue its march along the coast to Tripoli. The ground to be covered by the new advance had been carefully reconnoitred from the air, and the general topography of the country and the state of the roads had formed the subject of many air reports: very little enemy movement had been seen. The station at Homs was bombed on the 9th, 10th, and 12th of October by aeroplanes from Haifa aerodrome, the pilots landing at Damascus on the way to replenish with fuel. On the 13th of October the XXI Corps reached Tripoli, and two days later the cavalry occupied Homs. General Allenby thereupon decided to send the 5th Cavalry Division and armoured cars forward in co-operation with the Arab army in a spectacular dash to capture Aleppo, some three hundred miles distant from the line along which the operations had originally opened.

The advance to Aleppo began on the 20th of October. The indications were that the town was occupied by about 20,000 Turks and Germans, but a majority of them were troops of the lines of communication, and the estimate was that no more than 8,000 were combatant soldiers and that these were more or less demoralized. On the 19th of October, before the advance began, two pilots of No. 1 Squadron, Australian Flying Corps, were flying about twenty-five miles south-west of Aleppo when they encountered an enemy two-seater aeroplane at 18,000 feet, the first which had been seen for many days. They attacked and forced the enemy to make a landing. Captain Smith, one of the Australian pilots, landed his Bristol Fighter nearby, and as he taxied towards the enemy aeroplane the German pilot and his observer jumped to the ground and stood with their hands above their heads. When the British aeroplane came alongside Captain Smith's observer fired Very lights into the German two-seater and set it on fire, and the Bristol Fighter then took to the air again leaving the two Germans standing because the ground was soft and if they had been taken on board there was small likelihood that the Bristol Fighter, overloaded, could have been made to rise.

The station and the aerodrome at Aleppo were bombed

and also attacked with machine-gun fire from the air on the 23rd of October.[1] On the same day one of the Australian Bristol Fighters found two enemy two-seaters over the aerodrome at Babannit, north of Aleppo. The British pilot promptly attacked and the enemy aeroplanes went down and landed alongside four others on the aerodrome: the Bristol Fighter, from a height of 200 feet, dropped bombs among the enemy two-seaters and also poured machine-gun fire into them.

On the evening of the 25th of October a detachment of the Arab Army entered Aleppo where they inflicted severe casualties upon the enemy troops still in the town. Early next morning armoured cars and a cavalry Brigade, moving forward on the west side of the town, gained touch with columns retreating from Aleppo along the road to Qatma, but the British detachment was not strong enough to round up the enemy and so complete the victory.

At noon on the 31st of October an armistice put an end to the hostilities. Between the 19th of September and the 26th of October, as a result of the most spectacular campaign of the war, the three Turkish Armies on the Palestine front had been annihilated: they had left in British hands almost their whole equipment together with 75,000 prisoners and 360 guns.

---

[1] The Mobile Flight of No. 1 Squadron, Australian Flying Corps, moved forward with the advance to aerodromes at Homs and Hama.

CHAPTER VI

MESOPOTAMIA, PERSIA, AND INDIA

[Maps, pp. 249, 264]

In the middle of March 1918 Lieutenant-General Sir W. R. Marshall received a telegram from the Chief of the Imperial General Staff in which the situation in the Near East was summarized in the light of the collapse of Russia and of Romania. One of the aims of Germany, it was said, had been to obtain control of central Europe and of the Near East with the object of expanding eastwards. British military successes, especially in Mesopotamia, had placed a barrier across the obvious route, by way of the Berlin–Baghdad railway, but the turmoil in Russia gave Germany an opportunity, of which she was undoubtedly hoping to take advantage, to establish a new route to the East by the Black Sea, the Caucasus, and the Caspian.

There were various reasons why this alternative scheme should be opposed, among them the immediately important one that if Germany was left free to penetrate into Persia the flank of the armies in Mesopotamia would be turned, and the whole situation in that country, as well as in India, consequently endangered. It was desirable, therefore, that Lieutenant-General Marshall should 'ex-'tend from Baghdad to the Caspian and build up local 'organizations on a foundation of military strength, work-'ing forward into the Caucasus in order to win over 'Armenia and make our influence predominate in the 'eastern ports of the Black Sea'.[1]

A few days after the dispatch of this telegram the German offensive was opened in France, and when the magnitude of the enemy effort was revealed it became necessary to reconsider British policy in the Near East. On the 28th of March Lieutenant-General Marshall was informed by the Chief of the Imperial General Staff that the role of the British army in Palestine would be changed from offence to active defence, but that it was hoped to build up a

---

[1] See the *Mesopotamia Campaign*, by Brigadier-General F. J. Moberly, Vol. IV, p. 138.

general reserve for the East in Palestine. Meanwhile there would be no reduction of the force in Mesopotamia, which appeared to be strong enough to secure the positions on the Persian frontier as soon as the passes could be opened.

Throughout April 1918 Mesopotamia was swept by heavy gales, and many communications were broken. The bad weather temporarily closed the way to Hamadan and so made it difficult to take steps to counter the threat resulting from the enemy movements towards the Caucasus and Persia. Furthermore, the Qasr-i-Shirin–Hamadan route had, by gold and propaganda, been made insecure. Using Kifri as a centre, German and Turkish agents had created unrest, and implanted hostility to the British, among some of the tribes in the area of the road. To make the way safe to Hamadan, Lieutenant-General Marshall decided to drive the Turks from the Tuz Khurmatli–Kifri–Qara Tepe area and to occupy the two first-named places.

When the plans were nearing completion, an opportunity was offered for a subsidiary operation which would help the main object. The Sinjabis, one of the tribes which had succumbed to enemy influence in the country north-east of Qasr-i-Shirin, became involved in a quarrel with the Kalhur and Guran tribes who were friendly to the British. On the advice of the local political officer, Lieutenant-General Marshall sent a small mixed column to assist the friendly tribesmen. Aeroplanes of No. 72 Squadron took part. On the 23rd of April reconnaissances were made of the Sinjabi country, and the camps which were discovered were attacked next day with machine-gun fire by two pilots who flew low. On the 25th a brief action took place which was successful, the morale of the tribesmen being shattered by four aeroplanes which performed aerobatics close above them and poured machine-gun fire into their ranks. As a result of the swift and decisive defeat of the Sinjabis, German influence among the tribes along the Persian border became of small account.

Orders for the operations to drive the Turks from the the Tuz Khurmatli–Qara Tepe area had been issued on the 12th of April. The plan was to simulate a converging attack upon Qara Tepe and Kifri, but to strike in reality at Abu Gharaib and Tuz Khurmatli in order to cut off the enemy forces south-east and east of those places. To make the plan effective, four columns, A, B, C, and D, were organized, with six reconnaissance aeroplanes (R.E.8's) of No. 30 Squadron attached to Column A, six of the same type from Nos. 30 and 63 Squadrons to Column B, three from No. 30 Squadron to Column C, and three from No. 63 Squadron to Column D. In addition, a Flight from each of the two squadrons, and a third Flight from No. 72 Squadron, were ordered to be in readiness to assist as required in the work of co-operation with the main Column, B.

The preliminary movements were delayed by rain, but by the early morning of the 25th of April the columns had reached their centres of concentration. The aeroplanes, meanwhile, unimpeded by enemy aircraft, had been employed to survey the area across which the columns were to advance, and to report in particular about the suitability of the roads and rivers for the passage of the various arms.

To deceive the enemy about the British intentions, a kite balloon section, No. 52, was moved to Mirjana on the Diyala river on the 17th of April, and was used for observation in that area, to convey an impression that operations were pending from Qizil Ribat. With the same object of mystification bombing attacks were twice made on the 21st of April by No. 63 Squadron on camps and a dump near the Fat-ha gorge on the Tigris. A German reconnaissance aeroplane which flew down the Tigris, possibly to ascertain what the bombing activity portended, was destroyed north of Samarra by an S.E.5 pilot of No. 72 Squadron. The various measures taken to deceive the Turks succeeded and the attack came as a surprise.

It appeared on the morning of the 26th, however, when the British columns began to advance, that the enemy had received warning and had taken fright, for an air observer said he had seen movements which appeared to indicate a withdrawal from Qara Tepe towards Kifri. Other observers who were sent out during the remainder of the day with orders to keep a special watch for further signs of a withdrawal, returned with reports which made it clear that the Turks were not going back. No more than a few scattered parties were seen on the Qara Tepe–Kifri road, and these were attacked with 25-lb. bombs and with machine-gun fire.

Column D, on the British left, had instructions to demonstrate against Abu Gharaib in order to induce the Turkish garrison to occupy its positions on the Jabal Hamrin where it could be surprised and destroyed by a part of B Column (B 1) on the 27th. Column C, which was not to advance from the Diyala until the 26th, was to close on Qara Tepe on the 27th and pin the garrison to its ground while the remainder of B Column (B 2) placed itself in a position to cut the line of withdrawal of the garrison.

Although the air reports on the 26th nourished a hope that the British plans would be duly fulfilled, a belated decision of the Turks changed the prospects. That decision was to take no chances, and in torrential rain during the night of the 26th/27th the Qara Tepe garrison withdrew hurriedly towards Kifri, and the Abu Gharaib force towards Tuz Khurmatli.

Soon after dawn on the 27th the Turkish troops who had abandoned the Abu Gharaib position were discovered from the air moving towards Kulawand, and they were subjected to air attacks in which the Bristol monoplanes of No. 72 Squadron played their first part in the action. These aeroplanes could carry enough petrol to keep them in the air only for one and three-quarter hours, and were not therefore suitable for reconnaissance work, but they were capable of rapid manœuvre and their pilots, by swift diving attacks from low heights, brought terror to the disheartened and war-weary Turkish soldiers.

An important body of the enemy troops was seen to take up a defensive position at Kulawand, and the information was conveyed to the general officer commanding Column A by a pilot who landed at his head-quarters at 9.30 a.m. Orders were at once issued for an enveloping attack, but difficulties subsequently arose because the enemy entrenchments, constructed more than a year before by

CAVALRY AND AEROPLANES

German engineers, had become so overgrown with grass that it was impossible for the observers, no matter how low they flew, to see to what extent the trenches were occupied, or to say whether they were guarded by wire entanglements, an obstacle which would effectively stop the advance of the cavalry. In consequence the attackers had to feel their way and it was not until about 12.30 p.m. that they were ready to assault. As the cavalry started forward the aeroplanes flew over the Turks, attacking them with bomb and machine-gun. When the horses broke into a charge, overriding many Turkish soldiers who had left their trenches to hold a dry water-course, success came quickly. Numbers of the enemy, taking advantage of the tangled nature of the country, escaped into the hills to the north, but about 200 lay dead, and 565 were taken prisoners.

After the place had been captured, the cavalry and light armoured cars of Column A reconnoitred towards Tuz Khurmatli and the Aq Su watercourse, where they found the Turkish garrisons alert in prepared positions. The reconnaissance party withdrew to join Column B south of Kulawand, and the two columns (A, B 1 and B 2) were then placed under the orders of Major-General Sir W. de S. Cayley for operations against the Tuz Khurmatli defences.

On the 28th, while the preliminary movements for the new attack were taking place, the enemy positions were reconnoitred from the air and by the cavalry, and many attacks were made by pilots on the Turkish troops and batteries. Major-General Cayley learned from his reconnaissance reports that enemy artillery was in position near Yanija Buyuk and north-east of Tuz Khurmatli, and that the crossing over the Aq Su, south of Tuz Khurmatli, was guarded by infantry and machine-gunners entrenched on the right bank of the watercourse. As soon as he was fully apprised of the general situation he issued his orders for the attack to be made next day, the 29th of April. Not long after his orders had gone out a hostile aeroplane appeared over Kifri, which had been occupied in the morning without opposition by Column C. This was the first appearance of an enemy pilot since the operations had begun.

The British attack, which started at daybreak on the 29th, was made with dash and was met with an unexpectedly stubborn resistance, but by 9 a.m. Tuz had been occupied and the major part of the Turkish defending force captured. More than 200 Turkish dead were buried by the attackers, and 1,300 prisoners, 12 guns, 20 machine-guns, and much ammunition were secured. Those who escaped in disorder along the road to Tauq were pursued and attacked by cavalry and by aeroplanes.

Observers who flew over the Turkish area early on the 30th of April reported that the enemy troops had withdrawn from Tauq and were retiring on Kirkuk. Lieutenant-General Marshall had not intended to go beyond Tuz Khurmatli, but the War Office had telegraphed on the previous day to say that it was certain that the Turks, who would shortly dominate Trans-Caucasia, intended to occupy Persian Azerbaijan, and that German agents, working with the connivance of members of the Persian Government, had made arrangements for a general rising against the British as soon as Turkish troops appeared in Persia. It was clear that Lieutenant-General Marshall could not maintain a sufficient force for an effective diversion to counter the Turks in Persia, and it was suggested that his best plan would be to strike at once in the direction of Kirkuk–Sulaimaniya in order to force the Turkish XIII Corps to call for reinforcements from the troops allotted to the Persian adventure.

Lieutenant-General Marshall accordingly planned the capture of Kirkuk, but he pointed out, in a reasoned telegram in reply, the maintenance, climatic, and other difficulties which would make it unprofitable for him to establish a hold so far forward from his bases.

Before the advance to Kirkuk could be undertaken, a reorganization of the force was necessary. On the 2nd of May 'C' Flight of No. 30 Squadron moved forward, with four R.E.8 aeroplanes, to Tuz Khurmatli, and four Bristol monoplanes of No. 72 Squadron moved in company in order to provide fighting escorts, as it was clear that some reinforcing Albatros aeroplanes had reached the German air service. The Flight of No. 63 Squadron, which had taken part in the forward movement to Tuz Khurmatli, was sent back from Baquba, at the same time, to rejoin its squadron on the Tigris at Samarra.

There was a possible element of danger which had to be guarded against. It will be clear from a reference to the map that the Turkish XVIII Corps, holding the Fat-ha position on the Tigris, constituted a threat, from the flank, to the impending advance to Kirkuk. The British I Corps at Samarra was therefore ordered to occupy Tikrit, to send forward a mobile column to seize the Ain Nukhaila pass across the Jabal Hamrin, due east of Fat-ha, and to reconnoitre towards Kirkuk. Aeroplanes of No. 63 Squadron, specially sent out on the 1st and 2nd of May, reported that there were no Turkish posts at Ain Nukhaila, and also yielded information about the nature of the country and the suitability of the roads and tracks for military movements.

The advance towards Kirkuk was timed to begin on the 4th of May. Wild weather accompanied by heavy rain impeded the initial movements. On the 3rd, armoured cars found a small Turkish force in position at Taza Khurmatli, and the enemy troops were seen from the air to be still holding their ground on the two following days, but early on the morning of the 6th an air observer reported that Taza Khurmatli had been abandoned, and the place was thereupon occupied by the British. The advance was continued until touch was gained with the enemy about two miles south-west of Kirkuk. During the night of the 6th/7th of May the rain was torrential and the roads became almost impassable. Orders were sent out at 6.40 a.m. on the 7th to say that the operations for the day would be limited to defensive reconnaissances, but owing to the break-down in communications as a result of the rainstorms, the message took three and a half hours to reach Major-General Cayley. By that time his advanced guard, which had been on the move since early morning, was already in Kirkuk, which was entered at 8.45 a.m. and had been found evacuated by the enemy. Three damaged enemy aeroplanes, much ammunition, and about 600 sick and wounded Turks were taken in Kirkuk. The town was in a filthy condition and the inhabitants were found to be starving: soup kitchens had to be started for them, and scraps, voluntarily given by the troops, themselves on half rations, were distributed. Some days later four German aeroplanes bombed Kirkuk and killed 26 mules and wounded four men. The carcasses of the mules, under the direction of the medical officer who was directing the soup kitchen, were put to use, but the inhabitants, perhaps a little less hungry than they had been, were not grateful.[1]

On the 9th of May it was reported from the air that there were Turkish camps near Altun Köpri, but that there were signs of a withdrawal in the direction of Erbil. A mobile column, sent forward on the 10th, made contact with the enemy troops at Altun Köpri where an explosion was reported at 7 p.m., at a time when the Turks were in retreat.

Meanwhile, concurrently with the operations in the Kirkuk area, troops of the I Corps had occupied Tikrit and the Ain Nukhaila pass, while the co-operating aeroplanes had bombed the Turkish positions. There was evidence that the enemy had withdrawn some part of his force from the Fat-ha entrenchments, and the temptation to attack this position was inviting, but it was not Lieutenant-General Marshall's intention to undertake further commitments and the forward troops of the I Corps began a steady withdrawal in the middle of May, and, by the end of the month, were back again in their positions about Samarra. At the same time the withdrawal from Kirkuk had also been completed. This withdrawal, which was made against the advice of the civil commissioner, was necessitated by a lack of sufficient transport to maintain a force strong enough to ensure its own safety.

[1] 'The Medical Officer who was running the soup kitchen thought this 'was a heaven sent opportunity of providing unlimited stock, so the car-'casses were cut up and boiled down. That evening an unusually savoury 'broth was being issued when it leaked out that the foundation was "mule", 'and then an uproar began which it was difficult to quell. Why this should 'have been I can't say as the people being fed were mostly Armenians who 'should have had no prejudices' (Major-General Sir W. de S. Cayley, in a letter to the Author).

While these movements were in progress there had been an exchange of telegrams with the War Office about the future role of the force in Mesopotamia. Lieutenant-General Marshall had stated his conviction that he could go forward and capture Mosul, and clear the country between the Tigris and the Persian border of Turkish control, but if he did his railhead would be much closer to the enemy railhead at Nisibin, and his force, moreover, would have no effect on the Turks in the Caucasus and at Tabriz, who could be supplied from the Black Sea. He had urged that, because of the heat of the summer, no operations should be undertaken before the middle of September. The War Office had agreed to this postponement and had stated that, in the meantime, Major-General L. C. Dunsterville's operations should be supported to the maximum strength of the transport available. On the 21st of May, in a further telegram, the War Office had said that the latest information from Tehran indicated that a prompt display of military strength in Persia would lead to the Persian Government according the British active support, and Lieutenant-General Marshall was therefore urged to maintain at Hamadan, and towards the Caspian, a force up to a cavalry regiment, an infantry brigade, armoured cars, and aeroplanes. It was important that a British force, no matter how small, should reach the Caspian during the summer.

At the end of May the units of the Thirty-first Wing of the Royal Air Force, under the Command of Lieutenant-Colonel R. A. Bradley, were disposed as follows:

No. 30 Squadron (less 1½ Flights) (Major J. Everidge).	Baquba
Half-Flight of No. 30	Kifri
'B' Flight of No. 30	Ramadi
No. 63 Squadron (Major F. L. Robinson) . . .	Samarra
No. 72 Squadron Head-quarters and half-Flight (Major O. T. Boyd)	Baghdad
Half-Flight of No. 72	Hamadan
'A' Flight of No. 72	Samarra
'C' Flight of No. 72	Mirjana
No. 23 Kite Balloon Company Head-quarters . .	Baghdad
No. 51 Kite Balloon Section	Samarra
No. 52 Kite Balloon Section	Ramadi
Aircraft Park	Baghdad

With the cessation of major active operations in Mesopotamia during the hot summer months, the work of the Royal Air Force squadrons, except the detachments engaged with the 'Dunsterforce', consisted mainly of classes of instruction and practice co-operation with artillery, infantry, and cavalry, in preparation for the autumn campaign. A programme of photographic work, covering hundreds of square miles of territory, was also systematically fulfilled for the map compilation section.

Persia and the Caspian Sea
[Map, p. 249]

It had been possible to open the road to Hamadan at the end of May, and troops were sent forward in Ford vans to Kazvin, covering Tehran, where they took over from Lieutenant-Colonel Bicharakoff's Partisan detachment which represented the rear-guard of the Russian troops in process of evacuating Persia. 'B' Flight of No. 72 Squadron, equipped with Martinsyde aeroplanes, was transferred to Kazvin from Baghdad.

It will not be possible to set out here the complex political and military situation in Persia and Trans-Caucasia: it may be read in the official military history of the campaign in Mesopotamia. The fighting on the Persian plateau and in the mountain passes, and along the ridges overlooking the waters of the Caspian, had little cohesion. It is a story of British detachments standing side by side with Russians, Armenians, Assyrians, and Persians, sometimes uncertain about the temper and reliability of their Allies, conscious that their long line of communications was precarious, waging a tenacious fight against odds. From the railhead in Mesopotamia to the Caspian Sea the road along which all supplies had to move meandered through rocky passes and across mountain streams for some 700 miles. West of Hamadan the road was not metalled, and when the British first went forward to Kazvin many of the bridges were broken and much of the country in the area of the road was stricken by famine.

On the 8th of June, after he had completed the hand-

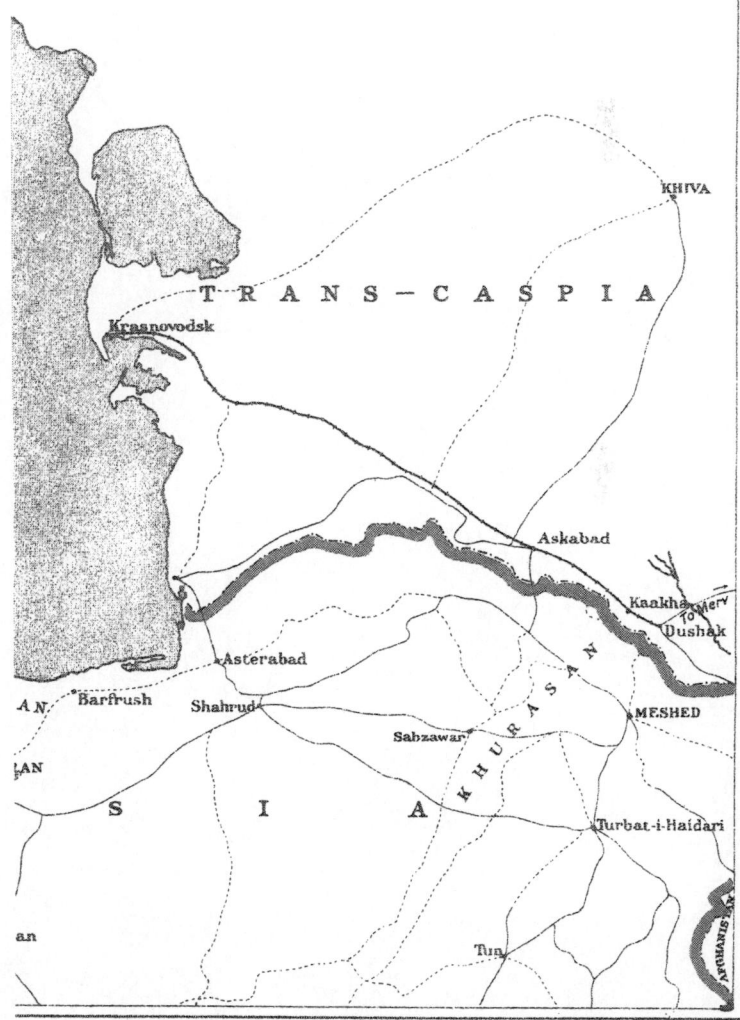

THE JANGALIS

ing over of Kazvin to the care of the British, Lieutenant-Colonel Bicharakoff marched out with his Russians, about 1,000 strong, for Enzeli with the object of taking ship for Baku where he had reason to believe the inhabitants would welcome his help in the defence of the town against expected Turkish attacks. The main interest of the British in Baku was in the oil supplies which it was desirable should not be made available to the enemy. As Major-General Dunsterville says: 'The capture of Baku by the enemy 'would give him ample stocks of oil for the running of the 'Caucasian railway lines and the Black Sea shipping (the 'oil is pumped in pipes from Baku to Batoum), and it would 'mean the control by him of the Caspian Sea, with all the 'valuable supplies obtainable from the various ports on its 'shores, and an open door to Asia and Afghanistan. Any 'enemy scheme of penetration into Asia through Turkestan 'would be greatly facilitated by the large numbers of 'released Austrian prisoners set at liberty in that country 'by the revolutionaries, and now wandering about ready to 'undertake any task that would procure them their daily 'bread.'[1]

A small British detachment, including a squadron of the 14th Hussars, and two armoured cars, accompanied the Russians. It was known that the Jangalis, under their leader Kuchik Khan and with German officers in their force, held entrenched positions guarding the bridge at Manjil. Attempts had been made to come to an agreement with Kuchik Khan to open the road to Enzeli and to give a guarantee that he would not interfere with the movements of British toops or convoys on the road. Nothing satisfactory had resulted, but it was considered possible that the Jangalis might yield at the last moment without fighting. All was ready for the attack on Manjil on the 11th of June, but it was arranged that two aeroplanes from Kazvin should first fly over the Jangalis positions. The presence of aircraft, it was thought, might help the tribesmen to a reasonable frame of mind, and the pilots were instructed to show themselves only, and not to open fire

[1] *The Adventures of Dunsterforce*, by Major-General L. C. Dunsterville, C.B., C.S.I., pp. 140–1.

unless they were attacked. When the aeroplanes came above the positions the Jangalis soon made their intentions clear. Widespread rifle fire was directed against the aircraft to begin the action of Manjil bridge. The pilots reported the details of the enemy positions.

Not long after the Russian and British troops had opened fire the Jangalis were overcome by panic, and victory was easily achieved. The Russians subsequently pushed forward to Enzeli while the British placed detachments at strategic points along the road to keep the route to Enzeli open.

The Jangalis derived a feeling of security from the well-wooded nature of their country, and they made a habit of finding points of vantage overlooking the way to Enzeli and of sniping at the convoys which moved along the road. In an attempt to put an end to this nuisance two Martinsydes made a bombing attack, on the 21st of June, on the barracks of the Jangalis at Kasma, where Kuchik Khan had his head-quarters, and it was afterwards known that seventy-seven of the tribesmen were killed or wounded. Similar attacks, with bomb and machine-gun, were made subsequently, from time to time, and they went some way to keep the Jangalis in check; in particular, the attacks made it easier for the small British detachment in Resht to maintain its position. In the words of Major-General Dunsterville: 'The situation of this detachment would 'have been precarious but for the aeroplanes, which pro-'duced a great effect by bombing and machine-gunning 'any concentration of the enemy; but this task was also 'rendered difficult by the density of the forest, which gave 'the enemy cover from view. The casualties inflicted were 'therefore slight, but the moral effect was great.'[1]

By the middle of July, however, the Jangalis had been roused to fresh efforts. On the 20th about 2,500 of the tribesmen, with the help of a few Germans and Austrians, attacked the small British detachment at Resht. Fierce fighting followed, some of it taking place in the narrow streets of the town, but the Jangalis were heavily defeated. 'The operations during the next two days consisted of

[1] *The Adventures of Dunsterforce*, p. 165.

'getting the Jangalis out of the town. This involved a good
'deal of street-fighting, but success was mainly achieved by
'aeroplane bombing, which soon rendered their retention
'of the various hotels and public buildings impracticable.'[1]
The aeroplanes which were responsible for the bombing of
Resht were two of No. 72 Squadron.

To make air attacks on the Jangalis easier, and as a
further step towards consolidating control of the port itself, an air base was opened on the 30th of July at Enzeli
with two aeroplanes flown from Kazvin by pilots who
bombed the tribesmen on the way. For ten days the aeroplanes kept up their bombing and machine-gun attacks
which, reinforcing the severe defeat inflicted on the Jangalis at Resht, induced Kuchik Khan to open negotiations
for peace. The Royal Air Force was requested to abstain
from bombing while the talks were proceeding and, on the
1st of September, an agreement was duly signed by which
the Jangalis undertook to give no further assistance to the
Turks.

The Christians of Urmia
[Map, p. 249]

In the town and district of Urmia, lying west of the
lake of that name, there was a population of some 80,000
people, most of them Christians of the Armenian or Assyrian churches: the Assyrians had the tribal name of Jelus.
The district had been surrounded for a year by two weak
Turkish divisions, against which the Christians of Urmia
had fought with stubborn ingenuity. They had, however,
expended largely of their resources and they had sent a
message to the British asking for arms, ammunition, and
money. To help them in their fight against the Turks
it was considered desirable to give the Jelus what they
asked, but a difficulty was that Turkish troops at Sauj
Bulag, south of Lake Urmia, barred the way. It was
decided to send an aeroplane to Urmia with a message
saying that a convoy of arms and ammunition would be
sent, and instructing the Jelus to fight their way through
the Turkish cordon to meet the convoy on a fixed date at

[1] *The Adventures of Dunsterforce*, p. 204.

Sain Kala. Lieutenant K. M. Pennington, with the Kazvin detachment of No. 72 Squadron, volunteered to make the flight, and fuel was provided for him on a roughly prepared forward landing-ground at Mianeh, where a British post had been stationed for some time. When Lieutenant Pennington set out from Mianeh on the 8th of July there were rumours that Urmia had been captured by the Turks. As soon as he arrived over the town he became aware that his appearance was stirring the inhabitants to great excitement, and he was subjected to desultory rifle fire. He flew low for some time, but found it impossible to decide whether the town was in the hands of the Turks or not. The rifle fire, he thought, might be explained by the fact that the Jelus were uncertain about his identity and intentions. When he flew over the building of the American Mission and his wave of the hand was vigorously answered he decided to take a chance and land, which he did with some difficulty. When the inhabitants learned that the pilot was British he was joyously received, and after delivering his despatches he made a safe return to Mianeh.

The British ammunition convoy reached Sain Kala as arranged on the 23rd of July, but the Jelus had been delayed and they did not arrive to take the ammunition over until after ten days had passed. By that time the Turks had entered Urmia where they massacred many Assyrians, and they pursued those who fled along the road to Sain Kala until checked by the British troops. The stream of Assyrian refugees continued to pour along the road to Bijar until eventually some 50,000 had assembled at the latter place. They were gradually evacuated by way of Hamadan to refugee encampments provided by the British at Baquba.

The Caspian
[Map, p. 249]

Meanwhile, Colonel Bicharakoff had, on the 3rd of July, sailed from Enzeli for Alyat, thirty-five miles south-west of Baku. This Russian officer had decided to join the Bolshevik revolutionaries because he believed there was no other way by which he could obtain a footing in the

Caucasus. He was, at first, well received, and he accepted the post of commander-in-chief of the so-called Red Army of the Caucasus. He was not anxious, however, to take his own detachment to Baku direct because he would there be too much at the mercy of the Bolsheviks, who might, he thought, turn against him at any time. That was why he chose Alyat which would give him some independence and would not prevent him from co-operating with the section of the Red Army which was actually in the field. Bicharakoff moved forward to take command of the Baku red army astride the Tiflis railway, but he found that the revolutionary troops were unreliable. By the end of July he had been forced back into Baku and the Turks were in possession of the heights commanding the town.

The Bolshevik Government at Baku, which had been opposed to direct British intervention, had been overthrown on the 26th of July, and a Centro-Caspian dictatorship had been set up in its place. The new régime at once appealed to the British for help. Bicharakoff, however, convinced that the new Government would be ineffective, and that it was, in any event, too late to prevent the Turks from occupying the town, withdrew his own men and moved along the Caspian coast towards Derbend. For a time only scant and conflicting news filtered through from Baku, but it gradually became clear that the Turks had missed a certain opportunity to take effective control of the town. The British were anxious to respond to the call for help which had been made by the new authorities in Baku, and a small mission of officers, with an escort of a platoon of infantry, was sent to report upon the general situation. They landed at Baku on the 4th of August and, few as they were, had an immediate tonic effect upon the inhabitants who were inspired to repulse a heavy Turkish attack on the following day. Major-General Dunsterville decided to send two aeroplanes to Baku for communication purposes and further to encourage the people of the town in their resistance. Two Martinsydes of No. 72 Squadron were accordingly flown from Kazvin to Enzeli on the 18th of August, and they continued to Baku when it was reported that the Russians could receive them on the aerodrome near the town: the British aeroplanes were ready for operations at Baku on the 20th of August.

As a result of the report made by the British mission, reinforcements were sent to Baku and they took over a part of the defended perimeter of the town. The British troops, however, found a state of affairs which was almost chaotic, and a feeling soon spread among the inhabitants that there was no longer need to bother themselves with defence now that British soldiers were about. On the 26th of August the Turks made an attack, supported by artillery, the brunt of which was borne by a British infantry company which, after an epic resistance, was forced to withdraw. On the 31st the Turks attacked again, but they were resisted by British and Russian troops until the latter were forced to give ground through the exposure of their flank by the withdrawal of Armenian battalions. On the 1st of September further ground was lost, but the Turks had to pay dearly for their advantage, and they were not again in a position to move until the 14th of September, following the arrival of reinforcements. In the attack on the 14th the Turks took possession of most of the high ground dominating the town, after a day during which both sides fought to a standstill. As the Turks had taken ground which placed the port and its shipping at the mercy of artillery fire, Lieutenant-General Marshall gave orders for the evacuation of the British detachment, and the move took place during the night of the 14th/15th of September. The intervention of the few British troops had kept the Turks away from the Baku oil-fields for six weeks, and had compelled them to divert an appreciable force for the capture of the town.

The two pilots who had worked with the Baku detachment were Lieutenants M. C. Mackay and R. P. P. Pope. They had no opposition from enemy aircraft to face, and they were mainly employed for reconnaissance duties, bombing, and for distributing propaganda reading matter. The report dealing with the work of the two pilots on the day of the evacuation of Baku, reads: 'About an hour 'before daybreak on the 14th September, the Turks

'attacked the Allied line west of Baku. Their main attack
'was concentrated on Wolf's Gap—a large break in the
'British ridge—through which ran a road. At dawn
'Lieutenant Mackay flew over this sector of the line and
'observed troops on the British ridge. Owing to clouds
'and mist at 1,000 feet the identification of these troops
'was difficult, and to avoid any mistake the pilot flew
'farther west to the Turkish ridge where enemy reserves
'were seen halted on the western slopes. Six drums from
'the Lewis were fired into these troops, and a report taken
'back to G.H.Q. as to their whereabouts. During the
'morning Lieutenant Pope did two reconnaissances—the
'first of thirty minutes, the second of fifty-five minutes.
'During the first, three drums were fired on to troops
'on the British ridge, who had now been identified as
'Turks. Owing to the gas regulator key falling away from
'his gun, Lieutenant Pope returned to the aerodrome,
'but the trouble having been remedied again took off and
'crossed the Turkish lines. Six drums were fired into
'Turkish troops who were now half-way between the
'old British ridge and Baku. Lieutenant Mackay crossed
'the enemy lines shortly after this and again fired six
'drums into the enemy reserves on the British ridge.
'The last three flights were carried out at 1,500 feet.
'Lieutenant Pope's machine had been unserviceable for a
'day or so previously and owing to shortage of mechanics
'and time required to be spent on the serviceable
'machines, only one machine flew on the 14th of Sep-
'tember. By 12.15 p.m. on this day the machine was
'really unfit to fly owing to hits from rifle and machine-
'gun fire from the ground, and at 3 p.m. orders were
'received from the G.O.C., British troops, Baku, to destroy
'the two machines, their flying to Krasnovodsk, Lenkoran,
'or Enzeli being out of the question. At 3.45 p.m. the
'machines were burnt, the engines being rendered useless
'by revolver bullets and an axe. At 4.15 p.m. Lieutenants
'Pope and Mackay left the aerodrome which was then
'under shell fire, taking away with them one (top) machine-
'gun and three cameras. The Royal Air Force personnel
'was ordered to take one of the remaining machine-guns

'and several drums of ammunition and join the British 'line which was then close to the northern end of the 'aerodrome. The third machine-gun was smashed. . . .' Eventually, after their spell of duty with the infantry, the survivors of the Royal Air Force detachment were transported to Enzeli, whence they were taken to the aerodrome at Kazvin.

While the desperate fighting had been in progress at Baku, employing the bulk of the 'Dunsterforce', there had been cause for alarm along the lines of communications. It had become known that large bodies of Turkish troops were assembling at Tabriz and at Urmia, on either side of the lake of Urmia. The British troops available to guard this flank of the Kermanshah–Enzeli line of communications fell far short of the numbers needed to ensure security. The most important of the routes, and the one along which it was considered probable the Turks would march, was the Mianeh–Kazvin road. To meet the Turkish threat there was a mixed British and Persian force, about 1,100 strong, based on Mianeh, with a forward detachment forty-five miles to the north-west. A range of hills known as the Kuflan Kuh, astride the road south of Mianeh, constituted a favourable position for the British to fight a delaying action. Air reconnaissances of the Turkish positions in the whole area were made from time to time, and information obtained towards the end of August and early in September amply confirmed a belief that the Turks would make an advance down the main Mianeh–Tabriz road. On the 5th of September the Turkish movement began with an attack on the outpost line, and the enemy pressure was such that the Allied detachment had been forced back to the Kuflan Kuh positions by the 10th of September. If this line fell the British troops between Enzeli and Kazvin would be in a precarious position, and their withdrawal was therefore ordered. There was fierce fighting in the Kuflan Kuh positions, but after a resistance lasting four days the British were compelled to make a further withdrawal, and they moved back to Nikhbeg on the 14th. It was on this day that the British troops at Baku were evacuated to Enzeli, and these troops, together with reinforcements from Mesopotamia, eventually brought the Turkish advance to a halt along a strongly established defensive line at Zenjan. The Turks, however, had really shot their bolt. By this time the victory of General Allenby in Palestine and Syria had changed the whole situation in the Near East, and the Turkish threat in the Caucasus could no longer be reckoned serious.

During the Turkish advance reconnaissances had been made at high pressure by two pilots who worked from a landing-ground at Zenjan. The pilots also subjected the Turkish troops and transport to machine-gun and bombing attacks from low heights.

On the 17th of September Major-General W. M. Thomson succeeded Major-General Dunsterville in the command of the troops in Northern Persia, the force being newly designated the 'Norper force'. On the same day three R.E.8's of No. 30 Squadron were flown from Kifri to Hamadan, across 200 miles of rugged country, to reinforce the small detachment of No. 72 Squadron working in Persia. The main work of the pilots and observers from now onwards was reconnaissance of the Turkish positions at Kuflan Kuh, supplemented by attacks on the demoralized enemy troops and by the dropping of propaganda. It was essential to plan every flight with care because spare parts and the facilities for repair were meagre, and the supplies of petrol had to be husbanded. Although the Royal Air Force detachment was small, those military officers who were best placed to judge were enthusiastic about the effect the aeroplanes had upon the campaign.[1]

[1] 'We were well informed of Allenby's progress and also of the Balkan 'advance, so it was easy to prophesy that the Turks' next move in Persia 'would be backwards not forwards. The whole of Northern Persia acces-'sible by aeroplane or otherwise was vigorously propaganda'ed and the 'Turkish withdrawal was confidently foretold. As a result much of their 'locally raised transport, drivers and animals, began to melt away and the 'rest of it stampeded when our aeroplanes bombed them in the Shabli 'Pass. With the rest of our widely scattered little Force unable to help, it 'it true to say that this small detachment of R.A.F. reduced the two 'Turkish Divisions south of Tabriz to chaos in a manner comparable with

An adventure which befell a pilot on the 6th of October is worth recording for its own interest and because of the light it throws upon the local conditions. Lieutenant T. L. Williams of No. 72 Squadron set out in a Martinsyde to escort an R.E.8 aeroplane on a reconnaissance flight along the Tabriz road. During the journey he lost sight of the two-seater, and while searching for it he came upon enemy troops in the Shabli Pass. After he had scattered them with his machine-gun, his engine suddenly failed and he was forced to land forty miles behind the Turkish lines. He set fire to his aeroplane and then, he says, 'fearing the 'Turks might arrive on the scene I made off as quickly as I 'could, leaving behind me in my hurry my water bottle, 'which would have been invaluable. I made for the nearest 'gap in the Buqgush Dagh, which was about six miles 'away, in an effort to avoid the enemy in a pass which was 'some three miles distant. Here I found myself among 'very high and particularly steep mountains without food 'or water, the procuring of which proved to be the greatest 'difficulty throughout my subsequent journey. Taking my 'direction from the sun I now walked as fast as the steep 'inclines permitted, becoming very exhausted by mid-day. 'I plodded along and at about 4 p.m. struck a Pass which 'I followed until it became dark, when, whilst seeking for 'a resting place for the night, I was hailed by a Persian to 'whom I explained my position as best my Persian vocabu-'lary would allow me, promising him 1,000 Tomans if he 'returned me safely to the British lines. Attracted by so 'large a sum he immediately agreed and took me to his 'house where I received some bread and water, spending 'the night in the same room as himself and his two wives.

'October 7th. The following morning I received visits 'from nearly all the local inhabitants who seemed deeply 'interested in my dress and appearance. At about mid-day 'four rough-looking persons arrived and deprived me of the 'following articles at the point of a revolver: 150 Krans in 'money, my watch, flying cap and goggles, shoes, topee, 'tunic, both collar and tie, and a few other things. The

that of Allenby's very much larger operations in the Jordan Valley' (Lieutenant-General Sir William Thomson in a letter to the Author).

'leader of these four men was a Pasha who I afterwards
'found out had notified the Turks of my whereabouts. In
'the meantime, I was given an old pair of Persian trousers,
'waistcoat, jacket, cap, and slippers. I also permitted my
'hair to be half-shaved in the approved Persian style,
'preparatory to starting out for our own lines which I did
'at 12 midnight with my Persian guide. Our intentions at
'this time were to arrive at Mianeh after ten hours' march-
'ing, to spend three hours there, and to pass through the
'town and over the Kuflan Kuh under cover of darkness,
'and from thence to Sarchem, where I expected to find
'our front line.

'October 8th. After walking hard until about twelve
'mid-day we rested outside a small village 20 miles from
'Mianeh where my guide left me to go and buy some food.
'Before parting he urged me to rid myself of everything
'English in case of capture, so I handed him my shirt,
'shorts and stockings, leaving myself with only a thin pair
'of old trousers, a waistcoat, a tattered jacket with hardly
'any sleeves, a Persian cap and a rotten pair of Persian
'slippers, through which some of my toes protruded. I
'now waited a good hour for the return of my guide, but
'his continued absence probably due to fear of being caught
'by the Turks soon decided me to move on alone and make
'straight for Mianeh which appeared in the distance. A
'little later I met two Turkish cavalry men whom I pre-
'sumed were on the look-out for me. I therefore en-
'deavoured to avoid them by walking inland a little and
'performing a certain duty but the ruse was unsuccessful
'and they hailed me talking and shouting for a minute or
'so. However, taking no notice of them I was permitted
'to continue my journey in which I next nearly walked into
'a Turkish camp where a patrol of about a dozen cavalry
'men were stationed, presumably guarding the cross-roads
'where the two rivers meet. By some promiscuous dodging
'I successfully evaded these men and arrived outside the
'town of Mianeh before dark. I remained in hiding in a
'ditch until dark, and then started off along the banks of
'the Karangu-So which runs north-east from Mianeh, thus
'avoiding the enemy as much as possible. After some six

'miles, having had nothing to eat all day, I was too tired
'to go on, and lay down on the open ground to sleep, but
'through lack of clothing I was unable to attain this object,
'and gladly welcomed the cold day of October 9th.

'October 9th. Proceeding along the banks of this river
'for about another eight miles I crossed it, and struck a
'pass which I was convinced would lead me to our lines.
'This day was the first day's journey across the Maman
'Kuh and Kuh Karawal, which mountains took me a total
'of three days to cross. I started off on an empty stomach,
'and with an unquenchable thirst, walking most of the way
'bare-footed, since the slippers bruised my feet badly. I
'passed a few Persians during the day, but none would give
'me anything to eat or drink though just before dark I
'discovered six berries which I ate one by one with the
'greatest satisfaction. As usual I failed to get much sleep
'or rest.

'October 10th. I started at dawn feeling very exhausted
'and weak, my feet becoming troublesome, owing to the
'ruggedness of the tracks. I now left the high mountains
'and came to rolling hills by which I knew I was not far
'distant from our lines. I was also convinced that the
'Kuflan Kuh and the Turks were well behind me, yet the
'journey was becoming very monotonous and tiring. During
'the day I passed a large number of Persians whom I ques-
'tioned as to my proper course, and from whom I tried to
'obtain something to eat, but without success. The night
'was spent as usual. Slowly and falteringly I continued my
'journey and hoping my destination was not far off. I soon
'heard the hum of an aeroplane which was a great relief.
'I tried to hasten my pace but my feet proved too sore and
'I trudged along at a very slow pace. About mid-day I
'passed the walls of a big village, but did not dare to go
'inside for food lest I should be detained there. Outside
'the village I picked up a single grape with greedy fingers
'and devoured it with the utmost satisfaction. Soon after
'this I saw the Zenjan–Mianeh road. I was quickly over-
'taken by a Sergeant Despatch rider, who assured me of the
'near proximity of some of our own R.A.F. tenders, for
'which I sat down to wait with a light heart. I now saw

'three of our machines returning to Zenjan and at 3.30 'p.m. one of our tenders appeared on the road. I now had 'the greatest difficulty in stopping the tender, the officer 'of the Gurkhas who was inside first of all suggested shoot-'ing me and finally trying to knock me down, which he 'nearly succeeded in doing, in my efforts to take up all the 'road. Finally by shouting in English I assured them of my 'nationality, and was conveyed back to the camp of the '2nd Gurkhas where I was received with most excellent 'treatment, and a good feed.'

The modesty of the report cannot conceal the fine spirit which alone enabled Lieutenant Williams to reach the safety of the British lines. There is irony in the circumstance that a few weeks later, when he was flying peacefully above Baghdad, the wings of his aeroplane folded back in the air and he was killed in the ensuing crash.

On the day that Lieutenant Williams reported to his squadron after his escape, three other officers were faced with a comparable adventure. On the 11th of October three R.E.8 aeroplanes, with an escort, left on a mission to attack Turkish columns. The escorting pilot, Lieutenant K. M. Pennington, after he had dropped bombs and used his machine-gun against enemy troops, was forced to land with engine trouble. Lieutenant A. E. Morgan, one of the R.E.8 pilots (observer, Lieutenant J. C. Chacksfield), landed and picked up the Martinsyde pilot, but the R.E.8 came to grief through hitting a large stone when taking-off again. The three officers set out for the hills, and after seven days of incredible hardship and danger, during which 120 miles were covered on foot, they walked into Allmazar, 'all more than glad to be safely back with the certainty of 'a good meal and an opportunity of tending rather blistered 'feet'.

Little more need be written here about the final operations in Persia. After the signing of the Armistice with Turkey, the Norperforce was concentrated at Enzeli for an operation to reoccupy Baku. This movement took place on the 17th of November 1918, but the story of the action is outside the scope of this history, and it will now be necessary to return to Mesopotamia for the final campaign.

The Autumn Campaign in Mesopotamia
[Map, p. 264]

On the 25th of September 1918 the War Office, in a telegram, thus summarized the military situation in the Middle East for the information of Sir Percy Z. Cox, newly appointed British Minister to Tehran: 'The complete 'destruction of the whole Turkish army in Palestine leaves 'Syria open to invasion. Every anti-Turkish element in 'the country will support the advancing British. The 'communications of the Turkish force in Mesopotamia are 'thus seriously threatened and in all probability it will 'be forced to abandon Mesopotamia altogether. Arabia is 'completely lost to them and the fall of Medina is now im-'minent. Turkey, in addition to being faced with the loss of 'three-quarters of her Asiatic territory, is gravely threatened 'in Europe by the Allied advance in the Balkans, which, 'since 15th September, has continued uninterruptedly. 'The Bulgarian army is in a critical situation and a slight 'further advance by the Allies will sever it in two. To meet 'all these dangers on so many fronts the Turks have only 'one army left, which is now in the Caucasus and Persia. 'General Allenby's victory has already compelled them to 'transfer to Constantinople a division which was destined 'for Tabriz; and the situation in the Balkans and Palestine 'will completely paralyse Turkish operations in the Middle 'East, and in all probability will lead very soon to the 'evacuation of Persia. Thus the whole situation has been 'transformed in the last few days and the Turks must now 'think only of protecting their own territory and not of 'further aggression.'[1]

Two days after this telegram was dispatched Bulgaria asked for an armistice, and it was reported that the German and Turkish troops would be withdrawn from the Caucasus. The general military situation and cooler weather made the moment ideal for a final offensive in Mesopotamia. On the 2nd of October Lieutenant-General Marshall was told, by telegram from the War Office, that Turkey might, because of the difficult position in which she found

---

[1] See *The Campaign in Mesopotamia, 1914–1918*, vol. iv, p. 254.

herself, ask in the near future for hostilities to cease. It was advisable in the circumstances that as much ground as possible should be gained up the Tigris. Furthermore, to help a possible advance by General Allenby's cavalry in the direction of Aleppo, a cavalry raid up the Euphrates should additionally be considered.

The main operations along the Tigris were entrusted to Lieutenant-General Sir A. S. Cobbe, commanding the I Corps. To protect his right flank a column from the III Corps, under the command of Brigadier-General A. C. Lewin, was to advance on the line Tauq–Kirkuk–Altun Köpri in order to prevent the Turks in that area from moving down the Little Zab.

No. 63 Squadron (less a half-Flight at Ramadi) and 'A' Flight of No. 72 Squadron, at Samarra, were to work with the I Corps. No. 30 Squadron (less a half-Flight at Zenjan, Persia) at Kifri, and 'C' Flight of No. 72 Squadron at Mirjana, were attached to Brigadier-General Lewin's column. Kite Balloons were judged to be unsuited to the projected warfare of rapid movement, and No. 23 Kite Balloon Company therefore was ordered to return to England: it left Mesopotamia on the 27th of October.

The main enemy position on the Tigris was at the Fat-ha gorge, thirty-five miles north of the British railhead at Tikrit. The position, naturally strong, had been developed during a year and a half, and Lieutenant-General Cobbe considered that to make a direct assault upon it would prove costly and indecisive. As, owing to lack of water, a turning movement round the Turkish right flank was not practicable, except for armoured cars, it was decided to turn the enemy's left, secure a crossing over the Little Zab, and drive the Turks across to the right bank of the Tigris where it was hoped that the major portion of the enemy force covering Mosul would be cut off and destroyed.

During the summer months the Royal Air Force, by photography, had provided the material for the making of maps of the country over which the advances were to take place. In connexion with the specific military plans, finally adopted, many special air reconnaissances were made to survey the passes and river beds to report upon their suitability for the movement of a force of all arms. Typical of the information sought is a request for a specified air reconnaissance which was to be made 'with special refer-'ence to roads, trails, and water'. The air observers were asked to state 'whether roads are fit for wheels, any serious 'obstacles, and also particular attention to be paid to 'wells [at places which were named], also whether country 'appears generally suitable for Ford vans'. Demands of this kind, general and comprehensive, called for a detailed survey. The reader would not be much helped if the resulting reconnaissance reports were reproduced, because they were compiled for staff study in conjunction with maps, air photographs, and general intelligence information, but a representative extract from one of the reports may convey some idea of the care with which the information was compiled. 'No wheeled traffic would be able to proceed 'south-west of a line B.B. 96 central to B.B. 50 central '[the references are to points on the map]. A good route 'would be as follows: Along Ain Nukhaila–Kirkuk road to 'a point about twelve miles north-east of Pass. After pass-'ing water-holes B.B. 96 b.–98 strike into desert on a 'bearing of about 320 degrees; on this route there are about 'five nullahs to cross; these are narrow water-channels 'usually with vertical banks a few feet high. The ground 'does not appear to slope down to them at all from either 'side, and they would not be serious obstacles. Ramping 'might be necessary in one or two cases. . . . At B.B. 62 'a. 27 a well-defined track from B.B. 61 a. 45 leading east 'to Kirkuk is crossed. A large mound here should be a good 'landmark. From B.B. 61 b. 29 to B.B. 61 b. 51 there is a 'large canal and the track crosses this at B.B. 61. a This 'crossing looks rather rough and steep. May be passable 'for wheels. By continuing north-west from the mound, 'this canal would be avoided and river bank would be 'reached about the village B.B. 50 d. 44. . . .'

A stranger might find it difficult to learn anything from the figures of fare stages set out upon the tickets of an omnibus in the service of the London Transport Board, but a driver or conductor might easily, from contemplation of a ticket, visualize a journey from one end of London to the other, picturing something of the scene and of the buildings along the route. The air reconnaissance reports of the war may be compared with fare tickets. Compiled in a sort of technical shorthand they seem almost meaningless, but they conveyed information of immediate use to the military staffs, and they also provided items of which the value might become apparent only after study, perhaps in conjunction with other and diverse clues. It would be false to dramatize the reconnaissance work for the reader, who should, however, remember that it formed a major activity of the air squadrons, and that upon the great numbers of reports regularly compiled by the air observers, and expertly assessed by the military staffs, much of the detail of the military plans was based.

On the 15th of October, by which time the preparations for the offensive were well advanced, the aeroplanes of No. 63 Squadron flew to the advanced aerodrome at Tikrit, where 'A' Flight of No. 72 Squadron was already installed. On the 18th Brigadier-General Lewin moved out from Tuz Khurmatli and occupied Tauq and the bridge four miles to the north-east, taking a few prisoners. By the morning of the 23rd the main preliminary moves had been completed, and Lieutenant-General Cobbe was in touch with the enemy on both banks of the Tigris, while Brigadier-General Lewin had reached Taza Khurmatli, twelve miles south-west of Kirkuk. Swift enveloping movements during the night of the 23rd/24th caused the enemy to abandon the Fat-ha position before daybreak. The pilots of 'A' Flight of No. 72 Squadron were in the air at dawn, and they found retreating Turks on the roads and they attacked them with machine-gun fire from a low height. One of the pilots was the first to bring back the news that the Turks were leaving the Fat-ha positions. The main air activity during the rest of the day was low-flying attack on the retreating troops. No opportunity was offered, such as had come the way of the Royal Air Force in the Nablus pass in Palestine, to induce a panic by means of bombing and machine-gun attacks concentrated in time and place, but although the air attacks during the advance to Mosul were necessarily diffused, the relentless pressure upon the retreating Turks was cumulative in its effect.

The complicated enemy and British movements throughout the 25th were well reported by contact patrol observers of No. 63 Squadron. In the morning a pilot and observer of the squadron found a Turkish column which they estimated at about 1,500 infantry with horse transport. They flew back to the advanced head-quarters of the I Corps to tell of what they had seen, and they also dropped messages on the way for the British cavalry. The opportunity offered for air attack upon the column was not missed. Two S.E.5 pilots and a Sopwith 'Camel' pilot of 'A' Flight of No. 72 Squadron at once set out in search of the Turks who were found east of the Humr bridge. The pilots repeatedly dived on the column as they fired their machine-guns, but the enemy troops revealed a fine discipline. They did not scatter in panic, as had usually happened in similar circumstances, but they kept their formation and brought fire to bear upon the aeroplanes, with the result that one S.E.5 was damaged and had to be landed near the British advanced cavalry, while the pilot in the Sopwith 'Camel' received a slight leg wound. The spirit of the Turks, however, was broken when they realized that if the easterly march was continued they would be enveloped by oncoming British cavalry. During the afternoon, therefore, the men turned back and recrossed the Tigris to the right bank, and they moved in increasing disorder as they were subjected to further attacks from the air, notably by the single-seater pilots of 'A' Flight of No. 72 Squadron.

On the 26th the Turks made a stand along the Mushak position, which was one of great natural strength, but during the night of the 26th/27th they further withdrew to a position covering Sharqat. British cavalry, however, guided by a local inhabitant, crossed the Tigris by a ford in the afternoon some fourteen miles above Sharqat and galloped to seize the Huwaish Wadi which they reached without meeting opposition. By the morning of the 27th two cavalry regiments, with two guns and a machine-gun squadron, were in a strong position across the Mosul road.

While these various movements were taking place on the 26th the aeroplanes, owing to the difficulties of communication on the ground, were mainly employed to report the changing dispositions of the British and Turkish troops.

All efforts were now directed to preventing the Turkish force from breaking through the cavalry screen in an effort to win through to Mosul. The Turks made a desperate attempt to get through on the morning of the 28th. Some 2,500 enemy troops, supported by guns and howitzers, attacked the 11th Cavalry Brigade, which had meanwhile been reinforced by the 1–7th Gurkhas from the 53rd Infantry Brigade. These attempts, and subsequent efforts to turn the right flank of the cavalry, were repulsed.

The British troops engaged had been marching and fighting in difficult country for days, and by the evening of the 28th they were exhausted. The moment, however, was critical, and it was imperative that the men should be called upon to make a final determined effort if the Turks were to be forced to surrender. If the pressure were relaxed there was every chance that the enemy force would open a gap to Mosul. There was fierce fighting during the night of the 28th/29th of October, when all enemy attempts to cut a way through to the north were frustrated. While the Turks were being held in the north the men of the 17th Division to the south were forcing the enemy rear-guards upon the main body in their position north of Sharqat. This position consisted of successive lines of hastily dug entrenchments commanding ravines which the British must cross to attack. In the afternoon of the 29th the attack was launched, and the Turks, fighting with the courage of despair, held a part of their positions until well into the night. When dawn came on the 30th it was clear the end was near. The way to Mosul was barred, and the force at Sharqat, hemmed in on all sides, packed into ravines raked by a murderous fire from which there was no escape, was in a hopeless position. Just when the British infantry were about to assault, white flags of surrender fluttered along the enemy lines. The last battle fought by the Turkish army in the war was over. The fighting had been characterized by a tenacity which reflected credit upon the skill and qualities of leadership of General Ismail Hakki Bey, the Turkish commander, the same officer who, in the spring of 1917, had shown a comparable stubbornness in command of the Turkish forces on the right bank of the Tigris opposite Kut al Imara.

After the surrender cavalry and light armoured-cars were ordered along the Mosul road, and they rounded up Turkish troops in the neighbourhood of Qaiyara. The total captures during the final operations amounted to 11,322 prisoners, 51 guns, 130 machine-guns, 2,000 animals, and war material of many kinds. The armistice with Turkey was signed at noon on the 31st of October 1918, and the war on the Mesopotamian front ended with Lieutenant-General Marshall's occupation of the Mosul vilayet.

War Operations in India

A central flying school was being formed to open at Sitapur in India in September 1914, but the outbreak of war ended the arrangements, and such staff and equipment as had already been allotted to the school were distributed for active service. The formation and work of the air force unit maintained by the Government of India for service during the early stages of the campaign in Mesopotamia have already been noted.[1]

In August 1915 the Viceroy of India was anxious to make use of aeroplanes on the north-west frontier where unrest had been caused subsequent to the entry of Turkey into the war. Accordingly a unit called 'A' Flight of No. 31 Squadron was formed at South Farnborough and left England with five B.E.2c aeroplanes for India at the end of November 1915, in company with a nucleus of personnel to form an Aircraft Park. The party arrived on Boxing Day and moved to a station at Nowshera where they stayed until March 1916, when a further move was made to Risalpur. 'B' Flight of No. 31 Squadron, provided by No. 22 Squadron, left England in February 1916, and the third Flight, 'C', drawn from the home defence brigade, followed from England in May. By October 1916 No. 31 Squadron,

---

[1] Vol. V, Ch. v.

together with the Aircraft Park, all under the command of Major C. R. S. Bradley, had been concentrated on the aerodrome at Risalpur.

No. 31 Squadron took part in operations on the Mohmand border in the latter part of 1916. Reconnaissances were made in October and November in co-operation with forces covering the establishment of wire-connected blockhouses along the border. A lashkar, that is to say a body of armed tribesmen, about 6,000 strong, was discovered from the air on the 13th of November in positions where it threatened Shabkadar. Major-General Sir F. Campbell, in command, thereupon issued orders for an attack to be made on the tribesmen on the morning of the 15th. Twelve aeroplanes from Risalpur, making use of an advanced landing-ground at Shabkadar, gave their help. During the morning wireless-fitted aeroplanes made it possible for the artillery to break up the enemy concentrations, and in the afternoon, when the tribesmen were in flight, they were bombed and attacked with Lewis guns from the air. By the evening of the 15th, when the aeroplanes left to return to Risalpur, it seemed that the tribesmen had been effectively dispersed, and air reconnaissances next day confirmed that this was so. Some small scattered bodies were found and bombed on the 16th, but reconnaissances on subsequent days failed to find any traces of the tribesmen who, it was clear, had gone back to their homes.

Towards the end of January 1917 'A' Flight of No. 31 Squadron was transferred to Bannu for work with the Bannu and Derajat Brigades in North Waziristan and the adjacent province of Khost, where unrest was marked. Rumours that flying chariots existed had spread among the the tribesmen, but there were apparently few who believed. The arrival of 'A' Flight was therefore reported to have created a disturbing impression. After reconnaissances had been made over a wide area of Mahsud country the Flight returned to Risalpur on the 11th of February. At the end of the month, however, there came news that a Mahsud lashkar was on the move towards Sarwekai, a post garrisoned by South Waziristan Militia, and three aeroplanes were sent to Tank to investigate. Not long after their presence became known the tribesmen dispersed, and by the middle of the month the air detachment was back again at Risalpur.

During ensuing weeks, however, the Mahsuds became more brazenly troublesome, encouraged by an apparent immunity from punishment. The aeroplanes, objects of dread before they had revealed themselves, had appeared to the Mahsuds as of no account, the only effect which resulted from their passage being the casting of a shadow across the ground. It was obvious that some decisive action was necessary in order to prevent the tribesmen from getting out of hand, and on the 19th of May the Government of India sanctioned punitive measures. Meanwhile, on the 5th, three B.E.2c's from 'B' Flight of No. 31 Squadron had been transferred to Tank for routine work with the forces in the Derajat command. There were daily reconnaissances, and on the 12th a few drums of ammunition were fired from the air into a blanket and tent encampment discovered by one of the B.E.2c's. The machine-gun fire sufficed to scatter about 1,000 Mahsuds, and a small bombing attack next day caused the camp to disappear. 'B' Flight continued to co-operate from Tank until the end of May when it was relieved by 'C' Flight for the special punitive operations.

As a preliminary the area was photographed, and from the photographs a map was made for the use of the general officer commanding the South Waziristan Field Force at Jandola. While the operations were taking place, in the week beginning on the 20th of June, the aeroplanes bombed the tribesmen, whose villages in particular suffered heavily through fires caused by the bombing. When the Mahsuds made their submission they were frank about their dread of air attack as a form of Government action against which they were entirely powerless. That the bombing helped to bring a quick ending to the operations was indicated in a telegram on the 27th of June, ordering the air attacks to cease. This said: 'G.O.C. Forces congratulates Royal Fly-
'ing Corps on successful bombing raids in Mahsud territory.
'These raids have had great effect and this morning a
'messenger arrived from Koniguran asking that they might
'be stopped while peace terms were being considered. He

says one bomb killed 12 men, wounded a number and 'destroyed some cattle. If Mahsuds now come to terms a 'full share of the credit will be due to Royal Flying Corps.'

The Mahsuds ratified the terms at a fully representative Peace Jirga held on the 10th of August, and peace was formally declared two days later. Subsequently, where sections of the tribe proved slow in keeping to the terms, or showed obstinacy, a demonstration from the air led to quick settlements. By the 18th of August the presence of aeroplanes was no longer deemed necessary and 'C' Flight of No. 31 Squadron therefore returned to Risalpur. The military authorities were so impressed with the effect of air attack on the morale of the tribesmen that it was decided to form another squadron, and this was done in September when No. 114 Squadron was formed at Lahore with a nucleus provided by No. 31 Squadron.

There was quiet on the north-west frontier during the final months of 1917 and in the beginning of 1918, and the flying personnel were mainly concerned with the routine of training and the work of a general survey of landing-grounds. In February 1918, however, the Marri tribes in Baluchistan began to stir and, on the 19th/20th, they made an attack, which proved unsuccessful, on Gumbaz fort. The Khetran tribes, stimulated by the Marris, burnt and looted the Government buildings at Barkhan on the 7th of March. Meanwhile aeroplanes had been dispatched to the troubled area, two to Sibi, two to Duki, and five to Deri Ghazi Khan. Reconnaissances had been made of the Sibi plains, and of the passes to the Marri hills, in the days following the attack on Gumbaz, but no signs of the tribesmen had been discovered. On the 1st of March an alarm was received at Sibi that some 3,000 Marris were making their approach from Chandia, fifteen miles away. One aeroplane, armed with a Lewis gun and four small bombs, set out to stop the advance, but no enemy could be found, and it was afterwards known that an efflux of spectators from a Chandia sports meeting had given rise to the rumours of Marris on the move.

In connexion with the military punitive measures the aeroplanes were employed to bomb villages and camps, and on the 22nd of March it was ordered that Kahan, capital of the Marri district, should be bombed daily. Dust storms were raging at the time the order was received, and it was not until the 24th that the bombing could begin. On this day three bombs were dropped, one of 112-lb. weight and two of 20-lb., and it was afterwards learned that they killed fourteen armed tribesmen. Subsequent bombing caused much damage in the village. By the end of March the Khetran tribes had submitted, and by the middle of April the more troublesome Marris had been subdued. Kahan was occupied on the 19th of April when the Marri Nawab and tribal headman made their unconditional submission. For the remainder of the year there was peace.

CHAPTER VII

THE ITALIAN FRONT

(Map, facing)

THE calamity which overtook the Italian army on the Caporetto front was sudden. Directed by the German general staff, the Austro-German offensive which was launched against the Italians on the morning of the 24th of October 1917 had for aim the crippling of the Italian army by means of one shattering battle, secretly prepared in all its details. On the flanks of the attack the Italians resisted, but at Caporetto the line broke, and the two Italian corps guarding the sector melted away, with the result that a wide gap was opened for a rapid exploitation of the enemy success. For a fortnight Italy was threatened with a major disaster, but Otto von Below, the German general in command of the offensive, had insufficient reserves to exact the maximum advantage from the victory he had won, and, on the 10th of November, the Italian retreat ended along the line of the river Piave.

The German air service had made a contribution to the victory. The maps, especially of the mountain districts, had been found to be inaccurate, and the task of providing the general staff with maps, upon which precise military plans could be based, fell upon the German pilots and observers. 'The squadrons of the German Air Force 'attached to the German troops in this district helped the 'General Staff out of their dilemma in the shortest possible 'time. A few days sufficed for our fighting pilots, with the 'daring and experience they had acquired on the Western 'front, to drive all the Italian airmen from the air, parti-'cularly as the Italians had hitherto only been confronted 'by the Austrian Air Force, which was at that time provided 'with inferior machines. Consequently our reconnaissance 'machines were ensured command of the air over the 'battle-fields, and were therefore able to carry out their 'work unhindered. Before long they had completed a photo-'graphic survey of the districts on both sides of the lines, 'and had provided the General Staff with a complete picture

2504.6　　　　　　　　T

'of the enemy's railway system, the distribution of his forces, 'and the disposition and strength of his flying units.'[1]

On the 26th of October the British and French Governments had agreed to send divisions from the Western front to help the Italians, and three days later a British detachment, consisting of the head-quarters of the XIV Corps, together with the 23rd and 44th Divisions, had been ordered to entrain for Italy. General Sir Herbert C. O. Plumer arrived to take command of the British troops in Italy on the 10th of November and he established his head-quarters at Legnago, but shortly afterwards moved to Padua.

For air co-operation, No. 28 Squadron, equipped with Sopwith 'Camels', and No. 34 Squadron, with two-seater R.E.8 aeroplanes, both withdrawn from France, were grouped to form a new wing—the Fifty-first—under the command of Lieutenant-Colonel R. P. Mills. In order to make the squadrons independent operational units they were each allotted one month's supply of petrol and oil, were given what was judged to be an adequate supply of transport and spares, and had their establishments increased to allow of immediate replacements of casualties. The first of the five trains in which the squadrons and the impedimenta were to travel left Candas on the 7th of November. There was nothing to be gained by sending the aeroplanes by air. In Italy all was uncertainty and the squadrons would in any event be unable to operate without their stores and transport. The organization at the Candas depot was such that the business of entraining the units could be done quickly and efficiently, and in the circumstances it was preferable that they should be dispatched to arrive complete.

While these arrangements were under way, an Allied conference assembled on the 5th of November at Rapallo, at which Mr. Lloyd George, the British Prime Minister, agreed, after consultation with the Chief of the Imperial General Staff, to send two additional British divisions to Italy, with two more aeroplane squadrons. Two Sopwith 'Camel' squadrons, Nos. 45 and 66, were chosen for transfer,

---

[1] Neumann, *The German Air Force in the Great War* (Eng. trans.), p. 236.

No. 66 moving first on the 17th of November. Meantime, the War Cabinet had decided to send yet a third detachment to Italy, consisting of the XI Corps headquarters and two divisions, and it became necessary in consequence to add another corps squadron, No. 42, equipped with R.E.8's. Nos. 42 and 45 Squadrons moved to Fienvillers on the 16th of November preparatory to dismantling and packing the aeroplanes for entrainment. The trains housing No. 42 Squadron left Candas for Italy on the 26th and 27th of November, and those with No. 45 Squadron on the 11th and 12th of December.

To administer the increased air detachment, it was decided to send to Italy a Brigade head-quarters under Brigadier-General T. I. Webb-Bowen, who left on the 16th of November and formed the VII Brigade at Mantua two days later. Brigadier-General Webb-Bowen, in a report at the end of November, proposed that a new army wing should be formed and that the existing Fifty-first Wing should include only the corps squadrons. He also asked for a balloon wing of two companies. The War Office stated in reply that the head-quarters of the Fourteenth Wing, together with No. 4 Balloon Wing, would be sent to Italy as soon as possible. These units left Candas on the 25th and 26th of December.

Meanwhile, the first squadrons to arrive had begun operations over the front. Nos. 28 and 34 Squadrons had reached Milan on the 12th and 14th of November, and, by working day and night, the squadron personnel had assembled and tested their aircraft on Milan aerodrome by the 14th (No. 28 Squadron), and the 17th of November (No. 34 Squadron). On the latter date the two squadrons, with the Fifty-first Wing head-quarters, moved to Ghedi and Montichiari, making a further move, five days later, to Verona. To provide a mobile source of supply for the squadrons, 'Z' Aircraft Park, which had been established at Milan on the 16th of November, sent forward lorries and trailers with two weeks' supplies of fuel and spares. This sub-Park, as it was called, was to travel in close proximity to the squadrons and was to draw fresh supplies from Milan as required. It moved to Verona on the 24th of November.

On the 28th further moves were made: the wing headquarters went to Villalta, north-north-west of Camisano, and Nos. 28 and 34 Squadrons moved to Grossa, north of the same town. Verona was occupied by No. 66 Squadron. On the 28th also an aeroplane supply depot was formed at S. Pelagio, south-south-west of Padua. 'Z' Aircraft Park and the sub-Park moved to the same area on the 29th of November and the 1st of December.

By this time the general situation had become clearer, and it was agreed that the British should take over from the Italians the Montello sector of the Piave, with the French on their left. The 41st Division went into the line on the 2nd of December from east of Nervesa to a point opposite Fontigo, and the 23rd Division relieved the Italians two days later from Fontigo to east of Vidor. No. 34 Squadron was accordingly transferred from Grossa to an aerodrome at Istrana, west of Treviso, on the 3rd of December.

The air situation when the British appeared on the front was unsatisfactory. The Austrian air service had been reinforced for the offensive by German squadrons, and the military victory which had been won over the Italians had made the enemy pilots aggressively confident. The first British flight over the Italian lines took place on the 29th of November when No. 34 Squadron attempted a photographic reconnaissance in the Montello area. Four Sopwith 'Camels' of No. 28 Squadron escorted the R.E.8's, but so persistently did enemy fighters attack the British aeroplanes that little photography was possible. One enemy single-seater, during a prolonged combat, was shot to pieces in the air by a Sopwith 'Camel' pilot.

On the 7th of December No. 42 Squadron arrived at Istrana, by way of Padua and San Pelagio, and began operations two days later. Meanwhile, the second fighting squadron, No. 66, had moved from Verona to Grossa on the 4th, thus making the strength of the Royal Flying Corps on the British front two fighter squadrons and two corps squadrons.

The British front settled to trench warfare, and the amount of work required of the two corps squadrons was unduly heavy because the area was new. In addition to the tactical duties on the corps front, daily strategical reconnaissances, visual and photographic, were required by general head-quarters. Three routes were allotted for successive days, in particular to enable watch to be kept upon the railway systems, and an escorting force of six Sopwith 'Camels' was normally provided. The two corps squadrons had also to undertake bombing operations as part of the offensive plan to force the enemy air service to adopt a defensive policy. It was discovered in December that the enemy pilots were using an aerodrome at San Felice, and this was bombed on the 15th and 16th by No. 42 Squadron: the aerodrome was seen a few days later to have been evacuated. The enemy air service retaliated with a daylight attack on the aerodrome at Istrana, 'every machine 'attached to the Army'[1] being impressed into the attack which took place on Boxing Day. An officer of No. 34 Squadron records: 'Our squadron was not operating at all 'that day, and only the squadron commander and a few 'clerks had gone to the aerodrome. The remainder of the 'squadron was in the village about one and a half miles 'away. About 11 a.m. I started to walk to the aerodrome. 'About half-way there I noticed that our anti-aircraft guns 'were firing. This was a most unusual occurrence, and 'when I looked to see what the target was, I could hardly 'believe my eyes. About five miles away, flying at all heights 'between 500 and 3,000 feet, was the most heterogeneous 'collection of aircraft I have ever seen. Making no attempt 'to keep together, but, on the contrary, widely scattered, 'thirty or forty Austrian machines were slowly approach-'ing us. Nearer and nearer they came. Every few hundred 'yards one would drop its bombs, and make for home. 'Finally, about twenty reached the aerodrome and bombed 'it. After bombing the aerodrome they did not go straight 'back, but becoming more dispersed they wandered all over 'the country at about 1,000 feet. When I arrived at the 'aerodrome I found that seven had fallen among our 'hangars and every machine had been hit. The damage 'was, however, trivial, and within one and a half hours all

[1] Neumann, pp. 238–9.

'were serviceable. The Italian squadron on the aerodrome
'had not been so fortunate, for although only one bomb
'had fallen amongst them, it had set a hangar on fire and
'destroyed two machines. We treated the raid lightly and
'thought no more of it. An amusing sequel lay in store for
'us. After lunch I and another officer set out to walk to
'corps head-quarters at Fanzolo for tea. It was about six
'kilometres away. As we climbed into a field over a hedge
'near C. Gritti Rizzi, we were astounded to see a small
'Austrian machine there, with the pilot apparently dead
'in his cockpit. On approaching it we heard snores, and
'found that the pilot was merely asleep. His machine-gun
'was loaded so we pointed it at him and awakened him. We
'talked to him in Italian, but finding that he talked perfect
'English, carried on our conversation in our own tongue.
'He soon realized his position and became quite affable.
'All that he remembered was that he had had a very good
'Christmas dinner at his squadron, and had put ten officers
'to bed at about 7 that morning. He himself had just got
'into bed when an order had come from Army head-quarters
'at Vittorio that every serviceable aeroplane in the army
'was to be loaded up with bombs immediately and proceed
'to bomb the aerodromes across the Piave by way of
'reprisal. The machine he had taken had not been filled up
'with petrol, and after forty minutes he had been forced to
'land. He had sent his mechanic to steal some petrol,
'hoping still to escape. We took him to corps head-quarters
'where we learned that five other machines had landed
'south of the Piave and several of the pilots were "not
'quite sober".'[1]

This description throws light upon the conditions of the time, but it may be remembered that the apparently haphazard way in which the attempt was made seems at least to be a proof of the lack of respect which the Austrian and German pilots had for such opposition as they expected to meet. They had been accustomed for some time to do in the air very much as they liked, and although the attack

[1] Two of the six aeroplanes which landed in the British area had been shot down by pilots of No. 28 Squadron. Italian pilots claimed an additional three destroyed on the Austrian side of the lines.

may impress the reader as a *jeu d'esprit*, fostered by the pouring of festive libations, at least it was prompted by spirits which were high. An enemy conscious of inferiority does not normally indulge in such adventures.

More serious bombing was undertaken by the German No. 4 Bombing Squadron which had been attached to the army head-quarters at the beginning of December. These bombers flew at night, and although they occasionally attacked aerodromes they chiefly directed their operations against the towns of Treviso, Padua, and Venice. As a member of the German air service who flew on the front says: 'In Padua, and in Venice, the grandchildren of the 'present generation will still be told the story of these 'northern "Barbarians", who, like the storm wind of the 'north itself, swooped down on their black pinions and 'carried terror and destruction in the stillness of night 'along the sleeping plains at the foot of the Alps.'[1]

The black pinions carried a measure of destruction to the aerodrome at Istrana at the end of December. During the night of the 29th, and again during the 30th, the aerodrome was bombed and a hangar with one aeroplane of No. 34 Squadron was destroyed, and several hangars together with six aeroplanes were damaged, as were workshop and photographic lorries.

Bombing and counter-bombing continued in January 1918, and air superiority definitely passed to the Allied air services. The Sopwith 'Camels', with their experienced pilots, whether employed as fighters or bombers, outclassed the enemy fighters. The 'Camels' undertook a bombing offensive against the aerodromes. In the early morning of the 19th of February eleven from Nos. 28 and 66 Squadrons, each carrying four 25-lb. bombs, attacked the aerodrome at Casarsa from about 200 feet and set fire to a former Italian airship shed. The attack was so successful that four Sopwith 'Camels' from each squadron were set aside for attacks on allotted enemy aerodromes. This type of attack, however, became less successful and more expensive, and it gave way to concentrated attacks, which proved to be effective and economical, on selected aerodromes.

[1] Neumann, p. 239.

By the beginning of March the Italian army, after four months of quiet, had progressed far towards recovery. Furthermore, it had been obvious for some time that the whole German preoccupation was with the Western front. Some of the British and French strength, therefore, was withdrawn from Italy to France. The 41st Division moved at the beginning of March and the 5th Division early in April. On the 10th of March Sir Herbert Plumer handed over the command of the remaining British troops in Italy to Lieutenant-General the Earl of Cavan, commanding the XIV Corps. The Fifty-first Wing head-quarters left for France on the 10th of March and was followed by No. 20 Balloon Company next day. On the 14th No. 42 Squadron moved. On the 26th of March Lieutenant-Colonel P. B. Joubert de la Ferté, of the Fourteenth Wing, took over the command of the Royal Flying Corps in Italy from Brigadier-General Webb-Bowen who, with the staff of the VII Brigade, returned to France. The reduction in the strength of the Royal Flying Corps had been important, and by way of compensation a Flight of Bristol Fighters was sent to Italy from England. It was first attached to No. 28 Squadron as a fourth Flight, but was soon afterwards transferred to No. 34 Squadron and called 'Z' Flight.[1] The Bristol Fighters relieved the R.E.8's of responsibility for distant reconnaissance work, a task which they had fulfilled, without loss under escort, for four months.

It was decided that the British troops should, during the summer, occupy a sector in the mountains. They were accordingly relieved by Italians on the Piave in the middle of March and took over a stretch of front on the Asiago plateau, between Asiago and Canove. The ultimate intention was to make an Allied attack from this position towards Val Sugana, but developments in France led to various postponements, and then, as a result of an Austrian offensive on the Italian front in June, the Allied attack was abandoned.

In accordance with the change of front, the head-quarters of the Fourteenth Wing moved from Villalta to

[1] When a second Flight was added to 'Z' Flight, in June, they became identified as No. 139 Squadron (on the 3rd of July).

ATTACK IMPENDING

Sarcedo on the 26th of March. No. 34 Squadron moved from Istrana to Villaverla on the 30th. No. 66 Squadron had moved from Limbraga to Casa Piazza on the 10th. On the 17th No. 45 Squadron flew from Istrana to Grossa.

While the British were changing position, patrols, usually by three Sopwith 'Camels', were maintained at 10,000 feet, from dawn to dusk, on both the Piave and the Asiago fronts to prevent enemy air observers from discovering the movements. When the transference of troops had been completed routine offensive patrols were ordered for the Asiago front, and areas were allotted for regular reconnaissance. The reconnaissances were made at first by single Bristol Fighters of 'Z' Flight, but on the 3rd of April the reconnaissance aeroplane failed to return, and subsequently an escort of three to six Sopwith 'Camels' was usually provided. Air fighting was intermittent, but occasionally intense. On the 30th of March a patrol of three Sopwith 'Camels' of No. 66 Squadron became involved with enemy fighters, which eventually aggregated nineteen. It appeared that six of them were destroyed, three by Lieutenant Alan Jerrard before he was himself shot down and made a prisoner; for his persistence in face of great odds Lieutenant Jerrard was awarded the Victoria Cross.

At the beginning of April there were indications that the Austrians were making a concentration of troops astride the Brenta, although there were no real signs of an impending offensive. The weather throughout April was for the most part stormy and unfavourable for observation, from the air or the ground: such air reconnaissances as were made revealed occasional unusual movements within the Austrian lines, but the visibility was never good enough for adequate investigation.

When the atmospheric conditions improved in May there was a notable activity in the air. Enemy pilots several times succeeded in crossing the British lines, and they dropped propaganda leaflets on the British troops. Reconnaissances disclosed Austrian preparations which seemed to indicate an attack in the Val Sugana area, and, to forestal the enemy, it was decided, in the middle of May, to prepare for an Allied offensive on the Asiago front.

Within a few days, however, the whole position was changed. There was a marked increase of enemy artillery and aircraft activity in the Piave area, held by the Italians, and it became known from intelligence sources, and through captured prisoners, that a large-scale Austrian offensive was planned: as a result it was decided to postpone the proposed Allied attack on the Asiago plateau.

On the morning of the 30th of May thirty-five Sopwith 'Camels' from Nos. 28, 45, and 66 Squadrons, dropped a ton of bombs and fired 9,000 rounds of ammunition on enemy hutments in the northern section of the Val d'Assa. The pilots bombed in column with about 100 yards separating the aeroplanes, and the attacks were made from under 500 feet.

In June enemy air activity showed a further increase, and reconnaissances were made of the British area. To put a stop to these reconnaissance flights the offensive patrol zones of the Fourteenth Wing were changed. On the 10th of June a close patrol of the line between Forni and Gallio was instituted, and pilots were instructed that they were not to leave their allotted line except to attack hostile aeroplanes in the immediate vicinity of the British front. In addition to this barrage patrol, a second patrol, known as the long offensive patrol, was maintained parallel with the first, but about five miles distant between Casotto and Cismon. The patrols were, in the main, effective in preventing the enemy from making useful reconnaissances of the British area. It was not an uncommon sight to see enemy pilots jump from a burning or disabled aeroplane and float safely to earth by means of a parachute, and one who landed in this way in the British lines explained that he had twice before similarly escaped after his aeroplane had been set on fire in combat with British pilots over the Austrian lines.

The increase of air activity was marked on the Piave front. Although the indications of an impending offensive seemed conclusive, a puzzling feature was an absence of rail and road activity in the back areas. Time and again in May and June special long reconnaissances were made to report upon the rail and road activity behind the immediate front, but nothing unusual was discovered.[1]

After a brief though violent bombardment the Austrian infantry attacked along the whole front from the sea to east of the Astico on the morning of the 15th of June. The battle thus involved the Italians in the Piave, the French on Mount Grappa, and the British on the Asiago plateau. The British line was penetrated at a few points, but, except on the left, the line was quickly restored. The Austrians were ejected from their gains on the British left by counter-attack on the morning of the 16th. In the mountain area, held by the British, there was rain and mist on the morning of the 15th and the pilots could do little to help. In the afternoon, when the weather became worse, the squadrons of the Royal Air Force were diverted to assist the Italians on the Piave front where the flying conditions were less unfavourable. The Austrians had attacked the Italians under cover of smoke screens and, accompanied by low-flying aeroplanes, they had succeeded in crossing the Piave, following which reinforcements of fresh troops had pushed forward south of the river.

The first news received by the British that the Austrians were crossing the Piave opposite the Montello had been brought in at 11.40 a.m. by the pilot in a Sopwith 'Camel' returning from patrol. Three 'Camels' of No. 45 Squadron left at 12.30 p.m., followed by three more at 12.40 p.m., and by three at 1.05 p.m. They each carried four 20-lb. bombs which were aimed at pontoon boats. One hit a pontoon loaded with men, and another destroyed a boat leaving the shore: troops were also attacked with machine-gun fire. The pilots returned with valuable information which showed that the Austrians were crossing the Piave in great numbers at several points. It was then decided to employ all the available British aeroplanes to help the

---

[1] It was known later that the Austrian command took great precautions to conceal their intentions. Chiefly, the attacking divisions were kept well behind the lines and were only sent forward into their battle positions early on the morning of the attack. The tactics adopted were similar to those employed by the Germans in connexion with their counter-attack at Cambrai on the 30th of November 1917.

Italian Army. At 4 p.m., for example, there were thirty-three Sopwith 'Camels' supplementing the work of the Italian air service by attacks on bridges, rafts, boats, and Austrian troops in the Piave sector. Captain W. G. Barker of No. 66 Squadron, who took part in the attacks, has recorded: 'The Austrians had been successful against the 'Italians. They had succeeded in crossing the Piave oppo-'site the Montello. The Montello, owing to its height, 'dominated the Venetian plain and under its cover they 'had thrown two pontoon bridges across the river. The 'leader selected the bridge farthest upstream and individual 'bombing commenced from about 50 feet. This bridge 'was quickly broken in two places and the pontoons, caught 'by the fast current, were immediately dashed against the 'lower bridge, carrying it away also. When this attack 'commenced these bridges were crowded with troops which 'were attacked with machine-gun fire. Many were seen 'to be in the water. This done, troops on small islands and 'in row boats were machine-gunned'. . . .

About 6 p.m. on the 15th, in another series of attacks, some 3,000 Austrian troops were caught on the river's edge in the process of embarking in boats: bombs were dropped among them and they were afterwards attacked with machine-gun fire. In all 350 bombs of 20-lb. weight were dropped during the day in an attempt to stem the advance on the Piave front. It has been said that this prompt voluntary action on the part of the Royal Air Force, doubly valuable because it was made early, prevented a second disaster comparable with what had happened at Caporetto. This is going too far. What is certain, however, is that the bombing of the bridges, and the disorganization among the Austrian troops resulting from the attacks made by the Italian airmen and by the Royal Air Force, imposed delays in the initial stages of the advance which appreciably prejudiced the chances of success for the enemy.

Under cover of darkness on the 15th/16th of June, the Austrian engineers made strenuous and successful efforts to bridge the river once more, and anti-aircraft guns were also brought up to protect the bridges. Throughout the

16th the bombing and machine-gun attacks were continued, and about two tons weight of 20-lb. bombs were dropped. On the 17th there were clouds and rain which impeded the low-flying attacks. The bad weather, however, which had brought rain in the mountains for some days, proved of important value to the Italians. From a river of peaceful flow, the Piave was turned into a swirling torrent. In the mountain regions were felled trees, piled by the river banks, stored until the time should be favourable to float them downstream to market. Many of these were carried away and they were swept down from the upper reaches until they came to the bridges thrown across the river by the Austrians into which they crashed. Most of the damage was done on the morning of the 18th of June, and a British air observer who reconnoitred the river in the early afternoon reported that all the bridges had been swept away except two near San Dona di Piave: two other bridges were nearing completion.

The Italian counter-attack began, and led to desperate fighting, but by the 20th the Austrian troops were being slowly but relentlessly pushed back towards the Piave. On the 22nd, General von Boroevitch, in command of the enemy operations, issued orders for a general withdrawal across the river and, by the 24th, the situation, as it existed before the offensive began, had been restored.

On the 23rd, when the Austrian withdrawal was in full progress, the whole Royal Air Force strength on the front was employed to help the Italian bombing squadrons to harass the retreating Austrian troops, as many as fifty British aeroplanes being engaged at one time (44 Sopwith 'Camels' and six R.E.8's).

The enemy effort had been an ambitious one. Austria had lost 20,000 prisoners and many guns, and the offensive power of the Austrian army had been definitely weakened. For the Italians the successful counter-attack marked an important victory. Caporetto had been avenged, and the morale of the Italian army and of the Italian people had been restored. The rupture of the Austrian bridge communications across the Piave was, we have seen, in the main an act of God, but on the critical opening day of the offensive the squadrons of the Royal Air Force had done much to hamper the free movement of the Austrian troops. An Austrian airman, shot down soon after the battle ended, had in his possession a cutting from a Vienna newspaper in which an Austrian correspondent had written of the early attempts to force the crossing of the Piave. His eyewitness account reads: 'Suddenly aeroplanes also appear. 'They come silently down from a great height in far-'reaching volplanes. Now their motors hum again and 'their machine-guns rattle. A hail of steel pelts down on 'the pontoons, which sink riddled. The guns of the defence 'bark from the bank and fragments of their shrapnel en-'danger the lives of their own men, men whom they wish 'to protect. One, two, three of the great Caproni bom-'barding aeroplanes descend, shot down on the mud of the 'Montello. A Nieuport comes down like a torch hurled 'from Heaven—the famous pilot, Major Barracca, is a heap 'of ashes. His list of victories is the same as that of his most 'victorious Austrian adversary, Captain Broumousky, who 'conquered 34 opponents. Lieutenant von Hoffman, in 'peace time a Ministerial official in Vienna, and his band, 'dash against the biplanes. Like raging bulldogs the Eng-'lish now advance on their furiously swift Sopwiths against 'our airmen, engineers, artillery, and infantry. Nothing, 'absolutely nothing, avails. The enemy pilots are too 'numerous, the enemy's shells too many. Like Sisyphus 'multiplied a hundredfold the bridge-builders work inces-'santly: they fall and disappear in the flood without a cry; 'they launch new pontoons; they think out new methods 'of transport from bank to bank—nothing helps; absolutely 'nothing avails. Six times are the bridges and footways 'completed, six times are they destroyed.'

In July there was quiet on the British front, but there was some co-operation between the Royal Air Force and the Italian air service. On the 2nd of July the Italian Third Army began an offensive action against the Austrians at the mouth of the Piave, and after four days' fighting gained its limited objectives. Because the Italians were short of aeroplanes and trained personnel a few British

R.E.8's were flown daily to the aerodrome at Malcontenta, and they worked from there under the orders of the Italians, mainly in co-operation with the artillery for which Italian air observers were flown: protection for the R.E.8's was provided by offensive patrols of Sopwith 'Camels'. The special co-operation ended on the 10th of July, but on the following day R.E.8's of No. 34 Squadron began to help the Italian Fourth Army in the Grappa sector. This help, because of the shortage of Italian aeroplanes, continued to be given to the Italian Fourth Army until September.

There were occasional bombing attacks on Austrian dumps, &c., in July and August, and there was some desultory, but often intense air fighting in which the Austrian pilots fought courageously, though with a consistent lack of success. On the 11th of August Sopwith 'Camels' of No. 28 Squadron, while bombing hutments, &c., in the Val d'Assa, exploded an ammunition dump. On the 31st of August a patrol of six enemy fighters crossed the British lines and was intercepted by three Sopwith 'Camels' of No. 45 Squadron, led by Captain J. Cottle. There was a sharp fight in which the Austrian pilots were outmatched, except in courage, and all six enemy fighters were shot down, five of them falling within the Allied lines: the Sopwith 'Camels' suffered no hurt. The reports of much of the fighting which took place in the air at this time are similarly one-sided, and the above episode is given not because it was exceptional in kind, but because the fight took place on the Allied side of the lines and there could be no question, therefore, about the result: it usually happened that the victims of the British pilots fell in Austrian territory and confirmation of a victory was often impossible to obtain. There was an occasion, on the 8th of August, when four Bristol Fighters of No. 139 Squadron, while on a routine reconnaissance, flew over the aerodrome at Pergine and were engaged by three Albatros fighters which were patrolling the area. The Bristol Fighter pilots destroyed two of the enemy aeroplanes in flames, but the third escaped. It was afterwards known that the combat took place while the Emperor Carl was paying a visit of inspection to the aerodrome, and that the Albatros fighters had been ordered to fly on protective patrol while the inspection was in progress.

In September a part of the British force was withdrawn from Italy to France, including No. 45 Squadron which left on the 20th and joined the Independent Force. The weather was often bad during the month, and such air operations as took place were of a routine kind.

At the beginning of October there were attacks of some interest on two Austrian flying training schools. One of these schools was at Campoformido, south-west of Udine, and it had been started to give a 'refresher' course to pilots whose flying on the front was deemed to be unsatisfactory: the school was expanded as a centre of advanced instruction also for observers, mechanics, and wireless operators. The second school was at Egna, south of Bolzano, where pilots received advanced training on service type aeroplanes. Campoformido was bombed by twenty-three Sopwith 'Camels' of Nos. 28 and 66 Squadrons, with three others as escorts, on the 4th of October. Ten 40-lb. phosphorous and seventy-seven 20-lb. bombs were dropped, and twenty-two hits were scored on the hangars and sheds. It was afterwards known that, in addition to miscellaneous stores, two hangars were demolished with ten new aeroplanes: three enemy fighters were also destroyed in combat. The flying school at Egna was attacked on the 5th of October by twenty-two Sopwith 'Camels' with twenty 40-lb. phosphorous bombs and forty-two of 20-lb. weight. A shed and hangars were burnt and some of the bombs, which were dropped from heights under 500 feet, exploded among aeroplanes lined up on the landing-ground. The Austrian aerodrome at Pergine was bombed by Bristol Fighters of No. 139 Squadron on the 7th of October.

The Battle of Vittorio Veneto

In October, General Diaz, the Italian Commander-in-Chief, was ready to strike a final blow at the Austrian armies, by which he was moderately outnumbered. He had at his disposal fifty-one Italian divisions, three British, two

French, one Czecho-Slovak, and also an American regiment. For the offensive Lord Cavan was entrusted with the command of the Tenth Army made up of the Italian XI Corps and the British XIV Corps (7th and 23rd Divisions). The British 48th Division remained in position on the Asiago plateau because it was desired to make as little change as possible in order to preserve secrecy, and it was incorporated temporarily in the XII Corps of the Italian Sixth Army.

At a conference on the 13th of October, General Diaz outlined his plan. His intention was that the Italian Tenth, Eighth, and Twelfth Armies should force the crossing of the Piave and advance to drive a wedge between the Austrian Fifth and Sixth Armies, and cut the communications between the Austrian forces in the mountains and those in the plains. The battle was to begin with a feint attack in the Grappa sector by the Italian Fourth Army. The task allotted to Lord Cavan's Tenth Army was to reach the Livenza between Portobuffole and Sacile in order to protect the flanks of the Eighth and Twelfth Armies in their northward advance. The British 7th and 23rd Divisions took over a part of the front from the Italian XI Corps, stretching from Salettuol to Palazzon, on the 21st of October. The British troops in the forward area wore Italian uniforms, and orders were given that no British guns were to fire before the general bombardment began. By these precautions it was hoped to conceal from the Austrians the presence of British troops in the Piave sector.

Before the British movements began the units of the Royal Air Force were concentrated in the Asiago area.[1] There was, however, no hurry to transfer these units to the Piave front because it was undesirable to show expansions on the aerodromes in that area. No. 33 Kite Balloon Section was withdrawn from the mountains to Grossa on the 2nd of October, and No. 139 Squadron moved to the

---

[1] At the beginning of October the units of the Royal Air Force were disposed as follows: Fourteenth Wing head-quarters and No. 28 Squadron, Sarcedo; Nos. 34 and 139 Squadrons, Villaverla; No. 66, S. Pietro in Gu (C. Piazza); No. 7 Kite Balloon Section, M. Cavalletto; No. 3 Kite Balloon Section, M. Mazze.

same place a week later. The Fourteenth Wing head-quarters took up new quarters in the Villa Margherita, north of Treviso, on the 19th of October, and No. 7 Kite Balloon Section went to Villorba on the following day. The Allied offensive was originally timed for the 25th of October, and No. 34 Squadron was transferred to S. Luca aerodrome, north of Istrana, and No. 28 Squadron to Limbraga, on the 22nd. At the same time the Fourteenth Wing head-quarters vacated the Villa Margherita and moved to Dosson.

There had been heavy rains which brought flood waters down the Piave, and the date of the attack was put back two days, to the 27th. The bombardment began on the evening of the 26th, and there was again a downpour all night which augured ill for the offensive, but on the morning of the 27th the skies cleared and they continued clear until the end.

The Piave, on the front of attack, was about one and a half miles wide, made up of many channels dotted with islands. The biggest of these, Grave di Papadopoli, three miles long and a mile broad, had been partly captured in the night of the 23rd/24th as a preliminary to the main attack, and the occupation had been completed two nights later. With this island in Allied possession the task of bridging the Piave had been made incomparably easier.

Mainly because of the need for secrecy, but partly also on account of the bad weather, there had been little flying by the Royal Air Force squadrons over the front of the attack before the offensive was launched. No photographs of the Piave sector were available, and No. 139 Squadron was given a programme of photography to cover the corps front. Attempts were made to comply with the orders, but until the 22nd the weather was unfavourable. On that day the whole corps area was covered, and the photographic section of the squadron, working at high pressure through the night, made 5,000 prints which, to save time, were distributed direct to the formations concerned. Although the orders were that no R.E.8's must appear over the Piave front before the battle, it was desirable that the pilots and observers in the contact patrol Flight of No. 34 Squadron, who would be required to keep close touch with the battle, should have knowledge of the ground. This they obtained by making use of two Bristol Fighters borrowed from No. 139 Squadron. It was arranged that, once the advance began, the contact patrol observers should, as necessary, call upon the Italian troops, as well as upon the British, to display flares or ground strips, and the observers were to drop messages for the Italian report centres. The Italian flying personnel, engaged on similar work of co-operation, could likewise call upon British troops to show flares.

The Tenth Army attacked at 6.45 a.m. on Sunday the 27th of October. Contact patrol messages received during the day showed the British troops across the Piave and pushing forward to their final objectives. A message flashed by panel from the ground from a party of British forward troops in the morning stated that they were short of ammunition, and six R.E.8's of No. 34 Squadron subsequently dropped 5,000 rounds of small arms ammunition in sacks attached to parachutes: it was seen that the sacks were recovered by the men. Enemy pilots were very active all day: in particular, they attacked the bridges across the Piave and the troops crowded in their neighbourhood. The bridge at Salettuol was shelled as well as bombed, but although there were appreciable casualties the bridge remained intact. Six of the aeroplanes of No. 34 Squadron were fiercely attacked at different times while co-operating with the British artillery or the infantry, and as a result the commanders of the two artillery Flights of the squadron were lost, one missing and the other wounded. By special arrangement nine Sopwith 'Camels', in patrols of three, had attacked the enemy kite balloons shortly after the offensive opened: three of the enemy balloons had fallen in flames. Pilots of the Sopwith 'Camel' squadron had been instructed also to watch for troop movements to and from the front at specified places and times throughout the day, and to make low-flying attacks as opportunity offered: many more targets were presented than the fighters could attack. An attempt was made to destroy a bridge over the Monticano river near Vazzola, but the bombs missed and, as it happened, it was well they did because British cavalry on the 29th surprised the Austrian garrison at the bridge, which was taken intact.

On the 28th the Allied advance continued, and it was reported in some detail by the aeroplanes of No. 34 Squadron. The fighter pilots were mostly employed in attacks on the Austrian columns in retreat along the main roads. On the 29th the Austrians resisted on the line of the Monticano, but the air observers reported an increase in the density of the retreating columns, and by the following day the retreat had become a rout, which ended on the 4th of November when an armistice came into effect.

As soon as the Austrian resistance had begun to crumble, the main concern of the squadrons had been to help shatter the enemy morale through bombing and machine-gun attacks. It was neither possible nor necessary for the corps squadrons to give detailed information about the final stages of the advance. So-called 'situation' flights were made by which the broad movements were reported. Nos. 28, 66, and 139 Squadrons were engaged almost to the full extent of their energies on low-flying attacks, supplementing the intensive bombing by the Italian air service.[1] The enemy aerodromes were over-run and there was increasing chaos along the lines of communication, with the result that opposition in the air ceased as soon as the rout began. In the few final days the one concern of the fighter pilots was to make a maximum number of journeys to attack the plentiful ground targets: it was all attack and no defence, terrible, but mercifully short.

[1] In the final advance the Royal Air Force squadrons dropped 20,000-lb. weight of bombs and fired 51,000 rounds of ammunition from low heights, at a cost of seven aeroplanes missing.

CHAPTER VIII

MACEDONIA

Final Air Operations, 1918

[Map, facing]

It will be recalled[1] that in September 1917 the Commander-in-Chief of the British Salonika force had urged the War Office to increase the air strength at his disposal by sending bombers and up-to-date fighters to enable him to extend his air operations. 'I am anxious', he had said, 'to 'widen the scope of the offensive measures undertaken by 'the Flying Corps, the more so as the size of my force pre-'cludes any other method of making our presence really 'felt in this country.' The response had not been encouraging. The War Office sent a few S.E.5a fighters in December 1917, but it was not until the spring of 1918 that enough had been received to bring about a change in the general air position.

With the formation of a fighting squadron, No. 150, in April 1918, air superiority passed to the British, and it was retained until the end of hostilities. No. 150 Squadron began with one Flight from each of Nos. 17 and 47 Squadrons, actually transferred on the 26th of April: the third Flight was formed independently on the 7th of May. The two original Flights took with them S.E.5a's and Bristol monoplanes, but the third Flight was equipped with Sopwith 'Camels'.[2]

The first of the bombers for which Lieutenant-General Sir G. F. Milne had asked were not received until August 1918, nearly a year after the request had been made. On the 21st of August No. 47 Squadron, which had worked with only two Flights of Armstrong-Whitworth's since the transfer of a Flight to No. 150 Squadron in April, was brought up to strength with the formation of a Flight of D.H.9 aeroplanes.[3] No. 17 Squadron worked with two

---

[1] Vol. V, p. 362.
[2] The strength of the squadron at the Armistice was 9 S.E.5a's, 7 Sopwith 'Camels', 1 Bristol monoplane, and 1 B.E.12.
[3] At the Armistice No. 47 Squadron had 10 Armstrong-Whitworths

Flights until the 14th of June, when a third Flight was formed, but the squadron remained under strength until September, when a Flight of D.H.9's arrived as reinforcements.[1]

During the summer of 1918, therefore, the two corps squadrons were not up to establishment, but the few up-to-date fighters of No. 150 Squadron so dominated the enemy air service that Nos. 17 and 47 Squadrons were enabled to increase their offensive bombing activities, in which they were helped from time to time by naval air detachments stationed at Thasos and Stavros. The two-seaters of Nos. 17 and 47 Squadrons, other than the D.H.9's, could be employed for bombing only if the observers were left behind, and protection was therefore provided by fighting escorts from No. 150 Squadron.

Notable bombing targets were the aerodromes at Hudova, behind the Dojran front, and at Drama on the Struma front. On the morning of the 8th of May, as an example, twenty aeroplanes from Nos. 17 and 47 Squadrons, escorted by fighters from No. 150 Squadron, bombed Drama. Eighteen of the same bombers attacked the aerodrome again in the afternoon, and sixteen naval aircraft also bombed the same target during the day: damage was done to hangars and to aeroplanes on the ground.

On the 13th of May ten aeroplanes from the detachment working at Thasos, under the orders of the Rear-Admiral, Aegean, flew to Marian aerodrome for two days' work in co-operation with Nos. 17 and 47 Squadrons. On the journey to Marian the naval bombers made a diversion to attack an enemy dump at Chepeldze, and after taking on a new load of bombs at Marian they attacked the dump at Marinopolje station, which had been previously bombed by fourteen aeroplanes from Nos. 17, 47, and 150 Squadrons. Next day the main targets were the dumps at Livunovo and Kakara, and the station at Demir Hisar, all squadrons taking part, after which the naval aeroplanes

and 6 D.H.9's. Major F. A. Bates had succeeded Major G. D. Gardner in command of the squadron on the 1st of August.

[1] At the Armistice No. 17 Squadron had 9 Armstrong-Whitworths, 6 D.H.9's, and 1 B.E.12.

flew back to their base at Thasos. On the 23rd of May sixteen aeroplanes from Nos. 17 and 47 Squadrons, escorted by eleven fighters from No. 150 Squadron, dropped $1\frac{1}{4}$ tons of bombs on the aerodrome at Hudova on the Dojran front.

Such bombing as that instanced above was in pursuance of Lieutenant-General Milne's wish to strike at the enemy through the only medium open to him. At the end of May, however, there were bombing attacks which aimed at helping Allied military operations west of the Vardar. General Guillaumat, Commander-in-Chief of the Allied Armies of the East, was planning an offensive on the Macedonian front, and by way of rehearsal, and with the further object of testing the quality of the Greek troops under his orders, he decided to capture about eight miles of front trench system, from north-east of Ljumnica to north of the village of Lunzi. To keep the enemy in doubt about the place of attack, artillery bombardments and raids were variously made by the French, the British, and by the Serbs. The British began with a bombardment on the front of the 22nd Division on the 28th of May, and the fire was extended to the front of the 26th Division next day. On the 29th, when the 7th South Wales Borderers made a raid on the Dojran front, ten aeroplanes, with an escort of eleven fighters, bombed the station, dump, and aerodrome at Hudova. On the same day an aeroplane observed for the fire of the 424th Siege Battery (8-inch howitzers) which had been loaned to the French for direct support on the main front. At 4.55 a.m. on the 30th of May the Greek infantry began their attack, and not long after they had started ten Royal Air Force aeroplanes again bombed Hudova, the objective being the aerodrome, where hangars were damaged and a petrol dump set on fire: these air attacks were part of the British activity to divert the attention of the enemy. The whole action was brilliantly executed, the enemy was taken by surprise, and the Allied troops captured all their objectives on the 30th of May, together with 1,812 prisoners. The victory, although a minor one, caused elation in Greece, where it helped to consolidate the position of M. Venizelos and to cement the unity of the Greek army.

From May onwards there were important changes in the dispositions of the British troops as a result of the taking over of a part of the Struma front by Greek divisions. The situation from the sea to the Vardar about the middle of July, when the movements had been completed, was as shown in the sketch, facing. While the moves were being made there were indications that the Bulgarians were preparing an offensive. Early in June air reconnaissance reports showed that Bulgar ammunition dumps behind the Dojran front had increased in size, as had camps and dumps in the Strumica valley. Furthermore, although enemy aerodromes appeared unchanged, there was more activity in the air than for some weeks, and many combats resulted. The signs that the Bulgars might be preparing an attack were confirmed from an unexpected quarter. Towards the middle of June deserters began to cross to the British lines in unusual numbers, and they brought with them the same story—that they had surrendered to avoid taking part in a battle which was about to take place between lakes Dojran and Tahinos. Lieutenant-General Sir C. J. Briggs, commanding the XVI Corps, with the approval of Lieutenant-General Milne, took full precautionary measures, but on the 17th of June newly arrived deserters gave the information that the attack, which had apparently been planned to coincide with the Austrian offensive on the Piave on the 15th of June, had had to be cancelled on account of a mutiny among the Bulgar soldiers. As soon as it was clear that there would be no enemy attack relief movements on the British front were resumed.

Meanwhile, the French General Guillaumat had been suddenly recalled to an appointment in France, and he was succeeded as Allied Commander-in-Chief by General Franchet d'Espérey, who formally took over on the 18th of June. Both generals were representative of the military genius of their country. Quiet, courteous, incisive, cautious in preparation, but swift and bold in action, each in his turn inspired confidence in the Allied armies on the Salonika front, and each contributed a share to the shaping of the final plan by which the enemy armies in Macedonia were subjugated.

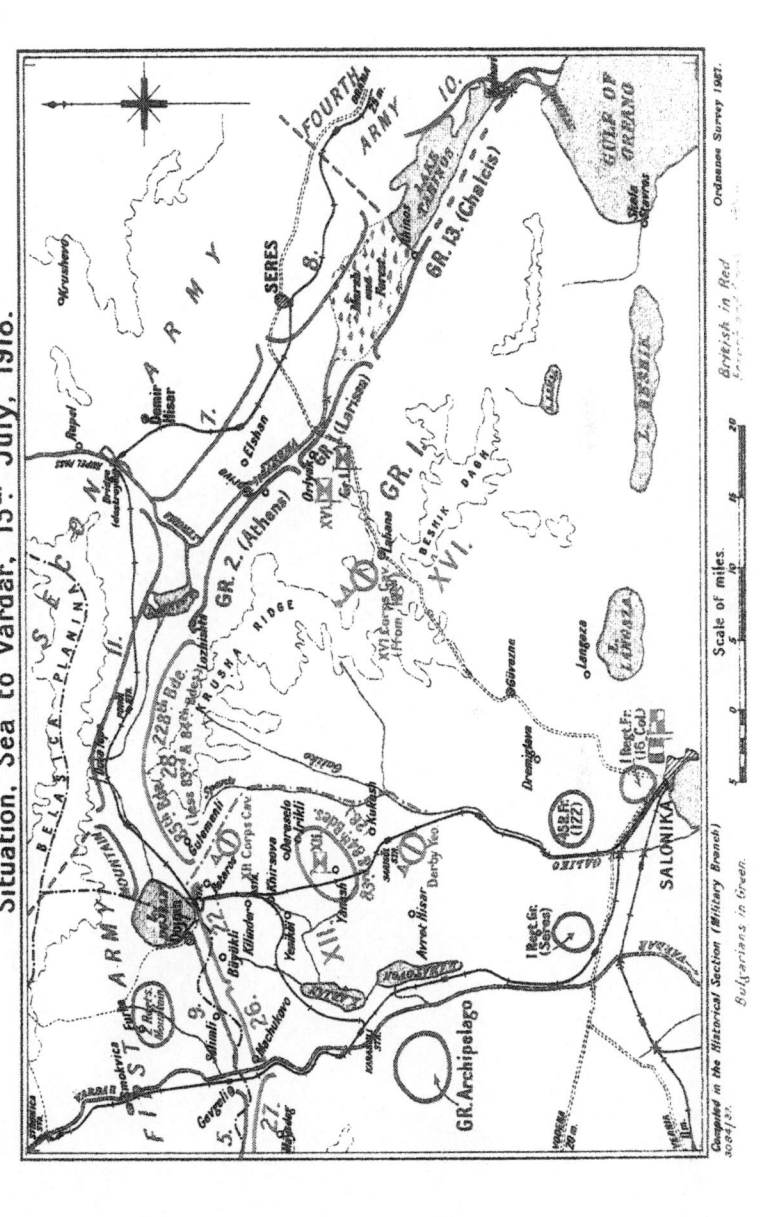

PLANNING THE OFFENSIVE

A change of command of the Royal Air Force is also to be noted. On the 19th of June Lieutenant-Colonel G. E. Todd succeeded Lieutenant-Colonel G. W. P. Dawes in command of the Sixteenth Wing.

During July and August there were no important operations on the ground, but the air squadrons did not cease from their bombing attacks, usually made by twenty or more aeroplanes at a time, on aerodromes, railheads, and dumps. In August the work of co-operation with the artillery gradually increased in volume, and the squadrons were also called upon to extend their photography of enemy territory. The reason for this expansion of the work of co-operation was the impending Allied offensive, destined to be the beginning of the end of hostilities. The authorities in England had, from the inception of the Salonika campaign, set their faces against a major offensive in the Balkans, and the strength of the British army in Macedonia had consequently never exceeded what was necessary to maintain a defensive role. How the Salonika front came to be the scene of the first decisive campaign of the war makes curious and interesting reading, for which the student is referred to the official military history of the campaign.[1] Although everything was ready, it was not certain until the 10th of September that the Allied Governments would agree to the offensive. On that day, however, General Franchet d'Espérey received a telegram sent by Monsieur Clemenceau in Paris to inform him that full agreement had at last been reached and that he was authorized to begin the Salonika operations when judged desirable.

General Milne, when expressing to the British War Office his adherence to the plans for the Allied offensive, had stated that success on the front allotted to the British army was unlikely if he did not receive necessary reinforcements. His demands were modest. He asked only for sufficient additional personnel to bring his units up to strength, and for a small reinforcement of artillery. He would, however, require a considerable increase of

[1] *Military Operations, Macedonia*, by Captain Cyril Falls, vol. ii, ch. vi.

ammunition, in particular of chemical shell. He was weak in heavy artillery for counter-battery work and it was his opinion that this weakness could best be mitigated through the employment of gas shell by which the enemy batteries, many of them sunk in elaborate concrete emplacements, might be neutralized. Finally, he stood in urgent need of spare parts for his mechanical transport, and of motor tyres and inner tubes. In the result the British Commander-in-Chief received only a modicum of what he asked for. 'What happened was that the British authorities 'at home gave their approval to the attack but did not 'supply the means which he declared to be necessary.'[1]

The task of the British Salonika army in the final offensive, difficult enough, was made more difficult by the failure to send the reinforcements and equipment judged by the British Commander-in-Chief to be essential. The anxieties of General Milne are sympathetically set out in the official military history and it would be out of place here to make further reference to the subject. What is of particular interest, however, is that those anxieties derived in some measure from the activities of German bombing squadrons on the Western front. On the night of the 11th of August 1918 German bombers destroyed No. 2 Base Mechanical Transport Depot at Calais, and the spare parts, tyres, and inner tubes for a majority of the British transport vehicles in service on the Western front became ashes.[2] The situation which resulted called for exceptional remedial measures, and indeed the disaster was on a scale which precluded any early possibility of attention to the wants, no matter how serious or urgent, of outside theatres of war.

How far the German bombers were also responsible for the shortage of shells on the Macedonian front cannot be exactly determined. Between the 19th and 22nd of May 1918, however, the bombers had destroyed more than 12,000 tons of ammunition as a result of successful attacks on two British main ordnance depots on the Western front.[3] This did not lead to a real shortage of ammunition in France, but the German success brought home to the

---

[1] *Military Operations, Macedonia*, vol. ii, p. 113.
[2] See pp. 429–31.   [3] See pp. 423–5.

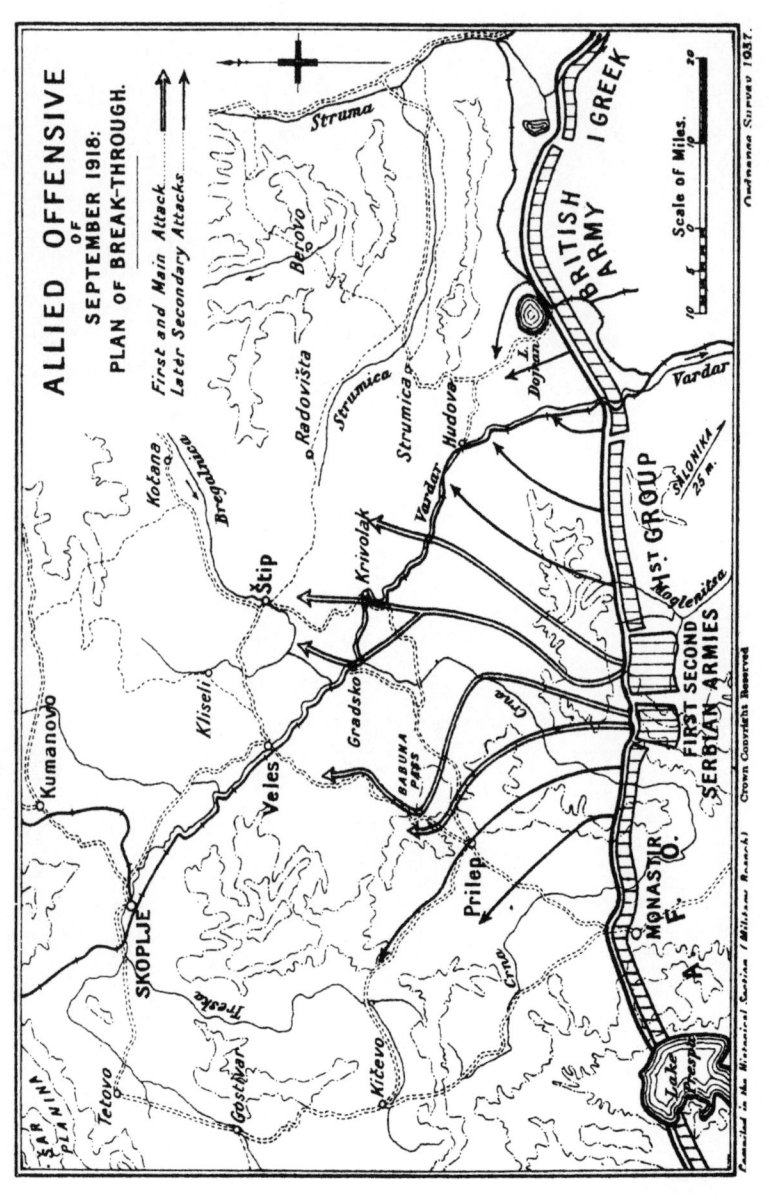

authorities the undue vulnerability of the ammunition depots, and, until steps taken to reduce this vulnerability should become effective, anxiety about the supply of ammunition to the Western front could not be allayed. The least that may be said is that General Milne's request would have received timely and more favourable consideration if the enforced pre-occupation of the home authorities with the ammunition needs of the armies in France had not existed. That air activity in northern France should have some effect upon military plans in Macedonia affords a striking example of the far-reaching results obtainable from successful bombing operations, *provided the targets are well chosen.*

In the offensive plan adopted by General Franchet d'Espérey the main role was allotted to the Serbian armies. The reader may the more easily appreciate the essence of the plan if he refers to the sketch, facing. The key point was Gradsko, situated at the junction of the Crna with the Vardar, and some thirty-five miles from the front line. If Gradsko could be rapidly taken the chief lines of the Bulgarian communications would be cut or threatened, the enemy forces would be divided, and the way would be opened for a decisive exploitation of the break-through. To advance against Gradsko along the narrow and difficult Vardar valley would be to attack the enemy where he was strongest, and where the chances of success, certainly of an early success, were remote. General Franchet d'Espérey therefore decided to attack from the mountains of the Moglena between the Crna and the Vardar, a formidable starting-point. On the chosen sector the Bulgars were holding forward positions which appeared to be impregnable, but if these could be carried by surprise in one rush the Serbian troops, fighting-fit and elated, would subsequently be hard to stop, more particularly if the enemy reserves could be pinned down on the remainder of the front.

The first of the secondary attacks which were to follow the main assault was to be made under the orders of General Milne against the Bulgar entrenched system on the high ground between Lake Dojran and the Vardar.

The group of divisions immediately west of the Vardar was to link the main Serbian attack with that at Dojran. The opposing forces along the whole front were approximately equal in strength, with the exception that the Allied armies had great superiority in aircraft, a total of about 200 aeroplanes against 80.

A preliminary operation on the British front, to make the enemy believe that a thrust up the Vardar valley was contemplated, took place on the 1st of September. The objective was a forward Bulgar position west of the river known as the Roche Noire salient, and the attack, which was reported by air contact patrol observers and proved entirely successful, was made by two battalions of the 27th Division at 5.30 p.m. At the moment when the infantry were launched four aeroplanes each dropped eight 20-lb. bombs on a regimental head-quarters in the village of Gevgeli, and each pilot subsequently fired a few hundred rounds of machine-gun ammunition at ground targets. One of the aeroplanes (pilot, Captain J. B. Walmsley; observer, Lieutenant R. D. de Pass) was struck by a bullet which exploded a box of Very lights alongside the pilot and set his coat alight. Under the impression that the aeroplane had caught fire the pilot spun earthwards, but his observer seized the extinguisher and put out the flames. The pilot thereupon came out of the spin and turned for home at a height of 500 feet, but he had not gone far when a tracer bullet hit the engine, which took fire. The observer played on the flames with the extinguisher while the aeroplane was piloted to the nearby aerodrome at Gorgop, where French mechanics finally overcame the fire with sand.

The British military and air activity brought out patrols of German fighting aircraft, but the combats which ensued were indecisive. For a day or two the enemy pilots continued to show themselves rather more than they had done for some time past. On the 3rd of September a formation of six fighters attacked a Royal Air Force photographic aeroplane and its Bristol monoplane escort near Lake Dojran. The monoplane was shot down into the lake, and the last that was seen of its pilot, Lieutenant J. P. Cavers, was when he was struggling in the water clear of his aeroplane under fire from the German aircraft: the reconnaissance aeroplane escaped. The final stages of the combat were witnessed by the pilots of four S.E.5a's as they were making their way home from escorting bombers during an attack on Miletkovo. The S.E.5a's, which were joined by two Sopwith 'Camels', dived on the Germans from 13,000 feet, and a general fight took place about 500 feet from the ground with the result that four of the enemy aeroplanes were destroyed. One British pilot pursued his quarry many miles behind the Bulgar lines and his final burst of fire, which caused the German aeroplane to crash, was aimed from a few dozen feet above the ground.

In preparation for the opening of the great offensive the work of the co-operating squadrons was mainly to help the artillery to register targets, and also photography of the enemy positions. The arrival of D.H.9 aeroplanes made extended reconnaissances possible, and it may be assumed that the passage of Royal Air Force aircraft a hundred miles or so from the front, over places where they had never before been seen, impressed the enemy people in a way which made them readier to throw their hand in after the Allied offensive had broken the defence lines. The D.H.9's set out on journeys which totalled as much as 300 miles, and photographs were taken of such distant centres as Kyustendil and Radomir. It is of interest that the latter town, no more than twenty miles south-west of Sofia, proclaimed a republic before the month had ended, and sent its menfolk, 6,000 or so strong, marching upon the capital.

The artillery bombardment, of great intensity, which preceded the Franco-Serbian assault on the main front, began at 8 a.m. on the 14th of September, and through the long day the mountains echoed and re-echoed with a thunder they had never known. At 5.30 a.m. on the 15th the assaulting divisions, French and Serbian, making up the Serbian Second Army, jumped from their trenches to begin the advance. Behind them were the supporting Serbian divisions, and on their left were the troops of the Serbian First Army, waiting for the right moment to intervene. Lean, skilful, steel-hard, fired and fortified by the conviction that they were about to free their country from the invader, the assaulting Serbs stormed the steep hillsides and won the whole of the Bulgar first line. The French were held for a time, but early on the 16th they, too, had completed their gains, and the front of attack was thereupon enlarged as planned. The advance made on the 16th took the troops forward an additional five miles, through the enemy second line of trenches, and by the end of the following day the attackers had progressed twenty miles from their starting-off places: the way to victory had been opened.

The attack on the British front began on the 18th of September. West of Lake Dojran were the British 26th and 22nd Divisions, the Greek Seres Division, and a French regiment, making up the XII Corps under Lieutenant-General Sir H. F. M. Wilson. East of the lake was the Crete Division and the British 28th Division under the XVI Corps commander, Lieutenant-General Sir C. F. Briggs. The order of battle of the Royal Air Force units on the morning of the 18th of September was as follows:

Sixteenth Wing Head-quarters . . . . . Salonika
   (Lieutenant-Colonel G. E. Todd)
   Advanced Head-quarters . . . . . Yanesh

No. 17 Squadron (Major S. G. Hodges)
   Head-quarters and 'C' Flight . . . . . Lahana
   (Armstrong-Whitworths)
   'A' and 'B' Flights . . . . Amberkoj
   (Armstrong-Whitworths and D.H.9's)

No. 47 Squadron (Major F. A. Bates)
   Head-quarters and 'C' Flight . . . . . Yanesh
   (Armstrong-Whitworths)
   'A' and 'B' Flights . . . . Hajdarli
   (Armstrong-Whitworths and D.H.9's)

No. 150 Squadron (Major W. R. B. McBain)
   Head-quarters and 'B' and 'C' Flights . . . . Kirech
   (S.E.5a's and Sopwith 'Camels')
   'A' Flight . . . . Marian
   (S.E.5a's)

No. 22 Balloon Company (Captain J. Y. McLean)
   26 Balloon Section . . . . Gulemenli
   27   ,,   ,, ... Yeniköi

Aircraft Park (Major C. H. A. Hirtzel) . . . . Salonika

The orders were that 'C' Flight of No. 47 Squadron would be responsible for artillery work, while 'B' Flight undertook contact patrol and close reconnaissance duties, all for the XII Corps; 'C' Flight of No. 17 Squadron was to work similarly for the XVI Corps, using the former aerodrome of No. 47 Squadron at Snevche as required. Protection for these co-operating aeroplanes was to be provided by fighters from No. 150 Squadron. 'A' and 'B' Flights of No. 17 Squadron were to be ready to answer calls from either of the two British corps for bombing and machine-gun attacks within four miles of the front, and 'A' Flight of No. 47 Squadron was to be responsible for strategical reconnaissance, and for bombing beyond the four-mile limit. No. 26 Balloon Section was at the disposal of the XVI Corps, and No. 27 Section at that of the XII Corps.

Meanwhile special preliminary air operations had begun on the 14th of September coincident with the opening of the bombardment on the main Franco–Serbian front of attack. On this day five aeroplanes bombed Hudova aerodrome, next day six attacked the station at Demir Kapija, and on the 16th five bombers again attacked Hudova aerodrome and dump. These attacks were on a small scale, but as their object was to help rivet the attention of the Bulgarians to the Dojran front there would have been little point in risking more aeroplanes than judged strictly essential, especially in view of the arduous work which lay ahead once the battle began. On the 17th, the eve of the battle on the British front, what little activity there was in the air was mostly confined to flights in co-operation with batteries engaged on registration.

The infantry attack on the Vardar–Dojran front was launched at 5.8 a.m. on the 18th of September. A distinguished French general who inspected the battle-field after hostilities had ended described it as the 'most terrible' position to assault which he had ever seen, and the author of this history, who knew the greater part of the Macedonian front as it appeared from the air, can testify that the Vardar–Dojran sector stood out as the most intricately formidable part of the Bulgarian line. Had the spirit of the Bulgar troops defending the front been weakened by news of the happenings west of the Vardar the assault would have had chances of success. Those troops, however, if they had knowledge of the real extent of the Franco-Serbian victory, which is doubtful, were unaffected. Their confidence, discipline, and skill were revealed as unimpaired. Nevertheless, the Greeks, who fought well, captured the foremost position and the intermediate position from Dojran Hill to Hill 340, while the 22nd Division took the enemy front work, known as O.6, on the 19th when the attack was renewed. No further ground was won. Although the attacks had failed of their immediate aim, which was to 'gain possession of the "P" ridge and the 'neighbouring high ground, and to exploit this success by 'all available means', they had achieved the object of pinning down the strong enemy concentration between the Vardar and Lake Dojran, and they had compelled the Bulgars to engage their local reserves. It has sometimes been said that an attack on a smaller scale would have had the same result, but, in the words of the military historian, 'the Bul-'garians, with their excellent observation posts, were in a 'position to distinguish at once between a demonstration 'and a genuine attack'.[1]

During the two days' fighting the aeroplanes did what was necessary in the way of reporting upon the movements of the attacking infantry and of the enemy, but the nature of the struggle was such that their chief usefulness was to indicate the positions of the active enemy batteries. Altogether 151 wireless calls for fire upon hostile guns were sent down from the air on the 18th, and 121 on the 19th, and many of the calls received adequate response. Owing to the smoke and the dust of the barrage fire the air observers could obtain their information, whether of the progress of the battle or about active hostile guns, only by flying near the ground, often below the line of the observation posts on the Grand Couronné and 'P' ridge. All the aeroplanes were hit by shell splinters or by bullets, but the wonder is that no more than one fell on the battle-field: it was directly hit by a shell and crashed in flames.

[1] Falls, *Macedonia*, vol. ii, p. 163.

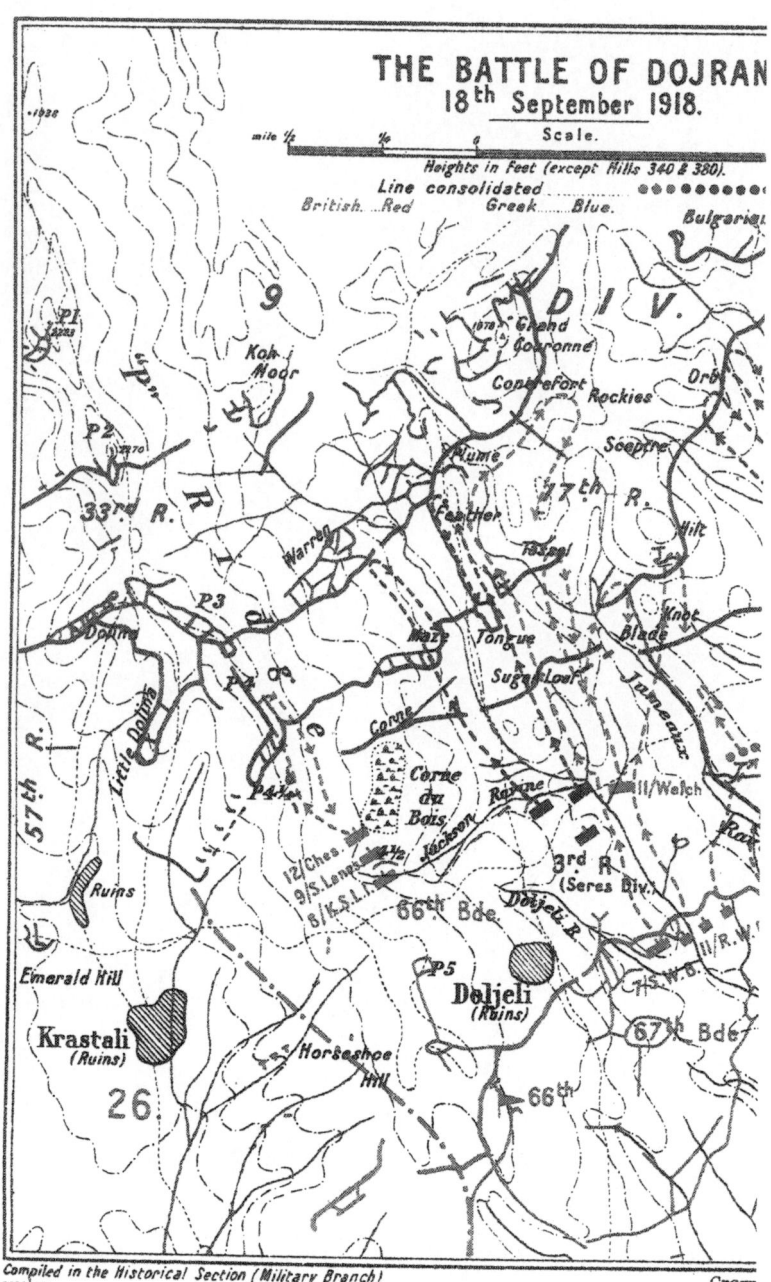

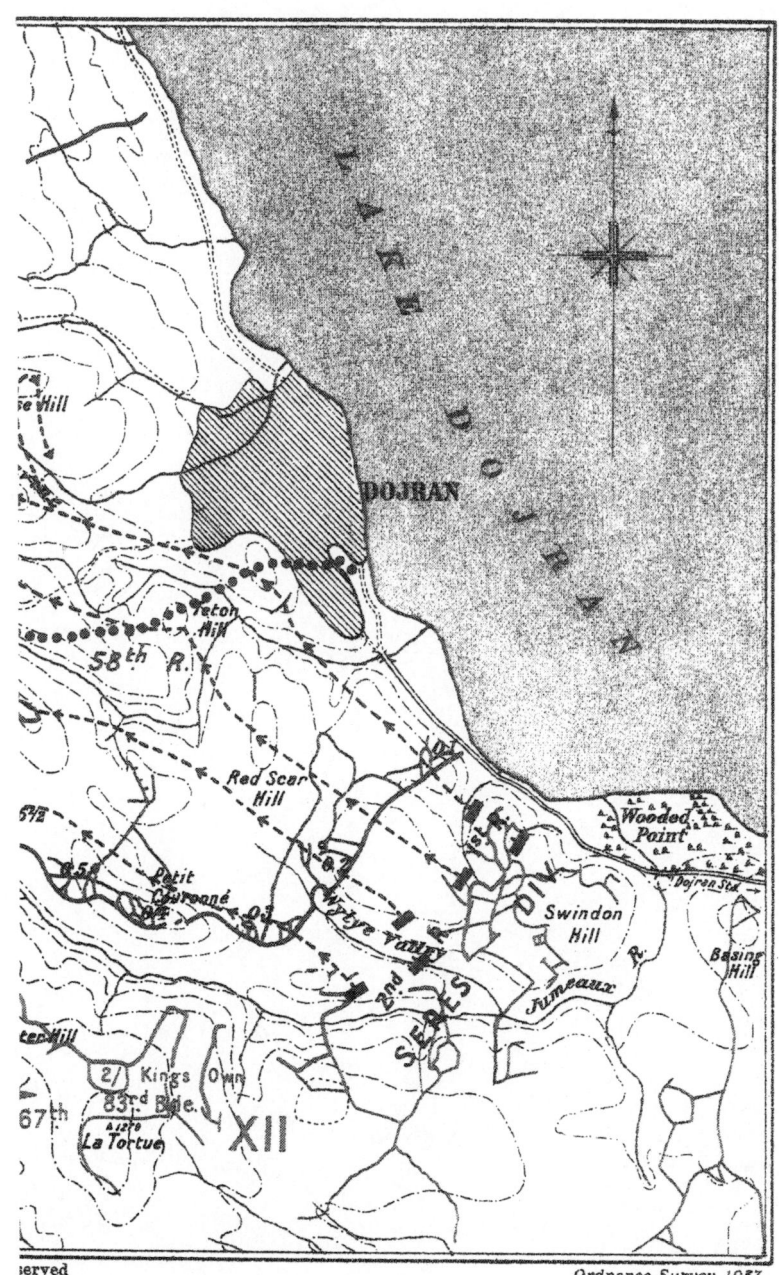

On both days there were bombing and low flying attacks with machine-gun fire in the immediate battle area, notably about the Grand Couronné, and bombing attacks on dumps behind the front. One D.H.9, fitted with wireless equipment which gave a range of about 100 miles, widely reconnoitred the Bulgar lines of communication in search of concentrations of troops or transport which might form suitable bombing targets: French bombers, using the British aerodrome at Yanesh, were ready to help those of the Royal Air Force as required. During the two days of the battle no exceptional bombing targets were reported, and the bombing attacks were therefore made on the dumps at Cerniste, Cestovo, Miletkovo, and Cinarli.

Little was seen of hostile aeroplanes during the battle. On the morning of the 18th a patrol of four fighters protecting the British contact patrol aeroplanes engaged five enemy single-seaters, which had others in support. Two of the hostile aeroplanes were sent down, and the remainder withdrew. This was the last encounter of its kind on the British Macedonian front: the enemy pilots henceforth left the air to the British.

There was an adventure of an unusual kind on the 19th. Two volunteers were called for to land two British infantry agents behind the enemy lines. The pilots chosen were Lieutenants James Boyd (No. 47 Squadron) and W. J. Buchanan (No. 17 Squadron). The passengers were Lieutenant R. Lamb, Royal Scots Fusiliers, and an unnamed sergeant, and their task was to obtain information about enemy movements in certain areas. Flying a B.E.2e, Lieutenant Boyd landed at dusk near the river Stara about five miles north of Strumica, apparently unseen. In less than a minute his passenger, Lieutenant Lamb, had set out on his mission, and the aeroplane had taken off again. The second aeroplane, which was last seen by the escorting pilots to be flying low down in the darkness in some sort of trouble, did not return.

The passengers who were landed carried four pigeons each, by which they were to communicate their information, but they had instructions that if capture appeared certain they were to release the pigeons without messages.

One had male pigeons, the other females, and on the 20th two of each sex returned with no messages. When the war had ended Lieutenant Buchanan was released from a prison at Philippopolis, and he related the story of his adventure. 'I left Yanesh aerodrome at 17.00 hours on the '19th September, 1918, with a sergeant who was to be 'landed near Petric, and crossed the enemy lines at 18.00 'hours at about 11,000 to 12,000 feet. I circled over the 'town of Petric several times and eventually selected a 'suitable spot to land about four miles due north of the 'town. I planed down and made a good landing in a field, 'but unfortunately a party of German troops proceeding 'along the Petric–Strumica road, whom I had not seen, 'had apparently noticed my approach and taken cover 'behind trees and hedges. As soon as I touched the ground 'they immediately opened fire at about 600 yards to 700 'yards range. My passenger at once got out of the machine 'and ran off towards some bushes, pursued by a party of 'Germans. I then got out of the machine myself and 'started my engine, which had stopped on landing; I also 'threw out the cage containing pigeons. I managed to 'take off and climbed to about 3,000 feet when my engine 'commenced to give trouble. I tried again and again to gain 'height to enable me to clear the Beles mountains, but I was 'obliged to descend and landed a second time, between 'Petric and Marinopolje. My engine then suddenly "picked 'up" and I again took off but could only reach 800 feet, at 'which height I essayed to travel through the Rupel Pass in 'order to avoid the hills. I had only covered a short distance 'when my engine completely gave out and I was forced to 'glide down and crashed in the bed of the river, having had 'one wheel shot away and two rifle bullets through a cylin-'der, presumably at my first landing. Bulgarian soldiers 'rushed towards me shouting "Bulgar or English?" On 'telling them that I was English they fired at me at point-'blank range, but the firing was very wild and the shots 'went in all directions, leaving me untouched. As they 'continued to fire I ran towards the hills, hoping to find 'cover, but they came after me and I was very soon over-'taken as I was hampered by the extra flying clothes I was

'wearing. I caught hold of the nearest soldier, gripping
'him by the shoulders, and called upon the others to stop
'firing. I handed my revolver to this man, but he im-
'mediately dropped it, being afraid of it. The others then
'came up and went through all my pockets, but only cleared
'my cigarette case. They then conducted me to a Regimen-
'tal H.Q. at Vetrina. . . .' He goes on to tell how he was
put on trial and informed that he would be shot, but how
he was eventually treated as an ordinary prisoner of war.

After the two-day battle of Dojran there was a brief
breathing-space. Both sides had suffered heavily, the
attackers more than the defenders, and on the 20th the
British and Greek troops were engaged in relief movements
and re-organization. Air reconnaissances on the 20th
reported no important enemy activity, except that there
were trains, with steam up, facing north in the stations at
Hudova and Demir Kapija: there was also a train at
Hudova alongside the aerodrome.

The operation orders issued to the squadrons on the
evening of the 20th allotted the usual artillery and close
reconnaissance duties to the co-operation Flights for the
next day. On the morning of the 21st, however, about
8 a.m., loud explosions were heard from the British lines
far into the enemy area, and it was not long before the
aeroplane observers were bringing back news which left
no doubt that the Bulgars were, at long last, turning their
backs upon the Dojran–Vardar defences. The most comprehensive information was given in a reconnaissance report
made by the observers in two D.H.9 aeroplanes which left
at 8.30 a.m. to inspect the Strumica Valley–Negotino–
Hudova area. The aeroplanes returned at noon and the
officers told of widespread movements. The hangars had
disappeared from the aerodrome at Hudova, the dumps
and buildings were burning at Cestovo, there had been a
notable clearance of military stores and camps at Demir
Kapija, there were fires blazing in Krivolak and Gradsko,
at Rabrovo there was much crowding of mechanical transport vehicles, and there were as many as 500 lorries and
wagons waiting their turn to move along the Kosturino
defile.

The XII Corps commander promptly issued orders that all defensive work was to cease, and that the troops were to be given a short rest preliminary to an advance. Every available aeroplane was ordered to bomb the enemy troops and transport. Thirty-two separate flights were made and a total of fourteen 112-lb. and two hundred and twenty-nine 20-lb. bombs were dropped. The main targets were the troops and crowded transport in the Kosturino defile on the Strumica–Rabrovo road, and when the bombs had been dropped the pilots and observers fired all their machine-gun ammunition into the luckless columns. Not many bombs failed to find a mark, so exceptional were the targets, and lorries, men, and animals were blown in all directions.

In the late afternoon two aeroplanes directed artillery fire on bridges near Furka: while these artillery observers were flying about their work they had a wide view of the destruction of military stores which was in progress in the enemy area, and one of them counted no fewer than sixty-four separate fires.

There was a gale blowing on the morning of the 22nd when the bombing was resumed. Seven 112-lb. bombs and a hundred and two of 20-lb. weight were dropped on enemy columns during the day, mainly in the Kosturino pass. At noon a telegram had been received from General Franchet d'Espérey saying that the enemy was in retreat along the whole front from Monastir to Lake Dojran, and that the retreat must be turned into a rout by an unceasing and resolute pursuit. General Milne's orders issued for the 23rd stated that the advance was to be continued with the greatest possible speed.

On the 22nd, and again on the 23rd, there were long-distance reconnaissances, nine on the 22nd and seven on the following day. The object was to find out as much as possible of the movements of the enemy, and to discover in particular whether the Bulgars were taking up any specific defensive positions. The information brought back by the observers was that there were no signs that the enemy troops intended to make a stand. It is easy to be wise in retrospect and it has been suggested that the D.H.9

aeroplanes, the most valuable bombing aircraft with the squadrons, should have been employed for offensive operations at this time, and that no more than the minimum strength should have been diverted to reconnaissance. There were, however, many reasons why the British command needed to be reassured about the enemy intentions. There were grave elements of danger if the Bulgars should make a counter-offensive, and no doubt the very full information provided by the air observers enabled the British Commander-in-Chief to push his troops forward in pursuit of the enemy faster, because with easier mind, than if he had received only scant knowledge of the hostile activities. The army command was in the best position to judge the needs of the situation, and its appreciation was that the aeroplanes were better employed on reconnaissance than on bombing attacks. About 40 light-weight bombs were dropped on the retreating columns on the 23rd, and a few thousand rounds of machine-gun ammunition were fired at troops.

On the 24th air reconnaissance reports showed that the enemy movements continued northwards in full force. On the Struma front, where reconnaissances were made by the single-seaters of No. 150 Squadron, a withdrawal was also reported to be in progress. Five of the Armstrong-Whitworths of No. 47 Squadron found targets of troops and transport in the neighbourhood of Strumica on the morning of the 24th and dropped thirty-six 20-lb. bombs which were seen to inflict casualties and damage. Two Armstrong-Whitworths of No. 17 Squadron attacked transport and troops again in the evening. None of the D.H.9's was in action on the 24th. On this day three aeroplanes from the naval contingent at Mudros arrived at Amberkoj, the aerodrome of No. 17 Squadron, to help in the operations. On the 25th there were fourteen bombing flights, during which a total of twelve 112-lb. and eighty 20-lb. bombs were dropped.

The Germans have stated that the Bulgarian First Army became demoralized as it retreated, and there can be no doubt that the British aeroplanes contributed much to this state of affairs. In the battle fought at Dojran on the

18th and 19th of September the Bulgarian First Army had suffered severe losses, although less severe than the British and the Greeks. The Bulgarian troops had revealed fine soldierly qualities, and it is known that their spirit remained high after the battle. As they proceeded to make their enforced withdrawal they might draw such comfort as they could from the knowledge that the difficulties of the country made it extremely unlikely that the British and Greek troops would be able to effect a rapid pursuit. Although the units of the Bulgarian First Army may have become aware, as they went back, of the demoralization in the ranks of the defeated Bulgarian Eleventh Army, it seems doubtful whether such well-tried soldiers would have collapsed so soon if it had not been for the air bombing offensive to which, as was made painfully clear to them by the disappearance from the air of German pilots, there could be no answer. By the 25th of September the demoralization was such that, in the words of the official military historian, 'the British and Greeks between Lake 'Dojran and the Vardar were troubled more by the nature 'of the country than by the resistance of the enemy'.

On the 26th the three bombers from Mudros (two D.H.9's and one D.H.4) attacked the aerodrome and railway sidings at Livunovo, and eight other pilots at intervals bombed troops and transport between Strumica and Yenikoi. On this day the Sixteenth Wing head-quarters moved with general head-quarters from Salonika to Yanesh, and 'C' Flight of No. 17 Squadron moved from Amberkoj to an aerodrome at Stojakovo. Next day there was considerable mist which impeded air work, but four aeroplanes bombed at various times, notably columns in the Kryesna pass on the Struma front. On the 28th air reconnaissances revealed that the Kryesna road was 'choked with transport'. Pilots made two or three journeys and there was a total of twenty-nine bombing flights during which one hundred and ninty-four light-weight and five 112-lb. bombs were dropped: all aeroplanes attacked also with machine-guns. Probably the greatest effect was obtained by six pilots of No. 47 Squadron when they bombed convoys in the Kryesna pass at 5.30 p.m. They carried forty-four bombs of 20-lb. weight, and half of these exploded directly among the transport, blowing some of it off the road, piling up wagons and causing a general panic. When making their way home from a reconnaissance flight which had taken them as far as Kyustendil, the pilot and observer in a D.H.9 saw twelve guns, oxen-drawn, among the retreating columns north of Kryesna. The pilot dived and machine-gun fire was opened from a height of 500 feet: some of the men and oxen were seen to fall. An American diplomat subsequently stated that he was in his motor-car on the road at the time the aeroplane attack was made and that he saw several of the oxen and drivers killed or wounded: he himself had a narrow escape.

On the 29th the mist was thick again. The first air observer over the Kryesna pass in the morning found that the traffic blockage had been cleared during the night, but that columns of transport and troops were on the move south of the pass. Seven pilots set out to attack these columns, and among the sixty-three bombs dropped were three of 112-lb. weight: many direct hits were made. This was destined to be the last offensive air operation and the martyrdom of the Bulgar troops was at an end. Mist and clouds throughout the remainder of the day prevented a continuance of the bombing, and at 10 p.m. a Convention was signed by General Franchet d'Espérey and by plenipotentiaries of the Bulgarian Government in accordance with which hostilities ceased at noon on the following day, the 30th of September. The activities of the Royal Air Force on the morning of the 30th were confined to reconnaissance flights, one of which was made to Sofia, which was found cloud-obscured.

It was possible near the end, and after hostilities had ceased, to gain a closer impression of the results of the bombing attacks. Staff officers who inspected the routes from Cestovo to Kosturino were awed by what they saw. Their observation was summarized in a telegram sent by advanced general head-quarters to the Sixteenth Wing, saying: 'The routes from Cestovo valley to Kosturino show 'signs of the indescribable confusion that must have existed 'in the retreat of the Bulgar army. Guns of all kinds, 'motor-cars, machine-guns, rifles, and every kind of war 'material abandoned. Dead animals are strewn every-'where, indicating that our R.A.F. must have contributed 'largely to bringing about this state of things.' The intelligence officer of No. 47 Squadron, who had been sent forward on the 26th of September to make such inspection as was open to him at that time, reported 300 transport wagons destroyed in one area with their horses and oxen lying dead. In a ravine there was 'a vast number of pack animals', and at the hospital at Rabrovo more than 700 human bodies had been collected for burial. Every few yards along the Rabrovo–Kosturino road were dead animals, derelict motor-cars, transport of all kinds, and in the nullahs near the road transport lay tumbled where it had crashed. First-hand evidence of the effect of the bombing in the Kryesna pass is lacking, but there is no reason to believe that it was less devastating.

Although Bulgaria had laid down her arms, the war was not over. The German supreme command, however, to whom the rapid collapse of Bulgaria had come as a surprise, had no illusions. They knew that the position of Austria-Hungary and of Turkey had been made extremely hazardous. General Franchet d'Espérey decided to direct his full attention to the Danube, rather than to Constantinople, and he ordered a bold forward movement. The British troops began to advance accordingly, but as the result of an interchange of views between General Milne and the authorities at home, and between the British and French Governments, the Allied plans were modified and the task allotted to a newly assembled army under the command of General Milne was to secure the passage of the Dardanelles to enable the Fleet to take action against Constantinople.

Before this decision was arrived at, the opportunity was taken to overhaul the aeroplanes, transport, and stores of the Royal Air Force squadrons. Some of the aeroplanes were employed to convey officials on important missions to Sofia and other places. When it was settled that the British army would move against Turkey, a Royal Air Force officer was sent to make a selection of suitable landing-grounds. Reconnaissances, meanwhile, were made by No. 47 Squadron from the former German aerodrome at Drama. It was decided to send a Flight from No. 17 Squadron for co-operation with the XVI Corps from an aerodrome near Philippopolis, and to organize a Composite Flight from Nos. 47 and 150 Squadrons for work with the XII Corps from an aerodrome near Gumuljina. An advanced convoy moved out to Philippopolis, on their 250-mile journey along bad roads, on the 19th of October, and two aeroplanes followed a few days later. The Composite Flight followed their transport to the aerodrome near Gumuljina on the 25th. On the 31st of October, before the various movements of the Royal Air Force units had been completed the armistice was signed with Turkey.

CHAPTER IX
THE MEDITERRANEAN IN 1918
[Map, p. 315]

'I REQUEST that the situation as regards aircraft in the 'Mediterranean may receive the earnest consideration of 'the Board', Vice-Admiral the Hon. Sir S. A. Gough-Calthorpe, British Commander-in-Chief in the Mediterranean, had said in a telegram to the Admiralty on the 15th of December 1917. The reader will recall that arising out of the representations made by the vice-admiral the air units in the Mediterranean had been expanded and reorganized, and that Wing Captain A. M. Longmore had been appointed to the staff of the commander-in-chief as senior air service officer with authority, under the vice-admiral, to move units as required from area to area in the Mediterranean.[1] There was, in other words, a unified air command and an assurance that the needs of the Mediterranean would be considered as a whole.

By the 1st of April 1918, the day on which the Royal Air Force was formed, the reorganization scheme had been nearly completed, and on that day the air units in the Mediterranean were:

Malta Group.
Head-quarters of Royal Air Force units in the Mediterranean	Malta
Seaplane Base	Kalafrana
No. 1 Balloon Base	Malta
No. 6 Balloon Base	Bizerta
Dockyard constructional unit	Malta

The aircraft carriers, *Engadine*, *Riviera*, and *Manxman* based at Malta. For local operations the units came under the orders of the Admiral Superintendent, Malta.

Adriatic Group.
Head-quarters, Taranto, with advanced head-quarters at Brindisi: under the orders of the Commodore commanding British Adriatic Force.
66th Wing (Wing Commander D. A. Oliver)	Otranto
²67th ,, (Wing Commander R. P. Ross)	Taranto

[1] Vol. V, pp. 395–7.
[2] Although formed with effect from the 1st of April 1918, this Wing did not begin operations until the end of June 1918. The first raid made by the Wing was on the 1st of July.

DISPOSITION OF UNITS

No. 224 Squadron . . . . Otranto
„ 225 „ . . . . Otranto
„ 226 „ . . . . Taranto
„ 227 „ . . . . Taranto
Seaplane Base . . . . Santa Maria di Leuca
No. 3 Balloon Base . . . . Brindisi
No. 4 Balloon Base . . . . Corfu
The aircraft on charge were: D.H.4, Sopwith 'Camel', Sopwith 1½ strutter; Short seaplane, F.B.A. (Italian) Flying Boat, Sopwith 'Baby', and Hamble 'Baby' seaplanes.

Aegean Group.
Head-quarters, Mudros: under the orders of the Rear-Admiral, Aegean.
62nd and 63rd Wings (Acting Wing Captain R. Gordon) Mudros
No. 220 Squadron . . . . Imbros
„ 221 „ . . . . Stavros
„ 222 „ . . . . Thasos
„ 223 „ . . . . Mudros
Seaplane Bases . . . . Suda Bay (Crete), and Syra
Airship Station . . . . Kassandra
Aircraft Carriers *Ark Royal* and *Peony*, based at Mudros.
The aircraft on charge were: D.H.4, Sopwith 'Camel', Sopwith 1½ strutter; Short and Sopwith 'Baby' seaplanes.

Egypt Group.
Head-quarters, Alexandria: under Rear-Admiral . . Egypt
Seaplane Base . . . . Port Said
Seaplane Base . . . . Alexandria
No. 2 Balloon Base . . . . Alexandria
Aircraft Carrier *City of Oxford* based at Alexandria.
The aircraft on charge were: Short, Sopwith 'Baby', and Hamble 'Baby' seaplanes.

Gibraltar Group.
Under the Senior Naval Officer, Gibraltar.
No. 5 Balloon Base . . . . Gibraltar
Aircraft Carrier *Empress* based at Gibraltar.

The operations of these air groups were almost entirely connected with the campaign against the U-boats. They may be broadly divided into (*a*) anti-submarine patrols and direct attacks on submarines at sea, and (*b*) a bombing offensive against the enemy ports and depots, particularly the submarine bases, and against the lines of communications. The work under (*a*) was mainly done by seaplanes, although aeroplanes also co-operated in the Adriatic and Aegean areas. It included protective escort duties with convoys, of which there was a great amount at the ports where there were seaplane stations, namely, Gibraltar, Malta, Alexandria, Port Said, and Taranto. The operations under (*b*), which included attacks on enemy aerodromes, were made by light bombers, mostly D.H.4's, usually with escorts of single-seater fighters.

Kite Balloons with Convoys

A notable feature of the war waged against the U-boat in the Mediterranean in 1918 was the increasing employment of kite balloons. The objection, advanced by some naval authorities, that a balloon was certain to advertise the presence of ships to the enemy long before they would otherwise become visible did not have much force in the Mediterranean where the air was usually so clear that the smoke from vessels in company could be seen from great distances, with the result that the presence of a convoy was betrayed whether or not a balloon was flown.

Opinion was divided about the position which the kite balloon ship should occupy relative to a convoy. Should the balloon be stationed some miles ahead of the ships, or should it be flown close to them? Those who advocated the first method claimed for it the advantage that a lurking U-boat would be forced to dive a long way from the convoy and might not, in consequence, be able to arrive at a favourable position in which to fire her torpedoes. Those who preferred that the kite balloon should keep station near the convoy argued that a submarine commander would be intimidated, and might therefore be disinclined to attack at all, or, alternatively, that he would fire his torpedoes only at long range and thus reduce the chances of a hit, more especially because the balloon observer would be in a position, and would have the necessary time, to indicate to the particular ship under attack how the oncoming torpedo might be avoided. Both methods were used, but there is not enough evidence to support a dogmatic assertion in favour of either one or the other. The available material and personnel did not permit of the two methods being employed together, but no doubt this would have become usual for the more important convoys had the war continued a little longer. There is little doubt that a balloon, no matter where it was flown, added to the security of the ships. It is fairly certain also that this result was achieved mainly by moral effect. To the U-boat commander the balloon represented a large all-seeing eye which it was the part of wisdom to avoid. The balloons were flown from destroyers or sloops, and the work of escort began in May 1918: from that time onwards those convoys in the Mediterranean which had a kite balloon in company were almost immune from attack. The stations where balloons were available for employment with convoys were those at Gibraltar, Bizerta, Malta, and Alexandria.[1] Other bases were in preparation at Genoa, Milo, and Port Said, and when they were ready it would be possible to supply escorting balloons for the principal convoy routes throughout the Mediterranean.

That the presence of a balloon was of help in warding off an attack seemed to be demonstrated by occasional happenings, involving unescorted ships, which took place after a convoy flying a balloon had passed on its way. It cannot be said that the episodes are conclusive, but an example or two will be given for what they are worth. For instance, the convoy from Bizerta on the 10th of August, escorted by the sloop *Snapdragon* with her kite balloon aloft, made the passage to Malta without incident, but when a few of the ships subsequently proceeded on their own to Marsa Scirocco at the south-east corner of the island they were attacked, and one of them was sunk by a torpedo. Again, two days later, the convoy from Milo, with the kite-balloon sloop *Penstemon* in company, handed over to an Italian escort at an appointed rendezvous that part of the convoy which was bound for Italy. The Italian section, which had no balloon or other escorting aircraft, had not gone far when it was attacked by a submarine and one of the ships was hit. The observer in the balloon saw what had happened

[1] The Adriatic balloon stations, at Brindisi and Corfu, were occupied with anti-submarine patrols north and south of the Otranto barrage.

and the *Penstemon* turned back to give such help as she could: no further attack on the convoy was made.

About the middle of May, probably on the 16th, the *U.39*, which had been cruising west of the Straits of Gibraltar, where she had attacked two ships, re-entered the Mediterranean. On the morning of the 17th a Short seaplane from the carrier *Empress*, which had arrived at Gibraltar on the 7th of May to lend her help in the protection of shipping, was on patrol east of Europa Point when the periscope of a submarine was sighted. The commander of the U-boat—the *U.39*—appeared to be positioning himself for an attack on eight ships which were proceeding in company. As the Short seaplane bore down upon the submarine it disappeared, but a 100-lb. bomb was dropped just ahead of the place where it had gone under: not long after the bomb had exploded a large oil patch began to form on the water. The seaplane pilot circled the area for a time, but he saw nothing more and he then flew with the ships for an hour. There is evidence that the *U.39* was attacked by aircraft again next morning, presumably French. Later, on the 18th of May, it was towed by another submarine into Cartagena and was there interned with its crew. This appears to be the only confirmed instance in any part of the British Mediterranean area in 1918, when direct aircraft attack put an end to the war activities of a U-boat.[1]

The Otranto Barrage

The main centre of anti-submarine activity in the Mediterranean was in the area of the Straits of Otranto, the comparatively narrow waters through which all the U-boats must pass on their way to or from their bases on the Austrian Adriatic coast. By the middle of April 1918 Vice-Admiral Gough-Calthorpe had assembled a sufficient force to enable him to put into execution his plans for perfecting the barrage. The dispositions of the ships varied from time to time, but the constitution of the barrage was

---

[1] The confirmed sinkings of U-boats in the whole Mediterranean area in 1918 were ten, additional to the above.

maintained without appreciable change. 'An outpost force 'of six submarines watched the approaches to Cattaro; to 'the south of them a force of destroyers patrolled a line 'drawn across the central part of the straits between point 'Samana, on the Albanian side, and Monopoli; by night 'they patrolled a line some twenty miles further to the 'south. A number of trawlers, fitted with hydrophones, 'occupied the narrowest part of the straits between Otranto 'and the coast to the south of Cape Linguetta; immediately 'to the south of them was what was called the main auxi-'liary patrol line of drifters and trawlers. It was thought 'that every passing submarine would be at least detected 'by the ships upon the first line that she crossed, and that 'from then onwards she would be pursued and harried 'without respite.'[1]

The part played by the Royal Air Force in the Otranto barrage scheme was varied. Brindisi was the earliest balloon base in the Mediterranean to begin work, and the first patrol started on the 2nd of May 1918 when a balloon with four officers and seven ratings was transferred to the sloop *Honeysuckle* about to set out on patrol of the Straits. Observers were sent up at 11.30 a.m. on the 3rd, and watch was kept without break during daylight hours until 6.30 p.m. on the 5th. On the evening of the 3rd the attention of the balloon observer was attracted by a suspicious oil patch, and forty minutes later an enemy submarine was sighted about seven miles away proceeding north on the surface. The *Honeysuckle* was directed towards the U-boat, which dived when the ship was still five miles distant. The sloop continued to the spot indicated by the balloon observer and dropped a depth charge, but nothing further of interest was seen. The Corfu station also began to supply balloons for the patrolling ships in May, and the above happening may be looked upon as typical of those in which the balloons from both stations were frequently concerned.

The seaplane base at Taranto was mainly used as a reception and erection depot for new aircraft, which were passed to the seaplane squadron at Otranto or to the sub-

[1] *Naval Operations*, by Sir Henry Newbolt, vol. v, p. 286.

station at Santa Maria di Leuca. The duties of the seaplanes were routine anti-submarine patrols, and special investigations when signals (code word 'Allo') were received of U-boats definitely sighted. In addition, as opportunity offered, the seaplanes were employed to escort convoys passing in the neighbourhood. One or two examples will help to illustrate the daily work of the seaplane personnel. On the morning of the 3rd of June the periscope of a submarine was sighted from a Short seaplane which was engaged upon a routine patrol. When the seaplane was still a mile and a half distant the U-boat went under, but a 230-lb. bomb was dropped on the position where it was estimated she would be: the bomb failed to explode. Calcium flares were then dropped to mark the spot, and three destroyers in the neighbourhood were informed by light signals and lamp messages of what had happened. A systematic search of the area then began, and some three hours later an oil patch appeared about two miles north of the original sighting. A 230-lb. bomb was dropped on the new position by the seaplane, which had replenished at its base, and the bomb duly exploded, but nothing more was seen. On the 15th of June a Short seaplane was on patrol along the barrage line when a signal was received at the home station requesting the help of aircraft to search for mines which had apparently been laid by a U-boat off Santa Maria di Leuca. A wireless call was sent out to the pilot of the patrolling Short seaplane ordering him to make a diversion in order to search the specified area: as a result a group of mines was found and their positions were reported. At 7.5 p.m. on the 19th of July a Sopwith 'Baby' seaplane set out upon a routine patrol. After the seaplane had been out some time a U-boat, camouflaged in green and black, was sighted with its periscope above water. The pilot dived, and 200 feet above the water the only bomb carried, of 100-lb. weight, was released: it exploded thirty yards from the submarine which began slowly to submerge. From the seaplane the U-boat was visible as it went down for about sixty feet. Two flares were dropped to mark the spot where it was last seen, and patrolling surface craft were signalled to take up the hunt, which proved unsuccessful.

Such incidents, unexciting and inconclusive, in the grim, baffling, and tedious warfare waged against the U-boats, were the common experience of the seaplane personnel in the area of the Otranto barrage.

More dramatic, and wholly offensive, were the bombing operations conducted against the U-boat bases at Cattaro and Durazzo by formations of D.H.4 and D.H.9 aeroplanes. To attack Cattaro, the most important base in the area, involved a journey totalling more than 400 miles over the sea. The bombing offensive, in which the Italian air service also took part, got under way in May, but as a beginning an attack had been made on Durazzo on the 23rd of April when five D.H.4's dropped two 230-lb. and sixteen 100-lb. bombs, which exploded among ships in the harbour and close to the seaplane base. The first attack of this period on Cattaro took place on the 11th of May, and between that date and the end of August there were twelve bombing attacks by British aeroplanes on Cattaro and seven on Durazzo.

The raid on Cattaro on the 11th of May was made by six D.H.4's which dropped bombs among submarines and destroyers in the harbour: one of the bombers landed with engine trouble and the pilot and his observer were later reported prisoners of war. The subsequent attacks were made by similar formations, and bombs to a total weight varying between one ton and two tons were dropped on each raid. Hits were reported from time to time on shipping both in Cattaro and Durazzo, and on the submarine head-quarters and barracks, the seaplane base, the arsenal buildings, and the dockyard at Cattaro, and on the seaplane base at Durazzo. The attacks, especially those on Cattaro, led to air combats from time to time, mostly of an indecisive character.

Evidence from the Austrian and German side of the exact results of the air bombing offensive, British and Italian, is not available. That it inflicted important damage is certain, but it seems clear that not enough was caused to exert any serious effect on the submarine campaign. Nor indeed can more be claimed for the whole elaborate Otranto barrage organization which required the services of nearly three hundred vessels of various kinds.[1] In April and May 1918 there had been fifty passages of submarines through the Straits of Otranto, and although all the submarines had been sighted, or detected by hydrophone, it was only possible on fourteen occasions to make some sort of attack, as a result of which no more than one submarine had definitely been sunk. That the barrage caused inconvenience to the U-boat commanders is obvious, and the passage was certainly a time of anxiety which possibly helped to fray the nerves of the U-boat personnel and so affect their morale.

In June 1918 the sinkings of Allied shipping in the Mediterranean were reduced by one-half. In July they rose very slightly, but in August the sinkings were down again, and they continued to fall as the war progressed to its end. It was considered at the time that this happy result was brought about by the elaborate offensive measures undertaken in the Mediterranean, and in particular by the Otranto barrage scheme, but the post-war view advanced by the official naval historian is that the defeat of the U-boat was due almost exclusively to a perfection of the convoy system.[2] He points out that although the enemy was not able to maintain quite as many submarines at sea in the Mediterranean area in June as in the previous month, the total number of days spent by submarines on cruise was not below the average. Yet, although the same amount of energy was expended by the U-boats, no more than 78,000 tons of shipping was destroyed in June against the 176,000 tons of a short time previously. This, in his judgement, was because the development of the convoy system led, in June, to more escortings of shipping, with longer and better protection for each escorted ship. (It may also be noted, in parenthesis, that a feature of this better protection was the provision of a kite balloon escort for the important convoys.) Though it may not be possible to

---

[1] In September 1918 the Otranto Barrage Force comprised 280 vessels, namely, 31 destroyers, 8 submarines, 6 sloops, 4 torpedo boats, 36 submarine chasers (American), 38 hydrophone trawlers, 14 trawlers, 101 drifters, 41 motor launches, and 1 yacht.

[2] See *Naval Operations*, by Sir Henry Newbolt, vol. v, ch. viii.

dispute the general conclusions of the naval historian, a doubt may perhaps be expressed whether sufficient weight has been given to the effect of the Otranto barrage organization, and of the air offensive. Both inflicted some damage, and much anxiety, and although the effect was far smaller than hope had encouraged, it was nevertheless ponderable and cannot rightly be left out of account when the causes which brought about the defeat of the U-boat campaign in the Mediterranean are enumerated.

The Aegean Group

The Aegean group consisted of a number of more or less isolated stations scattered over the Aegean area from Lemnos to Crete. The Air Ministry's intention was that each of the two wings should comprise a fighter (Sopwith 'Camel'), a light bomber (D.H.9), and a seaplane (Short '184' type) squadron, but the wings were below their allotted strength throughout most of 1918.[1] Actually, the aeroplanes of the Aegean group, which made up the Sixty-second Wing, were divided into three composite units consisting of two Flights of bombers and two of fighters. They were stationed at Stavros and Imbros, but one unit was kept mobile for work as required from Imbros, Thasos, Mitylene, &c. The two seaplane squadrons, which comprised the Sixty-third Wing, were distributed among the stations at Talikna (Lemnos), Skyros, Suda Bay, and Syra. The depot ship *Ark Royal* moved from Syra on the 16th of April to supply the Suda Bay and Syra stations. At Mudros, where the group head-quarters was situated, the central aircraft depot formed an erecting and distributing centre for aeroplanes to all stations of the Sixty-second Wing. Certain units of the Greek naval air service also formed part of the Aegean group for operations. The duties of the group may be set down as:

(*a*) Bombing attacks on enemy centres.

[1] At the end of August the two wings together had (serviceable) 30 light bombers, which were D.H.4 and D.H.9, and 48 fighters, with a collection of obsolescent aeroplanes mostly being used to give instruction to Greek pilots at Mudros. The seaplanes were 30 Shorts and 8 obsolescent single-seaters of the Hamble or Sopwith 'Baby' types.

(b) Routine patrols of the Dardanelles and Sea of Marmara to give warning of enemy naval activity, with occasional reconnaissances to Constantinople.
(c) Anti-submarine patrols, and
(d) Army reconnaissances on the Salonika front (by the Stavros unit).

The airship station at Kassandra employed only one airship, of the S.S.Z. type, which patrolled in search of submarines. A large airship programme for the Mediterranean was contemplated for 1919, with 29 airships and portable sheds variously distributed at suitable places throughout the Mediterranean (in Egypt, Crete, Sicily, &c.), in order to spread a wide network of airship patrols.

The objectives attacked by the bombers of the Aegean group included Galata aerodrome on the Peninsula, and the Nagara seaplane base, warehouses at Gallipoli, Chanak, the railway station and warehouses on the quay at Panderma, trains and stations on the railway lines of communication, bridges, notably those at Kuleli Burgas and Buk (on which a direct hit was made during a raid on the 22nd of September), and military targets at Constantinople. The last-named objective was bombed on three occasions in July, four times in August, twice in September, and once in October. This last attack, made on the 18th, involved two separate formations of seven and five de Havilland aeroplanes. All the bombers returned safely and they reported hits on the War Office, the railway, and on Haidar Pasha. Other objectives, in connexion with the Macedonian campaign, were the aerodrome at Drama, and military targets in the area of the lower Struma.

The enemy air service occasionally retaliated, but the bombing, with very few exceptions, was of a spasmodic kind and inflicted little damage. A notable exception was a series of attacks on the air station at Imbros which began at 8.40 p.m. on the 25th of July and continued until dawn on the following morning. A total of about sixty bombs were dropped, most of them scattered over the landing-ground and the quarters of the men: these were responsible for inconsiderable damage. One bomb, however, dropped from a height of fifty feet at 1.20 a.m., exploded in a hangar in which seven Sopwith 'Camel' fighters were housed. A fire was started which destroyed the hangar and its contents, and the loss of the Sopwith 'Camels' caused a shortage of fighters which was felt for some time. By way of answer to this attack the aerodrome at Galata was bombed during the night of the 25/26th of July, again next night, and by daylight on the 27th.

The Egypt Group

The Egypt group was organized as the Sixty-fourth Wing and consisted of the seaplane stations at Alexandria and Port Said, and the kite balloon bases. The air stations of the Egypt group came under the Rear-Admiral, Egypt, for operations, and were subsequently placed under the head-quarters of the Royal Air Force in the Middle East, with its head-quarters at Cairo, for administrative purposes. The work of the wing consisted entirely of anti-submarine and minefield patrols, and the escort of convoys to and from Egypt. Escort of convoys was the most important duty because the U-boat commanders did not apparently consider it worth while to operate near the Egyptian coast within reach of the British seaplanes, except on those occasions when convoys were on the move. A typical example of the usefulness of the seaplane work may be given. On the morning of the 8th of April a seaplane from the Alexandria base set out to escort an incoming convoy. Just when the seaplane picked up the first of the ships in the convoy, a submarine made an attack. The track of the torpedo, visible from the air, led to the periscope of the submarine, upon which the seaplane pilot dived and released a bomb. This exploded near the target, which turned. A second bomb, dropped just before the U-boat submerged, also failed to make a direct hit. Depth charges were dropped by escorting surface craft on the position indicated from the seaplane, but nothing more was seen: the convoy, meanwhile, proceeded safely into port.

Apart from the general naval air work briefly narrated above, the Royal Air Force in the Mediterranean was required to undertake special duties in connexion with military operations. At the beginning of July 1918 the Italian XVI Corps in Albania began an offensive against the Austrians. All British pilots and aircraft in the Otranto area, not specifically required for anti-submarine duties, were placed at the disposal of General Ferrero, the Italian Commander, who had his head-quarters at Valona. The Italian advance began on the 6th of July and was successful. It was made on a front of sixty miles to an average depth of ten miles and resulted in the capture of 2,000 prisoners, 26 guns, and 6 aeroplanes. The French meanwhile pushed forward the left of their Macedonian line to conform with the Italian advance.

The duties allotted to the British air service in connexion with the Albanian operations were (i) destruction of the Kuchi bridge in order to cut the enemy's only line of communication with Berat, (ii) to observe for the fire of the two co-operating British monitors, the *Earl of Peterboro'* and *Sir Thomas Picton*, (iii) to bomb the enemy aerodrome at Tirana, east of Durazzo, (iv) to provide fighting escorts for Italian bombing aeroplanes, and (v) to make low-flying attacks on road traffic, aerodromes, &c. In fulfilment of this programme the British aeroplanes dropped some three tons of bombs and fired about 3,000 rounds of machine-gun ammunition against ground targets.

During one of the attacks on the Kuchi bridge on the 6th of July, enemy fighters intervened, and the pilot in one of the D.H.9's was wounded and the engine in his aeroplane partly disabled by bullets: he was able, however, to return to his aerodrome. Another D.H.9 did not get back and when, on the following evening, Italian cavalry galloped forward and took possession of the enemy aerodrome at Fieri (against which low-flying attacks had been made by British aeroplanes on the previous day), they not only took prisoners five Austrian aviators and captured their aeroplanes, but they also rescued, from the Fieri hospital, the two British officers who had been brought down in their D.H.9 while bombing the Kuchi bridge on the 6th: one of them had been wounded in the foot.

The bombing attacks on the Kuchi bridge on the 6th

ITALIAN OPERATIONS IN ALBANIA, 1918.

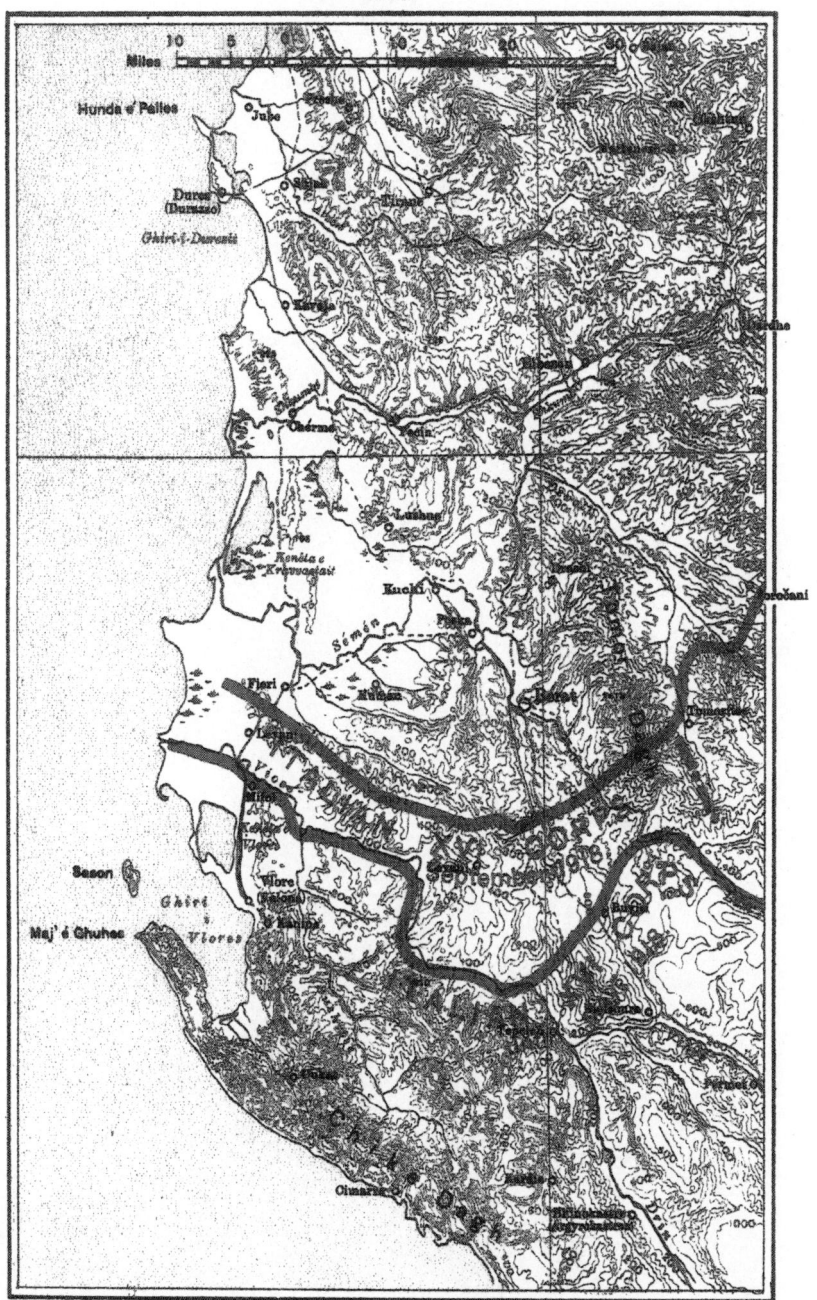

and 7th had proved unsuccessful, but as they seem to have been made, presumably under orders, from appreciable heights (some of them from 15,000 feet), this might not have been unexpected. On the 8th of July, however, the attacking pilots seem to have been allowed to use their own discretion. Two of them who attacked on that morning dropped their bombs from about 800 feet, and each obtained a direct hit with a 100-lb. bomb. It was clear from an air photograph, taken at the same time, that the damage inflicted had rendered the bridge useless for traffic, and the Italians were thereupon enabled to move forward to Berat. By the 10th the Italians had gained all their objectives, and the British aeroplanes returned to their bases, taking with them the grateful thanks of General Ferrero who paid generous tribute to the part which their help had played in the success of his operations. Subsequently, in August, Austrian counter-attacks against the Italians succeeded so well that they endangered the port of Valona, 'the capture of which by the Austrians would upset 'the whole situation in the Adriatic and render the main-'tenance of the Otranto Barrage impossible'.[1] Anxiety was ultimately relieved as an indirect result of the offensive launched by General Franchet d'Espérey on the Macedonian front in September.

On the 2nd of October a British and Italian fleet attacked Durazzo, and the bombing aircraft of the Sixty-sixth and Sixty-seventh Wings, operating from the aerodrome at Andrano, were given a special part. They operated in four formations. The first, of eight D.H.4's of No. 224 Squadron, escorted by four Sopwith 'Camels', arrived over Durazzo at 6.15 a.m. High explosive bombs of 100-lb., 112-lb., and 230-lb., to a total weight of 3,500 lb., together with eighty small incendiary bombs, were dropped. Just before the first formation of bombers returned to Andrano, the second formation, made up of six D.H.9's of No. 226 Squadron, left and they attacked Durazzo with 2,780-lb. weight of bombs at 10 a.m. On the outward journey this formation sighted the Allied fleet steering for Durazzo, and before they had finished dropping their bombs, the fleet had

[1] Falls, *Military Operations*, Macedonia, vol. ii, p. 119.

opened fire. The third formation, of four bombers of No. 226 Squadron, and the fourth, of seven, arrived over their objective at 10.50 a.m. and 11.30 a.m. respectively. Before the last of the bombers left, the bombardment by the Allied fleet had ended and Durazzo was burning fiercely in many places. A large *America* flying-boat and three Short seaplanes accompanied the fleet, and fighting formations of Sopwith 'Camels' patrolled over the town while the bombing attacks were in progress. This was the final concentrated bombing attack in the Otranto area; but before hostilities ended there were many low-flying attacks, mainly by the single-seater fighters, on retreating enemy columns on the Albanian front.

Aeroplanes from the Mediterranean took a part also in the final operations in Macedonia. At the request of General Sir G. F. Milne, the British Commander-in-Chief, four D.H.9's were sent to the aerodrome at Amberkoj to help bomb the retreating Bulgars. The bombing began on the 25th of September against troops and transport on the Strumica–Petric road: bombing flights continued daily until hostilities ended.

CHAPTER X
NAVAL AIR DEVELOPMENTS AND OPERATIONS, 1918

Home Waters

[Map, p. 380]

THE German U-boat campaign continued, throughout 1918, to influence, almost to the point of dictation, British naval developments. In the North Sea the measures taken to counter the submarine used up important elements of the first-line striking forces of Britain and were equivalent, in their total consequences, 'to a strategical division of the "Fleet".[1] For this reason, and for others set out by the official naval historian, Admiral Sir David Beatty, the Commander-in-Chief of the Grand Fleet, suggested early in January 1918 that, on the principle that trade must be protected, the strategy of the Grand Fleet should no longer be to endeavour to bring the enemy to action at any cost, but rather to contain him in his bases until the general position became more favourable: the Admiralty approved this suggested change of strategic method.

Action against the U-boats was defensive and offensive. The former included the system of convoys and of escorts, and the patrol of defined war channels around the British Isles. Offensive action lay mainly in organized hunts by flotillas of light craft, and in the placing of mine-fields.

Aeroplane versus U-boat

Following the introduction of the convoy system, German U-boat tactics were revised, and the change had an important effect on naval air policy in 1918. The submarine commanders found by experience that their operations had small chance of success unless they were conducted close to the shore where merchant ships might be caught on their way to a port of assembly or after they had dispersed from convoy. The charts kept in the Admiralty, on which the activities of the U-boats were plotted, clearly depicted the change in tactics. During the final quarter of

---

[1] *Naval Operations*, by Sir Henry Newbolt, vol. v, p. 206.

1917 the number of merchant ships sunk at a distance of ten miles or less from the land rose steadily, until the losses within this narrow belt reached sixty per cent. of the total sinkings. Furthermore, zones of particular danger were disclosed, mainly off the coasts of Devon and Cornwall, and between the Tyne and the Humber.

In consequence, the aeroplane, which could operate from any suitable aerodrome near the coast and with reasonable safety over inshore waters, took on a new importance as an anti-submarine weapon. At the end of January 1918 the Commander-in-Chief of the Grand Fleet asked for additional aircraft for patrol of the coastal area between the Tyne and the Tees where U-boat operations were intense, and early in March the Air Ministry, as a temporary measure, placed a Flight of F.E.2b aeroplanes of No. 36 Home Defence Squadron (Seaton Carew) at the disposal of the Admiralty. Two Flights of D.H.6 (training-type) aeroplanes were also established at Cramlington, near Newcastle, for anti-submarine work off the Tyne, and a further Flight, of F.E.2b's, at Ashington, was detached for patrol off the Northumberland coast.

These measures were of a makeshift kind. In the middle of March, however, a considered scheme was put forward by Captain R. M. Groves, R.N., the deputy-controller of the technical department of the Air Ministry. It aimed at the establishment of 'protected lanes' for merchant vessels where the trade routes approached within ten miles of the coast. The supposition was that U-boat commanders would not stay on the surface, nor operate with periscopes showing, if they knew that aeroplanes, which were potential bombers swift to act, were about. It was estimated that if sufficient aircraft could be provided for the passage of one aeroplane along the lanes every twenty minutes, the submarines would be forced into inactivity.

There was a shortage of efficient bombers and, in any event, aeroplanes capable of carrying heavy-weight bombs and manned by skilled pilots and observers were best employed on offensive operations. U-boat commanders, however, because of their known fear of aeroplanes, were susceptible to a reasonable measure of bluff, and types obsolete for other forms of air activity, in the hands of pilots unsuited for more exacting work, might still be employed with fair prospects of success on anti-submarine patrol. The main object, it was pointed out, was not so much to destroy U-boats, a matter calling for experience and skill, as to frighten them away from the protected lanes, which was considered to be comparatively easy of accomplishment. It happened that there were some 300 unwanted D.H.6 training-type aeroplanes. They suffered the disadvantage that they could not carry an observer as well as bombs, and that the engines with which most of them were equipped (90 horse-power Curtiss, O.X.5), were not very trustworthy.[1] On the other hand the D.H.6 could be flown with ease, even by pilots who for various reasons were not fitted for exacting service, and if it was forced down on the water through engine failure, which should not often happen because it would mostly be required to operate close to the land, then it had the advantage that it would not easily sink.[2]

The Air Ministry, while recognizing that the employment of the obsolete D.H.6 could be considered only a temporary expedient, offered, in pursuance of the scheme put forward by Captain R. M. Groves, to provide the Admiralty with 192 D.H.6 aeroplanes organized as thirty-two Flights, exclusive of those already operating at Seaton Carew and Cramlington. It was considered that twenty-seven of these Flights could be established at various coastal aerodromes by the end of June, and it was suggested that the remaining five Flights might be allocated to existing airship stations.[3] The Admiralty accepted the proposal while pointing out that the number of aeroplanes offered was inadequate to maintain vigilance over those coastal waters where continuous aeroplane patrols were deemed neces-

[1] Some had 90 horse-power Royal Aircraft Factory engines which were reliable.
[2] There were instances when a D.H.6 remained afloat for as long as ten hours.
[3] At the request of the Admiralty these five Flights were allotted to the United States Naval Air Service for patrols off the north-east coast of Ireland. The American air service had personnel available, but no aeroplanes.

sary. It was agreed that the Flights should be disposed as follows:

Humber to the Tees	5 Flights
Tees to St. Abb's Head	4 ,,
Portsmouth Group	4 ,,
South Western	8 ,,
Irish Sea	6 ,,

These Flights of D.H.6 aeroplanes were responsible for the main anti-submarine aeroplane patrol work to the end of the war. As a body they were the Cinderella of the air service. Many of the flying personnel suffered physical disabilities, some the result of service overseas. The repair facilities were never adequate, and the Flights were at no time up to strength in pilots, observers, or mechanics, so that the personnel were always overworked. For most of the time during which the Flights operated no armourers were available, nor any efficient bomb sights, and the bombs themselves were stored, more often than not, under tarpaulins in open fields, with the result that many failed to explode when dropped. Few Flights had regular observers and they had to rectify this deficiency by borrowing the services of trawler hands from local naval authorities.[1] These various troubles were of a trying kind, but the personnel suffered most perhaps from the housing conditions on the aerodromes. Many were under canvas, or else were scattered in billets at distances up to two miles from their stations. In October 1918 the Vice-Admiral Commanding the East Coast of England wrote to the Admiralty urging the immediate provision of huts. 'The matter', he said, 'is one that is of very great importance from a naval point 'of view, inasmuch as the absence of proper accommodation 'will undoubtedly react on the efficiency of the aerial 'escorts and anti-submarine patrols during the winter 'months.' The following extracts from the records of the Flights give an idea of the conditions under which they sometimes had to work:

[1] Patrol work was usually done by the D.H.6 flown as a single-seater and carrying bombs and light wireless equipment. For convoy work, however, a two-seater was considered essential with an observer trained in the use of the Aldis signalling lamp. The general proportion was 75 per cent. single-seaters and 25 per cent. two-seaters.

'Camp at Tynemouth, flooded out; all men's clothing 'and bedding wet through and in a disgraceful con- 'dition. Some of the tents blown down, others float- 'ing about. Endeavouring to billet the men in the 'meantime.'

'Officers' marquee at Elford collapsed during last 'night; impossible to re-erect as canvas is rotten. Men's 'field kitchen has no cover. Cooking only possible in 'boilers and field urns out in the open.'

'All tents at Seahouses flattened, messing being 'arranged in temporary billet. Whole situation most 'unsatisfactory, but am powerless to provide huts.'

The Air Ministry had placed orders for an adequate number of huts to serve as winter quarters many months before, but manufacturers, confronted with difficulties and delays in obtaining the requisite material and labour, could not keep to their promised dates for delivery and it was not until the end of the war that the first huts were dispatched.

In spite, however, of the unsatisfactory conditions under which the Flights worked, on the ground and in the air, they played their somewhat lonely and monotonous part with a will which more than once earned the admiration of the naval authorities with whom they co-operated. The opinion of naval officers who had the best opportunities to judge was that, in the patrolled areas, the U-boat commanders were continuously hampered in their operations. Off the north-east coast, during a period of four months in 1918, the greatest losses in merchant shipping occurred on a day when no aircraft could go out because of the strength of the wind. Off the coasts of Cornwall the experience was somewhat similar. There was a day in August 1918 when, in this area, merchant ships passed on their way unhindered so long as the air patrols were maintained, but in the afternoon, when the onset of heavy weather drove the aircraft patrols in, four ships were attacked and two of them destroyed. What the Lords Commissioners of the Admiralty thought of the patrols was set out in a letter to the Air Council in August 1918. 'They are of the 'opinion', said the letter, 'that considerable credit is due

'to pilots who first undertook the anti-submarine work,
'flying land machines over sea, particularly in the case of
'those using D.H.6 type, a training machine of poor per-
'formance, and by no means suited for this class of work.
'If the Air Council see no objection My Lords suggest
'that an expression of appreciation may be conveyed to the
'officers concerned—in addition to such other action as the
'Air Council may think desirable.'

Admiralty Air Requirements

Needless to say the D.H.6 organization did not meet the considered needs of the navy for anti-submarine work by aeroplanes. In April 1918 the Admiralty completed a statement of its general policy for the employment of aircraft in the U-boat campaign under the following headings:

I. *Coastal Areas.* An operational air group to be formed for each strategic area. The head-quarters to be in immediate touch with the senior naval officer and with the local base intelligence office, and linked by telephone with all air stations and wireless stations in the Group.

(*a*) Kite balloons to furnish an escort to convoys, and to work with hunting flotillas, as suitable surface craft for towing them become available.

(*b*) Airships to be employed principally for escort duties and in searching in advance of convoys; also to co-operate with hunting flotillas, in diverting traffic, and in searching for mines.

(*c*) Aeroplanes of a suitable type to maintain intensive patrol of an inshore zone up to 15 or 20 miles from the coast to assist in escort work, and to take it over in weather when airships cannot operate within that zone. A specially equipped squadron also to be maintained on a mobile basis to be disposed as necessary in relation to intelligence regarding the movements of enemy submarines. A Flight of the squadron to be prepared to leave at immediate notice to attack a submarine or to co-operate with surface-hunting craft anywhere within range, irrespective of whether the position was in the inshore zone or not.

(d) Seaplanes to work further to seaward, carrying out sweeps, escorting shipping, co-operating with hunting craft, and working hydrophones, when weather permits, in any area within range.

(e) The personnel to be specially trained in submarine hunting.[1]

(f) Each station to have its own wireless equipment to enable aircraft on patrol to communicate.

(g) A system of Direction-Finding Stations to be established.

II. *Barrage*. So far as their endurance permitted aircraft would patrol each barrage area, co-operate with surface craft, and endeavour to compel the U-boats to dive into deep mine-fields.

III. *Deep Sea Work*. In the first instance, work over deep sea areas would be undertaken by kite balloons. Experiments would also be made in fitting two auxiliary cruisers to carry seaplanes, and in towing airships from surface craft.

IV. *Attacks upon Enemy Bases*. Enemy bases in Belgium would be attacked as nearly continuously as possible. Attacks on bases in Germany would be made as opportunity offered, and as the range of aircraft operating either from towed lighters, from ships, or from the coast, developed.

In accordance with the above general scheme, strategical positions for air stations were provisionally selected, and a chart of the British islands on which the proposed dispositions of the aircraft were marked was sent to the Air Ministry.

The Admiralty stated that they did not expect that aircraft could be supplied in the immediate future, but that the dispositions shown represented what should be worked to as soon as possible.[2] The following points were made:

[1] A School for anti-submarine observers was opened at Aldeburgh. Books dealing with U-boat tactics, &c., were compiled by the Admiralty and issued to the air stations, which were also visited by expert lecturers.

[2] It was subsequently stated that the programme of expansion should be fulfilled by the end of 1918.

'1. *Aeroplanes.*

'(*a*) For the present, 27 Flights of D.H.6 have been 'arranged for patrol of various parts of the British coast 'and a further 5 Flights are being arranged for use by 'U.S. Air Force in Ireland. The use of D.H.6 machines 'is recognized as a temporary expedient until a type 'of machine specially designed for submarine hunting is 'available.

'(*b*) Proposals for the building of such a type of aero-'plane have been approved by Their Lordships and for-'warded to the Air Ministry.[1]

'(*c*) 36 squadrons of the latter type (648 machines) are 'eventually required for coastal patrol.

'This number is required on the basis of having one 'Duty Flight, one Stand By Flight, and one Stand Off 'Flight for each sub-area, and one Hunting Squadron for 'each area to be disposed in relation to intelligence received. 'To begin with, it is suggested that the various stations 'should only be equipped with two Flights each and fitted 'up in priority in relation to enemy activity to their full 'establishment.

'(*d*) It is proposed that the U.S.A. should supply the 'personnel and eventually the whole equipment of nine 'of the above squadrons, for use in Ireland, but to begin 'with all equipment except personnel would require to be

---

[1] The proposal was for a two-seater 'pusher', or twin-engined tractor, giving a clear view ahead and below, to carry one 500-lb. bomb or two 230-lb. bombs, machine-gun, and wireless transmitting and receiving sets. The aeroplane was to be fitted with a flotation gear, was to carry a minimum of four hours' fuel supply, to be capable of a slow landing on small aerodromes, and to be equipped with reliable and silenced engine, or engines. At the same time, specifications were communicated to the Air Ministry for the approved large flying boat, and for a small boat seaplane. The large flying boat (large America type), for long-distance reconnaissance, bombing, and hydrophone work, was to carry two 500-lb. bombs, be able to get off a rough sea, have silent engines easy to start or restart, and was to have an endurance of 600 miles for reconnaissance of the Heligoland Bight without the aid of lighters. The small single-engined flying boat was required for hydrophone work. It was to be capable of carrying one 500-lb. or two 230-lb. bombs, machine-guns, and wireless receiving and transmitting sets. The endurance was to be four hours and the cruising speed 60 knots.

'provided by the R.A.F. It is understood that the U.S.
'Air Force are willing to undertake this.[1]

'2. *Aeroplanes.*

'The above establishment is exclusive of the machines
'required for the Boulogne, Yarmouth, Ostend area, where
'machines must be able to defend themselves, and for that
'area 13 Flights of D.H.9 or other light bombers capable
'of self-defence are required.

'3. *Seaplanes.*

'(i) Float type or Small Boat. 180 machines or 30 Flights
'are required at present. Unless a machine of the above
'type is evolved of sufficiently good performance to justify
'its separate existence, it is intended that this type should
'die out, being replaced by the Large Boat type when the
'production of the latter type and facilities for housing
'at the various stations which now use Float Seaplanes have
'been arranged.

'(ii) Large Americas. 165 are at present required to be
'produced and maintained from British resources. When
'this number has been attained a further 180 are required
'to replace the Float Seaplanes now in use, the substitu-
'tion being made in such a manner that a total of not less
'than 363 seaplanes, including both small and large, are
'in commission at any one time. There are 12 Docking
'Lighters arranged for, and these can be used as temporary
'mobile bases for a similar number of Large Americas in-
'cluded in the above estimate. 54 Towing Lighters for
'Large Americas have also been ordered. Their function
'is for offensive operations against submarine bases, &c.,
'and it is anticipated that the wastage of aircraft used
'on this duty will be much heavier than in general patrol
'work.

'4. *Airships.*

'It is proposed to retain the present North Sea type
'until a Rigid type which is sufficiently good for working

[1] The U.S. Navy eventually found it impossible to supply the personnel for these squadrons.

'with the Fleet and for long-range reconnaissance is pro-
'duced. For the more local patrol work, it is proposed to
'concentrate on the small S.S. Twin type of Airship and
'when the present Coastal or C. Star Airships are worn out,
'to utilize the shed space for a further number of S.S.
'Twins, which have been included in the estimate.[1]

The factor which limited the expansion of naval air
units, as of all others, was engine output. When, in July
1917, the Government decided that the air services should
be doubled, the Large America flying-boat was enjoying
a gratifying success against the submarine and against
the Zeppelin. Towards the end of August 1917, therefore, when the Admiralty drew up revised plans for an
expansion of the naval air service to comply with the
Government decision, the number of Large Americas for
the 1918 programme was increased from 180 (as estimated
in May 1917) to 426. Of this number 150 were to be
allotted to stations in the Orkneys in accordance with the
scheme for a North Sea mine barrage, at that time in course
of development. In addition to the large flying-boats, the
expansion programme allowed for the provision of 413
float seaplanes, 122 'Baby' seaplanes, 431 light aeroplanes,
and 36 bombing aeroplanes.

The life of the Large America type was reckoned as six
months, so that 852 would be required in 1918 to maintain
an establishment of 426. It soon became clear, however,
that an output of this kind was impossible unless new
facilities for the construction of the flying-boats were provided. Eventually the United States Navy Department
agreed to help by equipping the seaplane stations at Brest,
Waterford, Queenstown, Berehaven, and at Lough Swilly.
Furthermore, the establishments of the English stations
were cut down, and as a result of these measures the total

[1] The first S.S. Twin was designed and built at Mullion. She was
wrecked on the 15th of March, a fortnight after her first flight. The S.S.
T.1. was completed at Wormwood Scrubbs in April 1918. The Twins
were equipped with two 75 horse-power Rolls-Royce engines. The car,
of watertight construction, was streamlined. Approval was given in June
1918 for the construction of 115 S.S. Twins and of 53 portable sheds,
delivery to be completed by July 1919.

number of Large Americas to be kept in commission in 1918 was reduced from 426 to 234. The original figure included 60 flying-boats for the Mediterranean, but it was decided that Large Americas required for this theatre of operations must be built at Malta, so that the figure of 234 applied only to home stations. The revised statement of requirements for 1918 (put forward in November 1917) was for 525 seaplanes (including flying-boats) and 66 aeroplanes for home and anti-submarine work; 116 seaplanes, 127 aeroplanes, and 100 torpedo-carrying aeroplanes for the Grand Fleet; 6 seaplanes and 240 aeroplanes for Dunkirk; and 264 seaplanes and 104 aeroplanes for the Mediterranean. This gave a total of 911 seaplanes and 637 aeroplanes, 1,548 in all. These figures, however, did not include aircraft required for training, practice, experiment, or reserve. In addition, special proposals were put forward for aircraft to photograph enemy naval bases (18 D.H.4's plus 6 in reserve); for a special striking force of 18 D.H.4's (plus 6 reserve), 18 torpedo aeroplanes (6 reserve), and 9 Large Americas (3 reserve) to be based at or near Yarmouth for attacks on enemy minesweepers, raiding forces, &c.; and, finally, for 50 Large Americas for bombing operations.[1]

The Air Board, however, stated that, because of the engine supply position, especially as it concerned Rolls-Royce engines, even this reduced programme could not be fulfilled. It was estimated that no more than 170 Large Americas could be provided by the end of May 1918,[2] and this number, added to 34 in service, gave a total of only 204, with no allowance for wastage. In accordance with this estimate the Board of Admiralty approved naval air requirements, of flying-boats, up to June 1918, as 133 Large Americas for anti-submarine work and for reconnaissance, and 36 for the North Sea barrage. In addition, 50 would be required for the proposed offensive operations from lighters.

[1] The intention was to convey these flying-boats within striking distance of their objectives. Some 54 lighters were ordered for this purpose, but the scheme was afterwards abandoned.
[2] By the end of May only 104 had been delivered.

The new statement of requirements put forward by the Admiralty to the Air Ministry in April 1918, to which reference has already been made,[1] asked for 459 seaplanes (including 114 Large Americas to be supplied by the Air Ministry only in the event of the United States finding it impossible to provide them) and 726 aeroplanes (including 162 for Ireland to be manned by U.S.A. personnel) for home and anti-submarine work; and for 8 seaplanes and 194 aeroplanes for the Grand Fleet. It was hoped that this programme would be fulfilled at the end of 1918. For purposes of comparison, the requirements, and the position as it was at the end of the war, so far as home waters are concerned, are tabulated below:

	Seaplanes, including flying-boats.	Aeroplanes.	Total.
Requirements for 1918 as estimated in November 1917	525	66	591
Revised programme of requirements for 1918	459	726	1,185
On Operations Stations on the 1st of January 1918	291	23	314
On Operations Stations on the 9th of November 1918	285	272	557

In April 1918 one squadron of Blackburn Kangaroo twin-engined aeroplanes was established on the East Coast, and this type of aircraft, with its good view ahead and fair speed, proved very successful. Between the 1st of May 1918 and the declaration of the Armistice these aeroplanes spent a total of 600 hours on patrol, during which they sighted twelve U-boats and attacked eleven of them. They thus sighted one submarine for an average of 50 hours flying, which compares with 196 hours for the Large America flying-boats, and with 2,416 hours for coastal airships. A few D.H.4 and D.H.9 aeroplanes had also been provided before the Armistice, and more were being substituted for the D.H.6 type when the war ended.

[1] p. 334.

Hydrophone Experiments

Experiments to detect the presence of submarines from the noise they made when under way were begun early in 1915 and resulted in the production of several hydrophones of a fixed, or non-directional, type. In 1916 hydrophone shore stations were established at a few places near which U-boat activity was pronounced, and a sea-service instrument was also evolved, but it could be used only when the listening vessel had been brought to a standstill. Gradually, however, the design was improved until detection was possible at low speeds. All that might be learned from these early instruments was that a submarine was in the neighbourhood, but in the spring of 1917 an apparatus with directional qualities was evolved, although it still suffered from the drawback that the listening vessels could obtain results only so long as they moved very slowly. Experiment, inside and outside the service, continued intensively, and in the summer of 1917 a new type of instrument, called the Fish Hydrophone, promised greater success, especially at fair speeds, than anything hitherto achieved. After modifications in the design, satisfactory trials with the Fish model were made in October 1917, and supply began shortly afterwards. In July 1918 a new towed directional-type instrument, known as the 'Porpoise', was produced at the Hawkcraig Experimental Station.

The possibilities connected with the employment of hydrophones by aircraft possessed strong appeal. Whereas a U-boat might hear surface craft engaged in a hunt, and go to the bottom to avoid them, nothing of the noise made by aircraft engines could be heard in a submerged submarine. Furthermore, aircraft might go to any point, where U-boat activity was reported, unaffected by intervening shoals or land, and could arrive before the slower-moving surface craft came upon the scene to confuse hydrophone listening. A drawback was that aircraft were more restricted in their work by the weather than surface craft. Experiments were made with seaplanes in the Aegean in the spring of 1917, but the hydrophones used were of the fixed type, and the value of the trials was accordingly limited. Early in 1918 experiments of promise were made at the Westgate Air Station, but it was proved that seaplanes of the float type, such as were employed during the trials, were not very suitable on account of their poor sea-going qualities, and the experiments were therefore transferred to Large America flying-boats.

In the design of apparatus ultimately adopted, a small, single-diaphragm, bi-directional hydrophone, of a total weight of 27 lb., was mounted at the end of a rattan, or hollow wood spar, free to revolve inside a streamlined outer casing attached by gymbals to a short outrigger. A handle at the top of the spar served to rotate the hydrophone and to indicate its direction. When in use, the hydrophone hung vertically from the gymbals and about ten feet below the surface of the water. By means of a tricing line, which also served as a steadying guy, the hydrophone could be hoisted up and braced to the side of the fuselage, a process which required no more than a few seconds. The upper end of the hydrophone was disconnected from the outrigger during flight and housed in a bracket above the gunport, where it offered negligible air resistance and in no way interfered with the handling of the aircraft. Hydrophones were fitted in a number of Large America type boats and also in a few float seaplanes. The necessity for stopping the engines while listening, however, and the uncertainty of re-starting after listening, coupled with the fact that the number of flying-boats available barely sufficed for ordinary patrol work, precluded any notable employment of hydrophones on service with heavier-than-air craft during the remainder of the war.

Towards the end of 1917 hydrophone experiments were made from airships. The trials began with the assumption that the airship must remain in the air while using the instrument, which must accordingly be towed through the water. There were many technical difficulties to be overcome before a suitable towed hydrophone could be evolved, but in the spring of 1918 a fair measure of success was achieved during trials in the Wash, when it was clearly demonstrated that, in fair weather conditions, listening was possible, with engines stopped, at a drifting speed up to eight knots. Other, and more promising trials were made at the Mullion airship station, where hydrophones came into fairly regular use on Zero type airships. They were sufficiently successful to induce the Admiralty to order a standardized 'single eel' type hydrophone for employment in all Zero airships, but the instruments had not been delivered when the war ended.

Anti-Submarine Aircraft Patrols

The total mileage flown by aircraft on anti-submarine patrol in home waters in 1918, as compared with 1917, was:[1]

| | Mileage. | |
	1917	1918
Seaplanes and aeroplanes	864,497	3,504,435
Airships	591,439	1,114,938
Kite-balloons	70,810	181,974
Total:	1,526,746	4,801,347

Submarines were sighted and attacked as follows:

| | Sighted. | | Attacked. | |
	1917	1918	1917	1918
Seaplanes and aeroplanes	139	163	90	117
Airships	28	23	16	13
Kite-balloons	2	6		1

It will be observed that the increase in the number of submarines sighted in 1918 was in no way proportionate to the increase in the mileage flown. A submarine was found by aeroplanes or seaplanes in 1917 for every 6,219 miles flown, but in 1918 for every 21,499 miles, and the mileage per effective attack by heavier-than-air craft jumped from 41,166 to 389,381. This increase was due in part to the employment of aeroplanes for inshore patrol. When U-boat commanders were operating close in during daylight hours they normally maintained diving trim in order that

[1] For a detailed table of anti-submarine air patrols from the 1st of May to the 12th of November 1918, see Appendix XVII.

they might get out of sight quickly. There is not much doubt also that the Germans made greater progress in tactics and appliances, aimed at avoiding attack from the air, than the air service did in making attack more effective. In 1918, for example, most U-boats were fitted with altiscopes through which they could, without coming to the surface, see whether aircraft were about. Even so, it is clear that excellent results were obtained by aeroplanes of a fair speed which had also a good view ahead and below,[1] and it is possible that had more of this type been available for patrol there would have been a reduction rather than an increase in the mileage per submarine sighted.

Although the mileage flown by airships was two and a half times greater in 1918 than in 1917, the number of submarines sighted and attacked was smaller. The reasons are probably the same as those given above for aeroplanes and seaplanes. In particular, it should be remembered that the size and slower speed of airships made it easier for them to be detected through the altiscope and therefore to be avoided.

It may be repeated that the respect paid by the U-boat commanders to aircraft meant that important stretches of sea were kept free for shipping. From some areas, which were closely patrolled, the U-boats were driven away altogether, and in others they were compelled to maintain a diving patrol, as a result of which it was calculated that the average length of a U-boat's cruise in the North Sea was reduced from seven days to five days. To sum up, the anti-submarine aircraft organization may be likened to that of a police force. The police are not to be judged only, or even mainly, by the number of miscreants they capture, but by the effectiveness of their prevention, or in other words, by the degree of protection afforded to the lawabiding citizen. If the number of hours spent on patrol in a year by the Metropolitan police, for example, could be set down beside the number of convictions obtained, the statistics might bear some resemblance to those for aircraft patrols and U-boats sunk. An increase of police patrol hours in any one year which was accompanied by a fall in the number of convictions, would probably be read as

[1] See Appendix XVIII.

proof of an increase in the effectiveness of the police service. It might be misleading to lay stress upon the similarities, but it is right to say that the value of the antisubmarine aircraft patrols in the war is to be judged in the light of the limitations they imposed on the activities of the U-boat commanders, and not by the number of submarines destroyed. Time and again the underwater craft were scared away from convoys by escorting aircraft, and that no more than six attacks were made in 1918 on convoyed ships during more than 7,000 air escort journeys is perhaps the best index to the efficacy of the air patrol work.

U-boats destroyed

Of the U-boats attacked by aircraft in co-operation with surface craft in 1918, there is not much doubt that six were destroyed, and about twenty-five damaged, most of them slightly. A brief account of some of the attacks on German submarines will here be given. On the 30th of May the s.s. *Dungeness*, while in a convoy off Sunderland, was torpedoed by a submarine, which was not identified. The U-boat was seen from a D.H.6 aeroplane, which bombed her, and she was afterwards attacked with depth-charges from surface craft. About three hours later the submarine was sighted awash off Seaham by a Sopwith 'Baby' seaplane which dropped a bomb close to her conning tower as she was going under. Light signals from the seaplane brought a destroyer and a Blackburn Kangaroo aeroplane to the scene, but the U-boat had disappeared, and she was not found again until the following night when, about 9.15 p.m., she was seen moving under the water near Seaham, from an F.E.2b aeroplane which had been sent out from the Seaton Carew air station to take part in a special hunt. The pilot dived and two 100-lb. bombs were dropped astride the blurred outline of the U-boat. The explosion of the bombs attracted the destroyer *Locust*, one of the hunting craft, which raced to the spot and dropped a depth charge. When the water thrown up by the explosion had subsided, the aeroplane observer could still detect the outline of the submarine beneath the surface, and he was able to indicate, by hand signals, where additional depth charges should be dropped. After the fourth had exploded, the conning-tower and side of the submarine suddenly broke surface, and she turned slowly over before sinking: it is possible that she had suffered some damage during the attacks on the previous evening.

In the early morning of the 12th of August four D.H.4's of No. 217 Squadron (Dunkirk), led by Captain K. G. Boyd, while on patrol in formation near Ostend, sighted a submarine, half-blown, heading towards the Belgian port. The patrol attacked in line, and eight 230-lb. bombs, with 2½ seconds' delay-action fuses, were dropped from heights between 200 and 1,000 feet. The first bomb, dropped by the leader, hit the port side of the submarine, which rolled over and lay bottom upwards while the other bombs were bursting about her. She sank within five minutes, and there is reason to believe she was the *U.B.12* which met her end in the southern part of the North Sea about this time in unknown circumstances.

A fortnight later there was another successful attack. Soon after midday on the 28th of August the s.s. *Giralda* was hit by a torpedo east of Kettleness, and three trawlers which went to help her found a faint ripple on the water, possibly caused by a hidden submarine. Depth charges were dropped and the position was buoyed. At 3.25 in the afternoon the pilot and observer (Lieutenants E. F. Waring and H. J. Smith) in a Blackburn Kangaroo aeroplane from Seaton Carew examined the area, and the account of their subsequent adventure reads as follows: 'I have the honour to report that whilst on anti-submarine 'patrol on Blackburn Kangaroo 9983, I sighted a long oil 'slick, close in shore, about five miles away from me, just 'as the south bound convoy was passing Runswick Bay. I 'altered course to investigate and sighted a submarine (sub- 'merged) in position 54–31 N. 0.40 W. She appeared to be 'lying on the bottom and did not alter her position. I got 'into position over her and released one 520-lb. bomb 'which detonated about 30 ft. from her starboard bow. 'Quantities of thick dark oil rose to the surface and a long 'succession of large bubbles, about 10 feet in diameter. We 'fired red Very Lights and H.M.S. *Ouse* came to the spot

'where bubbles were still rising and dropped 7 or 8 depth
'charges round the position. The last depth charge ob-
'served detonated directly on top of the hull of the sub-
'marine.' The destroyer *Ouse* rejoined the convoy to which
she was acting as part escort. About a fortnight later the
wreckage of the German submarine—the *U.C.70*—was
found by divers: she was lying on a rocky bottom in about
fourteen fathoms of water.

The *Ouse* helped also in the destruction of another U-
boat at the end of September. On the 29th a German
submarine was lying on the bottom of the sea, in twenty-
five fathoms of water, off Newbiggin Point. It was a
Sunday afternoon and the crew were perhaps taking a rest,
as they might do with quiet mind because the sea was so
calm there was small chance that they could operate, un-
discovered, against surface craft. It was the flat calm, however, which in the end led to their destruction. It happened
that while the crew were at ease, the tiniest of leakages in
one of the U-boat's tanks was causing a thread of oil to
carry a message to the surface of the sea. The patch formed
on the water was of the faintest, but the sea was so un-
troubled that the discoloration might just attract the
notice of an experienced air observer if one, by chance,
approached close enough. This condition was about to be
fulfilled. The Scandinavian convoy was on its way from
the Tyne escorted by destroyers and by armed trawlers,
and with the rigid airship *R.29*, from East Fortune,
overhead. At 1.25 p.m. the slight patch of oil attracted
the curiosity of the airship crew and a message, 'Oil patch
'rising below me', was flashed to the *Ouse*, the leading
destroyer. She at once altered course and raced for the
position, but she could see nothing and signalled: 'Drop
'light over it'. By way of reply a 230-lb. bomb was dropped
from the airship and the *Ouse*, when calm had been restored,
began to drop depth-charges. Other escorting destroyers
and trawlers joined in the attack, and a second 230-lb.
bomb was also dropped from the airship: at 2.30 p.m.
oil was reported rising to the surface in great quantities.
The convoy had by this time drawn away and the escorting
ships, except two trawlers fitted with hydrophones, left to

rejoin the merchant vessels. The *R.29* remained in the area of the oil patch until 4 p.m., when she also rejoined the convoy. The submarine may have been the *U.B.115*, which had left her base at Zeebrugge on the 18th of September for a cruise off the north-east coast of England and was never heard of again.

Earlier in the same month, on the 10th, the destroyer *Ophelia* was east of the Orkneys, flying a kite-balloon when, about 6.20 a.m., the observer (Lieutenant S. G. Mawdsley, R.A.F.) in the basket of the balloon reported a black object on the port bow. As the destroyer altered course and bore down upon the object it was revealed as the conning-tower of a submarine. The U-boat quickly disappeared under the water, but two charges, set to depths of 200 feet, were dropped through the oil patch which marked the position where she had been. The destroyer passed across the spot again and dropped a third depth-charge, after which she circled the position for some time. A few minutes after the explosion of the third depth-charge, the observer in the balloon telephoned to the ship that an upheaval had taken place under the water: the destroyer thereupon returned to the position and found much fuel-oil rising to the surface. The submarine was possibly the *U.B.83*, which never returned to her base.

In the next successful encounter a non-rigid airship, the s.s. *Z.1.*, from the Capel station, near Folkestone, took a part and the pilot was an American, Ensign N. J. Learned.[1] In the afternoon of the 16th of September, while the airship was making a routine patrol, a line of oil was seen to be slowly forming about seven miles from Capel. For half an hour the airship followed the line until it ceased in an extending patch of oil. The airship signalled patrol boats to investigate and a depth-charge dropped from one of them led to two explosions which, half an hour later, were followed by a third. Such was the end of the *U.B.103*.

Submarine Attacks on Convoys

It was not possible to provide aircraft along the coast in sufficient numbers or of the latest type to accompany

[1] Engineer, W. H. King; Wireless Operator, D. Paton.

all convoys, but when aircraft were present they contributed effectively to the security of the ships. An instance of an attack on a convoy escorted by aircraft occurred on the 26th of December 1917. On that day the airship *C.23A* had left her station at Mullion about 11 a.m. to search east of Falmouth to ensure that the way was clear for the starting out of a convoy of 24 ships. At 2.20 p.m. the convoy was in line ahead with its escort of two destroyers and ten armed trawlers on the starboard side and the airship on the windward (port) side. At 3 p.m., when the airship was steering east for the head of the line some distance away, it was seen that one of the leading ships had been hit by a torpedo. The *C.23A* moved at full speed towards the ship, which was about seven miles distant, and three minutes later saw a second ship torpedoed. At 3.10 p.m. the airship had reached the position, and within three minutes one of the two ships which had been hit, sank: the second torpedoed vessel was abandoned. The airship continued to patrol between the derelict vessel and the convoy; and at 3.40 p.m. a torpedo was seen to break surface astern of the last ship of the group. The airship at once sought the beginning of the torpedo track and dropped two 100-lb. bombs with delay-action fuses, but the sea was rough and no results were observed. The airship crew kept watch over the rear of the convoy for another hour, but no trace of the U-boat was discovered.

In 1918 air escort work in protection of convoys greatly increased. The statistics are as follow:

	No. of Escorts.[1]	Vessels attacked while in convoy.
Aeroplane and Seaplane	4,869	2
Airships	2,141	1
Kite-balloons	131	3

In comparing the number of the escortings by different types of aircraft it should be remembered that aeroplane

[1] The figures for the number of escorts do not refer to separate convoys, but to individual aircraft. One convoy, for example, might be picked up by relays of aircraft from different stations along the coast.

and seaplane escorts were of short duration, that airships kept company for longer periods, and that kite-balloon escortings usually extended to several days. A word or two may be said about the occasions on which vessels were attacked while in convoy. On a day in July 1918 a submarine was reported in the vicinity of a convoy by an escorting D.H.6 from the Redcar air station. Shortly afterwards a torpedo was seen to be approaching one of the leading ships, and the crew in the aeroplane dropped a flare, enabling the ship to alter course and avoid the torpedo. 'The aeroplane's prompt action undoubtedly saved 'the convoy', said the Vice-Admiral's report of the episode. Another instance of attack on a convoy when under escort by aeroplanes occurred in August 1918, in the area of the Farne Islands. An escorting D.H.6 was flying close to the convoy, in a rain-storm, when one of the ships, the Swedish s.s. *Jonkoping*, was hit and immediately sank. The pilot of the aeroplane flew seawards from the wreck and found a submarine faintly outlined near the surface. He dived and released a 100-lb. bomb, but the poor visibility due to the rain made it impossible to see what the effect of the bomb was. The one occasion in 1918 when an airship escort was present when an attack was made was during the assembly of a convoy off Trevose Head at a time when the airship was about five miles distant from the ships. In two of the three instances in which kite-balloons were concerned, the U-boat attacks were made at early dawn when the visibility was no more than 800 yards and when the balloons were being flown from ships some distance from the attacked vessel. It is of interest also that two successful attacks on convoys were made in 1918 very soon after kite-balloons had been hauled down.

Mine-fields in the Heligoland Bight

A broad belt of mine-fields had been laid across the Heligoland Bight with the original object of barring the passage of U-boats. The Germans, however, marked a numbers of channels by buoys and swept these channels as continuously as possible, with the result that the goings and comings of the U-boats had not been unduly restricted.

Although the vigilance of the enemy was successful in keeping the Bight open, the British Admiralty decided to maintain the mine barrage in 1918. The mines had not stopped the passage of the U-boats, but they had sunk several of them: the mines constituted a hindrance and a constant danger, and it was desirable that their pressure, though it fell far short of previous hopes, should be continued.

The movements and intentions of German vessels in the Bight area were often known in advance to the naval intelligence division in Whitehall. Air reconnaissances of the mine-fields, therefore, and of the German mine-sweeping activities, were only exceptionally required. On the other hand, if British aircraft rarely appeared the German authorities would, when they found precise British counter-action following upon sweeping operations, have cause for suspicion, and they might be led to form conclusions about the sources of the British information. It was desirable they should assume that the information came from the air, and reconnaissances extending to the outer portions of the Bight were therefore planned on the basis that the more the enemy mine-sweepers or other vessels saw of the British aircraft the better.[1]

The section of the mine barrage in the area of Terschelling was kept under observation by flying-boats operating direct from Yarmouth, that in the western Bight by flying-boats launched from towed lighters, and in the northern and eastern Bight by aeroplanes carried in the *Furious*.[2]

---

[1] The Germans assumed, as it was desired (and natural) that they should, that air reconnaissance gave the necessary information. 'The English were 'particularly anxious to know where we were sweeping for mines, the clear 'channels for our submarines, and how the boats were piloted in and out. 'Seaplanes were told off to obtain this information. . . . We could always 'take it for granted that whenever our minesweepers were observed at their 'work, the area which they had cleared would again become infested with 'mines during the next few days.' (Kapitänleutnant Moll in *Die deutschen Luftstreitkräfte im Weltkriege*, p. 550.)

[2] The *Furious*, the flagship of Rear-Admiral R. F. Phillimore, Admiral Commanding Aircraft, rejoined the Grand Fleet, after re-fit, in March 1918. See Vol. IV, pp. 34–6.

The suggestion that lighters should be used to carry flying-boats across the North Sea, and so increase their radius of action, had been put forward by Commander J. C. Porte at Felixstowe in September 1916. He had supplied a rough sketch of the type of special craft he had in mind which must, he stated, be strong enough to be towed at about twenty-five knots by a destroyer. His sketch showed a lighter which could be submerged by the flooding of tanks: after the flying-boat (each lighter was to carry one) had been floated in, the craft, through the ejection of water from the tanks by means of compressed air, would rise clear for towing. Admiralty representatives paid a visit to Felixstowe, and following a talk with Commander Porte a design had been begun without delay. It was decided that only the after end of the lighter should be submerged and that the flying-boat should be hauled up by a winch fitted on the fore deck. Steel construction was adopted in order that part of the hull might be used as an airtight trimming tank.

In January 1917 orders for four lighters had been placed, and the first was successfully tested at the builder's works in June. Towing trials which followed in the Solent were of such promise that the director of the naval air service proposed, in July, to order fifty additional lighters, but the Board of Admiralty thought it advisable that further trials should first be made in the North Sea. These took place, under the direction of Commodore R. Y. Tyrwhitt, at the beginning of September 1917, when a lighter, carrying a flying-boat, was towed at speeds up to thirty-two knots. As a result it was decided to build twenty-five more lighters immediately—a number subsequently increased to fifty. Their construction was undertaken at the new Government shipyard at Richborough by Royal Engineers, and the first had been completed in May 1918: thirty-one of the fifty had been delivered by the end of the war.

Some of these lighters were put to a use different from that which had been intended. In the summer of 1918 it was suggested that a few should be fitted with fixed wood flying-off platforms to accommodate a single-seater fighter aeroplane, and trials revealed that in suitable conditions of weather Sopwith 'Camels' could be flown off. The Admiralty attached much importance to this development because it promised a means of transporting fighting aeroplanes for daylight attacks upon Zeppelins in the North Sea, and upon German seaplanes near their bases. A total of twelve lighters were so fitted with flying-off platforms: they were equipped with a derrick to salve the aeroplane after flight, but, in practice, this seldom proved possible.

It was hoped eventually to employ the flying-boats, carried in the lighters, for a bombing offensive against the German naval bases in the North Sea.[1] Meanwhile, in order that experience might be gained in their handling, it was decided that they should first be used to extend the air reconnaissance in the Heligoland Bight, and in February 1918 standing orders were drawn up which made provision for two forms of air reconnaissance, called Scheme 'A' and Scheme 'B'. Where the area to be reconnoitred was within 150 miles radius of Yarmouth and therefore within range of Large America flying-boats operating from East Coast stations direct, Scheme 'B' was ordered. For areas outside this range, for which it was necessary to transport flying-boats by lighter, and to send a supporting naval squadron, Scheme 'A' was put into force.

The first operation under the latter scheme took place on the 19th of March 1918. At 5.30 a.m. three destroyers, towing flying-boats in lighters, arrived, with a supporting force, off the German coast. The three flying-boats were in the air at 7 a.m. and they proceeded on reconnaissance patrol until about 8.30 a.m., when two German seaplanes from the naval air base at Borkum made an appearance. The flying-boats shot one of the enemy seaplanes down in flames, and completed their reconnaissance without further interruption, after which they flew home to their base direct. The supporting force had not long been back in harbour at Harwich on the 20th, when the Admiralty

[1] Because of difficulties associated with forecasting the weather conditions in the North Sea, and because of technical progress made in the design of long-distance bombing aeroplanes, this project was abandoned in July 1918.

ordered that a similar operation be attempted next afternoon. Accordingly, at 6.30 a.m. on the 21st, the squadron sailed, and after picking up the destroyers with their lighters in tow, moved across the North Sea at 27 knots. Soon after midday the three Large Americas were in the air, and for about three hours they flew over mine-sweepers and destroyers in the Heligoland Bight, making careful note of the activity below them.[1] For part of the time two German seaplanes kept within sight, but out of range, of the flying-boats.

The air reconnaissance of the Bight disclosed, among other items of information, that mine-sweepers were clearing an area north of Ameland and Terschelling. On the 2nd of April a new mine-field was duly laid, and flying-boats on the two following days went across from Yarmouth to see if the Germans were again sweeping. No enemy craft were seen and, acting on a belief that they might be working under cover of darkness, the Harwich Force attempted a raid on the night of the 4th/5th of April, but nothing happened. A little later in the month, however, the Admiralty had reason to assume that another expedition would not meet with the same disappointment, and, on the morning of the 20th of April, the Harwich Force moved out of harbour. Two flying-boats, which had left Yarmouth at 8.55 a.m. to make a special reconnaissance, found, at 10.45 a.m., four German destroyers and four mine-sweepers at work north of Terschelling. Wireless messages giving the news were sent out from the flying-boats, but the signals were not picked up at Yarmouth air station. At 2.10 p.m., when the flying-boats had landed and reports had been made by word of mouth, the information about the enemy vessels was passed to the Harwich Force which at that time was nearing the Terschelling Light Vessel. Contact was made about 5 p.m., when British destroyers found the four German destroyers and fought a rapid action in which one vessel on each side was damaged.

Air reconnaissances early in May indicated that the

---

[1] The Admiralty expressed appreciation of the way in which the reconnaissances had been made, and said that the air reports had given valuable information.

Germans were sweeping a channel through the British mine-field north of the Frisian Coast, and Rear-Admiral Tyrwhitt was ordered to seek out and attack the enemy. The Harwich Force sailed on the 12th of May with three flying-boat lighters in the tow of destroyers. The ships assembled off Terschelling at 7 a.m. next morning, but a change in the weather, which became unfavourable for air reconnaissance, led to the abandonment of the enterprise.

Destruction of a Zeppelin

On the morning of the 10th of May 1918 the Zeppelin *L.62* set out from Nordholz to make a routine patrol over the Heligoland mine-fields. As she flew, her course was plotted in an office in the British Admiralty, and because she was a naval airship she was temporarily identified by a girl's name, *Clara*.[1] The drama of her destruction began with four successive code messages which told the air station at Killingholme of *Clara*'s progress across the squared chart of the North Sea. When the fourth signal was received, two minutes after midday, it was judged worth while to have a flying-boat ready to start upon receipt of the next message. More than an hour passed before this came in, at 1.08 p.m., and it gave what had been the position of the Zeppelin at 12.34 p.m. By this time an idea of the probable movements of the *L.62* had been obtained, and the flying-boat[2] left at 1.20 p.m. with some expectation that the airship would be intercepted. The story of what followed may be read in the report of Captain A. H. Munday, the second pilot. 'At 4.30', he said, 'I observed 'a German Zeppelin of the latest type on our port beam. 'It was about 1,500 feet above our machine and, approxi- 'mately, a mile away from us, and was proceeding due east 'in the direction of Heligoland. I pointed it out to Captain 'Pattinson and he at once put the machine at its best 'climbing angle. I went to the forward cockpit and tested 'the gun and tried the mounting, and found everything

---

[1] See Vol. III, p. 173.
[2] *Crew*: Captain T. C. Pattinson, first pilot; Captain A. H. Munday, second pilot; Sergeant H. R. Stubbington, engineer; Air-Mechanic Johnson, wireless telegraphy operator.

'worked satisfactorily. The engineer rating immediately
'proceeded to the rear gun cockpit and tested both port
'and starboard guns. At this time our machine was at a
'height of 6,000 feet. The hostile craft had evidently seen
'us first, and was endeavouring to get directly over us in
'order to attack us with bombs. When at a height of 8,000
'feet and the Zeppelin had climbed to a height of 9,000
'feet I opened the attack and fired about 125 rounds of
'explosive ammunition. The engineer rating also opened
'fire and fired about the same number of rounds. The
'Zeppelin was about 500 yards distant. All our fire appeared
'to hit the craft and little spurts of flame, our explosive
'bullets, appeared all over the envelope. I noticed much,
'what appeared to be water, ballast, and many articles
'being thrown overboard and then the nose of the hostile
'craft went up a few degrees from the vertical: this was
'apparently soon checked by the occupants, as the craft was
'righted and commenced to climb as much as possible. I
'had a gun stoppage and spent many minutes clearing it,
'being obliged to take the breech of the gun to pieces.

'The Zeppelin continued to climb and gain on us slightly
'and again endeavoured to get directly over our machine.
'The enemy succeeded and dropped five or six bombs. The
'engineer rating reported to the first pilot (Captain Pattin-
'son) that seven hostile destroyers were circling around
'beneath us. We were now at a height of 11,000 feet and
'the Zeppelin's height was approximately 12,500 feet. I
'opened fire again and fired another 130 rounds of explosive
'and tracer bullets. I noticed the propeller of the Zeppelin's
'port engine almost stop and the craft suddenly steered
'hard to port. I concluded that the port engine had been
'hit by our gunfire as well as other parts of the craft, as the
'envelope and gondolas seemed a background for all the
'flashes of the explosive and tracer bullets. There was
'much more outpourings of ballast and articles and con-
'siderable smoke. I concluded that we had finished the
'Zeppelin and informed Captain Pattinson that we had
'bagged it. But the craft again headed for Holstein in a
'crabwise fashion, emitting much smoke. I had other gun
'stoppages and one bad jamb. One of the explosive bullets

'exploded in the gun and flashed into my face and on to my
'hand but outside of a few scratches I received no injury.
'Our port engine commenced to give slight trouble and
'the engineer investigated. He reported that an oil feed
'pipe had broken and that it would not be long before it
'would break in two. As soon as I had my gun cleared of
'the trouble caused by the exploding of the explosive
'bullet I signalled to Captain Pattinson that I was ready to
're-attack and looked for the enemy craft. I saw it still
'proceeding due east in a crabwise fashion. It was losing
'height and emitting smoke which was of a black variety
'though parts of it were pure white. The hostile destroyers
'underneath opened fire on us and owing to engine trouble,
'lack of petrol for our return journey, and being only about
'60 miles off Heligoland we gave up the attack at 5.35,
'having been attacking for one hour and five minutes.

'The oil pipe broke in two and we were forced to glide
'and land in a rough sea. The engineer quickly climbed on
'to the top of the engine and repaired the break with tape.
'Fifteen minutes later we took off. As the machine was
'difficult to control, Captain Pattinson asked me to get
'out and endeavour to ascertain whether we had damaged
'the rudder or elevator in taking off and in looking back I
'observed the German destroyers steaming with all possible
'speed in our direction.'

Exactly what happened on board the *L.62* will never be known. Some time after the attack by the flying-boat the Zeppelin blew up, in flames: there were no survivors.

The Admiralty ordered a reconnaissance of the eastern section of the Bight to take place on the 18th of May. The towed flying-boats were to be off the Horn Reefs Light Buoy ready to take the air at 4.45 a.m., and after completing the reconnaissance they were to be met on the homeward journey by Large Americas from Yarmouth. Two flying-boats from Killingholme were under orders to leave at 2 a.m. to cover the withdrawal of the destroyers towing the empty lighters home. The operation passed off as planned and the reconnoitring flying-boats returned safely to Harwich after an uneventful flight of 470 miles.

Vice-Admiral Tyrwhitt, in the light cruiser *Curaçoa*, with two destroyers, broke away from the Harwich Force on the return journey to attend a conference at Rosyth. When the light cruiser was about fifty miles off Newcastle a flying-boat was sighted on the water, and one of the destroyers, sent to investigate, found on board two American Ensigns who had left their base at Killingholme to make a patrol, five days before. They had been forced down by engine failure five miles from the coast and had drifted seawards day and night: the flying-boat was towed into the Tyne by the destroyer.

The British offensive waged against the Zeppelins had made airship reconnaissance of the mine-field area hazardous, and throughout 1918, therefore, the importance of the German seaplane service increased. From the stations at List, Borkum, Heligoland, and Nordeney, seaplanes helped to guard the mine-sweeping flotillas from surprise attacks by enemy craft, and to guide the U-boats through the cleared paths in the mine-fields, and they hampered so far as they could the British mine-laying and reconnaissance expeditions. The stations were under the commander of the German Second Seaplane Division, who had his head-quarters at Wilhelmshaven. Although the German authorities had to practice a strict economy in the allotment of aircraft, they did not hesitate to expand the North Sea stations in 1918, and it became necessary to re-apportion the work of Borkum and Nordeney: the former station was made mainly responsible for fighting, and the latter for reconnaissance. They had the use of the carriers *Answald*, *Santa Elena*, and *Stuttgart*, and it was usual to send one or other of the carriers with the sweeping flotillas in order to give the seaplanes a wider radius of action than they had when operating from their base direct. 'Except in urgent and special instances', says a German authority, 'mine-sweeping was only carried out 'after preliminary air reconnaissance and with the pro-'tection afforded by aircraft patrols.'[1]

[1] Kapitänleutnant Moll in *Die deutschen Luftstreitkräfte im Weltkriege*, p. 549.

There is evidence that in 1918 the effective strength at Borkum averaged about 20 seaplanes, at Nordeney 48, Heligoland 24, and at List 32 (as compared with an average of about 12 for each station in 1917). The best-known types of seaplane used were a Friedrichshafener, with a 200 horse-power Benz engine, carrying a wireless-receiving as well as transmitting set, and equipped with two machine-guns; and a Brandenburger two-seater fighter monoplane with one fixed and one movable gun. In 1918 there were also in service, for long reconnaissance, Brandenburg and Gotha types with twin 200 horse-power Benz engines, and there was a Dornier experimental type with four 250 horse-power Maybach engines. The small fighting sea-planes were apt to break up on choppy water, that is to say, they were not particularly seaworthy, and they were therefore usually accompanied by a reconnaissance-type seaplane. Although the presence of the larger craft limited to some extent the activities of the fighters, which were compelled to throttle down in order to keep station, the accompanying seaplane could, when a fight took place, call for reinforcements by wireless, and was also at hand ready to pick up, when necessary, the occupants of a fighting seaplane forced down on the water.

The German seaplane units were many times in action with aircraft from the East Coast air stations. On the 30th of May two flying-boats from Yarmouth were making a reconnaissance of the Borkum area when one of them (F.2a. No. 8660) was forced down with engine trouble. The pilot flashed a message by Aldis lamp to say that the trouble was repairable, and the second flying-boat there-upon circled in the neighbourhood. After fifty minutes two German fighting seaplanes appeared, and a combat ensued, but when a few rounds had been fired the two forward machine-guns in the flying-boat jambed. The German pilots then turned for Borkum with the evident intention of seeking reinforcements. They were pursued by the British flying-boat, but the pilot soon realized that he was putting too much distance between himself and his companion on the water, and he therefore turned back, but although he made a long and careful search nothing could be seen of No. 8660. The pilot at last flew home, where he landed, after eight hours in the air, with no more than twenty minutes' supply of fuel. He arrived back at 4.45 p.m. and at 6 p.m. another flying-boat, piloted by Captain R. Leckie, set out for Borkum to make a further search.[1] This boat had not long left when a pigeon flew in with a message: 'F.2a. 8660 on water attacked by three 'Huns.'

What had happened can now be told. Soon after the two German seaplanes had originally appeared, the engine trouble in No. 8660 had been rectified and she had left the water; she had already gone some distance on her way when the second flying-boat returned from pursuing the enemy seaplanes and began to search for her. As soon as the German seaplane unit at Borkum received the news of the presence of the British flying-boats, five seaplanes left to intercept them. No. 8660, meanwhile, had stayed in the air for three-quarters of an hour and had then been forced down once again with engine trouble. She was found on the water by the German pilots who immediately attacked. They were met by fire from the machine-guns of the flying-boat, but the Germans were attacking a sitting bird, and after they had poured many bursts of fire into the flying-boat they noticed that three members of the crew had jumped overboard and were swimming. The German pilots thereupon ceased to attack, and they alighted on the water and picked up two of the swimmers: the third, possibly wounded, had been drowned. One German seaplane taxied alongside the flying-boat, and the German observer went on board and found a mechanic, who had been wounded in the head by splinters, and the British pilot dead in his seat. As it was impossible to tow the flying-boat home, the German pilot fired a few shots into the petrol tank and set it on fire: the flying-boat sank within ten minutes. The seaplanes returned to Borkum with their three prisoners.[2]

---

[1] This flying-boat returned at 11 p.m., having made a night flight, the first of its kind, across the North Sea. The search had been fruitless.

[2] The prisoners were: Ensign J. J. Roe, U.S.N.F.C.; Corporal F. Grant; and Private J. N. Money. The dead pilot was Captain C. L.

On the 1st of June one of the periodical sweeps by the Harwich Force, supported by units of the Grand Fleet, made with the object of rounding up the German minesweepers and their covering ships, failed, mainly because of a warning given by patrolling hostile seaplanes, which also aimed a few bombs at the ships. Sopwith 'Camels' were flown off the Australian light cruisers *Sydney* and *Melbourne*, and Lieutenant A. C. Sharwood from the *Sydney* caught up with one of the seaplanes and forced it down on the water, but gun trouble prevented him from following up his attack.

On the 4th of June five flying-boats from Felixstowe and Yarmouth, led by Captain R. Leckie, set out for the Haaks Light Vessel with one object, to fight enemy seaplanes.[1] The German pilots accepted the challenge and one of the biggest seaplane fights of the war took place off Terschelling in the afternoon. Before the action began a flying-boat (No. 4533) had alighted on the water, and a lamp signal had been made to inform the British leader in the air that the trouble was a broken petrol feed-pipe. As it was impossible that the flying-boat could get off the somewhat disturbed sea with only one engine working, Captain Leckie sent a message telling the pilot to taxi at full speed into Dutch waters, and to burn his craft before he himself was interned. Soon afterwards five German fighting seaplanes appeared, but they turned away when the flying-boats tried to engage them, and one left formation and flew to Borkum to call up reinforcements. For about half an hour the four British pilots circled over the crippled No. 4533 as she made her slow approach towards Dutch waters. When the expected German reinforcements arrived, numbering ten seaplanes, Captain Leckie turned to meet them head on, but only two of his flying-

Young, D.S.C., R.A.F., and the drowned mechanic Private W. F. Chase. The story of this episode (as of others in which Yarmouth aircraft were involved) is told in some detail in *The Story of a North Sea Air Station* (C. F. Snowden Gamble), pp. 388–91.

[1] The flying-boats, and their first pilots were: Nos. 4295 (Captain R. Leckie) and 4289 (Captain J. Hodson) from Yarmouth, and Nos. 4302 (Captain A. T. Barker), 4533 (Captain R. F. L. Dickey), and 8689 (Ensign J. A. Eaton, U.S.N.F.C.) from Felixstowe.

boats followed him, for one had gone away in pursuit of one of the German seaplanes which had first appeared on the scene: this flying-boat, with Ensign Eaton, U.S.N., at the controls, was eventually forced down in Dutch waters where the crew were taken off by trawler hands and interned in Holland. The three flying-boats which waged the main fight flew through and scattered the German formation. The action began at 4.35 p.m. and the account of what happened is told in the words of the leader as follows: 'The enemy consisted of three very large two-
'seater machines about the size of our 310 Short, but with
'wings of equal span, and carried synchronized guns. Four
'were of the usual two-seater type, the remaining three
'being scouts. In the middle of the action Captain Hodson,
'Corporal Beaumont, and Air Mechanic Taverner reported
'that a machine attacking them from under their tail was
'shot down. This machine was seen to side-slip and spin
'into the sea, and there is little doubt was destroyed. It
'was observed from No. 4295 [the leader's flying-boat]
'that a hostile machine broke off the fight and was com-
'pelled to land in the sea about 15 miles north of Ameland.
'This machine is believed to have been one of the large
'type already mentioned. His landing was observed by
'Major T. Haggerston, Captain Leckie, and Air Mechanic
'Chapman. He made a bad landing, bouncing very heavily,
'but the extent of his injuries cannot be stated. It is
'believed that the remainder of the squadron must have
'received considerable punishment as the encounter was
'fought at very close quarters, the enemy taking first oppor-
'tunity of steering east, and was last seen steering in this
'direction. At 5.15 p.m., knowing that the Felixstowe
'machines had only sufficient petrol left to bring them
'back to base, and as 4533 [the flying-boat with engine
'trouble making for Dutch waters] was then two to three
'miles from land, I decided to return to base. At this time
'the only machine with me was No. 4289, No. 4302 having
'been forced to land in Dutch waters between Terschel-
'ling and Vlieland. Repairs were effected promptly, and
'although wing tip float was crashed on landing, machine
'succeeded in getting off again, joining me at the Haaks.

'At 5.50 p.m. No. 4289 flashed a message stating that she 'saw a machine on the water behind, so immediately altered 'course east, and soon after picked up No. 4302 believing 'this to be the machine referred to by No. 4289. Again 'proceeded to base. On landing at base, Captain Hodson 'reported that the machine he saw was on the sea with a 'Dutch trawler standing by. It would appear to be evident 'that the machine he saw was Felixstowe boat No. 8689 'which must have developed engine trouble and landed 'among the Dutch fishing fleet at Haaks. . . . It is again 'pointed out that these operations were robbed of com-'plete success entirely through faulty petrol pipes. . . . It 'it obvious that our greatest foe are not the enemy, but 'our own petrol pipes. . . .'

Of the three flying-boats which returned to their base (at 7.10 p.m.) one brought home a dead officer, Lieutenant U. F. A. Galvayne, second pilot, who had been shot through the head. It is impossible to say what the German losses were, although there is evidence that some enemy seaplanes never returned to their base. All that is known for certain is that the wreckage of a hostile seaplane, carrying a pilot with a bullet through the heart, was washed ashore on one of the Dutch islands.

At 11 p.m. on the 17th of June the *Furious*, screened by destroyers, left Rosyth with the First Light Cruiser Squadron for a reconnaissance operation in the northern waters of the Heligoland Bight. At 6.45 next morning, off Lyngvig, the carrier was making ready to send off a reconnaissance aeroplane[1] when two German seaplanes appeared. Anti-aircraft gunfire was opened upon them, but they flew at 1,500 feet above the ships and seemed to take photographs: two or three bombs from the German seaplanes fell in the sea. Meanwhile, two Sopwith 'Camels' had been flown off the carrier, but when the pilots came within striking distance of the German seaplanes, the Sopwith 'Camels' developed machine-gun trouble, and the pilots had to break away and alight on the water from which, with their aeroplanes, they were picked up by destroyers.

[1] The *Furious* at this time carried Sopwith two-seaters (1½ Strutters) for reconnaissance, and Sopwith 'Camels' for fighting.

The light cruiser *Galatea*, which was sweeping to the south, also had an adventure with German seaplanes, which aimed bombs at her, but failed to obtain a hit. A Sopwith 'Camel' from the light cruiser set out in pursuit of the enemy, and its pilot eventually came upon a hostile seaplane in the act of alighting on the Ringkjöbbing Fjord. He dived and opened fire at short range, but after a few rounds the Vickers gun jambed: nor did a tray of ammunition fired from the Lewis gun have any apparent effect. A rainstorm swept across the scene and the disappointed British pilot turned back to find the *Galatea*, but he searched in vain, and he was at last forced to land on the shore at Fjaltring in Denmark, where he was interned. The *Galatea*, meanwhile, after unsuccessful search for her missing seaplane, had rejoined the *Furious*. At 12.30 p.m. two more German seaplanes appeared over the ships and they aimed four bombs at the *Furious*, which had to make quick use of her helm to avoid them. Two Sopwith 'Camels' flew off the deck of the carrier and one of them, piloted by Lieutenant G. Heath, forced a German seaplane down on the water, where it was found and sunk by the destroyer *Valentine*, which took the occupants, pilot and observer, prisoners: there was no further incident before the squadron turned for home.

The encounters with German seaplanes during the periodical expeditions to the Bight were episodes of a kind to be expected. There was not the same likelihood that Zeppelins would be encountered, but the sweeping squadrons always hoped that this might happen. On the 20th of May, excitement had been aroused in the First Light Cruiser Squadron when an airship had been seen in the far distance, and two fighting aeroplanes had been flown off the light cruisers *Phaeton* and *Royalist*, but the airship had quickly been lost to sight. As there seemed little chance of finding the Zeppelins in the air, the offensive temper of the navy turned to projects for destroying them in their sheds. Two special Flights equipped with Sopwith 'Camel' aeroplanes were formed, and the pilots were given careful training for the operation. Towards the end of June the Flights were embarked in the *Furious* and, in company with the First Light Cruiser Squadron, the carrier left Rosyth on the 27th, but two days later, when the ships were in readiness off the Danish coast, the weather was judged to be unfavourable and the attack was abandoned.

The force left Rosyth in a second attempt on the 17th of July, but when the ships were off the Lyngvig Light at 3.30 a.m. on the 18th, a thunderstorm broke and it was decided to postpone the attack for twenty-four hours. The *Furious* and the First Light Cruiser Squadron thereupon fell back upon the supporting force, a Division of the First Battle Squadron and the Seventh Light Cruiser Squadron. At dawn on the 19th, the carrier and her escorts were once more in position eighty miles north-west of the German airship base at Tondern, and soon after 3 a.m. the two Flights of Sopwith 'Camels', totalling seven aeroplanes, each aeroplane carrying two 50-lb. bombs, were in the air.[1] The first three pilots who attacked appeared to make hits on the northernmost of the two large double sheds at Tondern. One of the pilots, who first attacked by mistake a shed used, so far as is known, as an ammunition store, reported as follows: 'This was a low shed, very solidly 'built and looked semi-underground. It was about the 'same size as the large Zeppelin shed at East Fortune. No 'chimneys or outbuildings could be observed round it, so 'I decided to drop one bomb on it, which I did from a 'height of 700 feet, hitting it in the middle. I observed no 'signs of fire as a result of this hit, but many clouds of 'smoke. Immediately after this I saw Captain Jackson at 'about 3,000 feet above me and a good distance to the east 'of the town coming down in a dive, with Lieutenant 'Williams about half a mile astern of him. I climbed a 'little and joined in with them and then observed two very 'large sheds, larger by quite a considerable amount to the 'main shed at East Fortune Air Station, and also a smaller 'one. These were at least 5 miles to the north of the town 'and were standing up quite apart from anything else on 'flat ground. . . . There was absolutely no sign of life until

[1] Pilots, Captains W. D. Jackson, W. F. Dickson, B. A. Smart, and T. K. Thyne, and Lieutenants N. E. Williams, S. Dawson, and W. A. Yeulett.

'Jackson began diving on the shed when a battery on the
'Tondern–Hoyer road opened fire: besides this no other
'battery opened fire during our bombing. Captain Jackson
'dived right on to the northernmost shed and dropped two
'bombs, one a direct hit in the middle and the other slightly
'to the side of the shed. I then dropped my one remaining
'bomb, and Williams two more. Hits were observed. The
'shed then burst into flames and an enormous conflagration
'took place rising to at least 1,000 feet, the whole of the
'shed being completely engulfed. . . .' The writer of this
report returned safely to the ships, but his two companions
lost their way and eventually landed in Denmark.

The second 'Camel' Flight, led by Captain B. A. Smart,
was reduced from four to three before the objective was
reached, through one of the pilots being forced down on
the water with engine trouble.[1] The remainder bombed
their objective, but Captain Smart alone got safely back.
One of the other two was compelled to land in Denmark
and the second, Lieutenant W. A. Yeulett, was drowned.
The attack made by these three pilots, who came upon the
scene after the first shed had been destroyed, is described
in Captain Smart's report. 'I discovered the sheds', he
says, 'two large ones and one smaller, one of the larger
'having the roof partially destroyed and emitting large
'volumes of dense black smoke. When in position I gave
'the signal and dived on remaining large shed, releasing my
'bombs at 800 to 1,000 feet. The first fell short, but the
'second hit the centre of the shed, sending up a quantity
'of smoke or dust. Whether this burst into flames later I
'am unable to state, as the whole surroundings were thick
'with mechanics or soldiers armed with rifles and machine-
'guns, which gave so disconcerting a fire that I dived with
'full engine to 50 feet and skimmed over the ground in a
'zig-zag course to avoid it, and by the time I had got
'clear was unable to see the sheds on account of thick
'screen of smoke from first shed. The clouds were now very
'low and a general haze made visibility bad. I searched in
'all directions for the remainder of my Flight, but seeing
'nothing, I made straight for the pre-arranged rendezvous

[1] This officer was picked up by a British destroyer.

'at Brede. Here I slowed down to wait for the others, but 'after doing a circuit at slow speed and still nothing in 'sight, decided it was inadvisable to wait longer as I had 'already been in the air nearly two hours and wind had in-'creased: also the clouds were so low and thick as to give 'all of us, though separated, ample protection from superior 'forces of hostile craft.' Captain Smart eventually alighted alongside the destroyer *Violent*, but the last part of his journey had provided some anxious moments: for twenty minutes his engine had given only enough power for the maintenance of flying speed a few feet above the water. The operation, although at a cost, had had the success it deserved. In the shed which had been destroyed by fire lay the ashes of the Zeppelins *L.54* and *L.60*. The second shed was seriously damaged, but no other airship was lost.

Coastal Motor-boat Operations

The operations which next call for notice were of an unusual kind. Air reconnaissances and other sources of information had revealed that the German mine-sweeping vessels were usually accompanied by light forces and that, in support, capital ships were sometimes patrolling, or even anchored, in the inner Bight. A plan was drawn up to carry coastal motor-boats, of shallow draft and equipped to fire torpedoes, to the margin of the mined area, and there launch them for a dash across the mine-fields to the inner part of the Bight. With reasonable luck and the advantage of surprise, it might be possible to inflict important losses on the enemy, but whether this happened or not, the operations, at a modest calculation, were likely to create a feeling of anxiety sufficient to induce the German naval authorities to adopt a cautious attitude about the degree of support given to the mine-sweeping vessels.

The first attempt was made on the 29th of June, when the Harwich Force left harbour with three light cruisers, each carrying two motor-boats at their davits, and with a destroyer (the *Ulleswater*) flying a kite-balloon. Three destroyers, with flying-boats on lighters in tow, were also in company. Hopes were high as the ships moved across the North Sea upon their novel undertaking, but disappointment lay in wait. At 1 a.m.[1] on the 30th the force was in position about sixty miles north-north-west of Terschelling, and the motor-boats, each carrying one torpedo, set out, at thirty knots, on their adventure. They had orders to work in pairs, and one pair which made a sweep in the north-easterly direction found, at 3 a.m., ten minesweeping trawlers. Two of them were picked out for attack: one of the torpedoes failed to run, but the other scored a hit. The remaining motor-boats, meanwhile, had made a sweep in a south-easterly direction and had been attracted by smoke on the horizon towards which they had steered. At 3.25 a.m., when daylight broke with good visibility, the boats gave up pursuit of the smoke (no vessels were in sight) and returned to the supporting force, stopping on the way to pick up a Norwegian sailor found lying on a raft. All the coastal motor-boats were back at 4.40 a.m. and they were safely hoisted on board the light cruisers.

The help given by the flying-boats had been of no account. The pilots of the Large Americas had started off at 3 a.m. with orders to cut across the course taken by the motor-boats. They were not to journey more than sixty miles, were to return in any event if they saw the coastal motor-boats on the way home, were to send back news, by wireless, to the supporting force if enemy vessels were sighted or if anything appeared amiss with the motor-boats, and, finally, were to help guide the boats back to the cruisers. The flying-boats, however, themselves needed help. Because of a long swell and lack of wind, the pilots had trouble when they tried to get off the water, and one flying-boat had been wrecked and lost and another reshipped in a damaged condition. The third flew off late and made a brief reconnaissance, but it was wrecked through engine failure on its return. The kite-balloon flown in the *Ulleswater* proved of some use as a recognition mark by which the motor-boat crews were able to check their course back to the ships, but nothing of value was reported from the balloon basket.

To distract the attention of German seaplanes from the

[1] G.M.T. Local time 2 a.m.

area of the motor-boat operations, flying-boats from Yarmouth and Felixstowe patrolled off the Dutch islands. They found five fighting seaplanes, low down, near Vlieland, but the German pilots scattered as soon as they were attacked: there is some evidence that one enemy seaplane was damaged.

There was still another disappointing feature about the operation. From the motor-boats, two submarines had been sighted on the surface, but they had gone under before torpedoes could be fired at them, and because the coastal motor-boats did not carry depth-charges it had been impossible to take advantage of an exceptional opportunity. The Admiralty proposed that when next the motor-boats went out, half should carry depth-charges and half torpedoes, but Admiral Beatty said that the operations had been designed against surface craft, and that if attacks upon submerged U-boats were to be added, the original idea would be confused. After some discussion it was agreed that on the next expedition two of the six boats should be equipped with depth-charges.

This operation began just before midnight on the 7th of July, but on the following morning the boats cruised for some time without finding enemy vessels; it was impossible for the flying-boats to leave the water on account of a heavy swell. Another attempt was made on the night of the 17th/18th of July, but no flying-boats accompanied the force because it did not appear that the weather would be favourable. The destroyer *Ulleswater*, however, carried her kite-balloon aloft, but in the evening of the 17th a thunderstorm broke over the ships on passage across the North Sea and at 10.30 p.m. the balloon was struck by lightning and destroyed in flames, 'lighting up the whole blessed ocean for miles'.[1] At 11.40 p.m. the force had reached its destination and four motor-boats

---

[1] From a personal account by Commander E. K. Boddam-Whetham, R.N., who was in the *Ulleswater* at the time. 'As there were no observers 'in the basket, it being still dark', he goes on, 'I saw no point in making 'any obvious signals to Commodore (T), so I reeled in a bare end of wire and 'did nothing. About 10 a.m. I received a signal: "Flag—*Ulleswater*—Have 'you noticed you have lost your balloon?"'

were launched. While they were still out the storm broke again, and their crews had the greatest difficulty, low down on the water as they were, in finding their parent ships. By 7 a.m. three of the motor-boats had been picked up, but search for the fourth continued all day in vain, and at 6 p.m. the force gave up the search and returned to its base.[1]

On the 1st of August a similar operation took place, and once again a long swell made it impossible for the flying-boats to leave the water. At the moment the motor-boats were being launched, enemy wireless signals received in the ships revealed that the force was under observation, and shortly afterwards a Zeppelin was sighted some distance away through a gap in the clouds. The airship commander, making skilful use of the clouds to conceal his approach, bore down upon the light cruisers, and he dropped four heavy-weight bombs which fell close to the ships, but inflicted no damage. The clouds began to break up, and when anti-aircraft fire was opened on the Zeppelin she retreated. German seaplanes appeared soon after the airship had gone, but they were content to watch from a distance. By 9.30 a.m. the motor-boats, helped in their navigation by the kite-balloon flown in the *Ulleswater*, a valuable guiding mark, had been picked up, and the force, once more disappointed, made its way home.

There was one hopeful feature to offset the disappointment. It seemed that the Zeppelin commanders were losing their sense of caution, and that it would be worth while, next time, to take a fighting aeroplane in company. This recrudescence, if such it was, of airship boldness in the Bight coincided with the conclusion of experiments which promised to make it easier for fighting aeroplanes to be carried. Earlier in the year, Rear-Admiral Tyrwhitt had proposed that flying-boat lighters should be fitted with a flying-off platform, and Colonel C. R. Samson had worked on the suggestion. His idea was that a lighter, carrying an aeroplane securely fixed on board in flying position, might be towed by a destroyer steaming at thirty

[1] The crew of the missing motor-boat, after sinking their craft, had been taken on board a Dutch fishing vessel and given passage to Holland.

knots or more into the wind. The pilot would then run his engine to the full and, when he judged the moment was favourable, would free the aeroplane by means of a specially designed quick-release clip, and fly off. Colonel Samson had himself made the first trial on the 30th of May, when he had narrowly missed death. The experimental flying-off arrangement in the lighter consisted of two wooden troughs in which skids attached to the ordinary chassis of the aeroplane were to run. When Colonel Samson attempted to get into the air one of the skids on the Sopwith 'Camel' overran its trough, with the result that the aeroplane 'cart-wheeled' over the bow of the lighter. The towed lighter passed over the wrecked aeroplane which, with its pilot, was pushed under the water. After a grim struggle Colonel Samson succeeded in forcing his way out of his cockpit, and he regained the surface of the water and was eventually picked up by a whaler from the towing destroyer. The failure taught some lessons. The lighter took a very steep angle down by the stern when towed at full speed and it was obviously necessary that the flying-deck should dip forward to a corresponding extent when the lighter was at rest. The troughs had proved unsuitable, and a special flying-off deck was therefore designed, and skids were abandoned in favour of the ordinary aeroplane wheels. On the 31st of July 1918, when the modifications had been completed, Lieutenant S. D. Culley made a successful flight from the lighter's deck.

On the evening of the 10th of August the Harwich Force, with a fighting aeroplane in company, set out once again for the Heligoland Bight. Three of the light cruisers with the force each carried two coastal motor-boats, and one towed a kite-balloon. Three of the destroyers towed lighters carrying flying-boats, and one (the *Redoubt*) towed the lighter with the 'Camel' aeroplane on board. At 6.10 a.m. on the 11th the force was in position off Terschelling and the motor-boats were lowered for their cruise in search of enemy vessels. The weather conditions, from most points of view, were perfect. The visibility was exceptionally good, but, unhappily, a ground swell and an entire absence of wind made it impossible to get the flying-boats into the air. 'This was a calamity', Rear-Admiral Tyrwhitt subsequently reported, 'that had never 'crossed my mind as I considered the conditions ideal. 'Knowing, however, that the Yarmouth seaplanes were 'due, I had no misgivings regarding the coastal motor-'boats, which were already beyond recall.'

A few minutes after the motor-boats had started, four German seaplanes came into view, and for some time they kept watch on the ships. At 7.10 a.m. the three Yarmouth flying-boats arrived as arranged. The Rear-Admiral ordered that a signal should be made giving the position of the German seaplanes and, on receipt of the message, the flying-boats went off in search. The German seaplanes were visible from the ships and when, therefore, the Yarmouth flying-boats set a course in the air which took no apparent notice of the enemy seaplanes, it was assumed in the ships that the flying-boats had not received the message. The trouble was that although visibility on the surface of the sea was uniformly good, it was patchy in the air, because of an unusual diffusion of light, especially towards the sun, and the enemy seaplanes could not be seen from the flying-boats. After an hour the pilots returned to ask for further instructions and they were then told to seek out the motor-boats which, it was calculated, would be on their way back. A careful search was made, but no trace of the surface craft was found. While the search was still in progress a Zeppelin was sighted, and as it was undesirable that the flying-boats should break wireless silence, they flew back to the fleet to report by visual signal the presence of the airship.

Rear-Admiral Tyrwhitt had already been advised by wireless from the Admiralty in London that a Zeppelin was in his neighbourhood, and the airship had afterwards been sighted. The Harwich Force had turned at 8.30 a.m., to entice her seawards and, at the same time, smoke screens had been laid. The manœuvre seemed to excite the curiosity of the crew of the Zeppelin, which followed the ships. At 8.41 a.m. Lieutenant S. D. Culley flew off the lighter in the Sopwith 'Camel' and he climbed rapidly:

he was apparently not seen from the gondolas of the Zeppelin, which made a leisurely turn and proceeded towards Germany. At 19,000 feet he came up with her north of the island of Ameland, and he attacked head on from below: his orders had been to attack from above, but he had been unable to force his Sopwith 'Camel' higher. The watching eyes in the ships saw, at 9.41 a.m., a sudden burst of flame in the sky, followed by smoke and falling debris, and they knew that Lieutenant Culley's mission had succeeded. A smoke screen was made to guide the Sopwith 'Camel' pilot back to the ships, but it was not until two hours later that he was picked up with his aeroplane.[1] Rear-Admiral Tyrwhitt signalled the ships as follows: 'Flag-general—Your attention is called to Hymn 'No. 224, Verse 7', and those who took action on this cryptic message read:

> Oh happy band of pilgrims,
> Look upward to the skies,
> Where such a light affliction
> Shall win so great a prize.

The prize was the Zeppelin *L.53* (Kapitänleutnant Prölss). 'I consider', reported Rear-Admiral Tyrwhitt, 'that Lieutenant Culley's success is second to none of the 'many glorious deeds of the Royal Air Force, and an 'example of pluck, endurance, and great personal courage.' It is of interest that the Zeppelin made her last signal at 9.40 a.m., immediately before Lieutenant Culley attacked, and that her position at that moment, as it was calculated in Whitehall and communicated by wireless to Rear-Admiral Tyrwhitt, coincided with the actual position in which she was destroyed.

Before Lieutenant Culley was picked up the coastal motor-boats had become overdue, and Rear-Admiral

---

[1] It is possible that the peculiarities of the visibility led to the Zeppelin's destruction. Had her crew seen the Sopwith 'Camel' leave the lighter, the airship could almost certainly have got away in time. Lieutenant Culley himself nearly came to grief because of the variable visibility. He spent two hours searching for the ships and only saw them when he was less than two miles away, at the moment when his petrol was finishing. The debris falling from the Zeppelin had been visible to the crews in the ships fifty miles away.

Tyrwhitt had ordered destroyers and light cruisers to sweep in search of them. He also asked the Admiralty by wireless to send additional flying-boats from Yarmouth. In reply, the same boats which had been out in the morning were once more dispatched to Terschelling, and when they reached the Harwich Force, at 4.15 p.m., the pilots were ordered to make a search for the missing motor-boats to the eastwards. They saw nothing, and when they returned to the ships to report Rear-Admiral Tyrwhitt ordered them to return to their base. The Harwich Force, with great reluctance, also gave up the search and made its way home under abortive attack, until dark, from German seaplanes.

Enemy seaplanes had brought disaster to the motor-boats. After being launched from the light cruisers they had moved towards the Dutch coast and had then followed the coast-line at full speed about a mile outside territorial waters. Not long after the boats turned, six seaplanes appeared, but it was assumed that they were British until they came near enough for the black crosses on their wings to be discernible. The coastal boats immediately closed in order to concentrate fire from their Lewis guns, and they were soon fighting a machine-gun duel with the diving seaplanes, now increased to eight. Although the German pilots also aimed bombs at their swift-moving targets, the motor-boats held their own for half an hour, until the leader turned about to rejoin the Harwich Force. The German pilots from this time onwards had the sun at their backs, whereas the visibility eastwards from the motor-boats was blurred: furthermore, four fast fighting seaplanes, each equipped with two forward machine-guns, arrived to reinforce the attackers. The action developed into one of target practice for the enemy pilots. Keeping the sun directly behind them they roared down upon the coastal motor-boats, defined in clear detail, and the fire from the seaplanes, opened with fair accuracy at long range, was maintained without break and with increasing sureness of aim as they neared the luckless crews. After the fight had lasted fifteen minutes the British machine-guns were silent: some of the last rounds fired from the motor-boats struck one of the seaplanes at point-blank range and it crashed into the sea. The crews in the motor-boats had fought the action to the end, to the last bullet for each serviceable machine-gun, and almost to the last of the fuel supply for each engine.

The encounter took place three or four miles from the Dutch coast. One boat, with spluttering engines, reached the shore, another caught fire, but was navigated within half a mile of the shore before she was blown up, two more, with engines and guns useless, were sunk by their crews who took to the water for three hours until picked up by a Dutch torpedo-boat, while the remaining two, badly damaged, drifted into territorial waters from which they were salved by the Dutch. All the crews survived the adventure, although four of the officers and two of the men had been wounded. Two of the more severely wounded had been put overboard from the burning boat which had had to be blown up. Their peril was seen by three Dutch sailors stationed at Terschelling who made the half-mile swim from the shore and brought them back, an act of gallantry which came as a fitting end to one of the fastest and strangest actions ever fought at sea.[1]

It was not the naval way to let this disaster to the motor-boats go unavenged. Plans were quickly prepared, to be put into operation at a suitable opportunity, to strike an effective blow at the German seaplane service at Borkum and Nordeney. The attempt was made on the 24th of October by the Harwich Force in combination with flying-boats and Sopwith 'Camel' aeroplanes. The plan was for one of the light cruisers to send out fictitious signals, at full wireless strength, in the expectation that they would attract German aircraft to investigate. To deal with whatever enemy seaplanes might appear, four flying-boats and four Sopwith 'Camels' were in tow on lighters, while two

---

[1] The Dutch sailors, in recognition of their service, were awarded the Board of Trade Silver Medal for gallantry in saving life at sea. An account of the action, by an officer in one of the motor-boats, is given in 'The Sea and the Air', by Cedric Outhwaite, in *Blackwood's Magazine* for November 1927.

Flights, each of five flying-boats, flew across the North Sea from the air stations at Felixstowe and Harwich. Unhappily, the plan, long and carefully thought out, miscarried. The Harwich Force arrived at the rendezvous off Terschelling at 6.30 a.m., and half an hour later an attempt was made to launch the flying-boats. One of them, however, revealed engine defects, and it proved impossible to fly the others off the heavy seas: they were eventually re-shipped. At 8.30 a.m. a formation of five German seaplanes appeared, but when fire was opened on them from the ships they withdrew. Meanwhile, it had been discovered that three of the Sopwith 'Camels', because of defective tail-guides due to pounding by the seas on the outward passage, could not be made to fly. When the five flying-boats from Yarmouth arrived as arranged, they were informed that the enemy seaplanes had retreated eastwards, and were given orders to make a reconnaissance in that direction. The flying-boats from Felixstowe were ordered, by wireless, to come up in support of the Yarmouth Flight: two of them, however, had to turn back because of engine trouble, and the remaining three ran into fog and were eventually sent back to their base. The Yarmouth flying-boats, after patrolling for their allotted time without incident, received orders from Rear-Admiral Tyrwhitt to return to their station direct. They had not long started for home when sixteen German seaplanes approached the ships. Some of them passed over the Harwich Force in pursuit of the flying-boats while others attacked the ships with bombs. The seaplanes which had vainly pursued the Yarmouth flying-boats passed on their return journey near the fleet and disappeared towards their base.

Air warfare in the southern part of the North Sea was of a more continuous kind and did not involve squadrons of supporting ships. It was waged, on the German side, with a fine offensive spirit by the unit known as *Flanders I*, which operated from the naval air base at Zeebrugge. This unit was equipped with high-speed float-type seaplanes which could out-manœuvre and out-fight the British flying-boats, and were sufficiently seaworthy to enable their pilots to come down on the water, in fair weather conditions, to lie in wait for the British patrols.

On the 25th of April 1918 two flying-boats from Felixstowe were on patrol together when they were attacked by seven enemy fighting seaplanes from Zeebrugge. After the fight had lasted ten minutes, one of the flying-boats burst into flames, but the other, by skimming the water, succeeded in making its escape. On the 6th of June another flying-boat from Felixstowe was shot down by five German pilots, but the British crew, including the commanding officer of the Felixstowe air station, Lieutenant-Colonel E. D. M. Robertson, were taken from the wreckage, after clinging to it for eight hours, by Large America flying-boats sent out specially to find them. The Zeebrugge pilots were not only aggressive fighters, but they usually revealed themselves also as good sportsmen. They might, on this occasion, have continued their attacks on the flying-boat after it was wrecked, but, instead, one of the German pilots had landed alongside the British craft and had pointed in the direction of the shore, presumably to encourage a hope that help would be forthcoming.

Next day, the 7th of June, when a B.E.2c aeroplane from the Yarmouth air station was on anti-submarine patrol, five Zeebrugge seaplanes were sighted at 5.35 a.m. on the water south-east of Cross Sands. The German pilots at once flew off to attack the B.E.2c which carried bombs, but no machine-guns, and therefore represented an easy victim. The aeroplane pilot managed to elude the opening attack, and when the Germans were about to follow up, a Short seaplane came into view and the enemy pilots promptly turned to engage it. Making use of their superior speed they cut the Short off from land, headed it out to sea, and then closed in to attack. A machine-gun duel, in which the Short seaplane was outclassed, ensued at a height of 30 feet or so above the water. When the fight was approaching a climax the pilot of the Short sighted two vessels about seven miles away and he made for them direct. They proved to be patrolling motor-launches, and they at once opened fire on the pursuing

German seaplanes with 3-pounder Hotchkiss guns and with their Lewis guns. The Short alighted near the motor-launches, but the German pilots took up a circular formation and continued their attack, pouring almost continuous fire into the seaplane on the water from a height of a few feet. The observer in the Short, twice wounded, replied with his Lewis gun, but 'after the en-'gagement had lasted approximately ten minutes', says the report of the pilot, who also received a wound, the 'machine showed signs of sinking and we were so hope-'lessly outmatched that I gave the observer orders to cease 'fire and get into the water under the machine. We both 'climbed out of the machine into the water, between the 'floats, constantly ducking to avoid the bursts of machine-'gun fire. After about another five minutes' continuous 'attack, the enemy flew off in a south-west direction and 'we were picked up by motor-launch 129. . . .' The motor-launches had themselves come under attack from the German seaplanes, and one of them had been partly disabled by bullets which penetrated the engine-room.

In July the weather was often unfavourable for flying, but the German pilots lost no opportunity for activity. Four flying-boats from Felixstowe were on patrol near the North Hinder on the 4th of July when one of them, which had broken formation, was attacked and shot down by seven German seaplanes. The other flying-boats were soon involved and they all suffered damage, and two officers and two men among the crew were wounded. While the fight was at its fiercest an engine crank-case in one of the flying-boats was hit and the oil began to leak. The engineer, Second Air-Mechanic W. M. Blacklock, thereupon climbed out on the wing to stop the leak with his hand, and although fire from the German seaplanes was concentrated upon him, he stuck to his task and enabled his pilot to fly on until he came upon a fishing smack, alongside which he alighted.

On the 18th of July two Short seaplanes, with two Sopwith 'Camel' aeroplanes as escorts, were on patrol between the Kentish Knock and the Sunk Light Vessel when seven enemy seaplanes surprised them out of the sun. In the fight which followed one of the Sopwith 'Camel' pilots singled out one enemy seaplane and kept up his attack until it fell spinning into the sea.[1] Soon after the fight had begun the machine-guns in the other Sopwith 'Camel' had jambed and they could not be cleared, but the pilot continued to dive at the German seaplanes in order to confuse their aim. One of the Shorts went down and alighted on the water, and the other broke away and made full speed for its base at Westgate, but it never reached home and its destruction was claimed by a German pilot when he returned to Zeebrugge. It seemed that one of the German seaplanes alighted alongside the other Short which had been forced down on the water, where the two craft continued to fight, with the result that the Short was set on fire and sunk. The two 'Camels', much shot about and with their machine-guns jambed, returned safely to their aerodrome at Manston. Admiral F. C. D. Sturdee, Commander-in-Chief, The Nore, reporting to the Admiralty a few days later, said: 'This is the sixteenth occasion since '31st May, 1918, on which flights of German machines have 'been reported in this area, and the continual visits of these 'enemy craft show the great importance they attach to 'this district: this has been anticipated (*vide* my former 'submissions on this subject). On the 20th of July I sent 'the air officer on my staff to the Admiralty and Air 'Ministry to explain personally the serious situation of our 'air defences in this command. I understand that this is 'now appreciated by the air authorities at the Admiralty 'and the Air Ministry, so it is hoped that immediate steps 'will be taken to place our air defences at least on an 'equality with the probable enemy forces. Recognizing the 'strategic positions of Westgate and Manston with their 'proximity to the enemy air bases, the naval Flights at 'these stations, in order to be efficient in a real war sense, 'should be superior in number, type, and speed of machines, 'and staff for maintenance. Then these attacks will be met 'properly, and our command of the air will be assured; 'until this happens the enemy will continue their attacks,

[1] A semi-official list of seaplanes lost by the *Flanders I* air station during the war does not show any destroyed in this action.

'in the hope of destroying our weak patrols, daily or when
'the weather conditions allow. The present situation, with
'the consequent weak patrols, is so obviously unwarlike
'that it would seem only to require being mentioned to
'ensure it being rectified.'

The inferior equipment of the British air stations did not result from a lack of appreciation of their strategic importance. The main trouble, as has been told, was one of supply break-down. The complaint of the Admiral was similar in substance to those sent in from many other quarters. Because the *Flanders I* seaplane unit was equipped with aircraft often superior, and never inferior, in performance to those it met on the British side, and because the German pilots operated in formations which, though not large, were bigger than those sent out from the east coast air stations, it was enabled to inflict damage with disproportionate loss to itself. The average numbers of aircraft in service with *Flanders I* were: in 1915, 11; 1916, 20; 1917, 29; and 1918, 30. Apart from the routine patrols which gave valuable information in connexion with mine-sweeping operations and with the safe passage of U-boats, the records of the unit show that it shot down 26 Allied aircraft, destroyed six merchant vessels, took one into port as a prize, destroyed a British submarine and severely damaged another (the *C.25*), and destroyed two British non-rigid airships: the unit also made bombing attacks on Dunkirk, Calais, and Dover. The losses of the unit, in flying personnel, amounted to 27 killed from all causes, 4 missing, 18 taken prisoners, and 12 wounded.

THE BELGIAN COAST AND FLANDERS

The formation of the Royal Air Force led to some important changes in the Dover–Dunkirk command. In January 1918 the Air Council proposed to the Admiralty, 'that the 'air forces in the Dunkirk area should be re-organized on 'the following general lines:

'(1) A Wing will be attached permanently to the Dun-
'kirk–Dover Command for work in connection with the
'Navy, which Wing, for operation purposes, will come under

'the direct command of the Senior Naval Officer. Its
'maintenance as regards personnel, machines, stores, &c.
'would be arranged for by the Royal Flying Corps officer
'of the area.

'(2) Other air units, consisting of fighting, reconnais-
'sance, and bombing squadrons will be operating in the
'Dunkirk area under the command of the Field Marshal
'Commanding in France, their strength and composition
'varying from time to time according to the requirements
'of the naval and military situation.

'(3) The underlying principle will be that the units
'must be as mobile as possible, to enable a rapid concentra-
'tion to be made, either for attack or defence, and for this
'purpose immobile units should be reduced to a minimum.

'(4) The Air Council are aware of the importance Their
'Lordships attach to the attack of the enemy's maritime
'bases on the Flanders coast, and the necessity of checking
'the activity of the enemy's aircraft operating against the
'Fleet, and due weight will be given to these considera-
'tions in assessing the strength of the Air Forces operating
'in the Dunkirk area.

'(5) For purely local operations, and those of an im-
'mediate nature requiring the assistance of Air Force units
'to assist the Wing, the Senior Naval Officer, Dunkirk, will
'apply direct to the Royal Flying Corps Commander in the
'Dunkirk area.

'(6) For larger operations of a more important nature it
'is proposed that the Vice-Admiral, Dover, should apply
'direct for assistance to the Field Marshal Commanding
'in France.

'(7) For any major operations which Their Lordships
'may contemplate, necessitating a considerable concentra-
'tion of Air Force in the Dunkirk area, it is presumed that
'the Lords Commissioners of the Admiralty will com-
'municate with the Army Council and Air Council for the
'necessary arrangements to be made.

'(8) The Air Council propose that the establishment of
'the Dunkirk Wing shall be fixed as follows:

'1 Squadron of De Havilland 4 machines for recon-
'naissance work with the Fleet.

'1 Squadron of De Havilland 4 machines for anti-
'submarine work, the three flights being disposed
'either at Dunkirk, Dover, or Walmer, according to
'the requirements of the Vice-Admiral, Dover.
'3 Squadrons of fighting machines.'

In their reply the Admiralty accepted as a general principle the reduction of the naval air force at Dunkirk to one wing, but said: 'In view of the great importance that is 'attached to the work now carried out by the bombing and 'fighting machines which will pass from naval control, the 'Admiralty can only agree to the new arrangement on the 'clear understanding that the Naval wing will receive 'support when needed, and that offensive bombing will 'be carried out against naval objectives when necessity may 'arise, as indicated in paragraph 4 of your letter under 'reply.'

Accordingly, in March 1918, the Sixty-first Wing (Squadrons 201, 202, 210, 213, and 217) was permanently attached to the Dover–Dunkirk command for work with naval forces, while the Sixty-fourth Wing (Squadrons 203, 204, 208, and 209) and Sixty-fifth Wing (Squadrons 206, 207, 211, 214, and 215) were grouped as the VII Brigade and placed under the orders of Sir Douglas Haig, the Field Marshal Commanding-in-Chief.

The intention of the Air Council, at the time the above arrangements were made, was to organize a bombing force for large-scale attacks on German naval targets on or near the Belgian coast, notably the U-boat bases at Bruges and Zeebrugge. The force would, it was anticipated, operate under the orders of the Air Council as a northern bombing force, as a counterpart to a proposed southern bombing force to be constituted for attacks on German industrial centres. The latter force, the Independent Force, duly came into being, but the former was never established, at least as a British force. There were two main reasons for this, namely, the important effect of the German 1918 offensive which opened against the British in March, and British aircraft production failures.[1]

---

[1] See Chapter II.

When it had been arranged that General Head-quarters in France should take control of two of the Dunkirk Wings, it had not been intended that the squadrons should be moved away *en bloc* from the coastal area. Sir Douglas Haig had been told by the War Office of the importance which the Admiralty attached to the bombing of the submarine bases in Belgium, or such similar naval targets as the Vice-Admiral, Dover, might indicate, and it had been pointed out that the Air Council fully shared the Admiralty views. The Army Council had been willing to agree that certain of the squadrons transferred to the control of Sir Douglas Haig should be retained in the Dunkirk area, and it was impressed upon the Field-Marshal that further squadrons would be added, as material became available, in accordance with the policy of the Air Ministry to build up a northern bombing force.

In the storms and stresses of the March and April battles on the Western front the above hopes and intentions went by the board. All the squadrons which could be spared from the Dunkirk area were moved to the vital battle fronts. Furthermore, Vice-Admiral Sir Roger Keyes, who had succeeded Vice-Admiral Sir Reginald Bacon in command of the Dover Patrol on New Year's day 1918, offered on the 26th of March, when the Western front situation was critical, to place at the disposal of Sir Douglas Haig any or all of the squadrons in the Wing permanently allotted for naval air operations. The offer was gladly accepted and two fighter squadrons, Nos. 201 and 210, were moved at once. Owing to the almost continuous fighting which took place on the Western front from that time onwards until the end of the war it was never possible for Sir Douglas Haig to release squadrons for large-scale operations in the area of the Belgian coast, much to the disappointment, very natural in the circumstances, of Vice-Admiral Sir Roger Keyes.

It is probable that the reduction of the naval air strength at Dunkirk was effected without misgivings for the reason that there were expectations of important help from America. The United States naval authorities had agreed to form a bombing group which would have for particular object attacks on the German U-boat bases at Bruges, Zeebrugge, and Ostend. The plan made allowance for twelve bomber and fighter squadrons stationed at various places between Calais and Dunkirk. Owing to disappointments in connexion with the output of American aircraft, the number of squadrons allotted to the Northern Bombing Group (N.B.G.), as it was called, was reduced from twelve to eight, but production difficulties persisted and a part only of the reduced force, which had been placed under the orders of the Vice-Admiral, Dover, and drew its stores from the 5th Group, Royal Air Force,[1] had been assembled at the time of the armistice. The first bombing raid did not take place until the 14th of October 1918, but within a fortnight the Americans had made eight day and night raids on various objectives in Belgium. With the evacuation by the Germans of the submarine bases in Flanders the special reason for the activities of the American bombers no longer existed, and the services of the force were offered to General Pershing who replied, however, that he thought the group would best be employed to help the British operations in the Belgian area. Accordingly the American bombers worked with the Royal Air Force in support of the final advance of the British armies. The American northern group dropped in all, during its brief period of active service, about one hundred tons of bombs on various enemy targets, naval and military.

At the beginning of April 1918, when the various moves in connexion with the Dunkirk reorganization had been completed, there remained in the Dunkirk area, under naval control, No. 213 fighter Squadron, No. 217 anti-submarine Squadron, and No. 202 reconnaissance Squadron. There also remained in the area, under army control, No. 204 fighter Squadron,[2] No. 211 day-bomber Squadron, and Nos. 207, 214, and 215[3] night-bomber Squadrons.

[1] The instructions of Vice-Admiral W. S. Sims stated that the U.S. Naval Northern Bombing Group would, for administration and internal organization, be considered an independent unit, but that all operations would be controlled by the Vice-Admiral Commanding the Dover Patrol.

[2] No. 204 Squadron was transferred to the command of Sir Roger Keyes on the 21st of April.

[3] No. 15 Squadron, afterwards No. 215, had been formed at Coudekerque

The squadrons working directly for the navy, including the air units stationed at Dover, formed the 5th Group under the command of Lieutenant-Colonel F. C. Halahan, with Brigadier-General C. L. Lambe in command of the VII Brigade. Early in May, however, with the *de facto* reduction of the Dunkirk–Dover force, the VII Brigade was formally disbanded and Brigadier-General C. L. Lambe took command of the 5th Group, with Lieutenant-Colonel Halahan at Dover as his second in command.

The main activities of the Dunkirk air units in April and May 1918 were connected with the naval operations against Zeebrugge and Ostend, the object of which was to block the entrance to the canal at Zeebrugge, and to Ostend harbour, in order to close the waterway communications with the German inland naval base at Bruges. An up-to-date survey of the area of operations was a necessary preliminary, and it is probably true to say that the Royal Air Force had contributed the most important part of its share in the enterprise before the event. It was necessary to obtain the desired information for varying conditions of tide, and reconnaissances, and in particular photography, had to be multiplied accordingly. The work was done by No. 202 (D.H.4) Squadron which, over a period of some weeks, photographed and re-photographed the whole specified area. Plans and models of the coast and of the naval objectives, based on the photographs, were constructed and, in addition, a replica of the Zeebrugge mole was marked out for training purposes on the ground at Deal. As the naval blocking operations were to take place at night and under cover of smoke-screens, an important aspect of the air work was a survey of the buoys marking the channels by which the objectives could be reached.

The success of the exploit depended upon secrecy. The ships were to assemble some sixty miles from the Belgian ports, and because the passage to the objectives would require about seven hours there would at the beginning of the voyage be some hours of daylight during which the force might be surprised by German aircraft or by submarines.

on the 10th of March 1918, from personnel provided by Nos. 7 and 14 Naval Squadrons.

If this should happen failure was likely, and very careful arrangements were therefore made to screen the assembly and early movements of the ships. These arrangements included aeroplane, seaplane, and airship patrols, and seaward patrols by surface craft, all directed against possible submarines, and air offensive patrols, over the fleet by aircraft from Dover, and over the Belgian coastal area by Sopwith 'Camels' from Dunkirk. Low bombing attacks on the German aeroplane and seaplane bases at Zeebrugge were also ordered.

During the operation the Royal Air Force was required to divert the attention of the defenders by making bombing attacks on batteries in the area of the objectives. These attacks were to begin two and a half hours before the naval zero hour, and were to continue, with increasing intensity, until the block-ships, with their supporting vessels, reached the objectives. It was hoped that the bombing attacks would impel the crews of the German batteries to seek shelter in their dug-outs, and so leave the guns more or less unattended at the time when the expedition reached the coast, and it was also hoped that the searchlights would be diverted to the aeroplanes, away from the approaching fleet. During the final period of the approach journey, the aircraft were to drop a preponderance of incendiary bombs in order to cause fires which would illuminate the area, and immediately before the time of arrival of the ships the pilots were to release parachute flares for the same reason.

The enterprise was planned for the night of the 11th/12th of April 1918. At 10.40 p.m. on the 11th the first of the Handley Pages of No. 215 Squadron left its aerodrome, in bad weather, for Zeebrugge. For an hour, while bombs of 112-lb. weight were being dropped at intervals, the Handley Page was presented as a target for the enemy searchlights and anti-aircraft batteries, and it presumably received some damage because at 1.30 a.m., over the sea, one engine suddenly failed, and the aeroplane lost height and eventually crashed on the water seven miles off Ostend. The pilot, Captain J. R. Allen, was not seen again, but the observer, Captain P. Bewsher, and the gun-layer, Lieutenant M. C. Purvis, were picked up by a coastal motor-boat and taken back to Dunkirk.

About the time that the Handley Page crashed, the weather became worse, with rainstorms and poor visibility, and no more than three of the six additional Handley Pages of Nos. 214 and 215 Squadrons, allotted for similar bombing attacks, reached the neighbourhood of their objectives: one of them was forced to land in Holland and was interned with its crew. Meanwhile, the unfavourable weather had led to a decision for postponement of the naval attack, and the fleet accordingly withdrew.

After a further postponement, the operation took place on the night of the 22nd/23rd of April. The delay had some effect upon the help which the Royal Air Force was able to give. At the time when the fleet turned back on the morning of the 12th of April the position of the British Army on the Western front was critical. The Germans had broken through the line on the Lys, and they were pressing hard towards the capture of the Channel ports. The evacuation of certain northern bases and depots became a matter for urgent consideration, and Major-General J. M. Salmond put forward to the Air Ministry, as a precautionary measure, proposals for a dispersal to England, and to various parts of France, of the air units in the Dunkirk area. The suggestions were placed by the Air Council before the Board of Admiralty, who approved, and although the arrangements were never put into full effect, some important reductions were made in the Dunkirk bombing strength. The personnel of two Handley Page squadrons, Nos. 207 and 215, were sent to England, and the aeroplanes of the squadrons were allotted to No. 214 Squadron, which remained in the area, and also to No. 216 Squadron, which was part of the force stationed in the neighbourhood of Nancy for bombing attacks on German industrial and military targets.

The result was that when the naval attack was made on the 22nd/23rd of April there was a much reduced bomber force available for support. In the afternoon of the 22nd, when the fleet, escorted by aircraft, had set out for Zeebrugge and Ostend, the weather was clear. By the evening, however, the sky had clouded over and a drizzle had set in, but the strength and direction of the wind were favourable for the laying of smoke-screens and Vice-Admiral Keyes made a signal that the attack would take place. The bad weather, unhappily, kept the night bombers on the ground, and aeroplanes played no part in the blocking operations, which added some stirring pages to British naval history. On the 23rd, when the weather improved after early mists, the air squadrons took photographs of the scene of the naval operations, and made a series of bombing attacks with the object of hampering salvage work by the enemy: in these attacks bombs of 112-lb. weight were dropped by the Sopwith 'Camels' of No. 213 Squadron.

At Zeebrugge the naval effort had been successful in partly blocking the entrance, but at Ostend the attempt to seal the harbour had failed. The wind had veered at the last moment and had blown the smoke-screen back upon the ships, thus disclosing them to the enemy, as well as making navigation difficult, a difficulty which was made greater because the Germans had shifted, undetected, the important Stroombank buoy from which the block-ships were to steer for the harbour. The result was that the ships grounded to the eastward of the entrance.

Although Ostend was still open, air photographs showed a crowding of torpedo craft and submarines at Bruges. A second attempt to block the entrance to the harbour at Ostend by sinking the *Vindictive* was prepared, and meanwhile day-bombing attacks, dogged by bad weather, were directed by the limited resources available to the Vice-Admiral, Dover, against the shipping in Bruges, and also against Zeebrugge and Ostend. The weather was mostly unfavourable for night operations, but when night bombing was possible the targets allotted to No. 214 Handley Page Squadron, formerly under the Vice-Admiral, but now under the army, were military ones, namely the railway junctions of Courtrai, Roulers, Thourout, Tournai, and Lichtervelde, in connexion with the German offensive on the Lys.

The Vice-Admiral of the Dover Patrol felt cause for complaint at his lack of bombing resources. It seemed to him that there was a golden opportunity to concentrate bombing attacks against the torpedo craft and U-boats which the air photographs revealed to be lying at Bruges subsequent to the Zeebrugge attack. He yearned for some of the squadrons which had passed from his control, and he wrote to the Admiralty on the 1st of May pleading that two day and two night-bombing squadrons should be placed under his direct command. The Admiralty forwarded the letter to the Air Ministry on the 3rd of May, saying: 'Consequent on the successful operations lately 'carried out by the Navy on the Belgian Coast, My Lords 'have found it necessary to reconsider the opinion expressed 'by them in their letter of the 16th February, and they 'request that two day and two night-bombing squadrons 'may be placed under the direct orders of the Vice-'Admiral, Dover, at the earliest possible moment. . . .' To this request the Air Ministry replied on the 16th of May that No. 214 Squadron would be requested to help, but said: 'It is regretted that, in view of the extreme urgency 'of the demands for long-distance bombing squadrons else-'where, it has not been found possible to provide the 'additional squadrons of this type which were asked for in 'your letter. . . .'

Meanwhile bad weather had delayed a renewal of the attempt to block Ostend, and it was not until the 9th of May that the conditions of weather, tide, and wind proved suitable. For the new attempt it was arranged that the ships should withhold their fire and the aeroplanes their bombing until the presence of the ships became known to the enemy. It was ordered that the aeroplanes should be in the air, ready to bomb the coastal batteries at Ostend, about forty minutes before the *Vindictive* was due to arrive at the harbour entrance: the signal for the aeroplanes to begin to drop their bombs would be the opening of fire by the monitors. Parachute flares were to be dropped from the air on pre-arranged positions.

Air reconnaissances had been hampered by poor visibility for some days before the operation took place, but late on the 9th of May, when the expedition was already on its way, aeroplanes which had been making a seaward patrol returned to Dunkirk with news that the buoys usually off Ostend had apparently disappeared. Although darkness was setting in Major Ronald Graham and Lieutenant G. C. Mackay, in Sopwith 'Camels' of No. 213 Squadron, left at once, and they were able to satisfy themselves, from a low height, that the buoys had been taken away. Such a disconcerting possibility, although considered to be unlikely, had not been overlooked, and when Major Graham returned with his information action was taken at once to lay a special light buoy. This was done in good time, and the light formed a satisfactory point in connexion with the laying of smoke screens and for course-setting by the block-ships.

At 1.43 a.m. on the 10th of May, as the *Vindictive* approached the entrance to the harbour at Ostend, the pre-arranged signal to open fire was given and response was promptly made by the ships, by siege guns on land, and by the aeroplanes. The last-named were seven Handley Pages of No. 214 Squadron, and they began to bomb at 1.45 a.m. For forty-five minutes the bombing continued, during which time six 550-lb., fifty-three 112-lb., and twenty-six 25-lb. bombs were aimed at the German batteries. Each aeroplane, in addition, from 2 a.m., when the *Vindictive* was timed to be in position at her objective, dropped, at intervals, six parachute flares mainly with the object of illuminating the pier-heads in the harbour entrance. As soon as the operation started a fog came up, but the pilots were able, by flying low, to fulfil their tasks. On their return, however, the fog had deepened, and it obscured the ground with the result that four of the pilots were forced to land away from their aerodrome: one crashed on landing near St. Omer and the aeroplane was wrecked and two members of the crew were injured.

A low reconnaissance on the morning of the 10th of May, made by Sopwith 'Camels' of No. 213 Squadron, reported that the *Vindictive* was lying high out of the water between the piers at Ostend, where it seemed that she was obstructing about one-third of the channel. What had happened was that the fog and smoke had made it difficult for the *Vindictive* to feel her way to the entrance, and when she arrived it had been discovered that she was too close to the eastern pier to swing across the channel, as had been planned. She grounded to make an angle of about twenty-five degrees with the eastern pier, leaving a useful passage between her stern and the western pier.

The Admiralty continued, after the second blocking attempt, to press the Air Ministry to allocate bombing squadrons to the Vice-Admiral of the Dover Patrol. On the 23rd of May, as a result of representations made by the Air Ministry to the War Office, a telegram was sent to Sir Douglas Haig saying: 'There is at the present 'moment, as a result of recent successful naval operations 'against Zeebrugge, a large accumulation of enemy sub-'marines in Bruges Docks which have no egress to the sea 'at present, and it is of vital importance that this unique 'opportunity of destroying enemy craft in their harbours 'should be exploited to the full. It has been decided, 'therefore, after careful consideration, that the bombing 'units of the 5th Group should be reinforced temporarily 'from units under your command. Kindly arrange to hand 'over to the G.O.C., 5th Group, for such period as may be 'necessary for this specific operation two de Havilland 9 'Squadrons, one of which should be No. 211.'

Sir Douglas Haig replied that No. 211 Squadron could not be spared, and the Air Ministry thereupon came to the help of Vice-Admiral Keyes by placing temporarily at his disposal, on the 31st of May, one of the home defence squadrons, No. 38, equipped with F.E.2b's, suitable for light night-bombing. Sir Douglas Haig contributed No. 98 (D.H.9) Squadron on the 25th of May. Meanwhile No. 214 Handley Page Squadron had been requested, as from the 16th of May, to bomb Bruges on every available occasion. Vice-Admiral Keyes, in a telegram to the Admiralty on the 30th of May, stated his opinion that the F.E.2b's about to arrive at Dunkirk would prove of little real value, and he pointed out that No. 214 Squadron, which was supposed to be helping him, had no more than six Handley Pages available. He said: 'It is deplorable that such a 'golden opportunity should be allowed to pass, but it is 'not too late to make up some lost ground in the next few 'days if a concentrated effort is made at once, for, from 'yesterday's photographs it appears that the same craft are 'still blocked at Bruges in the Canal and there is indica-'tion that the southern lock gate at Zeebrugge has been 'damaged.' He recommended that No. 214 Squadron should be strengthened and placed under his direct orders. This was agreed to and No. 214 Squadron accordingly came under the control of Sir Roger Keyes on the 4th of June when a new Wing, the Eighty-second, was formed. On this date the vice-admiral had under his direct command two fighter squadrons, one anti-submarine squadron, one reconnaissance squadron, two day-bomber squadrons, and two night-bomber squadrons. One of the day-bomber squadrons, however, No. 98 (D.H.9), returned to the control of the G.O.C., Royal Air Force, on the 6th of June.

It seems fair comment that insufficient weight was given to the importance of bombing the exceptional target presented by Bruges dockyard. The attention of General Head-quarters in France was riveted to the Western front. It can be understood that in April, while the critical battle of the Lys was still raging, Sir Douglas Haig could contemplate no diversion of his somewhat slender bombing resources for attacks, no matter how desirable, against naval targets in Belgium. At the end of April, however, the enemy offensive in Flanders had been brought to a standstill. German offensive action did not reopen, against the French on the Chemin des Dames, until towards the end of May. It is true that Sir Douglas Haig had still to face the probability of another major offensive against the British army. It is true also that opposite the British front there were more targets of first-class military importance than the Commander-in-Chief had the bombing resources to attack systematically. When all is said, however, the fact remains that during May there was a lull in the Western front battles. When the circumstances of the time are fully considered, it seems clear that a temporary concentration of bombing aircraft could, and should, have been made with Bruges dock for target.

The matter was one which might properly have been placed before General Foch, the Generalissimo. Before

May was ended, he was himself calling upon Sir Douglas Haig to help the French with bombing and fighting squadrons. He also arranged for reciprocal help, from the French air force reserve, should the need arise as a result of a possible German attack on the British front. That is to say, his vision was ranging over the whole Western front and he was thinking in terms of an air concentration, irrespective of national divisions, according to the changing needs of the general situation. Although the target at Bruges was a naval one, and not therefore a strict concern of General Foch, it seems that the occasion was one when a broader view could have been taken because of the apparent unusual and fleeting opportunity to strike a blow which was calculated to have an important effect upon the enemy's naval war operations.[1] It may be remarked, in conclusion, that such targets, whether they might be naval or military, would be a proper concern for the staff of an air-striking force.

Such bombing forces as were made available to the Vice-Admiral, Dover Patrol, attacked Bruges, Zeebrugge, and Ostend, as opportunity and weather offered, and during the month of May thirty-six tons of bombs were dropped on Bruges, thirty-two on Zeebrugge, and nine tons on Ostend. There is no evidence that the attacks on Bruges dockyard or on Ostend caused any irreparable damage. At Zeebrugge results of some importance were achieved by two novel attacks which took place on the 28th of May. At 2.25 a.m. a Handley Page of No. 214 Squadron, piloted by Captain C. H. Darley, glided over Zeebrugge from the sea, with engines silent, and arrived over the lock-gate at a height of about 200 feet. The Handley Page dropped three bombs of 520-lb. weight, one of which exploded close to the northern gate, while the others fell in the lock. Ten minutes after the Handley Page had bombed, Lieutenant-

[1] Since the above was written, it has come to light that Foch learned of congestion in the ports of Bruges and Zeebrugge from French naval air reconnaissances, and that he asked Sir Douglas Haig, on the 21st of May, to concentrate squadrons for intensive bombing in order to 'conclude the work so happily begun by the British Navy'. The reply from British G.H.Q. sent next day stated that all available squadrons had been placed at the disposal of the Vice-Admiral, Dover Patrol.

Colonel P. F. M. Fellowes, commanding the Sixty-first Wing, left his aerodrome in a D.H.4 (Observer Sergeant H. Pritchard) to attack the lock-gate from a low height at dawn with two 230-lb. bombs. There is evidence that one or both of the bombs hit the target: the aeroplane was shot down and the occupants were made prisoners.

The bombing of the German naval bases in Belgium brought retaliation. During the nights of the 4th, 5th, and 6th of June strong attacks were made on the aerodromes in the Dunkirk area, and on the night of the 5th/6th, in particular, when about two hundred bombs were dropped, two hangars and two aeroplanes were destroyed, and one hangar and thirty-seven aeroplanes slightly damaged. On the night of the 6th/7th, when Coudekerque was attacked by about thirty aeroplanes, it happened that all the serviceable Handley Pages had left for a raid, and that three unserviceable aeroplanes had been moved to safer quarters. Although no aeroplanes were therefore bombed, two hangars were destroyed, and six were damaged together with various aerodrome buildings. The general damage was such that Coudekerque was forthwith abandoned, except as a landing-ground. In the same night at Teteghem aerodrome, which was bombed by the light of parachute flares, two hangars were destroyed and nine fighting aeroplanes somewhat seriously damaged.

Sir Roger Keyes at once asked the Admiralty for reinforcements of one Handley Page squadron, one day bomber squadron, and one fighter squadron, and in his telegram he pointed out that German bombing had, in three nights, put forty-two aeroplanes out of action. He also asked for anti-aircraft guns and these were eventually supplied to him, but the Admiralty stated, in reply to the request for additional squadrons, that as an American bombing group was shortly to be placed under his orders it would be impossible to obtain further help from the Royal Air Force. The Admiralty added, hopefully, that, in any event, the American squadrons would be available before any additions could be provided from Royal Air Force resources.

By way of reply to the enemy attacks many raids were

made against targets at Bruges, Zeebrugge, and other centres in Belgium. During one night, the 10th of June, No. 214 Handley Page Squadron dropped sixteen 112-lb. and four 250-lb. bombs on Thourout railway junction, four 112-lb. on Bruges docks, sixteen of the same weight on the La Brugeoise power-station and steelworks on the outskirts of Bruges,[1] fourteen 112-lb. bombs on the Zeebrugge–Bruges canal, and three of 550-lb. weight on the Zeebrugge lock.

It appeared that the naval air bombing induced the enemy to strengthen his air fighting units in Belgium. Enemy opposition noticeably increased throughout July and when, early in August, it became known that aircraft reinforcements had reached the important aerodrome at Varssenaere, west of Bruges, it was decided to make a large-scale attack on the aerodrome. The plan was to bomb at dawn with fighter aeroplanes, British and American, and to attack an hour later with British D.H.9 day-bomber squadrons. The squadrons which took part were Nos. 210 and 213, and No. 17 U.S. Aero Squadron, all equipped with Sopwith 'Camels', and Nos. 211 and 218 D.H.9 Squadrons. In addition No. 204 Sopwith 'Camel' Squadron, after accompanying the bombing formation over the target, had orders to patrol at 5,000 feet against attempted attacks by hostile aircraft.

After much practice, the operation took place on the 13th of August. A total of fifty Sopwith 'Camels' set out at dawn and took up formation over Dunkirk harbour whence they proceeded, in two long lines, parallel with the coast about seven miles out to sea. Near Ostend, on a light signal from the bombing leader, Lieutenant W. E. Gray of No. 213 Squadron, the Sopwith 'Camels' turned inland and dived for their objective from 5,000 feet. As the bombers neared the aerodrome it was seen that three Flights of Fokkers were lined up on the ground with engines running, and that officers and mechanics were stand-

---

[1] An attack by a Handley Page of No. 214 Squadron on the La Brugeoise works on the 30th/31st of May had caused the explosion of an ammunition dump alongside the works. The concussion effect was felt throughout the town and is said to have caused great alarm.

ing about. The surprise was complete and the Germans could do nothing before the bombs began to explode. For ten minutes the scene was one of chaos. Flames leaped from hangars and aeroplanes and from a petrol dump, buildings collapsed, and the rattle of the machine-guns of the Sopwith 'Camels' mingled with the noise of the exploding bombs. Particular attention was paid to a local chateau which served as quarters for the flying officers. As the bombers turned away after their intensive ten minutes, during which one hundred and thirty-six 25-lb. and six 40-lb. phosphorus bombs had been dropped, they saw desolation below them. All the Sopwith 'Camels' returned safely at a low height, and one enemy fighter which was encountered by chance was destroyed over the sea. No. 211 Squadron subsequently bombed the aerodrome again, as arranged, with fourteen 112-lb. bombs and one of 230-lb. weight, but an attempted attack by the D.H.9's of No. 218 Squadron was frustrated by enemy fighter formations.

The damage inflicted as a result of the raids on Varssenaere cannot be exactly stated, but it is known that one of the bombs dropped by No. 211 Squadron made a direct hit on the officers' chateau, destroying the upper parts of two wings, that eight aeroplanes on the aerodrome were wrecked, that heavy casualties were caused, and that an additional twenty or thirty aeroplanes were destroyed in the hangars. It is also known that the aerodrome long remained entirely disorganized.

The subsequent story of the Dunkirk air units properly belongs to the narrative of the final Allied offensives on the Western front, as a result of which the German Army sued for peace.

CHAPTER XI
PRELUDE TO VICTORY
The Battle of the Aisne, 1918
[Maps, p. 414 and at end.]

THE German onslaught against the British on the Somme in March, and on the Lys in April, 1918, had caused about 250,000 British casualties. Some divisions had been so depleted that they could not again be made fit for active operations unless they could be given a period of quiet in which to reorganize and to train the newly arrived drafts, mainly composed of young recruits. At the suggestion of General Foch it was agreed, after some hesitation, that five British divisions which had suffered heavily, namely, the 8th, 19th, 21st, 25th, and 50th, should change places with French divisions on a part of the front near Rheims where it was not expected that there would be any abnormal activity. The divisions, under the G.O.C. and staff of the IX Corps, moved south in May, to the area of the French Sixth Army, and No. 52 (R.E.8) Squadron flew to an aerodrome at Fismes to provide the necessary air co-operation. Those British troops who had known the stricken battlefields in the north were impressed by the quiet, by the comparative comfort, and by the gentle pleasantness of the new landscape: it seemed too good to be true.

And so it proved. The British infantry and field artillery had not fully settled in when the crash came. There was no indication of what was in store. The R.E.8's of No. 52 Squadron made reconnaissances, but the enemy side of the Ailette was thickly wooded and the air observers saw nothing suspicious, with the exception that in the early morning, and again in the late evening, of the 22nd, the 23rd, and the 24th of May, distant clouds of dust were reported on the roads leading towards the front. It does not appear that these observations aroused particular interest. Had they done so, and had aeroplanes been sent out specially to investigate, it might have been discovered that the dust clouds were mostly being thrown up by heavy artillery moving into the area. In fact, the first news of the German plan was conveyed by two prisoners who were captured by the French in the late afternoon of the 25th of May, and if any doubts still remained they were finally set at rest at 1 a.m. on the 27th, when the peace of the Aisne was suddenly shattered by the opening of one of the greatest bombardments of the war.

The Germans achieved surprise in that they had concentrated more than 1,000 heavy guns, with ammunition, undetected. The precautions which they took to ensure secrecy were thorough, and were made easier because of the well-wooded nature of the country in the enemy back and forward areas. Furthermore, the Germans had unexpected allies in the river which ran part of its course through no-man's land. The Ailette was the home of numerous frogs whose nightly chorus of croaking excluded more distant sounds, such as must have resulted from large-scale movements of guns and material, from reaching the ears of front-line listeners. The Ailette, moreover, was unfordable and prevented the French from making raids to obtain prisoners for intelligence purposes.

So far as No. 52 Squadron was concerned there is not much to be said. The reconnaissance area of the squadron covered only the front of the British IX Corps, and, in any event, the pilots and observers were flying over country which was new to them, as it was to the British Corps staff. A measure of familiarity with local conditions, with the habits and dispositions of an enemy, is necessary before the significance of changes, if any, may be adequately assessed. It was, moreover, the conviction of the Allied command that when the next German large-scale offensive was made it would take place in the Somme area as a continuation of the March attack. The Rheims front was therefore looked upon as more or less above suspicion, and complacency is not a state of mind which helps to elucidate the well-obscured intentions of an enemy. It is possible that had the IX Corps been on the British front the Royal Air Force long-distance reconnaissance squadrons would have been ordered to investigate the dust-clouds reported by No. 52 Squadron. As it was, the matter was one for the French Sixth Army command and it may be that the conviction that the Germans would attack elsewhere, coupled with the fact that the British were still in the process of settling in—and adequate liaison between Allies requires time for its effective development—suffice to explain why no action was taken about the reported dust-clouds.[1]

The German bombardment began at 1 a.m. on the 27th of May on a front of twenty-seven miles, from Brimont to Leuilly, and, at 3.40 a.m., the enemy infantry assaulted. The Allied sector which was attacked was weakly held, the bombardment was devastatingly effective, and before the day had ended the Germans had penetrated the Allied area to a maximum depth of twelve miles. The British 8th and 50th Divisions had ceased to exist except for scattered parties, but the 21st Division on the right, less heavily involved, was not in such dire plight. Only the 25th Division, in reserve, remained intact, and it was compelled to take over the defence of the greater part of the IX Corps front.[2]

The aeroplanes of No. 52 Squadron, under conditions of great difficulty, flew over the battle-field to report the German advance. They encountered opposition from formations of fighting aeroplanes which patrolled at low heights ahead of the German troops: the first British aeroplane out, at dawn on the 27th, was shot down. There was little co-operation with the artillery because many guns were lost or disabled, and few of the batteries which escaped had their aerials intact, or, if intact, erected. The air observers dropped message bags from time to time telling batteries of excellent targets of marching columns, but on the whole the co-operation with the artillery may be said to have broken down. The aerodrome at Fismes was increasingly shelled as the day passed: some transport and two aeroplanes were hit, and there were casualties. In the afternoon

[1] There is evidence that the General Officer Commanding the British IX Corps was uneasy about the possibility of a German attack, but the representations which he made at French Sixth Army head-quarters were rejected.

[2] The British 19th Division was in reserve in the neighbourhood of Chalons under the French Fourth Army. During the night of the 28th/29th of May it was transported in buses to the IX Corps sector to fill a gap in the French line across the Ardre Valley.

No. 52 Squadron was forced to move back to an aerodrome at Cramaille, already overcrowded with French aeroplanes. The personnel of the squadron took rest where they could, and the R.E.8's were left out in the open. At dusk the German pilots began to bomb Cramaille aerodrome, and until dawn next morning the attacks were maintained with little intermission: as a result ten French aeroplanes were destroyed by fire. At daylight on the 28th No. 52 Squadron was ordered by the French to move again. The aeroplanes were flown first to La Ferté and then to Trècon, south of Rheims, and the transport moved by a different route, joining the aeroplanes at Trècon on the evening of the 29th. During the confusion of the moves there were no flying operations, but on the 30th the squadron came into action once more, when low bombing and machine-gun attacks were made.

By the evening of the 30th of May the German troops had reached the Marne on a front of ten miles, but the worst was over. For some days afterwards there was bitter fighting, but by the 6th of June, by which time General Foch had sent nearly thirty divisions to the assistance of the French Sixth Army, the way had been barred to a further advance, and the battle came to an end. The British troops were gradually withdrawn from the French area, and No. 52 Squadron, after resting at Trècon from the 19th to the 30th of June, moved to Auxi-le-Chateau to join the III Brigade. The squadron had been able to do little that was useful once the German attack had begun, and may almost be said to have been in the way. This was partly because the attack had taken the Allies by surprise, with the result that no precautionary arrangements for withdrawal were in existence, and partly because the French army had no room, during an emergency, for a British squadron untrained in French methods of co-operation.

The Battle of the Matz
[Map, p. 414]

It was assumed that the Germans would not long stay their hand. There was good evidence that there would be an attack on the immediate right of the German armies engaged in the Aisne battle, and that the objective would be Compiègne. Late on the 7th of June a telegram from General Foch informed British General Head-quarters that there were strong signs of an attack impending on the Montdidier–Noyon front, where German pilots were active over the French lines. The Generalissimo asked that the greatest possible concentration of British fighting and bombing air strength, additional to the units already attached to the French, should be directed towards the area Nesle–Roye. The time when these air units might intervene most effectively would be communicated later. The British reply, on the 9th of June, stated that the air units with the British Fourth Army had been increased to a total of eight fighter squadrons, three day bomber squadrons, and four night bomber squadrons, and that orders had been given that the maximum possible of this air strength was to be employed, when required, in the direction indicated.

The Royal Air Force detachment referred to in the telegram from General Foch as already with the French was the Head-quarters IX Brigade. As a step towards ensuring air superiority in the neighbourhood of the possible German attack, General Foch had asked on the 29th of May that the Royal Air Force should hold five fighter squadrons and three day-bomber squadrons in readiness to move into the Beauvais area for operations in the direction of St. Quentin and Laon. At the same time he had said that he would himself hold twelve French fighter squadrons and nine day-bomber squadrons ready to move north to help the Royal Air Force if the German attack should come not against the French, as expected, but against the British west of Hebuterne.

On the 2nd of June there were no longer any doubts about where the blow would fall, and General Foch, by telegram on this day, had requested that the British squadrons, to receive which full arrangements had been made, should move south as soon as possible. The squadrons had accordingly moved next day; they were Nos. 27, 32, 49, 73, 103, 2 A.F.C., 43, and 80, together with the head-quarters of the two Wings (the Ninth and Fifty-first), and their parks and ammunition column.

In the threatened area the French also had made a special concentration of squadrons. On the 1st of March 1918 the French offensive air units had been grouped to form two mobile detachments known as the *Aviation Reserve* of the Group of Armies of the North, and as *Escadre* No. 11. The latter unit, of a strength approximating 250 aeroplanes, mostly operated in the eastern part of the French front. The *Aviation Reserve* was reorganized, early in June, as the *1st Air Division*, which consisted of bombers (*Escadres* 12 and 13, representing three groups of three squadrons each), and fighters (*Escadres* 1 and 2, or three groups of four squadrons each). The *Air Division*, which was a true strategic reserve available for intervention wherever operations of vital importance were taking, or were about to take, place had, at the time of the German attack in June 1918, a total of 600 bomber and fighter aeroplanes.[1] The offensive strength of the Royal Air Force, available for supporting the French on the front of twenty miles which was attacked, was approximately 200 aeroplanes.

The IX Brigade had, when it moved south, come under the orders of Commandant L. Picard, the air commander of the French group of reserve armies (*G.A.R.*), and subsequently worked in direct co-operation with the French *Air Division*.[2] Orders issued by Commandant Picard for the 5th of June, in anticipation that the German attack would take place at any moment in the area Montdidier–Lassigny, stated that the main fighting strength of the IX Brigade would be held ready for offensive operations as soon as the battle should begin, but called for bombing attacks on Roye, where concentrations of enemy troops must be expected. In accordance with these orders the British day-bomber squadrons had released five tons of bombs over Roye on the 5th. The bombing attacks were switched next day to Ham and Chaulnes, and on the 7th there was a further

---

[1] By the 1st of August 1918 the strength of the French 1st Air Division had increased to 630 aeroplanes, and by the armistice to 732.

[2] See the French official history, *Les Armées françaises dans la Guerre*, Tome VI, 2ᵉ Volume, Annexes, 2ᵉ Volume.

change when the allotted targets were Flavy-le-Martel and Nesle: dumps in the last-named town were set on fire by the bombers of No. 103 Squadron. On the 7th, in particular, there was enemy opposition, the bombers, two of which were lost, encountering formations of twenty-five to forty German fighters. Such large formations were unusual on the French front, and the operation orders issued on the evening of the 7th for the following day took note of the change. The bombing targets allotted to the IX Brigade were Ham and Fresnoy-les-Roye, and the full available fighting strength of the brigade was ordered to be sent as an escort to the bombers. The attack on Ham was abandoned because of clouds, but Nos. 49 and 103 Squadrons, heavily escorted, bombed the second target without meeting opposition.

The German offensive was launched at 3.20 a.m. on Sunday the 9th of June between Montdidier and Noyon. It was made by eleven divisions in the front line with seven in support, and was met by eight French forward divisions with four in support. The French defences were organized as three positions, front, intermediate, and main, with the front lightly held. The attack achieved a local success in the centre, along the Matz, and there was some further progress on the 10th, but French counter-attacks next day with five fresh divisions retook some of the ground which had been lost and induced the enemy command to believe that nothing could be gained by prolonging the battle. The Germans had made a maximum penetration of six miles, and they had captured guns and prisoners, but the success achieved was small in comparison with previous offensives, and the main reason was that the French knew what was coming and were fully prepared: nor did they use the front line as the line of resistance.

The IX Brigade was employed during the three days of the main battle on low-flying attacks, during which a total of sixteen tons of bombs were dropped and 120,000 rounds of machine-gun ammunition were fired. The reports of the pilots reveal that targets of troops and transport were plentiful, and it would appear certain that heavy toll was taken. In connexion with the French counter-attack on the 11th, it had been arranged that the British fighters should attempt to destroy the enemy observation balloons along the line Montdidier–St. Maur three hours before the French infantry were due to begin their advance. Seven German balloons were flying on the front specified, but they were protected by German fighter formations which succeeded in preventing the British pilots from getting within striking distance of the balloons: in the many combats which resulted six German aeroplanes were reported to have been destroyed.

During the battle, which was intense and confused, there were instances of British pilots attacking French troops, and of French pilots and infantry firing upon Royal Air Force aeroplanes. One British pilot was wounded and forced to land by a French two-seater which did not cease to attack even when the aeroplane was on the ground. There was an occasion on the day of the French counter-attack when a British pilot who reported a concentration of German troops and transport in a wood was allowed to lead a formation to bomb the enemy, with the result that eight French officers were wounded and seventy-five horses were killed. Consequent upon this very regrettable happening orders were issued by the IX Brigade which made Royal Air Force squadron commanders personally responsible for ensuring that each pilot, before he set out upon a mission, was provided with a map showing the battle line according to the latest available military information. There had been precautions against the danger of British aeroplanes being mistaken for those of the enemy. When the squadrons of the IX Brigade had arrived in the area, aeroplanes had been flown to the French aerodromes to give the French pilots an opportunity of studying them at close quarters, and they had also been flown low above the French infantry for a similar reason. There would be no profit in recounting the above episodes except to illustrate the imperative need, when allies are called upon to work together in unusual circumstances, for close and continuous liaison. It seems obvious that the British pilots could not have been kept informed, on the day of the French counter-attack, of the changes in the position on the ground: if they had been, the mistaken bombing attack could not have been made.

While the battle of the Matz was still in progress Major-General J. M. Salmond issued a memorandum to his brigade commanders in which he said it was probable that the enemy would make a supreme effort to overwhelm the British front. 'His attacks since the 21st of March on the 'Somme, on the Lys, on the Aisne, and on the present 'battle front', he said, 'have without doubt been made 'with the object of forcing the Allies to use up their avail- 'able reserves. He has to a great extent succeeded in this 'object. He has, at the same time, been making prepara- 'tions along the whole of the British front for an attack on 'a large scale. These preparations are now complete. No 'further indications can be obtained of his selected point of 'attack by means of increased dumps, light railways, &c., 'since these are already in position and are uniform along 'the whole front. In order to prevent surprise, such as 'apparently occurred on the last attack on the Aisne, it is 'a vital necessity that his approach march be discovered. 'The time during which this approach march takes place 'is, without doubt, during the night, and the very early 'hours of the morning during any period up to five nights 'of the day selected for the attack.' The Royal Air Force brigade commanders were therefore instructed to see that all likely approach routes were reconnoitred twice nightly, and they were told that although little that was definite might be discovered, even slight indications could prove to be of vital importance. Furthermore it was desirable that the same areas as were reconnoitred in the dark should be surveyed again immediately before dawn, and it would be necessary, because of the restricted visibility at that hour, for pilots to fly close to the ground to make the task of their observers easier. 'Responsibility that the British 'army is not surprised is on the Royal Air Force' was the concluding sentence of the paper.

Two days later, in a personal memorandum which was sent to Sir Douglas Haig, General Foch made a comprehensive survey of the disposition of the German forces, and stated his conclusion that the enemy had three possibilities open to him, namely, (i) an offensive in a sector of the front between the sea and the Somme, (ii) a continuation of the attacks between Montdidier and Rheims, and (iii) a surprise assault on some other part of the front, in Champagne, at Verdun, or in Lorraine. So far as concerned the first two possibilities the Germans could, because of the existing dispositions of their reserves, make a concentration by means of night road marches as they had done immediately before their offensives in March and May. It was necessary, therefore, that all the approach routes to the front between the sea and Rheims should be carefully watched, particularly at night from low heights. The third plan, of a surprise assault, could not be adopted without a considerable movement of troops, &c., by rail, and the air services should therefore arrange for reconnaissance of the more important transverse railways, as well as of the enemy back areas between the sea and Champagne.

In accordance with the memorandum of General Foch a detailed plan for day and night reconnaissance of the railway systems, which aimed at assessing the density of the traffic along the whole German front between Flanders and Alsace, was drawn up by the French staff for French squadrons. The Royal Air Force was consequently absolved from this particular duty on the British part of the front. It still had the responsibility, however, of keeping a close watch upon the general enemy area opposite the British armies, and it was considered that best information about the German intentions would be obtained from a systematic photographic reconnaissance of enemy billeting areas. Maps, specially prepared by the intelligence branch at General Head-quarters, on which the important German billeting areas were marked, together with the roads by which enemy artillery might be expected to move into the area opposite the British from other parts of the front recently active, were issued, and the Royal Air Force photographic reconnaissances were based upon these maps. Air observers, while engaged upon photographic duties, were given instructions to keep a general look-out for abnormal train activity, and for any movement of heavy artillery along the roads distant from the front.

Bearing in mind the possibility of an attack being made against the British front, Major-General J. M. Salmond suggested to General Head-quarters on the 15th of June that the French should be asked to hold the IX Brigade in readiness for immediate return. In the result, the squadrons of the IX Brigade moved north into the British area on the 21st of June, the Ninth Wing of the Brigade being reinforced by Nos. 25 and 62 Squadrons from the Eighty-first Wing, which was temporarily disbanded.[1]

As soon as the head-quarters IX Brigade once more came under British orders, a concentrated bombing scheme was initiated. The problem of dislocating the enemy railway communications by means of bombing attacks had been studied from the early days of the war, and the study had been intensified during 1918. In April memoranda upon the problem had been placed before the Supreme War Council by the British and French sections of the Inter-Allied Transportation Council, and in these papers principles were set out upon which, it was suggested, the selection of railway bombing targets should be based. It appeared impracticable, it was said, to cut the German railway communications at a distance of more than fifty miles from the front because of the multiplicity of lines available. Suitable objectives could be divided into (i) junction stations and large depots, (ii) wayside stations, and (iii) sections between stations. Damage to the track or to a train in a large junction station might not have much effect upon traffic because there would be many lines, and because gangers would normally be at hand to begin the work of repair without loss of time. Although hits might be made on workshops or engine-sheds, with resultant damage to locomotives or machinery, there would be little or no consequent interruption of local traffic. Nor was it to be expected that the damage inflicted would be on a scale large enough to affect the enemy's general rail-

---

[1] The Eighty-first Wing was re-formed as a Corps Wing on the 1st of July 1918. On the 24th of June the IX Brigade again took over the Fifty-fourth (Night) Wing.

way transport position. If the watering arrangements in a junction station could be destroyed the interruptions of traffic would be immediate and important, but a water tower offered too small a target for definite attack.

The bombing of wayside stations did not appear to present a greater prospect of useful results for the reason that they also, like the larger stations, were usually equipped with a number of lines, and had repair gangs at hand or quickly procurable. It seemed, therefore, that traffic could most effectively be interrupted if a line was destroyed between stations. The destruction of a bridge, viaduct, or running train, offered the best results, but targets so small were difficult to hit. A straight stretch of line, however, formed a fairly easy mark, and if it could be hit where it ran through a cutting it was obvious that considerable dislocation of traffic must ensue. The enemy would normally be making the greatest use of his railway system, at a distance from twelve to fifty miles behind the front, just before sundown and just after dawn, and if therefore it was not possible to maintain bombing attacks throughout the twenty-four hours, they would offer the best results if they began about one hour before dusk and were continued at intervals throughout the night until an hour after daybreak. In pursuance of these general assumptions the members of the Inter-Allied Transportation Council had put forward a comprehensive selection of targets on the German railway system. 'It is considered', said the memorandum dealing with the front opposite the British armies, 'that almost complete interruption can be 'effected by cutting railways between Marcoing and Cam-'brai, between St. Quentin and Busigny, and between Ter-'gnier and Laon', and the sections along these lines most suitable for bombing attack were specifically indicated. The various papers had been forwarded to Royal Air Force head-quarters which had decided, after due consideration, that in the existing circumstances it was impossible to bomb effectively, and to keep under bombardment from the air, the small targets indicated.

At the beginning of June the matter had been raised again, this time by General Plumer, commanding the

A BOMBING SCHEME

Second Army. In a memorandum which he submitted to General Head-quarters he pleaded for concentrated bombing attacks upon carefully selected points on the railways. To achieve success, he said, the same targets, which should be few, must be attacked continuously over a period, at least for six or seven successive nights. He suggested two suitable points on the system opposite the Second Army, namely, Armentières station and the railhead between Comines and Wervicq. British General Head-quarters had been well disposed towards the suggestions put forward by General Plumer, but because the head-quarters IX Brigade was at the time working under the orders of the French it had not been possible to proceed further.

When, however, the IX Brigade returned from the French area on the 21st of June the matter was reviewed, and it was then decided to concentrate bombing operations against a few selected points of the enemy communications. On the 23rd of June General Head-quarters issued instructions, based on a memorandum by Major-General J. M. Salmond, giving the following targets, specifically chosen to hinder an enemy concentration on the approximate line La Bassée–Ypres.[1] The squadrons to take part were Nos. 49, 29, 98, 103, and 107 (day bombers), and Nos. 58, 83, and 207 (night bombers).

(i) Valenciennes railway junction and the line Valenciennes–St. Amand.
(ii) Tournai junction and the line running east from that town.
(iii) The Fives junction south of Lille, and the line Lille–Roubaix, and
(iv) Courtrai junction, and the line running to the north.

The operations, which began on the 24th of June, were looked upon as experimental. It was agreed that the intelligence branch at General Head-quarters should compile the fullest possible information about the bombing results, and that frequent discussions upon the subject should take

[1] Three other schemes were prepared about the same time to meet concentrations against other possible fronts of attack.

place between the army and air staffs. Royal Air Force head-quarters hoped that the operations might provide material for decisions upon the following points:

  (i) to what extent it was possible to interrupt communications by means of attacks on selected lengths of railway line,
  (ii) whether it was better for pilots to fly in close formation and drop their bombs together at a signal from the leader, or to follow one another, each taking his own aim, and
  (iii) how the material effects of comparatively low bombing by night compared with those obtained as a result of day attacks from a height.

The bombs used were mostly of 112-lb. weight, and in a typical attack by day some thirty bombs of this weight were dropped. The night bombers carried a similar weight, except the Handley Pages of No. 207 Squadron which in a single night dropped a total of one hundred and sixty 112-lb. bombs. In the period from the 24th of June to the 2nd of July the four day-bomber squadrons, from heights varying between 11,000 and 14,000 feet, dropped 19 tons of bombs on their allotted objectives of railway junctions and lengths of line, and 10 tons on miscellaneous targets when, for various reasons, the railways could not be reached. The three night squadrons dropped 42 tons of bombs on their railway objectives, and 5 tons elsewhere. At a conference on the 1st of July air photographs and all available information about the results of the bombing were studied and the conclusion was reached that attacks upon sections of railway line should cease. Pilots and observers had contended that bombs which exploded quite close to a length of line did no apparent damage, and the air photographs supported this view. It was therefore decided to concentrate the attacks upon the four railway junctions, but to include any trains which might be seen on the lines radiating from the junctions. In the next four days, which were not very favourable because of wet weather, $3\frac{3}{4}$ tons of bombs were dropped by day (plus $1\frac{1}{2}$ tons on targets other than those allotted), and 9¼ tons at night (plus ¾ ton). On the 6th of July a further experiment was ordered with the object of testing whether better results would be obtained by day bombers who dropped their bombs in formation at a signal from the leader, or from those who attacked as individuals. The weather, however, continued to be unfavourable, and as there were only a few attacks, made from 12,000 feet or higher, there was not much to be learned.

The total weight of bombs dropped during the course of the various experiments was 106 tons, of which about twenty tons were not aimed at the allotted targets. In a report dealing with the experiments, Major-General J. M. Salmond pointed out that they were cut short owing to the transfer of the IX Brigade to the French front. 'No 'reliable data have, therefore, been obtained,' he said, 'but 'so far as experience goes it seems that more interruption 'can be caused to communications by bombing important 'junctions than by attempting to destroy lengths of rail-'way line. Damage to the latter is nil unless the bomb 'explodes within a very few feet of the track and in any 'case is quickly repaired. In a junction, in addition to the 'tracks, there are other objectives, such as signal boxes, 'engine sheds, &c., the destruction of which is bound to 'dislocate traffic more or less. The results of experiments 'are also inconclusive as to whether it is best to drop bombs 'in formation on a signal from the leader or for each pilot 'to take his own aim, but it appears likely that the former 'will usually give the better results when bombing by day 'from a height. It may sometimes be best for each sub-'formation of 3 to 6 machines to drop its bombs simul-'taneously on a signal from its leader in place of the whole 'formation doing so. No reliable data have yet been 'obtained as regards the comparative results of bombing by 'night and from a height by day.'[1]

[1] Experiments were also made at home throughout 1918. For a paper setting out general conclusions as a result of the home experiments as well as of experience on the Western front, see Appendix XXIII, *Methods of Bombing*. See also the section dealing with 'German Night Bombing', pp. 419–32.

The Second Battle of the Marne
[Map, p. 414]

The squadrons of the IX Brigade, it will be observed, had been moved back to the French front, and the reason for this must be explained. The main German reserves, amounting to twenty-five divisions, were concentrated under Prince Rupprecht of Bavaria on the German right, opposite the British front in Flanders. It was, however, the opinion of General Foch, as expressed by him in a *directive* issued on the 1st of July, that if a German attack took place in Flanders it would be a subsidiary one, and that the main enemy offensive would be made between Lens and Chateau Thierry, with either Abbeville or Paris for objective. An alternative, or possibly subsidiary, attack might be made in Champagne. July was not many days old before the reports of French air observers, supplemented by air photographs, fixed the attention of General Foch to Champagne. So definite and comprehensive were the indications that, on the 12th of July, in a further *directive*, General Foch revised the views he had put forward at the beginning of the month. He was now of the opinion, he said, that the attack in Champagne, obviously impending, was being planned as a decisive blow against the French armies. On the 10th he had, as a precautionary measure, asked Sir Douglas Haig to hold a group of fighter and bomber squadrons ready to reinforce the French air service in the Champagne sector, and in the early hours of the 13th he sent a telegram requesting that the squadrons should move to named aerodromes (Rozoy-en-Brie, Orneaux, Pezarches, Chailly-en-Brie) as soon as possible. Through rainstorms on the 14th of July Nos. 32, 49, 43, 54, 73, 80, 27, 98, and 107 Squadrons flew south to join the French, and the head-quarters of the IX Brigade opened under the orders of the French Group of Armies of the centre.

General Foch also wished to be supplied with reinforcements of British divisions, and on the 12th and 13th he asked for six to be moved without delay, and he quickly submitted a request that four more divisions should be held ready to move when wanted. Two divisions, the 12th and 13th, accordingly moved south on the 13th of July, and two others, the 51st and 62nd, began to entrain the following day, together with the head-quarters of the XXII Corps, to which No. 82 Squadron was allotted: the squadron flew from Le Bourget to Haussimont on the 17th of July. Sir Douglas Haig was not happy about meeting the further demands of General Foch because the indications still pointed to the launching of an important German offensive on the British front, between Ypres and Hazebrouck, some time about the 20th of July.[1] At a personal interview on the 15th, however, between Generals Haig and Foch, it was decided that two additional British divisions, the 15th and 34th, should be sent to complete the British XXII Corps with the French. Sir Douglas Haig had been requested, on the 13th, to extend the fighting patrols of the Royal Air Force to cover the somewhat denuded front of the French First Army next to the British. He had accordingly undertaken to extend the patrol area of the British Fourth Army fighting squadrons as far south as Montdidier, but he pointed out that, in the absence of the IX Brigade, it would be impossible, if the German air service should become unusually active on the British front, for the British air squadrons to operate south of Moreuil.

Meanwhile at midnight on Sunday the 14th of July the German bombardment had opened with a crash that awakened the inhabitants of Paris to a new attempt to possess their city. At dawn, 4 a.m., on the 15th, the German infantry moved. For three days the opposing armies were locked in a bitter struggle, with American divisions assisting the French. The progress of the fighting demonstrated that the tide was already on the turn, and by the evening of the 17th, when the attacking divisions had already shot their bolt, the maximum

[1] It can now be stated that the German supreme command planned to make such an attack on the date named, and that all preparations had been made. Before the German attack could be launched, however, General Foch had taken the offensive, which compelled the German command to abandon its Flanders plan.

advance, the result of long planning and of great sacrifice in battle, had taken the German troops no farther than six miles from their jumping-off places.

The Royal Air Force squadrons of the IX Brigade helped the French *Air Division* to stem the German offensive. The British squadrons were mainly engaged in attacks against ground targets from low heights, and, in particular, in attacks on the numerous footbridges thrown by the enemy across the Marne, some of which were destroyed by bombing. The German single-seater pilots strenuously contested the Allied low-flying activities, and during the three days of the struggle eleven British aeroplanes were shot down within the enemy lines and four were wrecked after being damaged in combat: in addition, one officer was killed and thirteen officers were wounded.

On the 18th of July General Foch, at the suggestion of General Mangin, launched a tentative counter-offensive against the western shoulder of the salient on the front between Chateau Thierry and Soissons, with subsidiary assaults against other parts of the salient. The offensive, in which American, British, and Italian troops fought with the French, succeeded so well that, after three days, the German supreme command was compelled to order a withdrawal. By the beginning of August the German gains on the Marne, made as a result of the offensives in May and June, had been abandoned. More important, the initiative had passed from the enemy, exhausted by his many offensives, to the Allies.

In the Allied counter-attack which began on the 18th of July No. 82 Squadron co-operated with the British 51st and 62nd Divisions. The task of the squadron was to report the forward movements of the infantry, but German troops were also attacked as opportunity offered. The bomber and fighter squadrons of the IX Brigade were employed against ground targets so long as the Allied troops were advancing and there was confusion within the German lines, but when the forward movement began to slacken the bombers were switched to attacks, from high altitudes, on enemy dumps and aerodromes and on targets along the lines of communication.

As a result of the Allied success on the Marne the German supreme command had been compelled to withdraw divisions from its reserve concentration in Flanders. In consequence a German offensive against the British armies had, from being probable, become unlikely. At an Inter-Allied conference held on the 23rd of July, when the success of the Allied counter-attack on the Marne was already assured, General Foch expounded plans for increasing the pressure upon the enemy by means of co-ordinated local offensives with definite limited objectives. It is of interest that on the same day Royal Air Force head-quarters in France cancelled the scheme for systematic photography of the enemy billeting areas, which had been in progress since the middle of June, and ordered that watch be kept instead on the main enemy railway communications.

Minor Operations

Early in June, at the time when the French were being attacked on the Aisne, General Foch had written to Sir Douglas Haig to point out that it would be of advantage to pin down the German reserves by means of offensive operations north of the river Somme. Whatever operations were undertaken should, he suggested, have a well-defined object in view, such, for example, as the elimination of the bulge east of the forest of Nieppe, and in order to ensure economy in the numbers of troops employed it was important that the plans should be adequately prepared beforehand with particular attention to the use of tanks. Consequent upon the memorandum of General Foch, Sir Douglas Haig had instructed his army commanders to put forward their proposals. Arising out of the proposals submitted, minor attacks took place on the 28th of June, when the British line was advanced east of the Nieppe forest, and on the 4th of July, when an action was fought at Hamel which greatly influenced the British tactics in the subsequent battle of Amiens.

Sir Henry Rawlinson and the staff of the Fourth Army planned the Hamel attack with fine imagination.

Objectives, the capture of which would improve the line of the Fourth Army, were selected, and to attain them Sir Henry Rawlinson decided to employ a comparatively small force of infantry—ten battalions—on a wide front, with sixty tanks in support. To overpower the noise of the tanks while they were assembling, the F.E.2b's of No. 101 Squadron flew at night about the front line area. At 1 a.m. on the 4th of July the tanks were along their starting-line, and at 3.10 a.m. the artillery barrage opened. The date for the attack—Independence Day—had been tactfully chosen by Sir Henry Rawlinson because four companies from an American division had been incorporated, by platoons, among the attacking troops. This was the first time in the war when American soldiers went into action side by side with British infantrymen, and the beginning was a favourable one because the execution of the plan of attack came near perfection. As the artillery barrage opened the infantry and the tanks moved, and so complete was the surprise that by 5 a.m. all battalions except one had reached their final objectives.

No. 3 Squadron, Australian Flying Corps, was mainly responsible for the work of tactical co-operation with the assaulting troops, and No. 8 Squadron for similar duties with the tanks, while No. 9 Squadron had the special task of dropping small arms ammunition at pre-arranged points for the use of the forward infantry. This supply work was, within its limits, an unqualified success. There were six centres where, by pre-arrangement, ammunition was to be dropped, and when the advancing infantry reached these centres they were instructed to display the letter 'N' for purposes of identification and as a signal to the aeroplanes of No. 9 Squadron: in addition, machine-gun posts were to be supplied if they displayed the letter 'V'. An aeroplane carried two boxes, each containing a total of 1,200 rounds, which were attached to cylinders holding parachutes on modified bomb release gears. Eight aeroplanes were made responsible for carrying to the dumps, and four were allotted for answering 'V' calls from the machine-gun posts. About thirty minutes sufficed for the double journey from the aerodrome to the forward dumps, and ninety-three boxes of ammunition were dropped during the day of the attack, at a cost of two R.E.8's missing.

On the night before the attack selected enemy billeting areas had been bombed by No. 101 Squadron (nine 112-lb. and three hundred and fifty 25-lb. bombs), and on the day of the action dumps and bivouac areas were bombed by No. 205 Squadron. The fighter squadrons flew low over the enemy lines as soon as the assault had begun, and the pilots made many attacks on infantry, guns, and transport, often from a height of about 200 feet. German aeroplanes did not appear over the battle front until about 9.30 a.m., when, and subsequently, they made desultory attempts to interfere with the work of the Royal Air Force: five British aeroplanes did not return to their aerodromes, and five German fighters and one balloon were destroyed.

In a minor operation in the north on the 19th of July, which led to the occupation of the village of Meteren and of ground which had given the enemy good observation of the approaches to the village, the attacking infantry made use of tin disks, worn on the back, which proved easy to see from the air and enabled the observers accurately to report the progress of the troops.

Meanwhile, all armies had been instructed by Sir Douglas Haig to prepare plans for a resumption of the offensive. In accordance with these orders, General Rawlinson, the Fourth Army Commander, considered schemes for an attack south of the Somme with the object of freeing Amiens and the Paris–Amiens railway. After the failure of the German Rheims attack on the 15th of July, General Rawlinson urged strongly, in an interview with Sir Douglas Haig on the 16th, that he should be allowed to proceed. The Commander-in-Chief gave his provisional approval, and next day the Fourth Army Commander was told to go ahead with his preparations. There was a conference on the 23rd, called by General Foch, who said he was anxious that the British attack should be made at the earliest possible moment, and indicated that the French First Army would co-operate. The attack was fixed to begin on the 10th of August, but on the 28th of July General Foch sent a letter to Sir Douglas Haig in which he pointed out that the Germans were falling back from the Marne with increasing speed, and he said they would doubtless establish themselves behind some river in order to obtain time for reorganization. In the circumstances, said General Foch, it would be of advantage if the British Fourth Army and the French First Army began their proposed operations as soon as possible, because every day gained would mean that the enemy would be less prepared to withstand the blow. As it was desirable that the operations of the two armies should be under a single command, he asked Sir Douglas Haig to take control. As a result of the representations made by General Foch, the date for the attack was put forward from the 10th to the 8th of August.

Orders issued by British General Head-quarters on the 29th of July set out the objects of the attack. When the line of what had been the Amiens outer defence system was reached, the Fourth Army, keeping its left flank on the Somme, was to push forward to Chaulnes, while the French First Army, resting its right on the Avre, similarly pressed the enemy towards Roye. On the 3rd of August the British plans were extended. The Germans were still rapidly falling back from the Marne, and Allied optimism had grown, and on that day Sir Douglas Haig told General Foch that he had given Ham, fifteen miles beyond Chaulnes, as the ultimate objective. At a conference two days later, attended by his subordinate commanders, Sir Douglas Haig explained that if all went well with the British and French attack the Generalissimo intended to employ more French reserves south-east of Montdidier, and it was clear that the operation might well develop into one of great magnitude. In order that rapid advantage might be taken of whatever success was gained, Sir Douglas Haig said he had assembled three British divisions in general reserve close behind the battle front, and that further divisions were being held behind the remainder of the British front in readiness to move.

German Night Bombing
[Map, at end]

While the business of preparation for a large-scale offensive was proceeding, with the whole crowded area behind the front alive with activity, German bombing operations created some anxiety. The enemy advance against the British on the Somme and on the Lys in March and April had endangered the railway system. 'The culmination was 'reached in May 1918, when the great lateral line from 'St. Just, via Amiens, to Hazebrouck had to be abandoned 'as a railway route owing to enemy shell fire. Our armies 'were then penned into a narrow strip of country, possess-'ing only one lateral railway communication, through 'Abbeville and Boulogne. Most of the forward engine 'depots had been lost, and several of the important engine 'depots remaining were so close to the enemy as to be 'practically useless, and our one lateral, along which all 'reserves and reinforcements drawn from one part of the 'front to be thrown in at another had to be moved, was 'threatened daily and nightly by persistent air attacks on 'the bridge over the Canche river at Etaples.'[1]

The Germans knew the importance of destroying, and the British of protecting, this line of communications. Every bridge, from Dunkirk to Abbeville, was separately considered, no doubt by the commands on both sides, but certainly by the British. Where there were masonry viaducts, overhead cover, designed to cause the bombs to explode on the surface, was provided. At important points alternative routes were surveyed, and the material necessary for creating a loop-way was assembled in the neighbourhood. A specially vital point, other than the Etaples bridge, was the lofty bridge at Wimereux, near Boulogne, where survey revealed that it would be impossible to make a useful deviation. Here a compromise was made by placing a bursting cover of steel rails on the bridge and by erecting massive timber supports under the arches in

---

[1] 'Land Transportation in the Late War', by Colonel M. G. Taylor, C.M.G., D.S.O., in the *Journal of the Royal United Service Institution*, November 1921.

order to prevent them from collapsing if a hit should be made.

The Etaples bridge over the Canche Estuary, which carried about one hundred military trains each day, was a long masonry viaduct. When the German advance enhanced the military importance of this line, already great, it was decided to construct an alternative line about a mile above the existing bridge, and there ensued a race against time which the German air force came near to winning. During the night of the 19th/20th of May, at the time when the last of the German aeroplane raids was being made on London, fifteen bombers attacked the Etaples bridge. Only one bomb fell close and this did no damage: most of them exploded in neighbouring hospitals and camps with terrible effect, for the killed numbered 182 and the wounded 643, while 10 persons were not accounted for. One of the German bombers was shot down, and the captured crew insisted that they did not know that hospitals were situated near the railway. They also expressed surprise, not without reason, that large hospitals should be placed close to air targets of first-rate military importance.[1] In another attack on the 30th/31st of May, when 41 civilians and 3 soldiers were killed, and 4 soldiers wounded, a direct hit by a bomb of heavy weight was made, soon after 11 p.m. on the 30th, on the Etaples bridge, a span of which collapsed. The German offensive against the French on the Chemin des Dames had opened three days earlier, and the railway was being worked to its full capacity to provide for the rapid movement of two French reinforcing divisions from Flanders to the threatened area. It happened that the construction of the alternative line had already progressed to the point when it was possible to make it temporarily usable, and the French troop movements were resumed, by way of the

[1] An inquiry into the matter of the bombing elicited, in a report made by the Director of Military Operations at the War Office, the statement: 'We have no right to have hospitals mixed up with reinforcement camps, 'and close to main railways and important bombing objectives, and until 'we remove the hospitals from the vicinity of these objectives, and place 'them in a region where there are no important objectives, I do not think 'we can reasonably accuse the Germans.'

alternative bridge, at 3 a.m. on the 31st of May. Furthermore, the railway construction troops in the neighbourhood, who had been warned that they must hold themselves ready for repair work at a moment's notice, had been able to make the damage to the original bridge sufficiently good for traffic to be resumed at 10 p.m. on the 31st. Less than an hour after the repairs had been completed the bombers came again, and although they failed to hit the bridge, they succeeded in cutting a part of the line, and they also set fire to a hospital train with the result that 27 patients and attendants were killed and 79 wounded, and eleven trucks of medical stores were destroyed. Additional casualties outside the hospital area were 8 killed and 36 wounded: the railway line had been made fit for traffic once more by 8 p.m. on the 1st of June. There were many similar attacks on the Etaples bridge: the line was broken for a few hours on the 30th of June, and again with more serious effect on the 24th of July. On the latter occasion a bomb exploded on the main track near the Etaples station, and an empty goods train from Abbeville plunged into the crater with the result that there was much confusion and delay to traffic. The usual practice, as noted below, was to bring trains to a halt when they came near a station which was under attack, but on the night of the 24th of July, for some unexplained reason, this precaution was not taken. Nor was it only the railway system which was affected. No. 3 Medical Board Depot Camp, near the station, suffered heavily. The military casualties in the camp were 39 killed and 91 wounded and, additionally, 12 civilians were killed and one was wounded. Apparently one bomb sufficed to inflict these serious casualties: it was of a heavy type and seems to have burst above the ground, radiating destruction in all directions: no bomb crater was made.

A word must be said on the subject of warnings and of general precautionary measures, so far as they concerned the railways. The night traffic required for the maintenance and movement of the armies on the Western front, especially from March 1918 onwards, when a succession of battles on a big scale were fought in different areas, was prodigious. The traffic had to be kept moving, even at some expense to safety. The general orders were that trains must keep running between stations, but that they must halt when they approached a station which was actually being bombed. On the *Nord* system information about night raiding enemy aircraft was telephoned to the *Commission de reseau* which thereupon instructed, by code telephone signal, the particular stations, which the movements of the raiders indicated might be affected, to put out their lights. As the bombers passed on their way, a warning message was progressively sent out ahead of them, while an 'all-clear' signal was given to stations no longer threatened. The efficiency of the French railway warning scheme was greatly helped by the regular habits of the German bombers, which made it possible after a time for the French railway authorities to forecast with fair accuracy the probable enemy objectives on each specific occasion. The ideal aimed at by the French was the sweeping of the country-side with an area of darkness which would always be under the bombers, and would endure no longer, nor be more extensive in area, than was strictly essential for the confusion of the attacking pilots.

It is obvious that how far such an ideal may be possible of achievement must depend upon the efficiency and the speed with which information about the movements of enemy bombing aircraft is collected and distributed. The restriction of such interference with general activities as the passage of hostile aircraft may achieve is a question of considerable importance. There seems little doubt that some such system as that elaborated to deal with military railway traffic in France, whereby warning precautions were given and relaxed with a rapidity which aimed at keeping pace with the raiders, will come to be recognized as generally desirable. In this matter the defence enjoys the abiding advantage that the waves by which information may be communicated, whether wireless or telephonic, travel at a speed which no bombers will attain. This basic fact makes the efficiency of any warning system a matter mainly of organization. It may appear tempting, in times of peace, to pay no more than perfunctory attention to this problem, but it must be apparent that neglect carries with it ponderable risks. It would be a matter of grave difficulty to improvise, in the confusion of war, a warning organization which would work with that degree of efficiency essential if one of the most serious of the indirect effects of the bombing threat is to be kept at a minimum. The organization must be perfected as an ordinary defensive measure under peace conditions, and a study of the day-to-day working of a railway system would appear to offer suggestions adaptable to the organization of an air raid warning scheme suitable for the emergency of war.

Although the damage inflicted by the German railway bombers was not vital, it should be remembered that the threat was continuous during the months of anxiety when the German armies were battering the Western front. News might come on any night of lucky hits which would lead to traffic dislocations on a scale big enough to affect British military plans. There were also other reasons for disquiet. The German advance had compressed the area in which the vast business of supply had to be conducted. In many depots there was congestion which little could be done to relieve. Within a short journey of the enemy aerodromes there were many targets of first-class military importance and of a vulnerability which placed them very much at the mercy of air bombers. The targets indeed were far too numerous for the attenuated German air service to deal with at all adequately. The German armies had created, by their deep advance in March and April 1918, a situation which was so favourable for air action that the German air service, had it been strong enough to take advantage of the situation, might possibly have changed the course of the war. Happily for the Allied cause, the German air service was far too weak, comparatively, to do any such thing, but, as shall be told, the damage which it was able to inflict was sufficiently serious.

Between 10.15 p.m. on the 19th of May and 1.25 a.m. on the 20th, about 500 bombs were dropped on No. 12 Ordnance Depot at Blarges, and on No. 20 at Saigneville, north-west of Abbeville. Twenty-two officers and men were killed and 78 wounded, and there was much miscellaneous material damage, some of it to an ammunition store, but there were no explosions. At 10.15 p.m. on the 20th the bombing was resumed, and it continued until 4 a.m. on the 21st. Soon after the attack started an incendiary bomb hit a hangar containing cordite in the ammunition depot at Blarges, and flames lighted the country-side throughout the remainder of the night. It was therefore a comparatively simple matter for the German pilots who came after to choose their targets, and it was not long before the depot was burning in many places. When the ammunition began to explode the whole area became an inferno. One shed, stocked with trench mortar bombs, which was directly hit, disappeared with a roar that assailed all ears for miles around, leaving only a crater fifty yards wide and ten yards deep. Throughout the 21st of May the explosions in the depot continued, and when at last they came to an end and it was possible to take stock of the damage it was found that 6,000 tons of ammunition, out of an original total of 27,000 tons, had been destroyed with many buildings. The casualties were no more than 3 killed and 8 wounded, and they were light because the bombing attack on the previous night had induced the authorities to move the quarters of the personnel some distance from the depot, a movement which was just completed in time. General Foch, who heard of the attack with some concern, sent an officer to seek full information about the happening.

Next night, the 21st/22nd of May, the bombers turned their attention to No. 20 Ordnance Depot at Saigneville, where 40,000 tons of ammunition were stored. As they had done at Blarges, they attacked in relays over a period, and once again they had early luck. One of the first bombs to fall exploded in a shed stacked with small arms ammunition, which caught fire. Shortly afterwards cartridges for 60-pounder and 6-inch howitzer shells were hit, and when they were fully alight the blaze was visible forty miles away. Five thousand six hundred tons of ammunition were destroyed, including the whole stock of sixty-nine million rounds of small arms ammunition.

On the 18th and 19th of May a dump containing 1,000 tons of shells had been blown up at Campagne in the Second Army area, so that during four successive nights the enemy bombing pilots destroyed a total of 12,500 tons of ammunition.

It was about this time that the Germans ceased to bomb England. No doubt the increasing efficiency of the defence measures at home had something to do with this decision, but German authorities have stated that from May 1918 onwards the Western front claimed their full attention, and that it was mainly for this reason that the air attacks on England ceased. It may be that the destruction, on successive nights, of two British depots in France illuminated, for the German general staff, targets of great military importance on the Western front which were being left undisturbed because energy was being dissipated in attempted attacks, of a military value which it was difficult at the time to assess, on London and other English cities. It may be argued that the German bombers had luck on their side when they exploded the ordnance depots in France, and that a similar success with, say, Woolwich Arsenal, might have had incomparably greater results. There are those who believe in the so-called strategic bombing of industrial centres and similar targets, with no more than a minimum diversion of force for the duties of military co-operation, and those who assert, on the other hand, that the object, in a land war, is to defeat the enemy army and that, as a corollary, the maximum force must be made available to support the army in the field. An archangel perhaps might give definition, in this connexion, to the words 'minimum' and 'maximum'. The matter, surely, is not one for dogmatic assertion either way, with schools of thought in exacerbated opposition. Rather is the question one of common sense, to be decided according to all the relevant circumstances. In 1918 the German command sought a decision on the Western front. The supreme effort failed, and subsequently until the end the German armies were fighting for their very existence. From March 1918 onwards the Western front dominated the whole war panorama, a fact which made essential the concentration of every energy in furtherance of what was the decisive campaign. The material for a bombing offensive against England on a scale which would offer important results, in strict co-ordination with the military offensives in France, was not available. As a result of such attacks as Germany had been able to make, Britain had already been compelled to take elaborate defensive precautions which had diverted men, guns, and equipment for home defence. From a military point of view all Germany needed to do was to keep the threat alive sufficiently to ensure that the defence personnel and equipment in England would not be dispersed to more active theatres. It seems clear that from the moment when the German high command decided to make a grand offensive on the Western front, every resource had to be put into the battle which must prove decisive, one way or the other.

It will be apposite here to refer to some comment on the subject of the strategical employment of the German bombing resources put forward in an earlier volume[1] when the general and specific effects of the German air raid campaign against Great Britain were analysed. It was suggested that the enemy night-raiding campaign which began in September 1917 represented to some extent a waste of effort because it led to a dissipation of strength. The comment was offered that the German command should have waited, and should have co-ordinated the night campaign against England with the military offensive which was launched against the British armies in March 1918. The following words, however, were included by way of qualification: 'Provided always that the Germans 'intended to employ part of their bombing strength against 'England, and not to concentrate their entire resources on 'attacks on military objectives on the Western front.' These words were expressly inserted in order that the matter might be left open for further consideration in the light of the bombing attacks on military objectives in France as set out above. The reader now has the main facts before him and he will no doubt conclude that, so long as targets of first-class military importance in France

[1] Vol. V, pp. 152–9.

lay wide open to attack at a crucial time, a continuance of the bombing campaign against England, whether coordinated with the military campaign in France or not, was an unjustifiable dissipation of effort. The one possible exception was, as already suggested, such action, on a strictly economic basis, as might be judged essential to stay any suspected or ascertained dispersal of British home air defence units.

For the Allies there were special circumstances which made attacks on German industrial centres seem to offer a prospect of important results, moral rather than material. So long as the German offensive endured, with the perils which it brought in train, so long was it imperative for every Allied resource to be concentrated on the decisive front to bring about the defeat of the enemy purpose. No profit would have resulted from attacks on distant targets in Germany if the German armies had broken through the Western front. When, however, the onslaught ended, there was much to be gained from a judicious employment of the air weapon against military targets in Germany. The German people, blockaded, had sustained a long war and they were more afflicted with war weariness than the Allied peoples. It was obvious to the Germans that their resources were exhaustible, and when the great offensive in France came to its indecisive end, every intelligent German must have become aware that his country, cut off from the world and facing enemies who had the vast resources of America at their disposal, had shot her bolt. The farther bombing aeroplanes penetrated into Germany, the more was the general ascendancy of the Allies brought home to the German people. The war had been fought on Allied territory and, so long as Germany itself had remained inviolate, the spirit of the people had not failed. It was the Allied aeroplanes which carried the war into Germany, and when hopes of a military victory on the Western front had been shattered the outlook of the people was such that the maximum moral effect was assured for aircraft bombing.

The targets open to aircraft attack are, and will always be, almost illimitable. The art of air warfare is mainly a question of choice of the right targets at the right time. The temptation to dissipate effort will invariably be great. The commander or Government most successful in resisting sentimental or similar motives for action, whose choice of objectives is governed to the greatest extent possible by pure military considerations will fail, if failure comes, from causes other than faulty war policy.

In view of the increase in the enemy bombing activity in France in May 1918, a night-fighter squadron, No. 151, was hastily formed in England from home defence Flights for service on the Western front. The squadron, which was equipped with Sopwith 'Camels', arrived in France on the 21st of June, and up to the time when the British offensive opened on the Somme on the 8th of August its main task was night defence of the Abbeville area. An elaborate defence system, which employed many searchlights and anti-aircraft guns, was evolved, and the squadron was placed in wireless touch with the anti-aircraft defence commanders, from whom an early warning of the passage of night raiders was obtainable. For some time after the arrival of the squadron, indeed almost to the end of July, the weather was more often than not unfavourable for night attack. The first definite success of the night fighters came on the 23rd of July when Captain A. B. Yuille so damaged a Gotha-type aeroplane over Etaples that it was subsequently forced to land, and its crew of three were captured. On the 10th of August the same officer shot down a five-engined Giant in flames near Talmas: this aeroplane, the first of its kind to fall in the British lines, carried a crew of nine.

Searchlights and guns were disposed at other strategic points within the British area, at Doullens, Arras, &c., but as the single-seater fighters were not equipped with wireless receiving sets, and because they were too few to afford adequate protection for each separate area, the possibility of making contact with the enemy raiders was too much a matter of chance. Eventually a scheme was evolved whereby a wide belt, or barrier, of searchlights and guns was established in two lines nearer the front, from the north of Arras to the Foucaucourt–Amiens road. This light and gun barrage, with which the activities of the air fighters were closely co-ordinated, proved effective. No. 151 Squadron, which had moved to an aerodrome at Vignacourt, north of Amiens, was enabled to pass from purely defensive patrolling to the offensive. The Sopwith 'Camel' pilots would, as occasion offered, visit the German aerodromes to await the return of the raiders in order to attack them as they attempted to land. In all, in the space of its five months' service in France, No. 151 Squadron shot down sixteen German bombers on the British side of the lines, and ten on the German side, for which there was confirmation of four. No. 151 Squadron did not itself suffer a single battle casualty—a truly remarkable record.

The account of No. 151 Squadron has gone ahead of the story, and it will be necessary to go back a little to tell of another appreciable success achieved by the German bombers. Between 10.38 p.m. and 11.37 p.m. on the 11th of August some nine aeroplanes attacked Calais. The military casualties, British, French, Belgian, and Portuguese, amounted to 16 killed and 31 wounded: in addition 3 civilians were killed and 10 wounded. In the northern area of the town the building and machinery of the pumping station were wrecked, the Belgian mechanical transport depot was gutted by fire and destroyed with 100 vehicles and a quantity of spare parts, and railway wagons and workshops were damaged. Far more serious was the damage inflicted in the southern part of the town. There a timber yard, belonging to a French Government contractor, and the British No. 2 Base Mechanical Transport Depot were set on fire. The timber yard was ablaze before the depot was attacked, and there were also two other fires caused by the bombing in different parts of Calais, with the result that when flames appeared at the British Base Depot all the Calais fire engines were engaged elsewhere. The fire was enabled to get out of hand and to pass unimpeded from shed to shed. How serious this was, and why, is apparent from the following extract from the relevant War Diary. 'Unfortunately we had all our eggs in one basket 'because during March, 1918, we were obliged to evacuate

'Abbeville owing to the advance of the enemy, and the
'advanced Mechanical Transport Depot in which, up till
'then, a proportion of spares of all makes (of vehicles)
'had been stored, was moved to Calais where accommo-
'dation was so limited that we had to transfer the stock
'to No. 2 Mechanical Transport Depot. It had always
'been the intention to return to Abbeville, but the move
'was held in abeyance until the tactical situation was
'clearer.'

The German bombing attack made any further consideration about moving the stores unnecessary. Spare parts for 6,497 motor-cars and ambulances, for 12,270 lorries, and for 799 tractors were destroyed. These figures represented about 55 per cent. of all motor-cars and ambulances on service with the British armies on the Western front, 40 per cent. of all lorries, and 93 per cent. of tractors. About 26,000 inner tubes and 16,000 tyres also disappeared. The monetary value of the goods destroyed amounted to one and a quarter million pounds sterling. It may be noted, in passing, that this compares with an estimated monetary value of £1,434,526 for the damage caused by all of the fifty-two day and night aeroplane raids on Great Britain.

The very serious losses made the transport position on the Western front immediately grave. Delay in replacing the spares threatened the maintenance of a major part of the mechanical transport in the field. An urgent telegram sent by the Quartermaster-General in France to the War Office resulted in an order being given to home manufacturers whereby an absolute priority was accorded to all outstanding orders for spare parts for transport. At the same time the dispatch from England to Eastern theatres of war of spare parts for the types of vehicle mainly concerned was suspended, units at home were called upon to surrender whatever was not barely necessary to keep them going, and mechanical transport units in the field were ordered to send in all spare parts except those few wanted for vehicles actually under repair at the time. It happened that British war industrial development had reached a stage by the middle of 1918 which made it possible to build up once more a reserve of supplies, and so far as the Western front was concerned the effect of the destruction of the Calais depot may be described as one of very serious inconvenience, although it might easily have been critical. An indirect effect, however, of some importance, was felt in Macedonia where the part played by the British Army in the final offensive in that theatre of war was to some extent conditioned by a lack of spare parts for transport, particularly of tyres and inner tubes.[1]

The reader may ask how it came about that targets of the kind and vulnerability noted above were offered to the German air service. Because the advance of the German Armies in March and April 1918 had compressed the vast impedimenta of the armies, it was no doubt difficult and harassing enough to make the mere physical arrangements necessary to keep the armies supplied, without taking into account the need for cover and dispersion or other precautionary measures imposed by the threat of air attack. If the threat from the air had also to be allowed for, it might have been impossible for the supply organization to keep going at all. There was, furthermore, at the best of times, keen competition for all suitable military sites behind the lines in France, and when the British armies were forced back that competition became more fierce. When all is said, however, it can hardly be doubted that risks were taken which it is difficult to justify. No longer away in time from the enemy aerodromes in Belgium than a London suburban train journey were concentrated, unprotected, the greater part of the Western front mechanical transport spares. Close to the Etaples railway bridge, one of the important military targets in France from the spring of 1918 onwards, were placed great hospitals and other camps. It must be admitted that we showed a general reluctance to make allowance for the bombing menace. Surveying the whole field of war, it can be argued that the likelihood of a hit on this or that particular objective was small, and the British character inclines to the taking of a sporting chance in preference to making fussy and apparently endless preparations for something which may never happen. Such

[1] See p. 298.

an attitude of mind has its advantages, but it can also be merely stupid, or worse.

In July 1918 the Royal Air Force lost two of its best known fighting pilots. One of them, Major James Thomas Byford McCudden, has already been introduced to the reader,[1] and has often found mention in this history. He was officially credited, between September 1916 and March 1918, with fifty enemy aeroplanes destroyed, and in April 1918 he was awarded the Victoria Cross. He was appointed to the command of No. 60 Squadron, and when flying to join the squadron from England, where he had been on duty for some weeks, he was accidentally killed on the aerodrome at Auxi-le-Chateau on the 9th of July 1918.

The other pilot, Major Edward Mannock, makes his appearance in these pages for the first time. He was commissioned in the Royal Engineers in April 1916, and transferred to the Royal Flying Corps in August of the same year; he graduated as a pilot in February 1917, and was posted to No. 40 Squadron in France in April. His first success came on the 7th of May 1917 when he shot down an enemy kite balloon, and a month later he destroyed his first enemy aeroplane. In January 1918 he returned to England, but he was in France again at the end of March as a Flight Commander in No. 74 (S.E.5a) Squadron. In June 1918 he was appointed to command No. 85 (S.E.5a) Squadron which had recently arrived in France from England. On the 26th of July, when returning to his aerodrome after destroying an enemy aeroplane, he was shot down by fire from the ground and fell in flames. Edward Mannock was a great formation leader who had the gift of inspiring those who flew with him. He had a keen, analytical mind, and pilots who served under him have testified that he was always thinking out schemes for the tactical handling of a fighting formation. His main successes were won between May and July 1918, and when allowance has been made for the time during which his powers and his opportunities were at their height, and for his influence upon his contemporary

[1] Vol. II, pp. 316–17.

pilots, there are grounds for the claim which has been made that he was the greatest fighting pilot of the war: he was posthumously awarded the Victoria Cross.[1]

Air preparations for the battle of Amiens

Secret instructions issued by General Head-quarters on the 27th of July set out the methods to be followed in order to obtain surprise in the impending battle. To attract the attention of the enemy to Flanders the Royal Air Force was ordered to occupy additional aerodromes in the area of the Second Army, and steadily to increase activity in that neighbourhood until the 6th of August, that is, until two days before the British offensive was to open on the Somme.

On the 1st of August Major-General J. M. Salmond submitted for the approval of General Head-quarters a memorandum in which he gave, in general terms, his proposals for the employment of the Royal Air Force squadrons in the battle.[2] He said that during the two days before the opening of the offensive it was desirable to show activity in the air on the fronts of the First and Fifth armies. On the night preceding the attack (Z–1 night) Handley Page aeroplanes would patrol the front line area in order to drown the noise of assembling British tanks.[3] On the first day of the battle the work proposed was:

(i) At daybreak the day bomber squadrons were to attack aerodromes on the Fourth Army front, with the fighter squadrons giving their support.

[1] The career of Edward Mannock is told in *King of Air Fighters*, by Flight Lieutenant Ira Jones, D.S.O., M.C., D.F.C., M.M.

[2] Corps squadrons: Nos. 3 (Australian Corps), 35 (III), 5 (Canadian Corps), 6 (Cavalry Corps), 8 (Tanks Corps), 9 (dropping ammunition, &c.).

Army squadrons: 1 day bomber and reconnaissance squadron, 1 night bomber, and 7 fighter squadrons, 3 of which were suitable for low-flying operations.

Balloons: 4 companies of 2 balloons each.

The IX Brigade was to consist of 1 reconnaissance squadron, 4 day bomber squadrons, 2 night bomber squadrons, and 6 fighter squadrons.

[3] During the night preceding the attack the weather conditions were very bad, but one pilot (Lieutenant G. A. Flavelle) of No. 207 (Handley Page) Squadron accomplished a fine feat in patrolling the allotted area for about three hours.

(ii) The fighter squadrons afterwards were to stand by ready to operate on the Fourth Army front if enemy air activity became important, and

(iii) The day bomber squadrons were to attack in the evening, with the help of the fighter squadrons, the railway stations at Péronne and Chaulnes.

The day bomber squadron with the Third Army was to assist by attacking Bray, while the fighter squadrons of the Third Army were to be ready to help on the Fourth Army front if the Germans should become unduly active in the air. When darkness closed over the battle-field on the first day of the offensive the two night bomber squadrons of the IX Brigade were to attack Péronne and Chaulnes, while the night bomber squadron of the Third Army attacked billets and road or railway movements north of the Somme.

The reasons underlying these proposals, which were approved by Sir Douglas Haig, are obvious enough. There was to be no abnormal air activity on the front of attack before the opening of the battle in order that the enemy might be kept free of suspicion; the bombing of German aerodromes in the early morning was calculated to reduce enemy air activity; and the attacks on the railway junctions were not to take place before the evening because it was deemed improbable that rail movements, set in motion by the offensive, would develop until twelve hours after the battle opened.

The British battle front was not reinforced with squadrons until a few days before the attack was due to begin. On the evening of the 7th of August, the eve of the offensive, the British air strength available for the battle, although not all of it was in the actual area, totalled 800 aeroplanes, made up as follows:

V Brigade	Aeroplanes
6 Corps Squadrons of the 15th Corps Wing	110
8 Fighter Squadrons of the 22nd Army Wing	164
1 Fighter Reconnaissance Squadron of the 22nd Army Wing	21
1 Day Bomber Squadron of the 22nd Army Wing	20
1 Night Bomber Squadron	17
Total	332

AIR CONCENTRATIONS

IX Brigade
- 6 Fighter Squadrons (including 1 night fighter) . . . 130
- 4 Day Bomber Squadrons 71
- 4 Night Bomber Squadrons 57
- 2 Fighter Reconnaissance Squadrons 36

Total 294

III Brigade (available)
- 4 Fighter Squadrons 82
- 1 Day Bomber Squadron 18
- 1 Night Bomber Squadron 18
- 1 Fighter Reconnaissance Squadron 18

Total 136

I Brigade (available)
- 1 Day Bomber Squadron 19

X Brigade (available)
- 1 Day Bomber Squadron 19

Total British aircraft strength available for work over the active front: 110 Corps aeroplanes, 376 Fighters, 147 Day Bombers, 92 Night Bombers, 75 Fighter Reconnaissance aircraft.

The French also made a secret air concentration. On the 5th of August General Debeney, commanding the French First Army, requested the support of the *Air Division*, which had been taking part in the Champagne offensive and counter-offensive. General Pétain agreed, and the *Air Division* moved on the 7th: it disposed of a total of 432 fighters and 195 day bombers. In addition, the fighting group with the French First Army, temporarily reinforced, comprised 180 fighters. Fifty-two night bombers were also placed at the disposal of the French First Army, so that, together with the 245 two-seater reconnaissance, &c., aeroplanes, there were 1,104 French aircraft available on the front of attack of the French First Army.

Thus the total British and French air strength ready for service on the 25-mile front of the August offensive, from Courcelles to Albert,[1] was:

- Corps aeroplanes 290
- Fighters 988
- Day Bombers 342
- Night Bombers 144
- Fighter reconnaissance 140

1,904

[1] On the opening day the attack involved a part only of the French First Army, extending to Braches, about seventeen miles in all. The battle later involved all the French First Army and part of the French Third Army.

The Germans held the front opposite the British Fourth and the French First Armies with the German Second Army and about half of the Eighteenth Army. These two German armies together had, when the battle opened:

Corps aeroplanes	171
Fighters	140
Bombers	36
Battle fighters	18
	365

There was, therefore, an overwhelming Allied air concentration. The main German air strength was still in Champagne where the German Sixth and Seventh Armies had 850 aircraft, of which 430 were single-seater fighters.

On the 5th of August Brigadier-General L. E. O. Charlton, commanding the V Brigade, Royal Air Force, the brigade working under the orders of the Fourth Army, drew up a memorandum to be communicated to all pilots and observers on the afternoon before the opening of the offensive. In this the plan of the battle was lucidly explained, because 'each pilot and observer should be fully informed of 'the general plan in regard to the preliminary operations, 'such knowledge helping him to a wider appreciation of the 'course of events as they unfold and rendering more valuable 'in consequence his action and reports'. This appears to be one of the few occasions so far as can be judged from the official records when a formal considered attempt was made to take the pilots and observers into the confidence of the General Staff. 'The more they know, the better they will work' might well be chosen as a motto for the guidance of the staff when dealing with the personnel of army co-operation squadrons.

CHAPTER XII
THE AMIENS OFFENSIVE
[Maps, facing, p. 550, and at end]

AT 4.20 a.m on the 8th of August the bombardment opened, and within a few minutes the tanks, armoured cars, armed lorries, and infantry moved forward. There was a thick ground mist, as there had been when the Germans had counter-attacked so successfully at Cambrai in November 1917, and again when they had begun their offensive against the British on the 21st of March 1918. The enemy was taken completely by surprise, and at the end of the day the British troops had advanced about seven miles, and, except at Le Quesnel, had regained the Amiens outer defences on the front of attack. The whole German army was shaken by the rapidity and by the extent of the success, as is clear from Ludendorff's description of August the 8th as the 'black day' of the German army in the war, and by the word 'catastrophe' in the title of the German official monograph dealing with the battle.[1]

The early mist, which screened the movements of the British infantry and of the tanks, made useful air co-operation impossible: the aeroplanes could not enter fully into the battle until after 9 a.m. As the mist cleared it was revealed that there was great confusion within the German lines, and exceptional targets were offered to the low-flying single-seater pilots. The battle-field became alive with aeroplanes, and a mere summary of the air attacks would require many pages. A few examples must suffice to picture for the reader the confusion of the morning, and of the part played by the low-flying pilots. At about 10.30 a.m. two pilots of No. 201 Squadron, flying in search of targets east of Harbonnières, saw three trains near the village. It ap-

[1] *Schlachten des Weltkrieges 1914–1918: Die Katastrophe des 8. August 1918*. 'When darkness came on the 8th of August over the battle-field of 'the Second Army', says the German monograph (pp. 196–7), 'the heaviest 'defeat suffered by the German Army since the beginning of the war had 'become an accomplished fact. . . . Almost everywhere it was obvious that 'German soldiers had surrendered to the enemy, arms and equipment had 'been thrown away, trench mortars, machine-guns, and guns, had been 'abandoned, and men had sought safety in flight.'

peared that they might be loaded with ammunition, and each pilot dropped four 25-lb. bombs from a height of 100 feet. The aeroplane attack was watched by a squadron of the 5th Dragoon Guards who, seeing fire break out among the trains, galloped towards the position. As they bore down upon the scene two of the trains, which were of narrow gauge, steamed away, but the third, of standard gauge and badly damaged, could not move. It was surrounded by the Dragoon Guards and by other patrols, and the passengers, many of whom it was learned had just arrived at the front from leave, were taken prisoners after a brief resistance.

In the same neighbourhood an 11·5-inch gun, with two ammunition trucks, was also captured as a result of air attack. 'Early on the 8th of August', wrote General Sir A. Montgomery, 'some low-flying aeroplanes dis-'covered an 11-inch long-range railway gun, which had 'been used in the bombardment of Amiens, busily firing 'although our infantry was advancing within 1,000 yards 'of the position. Swooping down close to the gun our air-'men dropped a number of bombs on it with such effect 'that when the troops of the 5th Australian Division arrived 'on the spot they found the whole gun's crew either killed 'or wounded.'[1] A small party from the 8th Field Company, Australian Engineers, of the 5th Australian Division, uncoupled a burning part of the train, filled the boiler of the engine, raised steam, and drove the gun into the British lines. It was afterwards, at the wish of General Foch, placed on show to the people of Paris.

The squadron responsible for this fine piece of work cannot be identified with certainty, but it is possible that the gun train was one of the targets attacked by two Sopwith 'Camel' pilots of No. 201 Squadron whose reports state simply that bombs were dropped on a burning train near Harbonnières. The pilots were unable to see what happened after the bombs exploded because their attention was diverted by the arrival of an enemy two-seater, which they attacked and forced to land. They were subsequently attracted to a wood near Proyart which was seen to be 'swarming with troops', and for about an hour

[1] *The Story of the Fourth Army*, p. 50.

the two pilots made diving attacks on the luckless German infantry. At first the enemy troops answered the machine-gun fire from the air, but they lost heart and rushed about aimlessly as the Sopwith 'Camels' repeatedly swooped down upon them.

An S.E.5a pilot of No. 24 Squadron dropped his bombs among about 300 German infantry and fired upon them. Another pilot of the same squadron attacked a similar number of enemy troops moving across a field, and many fell when his bombs exploded among them. The pilot subsequently saw eight British armoured cars which had been stopped by fire from an anti-tank gun. After he had made three attacks the enemy gun was silenced, and the armoured cars were enabled to proceed. A little later the same pilot, while attacking troops, had the main petrol tank in his aeroplane pierced by a bullet. He landed in the belief that the ground he had chosen was clear of the enemy, but a party of about twenty-five Germans ran towards him from hiding. He fired a revolver bullet into the nearest German at twenty yards range, switched on the gravity tank in his aeroplane, and was just able to get into the air again and fly as far as an advanced party of British cavalry. The pilot informed the troopers of the whereabouts of the Germans who had approached his aeroplane, and the cavalry galloped forward and captured them.

A pilot of No. 209 Squadron, after dispersing infantry with bombs, had the engine and controls of his Sopwith 'Camel' so damaged by fire from the ground that he was forced to land in front of British cavalry outposts. He joined the cavalry and, shouldering a rifle, took a part in the fighting.

So one might go on. On the 8th, and up to 4 p.m. on the 9th, there were many hundreds of similar attacks by individual pilots;[1] transport was blown off the roads; machine-gun posts which were holding up parties of

---

[1] From the opening of the battle until 4 p.m. on the 9th, the nine fighter squadrons of the V Brigade dropped a total of one thousand five hundred and sixty-three 25-lb. bombs, and fired 122,150 rounds of machine-gun ammunition on ground targets.

cavalry or infantry were silenced and the crews were subsequently captured with their guns by the advancing British troops; motor-cars were bombed and the occupants fired upon when they jumped from the cars; horse-drawn transport was stampeded; and time and again parties of infantry were scattered in panic, leaving dead and wounded behind them.

A feature of the air co-operation in the morning was the laying of smoke screens. Owing to a scarcity of 60-pounder smoke shells, and because guns or howitzers of smaller calibre had not the range to reach the places which it was desired to screen, it had been planned that aeroplanes should drop phosphorus bombs, with contact fuses, in front of certain fortified villages and woods in order to cover the approach of British tanks. The bombs were to be dropped at stated intervals from about four hours after zero, but because of the morning mist the smoke bombing was a little late in beginning. From 9 a.m., however, Nos. 9, 3 A.F.C., and 5 Squadrons laid a number of screens on the fronts of the Australian and Canadian Corps. One such, put down by six R.E.8's of No. 9 Squadron, which dropped a total of twenty-four 40-lb. phosphorus bombs at 11.20 a.m. in the neighbourhood of Proyart, was stated by the 4th Australian Division to have been particularly effective. An official report commenting upon this aspect of aircraft co-operation said: 'The success of the smoke 'screens during the 8th of August showed that such screens 'could be adequately produced on limited objectives for a 'short period from the air. Approximately three aero-'planes per objective (e.g. a village), and renewed every 'quarter of an hour, was required. The work, however, 'was too much for a corps squadron engaged on the line.'

The main air work throughout the morning of the 8th was, as already explained, directed against ground targets, but in the afternoon the character of the operations changed. About midday pilots and observers reported that the roads leading to the Somme crossings were becoming crowded with retreating German troops and transport. If the bridges, gateways to and from the field of battle, could be broken, the enemy troops west of the Somme would find themselves compressed within the pocket of land made as a result of the abrupt change of course which the river Somme takes at Péronne. The confusion within the ranks of the German Second Army would be magnified, and there would be countless targets presented for low-flying attack. More important, the closing of the ways by which help might come to the troops west of the river would bring the German army in the Somme area face to face with a major disaster. The most hopeful supporters of air warfare did not believe that a success so complete was possible, but although the bigger prize might prove to be out of reach it was believed that every interruption of traffic which air bombing achieved would be richly and disproportionately rewarded.

Major-General J. M. Salmond, presumably on the instructions of General Head-quarters, cancelled, by telephone, all existing arrangements for bombing in the afternoon of the 8th of August, and ordered, instead, attacks upon the Somme bridges, which were to be bombed 'as long as weather and light permits': the fighter squadrons were to take part by dropping bombs of 25-lb. weight.

These orders led to a conflict which was as dramatic as any in the war in the air. The bridge at Brie was attacked by Sopwith 'Camels' of No. 54 Squadron, by D.H.9's of No. 107 Squadron, and by D.H.4's of No. 205 Squadron: some of the pilots made three journeys, and fifty-six 112-lb. and one hundred and nineteen 25-lb. bombs were dropped. The Péronne road and railway bridges were bombed by D.H.9's of No. 98 Squadron, Sopwith 'Camels' of No. 43, and S.E.5a's of No. 1 Squadron, with fifteen 112-lb. and sixty-eight 25-lb. bombs. The bridge at Bethencourt was twice attacked in the afternoon by D.H.9's of No. 49 Squadron and S.E.5a's of No. 32. In the first attempt on Bethencourt ten D.H.9's and twelve S.E.5a's took part, but German fighters engaged the bombers before the objective was reached, and no more than four D.H.9's and three S.E.5a's attacked the bridge: the remainder dropped their bombs on divers places. German fighters also appeared upon the scene during the second attack, made by seven D.H.9's and eleven S.E.5a's of the same two squadrons. The Germans intercepted the British pilots at about 1,000 feet, just when they were diving on the target, and the result was that the bombs could not be aimed with precision: one bomb, however, of 112-lb. weight, appeared to explode on the bridge. The bridges at Voyennes, Pithon, and Offoy, were attacked by D.H.4's and D.H.9's of No. 27 Squadron, accompanied by Sopwith 'Camels' of No. 73 Squadron.

The total number of individual daylight bombing flights (including light bombing by single-seater fighters) made in the attempt to damage the Somme bridges on the 8th of August was 205, during which twelve tons of bombs were dropped. The air fighting which impeded the attack on Bethencourt has been mentioned, but it should be stated that the German pilots fought generally with a reckless courage to take toll of the bombers, even though they could not prevent the attacks. Eight of the bombing two-seaters and a similar number of single-seaters were lost. At midday on the 8th the German army command had ordered the fighter squadrons to leave the upper air and to direct all their efforts towards making it possible for the German artillery and contact patrol aeroplanes to fulfil the tasks demanded of them. It would appear that it was this order, rather than any specific command to protect the bridges, which ensured the presence of German fighters in the area, and at the height, where they were able to intercept the early bombing attacks. Thereafter protection of the bridges became a first charge upon the activities of the *Jagdstaffeln*. In the same order in which the German fighters were told to fly low over the battle-field it was said that *Jagdstaffeln* from neighbouring armies, and from Flanders, were on their way to help, among them the Richthofen squadron.[1]

The only means by which the German fighting pilots could redress in some degree their inferiority in numbers was to spend the minimum of time upon the ground. Many

[1] Commanded by Hauptmann Hermann Göring. After Richthofen's death on the 21st of April, Hauptmann Reinhard had assumed command of the squadron, but he had been killed when testing a new type aeroplane in June, and had been succeeded by Hauptmann Göring.

of them were in the air on the 8th of August for ten hours, taking part in combat after combat. Two Flights of the Richthofen squadron were in action over the battle-field on the 8th, and among those who fell was Leutnant Loewenhardt, whose fifty-first victory was announced the same day and who wore the order *Pour le mérite*: and 'many 'more were to follow him in the subsequent days.'[1] The squadron was reduced within a short time from fifty aeroplanes to eleven, suffering losses which have been described as 'terrible' (*fürchterliche Verluste*).[2]

Hauptmann Göring rallied the remnants of the squadron and again took them into the air, but four more aeroplanes were lost. The Richthofen circus which, for nearly two years, had been the head and front of the German air fighting formations in the West, had been fought almost to destruction. What remained of it was withdrawn from the battle (*gänzlich aus dem Kampf gezogen*).[3] Although Hauptmann Göring was given some young pilots, and was subsequently able to get going once more with the help of his former flight commanders, it was impossible for the unit to recover its glory in the few weeks of active life which remained. The eclipse of the squadron suggests a point or two of interest in connexion with the subject of a defensive policy in the air. It was said in a former volume that the tactics of Manfred von Richthofen were perfectly suited to the conditions under which the German armies fought on the Western front. It was written: 'If 'it was the part of wisdom to avoid or to break off a fight, 'Richthofen would never hesitate. The "Circus" was, there-'fore, not only extremely active, but also extremely elusive.'[4] Hauptmann Göring, a leader of proved worth, was possibly gifted with a temperament more offensive in quality than that of his predecessor, or it may be that the German air service, sensing that the whole background of the war was changing, was impelled to throw its weight into the battle heedless of cost or danger. There does not seem much doubt that the irrecoverable losses suffered by the enemy

[1] *In der Luft unbesiegt*, p. 207.
[2] *Hermann Göring. Ein Lebensbild*, by Martin Sommerfeldt, p. 32.
[3] Idem. [4] Vol. IV, p. 396.

air service in the fighting which began on the 8th of August resulted from the fact the German pilots, for the first time in the war, stayed to fight without calculation. Their normal tactics, akin to those of guerrilla warfare on the ground according to which it is unwise to stay longer than is strictly useful, were abandoned. 'With a real con-'tempt for death the squadron rushed against the enemy's 'superiority of numbers and suffered terrible losses owing 'to its reckless behaviour. . . .', says Hermann Göring's biographer. When a general comparison is attempted between the relative costs of the British offensive and the German defensive air policies, August 1918 is a period which might be specially examined. With the opening of the Amiens battle the Germans began to execute their defensive policy with that indifference to caution which so often characterized the employment of the British squadrons, and the German losses, in consequence, were 'severe'.

The truth probably is that no definite comparison between the British and German air policies is possible, because the British air offensive was never dominated by the element of economy as was the German air defensive. It was presumably the available cloth which dictated the pattern of the German coat. The British garment was generously designed on the assumption that the necessary cloth would be forthcoming. Due weight, furthermore, must be given to the question of national characteristics. 'The English . . . absolutely challenged us to battle, and 'never refused fighting', or again: 'Frequently the daring 'of the latter [the British] can only be described as stupidity. 'In their eyes it may be pluck and bravery', wrote Manfred von Richthofen from a rich experience of encounters with British opponents.[1] That 'he who fights and runs away may live to fight another day' is not one of those sayings which has appealed to the British character. Although a military historian must commend the judgement of Richthofen, that recklessness in battle can be mere stupidity, it is difficult for an Englishman not to applaud the spirit which never acknowledges defeat.

[1] *The Red Air Fighter*, pp. 79 and 88.

TECHNICAL SUPERIORITY

The plight of the German air service would have been grave indeed, during the remainder of the war, had it not been for the timely appearance of an engine of remarkable performance for its time. It has often been revealed in this history that technical superiority, not necessarily of great degree, is a dominant factor in air warfare. In May and June 1918 some of the German fighter squadrons in France were re-equipped with the Fokker D.VII biplane. The first aeroplanes of this type seem to have been fitted with Mercedes engines of 160 or 180 horse-power, but it was not long before a new engine, of 185 horse-power, built by the *Bayerische Motoren-Werke*, and known as the B.M.W., was in production, and this engine so improved the performance of the Fokker D.VII as to make it almost a new design. With the B.M.W. engine, which was of first-class reliability, the D.VII had a speed of 125 miles per hour, and a better rate of climb than any contemporary Allied aeroplane actually in service.[1] It could reach 6,600 feet in 4 minutes, 13,200 feet in $10\frac{1}{4}$ minutes, 16,500 feet in 14, and 19,800 feet in $18\frac{3}{4}$ minutes.[2] The German writer Sommerfeldt says: 'Without this mag-'nificent weapon the tenacious and successful resistance 'offered in the final months of the war would have been 'impossible.'[3]

The Royal Air Force casualties on the 8th of August had been heavy. Forty-five aeroplanes were lost, and fifty-two more were wrecked or damaged and had to be struck off the strength of the squadrons. This was of a total of about 700 serviceable day-flying aeroplanes, and the wastage rate,

---

[1] It was outclassed on the British side by the Martinsyde F.4, so far as is known the aeroplane with the highest performance produced anywhere in the world in the war. The Martinsyde F.4, fitted with a 300 horse-power Hispano-Suiza engine, had a speed of 144·5 miles per hour at 6,500 feet, and of 136·5 at 15,000 feet. It could reach 6,500 feet in 4 minutes, 10,000 feet in 6·9 minutes and 15,000 feet in 11·75 minutes. Its service ceiling was 26,000 feet. None of these aeroplanes had arrived in France before the war ended.

[2] For tables giving the technical data of German war-time aircraft, see pp. 108–13 in *Die deutschen Luftstreitkräfte im Weltkriege*. For particulars of British aeroplanes see Appendix XXVII.

[3] *Hermann Göring*, p. 33.

therefore, was more than 13 per cent. for the day. The losses in flying personnel were 57 missing, 4 killed, and 19 wounded, or approximately one casualty for every 20 hours flown on the active front. Of the total of 97 aeroplanes deleted from the strength, 70 belonged to the bomber and fighter squadrons engaged on low-flying attacks against the Somme bridges or ground targets. As the number of aeroplanes so employed was about 300, the rate of wastage for low-flying aircraft was approximately 23 per cent.

The orders issued by the IX Brigade head-quarters on the evening of the 8th of August for the following day said: 'It is reported that during the day's operations, 'enemy aircraft scouts molested our bombers by diving on 'them from the clouds and preventing them from carrying 'out their missions effectively. Wing commanders will, 'therefore, detail scouts for close protection of bombers to 'ensure that the latter are not interfered with by enemy 'aircraft while trying to destroy bridges. This is the sole 'duty of these scouts who will not, therefore, carry bombs.'

The attacks on the bridges continued during the night, when six tons of bombs were released by forty-five F.E.2b's and five Sopwith 'Camels'. The first daylight raiders on the 9th set out about 5 a.m. The operation orders stated that all available aeroplanes from No. 27 Squadron were to attack the bridge at Voyennes from 500 feet or lower, and that those of No. 49 Squadron were similarly to bomb the bridges at Falvy and Bethencourt. Close protection was to be provided by Sopwith 'Camels' of No. 73 Squadron, half of which were to fly with the bombers of No. 27 Squadron, due to set out at 5 a.m., and half with No. 49 Squadron, timed to leave the ground at 5.15 a.m.

For some reason which is not apparent in the official records, the single-seater pilots took no part in the fighting in which the bombers were involved. Presumably the Sopwith 'Camel' pilots failed to find the bombers, or else, having found them lost touch, and they returned with nothing to report. More than half the bombs were aimed at targets other than the bridges, but, although enemy pilots were successful in confusing the aim of the bombers,

AN AIR FIGHT

none of the D.H.9's was shot down. It was claimed that four of the enemy were shot down by one of the D.H.9's of No. 49 Squadron (pilot, Lieutenant J. A. Keating, U.S.A.; observer, Second Lieutenant E. A. Simpson). Their combat report may be quoted as illustrative of the fighting of this time: 'When formation approached 'objective, 10 to 15 enemy aircraft attacked from south-'east. They followed us over objective, when bombs were 'released. As formation turned west a further 10 to 15 'enemy aircraft came from easterly direction and a run-'ning fight ensued. We were persistently attacked by a 'large number of enemy aircraft; observer fired a good 'burst into the first enemy aircraft which was only 50 feet 'from our tail, and it turned over on its back and burst into 'flames: this was over Marchelepot. Another enemy aircraft 'dived on us and when he got to about 60 or 70 feet dis-'tance, observer fired about 100 rounds into him, when 'large quantity of flames burst out and machine went down 'ablaze near Ablaincourt. When over Soyecourt, observer 'fired a further long burst into another enemy aircraft at 'a very short distance which stalled, went into a spin and 'went down hopelessly out of control, and was seen to 'crash near Soyecourt. Immediately after this machine 'disappeared observer saw another enemy aircraft diving 'on our tail, and before he could change drums the enemy 'aircraft had approached to within 40 feet of our machine. 'Observer then fired about 60 rounds straight into this 'enemy aircraft which fell over on its side and spun right 'into the ground west of Soyecourt. During the combat 'our machine was so badly shot about that we were forced 'to land near Lamotte-en-Santerre with damaged engine, 'tail, propeller and under-carriage. Captain C. Bowman 'confirms seeing an enemy aircraft go down in flames over 'Marchelepot.'

At the same time as the attacks were being made by the squadrons noted above, other squadrons were bombing bridges farther north. Six D.H.9's of No. 98 Squadron, closely escorted by five Sopwith 'Camels' of No. 43 Squadron, attacked the bridge at Feuillères, but the raid was contested and no hits were reported: one D.H.9 and one German fighter were shot down. The bridge at Brie was allotted to No. 107 Squadron with orders that three formations of five D.H.9's, with Sopwith 'Camel' escorts provided by No. 54 Squadron, should set out at intervals of thirty minutes, beginning at 4.30 a.m., to attack the bridge from a height of 3,000 feet or under. The first formation actually left at 5 a.m., and was assailed when nearing the objective by twelve Fokker biplanes. As a result of the fighting, during which one German aeroplane and one bomber were shot down, no more than four 112-lb. bombs were released over the target, without making hits. The second formation had also to fight its way out and home and lost one of its number, but six bombs of 112-lb. weight were aimed at the bridge without apparent result. The third formation, of five D.H.9's with four Sopwith 'Camels' as escorts, which left at 6.20 a.m., was met by patrolling German fighters over the objective. The British formation was attacked from all directions and the separate combats were fought to an end; three German aeroplanes fell in flames, and three of the five D.H.9's and two of the four Sopwith 'Camels' were shot down: one of the two remaining D.H.9's crashed within the British lines with a wounded pilot.

No. 205 Squadron, equipped with D.H.4 aeroplanes, also attacked the bridge at Brie in the morning. Sixteen pilots of the squadron dropped twenty 112-lb. and thirty-six 25-lb. bombs from about 11,000 feet, but no hits were seen. Early in the afternoon the same squadron attacked the bridge at Brie again, and also the bridge at St. Christ, but from lower heights. At Brie seven D.H.4's dived in formation through the clouds and dropped fourteen 112-lb. bombs from 2,000 feet. A hit was made on the west end of the bridge, and another on transport crossing over. A similar formation bombed the bridge at St. Christ from 5,000 feet, but without definite results. Further attacks on the same bridges were made by No. 205 Squadron in the evening, but from 12,000 feet and without effect. During the day's operations, eighteen pilots of this squadron were in the air for a total of 95 hours, during which they dropped, in all, $5\frac{1}{4}$ tons of bombs. They were not attacked

BOMBING THE BRIDGES

and suffered no losses, and, as German fighters were in the close neighbourhood of the objective during at least one of the raids, it would appear that the Rolls-Royce D.H.4 was rightly held in greater respect than the D.H.9 aeroplane.

The task of destroying the bridge at Péronne had been allotted to No. 57 Squadron of the III Brigade. At 7 a.m. ten D.H.4's, in two formations, escorted by five Bristol Fighters of No. 11 Squadron, set out. On the way the escorting aeroplanes were attacked by eight Fokkers, and they became detached from the bombers, whose leader thereupon decided that it was inadvisable to attempt an attack on the bridge from a low height. The bombs were therefore aimed at the Péronne railway sidings from 12,000 feet, and although German pilots attacked at the moment when the bombs were being dropped, the D.H.4's returned safely.

As a result of the experiences of the morning, there was a change of tactics in the afternoon. No. 49 Squadron was ordered to attack the bridge at Falvy, No. 27 Squadron, Bethencourt, No. 107 Squadron a bridge between Cappy and Péronne, and No. 98 Squadron the bridge at Brie. Every available aeroplane from each squadron was to be employed, and each formation was ordered to be over its objective at the same time—5 p.m. 'Accurate timing', it was said, 'is of the utmost importance.'

The arrangements for protection were elaborate. The orders of the head-quarters IX Brigade stated: 'All avail-
'able machines of both wings[1] will be detailed to afford
'close protection of the bombers. By close protection is
'meant that scout machines are to fly at about the same
'level as bombing machines, and to remain in their im-
'mediate vicinity till completion of the operation. The
'machines of 62 Squadron detailed for the 4–5.30 p.m.
'patrol will spend the last half hour of their patrol over
'the line Péronne–Bethencourt. Four squadrons of the
' I Brigade will be patrolling from 4.30–6 on approximately
'the following lines—Cappy–Brie; Maurepas–Péronne–
'Athies; Marchelepot–Nesle; Ennemain–Matigny. Each

[1] That is, the Ninth and Fifty-first wings of the IX Brigade.

'of these patrols will be of approximately squadron 'strength, and they will fly just above the clouds. Our 'scout machines are therefore free to escort the bombers 'closely.'

The word 'our' in the above orders refers to the fighter squadrons of the IX Brigade. This was because the line patrols above the clouds were, as stated in the order, to be provided by squadrons (Nos. 19, 22, 40, and 64) of the I Brigade specially brought down from the north for the operation.

When the bombing attacks were made the clouds were at 2,000 to 3,000 feet. No. 27 Squadron sent nine D.H.9's and two D.H.4's to Bethencourt under escort by eleven Sopwith 'Camels' of No. 73 Squadron. As the bombing formation, flying at 2,000 feet, approached the objective, eight Fokkers attacked, and they continued to make spasmodic attacks while the bombs were being dropped and during a part of the homeward journey. One of the enemy fighters was shot down and seen to crash, but the bombers returned safely, though with one of the observers wounded. It would appear that the escorting Sopwith 'Camels' must have lost touch with the bombers because the reports show that the fighters saw only one enemy aeroplane, which they engaged at long range. Owing to the action of the enemy pilots over the objective the aiming of the bombs was uncertain, but bursts were seen at both ends of the bridge.

Seven D.H.9's of No. 49 Squadron were turned back before they reached Falvy by about twenty hostile fighters, which dived on the bombers from the clouds. The bombs were dropped in the neighbourhood of Fresnes, and the D.H.9's fought their way home without loss: one of the German fighters was shot down in flames. The escorting S.E.5a's of No. 32 Squadron, once again, so far as can be judged from the official reports, lost touch with the bombers. The fighters seem to have flown above the clouds, where they attacked two formations of eight and twelve hostile aeroplanes which dived away in an easterly direction, and it was apparently these German fighters who attacked the bombers of No. 49 Squadron. The attacks on the bridges at Eclusier and Brie met with no opposition, but no direct hits were reported. The four fighting squadrons of the I Brigade which, it will be recalled, had been ordered to make their patrols immediately above the clouds during the time the bombers were on passage, saw few German aircraft and had no encounters of importance. An analysis of the concerted afternoon effort to damage selected Somme bridges shows that 35 bombs of 112-lb. weight were aimed at the objectives. The force employed was 30 bombers (carrying a total of 60 bombs), with 50 fighters in escort, and with an additional 74 fighting aircraft on patrol in support immediately above the clouds.

While the drama of the Somme bridges was being fought out in the air on the 9th, the Allied advance on the ground continued. By nightfall Bouchoir, Rouvroy, Morcourt, and Framerville were in British hands, and the outskirts of Lihons and Proyart had been reached. North of the Somme, where the British III Corps had attacked in the afternoon, the line Chipilly–Morlancourt–Dernancourt had been gained, while on the British right the French First Army had progressed nearer to Roye. Owing mainly to the activities of the German fighter aircraft which had reinforced the battle front, the fighter squadrons of the V Brigade were employed less on low-flying attacks on the 9th and more on offensive patrols than they had been on the first day of the battle: there were many combats at about 2,000 feet or under in which both sides lost aeroplanes. The losses suffered by the Royal Air Force on the 9th were fewer than on the previous day. The casualties totalled 47, of whom 36 were killed or prisoners, and the aeroplanes written off numbered 45. The attempts made to destroy the bridges accounted for seventy-five per cent. of the total losses.

The attacks on the Somme bridges continued during the night of the 9th/10th when 106 aeroplanes dropped a total of $16\frac{1}{2}$ tons of bombs. Among the bombers were seven Handley Page aeroplanes of No. 207 Squadron which together dropped one hundred and twenty 112-lb. and forty 25-lb. bombs from heights between 4,000 and 5,000 feet. The results of the attacks were not closely observed, but two hits on the bridge at Voyennes were claimed. The attacks by the day bombers of the IX Brigade were not continued on the 10th, but the D.H.4's of No. 205 Squadron attacked the bridges at St. Christ and Brie from about 12,000 feet, and a hit upon each was claimed. Two raids were made, and during the second, in the afternoon, about fourteen German fighters attacked the bombers. A German aeroplane fell in flames, and several D.H.4's were hit by bullets, but all reached home safely, one of them with a wounded observer. Night bombing of the Somme bridges was continued, with decreasing intensity, until the 13th/14th of August, and thereafter intermittently.

The bombing had failed to achieve its object. Some of the bridges suffered minor damage, but not enough to make them unsafe for traffic. From the 8th to the 14th of August, by day and by night, there were 700 aeroplane flights, including escorts, in strict connexion with the bombing of the bridges, and fifty-seven tons of bombs were released over the objectives. The frequent passage of the bombers no doubt affected the morale of the German soldiers, and, in the crowded area of the bridges, the bombs often inflicted damage when they fell wide of their target. The bombing, however, because it failed in its main object, exerted no real influence on the battle. It is possible that greater value for the energy expended would have been obtained if the Royal Air Force had kept to its plan for attacks on the main enemy railway junctions.[1] It was not, however, until the morning of the 10th of August, forty-eight hours after the offensive had begun, that the railway communications were seriously bombed.

The railway bombing on the morning of the 10th of August was directed against the stations at Péronne and Equancourt on the Bapaume–Epehy railway. The bombs were dropped from a height of 12,000 feet and few hits were seen. The Péronne bombers, twelve aeroplanes of Nos. 27 and 49 Squadrons, with an escort of forty fighters from Nos. 32 and 62 Squadrons, were attacked over the

---

[1] See pp. 433-4.

objective by about fifteen Fokkers. A patrol of seven S.E.5a's of No. 56 Squadron joined in the fight, which was fiercely contested. The Fokkers were well handled, and it was demonstrated that their technical qualities were just sufficiently superior to those of the British fighters as to give the German pilots an advantage at close quarters which enabled them time and again to extricate themselves from difficult positions. One German aeroplane fell in flames and others went down apparently out of control, but before the fight had ended one British bomber and four single-seaters had fallen in the German lines: another single-seater, although it returned safely, had been so damaged by bullets that it had to be struck off the strength of the squadron. Péronne was bombed again in the evening of the 10th when bursts were seen in the station sidings: German fighters which attacked were driven off after two had fallen in flames.

Ninety additional British fighting aeroplanes were brought into the battle area on the 10th, and, on this day, the total concentration of British single-seater fighters for the battle was 480, which represented seventy per cent. of the existing Royal Air Force fighter strength on the Western front. The bombing of Péronne continued throughout the night of the 10th/11th of August when 200 bombs, mostly of 112-lb. weight, were aimed at the station from heights between 1,000 and 6,000 feet: an explosion occurred among trains in the sidings. The main bombing targets of the squadrons of the IX Brigade on the 11th were the stations at Péronne, Cambrai, and Equancourt. The two first-named objectives were attacked without incident, and effective hits were reported, but the Equancourt bombers were reduced in strength through engine trouble, and the escorting formations, hampered by the cloudy weather, did not keep good touch with the bombers. Owing to the intervention of enemy fighters, the majority of bombs were aimed at targets other than that allotted, and two of the bombers were shot down.

The D.H.4 day bombing squadron of the V Brigade, No. 205, three times attacked Péronne on the 11th of August, and dropped a total of four tons of bombs. Hits on the station were photographed, and although German pilots attacked the bombers during each raid, No. 205 Squadron had no loss to report, whether of personnel or aircraft, as a result of the day's operations. On the other hand, three German aeroplanes were sent down out of control, one of them after collision with a falling bomb which caused a wing of the German fighter to be torn off. The sixteen available pilots of No. 205 Squadron flew a total of 88 hours on the 11th of August, a fine day's work, and while tribute should be paid to the spirit and efficiency of the squadron personnel, in the air and on the ground, note must be taken of the aeroplanes with which the squadron was equipped. The D.H.4, fitted with the 275 horse-power (Eagle VI) Rolls-Royce engine, was splendidly reliable. In the four days of intensive fighting, from the 8th to the 11th of August inclusive, the D.H.4's of No. 205 Squadron were in the air for a total of 324 hours 13 minutes, and dropped sixteen tons of bombs. Every aeroplane returned from its mission, and no more than one had to be struck off the strength of the squadron. This aeroplane, which had been hit in combat, was too badly damaged to be reconstructed in the squadron and had to be sent to the depot. By way of comparison, a typical D.H.9 Squadron flew a total of 115 hours in the same period and dropped four and a half tons of bombs. During the operations seven of the D.H.9's were lost and two others were wrecked, and ten pilots had to leave formation, without dropping their bombs, through engine trouble. A further sidelight on the engine question is in the fact that in the same four days pilots of No. 205 Squadron required no more than a total of $3\frac{1}{2}$ hours in all on test flights while those of the D.H.9 squadron spent 21 hours in the air on similar duties.

The Bombing of the Somme Bridges: a Commentary

The operation orders issued by Fourth Army headquarters on the 11th of August stated that as the enemy resistance was becoming increasingly effective the British advance would not be continued until artillery could be brought forward, and also an additional allotment of tanks made to the army corps. There was talk of proceeding on the 15th, but owing to an expansion in the enemy strength, and because of the devastated nature of the old battle-field area which lay in front of a further advance, Sir Douglas Haig decided to postpone the operations indefinitely, and the battle thus ended. General Foch was not at first in favour of this decision, but he eventually agreed, and the French First Army ceased to be under the general command of Sir Douglas Haig at noon on the 16th of August. After the jump forward on the first day of the battle progress had been comparatively slow, and the high hopes with which the offensive had opened had not been fulfilled. Nevertheless, the advance had penetrated to a total depth of more than twelve miles and the old line of the Roye–Chaulnes defences had been reached, with the result that the important centre of Amiens, with its railways, had been made safe from artillery fire. The prisoners taken by the British numbered 22,000, and 400 guns had been captured. Gains of territory and material, however, were not the most important items in the profit and loss account of the battle. On the evening of the 8th of August, for the first time, fear entered the minds of the German soldiery that all was not well, and that it was only a matter of time before peace would have to be sought.

It is significant that orders were given some time in August for the air raid campaign against London and Paris to cease. It may be worth noting, in parenthesis, that the German bombing squadrons were planning large-scale attacks on the French and British capitals with small bombs, of 1 kilogram weight, of high incendiary qualities. It was said that they were unaffected by water—that water, indeed, was fuel for them—and as thousands were to be dropped during each raid it was hoped the effect would be great, more particularly because such fire brigades as were available, necessarily few in comparison with the number of fires which it was hoped would be started, would be unable to overcome the basis of the fire—the incendiary bomb—with water. London and Paris were spared this attempt at 'frightfulness' on 'humanitarian grounds', and all that need be noted is that defeat, no less than victory, may teach the wisdom of showing mercy to an enemy. It is less difficult to overcome a temptation to commit what may be a crime when punishment, which if inflicted is certain to be condign, is seen also to be inevitable.

The air operations during the battle had important though unexpected results. The British losses were heavy, but so were the German. Indeed the German air service was so roughly handled that it was never able fully to recover. There can be no gainsaying the fact that the German pilots fought magnificently. On the actual battle-front they had been reinforced as soon as the battle had opened. The Richthofen *Jagdgeschwader* (No. 1, with Flights 4, 6, 10, and 11) flew to Ennemain from the area of the German Seventh Army east of Laon, and No. 2 *Jagdgeschwader* (Flights, 12, 13, 15, and 19) flew to Foreste from the area of the German Ninth Army. The German aerodromes housing the fighter Flights were almost within sight of the Somme bridges. Because the bombing of the bridges was perforce attempted mainly from low heights, it was possible for the German pilots to fly off their aerodromes and to be over the bridges level with the bombers within a few minutes of a warning message. The German fighters, in attempting to prevent the bombers from hitting the bridges, were protecting, as it were, a series of pin-points. The position was unlike anything that had happened before. In the past the German pilots had been able to suit their tactics to the general conditions. The air forces opposed to them were numerically stronger, and it was sound tactics to seek every advantage, to choose the moments for intervention, to break off an action when the advantages, whether of surprise or arising from conditions of the sun or the light, had disappeared. It had never been possible for the German air service to prevent the Royal Air Force squadrons from working. All it could hope to do was to make those squadrons pay as dearly as possible, and this could best be done by seeking out the weaker elements and avoiding the stronger. So long as the German fighters could take what might be called a 'general' view of the air war, so long might they intervene at their particular discretion. The bombing attacks on the vital Somme bridges, however, forced the German air service to give specific battle. It was not possible, if the bombing was to be prevented, to break off an action with the knowledge that other and easier opportunities of taking toll of the enemy would be freely offered. The German pilots could, in this instance, fulfil their duty only if they fought to the end. Many of the bombers were shot down, but those that fell must have taken with them some of the flower of the German air service. Although, when the bombing had ended, the bridges remained intact, in their neighbourhood lay the wreckage of some of the best of the German aeroplanes which had carried to destruction with them pilots irreplaceable for their experience and character.

It is worth examining whether the sacrifice was as essential as appeared at the time, that is to say, whether, without the resistance offered by the German pilots, it would have been within the power of the Royal Air Force to achieve what it set out to do. Although the question cannot be definitely answered, there is not much doubt that the reply should be in the negative. The official records setting out the full technical details of the Somme bridges which came under attack cannot be found. Even though some of the bridges had been badly damaged in the March retreat and only temporarily repaired, it is still true to say that they represented a most difficult kind of bombing target. Appreciable damage might be inflicted only as a result of a direct hit upon an unsupported part of a bridge between the piers. A miss by no more than a foot or so meant that the bomb would explode in the river bed or on the embankment with no lasting effect. Under the most favourable conditions for aiming, therefore, there would have been much uncertainty about success. Furthermore, the bombs which were dropped, mostly of 112-lb. weight, were not heavy enough to ensure vital damage even if a hit were made. The Royal Air Force bombers, undisturbed by the German fighters, would still have needed an undue measure of luck as an element even of partial success. Critics, looking back, have condemned the attempt to destroy the

Somme bridges as misguided. This is probably putting the matter too strongly. As it happened, the attempt may partly be justified on the score that it served to force the German air service to give battle and to make sacrifices which it could not afford to make. It is true that this was an unexpected result, which was not taken into account at the time, but from the point of view of possible military advantages the attempt may also to some extent be defended. The German army in the battle area on the 8th of August was on the run. Help might come only by way of the bridges, which were also the bottle-necks on the lines of retreat. If they could have been shattered, the Germany army on the Western front would almost certainly have been faced with a major disaster. Risks, whether of chance or casualties, would seem to weigh little in the balance when the prize to be won as a result of success appeared so glittering.

It may not be out of place to offer a word of comment about the handling of the squadrons. It was probably not expected that the German fighters on the battle front would be reinforced to any notable extent on the first day of the offensive, and the intervention of some of the *Jagdstaffeln* flights, newly arrived from neighbouring armies on the afternoon of the 8th, achieved surprise. It is unlikely that had such a stiffening of opposition been looked for, the bombing operations would have been conducted in the way they were. The bridges were near the aerodromes, notably Ennemain and St. Christ, which housed the main German fighter formations. One must assume that once the extent of the British and French success became clear, the importance of the bridges would be apparent to the German command, and that the German air service would be given the task of protecting them. Because the clouds were at 2,000 feet or so, and because the targets were small and difficult to hit, it seemed obvious that protection could best be attempted by German patrols, at a comparatively low height, which could quickly be reinforced by aeroplanes from the adjacent aerodromes. It will be remembered that the aerodromes had been allotted as targets for attack on the morning of the 8th. The mist, however, had made the task of the bombers difficult. Fourteen D.H.9's of No. 27 Squadron which set out at dawn on the 8th to attack St. Christ aerodrome failed to find their objective and bombed ill-defined targets in the Péronne area instead. Eight D.H.9's of No. 98 Squadron had better luck and dropped sixty-two 25-lb. bombs on the aerodrome at St. Christ. The aerodrome at Bouvincourt was found by one of two formations of D.H.4's of No. 205 Squadron (the second formation bombed Chaulnes station instead), but the bursts of the bombs were not observed. Moislains aerodrome, north of the Somme, was attacked by ten D.H.4's of No. 57 Squadron.

There were no subsequent attempts to bomb the main German aerodromes. Furthermore, the British fighters which escorted the bombers for the attacks on the bridges on the 8th were ordered to carry 25-lb. bombs, with the result that where their full attention was needed to defend the bombers, that is over the targets, they became bombers themselves and could not in consequence provide efficient protection. Royal Air Force head-quarters was quick to read the lessons of the 8th, and the orders for the 9th absolved the fighters from carrying bombs, and stated that they were to keep in the closest touch with the D.H.9's. When this type of attack also proved a failure, there was a change to the concentrated onslaught at 5 p.m. in the afternoon of the 9th, but once again no attempt was made to attack the German aerodromes as part of the general tactical scheme: furthermore, the main fighting formations were ordered to fly just above the clouds. The reason was that the German single-seaters had made many of their attacks by diving through the clouds, and it was no doubt considered desirable that the British fighters should engage them in the upper air. In one instance enemy pilots were met and engaged above the clouds, but they promptly dived through the cloud layer, attacked the bombing formation below, and drove them away from their target and back to the British lines.

It is apparent from the reports of the pilots engaged, bombers and fighters, that it proved extremely difficult to maintain touch between the single-seaters and the two-seaters. Close escort work of the kind ordered was something new, and there had been no opportunity for practice, so necessary when formations of aircraft of different performances are required to fly in company. The weather conditions on the 9th of August in particular were difficult, and the bombers did not have the support of the fighters at the critical times and places.

A comparison with the attack on the lock gates at Zeebrugge, a somewhat similar target,[1] suggests that success against the bridges might have been more likely if D.H.4's or Handley Pages had been employed singly at dawn on the 9th. They might have been ordered to make their approach from the east instead of from the west. That is to say, they could have been over the German back areas while it was still dark and then, just when it was light enough for the targets to be distinguishable, each pilot might have dived, with engines quiet, and have released one or two 500-lb. bombs, continuing his homeward journey at full speed. A series of such attacks, carefully timed, with different pilots allotted to the various bridges, would possibly have provided a chance of success at small cost. No doubt the reader may think of other ways which would appear to have offered opportunities for success. Certainly the attempt to damage the bridges provides excellent material for a staff exercise; the student, however, should be suspicious of an easy solution.

It is now important to consider whether the desired results might have been achieved through attacks on carefully selected objectives on the lines of communication. It seems probable that the choice of the Somme bridges as targets was originally made chiefly with a view to impeding the enemy retreat, and that the idea of cutting off the arrival of enemy reinforcements was a secondary one. On the opening day of the battle, when the full benefits of surprise were obtained, the advance made by the Allied armies was considerable and the German forces on the Amiens front were thrown into confusion. The enemy resistance, however, stiffened, at first gradually and then with rapidity until, by the 11th of August, the end of the

[1] See pp. 393-4.

battle was in sight because there was 'no intention to try 'and break through regardless of loss'.

In other words, the Allied success was limited by the timely arrival of adequate German reinforcements. In fact, by the evening of the 11th of August, sixteen German divisions, additional to the eight already in line opposite the British Fourth Army on the morning of the 8th, had been identified in the area, and twelve of these divisions had been brought in from the fronts of other German armies. The question arises whether the main bombing offensive, French as well as British, should have been directed towards isolating the battle-field in order to delay the arrival of these reinforcements which successfully prevented a 'break through'. The dispositions of the German divisions on the whole western front before the battle began were known with fair accuracy, and those which, as seemed likely, would be rushed to the threatened front were listed. Furthermore, aircraft were available for reconnaissance to help determine the actual strength and direction of the enemy reinforcing movements once the offensive had opened. From a close expert study of all the information available before the offensive began, coupled with such knowledge as might have been acquired from the reports of specifically ordered reconnaissances, it would have been possible to indicate objectives along the enemy lines of communication where successful bombing would have offered a reasonable chance of blocking, temporarily, the main approaches to the battle area. An analysis of the whole battle, of a kind suitable for adequate staff study, cannot be attempted within the scope of this history. In this connexion the reader may profitably refer to the account given by Wing Commander J. C. Slessor in his book *Air Power and Armies*,[1] from which the following extract is taken: 'From a glance at the map the idea 'of a sort of barrage on the Somme bridges looks, at 'first sight, attractive. But from Bray to Pithon there are 'fourteen permanent road and rail bridges, apart from a 'number of foot bridges and military bridges which existed 'at the time; and by the time they reached the Somme

[1] Chapters VIII, IX, and X.

'enemy columns could afford to split into many smaller
'groups, and in effect the targets presented, instead of being
'like a hose-pipe, became like the nozzle or spray at the end
'of it, and were correspondingly far more widely scattered
'and less vulnerable. Moreover, the Somme crossings were
'only a few hours' march from the front; and though un-
'doubtedly the Germans suffered severely under the bomb-
'ing, there were constant long pauses during which no
'bombing took place, and the enemy columns could—and
'in fact did—pour across the bridges and on to the front
'line. Very much the same thing applies to the detraining
'stations such as Péronne, Nesle and Equancourt; it is true
'that troops detraining are very vulnerable, but they are
'equally vulnerable when entraining. In summary it
'amounts to this, that, if the aim is to prevent the flow
'reaching its destination, it is better to block it at the
'cistern or the tap or to cut the hosepipe than to try to
'block up all the holes in the spray.'

Tribute has been paid to the German pilots for their fine resistance. In addition, they made their presence felt in the front line area, and there were attacks, with bomb and machine gun, by day and by night, on British troops. It was at this time also that the German night bombers scored an outstanding success by destroying No. 2 Mechanical Transport base depot at Calais.[1]

There was an episode worth noting which took place on the 13th of August. Seven D.H.4's of No. 18 Squadron, with Bristol Fighters of No. 22 Squadron acting as escort, were climbing to gain height for a bombing attack on Somain when a German two-seater was seen to be cruising at about 20,000 feet near the lines. The two-seater flew eastwards, ahead of the British formations, and fired lights, with the result that German fighter aeroplanes were seen to leave the aerodromes near Douai. A long engagement resulted in which, it was reported, five enemy aeroplanes were destroyed, one of them in flames: a D.H.4 bomber failed to return. This attempt to obtain and pass on warning of an impending bombing attack represented tactics of a kind which might be used only sparingly. A

[1] See pp. 429-31.

warning given in this way was received on both sides of the trench lines, and it would be an easy matter, as Major-General J. M. Salmond pointed out to his brigade commanders, to arrange for an overwhelming number of fighting reinforcements to arrive unexpectedly at the moment when the German fighters became committed.

Some Lessons of the Battle

The general work of the squadrons in the battle, apart from what has already been considered, taught some lessons. The Fourth Army commander, in a memorandum issued after the battle, said: 'The important part played 'by the 5th Brigade, Royal Air Force, in the battle of the '8th August has filled me with admiration. . . . The action 'of low-flying machines on "Z" day, though it entailed 'heavy casualties, had a serious effect in lowering the 'enemy's morale and inflicting actual losses, as is shown by 'captured documents. The damage done by bombing 'squadrons both by day and night, the reports of the con-'tact patrols, and the constant and hazardous work of the 'artillery machines had a very marked influence in bring-'ing about the unqualified success of the operations. I 'have been particularly struck by the vigour with which 'the balloons were rapidly pushed forward in close support 'of the firing line and the valuable assistance they rendered 'to the staff and to the artillery. . . .'

Let us look a little more closely at some of the activities referred to by General Rawlinson. All the evidence seems to show that the low-flying operations against ground targets during the first morning of the battle were more successful than any similar attacks had been in the past. It was made clear, however, that success depended very much upon the degree of knowledge possessed by the low-flying pilots about the area in which they were operating, and about the general and changing situation upon the ground. The better they knew the lie of the land, and the more they knew about what was happening in the battle, the more effective their attacks proved to be. The progress of events on the 8th showed that so long as the advantages of surprise existed so long was it profitable to employ every available aeroplane upon low-flying attacks. As soon as the enemy reorganized his air defence it became necessary to employ fighting squadrons to defeat the German squadrons in the air. Furthermore, as the resistance on the ground stiffened, after the first onslaught, it was revealed that low-flying attacks were calculated to achieve increasingly less at higher cost. A memorandum issued by the officer commanding the 22nd Wing stated: 'After the first rout 'of the enemy a time comes when he will organize his 'defence and our progress will slow down. This is a time 'when low-flying scouts must be sparingly employed, and 'then only on reliable information on the situation on 'points where local counter-attacks are developing or where 'our troops are held up at strong points. Indiscriminate 'low-flying must cease at this period, or casualties will be 'excessive. . . . At this period also the physical powers of 'the pilots must be taken into consideration, as no pilot 'can stand an excessive strain of low-flying. The final 'period to be hoped for is the complete rout of the enemy, 'when, in spite of everything, all scouts must be again em-'ployed low. A point which should be impressed on all 'pilots is that they are less vulnerable very low than at 'heights of 3, 4, or 500 feet. Thus, after picking their 'targets at about 1,000 feet and diving, they should remain 'very low until clear, and then climb again.'

Co-operation with the tanks, satisfactory up to a point, showed an imperative need for closer and more detailed liaison with the Tank Corps. No. 8 Squadron (Major T. L. Leigh-Mallory), equipped with eighteen Armstrong-Whitworth aeroplanes, had been attached to the Tank Corps on the 1st of July 1918 for experiments in co-operation. There was an immediate interchange of officers between the squadron and the tank units, the former being given opportunities to ride in tanks, and the latter to fly. The first needs of efficient co-operation, understanding and friendship, were thus early achieved. Experiments were made with wireless telephony by which the air observers might communicate information, but it was found that talk from the air could be heard inside a tank only under the most favourable conditions and so long as the aeroplane was within a quarter of a mile of the tank at a height not greater than 500 feet: it was accordingly decided that this means of communication was of no immediate practical use. At the end of July tests with wireless telegraphy proved successful, messages being clearly received in the tanks from aeroplanes which were 9,000 yards away and at 2,500 feet altitude. It was too late, however, to perfect the organization, equipment, and methods of liaison, by which advantage could be taken of this success. Reliance was mainly placed upon methods of disk signalling, and a comprehensive code of signals was evolved by which the air observers could communicate in a simple way the nature and direction of a target.

In the battle visual signalling proved of little practical use. To read code messages accurately, a high degree of concentration is necessary and there were too many distractions under battle conditions to make this more than occasionally possible. Much useful information, however, was conveyed to the Tank Corps by means of dropped messages. There was some difficulty in knowing when a tank was out of action, and the need for a special signal was disclosed to avoid the danger that tanks which had temporarily halted would be reported as disabled. It seemed obvious that, pending the general introduction of wireless, and perhaps even as supplementary to it, some kind of percussion bomb, which would give a good volume of smoke for some minutes, would be useful for indicating targets. There was difficulty during the fighting in locating anti-tank guns, and in taking action against them. The tanks suffered heavily from gun-fire, and one of the lessons of the battle was that it was imperative to allocate a special fighting squadron to the Tank Corps in order to develop liaison and offensive plans for dealing with the anti-tank guns in the next attack.[1]

One of the pilots of No. 8 Squadron gained a Victoria Cross in the battle. Captain F. M. F. West, an officer of long flying experience in France, had obtained some useful information through gaps in the mist while on tank contact patrol early on the 8th of August, and had after-

[1] No. 73 Squadron was so attached: see pp. 469 and 477.

wards made a crash-landing on the fog-bound aerodrome, towards which he had been directed by rockets. His lip had been cut and the knee of his observer, Lieutenant J. A. G. Haslam, had been damaged, but the two officers, after attention at a casualty clearing station, had insisted on returning to their squadron. Next day they were out on similar contact patrol duties, and while attacking, from a low height, enemy troops which were surrounding four of the tanks, the engine in their aeroplane was shot out of action from the ground, and the pilot was with great difficulty able to reach the British front-line area where a safe landing was made. On the morning of the 10th of August Captain West and Lieutenant Haslam had the task of co-operating with tanks making for Roye. The pilot was attracted by German movements near Roye, and he flew on and attacked the enemy troops and transport with bombs and machine-gun fire. On the homeward journey enemy fighters appeared and one of them attacked at close range. An explosive bullet hit the left leg of Captain West, smashing the femur and cutting the femoral artery. The leg 'flopped round' the control lever, and the aeroplane could not be properly controlled until the pilot had taken his leg and fixed it out of the way. Meanwhile the enemy continued to attack, and Lieutenant Haslam, who had maintained a good fire, was also wounded. He continued to fire on the enemy while his pilot, with fine skill, went down to make a good landing on his own aerodrome.

Contact patrol work in co-operation with the infantry had been effective on the 8th of August, the first day of the battle, when enough flares were lighted to enable the air observers, once the fog had cleared, to follow the rapid advance with fair accuracy. Subsequently, however, owing to difficulties of supply, there was a shortage of flares in the forward areas, and reliance had to be placed upon metal disks and white flaps displayed by the infantry. The flap was that of the haversack carrying the respirator, on which a patch of white shiny cloth had been sewn. This proved fairly easy to see from the air, whereas the metal disk, apt to rust or tarnish quickly, sometimes proved difficult to locate. Prearrangement, whereby signals were to be made asking for flares to be lighted at specified times and places, was found of little use. With the situation changing rapidly, and with the depth of the advance varying greatly along different parts of the line, the only safe method of finding the infantry was for the contact patrol pilot and observer to begin at the last known position, and to work forward methodically, noting all positions captured and held, until the enemy was seen, or his presence betrayed by fire directed at the aeroplane. The contact patrol pilot then turned, and his observer endeavoured to plot, with the help of flares, disks, or by direct observation, the approximate line reached. With enemy strong points holding out even though surrounded —hostile islands created by the forward sweep—and with British patrols in irregular advance of any formed bodies of troops, it was obviously easy for the air observers to jump to conclusions. It was found that those who had good knowledge of the organization of the army, and who had come to their task of observation with experience which helped them to appreciate the flow of a battle, produced, in general, the reports of best value. In the words of the corps wing commander, written after the battle: 'Nothing at present in the training of corps contact ob-'servers can compensate for the lack of army experience— 'in default of this he cannot appreciate the situation. As 'an example, the enemy puts down a barrage—the observer 'does not connect this with a raid or counter attack and 'misses the approach of the enemy infantry.'

The French Air Service[1]

The French air division was employed during the battle in the area of the French First Army. General Debeney's orders, issued on the evening of the 8th of August, allotted the stations at Ham, Hombleux, Roye, Fresnoy-les-Roye, and Fransart as bombing targets during the night of the

---

[1] The particulars of the French air division are taken from the French official military history: *Les Armées françaises dans la Grande Guerre*, Vol. VII, 1 and annexes. See also *La Doctrine de L'Aviation française de Combat, 1915–18*, by Général Voisin.

8th/9th. The same stations were to be attacked by day on the 9th with, in addition, the cantonments of Tilloloy, Beuvraignes, and Bus. The fighter squadrons were to attack enemy balloons, troops in the neighbourhood of Bus, Fescamps, and Boulogne-la-Grasse, and were to maintain control of the air over the French First Army as far as Rollot.

For the night of the 9th/10th the bombing targets were the stations at Ham, Hombleux, and Guiscard, but for daylight bombing during the 10th the objectives were Roye Junction and the station and Somme bridge at Ham. The fighter squadrons during the 10th were to make offensive patrols, and to attack enemy troops in the neighbourhood of Boulogne-la-Grasse, Bus, and Guerbigny.

For the night of the 10th/11th, the targets were Ham, Tergnier, Saint-Quentin, Hombleux, and Guiscard, and for day attacks on the 11th, the junctions at Ham and Guiscard. The fighters, as before, were to maintain air superiority and to attack ground targets. The same orders were issued for the night of the 11th/12th and for the day of the 12th.

CHAPTER XIII
THE BATTLE OF BAPAUME
[Maps, pp. 437, 550, and at end]

It was the wish of Marshal Foch that the next British blow should be directed against the Roye–Chaulnes position, but Sir Douglas Haig was anxious to extend the front of his offensive northwards, between the Somme and the Scarpe, and Marshal Foch eventually agreed. Sir Douglas Haig's reasons were that a successful attack between Albert and Arras, where the ground was suitable for the employment of tanks, would turn the line of the Somme south of Péronne and would be a step towards the strategic objective St. Quentin–Cambrai. Furthermore, the salient in which the Germans found themselves was already threatened from the south, and they did not seem prepared to meet an offensive on its northern shoulder.

Sir Douglas Haig's plan was to stage a preliminary operation on the morning of the 21st of August with the object of recovering the Arras–Albert railway, and to follow this with a general attack two days later by the Third and Fourth Armies north of the Somme. The proposed new battle sector was so close to the scene of the Amiens offensive as to make unnecessary any great alterations in the disposition of the air units. A few squadrons which had been working at high pressure changed places with squadrons in quiet parts of the line, and some others moved across the river, including No. 6 Squadron for work with the Cavalry Corps, and No. 8 Squadron attached to the Tank Corps. A fighting squadron, No. 73 (Sopwith 'Camels'), was also placed at the special disposal of the Tank Corps commander for low-flying attacks against anti-tank guns: a map showing where it was thought these guns were likely to be found had been prepared. Two American fighting squadrons, No. 17 from the X Brigade and No. 148 from the V Brigade, were moved to the Third Army area, and four British fighting squadrons were added, by which the fighting strength of the III Brigade was brought up to ten squadrons[1] on the eve of the battle.

[1] Nos. 1, 3, 54, 56, 60, 73, 87, and 201, and Nos. 17 and 148 American.

Furthermore, the four fighter squadrons of the neighbouring I Brigade had orders to provide high offensive patrols in the battle area. The army Wing of the III Brigade was strengthened by No. 11 Bristol Fighter reconnaissance squadron, by No. 57 D.H.4 day bomber squadron, and by No. 102 short-distance night bomber squadron.

Brigadier-General C. A. H. Longcroft, the III Brigade commander,[1] issued his detailed operation orders on the 19th of August. The success of the military plans depended upon surprise, and great care, he said, must be taken to ensure that there was no air activity of a kind to attract the attention of the enemy. Not until the last of the patrolling aeroplanes had landed on the eve of the battle were the squadrons to be informed that the attack would take place on the morrow. To overcome the noise which would be made by the tanks as they assembled during the night of the 20th/21st of August, aeroplanes were to fly on the front of the Third Army, but, in order that the enemy might be kept in doubt, night flying was also to take place along the fronts of the neighbouring Fourth and First Armies. On the same night No. 102 Squadron was to bomb Bapaume, Achiet-le-Grand, and Achiet-le-Petit.

No more than three fighting squadrons were allotted for attacks against ground targets, one to each corps front. They were No. 3 Squadron to the front of the IV Corps, No. 60 to the VI Corps, and No. 56 to the V Corps. Each squadron was to send its aeroplanes away in pairs at half-hourly intervals, beginning thirty minutes after zero hour, and the pilots were to pay attention to specified routes by which it was expected that resting battalions would approach the battle. Offensive patrols up to a height of 10,000 feet were to be provided by the two American Squadrons and by Nos. 87 and 11 Squadrons. The patrols by the fighter pilots of the neighbouring I Brigade were to be made above this height. Two squadrons of the headquarters IX Brigade, Nos. 1 and 54, which had been placed under the temporary orders of the III Brigade, were to be held in reserve for employment against enemy

[1] Brigadier-General Longcroft had returned to France, from commanding the Training Division in England, in April 1918.

balloons, and to reinforce the offensive patrols. No. 201 Squadron, which was temporarily resting, was given no specific duties. There were to be bombing attacks on German aerodromes and German head-quarters, special reconnaissance flights, and attempts to cut the enemy rail communications.

Such in outline were the intentions, but a ground mist and light rain, which set in during the night of the 20th/21st of August and continued until some hours after dawn, put the air service to some extent out of action. There is evidence that the noise of the tanks moving to their assembly places was heard in parts of the German lines, but in general the attack took the enemy by surprise, and the front line was carried at the first rush: by the evening the advance had reached a depth between two and three miles. Not until about 10 a.m. had the mist, which on balance had been to the advantage of the tanks and the assaulting infantry, cleared. By this time the tanks had completed their main tasks, but No. 73 Squadron, which had been given the duty of watching for anti-tank guns, arrived over the battle-field in time to attack a few enemy batteries which were firing on some of the tanks. 'August '21', wrote Brevet-Colonel J. F. C. Fuller, 'was the most 'disappointing day No. 8 Squadron experienced whilst 'attached to the Tank Corps. The morning was very foggy 'and it was quite impossible for the machines to leave the 'ground until 11 a.m., a little over six hours after Zero, 'which was at 4.55 a.m. In spite of this the counter-gun 'machines were not too late to carry out useful work against 'several batteries; this work was chiefly carried out by No. '73 Squadron, which was quite new to the work. The 'value of the experience gained on this day was amply 'demonstrated by the effective work carried out by this 'squadron on the 23rd, when many hostile guns were 'attacked and their crews scattered.'[1]

There were some bombing attacks in the morning of the 21st on enemy head-quarters, and in the afternoon on railway objectives at Aubigny-au-Bac, Marquion, and Roisel, but the afternoon attacks, which were made from

[1] *Tanks in the Great War, 1914–18*, p. 248.

13,000 feet, did not appear to be effective. There was little opposition in the upper air, but the German pilots were active low down over the battle-field.

The night of the 21st/22nd of August was fine and the night-flying reconnaissance and bombing squadrons had little rest. The railway bridge over the Sensée river at Aubigny-au-Bac was hit, and a bomb on sheds at Marcoing station caused explosions and fires. Four Sopwith 'Camel' pilots of the night-fighting No. 151 Squadron, each carrying four light-weight bombs, attacked the German aerodromes at Moislains and Offoy, setting fire to some hangars at the latter place. A pilot of the same squadron destroyed an enemy night-flyer which fell in flames near Arras. The biggest attack of the night was made on Cambrai railway junction by Handley Pages of No. 207 Squadron which dropped a total of twelve tons of bombs.

At 4.45 a.m. on the 22nd of August the III Corps, together with the 3rd Australian Division, assisted by tanks, resumed the attack on a front of 10,000 yards from the Somme to Albert. The enemy resisted stoutly, especially in Albert, but the town was captured by the 18th Division and the line was pushed forward beyond the village of Méaulte.

The air bombing on the 22nd was mainly directed against the railways radiating from Cambrai towards the front, the attacks being made from heights varying between 10,000 and 15,000 feet. Some of the raids were contested, the most determined of the enemy efforts being that which was made to prevent a morning attack on Cambrai by ten D.H.9's of No. 27 Squadron, escorted by fifteen Bristol Fighters of No. 62 Squadron. There was much confused fighting in the neighbourhood of the objective, and four German aeroplanes were shot down, two of them in flames, and two Bristol Fighter pilots were wounded, but were able to make landings within their own lines.

As a result of the infantry advance made in the two days of preliminary fighting, the way had been cleared for the main battle. This began on the morning of the 23rd of August and involved thirty-three miles of British front,

CHANGE IN OUTLOOK

from the junction with the French at Lihons to Mercatel, near where the Hindenburg line joined the old Arras–Vimy defence system of 1916. On the right of the British the battle was extended along the French front as far as Soissons. The opening of the main offensive was marked by a change in the conduct of the war—a change which had been notified to the army commanders in a remarkable telegram sent by Sir Douglas Haig on the evening of the 22nd for communication to subordinate leaders. After pointing out the necessity for bold and resolute action to obtain full advantage from the existing favourable position, Sir Douglas Haig said: 'The effect of the two 'very severe defeats, and the continuous attacks to which 'the enemy has been subjected during the first month has 'been to wear out his troops and disorganize his plans. 'Our Second and Fifth armies have taken their share in 'the effort to destroy the enemy and already have gained 'considerable ground from him in the Lys sector of our 'front. To-day the French 10th Army crossed the Ailette 'and reports that a Bavarian Division fled in panic carry-'ing back with it another division which was advancing to 'its support. To-morrow the attack of the Allied armies 'on the whole front from Soissons to Neuville Vitasse (near 'Arras) is to be continued. The methods which we have 'followed hitherto in our battles with limited objectives 'when the enemy was strong are no longer suited to his 'present condition. The enemy has not the means to 'deliver counter-attacks on an extended scale nor has he 'the numbers to hold a continuous position against the 'very extended advance which is now being directed upon 'him. To turn the present situation to account the most 'resolute offensive action is everywhere desirable. Risks 'which a month ago would have been criminal to incur 'ought now to be incurred as a duty. It is no longer neces-'sary to advance in regular lines and step by step. On the 'contrary each division should be given a distant objective 'which must be reached independently of its neighbour 'and even if one's flank is thereby exposed for the time 'being. Reinforcements must be directed on the points 'where our troops are gaining ground, not where they are

'checked. A vigorous offensive against the sectors where
'the enemy is weak will cause hostile strong points to fall
'and in due course our whole army will be able to continue
'its advance. This procedure will result in speedily break-
'ing up the hostile forces and will cost us much less than
'if we attempted to deal with the present situation in a
'half-hearted manner. The situation is most favourable:
'let each one of us act energetically and without hesitation
'push forward to our objective.'

The Allied line sprang into action at 4.45 a.m. on the 23rd of August. The Royal Air Force brigades mainly involved were the III working with the Third Army, the V with the Fourth Army, and the head-quarters IX Brigade. The two first-named were concerned with the tactical areas of their respective armies, and their direct co-operation with the infantry, tanks, and artillery, was of a normal kind and does not call for close examination.

There was, however, one innovation which must be noticed. This had been brought about by experience during the fighting which began on the 8th of August. On that day and on subsequent days many targets eminently suitable for low-flying attack had been notified from the air, but owing to delays in communication the low-flying squadrons had sometimes missed opportunities to concentrate their full weight upon the targets. As an example, a pilot on the 8th of August had discovered columns of transport in a state of crowded confusion along the Amiens–Brie road, and he had himself engaged them with his machine-guns, but no news of the target was received in the British lines until the pilot landed nearly two hours later.

To accelerate the collection and distribution of information of this kind, a Wireless Central Information Bureau (known as C.I.B.) had been set up near Villers-Bretonneux. Although the main duty of the bureau was to report targets favourable for bombing and machine-gun attacks, it was also made responsible for keeping a watch upon enemy air activity and for giving news about this activity to air fighting units. The working of the bureau may be best illustrated by two examples, one of each kind. An observer in an aeroplane engaged in the work of co-operation with the infantry or artillery who sighted a formation of hostile aircraft at once tapped out a wireless code message, prefaced by the identity letter of his squadron, giving the number, height, and approximate position and course of the enemy. The information was immediately passed by the bureau on a continuous wave wireless set for reception by nearby fighting squadrons, and the attention of pilots who might already be in the air within view of the station was attracted by the placing of a distinctive arrow on the ground, pointing in the direction where the enemy aeroplanes had been seen. For communicating information about ground targets favourable for air attack the procedure was somewhat similar, but the observer who discovered the enemy used the 'L.L.' call and gave the pin-point position of the target, together with a brief indication of its nature. The bureau passed the news by wireless to the units allotted to attacks on ground targets. In both instances, whether the enemy was in the air or on the ground, the air observer concerned fired a red light to attract any British pilots who might be in his neighbourhood.

The wireless calls from pilots and observers of the corps squadrons sent down from the battle area to the Central Information Bureau would, it was said, largely control the action of low-flying pilots once a battle had begun. It was also said that the new system was an important step towards closer co-operation between the corps wing and the army wing of a brigade, and was calculated to economize energy in general and to ensure a more efficient application of force in particular.

The attention of all pilots was specially called to the need for taking action against anti-tank guns. There was an occasion not long after the battle had opened on the 8th of August when a single gun had disabled eight tanks in succession and had in consequence brought the infantry attack in its area to a standstill. 'It was not 'too much to say', wrote Brigadier-General L. E. O. Charlton, the V Brigade commander, in a memorandum in which he laid stress upon the individual responsibility in the matter of each pilot and observer, 'that without the 'anti-tank guns the advance of our line would have been 'irresistible'.

The so-called strategical bombing by the squadrons of the head-quarters IX Brigade was concentrated against the railway junctions at Somain, Valenciennes, and Cambrai (ville), beginning during the night before the attack. On this night, 22nd/23rd of August, the moon shone from a clear sky, and No. 58 Squadron bombed Somain, No. 83 Squadron Cambrai, and No. 207 Squadron Valenciennes. Although the greatest weight of bombs was dropped on the last-named centre it appears that most damage was inflicted at Somain, where a train containing ammunition was hit, among others, and set on fire. While this moonlight railway bombing was in progress, pilots of No. 102 Squadron of the III Brigade were going backwards and forwards making attacks on troops and transport and on the billeting villages in the neighbourhood of Bapaume, and those of No. 101 Squadron of the V Brigade were bombing similar objectives in the Fourth Army area. As soon as it was daylight the attacks on the three railway junctions were taken up by the day bombers of Nos. 27, 49, and 107 Squadrons.

The British infantry moved steadily forward on the 23rd. The Australian Corps, south of the Somme, took Herleville, Chuignolles, and Chuignes, together with more than 2,000 prisoners, and north of the river the III and V Corps gained the high ground east and south of Albert. North of the Ancre the Third Army attack between Miraumont and Neuville Vitasse found the enemy disorganized and forced him back in some confusion. During the morning Bihucourt, Ervillers, Boyelles, and Boiry-Becquerelle were captured with 5,000 prisoners and many guns.

On the Third Army front low-flying attacks were made by No. 3 Squadron and by No. 17 American Squadron, and by the three squadrons (Nos. 1, 54, and 73) of the head-quarters IX Brigade which had been temporarily attached to the III Brigade. No. 73 Squadron co-operated with some success with the advancing tanks, and the pilots were able, by diving attacks on anti-tank batteries, to silence the guns long enough to enable the tanks to advance.[1]

The low-flying attacks by the single-seaters on the 23rd of August were supplemented, as usually happened, by the pilots and observers in the co-operating corps aeroplanes. As an example of their work the experiences of a pilot and observer in an R.E.8 of No. 59 Squadron may be given. They were patrolling over the battle-field in the afternoon, keeping watch to note the positions of active enemy guns, when they saw that a British barrage was being placed in front of the New Zealand Division between Irles and Bihucourt. It happened that at the time there was no contact patrol aeroplane in the neighbourhood, and the pilot of the R.E.8 therefore went down within about fifty feet of the ground in order that his observer might watch events. The New Zealanders could be recognized as they moved forward close behind the barrage, and shortly afterwards the pilot dived upon a German machine-gun which was seen from the air to open fire upon the advancing infantry. The enemy gun was silenced, and it was then observed that flares of distress were being sent up from the German line; the aeroplane pilot put a few bursts of

[1] 'The tactics adopted in this counter-gun work are interesting. To 'send down zone calls was useless, as the German gunners opened fire, as 'a rule, when the tanks were but 1,000 yards away. Immediate action 'was, therefore, necessary, and this was taken by bombing and machine-'gunning hostile artillery until the tanks had run over the emplacements. 'The method of locating the hostile gun positions consisted in carefully 'studying the ground prior to the attack by consulting maps and air 'photographs, and from this study to make out a chart of all likely gun 'positions. On September 2nd a most valuable document was captured 'which set forth the complete scheme the Germans had adopted in con-'nexion with the distribution of their guns for anti-tank work; further, in 'this document were described the various types of positions anti-tank 'gunners should take up. By the aid of this document and a large-scale 'map it was possible to plot beforehand the majority of possible gun posi-'tions. As each of our aeroplanes had only about 2,000 yards of front to 'watch, the result was that all likely places were periodically bombed. In 'this way, by selecting the likely places beforehand, a great number of anti-'tank guns were spotted as soon as they opened fire, and thus immense 'service was rendered to the tanks.' *Tanks in the Great War*, by Brevet-Colonel J. F. C. Fuller, D.S.O., pp. 247–8.

machine-gun fire into the enemy positions, and subsequently watched the New Zealanders enter the German line where men could be seen holding their arms above their heads in token of surrender. Some enemy troops who were seen to run forward from a nearby disused gun pit were fired upon from the air, and they also surrendered to the New Zealanders, who signified their thanks for the help they had received from the R.E.8 by waving handkerchiefs as the aeroplane left the line: the R.E.8 had been hit by many bullets fired from the ground, but the pilot was able to return safely to his aerodrome. Low-flying attacks on the Fourth Army front were made chiefly by Sopwith 'Camels' of No. 203 Squadron.

The Third and Fourth Armies resumed the attack at 1 a.m. on the 23rd/24th of August, and although German rear-guards made a stubborn resistance the advance could not be stayed, with the result that when darkness closed over the battle-field on the 24th the whole of the Thiepval ridge had been cleared and many thousands of prisoners had been left in British hands. The line which had been reached ran from La Boisselle–south-east of Pys–south of Grévillers–east of Biefvillers–west of Sapignies–west of Béhagnies–Mory–west of Croisilles–St. Martin–north-east of Neuville-Vitasse.

While the battle was being continued during the night of the 23rd/24th the clouds were low and there was some rain. The head-quarters bombing squadrons did not fly, but Nos. 101 and 102 Squadrons attacked various targets, mainly troops and transport, in front of the Third and Fourth Armies. The visibility continued to be poor until about midday on the 24th, and the air work was consequently restricted while the infantry were moving forward in the morning. The head-quarters day-bombing squadrons took a rest throughout the 24th, but those attached to the III and V Brigades made attempts upon the stations at Péronne and Velu. The attacks, however, were made from about 13,000 feet, from which height the targets were invisible, and the bombing, therefore, was probably of no practical military value. The attempts may be looked upon as an expression of the will of the pilots and observers to take an outside chance to help the attacking infantry. The Péronne bombers and their escorts came into brief conflict with German fighters, one of which, a Fokker, was shot down in flames. Apart from this fight there were few air encounters throughout the day.

The night of the 24th/25th of August was moonlit, and the bombers, German as well as British, were busy. The railway junctions at Somain, Cambrai, Douai, and Valenciennes, were the main targets for the British pilots, but some of the bombs were aimed at billets, troops, and transport in the area of the battle. At Somain, which was attacked by No. 58 Squadron from 800 feet, hits were made on the station buildings, and a train was set on fire and later exploded. Hits on the junction at Cambrai were made by No. 83 Squadron, on Douai by No. 207 Squadron, and on Valenciennes by the same squadron, and by No. 148 Squadron of the I Brigade.

An example, typical of the attacks upon troops and transport, may be quoted from the records of No. 102 Squadron, which dropped more than three tons of bombs during the night. A pilot and observer of this squadron, in their F.E.2b carrying fourteen 25-lb. bombs, were southwest of Cambrai at 10.30 p.m. on the 24th when they saw a column of horse and motor transport moving into Metz-en-Couture from the direction of Ruyaulcourt. The pilot waited until the transport had halted in the middle of the village and then, from a height of 200 feet, he fired down Very lights. As they flared up, throwing grotesque patterns across the transport, the pilot passed and re-passed over the column, releasing his bombs two or three at a time, and attacking with machine-gun fire. When all the ammunition had been expended the F.E.2b was flown close above the village street on a flight of inspection: it was seen that dead and wounded horses were lying on the road and that order had gone from the column, in which there were many gaps.

The German night raiders, although they made fewer flights than the British, had some success. Among the places attacked was Boulogne, on which thirty-seven bombs fell, causing destruction to twelve lorries and damage to military huts: three of the German bombers were intercepted by night-fighting pilots of No. 151 Squadron who destroyed two of them. Most damage during the night was inflicted by five German pilots of No. 16 *Schlachtstaffel* who dropped an inconsiderable number of bombs on the aerodrome of Nos. 48 and 84 Squadrons at Bertangles. Hits were made on the wooden hangars housing the aeroplanes of No. 48 Squadron, and fires resulted which destroyed five hangars together with nine Bristol Fighters. The one remaining hangar of the squadron was also partly burnt and two Bristol Fighters inside were damaged. This was not the sum total of the destruction, for one more aeroplane of No. 48 Squadron was wrecked by a direct hit from a bomb, office and stores huts, with six transport tenders, were consumed by flames, and part of a hangar belonging to No. 84 Squadron was burnt with an S.E.5a aeroplane. No. 48 Squadron had to be withdrawn from the line to Boisdinghem to be re-equipped, but the squadron was flying again within forty-eight hours on the front of the II Brigade.

By way of retaliation for this attack, the day bombers of the head-quarters IX Brigade were given German aerodrome targets on the 25th of August. The aerodromes chosen were at Étreux, south-east of Le Cateau, and Mont d'Origny, east of St. Quentin, which respectively housed Nos. 1 and 4 *Bombengeschwader*. Nos. 27 and 49 Squadrons attacked Étreux, and Nos. 98 and 107 Mont d'Origny. Nos. 32 and 43 fighter Squadrons had orders to patrol the Marcoing and St. Quentin areas while the bombing was in progress, and subsequently to escort the bombers on their homeward journeys. In addition, No. 62 Bristol Fighter Squadron was ordered to provide patrols over the two target aerodromes while the attacks were being made. The bombing of Étreux took place at 4 p.m., when 144 bombs of 25-lb. weight were dropped from heights varying between 10,000 and 13,000 feet: one of the hangars was seen to burst into flames. There was considerable air fighting of a confused kind, some of it taking place during a thunderstorm on the homeward flight, as a result of which two D.H.9's of No. 49 Squadron were shot down and one German aeroplane fell in flames. The S.E.5a's of No. 32 Squadron became involved in a fight with Fokker biplanes some distance south of where it had been arranged the S.E.5a's should meet the bombers for homeward escort. Two of the Fokkers were destroyed, and from one of them the pilot jumped with a parachute which was seen to bear him safely to earth.

The attack on the Mont d'Origny aerodrome proved disappointing. Thirteen D.H.9's of No. 98 Squadron had set out at 4 p.m. and eleven of No. 107 Squadron forty minutes later. No more than eight aeroplanes, all from No. 98 Squadron, reached the objective, at which 53 bombs of 25-lb. weight were aimed from 13,000 feet. The visibility, according to the bombing reports, was poor and no results were observed. Five D.H.9's of this squadron had turned back because of engine trouble, as had three of No. 107 Squadron for the same reason. The remaining aeroplanes of the latter squadron, unable to reach the enemy aerodrome owing to the bad weather conditions, bombed miscellaneous targets with no apparent results. They were attacked while dropping their bombs, but the German fighters, possibly disheartened by a lack of success, moved away and attacked the returning D.H.9's of No. 98 Squadron, against whom they had no better luck. A patrol of fifteen Sopwith 'Camels' of No. 43 Squadron, which had set out to meet the Mont d'Origny bombers, flew into clouds and did not see the D.H.9's.

On the 25th of August and subsequent days the infantry advance continued steadily. On the 25th itself Favreuil, Sapignies, Behagnies, and Mory were taken. Next day the French, on the British right, captured Fresnoy and caused the enemy to evacuate Roye, which was entered on the 27th. The Germans gave up Bapaume on the morning of the 29th, and by the night of the 30th the line of the Fourth and Third Armies north of the Somme ran from Clery on the Somme, past the western edge of Marrière Wood to Combles, through Lesbœufs, Bancourt, Fremicourt, and Vaulx-Vraucourt, to Écoust, Bullecourt and Hendecourt. During the night of the 30th/31st of August the 2nd Australian Division stormed Mont

St. Quentin which commanded Péronne and the Somme crossings and, although the opposition was determined, the positions were secured and held against counter-attacks and, on the 1st of September, the Australian troops entered Péronne. This day marked the end of the second stage of the offensive, during which the enemy had finally been driven back across the old Somme battle-fields and, in addition to heavy losses in killed and wounded, had left 34,000 prisoners and 270 guns in Allied hands.

Clouds lay over the battle-field during much of the time when the British infantry were moving forward, and the work of the bombing squadrons in particular had been hampered. Low-flying attacks on ground targets were, however, maintained and in these the three head-quarters fighter squadrons, Nos. 1, 54, and 73, had played a notable part.[1]

The corps squadrons, by contact and artillery patrols, had kept touch with the advance. Two episodes from the record book of No. 59 Squadron may be quoted to illustrate the activities of the corps pilots and observers. The particular episodes are chosen not because they were unusual in themselves, but because of the opportunity they give to mention a pilot and observer who had a consistently good record of work. The two officers were Captain D. H. M. Carbery and Lieutenant J. B. V. Clements, whose reports time and again provided valuable material for the staff of the corps with which the squadron co-operated. In the afternoon of the 25th of August they were on contact patrol in their R.E.8 aeroplane from 2.50 p.m. until 6 p.m. At 3.15 p.m., not long after they had reached the German lines, an enemy battery was seen to be firing. Its position was notified to the British artillery by N.F. wireless call, and it was not long before neutralizing fire was opened which silenced the enemy guns. Twenty minutes later a limbered gun was seen from the aeroplane to be moving at a walking pace towards Bapaume. The pilot dived and opened machine-gun fire from a low height: the gun moved off across country, leaving eight members of

---

[1] Nos. 54 and 73 Squadrons had been transferred from attachment to the III Brigade to the V Brigade on the 26th of August.

the crew lying on the road. At 4.28 p.m. another German battery was seen active and an N.F. call once more brought retaliatory fire to bear which silenced the enemy guns within seven minutes. At 4.50 p.m. the R.E.8 passed over an exploding dump and, five minutes later, about fifty German infantry were seen. Their position, preceded by a 'fleeting target' call (G.F.), was sent out by wireless, and shells were soon exploding among the German troops. At 5 p.m. the pilot and his observer engaged with their machine-guns about twenty soldiers who were seen standing about in the square at Bapaume. Ten minutes later the R.E.8 officers saw a gun, which had been brought forward by a team of six horses, suddenly open fire and, while they were waiting for the British artillery to respond to their N.F. call, they themselves attacked the enemy gun team with machine-gun fire from 200 feet: it was not long, however, before the N.F. call was answered and the German gun ceased firing.

The same two officers were out again at 6.40 a.m. next morning, the 26th, but the clouds were at 300 feet and there was rain, which made effective co-operation impossible. They took the air once more, in improved weather, at midday in order to watch the progress of the advance by the IV Corps. At 12.58 p.m. a concentration of about 500 enemy troops was observed from the R.E.8 north-east of Beugnâtre, and it was further seen that huts and dug-outs in the area were crowded with soldiers. A 'fleeting target' call was made at once and shells were soon exploding among the enemy. At 1.20 p.m. about 1,000 German infantry were found crowded in trenches south-west of Beugnâtre, and in the interval before a 'fleeting target' call was answered the Germans were fired upon from 800 feet by the R.E.8's machine-guns. Yet another call for fire on a party of infantry was sent out at 1.30 p.m., and subsequently the two officers engaged various ground targets with their machine-guns until all their ammunition had been expended.

The above examples may be looked upon as typical of those, recorded in many hundreds of reports, which picture the work of the pilots and observers of the corps squadrons during the battle. The squadrons also delivered, by parachutes, from 30,000 to 60,000 rounds of small arms ammunition each day to British troops in forward positions.

The activity of the German air service during the battle was intermittent, but when the enemy fighting pilots intervened the technical superiority of their Fokker biplanes brought advantages. On the evening of the 26th of August a formation of brightly painted Fokkers attacked nine Sopwith 'Camels' of No. 17 American Squadron which were making an offensive patrol over the Bapaume–Cambrai road at 5,000 feet. In a stern encounter, during which the Americans fought with fine gallantry, one Fokker was destroyed, but six of the American pilots were shot down in enemy territory, and one of the three who returned landed a damaged aeroplane with difficulty.

The Battle of the Scarpe

The operations of the Third and Fourth Armies have, for convenience of narration, been recounted up to the end of a phase on the 1st of September. On the 26th of August, however, the British First Army, under General Sir H. S. Horne, on the left of the Third Army, had opened an offensive which was in effect an extension of the general battle. Striking eastwards from Arras, with its left covered by the Scarpe and Sensée rivers, the valleys of which had been inundated by the Germans, the object of the First Army was to turn the enemy positions on the Somme battle-field. The preparations necessary to make possible the launching of such an action at short notice had been under way for some time.

The advance was entrusted to the Canadian Corps which had been specially transferred from the Fourth Army, and to which the Third Tank Brigade had been allotted. The First Army was also reinforced by the Cavalry Corps, less the Second Cavalry Division, from the Third Army, and by the 4th Division from the Fifth Army.

There were transfers also of air squadrons. Nos. 8 and 73 Squadrons, experienced in the work of co-operating with tanks, moved into the First Army area where they came under the orders of the I Brigade. No. 5 Squadron moved with the Canadian Corps which was additionally given the services of No. 52 Squadron, and No. 6 Squadron moved with the Cavalry Corps. An extra fighter squadron, No. 54, one of those belonging to the head-quarters IX Brigade, was transferred to the First Army front from temporary attachment to the Third Army. Thus the I Brigade, for the opening of the offensive, was made up of five fighter squadrons (Nos. 40, 54, 64, 208, and 209), one fighter reconnaissance squadron (No. 22), one day bomber squadron (No. 18), one night bomber squadron (No. 148), two squadrons (Nos. 73 and 8) allotted for work with the tanks, Nos. 5 and 52 Squadrons for tactical work with the Canadian Corps, and No. 6 Squadron for similar air co-operation with the Cavalry Corps.

Sir Douglas Haig, during a visit he paid to Canadian Corps head-quarters on the 24th of August, discussed the details of the proposed operations at some length. The initial task of the Canadians, reinforced by other British divisions as necessary, was to break the Drocourt–Quéant line and reach the line of the Canal du Nord. When this had been achieved the corps was to sweep southwards behind the Hindenburg Line.

The plan involved the overrunning of three German main defensive positions, each of which was to mark a stage in the advance. Zero hour was to be at 3 a.m. on the 26th of August. The air operation orders issued by the Tenth (Army) Wing for the 26th stated that Nos. 208, 209, 64, and 54 Squadrons would, consecutively, attack ground targets, beginning with No. 208 Squadron at dawn. The last specified patrol, by No. 54 Squadron, was to start at 7 a.m. Subsequently, throughout the day, the four squadrons were to work from the aerodrome at Izel Le Hameau under the special order of Major B. E. Smythies, a step forward of some interest because, for the first time, one officer was made responsible for directing the low-flying attacks according to the variations of the situation. The only condition laid down was that the attacks were to be made from as low a height as possible, and never from above 1,000 feet. It was suggested that targets suitable for this form of attack were guns in emplacements or in the open, troops concentrating for action, and men and transport on roads and bridges.

The duties allotted to Nos. 40 (S.E.5a) and 22 (Bristol Fighter) Squadrons were offensive patrols, at two-Flight strength, to be made from dawn onwards at heights varying between 4,000 and 8,000 feet. The object of the patrols was to prevent useful observation from enemy balloons in the battle area, to keep enemy aeroplanes at a distance, and to afford general protection to the low-flying aeroplanes. The day bomber squadron of the I Brigade, No. 18, was to attack Aubigny-au-Bac and specified railheads at 7 a.m. and at 3 p.m.

The day bomber squadrons of the head-quarters IX Brigade were to bomb German aerodromes north of Cambrai, opposite the front of attack, at daybreak. One squadron had the aerodrome at Epinoy for target, another Ermerchicourt, and a third, Haynecourt. In the afternoon, after 3 p.m., the allotted objectives were Seclin, Somain, and Valenciennes, on the line of railway communications from Lille to Valenciennes. The X Brigade, working with the Fifth Army on the left of the First, was called upon to extend the area of its offensive patrols to a line due east of Lens, and the II Brigade, with the Second Army on the left of the Fifth, was to make a compensating southerly extension of its offensive patrol area to the river Lys.

At 3 a.m. on the 26th of August the 2nd and 3rd Canadian Divisions attacked on a front of 6,000 yards south of the Scarpe, and at 9 a.m. the 51st Division came into action on a front of 2,000 yards north of the river. Wancourt, Guémappe, and Monchy were captured, and by nightfall the outskirts of Roeux had been reached.

The advance was made in bad weather with low clouds, rain, and a strong south-westerly wind. The bombing operations ordered for the head-quarters IX Brigade squadrons could not be accomplished, but in the area of the battle the I Brigade squadrons, together with those attached, attempted all that was asked of them, beginning at 6.50 a.m. The pilots and observers of the two corps squadrons, Nos. 5 and 52, were in the air during the day for a total of 91 hours. From a height of 200 feet or so they kept watch upon the advancng infantry and dropped messages and maps from time to time giving particulars of the progress made; they sent down wireless calls for fire upon active German batteries, anti-tank guns, troop concentrations, and upon machine-gun nests; and themselves made many attacks, with bombs and machine-gun fire, upon such targets.

The first of the fighter pilots whose special task was to attack ground targets left in a rainstorm at 6.50 a.m. By 7.20 a.m. No. 209 Squadron had eighteen Sopwith 'Camels' in the air, each carrying four 25-lb. bombs. The pilots attacked machine-gun emplacements, troops, and transport, but three of the aeroplanes were shot down by fire from the ground, one of them falling on enemy territory. The Sopwith 'Camels' were followed at 8 a.m. by S.E.5a's of No. 64 Squadron, with Sopwith 'Camels' of No. 54 Squadron relieving them at 10 a.m., and the same type aeroplanes of No. 208 Squadron going out at 10.30 a.m. Through the remainder of the day the single-seater fighters went backwards and forwards between the aerodrome at Le Hameau and the battle-field, but they did not fly merely hoping that good targets would be found. They were given specific objectives, chosen in accordance with the wireless messages, telling of enemy movements and concentrations, sent back by the observers in the corps aeroplanes and noted in the Central Information Bureau. Furthermore, twice during the day, morning and afternoon, Major B. E. Smythies, who was generally responsible for the intervention of the fighter squadrons, flew over the battle-field to make a rapid personal survey of the situation. A total of 553 bombs of 25-lb. weight were dropped by the low-flying pilots, and 26,000 rounds of machine-gun ammunition were fired on ground targets. The cost was comparatively small: one aeroplane was missing, three pilots returned wounded, and four aeroplanes were wrecked. There was little opposition from German aircraft throughout the day, and the patrolling Bristol Fighters and S.E.5a's of Nos. 22 and 40 Squadrons had nothing of interest to report until the evening when No. 40 Squadron had a brief encounter with a Fokker formation over the Scarpe, during which one of the enemy fighters was apparently shot down out of control.

One of the objectives bombed during the day was the station at Brébières where air observers had reported notable train movements: it was attacked again in the rain-swept night of the 26th/27th of August by No. 58 Squadron of the head-quarters IX Brigade. Marquion station and village received a hundred and five 112-lb. and thirty-seven 25-lb. bombs from the Handley Pages of No. 207 Squadron, while night bombers of No. 148 Squadron attacked the billeting villages of Vis-en-Artois and Etérpigny.

At 4.55 a.m. on the 27th of August the 2nd and 3rd Canadian Divisions continued their advance. By 9.30 a.m. the 3rd Canadian Division had captured the Bois du Vert and had reached the Bois du Sart, but it soon became clear that the Germans intended to make a desperate bid to delay the advance. Not until the next afternoon, and after an intense bombardment followed by heavy fighting, were the Canadians able to capture the strong Boiry–Fresnes–Rouvray defences: Pelves and the stubbornly defended Jigsaw Wood were also taken. Meanwhile, on the 27th, the 51st Division had won Roeux, Plouvain, and Gavrelle. During the last days of the month the advance continued, and by the evening of the 30th the First Army was within assaulting distance of the strongly fortified trench system which had been built to connect the Hindenburg Line at Quéant with the old German front at Drocourt, south of Lens. The rupture of the Drocourt–Quéant switch would turn the Hindenburg Line.

The arrangements for the co-operation of the Royal Air Force squadrons on the 27th of August were similar to those for the previous day, except that the fighter low-flying patrols, up to 7.30 a.m., were ordered to be made at squadron strength. Between 5.15. a.m. and 7.30 a.m. sixty-six single-seater pilots were engaged on low offensive work, including twelve from No. 73 Squadron specially concerned with anti-tank guns, in the comparatively narrow area from the Scarpe river to the Arras–Cambrai road. From 7.30 a.m. onwards until 5 p.m. two Flights from each low-flying fighter squadron went out consecutively at intervals of about an hour. Between 5 p.m. and 7 p.m., in spite of low clouds and rain, the squadrons once more flew at full strength, dropping bombs and attacking enemy troops, transport and batteries, from a few dozen feet above the ground. During the day the five single-seater squadrons (including No. 73), although the weather conditions were always difficult, dropped a total of six hundred and forty-six 25-lb. bombs and fired 47,570 rounds of machine-gun ammunition at ground targets, mainly German troops in the battle area.

The pilots and observers of the two corps squadrons, Nos. 5 and 52, flew close above the battle-field from dawn to dusk, reporting the progress of the advance and calling for fire on active German batteries. The R.E.8's of No. 52 Squadron, in addition, three times attacked troop concentrations at Biache St. Vaast on which they dropped a total of one hundred and three 25-lb. bombs. Enemy fighter patrols attempted to interfere from time to time with the work of co-operation, but they were given little scope by the offensive patrol formations of Nos. 40 and 22 Squadrons. During the day, one patrolling Bristol Fighter was shot down, five single-seaters failed to return from their low-flying missions, and three enemy aeroplanes were destroyed.

The head-quarters bombing squadrons did not fly on the 27th because of the unfavourable weather, but nine D.H.4's of No. 18 Squadron, I Brigade, attacked Cantin railhead, south of Douai, as ordered, at 10.30 a.m. from 13,000 feet, and reported bursts on the railhead and dumps.

On the 28th of August the low clouds persisted, and there was, in addition, a ground mist which curtailed the work of co-operation of the corps pilots and observers. Next morning, the 29th, when the weather conditions improved, the head-quarters IX Brigade day-bombing squadrons, heavily escorted, came into action once more with attempted attacks on the stations at Cambrai, Valenciennes, and Somain. Six of twelve D.H.9's which set out for the first-named station turned back with engine trouble, but the others, together with one D.H.4, dropped their bombs from 12,500 feet and one or more started a fire in Cambrai station buildings: enemy fighters who attacked the bombers over the target were driven off. Two D.H.9's of No. 107 Squadron turned back with engine failure after setting out for Valenciennes, but the remainder of the formation, ten in number, bombed the objective and caused a fire to break out. Fifteen Bristol Fighters of No. 62 Squadron who accompanied the bombers had an encounter at long range with a Fokker formation. The attack on Somain, attempted by twelve D.H.9's of No. 98 Squadron with fifteen Sopwith 'Camels' of No. 43 Squadron as escort, was frustrated. As the bombers approached the objective they were assailed by about twenty German fighter pilots. The bombs were dropped at once, but as the D.H.9's turned back a severe engagement began. Two enemy aeroplanes were destroyed by the bombers of No. 98 Squadron and two by Sopwith 'Camels' of No. 43 Squadron, but of the latter, which fought fiercely to protect the bombers, five failed to reach home. It was afterwards known that one of the pilots had been killed in the air, and that the other four, shot down within the enemy lines, had been made prisoners. All the bombers reached the British lines, but one, much shot about, made a forced landing, and another, containing a wounded pilot and a dead observer, fell and was wrecked near Albert. A third D.H.9, which crashed near the front-line trenches with its pilot and observer wounded, had had a remarkable flight. Slight engine trouble had prevented the pilot, Lieutenant J. N. Brown, from keeping formation and he had been pounced upon by a Fokker which shot away the elevator controls of the bomber. The D.H.9 pilot dived, and three or four German aeroplanes dropped down in pursuit. Bullets from them wounded the observer, Second Lieutenant H. Lawrence who, however, kept his gun going and, at 9,000 feet, set one of the enemy fighters on fire and hit another, which began to fall out of control. The D.H.9 was further hit, and when the observer was again wounded and his guns were jammed, the position seemed desperate, but clouds enabled the pilot to elude his remaining adversaries: the D.H.9 crashed near Mory. It would appear that the same German fighters who fought the Somain bombers and their escort had just previously attacked and shot down two D.H.4's from a formation of No. 57 Squadron of the III Brigade at a time when they were bombing the station at Ytres.

On the 30th of August the junction at Valenciennes was again attacked by No. 98 Squadron, some of whose twenty 112-lb. bombs burst in the station sidings. Twelve German Fokkers which attempted to interrupt the bombing were driven off by sixteen escorting S.E.5a's of No. 1 Squadron. On the same day No. 27 Squadron, prevented by heavy clouds from reaching its allotted objective at Solesmes, dropped thirteen 112-lb. bombs on Le Cateau from 13,000 feet without definite result. On the 29th and 30th the low-flying attacks by the single-seater fighters on ground targets in the battle area were continued, but on a reduced scale, and there were bombing attacks, by day and by night, notably on Cantin, Douai, and Pont-à-Vendin. The pilots and observers of the corps squadrons, on these two days, maintained their work of co-operation with the advancing troops.

August had been a disastrous month for the German army. During that month the Royal Air Force played a dominant part among the Allied air services, a part which it was called upon to sustain until the end.[1] The statistics given below

1918	Aeroplanes missing. (all duties).		Bombs dropped (in tons).	
	Br.	Fr.	Br.	Fr.
March	145	24	420	228
April	93	29	444	215
May	128	46	686	530
June	107	64	674	642
July	128	67	577	500
August	215	55	948	550
September	235	59	667	363
October	164	46	654	523

[1] British aircraft production in August did not keep pace with the casualties on the Western front, and some squadrons had to operate below strength. The reason for the shortage was an insufficiency of suitable engines.

for the French and British air services (excluding the Independent Force) are of some interest as indicating the strength of the British effort during the whole period of the heavy fighting on the Western front from March 1918 onwards.

The Drocourt–Quéant Switch

It will be recalled that on the 1st of September the Australians had entered Péronne as a result of their fine feat of the day before when they had rushed the key position of Mont St. Quentin. On the 2nd, while the Fourth Army was taking advantage of this success and was making rapid progress east of Péronne, the First and Third Armies were making their great attack astride the Arras–Cambrai road against the Drocourt–Quéant switch line. The divisions directly concerned at the beginning were the 1st and 4th Canadian and the 4th British, of the Canadian Corps of the First Army, and the 52nd, 57th, and 63rd (Naval), comprising the XVII Corps of the Third Army. Two companies of tanks were allotted to each attacking division with the object of helping the infantry into the Drocourt–Quéant line: they were not to be further employed after the first objective had been captured. An independent force of armoured cars, Canadian motor machine-gun units, and cavalry, which had been highly successful on the Fourth Army front on the 8th of August, was given the task of pushing through the first objective three hours after the assault had been launched and of moving rapidly down the Arras–Cambrai road to secure the important bridge over the Canal du Nord at Marquion, and other bridges in the immediate neighbourhood. The force was to establish a bridge-head astride the Cambrai road, but as soon as the infantry arrived to take over, the mechanical and cavalry units were to go ahead again, if possible to Cambrai.

The work of co-operation of the Royal Air Force was to begin during the night before the attack. The I Brigade F.E.2b night bomber squadron, No. 148, was ordered to bomb the important defended villages of Saudemont, Écourt St. Quentin, and Palluel. The aeroplanes, on their way to and from the objectives, were to be flown over the front where the attack was to take place in order to overpower the noise of the assembling tanks, but the I Brigade was to make such additional arrangements as appeared necessary to maintain aeroplanes over the front line area while the tanks were on the move. The F.E.2b squadron, No. 102, of the III Brigade had similar objectives of billeting villages in front of the Third Army. The night bomber squadrons of the headquarters IX Brigade were given Cambrai (ville) station and the German aerodromes at Étreux and Mont d'Origny.

From the time the attack was launched No. 8 Squadron was, as before, to be responsible for the work of tactical co-operation with the tanks, while No. 73 Squadron had the special duty of offensive action against anti-tank guns. No. 6 Squadron was to co-operate with the cavalry, and Nos. 5 and 52 Squadrons with the attacking divisions, including the independent armoured car force.

The task of the XVII Corps (No. 13 Squadron) of the Third Army was to give the Canadian Corps artillery support, and to advance its own left in order to turn Quéant from the north. The other corps of the Third Army were to act energetically to help the main object, and the operation orders issued by the general officer commanding the III Brigade stated: 'The importance of this 'attack by the First Army cannot be over-estimated and 'the measure of co-operation afforded by III Brigade, 'Royal Air Force, must be in proportion to the importance 'of the attack'.

The day bomber squadrons of the head-quarters IX Brigade, escorted by the fighter squadrons, were to attack, between 6.30 a.m. and 9 a.m., Douai station, Aubigny-au-Bac, Marquion, and certain bridges over the Sensée river. If the weather conditions made it impossible for the attacks to take place before 9 a.m., the objectives were not to be bombed subsequently without reference to Royal Air Force head-quarters. The targets allotted for the afternoon for the head-quarters bombers were the stations at Douai, Cambrai, and Valenciennes.

The II Brigade had orders to extend its offensive patrol

area as far as the Bethune–La Bassée Canal, and the X Brigade to the Arras–Douai road. Each of these two brigades was also to send fighter aircraft at daybreak to attack from low heights an enemy aerodrome on its front.

The army squadrons of the I Brigade were to be employed as in the earlier attack. Low-flying fighters at squadron strength were to leave at dawn (No. 54 Squadron), 5.45 a.m. (No. 208 Squadron), 6.15 a.m. (No. 64 Squadron), and at 7 a.m. (No. 209 Squadron). Their targets were assigned in advance: from zero hour, the time of the opening of the offensive, until three hours afterwards, the main objectives for the low-flying pilots were the defended villages of Saudemont, Écourt St. Quentin, Rumancourt, and the Cambrai road from north of Villers-les-Cagnicourt eastwards to the Canal du Nord, but the pilots were also to attack kite balloons as opportunity offered. During the next three hours, from zero plus 3 to zero plus 6, the attacks were to be made against the Canal du Nord villages of Palluel, Sauchy-Cauchy, and Marquion. In addition, two or three aeroplanes from each formation were to be detached for attacks on trains on the Cantin–Aubigny-au-Bac railway in co-operation with offensive patrols. The general scheme for the employment of the low bombers had been worked out as complementary to the programme arranged for the heavy artillery. Offensive patrols, at two-Flight strength, were to be provided by Nos. 40 and 22 Squadrons, which were to provide protection for the low-flying aircraft, and, in particular, between zero and zero plus 5 hours, were to attack German kite balloons in the area. They had the further task of keeping watch for German aeroplanes which might attempt to attack the independent armoured car force operating along the Cambrai road. The I Brigade day-bombing Squadron, No. 18, was to attack Palluel at 7 a.m. with half its strength, and again at 8 a.m. with the other half. Subsequently the squadron was to concentrate its attacks upon the railway at Aubigny-au-Bac. Contact patrol aeroplanes were to fly over the battle-field to make reports of the general progress of the attack at zero plus $2\frac{1}{2}$ hours, and afterwards at intervals of three hours. The employment of the I Brigade was concerted direct with Canadian Corps head-quarters in accordance with special orders issued by the First Army.

The bombing attacks by No. 148 Squadron against the defended villages opposite the front of the First Army started at 9 p.m. on the 1st of September and were continued until the beginning of the infantry advance next morning. There were clouds and some rain, but many pilots made three journeys, and nearly 300 bombs were dropped: the most apparent result was the explosion of ammunition dumps at Palluel. Night reconnaissance flights were also made by the squadron, covering the whole First Army front, but no enemy movements were reported. The bombing attack on Cambrai was not made as ordered because of the unfavourable weather. No. 207 Squadron, which had been allotted Étreux aerodrome as an objective, was directed instead against Marquion, on which the Handley Pages of the squadron dropped sixty-five 112-lb. and thirty-two 25-lb. bombs.

The Attack
[Map, p. 437]

Zero hour was 5 a.m. on the 2nd of September. The attack achieved a remarkable success, and by noon the whole of the defences of the Drocourt–Quéant system had been captured, from the western outskirts of Cagnicourt to Étaing on the Trinquis brook. Further advance, however, met with stern resistance from machine-gun nests in woods, in Villers-les-Cagnicourt, and on the reverse slopes of the Cagnicourt–Dury ridge: the armoured car force was delayed at the cross-roads north of Villers-les-Cagnicourt. Hard fighting proceeded throughout the day, and by dusk the attacking troops had reached the general line Buissy–Villers-les-Cagnicourt, and Étaing. The supporting attack by the XVII Corps of the Third Army, which had been launched at the same time as the First Army attack, had for its chief object the knot of fortifications at the junction of the Drocourt–Quéant switch with the Hindenburg Line. By the evening of the 2nd the XVII

Corps had captured the knot and was on the line of its final objective well to the east. The 63rd (Naval) Division of this corps lay along the railway, from east of Quéant to the Bois d'Inchy, and the 57th Division was moving on Quéant and Pronville from the north.

The low-bombing attacks on the morning of the 2nd had been begun by seventeen Sopwith 'Camels' of No. 54 Squadron, and the squadrons flew in rotation throughout the day, although at one time in the morning, when there was some overlapping, ninety low-flying single-seater fighters were attacking German infantry, battery, and transport targets in front of the Canadian Corps. The low-flying pilots, five of whom were shot down within the enemy lines, dropped more than 8 tons of bombs (seven hundred and twenty-eight 25-lb.) and fired nearly 50,000 rounds of machine-gun ammunition.

The activity of enemy aircraft was spasmodically intense, and the British co-operating two-seater squadrons attracted attention. In the four corps squadrons on the First Army front, Nos. 5, 6, 8, and 52, four officers were missing and ten returned with wounds: fifteen aeroplanes, missing or wrecked, were struck off the strength of the four squadrons. Stress has occasionally been laid in this history on the value of the reports made by the corps squadron observers, usually obscure junior officers. Opportunities came their way which, if accepted, could, and did, have an important effect upon the military operations. That is to say, the air observers (and the term is used to include pilots whenever they were responsible for making the observations, as they were to an increasing extent in 1918) had scope, especially under the changing conditions of a battle, for the full employment of such initiative, judgement, and experience as they possessed.[1]

[1] It is of interest that in a letter of comment dealing with the Somme battles in 1916, written to the official military historian, a former staff officer called attention to the 'really sublime work by young contact pilots'. 'I remember', he wrote, 'a young pilot whose reports were rendered in 'the writing and spelling of a child of eight (they were beyond all praise in 'other respects) . . . and they constituted on several occasions far the most 'reliable and frequent information we got at 6th Divn. H.Q. He was, of 'course, killed. I remember his name was Scaife.' The author of this history

VALUABLE AIR REPORTS

There was an example, on the 2nd of September on the Third Army front, of a piece of air observation which had results of the kind mentioned. The task of the XVII Corps, as already told, was to assist the First Army attack by taking the triangle of defences at the junction of the Drocourt–Quéant and Hindenburg lines. The left division of the corps, the 57th, was to form immediately behind the right of the 1st Canadian Division and was to follow the waves of that division closely. If the Canadian division penetrated the Drocourt–Quéant line, the 57th Division, going through the gap, was to turn southwards and work its way down the trenches which formed the apex of the Quéant triangle. The 63rd (Naval) Division of the XVII Corps was to follow the 57th Division, pass through the gap in the Drocourt–Quéant line, and push forward in an easterly direction in conformity with the advance made by the 1st Canadian Division on its left. 'The task assigned to '63rd Division', says the XVII Corps war diary, 'demanded 'very careful timing and adjustment.' It was also stated that the orders for the division to push through would be issued by the XVII Corps head-quarters, and that: 'Con- 'tact planes will be sent out by the Corps whose sole duty 'will be to report the progress of the right of the Canadian 'attack and the progress of the 57th Division.' The air observers had orders to drop their messages, by bag, at the dropping-station of the 63rd Division as well as at that of the XVII Corps. Two R.E.8's of No. 13 Squadron (pilots, Captain G. B. Bailey and Lieutenant T. S. Symonds; observers, Lieutenants R. A. B. Pope and A. D. Vaughan) left about 5 a.m. to make the contact patrols as ordered. To obtain their information the two pilots were compelled to fly low down through the barrage of the heavy artillery. 'The reports they dropped at Corps 'head-quarters', reported the officer commanding No. 13 Squadron, 'were concise, accurate, and clear. Relying on 'these reports, the Corps Commander ordered the 63rd 'Division to advance with the result that the Corps

had, some years before the above letter was written, reached a similar conclusion from an independent examination of the official records, and he paid a tribute to Second Lieutenant T. E. G. Scaife in Vol. II, p. 290.

'achieved such success that it was able to capture Quéant, 'Pronville, and Inchy on the following day. On the even-'ing of the 2nd instant the Corps Commander rang me up 'and told me that the success of the operations depended 'very largely indeed on the information obtained from the 'air. . . .'[1]

The spasmodic activity of the German pilots, already referred to, led to a number of encounters, involving the offensive patrols of the III as well as of the I Brigade.[2] There was a bitter engagement which began near Marquion about 9.30 a.m., and in which S.E.5a's, Sopwith 'Camels', and Bristol Fighters fought a large formation of Fokkers and Pfalz Scouts: six aeroplanes were shot down, three from each side. There was another engagement in the same area at 11.50 a.m. which began with a clash between escorted low-flying formations. Ten S.E.5a's of No. 64 Squadron were being escorted by four Bristol Fighters of No. 22 Squadron when about fifteen German fighters in two layers were met. The lower German layer was firing into British advanced positions while the upper formation kept guard. Issue was at once joined, and soon after the fight began nine Sopwith 'Camel' pilots of No. 148 (American) Squadron, who were on offensive patrol, and some R.E.8's of No. 5 Squadron engaged on artillery patrol, became involved, as did additional enemy aircraft. The combats were of a confused kind, during which five German aeroplanes were shot down, three of them by the American pilots. Four of the Sopwith 'Camels' of No. 148 (American) Squadron were shot down in the enemy lines and two others which returned had been so shot about that they had to be rebuilt; an R.E.8 of No. 5 Squadron was damaged in combat and the pilot was compelled to make a forced landing just inside the British line with a wounded observer. The combat

---

[1] The actual reports dropped by the air observers are not included in the relevant war diaries. There is evidence that the Corps Commander, supplementary to the air reports, had some information from the 1st Canadian Division which appeared to show that the Canadians had penetrated the Drocourt–Quéant line.

[2] The fighter squadrons of the I Brigade, as well as Nos. 22 and 40 Squadrons, covered the Canadian corps front.

report of one of the American pilots may be quoted as an example of its kind, and it is also of interest as showing British and American pilots in action together. The report of Lieutenant Elliott W. Springs reads: 'At 11.45 a.m., 'with three machines I attacked four Fokker biplanes on 'the Arras–Cambrai road about four miles south-west of 'Haucourt. Three more came down out of the clouds and 'we were forced to withdraw. Seven more enemy aircraft 'came up from the north-east, and after some manœuvring I 'attacked another enemy aircraft south-east of the road, but 'we, in turn, were attacked by a large number. Succeeded 'in drawing enemy aircraft closer to our lines and went in 'again. Our top flight attacked from above us and a dog-'fight ensued. We were badly outnumbered. Took one 'enemy aircraft off tail of a 'Camel' and was, in turn, 'attacked from above. Saw one enemy aircraft attack an 'R.E.8 and attacked him. Assisted by a Bristol attacked 'another enemy aircraft very low. We succeeded in prevent-'ing enemy aircraft from attacking R.E.8, and eventually 'drove them all east. Enemy aircraft finally disappeared 'in clouds over Cambrai. Very heavy clouds of 4–5,000 'feet, but visibility good underneath. Fokker pilots very 'good, but poor shots. About 25 enemy aircraft seen.'

The total casualties in the I and III Brigades were 36 officers (22 missing and 14 wounded), and the number of aeroplanes deleted from the strength was also 36, of which 18 were missing. Three British balloons were shot down by German pilots.

During the night of the 2nd/3rd of September the German infantry fell back rapidly in front of the right of the First Army and along the whole front of the Third Army. A contact patrol aeroplane of No. 5 Squadron, which was flown at 300 feet over the battle-field early on the 3rd, reported that there were no German troops west of the Canal du Nord, and infantry patrols were consequently pushed rapidly forward on the Canadian Corps front. It was later seen from the air that the enemy was blowing up the bridges over the canal. By the end of the day the British had taken up the general line of the Canal du Nord from Péronne to Ytres, and thence to Hermies,

Inchy-en-Artois, Écourt St. Quentin, and the Sensée river east of Lécluse.

It soon became clear that the Germans intended to stand along the eastern bank of the Canal du Nord, and that a strong attack would be necessary to dislodge them. On the First Army front, therefore, there was a halt in the operations, but farther south the Germans withdrew from the eastern bank of the Somme below Péronne, and the river was crossed by the British Fourth Army and by the French on the 5th of September. By the 8th of September the German line ran from Vermand through Epéhy to Havrincourt, and thence along the eastern bank of the Canal du Nord.

During these days of retirement the German troops and transport were harassed by the low-flying fighter aircraft, particularly on the front of the British Fourth Army. From the 5th of September, however, the low-flying activities of the fighter squadrons were generally curtailed in accordance with orders issued to all brigade commanders by Royal Air Force head-quarters as follows:

'1. Orders have been issued to Armies to press the enemy 'with advanced guards with the object of driving in his 'outposts and rear-guards and ascertaining his dispositions, 'but to undertake no deliberate operations on a large scale 'for the present. Troops are to be rested as far as possible 'and our resources conserved.

'2. The G.O.C. wishes brigadiers to adopt a similar 'policy in the case of the R.A.F. which has now been work-'ing at high pressure for many months. Should the enemy 'adopt an aggressive policy in the air, it will, of course, be 'necessary to continue a vigorous offensive, but, provided he 'keeps well back at a distance behind his lines, the policy of 'seeking out and destroying his machines will be less actively 'pursued and offensive patrol work will be restricted to 'keeping back his artillery and reconnaissance machines 'and enabling ours to do their work.

'3. To carry out the above policy the G.O.C. wishes 'brigadiers to reduce the number of fighting squadrons 'working over the lines to a minimum each day, and to 'take individual squadrons definitely off this work for a day 'or more at a time, during which they will carry out train-'ing only.'

On the night of the 3rd/4th of September the bomber squadrons of the head-quarters IX Brigade had taken a part in the battle with attacks on the stations at Douai, Denain, and Cambrai (ville). On the 4th the head-quarters day bombers had Valenciennes, Douai, and Cambrai (ville) for targets. Escorts for the day bombers were provided by Nos. 32 and 62 Squadrons, and there was fierce fighting during which nine enemy aeroplanes were destroyed and seven British aircraft fell in the German lines.

It was possibly some of the same enemy fighting formations as attacked the bombers and their escorts which took heavy toll of No. 70 Squadron, temporarily attached from the II Brigade for work over the front of the First Army. While engaged on offensive patrol, the squadron met many Fokkers, said to number thirty in all, and in a tense fight, in which the Sopwith 'Camels' were outnumbered, two German and eight British aeroplanes fell, and one among the pilots of No. 70 Squadron who returned was wounded: of the eight pilots who did not get back three died of wounds as prisoners of war.

A survey of the work in the battle of the squadrons co-operating with the First and Third Armies reveals that about eighty per cent. of all the locations made of enemy batteries were obtained through $N.F.$ wireless calls from the pilots and observers of the corps squadrons. These calls were dealt with in the same way as $G.F.$ calls, that is to say they were answered by an intensive fire for five minutes by every British battery in whose normal zone the target was situated. The call was repeated from the air if it was judged that a further burst of fire was desirable. The military war diaries show that seventy-five per cent. of the calls sent down were answered, even though the answers were not always observed from the air, and it is stated in the same diaries that the resultant neutralization of the enemy batteries was very effective. The work of the artillery, as might be expected, was most helpful in the early stages of the advance, but became less so as the advance proceeded, mainly because it was difficult to move guns forward.

From the reports of the contact patrol observers it is clear that too few flares were lighted. In order to obtain information which could be relied upon, pilots had to fly low enough for their observers to recognize the nationality of the troops below. It would also appear that it had not been found possible to supply the infantry, as an aid to identification, with a sufficient number of white linings for the flaps of the gas-mask haversack. In one corps, which was unprovided with these linings, the advancing troops, when their flares had been exhausted, made use of the lids of their mess tins to indicate the positions they had reached, an improvised method of signalling which proved of value. There can be little doubt that flares, no matter how suitable in theory, did not give the desired results in battle. The infantry could not put away a belief that flares were revealing to the enemy, and this was a view with which the Royal Air Force had some sympathy because there were occasions when the British air observers were enabled to plot German forward positions by noting flares lighted in response to calls from German aeroplanes. It seemed fairly agreed that a white lining, with a tin disk attached, in the flap of the gas-mask haversack, would provide the best means of identification during battle. This method had the advantage that the already burdened infantry would not be called upon to carry additional equipment, and that the gas-mask flap was at hand ready for use at any time.

The information in the messages and maps dropped by the contact patrol observers proved to be of a high general degree of accuracy, but there was an occasional tendency to show more than was seen. This arose from an attempt to link observations, by inference, in order to depict a rough line, presumably a result of inexperience of warfare of the kind being fought in which, in the words of Sir Douglas Haig's telegram, it was 'no longer 'necessary to advance in regular lines and step by step'.[1] It was impressed strongly upon the officers of the corps squadrons that they must not report anything which they did not unmistakably see.

[1] See p. 473.

AMMUNITION BY PARACHUTE

There were many calls, generously answered, from the infantry during the battle, for ammunition to be dropped by parachute. Stress was laid upon the future need for a strict economy in this method of employing aircraft because aeroplanes so used were diverted from offensive work. It was justifiable only in emergency when ammunition could not be transported to forward troops by other means, and those concerned were requested to resist any tendency to call for deliveries of ammunition by parachute mainly because the aeroplane was a speedier alternative means of transport.

The work of the artillery and counter-attack patrols was closely co-ordinated, together with that of the low-flying fighting aircraft, by the Central Information Bureau. The wireless signals from the air calling for fire on enemy fleeting targets were passed to the counter-battery staff officer who took immediate action on those messages which could be dealt with by artillery fire, and transmitted the remainder by wireless to the army wing head-quarters for such action as the wing commander judged necessary. If the counter-battery staff officer received information about enemy movements from sources other than the air, he himself sent a message to the army wing commander.

While the advance was in progress the positions of the German batteries changed, and no attempts were therefore made to photograph the counter-battery area. In this period, however, there were many demands for oblique photographs picturing the lie of the ground in front of the advancing infantry, and prints were often dropped at divisional dropping-stations, usually within about four hours of the photographs being taken. In order that air casualties which might interrupt or lead to delays in important work should be known, artillery and contact patrol pilots had instructions to make a routine call to the Central Wireless Station (where usually the Central Information Bureau was established) every half hour. If the call ceased the squadron commander could assume that the aeroplane had for some reason been forced down, and judge whether he must at once send another aeroplane to complete the task.

The Battle of Havrincourt and Epéhy

[Map, p. 437]

In advance of the Hindenburg line of defences there were positions about Havrincourt and Epéhy which it was necessary to capture before the main system could be assaulted. Preliminary operations were opened by the IV and VI Corps of the Third Army on Thursday, the 12th of September, and they ended on the 17th along a line stretching roughly from Gouzeaucourt on the left to Holnon on the right.

While these preparatory actions were taking place rain and poor general visibility curtailed flying. On the 15th of September, during a temporary improvement in the weather conditions, the German pilots made many concerted attacks upon British balloons along the fronts of the First and Third Armies, by which six balloons were destroyed and four damaged. In reply the Royal Air Force shot down three German balloons in flames and damaged three more. It is possible that the German attacks were themselves in retaliation for an episode which had taken place on the previous day. Six balloons of No. 1 Balloon Wing on the First Army front had been destroyed under conditions which made it appear that the same German pilot was concerned, and it had been decided to set a trap for him similar to one which had been successfully employed in November 1917 on the Macedonian front.[1] Five hundred pounds of high explosive were packed in a balloon basket, and on the 14th of September when the balloon, so loaded, was attacked in the air, the charge was fired electrically, but although the German aeroplane was thrown into a spin by the force of the explosion the pilot was able to regain control near the ground and return to his lines.

In further reply to the enemy activity, aerodromes opposite the front of the First and Third Armies were attacked. In the afternoon of the 15th of September, ten S.E.5a pilots of No. 56 Squadron dropped 34 bombs of 25-lb. weight on the aerodrome at Estourmel, south-east of

---

[1] See Vol. V, pp. 361-2.

Cambrai, and fired 1,800 rounds into the hangars from low heights. It was reported that a hangar was destroyed in flames, that a direct hit wrecked a shed, and that four hits were made on the officers' quarters.

On the 16th of September activity in the air was again intermittently intense, and reconnaissance flights were made by enemy aeroplanes over the back areas of the British Third Army. Many combats resulted and eight German aeroplanes were destroyed, four of them in flames, while four British fell within the enemy lines. Next day, the 17th, Nos. 64 and 209 Squadrons, escorted by Bristol Fighters of No. 22 Squadron, attacked the German aerodrome at Emerchicourt. The attack was made from a low height and about 100 light-weight bombs were dropped and 4,500 rounds of machine-gun ammunition fired: bombs fell among aeroplanes on the landing-ground and also caused fires in aerodrome buildings and tents. A Sopwith 'Camel' of No. 209 Squadron and an S.E.5a of No. 64 Squadron failed to return.

The main attack against the Epéhy and Havrincourt positions was opened by the British Fourth and Third Armies at 7 a.m. on the 18th of September along the front of about seven miles from Holnon to Gouzeaucourt, with the French First Army acting in co-operation south of Holnon. A few tanks were employed in the attack, which took place in heavy rain, and an advance of about three miles was made through the well-organized defensive belt formed by the old British and German trench systems. On the extreme right, and in the left centre about Epéhy, the enemy resistance was determined, but by nightfall on the 18th, after bitter fighting, this resistance had been largely overcome: local action during the following days secured all the remaining points which it was necessary to hold before the Hindenburg defence system could be assaulted.

The night had been fine, with a clear moon until 1 a.m. on the 18th, and Nos. 101 and 102 Squadrons made many bombing attacks on defended villages opposite the Fourth and Third Armies. German pilots were also active against the British lines of communication, but many were intercepted by single-seater fighter pilots of No. 151 Squadron who destroyed three of the bombers.[1]

Rain set in before dawn on the 18th and the clouds were low. The main feature of the day's flying was a determined attempt to assist the artillery, and many wireless calls for fire on active hostile batteries, and upon troops and transport, were answered. Attacks planned to take place on enemy aerodromes and upon the railway junctions of Busigny and Bohain could not be made. The weather was poor again on the 19th, but on the 20th bright intervals brought strong formations of German fighters into the air and there was one protracted encounter on the Fourth Army front which involved about twenty Fokker biplanes and seven Bristol Fighters of No. 20 Squadron with eleven S.E.5a's of No. 84 Squadron. Eight of the German fighters were destroyed, six of them by the Bristol Fighters, two of which were also lost. The German air service was again very active on the 24th, and on the whole British front eighteen enemy aeroplanes were destroyed in combat, six of them falling to No. 148 American Squadron, and five to No. 17 American Squadron.

Brigadier-General C. A. H. Longcroft, commanding the III Brigade, issued instructions on the 22nd of September which may be quoted for the light they throw upon the tactical employment of fighter aeroplanes at this period. 'The present policy of the enemy air patrols on this front', he said, 'seems to be to put very strong patrols (20 to 40 'machines) into the air at varying periods during the day 'with a view to making offensive demonstrations and 'occasionally attacking small patrols of our machines when 'obviously at a disadvantage. This system makes the work 'of our small patrols difficult, as either they are not in 'sufficient strength to attack the enemy or no enemy are 'found in the air to attack. In order to deal with this

[1] No. 151 Squadron had been relieved of its specific responsibility for the defence of Abbeville on the 14th of September, and from that time onwards it operated at night over the forward areas, newly provided with a searchlight barrier system, of the British First, Third, and Fourth Armies. The idea was that a barrier system in the forward areas provided general protection for all the localities in the rear at a less cost in equipment than if each important centre was given a separate defence. See pp. 428-9.

'situation the following policy in carrying out offensive 'patrols will be adopted:

'(*a*) Offensive patrols will normally consist of two or 'more fighting squadrons. The same squadrons should 'work together whenever possible, and the patrol should 'be comprised of an S.E.5 or "Dolphin" squadron above, 'with one or more "Camel" squadrons below.

'(*b*) Squadrons will always be divided into flight forma-'tions working at varying heights.

'(*c*) Squadrons above are responsible for keeping in 'touch with the squadron immediately below. The leader 'of the lowest squadron is the leader of the whole patrol.

'(*d*) The primary object of each patrol is to find and 'attack enemy formations in the air. The lowest squadron 'is responsible for initiating the attack. During periods 'of slight enemy activity, "Camel" squadrons should carry 'bombs with a view to carrying out attacks on hostile aero-'dromes, and if the air seems clear of the enemy the leader 'of the formation may initiate an attack on an aerodrome by 'firing a "Very" light signal. Certain aerodromes should 'be told off to each formation and photographs supplied to 'squadrons concerned. These attacks will be carried out 'by bombing and machine-gun fire from the "Camels", the 'S.E.5's or "Dolphins" being held responsible for warding 'off attacks by hostile machines. When bombs are being 'carried by "Camels", but an opportunity occurs of attack-'ing a hostile formation, the "Camels" should release their 'bombs over the enemy country before initiating the attack.

'(*e*) The duties of the various sub-formations of a patrol 'are as follows:

'(i) Top sub-formation will watch the upper air and 'is responsible that the formation is not surprised.

'(ii) The lowest sub-formation (as stated in (*d*) above) 'is responsible for initiating attacks and will search 'for hostile formations below or on the same level.

'(iii) Intermediate sub-formations will ensure that no 'hostile machines dive below them without being 'attacked.'

While the operations were in progress on the Epéhy and Havrincourt front the Royal Air Force co-operated also with Allied attacks elsewhere. On the 12th of September, the day the preliminary movements began on the Third Army front, the First American Army, assisted by French divisions, had opened the offensive which drove the Germans, with heavy losses, from the St. Mihiel Salient. Marshal Foch had requested bombing help from the Royal Air Force to which he had allotted targets in the area Valenciennes–Le Cateau–Busigny. The French air service would, he said, attend to the sector St. Quentin–Mézières and the neighbourhood of Conflans, and the Independent Force would temporarily divert its attention to specific objectives on the Lorraine front. The bombing was timed to begin on the night of the 12th/13th of September, but the weather made this impossible and it was not until the next night that the bombers of the Royal Air Force head-quarters IX Brigade were able to go out. The Handley Pages of No. 207 Squadron, which flew through heavy rain, attacked Le Cateau station with one 1,650-lb. bomb, forty-eight 112-lb. and thirty 25-lb. bombs. No. 83 Squadron had to turn back from an attempt to bomb Busigny station on account of the weather, which again made operations impossible on the following night.

Marshal Foch had told Sir Douglas Haig on the 12th of September that he possessed information which showed a German intention to attack Paris with large numbers of small incendiary bombs. Every available German bombing aeroplane would be employed, and after Paris had been dealt with the Germans would turn their attention to London. As a result of this information General Pétain had arranged to bomb the aerodromes of the German Nos. 2 and 4 Night-Bombing Squadrons, and Marshal Foch asked that the Royal Air Force should be instructed to attack Étreux aerodrome, which housed No. 1 Bombing Squadron, and other night bomber landing-grounds in the neighbourhood of Cambrai and St. Quentin. Major-General J. M. Salmond subsequently pointed out that the only aerodrome in the area of Cambrai–St. Quentin known to accommodate night bombers was Bazuel, east of Le Cateau, which would be attacked by the Royal Air Force in addition to Étreux. The aerodrome at St. Maur, south of Tournai, which also housed night bombers, would form a third objective. The bombing of the three aerodromes, Étreux, Bazuel, and St. Maur, was begun on the night of the 15th/16th of September by Nos. 58, 83, and 207 Squadrons, and was continued on subsequent nights.[1]

[1] The information received by Marshal Foch was true in substance, but the Kaiser had given an order in August, 'on humanitarian grounds', that the attacks with incendiary bombs must not take place. See p. 455.

CHAPTER XIV
VICTORY

Breaking the Hindenburg Line

[Maps, pp. 437, 550, and at end]

By the 24th of September the British and French armies, from the Scarpe to the Oise, were close against the last of the German organized defence lines. In Macedonia, in Palestine, and in Mesopotamia the enemy resistance was already fast crumbling. The time had arrived for a final supreme effort on the Western front in order to end the war before the winter. The only comfort which the Germans might draw in the west was from the vaunted impregnability of the Hindenburg Line, a 'granite wall' as it was termed, against which the Allied Armies might be expected to batter in vain.

The plans of Marshal Foch, made after consultation with the British and American commanders, provided for four convergent Allied attacks to be made simultaneously. The Americans, under General Pershing, were to push west of the Meuse in the direction of Mézières; the French, under General Gouraud, were to attack west of Argonne in close co-operation with the Americans and with the same general objective; the British were to attack on the St. Quentin–Cambrai front in the direction of Maubeuge; and the Belgians, together with the British left (Second Army), under the general command of His Majesty the King of the Belgians, were to advance in Flanders in the direction of Ghent.

The valley of the Meuse, down which the Americans and the French must move towards Mézières, was difficult ground for military operations, and this area of wooded uplands and masked valleys, naturally formidable, together with the Hindenburg defensive zone, constituted the main problems of the Western front. If the Meuse attack succeeded the German troops would be forced back towards the broken and heavily wooded country of the Ardennes, and, if the British offensive was likewise successful, the enemy lines of communication, by which retreat must be effected, would be threatened and the German armies on the Western front would face disaster. The object of the attack to be made in Flanders was to clear the Belgian coast and to complicate the enemy retirement.

Between St. Quentin and the village of Bantouzelle, opposite the British, the main Hindenburg defences lay partly to the west, but more generally to the east of the line of the canal de St. Quentin. The positions on the west bank of the canal had been skilfully chosen specially to deny to the attackers any effective artillery support. The line of the canal offered natural shelter to the outpost garrisons during a bombardment, and the Germans had made the cover ingeniously effective. The sides of the deep cutting along which the canal ran north of Vendhuille had been studded with dug-outs and concrete shelters, and on the top edges of the cutting there were concealed armoured machine-gun emplacements. Between Vendhuille and Bellicourt the canal passed for 6,000 yards through a tunnel which provided living accommodation for the troops, who could rapidly move by way of shafts to the trenches above ground. South of Bellicourt the cutting became shallow, and at Bellenglise the canal was at ground level. Parallel with the canal about a mile on the western side, south of Bellicourt, ran two intricately organized defence lines, heavily wired. Except in the tunnel sector the double line of trenches forming the Hindenburg Line proper lay immediately east of the canal, but they were linked with the lines to the west of the canal by numerous communication trenches. There was a multitude of subsidiary defences, and the whole zone, east of which lay open country, was about five miles deep.

On the evening of the 26th of September, between St. Quentin and the Sensée river, the British Fourth, Third, and First Armies, in the order named, held a line running from the village of Selency, through Gricourt and Pontruet, east of Villaret and Lempire to Villers Guislain and Gouzeaucourt, northwards to Havrincourt and Mœuvres, and thence along the west side of the Canal du Nord to the flooded country of the Sensée river at Écourt St. Quentin.

On the front of the First and Third Armies the Germans

held strong positions covering the approaches to Cambrai between the Nord and the Schelde[1] canals, including a section of the Hindenburg Line itself north of Gouzeaucourt. The enemy trenches in this sector faced south-west, looking towards the area in which the preparations for the main attack on the Hindenburg Line were taking place, and it was desirable that the northern defences should be captured in the early stages of the operation in order to make it easier for the artillery of the Fourth Army to get into position. On the Fourth Army front, where the main blow was to fall, the fortress-like strength of the German positions made a prolonged artillery bombardment necessary.

Sir Douglas Haig decided to open a general bombardment along the front of all three armies during the night of the 26th/27th of September, and to attack on the First and Third Army fronts on the morning of the 27th. In this way the enemy might be puzzled to know where the main blow would fall, while the First and Third Armies would be enabled to get nearer to their final objectives and, in doing so, make the task of the Fourth Army easier. Meanwhile, on the morning of the 26th, the American and French attack had opened down the Meuse.

Air Plans

From right to left of the whole British line the Royal Air Force Brigades with the armies were:

Fourth Army	V Brigade
(Gen. Sir H. S. Rawlinson)	(Brig.-Gen. L. E. O. Charlton)
Third Army	III Brigade
(Gen. the Hon. Sir J. H. P. Byng)	(Brig.-Gen. C. A. H. Longcroft)
First Army	I Brigade
(Gen. Sir H. S. Horne)	(Brig.-Gen. D. Le G. Pitcher)
Fifth Army	X Brigade
(Gen. Sir W. R. Birdwood)	(Brig.-Gen. E. R. Ludlow-Hewitt)
Second Army	II Brigade
(Gen. Sir H. C. O. Plumer)	(Brig.-Gen. T. I. Webb-Bowen)

The northern advance into Belgium involved, in addition to the Belgian and French air services in that area,

---

[1] The Schelde is also known as the Canal de L'Escaut.

the II Brigade and the Fifth Group (Dunkirk) units of the Royal Air Force. The bombing strength of the Independent Air Force in the south was to be employed in support of the American and French offensive down the Meuse.[1] The head-quarters IX Brigade (Brigadier-General R. E. T. Hogg) was to be employed as required.

It was in the area of the Hindenburg Line that the main British air strength was concentrated. The V Brigade with the Fourth Army was increased before the battle to a total of seventeen squadrons, representing 337 aeroplanes. The III Brigade with the Third Army had fifteen squadrons, plus one Flight, or 261 aeroplanes, and the I Brigade with the First Army had twelve squadrons plus two Flights, or 236 aeroplanes. The attack in the area of the Hindenburg Line also had the support of the thirteen squadrons of the IX Brigade (224 aeroplanes).

Thus for the operations officially known as the Battle of Cambrai and the Hindenburg Line, the three British Armies concerned had the immediate support (excluding help from the flanks) of 1,058 aeroplanes,[2] namely 27 fighter squadrons, 4 fighter-reconnaissance squadrons, 7 day bomber, 6 night bomber, and 13 corps squadrons, plus 3 Flights.

The advance of the First and Third Armies on the 27th of September was to be made along the thirteen miles of front from Gouzeaucourt to the neighbourhood of Sauchy-Lestrée in the general direction of Cambrai. The northern section of the Canal du Nord constituted an obstacle too formidable to be crossed by direct assault, and it was therefore necessary for the attacking divisions to force a passage on the narrow front about Mœuvres, and afterwards to spread fanwise. The main task was again allotted to the Canadian Corps which was to have the co-operation of the XXII and XVIII Corps of the First Army on its left. The XVII and IV Corps of the Third Army were to attack on the right.

The success of the operations depended upon the ability of the Canadians to secure the crossings in the neighbour-

---

[1] See pp. 148–9.
[2] One hundred and thirty-five of these were shown as temporarily unserviceable on the opening day of the battle.

hood of Mœuvres. After making the passage of the canal, the Canadian Corps was to capture the Marquion line of defences, and Bourlon village and wood, and to secure the general line Fontaine–Notre-Dame–Sauchicourt farm–the railway crossings over the Canal du Nord. From this line the operations were to be developed without delay to capture the high ground about Sailly–Haynecourt–Épinoy–Oisy-le-Verger. The eventual objective of the Canadian Corps was the general line Morenchies–Blécourt–a factory east of the Épinoy–road to Aubencheul-au-Bac.

The Corps squadrons concerned in the attack were:

Canadian Corps	No. 5 Squadron
XXII Corps	„ 52 Squadron
XVII Corps	„ 13 Squadron
VI Corps	„ 12 Squadron
IV Corps	„ 59 Squadron.

On the front of the Canadian Corps No. 5 Squadron was to send out contact patrol aeroplanes at zero plus 2, plus $4\frac{1}{2}$, plus $6\frac{1}{4}$, and plus $8\frac{1}{2}$ hours, and thereafter at intervals of three hours. On the left of the Canadian Corps No. 52 Squadron was to report the general position on the front of the XXII Corps at intervals of three hours from daylight to zero plus 6 hours, and subsequently was to arrange for special reports as follows:

(a) the situation at zero plus 6 hours, in particular whether the Canadians on the right of the XXII Corps had reached their third objective between the Canal du Nord and Sauchicourt Farm;

(b) the situation at zero plus 9 hours, whether the attacks by the 56th and 11th Divisions had begun, and

(c) the situation at zero plus 11 hours, the progress of the attacks by the 56th and 11th Divisions.

One aeroplane of No. 52 Squadron was to be in the air all day to watch for enemy counter-attacks, and additionally there were to be three aeroplanes over the front without intermission to report active hostile batteries and other targets to the artillery in accordance with arrangements made directly between the squadron and the General Officer Commanding the Royal Artillery of the XXII Corps.

Extracts from the detailed orders issued by the XVII Corps of the Third Army, on the right of the Canadian Corps, for contact patrol work required of No. 13 Squadron are worthy of quotation as illustrating the careful staff work of the period, and because they show how it was possible to simplify the task of the air observers and consequently to increase the chances of good results. The orders stated that the aeroplanes of No. 13 Squadron would call upon the infantry to light flares, or otherwise obtain information, in accordance with the following particulars.

(i) At zero plus 90 minutes (1½ hours)

The reply to this call will let commanders know how much of the Hindenburg Support Line, the Canal, Hindenburg Front Line, and Leopard Avenue is definitely in our possession.

(ii) At zero plus 140 minutes (2 hours 20 minutes)

At this hour the left division (63rd) should be on the 2nd objective in E.23a and the right along Tiger Trench in E.28a. The right division (52nd) should possess the whole of the Hindenburg Front line and the Canal, be established in Lion Trench (E. 27), and possibly have commenced mopping up the area east of the Canal in E. 27c and d and K. 3b.

(iii) At zero plus 270 minutes (4½ hours)

At approximately this hour our troops should be generally on the line of the 2nd objective, having captured Graincourt and Annexus.

(iv) At zero plus 300 minutes (5 hours)

The 57th Division is due to pass through the 63rd Division on the 2nd objective, both from the direction of Graincourt and Annexus, at zero plus 290 minutes. The contact plane will watch the movements of this division and report its progress at zero plus 360 minutes.

(v) At zero plus 500 minutes

Flares will be called for from the 3rd objective.
If, from previous reports, it seems very improbable that the 3rd objective will be captured on 'Z' day, the O/C Squadron will ask Corps for instructions regarding this plane.

From zero plus 2 hours onwards throughout the day No. 13 Squadron was, in addition, to arrange for low-flying aeroplane patrols to report the possible developments of hostile counter-attacks, and to give information of fleeting targets to the artillery. The air observers of the squadron were to warn the British infantry, directly concerned, of counter-attack movements by means of magnesium 'wing tip' flares and by dropping a red smoke bomb in the area where it was seen that the enemy troops were assembling or attacking.

Arrangements somewhat similar in kind were made for the other corps squadrons, while No. 8 Squadron settled the details of co-operation direct with the tank battalion.

Low-flying Attacks

There were different schemes in the two Brigades for the employment of low-flying aircraft. The I Brigade with the First Army adopted an organization similar to that which had been in force for the earlier attacks. That is, five squadrons (Nos. 40, 54, 64, 203, and 209), immediately after their first morning patrol, were to concentrate on the aerodrome at Le Hameau under the orders of Major B. E. Smythies of No. 64 Squadron. The main objectives for low-flying attacks were the crossings over the Senseé and de L'Escaut canals, and in particular the crossings at Fressies, Hem-Lenglet, and Wasnes au Bac. Pilots were instructed to fly in an easterly direction along the Sensée canal, and on returning to wheel south between Wasnes au Bac and Paillencourt and attack any enemy troops and guns seen retiring east and north-east to the line Fressies–Abancourt–Bantigny–Ramillies: special attention was to be paid to the road and valley between Wasnes au Bac and Bantigny. The pilots were also told it was important that enemy balloons should be kept down from zero to zero plus 5 hours, and they were to attack them so far as it was possible to do so.

On the Third Army front only one squadron, No. 201 (Sopwith 'Camel'), was ordered to make low-flying attacks. Whereas on the First Army front the low-flying pilots were given special tactical objectives, those of No. 201

squadron were told, for their first patrol, to watch the advance and assist as they could, and to pay particular attention to any strong points which might be holding up the attack. After the first patrol had been completed the squadron was, during the remainder of the day, to operate from an advanced landing-ground in accordance with information of favourable targets received through the Central Information Bureau.

Offensive Patrols

The First Army offensive formations, to be provided by Nos. 19 and 22 Squadrons, were to patrol between 4,000 and 8,000 feet to protect the low-flying aircraft and day bombers,[1] and were also to attack German aeroplanes and balloons in the area of operations. The squadrons were to fly in company as one large formation and go out at stated times, namely 6 a.m., 11.30 a.m., and 5 p.m. This scheme for putting the full strength of the two squadrons into the air at definite times was presumably influenced by the German policy of mass employment of fighters, but if this was so it might have been more profitable if the squadrons had been ordered to stand by ready to go up on receipt of a warning that the German fighting formations were in the air.

On the Third Army front Nos. 3 and 56 squadrons were to leave the ground at dawn to attack enemy kite balloons and were subsequently to fly on offensive patrol. At 7.30 a.m. No. 148 American (Sopwith 'Camel') Squadron and No. 60 (S.E.5a) Squadron were to set out on offensive patrol, but the American pilots were to carry bombs and fly below the British S.E.5a's in order to attack suitable ground targets, particularly any which might be seen approaching the crossings of the Canal de l'Escaut. At 8.30 a.m. No. 17 American Squadron, carrying bombs, and No. 87 Squadron, were to fly in company on a similar mission. It was ordered in each instance that when specially good targets were seen the bombers were to make their attacks from

[1] No. 18 Squadron was to make three attacks on Wasnes au Bac while the offensive patrols were in the air.

a low height. Afterwards, the squadrons were to fly together on ordinary offensive patrol. No. 11 Squadron was in addition ordered to provide offensive patrols at the maximum possible squadron strength. The day bomber squadron, No. 57, attached to the Third Army was allotted the target of Rumilly and certain German head-quarters.

The Head-quarters IX Brigade

The night bombers of the head-quarters brigade were ordered to attack the stations at Denain (No. 58 Squadron), Busigny (No. 83 Squadron), and Le Cateau (No. 207 Squadron) during the night preceding the attack, and to reconnoitre the area Lille–Tournai–Valenciennes–Douai (No. 58 Squadron) and Cambrai–Le Cateau–Busigny–Wassigny–St. Quentin (No. 83 Squadron). On the opening morning of the attack the allotted objectives were the enemy aerodromes at Emerchicourt, Bévillers, and Bertry, but for the afternoon the targets were the stations at Denain and Le Cateau. Offensive patrols were to be sent out in conjunction with the daylight bombing attack at the discretion of the brigade commander. No. 25 Squadron was made responsible for strategical reconnaissances and for photography.

The Battle of the Canal du Nord
[Map, p. 511]

At 5.30 a.m. on the 27th of September, just when it was light, the First and Third Armies went into action along the thirteen miles of front from Sauchy–Lestrée to Gouzeaucourt. The attack progressed according to plan. By the end of the day the troops were everywhere across the canal du Nord, and were close upon the Schelde canal south of Cambrai: ten thousand prisoners and 200 guns had been left in British hands. Next day, the 28th, the advance was continued and Gouzeaucourt, Marcoing, Noyelles-sur-l'Escaut, Fontaine-Notre-Dame, Sailly, and Palluel were taken. At Marcoing, after a severe struggle, troops of the VI Corps of the Third Army established themselves on the eastern bank of the Schelde canal. Cambrai was now threatened from two sides and could no longer be used as a railhead.

Although the sky was clear when the attack started on the morning of the 27th, rain had been falling during most of the preceding night. The night bombers of the III Brigade had nevertheless attacked the allotted objectives of German head-quarters on the Third Army front, while No. 83 Squadron of the head-quarters IX Brigade had bombed the station at Busigny.

At 5.50 a.m. on the 27th, twenty minutes after the infantry advance had begun, the aeroplanes of the corps squadrons were flying over the battle reporting those enemy batteries which were active. They also reported many known batteries which had become silent—information of value because it enabled the British counter-batteries to switch their fire to other targets. The task of observation was made difficult by smoke screens and by exploding shells. Many calls to the artillery sent out by the air observers were promptly answered, and as a result some German guns were put out of action and infantry concentrations were dispersed. The contact patrol aeroplanes flew according to programme, and their written reports and marked maps kept the corps staffs informed of the general progress of the attack. The pilot and observer in one contact patrol aeroplane of No. 13 Squadron, who were making a call for flares to be lighted on the XVII Corps front at 6 p.m. on the 27th, saw German infantry forming for a counter-attack in the neighbourhood of Anneux. An S.O.S. call was sent by wireless to the artillery and, in addition, wing-tip flares were lighted and a smoke bomb dropped among the enemy troops, in accordance with the prearranged scheme. The warning was correctly interpreted by the 63rd Division and by the forward troops of the 57th Division. A protective barrage was put down by the artillery and this, coupled with machine-gun and rifle fire, broke up the attempted German attack.

A pilot and observer of the same squadron had had an adventure over the same part of the front a little earlier in the evening. While engaged on artillery and counter-attack patrol they had dived upon a party of about thirty Germans huddled together in a trench, but just when the pilot was about to press the lever to bring his machine-gun into action some one had waved a white handkerchief from the trench. The pilot withheld his fire as he shot past the mark, and then returned to dive again, and this time handkerchiefs fluttered from the whole party. The pilot thereupon flew back to the nearest British troops, a few hundred yards away, and, from close above them, waved his arms to indicate that they should go forward to the German position. His signs were understood and the British infantry, who belonged to 'B' Company of the *Hawke* Battalion of the 63rd (Naval) Division, moved forward and took the German party prisoners while the aeroplane flew overhead ready to intervene at any sign of a change of mind.

The main air offensive against the German troops on the First Army front was made by the five fighter squadrons specially allotted to low-flying attacks under the general command of Major B. E. Smythies, who himself accompanied attacking formations twice in the afternoon. Seven hundred 25-lb. bombs were dropped by the single-seater pilots of these five squadrons and some 26,000 rounds of machine-gun ammunition were fired, the main targets being troops and transport on or near the bridges across the Sensée and Schelde canals. The object of the attacks, it will be recalled, was to deny as far as possible the use of the crossings to the enemy, and there can be no doubt that the moral as well as the material effect of the low-flying offensive was important. In addition to these attacks by the single-seaters, two high bombing raids each were made by No. 18 Squadron of the I Brigade and by No. 103 Squadron of the X Brigade on Wasnes au Bac.

On the Third Army front, where the low-flying single-seater pilots flew in Flights instead of squadrons, the attacks were co-ordinated with the movements of the advancing infantry and tanks, but they were rather more spasmodic than on the First Army front in the sense that the pilots in general attacked troops and transport at their discretion. There were, however, occasions when targets were definitely allotted, notably in the afternoon and evening when the low-flying attacks were directed against positions in the village of Gonnelieu and at Cantaing which were holding up the advance.

The day bombers of the head-quarters IX Brigade, closely escorted, attacked the German aerodromes at Ermerchicourt, Bévillers, and Bertry, and some intensive fighting resulted, during which it was claimed that five German aeroplanes were destroyed and many sent down out of control. Elsewhere on the front throughout the day the German pilots were intermittently active, usually in large formations, one of which, in the morning, flew low and made machine-gun attacks upon forward troops of the 63rd Naval Division.

During the night of the 27th/28th of September the clouds were low again, and there was rain, but bombing attacks were made against the enemy railway communications. The most notable were directed against the junction at Busigny, on which more than six tons of bombs were dropped by the Handley Pages of No. 207 Squadron. The night flyers reported an almost continuous stream of transport along the road between Beauvois and Cambrai, and much transport also on the roads from Le Cateau to Bavai: Cambrai station was seen to be burning, as was Rumilly where the fire had been started by air bombing.

The weather continued to be poor on the 28th, the second day of the advance, but the aeroplanes were out early over the active front. As an example of a valuable piece of co-operation work the activities of a contact patrol aeroplane of No. 13 Squadron may be noted. Captain G. B. Bailey and Lieutenant J. W. G. Clark of this squadron had been instructed to report upon the progress made by the 57th Division in its advance towards the Schelde canal. At first the division had made rapid progress, but it had subsequently been held for a time by stubborn enemy resistance near the villages of Cantaing and Fontaine Notre Dame. Soon after 10 a.m. this resistance had been overcome, and by 11 a.m. the division was moving steadily towards the canal. Captain Bailey and Lieutenant Clark were at this time reconnoitring the area from a height of 400 feet, and they came to the conclusion that the Germans had withdrawn to a line east of the canal and that it was no longer necessary for the 57th Division to feel its way forward. They therefore dropped a message upon the forward troops of the division telling them they would encounter no opposition west of the canal, and urging that they should press on at once. The aeroplane was then flown over the divisional report centre where a message was dropped to tell of what had been done. When the officers returned to the line they found that the 57th Division had accelerated its rate of progress: it quickly reached the canal, but the enemy had already blown up the bridges, and as most of the immediately available bridging material had been used to bridge the Canal du Nord, leaving little for the Schelde canal, the 57th Division could not pursue the enemy beyond the canal line. Before they left the battle-field the two officers of No. 13 Squadron took photographs of the locks and crossings over the canal, and when the plates were developed the extent of the damage at each crossing was disclosed, and it was also revealed where material was lying which might be used for the repair of the bridges.

There was an incident worthy of record on the 28th of September. Captain D. H. M. Carbery (observer, Lieutenant J. B. V. Clements) set out in an R.E.8 of No. 59 Squadron at 6.5 a.m. to make a counter-attack patrol. At 7.15 a.m., while flying over the front, the officers saw a limbered gun which was being galloped away, and when their call for fire to the British artillery went unanswered they dropped four 25-lb. bombs on the limbers which were hit and disabled. The pilot then attacked the gun crew with machine-gun fire, inflicting casualties on them, and on the horses, with the result that the gun was left in the road. The British infantry subsequently advanced and took charge of the gun, which was presented to the Royal Air Force as a trophy.[1]

The low-flying attacks on the 28th of September on the First Army front were confined to the three Sopwith 'Camel' Squadrons (Nos. 54, 203, and 209). The two

[1] The gun is in the possession of the Royal Air Force College, Cranwell.

S.E.5a squadrons, Nos. 40 and 64, which had been allotted on the first day to low bombing, were employed on the 28th on offensive patrols with orders to pay special attention to the enemy observation balloons, but neither the German pilots nor balloon personnel were very active and the offensive patrols were made with little incident. The low-flying attacks on the 28th by the Sopwith 'Camels' were mainly directed to the neighbourhood of the canal crossings. During one of these attacks in the evening ten pilots of No. 209 Squadron discovered a large enemy column of troops and transport on the Cambrai–Le Cateau road. The pilots concentrated their attacks upon the column from a low height, dropping thirty-six bombs and firing some thousands of rounds of machine-gun ammunition, as a result of which the column was thrown into confusion.

The D.H.4 day bomber squadron, No. 18, attached to the First Army, was employed on the 28th on photographic duties over the country east and north-east of Cambrai. On the Third Army front No. 57 Squadron attacked a German head-quarters at Awoingt, south-east of Cambrai, while No. 49 Squadron of the head-quarters IX Brigade bombed Rieux, east of Cambrai.

The Capture of the Hindenburg Line

At 5.50 a.m. on Sunday, the 29th of September, after two days of preparatory bombardment, the Fourth Army began its advance against the Hindenburg defences between Bellenglise and Vendhuille, with the general line Lehaucourt–Magny-la-Fosse as the first objective, called the Green Line, and Le Tronquoy–Levergies–Waincourt–Beaurevoir as the day's final objective, or Red Line. The right wing of the Third Army (the V and IV Corps) was also engaged between Marcoing and Vendhuille, as was the French First Army between St. Quentin and Cerizy.

The corps engaged on the Fourth Army Front were the III, IX, XIII, Australian, II American, and Cavalry. The attack was supported by 1,634 guns and howitzers, and by the 3rd Tank Brigade (50 Whippet tanks), the 4th Tank Brigade (70 to 80 tanks), and by the 5th Tank Brigade (84 tanks). The tanks were allocated mainly to the fronts of the Australian and American Corps. The V Brigade, Royal Air Force, working with the Fourth Army, had 9 fighter squadrons, 1 fighter reconnaissance squadron, 1 day bomber, 1 night bomber, and 5 Corps squadrons, which, on the morning of the 29th of September, had on their charge a total of 337 aeroplanes (of which 48 were listed as temporarily unserviceable).

An important feature in connexion with the attack was the possession of a complete knowledge of the organization of the enemy defences. Captured German documents and maps confirmed or corrected what was already known and added whatever was missing of detail, and as a result British maps, specially printed for the attack, included precise information about machine-gun and trench-mortar emplacements with their direction of fire, about engineer parks, ammunition and supply dumps, telegraph and telephone centres, signal stations, unit head-quarters, observation posts, batteries, dug-outs, and—of supreme importance —the detailed organization of the tunnel defences with their exit points in the Hindenburg defence system. The intricacies of the most formidable zone of fortifications of the war were an open book to the troops whose task it was to capture them.

Scheme of Air Co-operation

The spear-head of the attack was formed by the Australian Corps, the American Corps, and the IX Corps. With the two former, No. 3 Australian Squadron worked in direct co-operation, while No. 9 Squadron was similarly employed with the IX Corps. In the Australian Corps area No. 8 Squadron and No. 73 (Fighter) Squadron worked with the tanks. No. 6 Squadron was attached to the Cavalry, ready to exploit success. On the left of the main attack No. 35 Squadron was with the III Corps, and No. 15 Squadron with the V Corps of the Third Army. In addition to the usual instructions for contact and counter-attack patrols, and for co-operation with the artillery, arrangements were made for smoke screens to be laid by aeroplanes at specified times on sectors of high ground which gave the enemy good points of observation.

Brigadier-General L. E. O. Charlton, commanding the V Brigade with the Fourth Army, issued a memorandum to the 22nd Wing on the objects of the impending battle, with orders that its contents be communicated to all officers on the evening of the 28th of September. 'The 'attack to be delivered on the Fourth Army front on 'September 29th', he said, 'is expected, if successful, to 'have wide and far-reaching results, and may well be 'decisive of events on the Western Front'; and among the points upon which he laid stress were: '(i) The destruc-'tion of hostile balloons assumes extra importance on the 'day of attack. This is because a number of the enemy 'battery positions in the Hindenburg system can only be 'served by aerial observation. Systematic measures must 'therefore be devised for this end; (ii) Reconnaissances 'during the battle, especially of the battle area and the 'country immediately in rear of it, will be urgently required. 'Such reconnaissances must be continuous and must be 'undertaken at such a height as will permit of road activity 'being seen and noted. The pilots and observers of the 'Army two-seater squadrons must be imbued with the im-'portance of this as the only means of providing against 'surprise by counter-attack; (iii) Low-flying attack will be 'ordered on the Central Information Bureau system under 'which machines are directed to a locality where targets of 'sufficient importance are known already to exist; and (iv) 'If in course of a low-flying attack an enemy battery is 'encountered in action in the open, it will be justifiable to 'leave all in order to attack it: this should be particularly 'impressed.'

These considerations, with others, were translated into detailed orders issued from the 22nd Wing head-quarters on the eve of the battle. It may be noted that offensive patrol pilots were warned that the army battle area was from Honnecourt to St. Quentin and that they must on no pretext allow themselves to be inveigled outside these defined limits: nor were they to fly so far east of the immediate battle area that enemy aircraft would have opportunity to pass them unseen. The night bombers of No. 101 Squadron were to attack enemy villages opposite the Fourth Army front, before the battle opened, and were also, as on previous occasions, to keep flying about the front-line area in order to drown the noise of the assembling tanks.

For the night preceding the attack the bombers of the head-quarters IX Brigade were given the targets of the fortified villages of Villers-Outreaux and Fresnoy-le-Grand, and the railway stations of Bohain and Busigny. One head-quarter night bomber squadron, No. 58, was allotted Inglemunster junction as an objective in connexion with the battle in Flanders.[1] The day bombers of the IX Brigade were, on the 29th, to attack the enemy aerodromes at Busigny and Montigny as early as possible, and in the afternoon (3 p.m.) were to bomb the railway stations at Bohain and Busigny.

The Attack
[Map, p. 530]

The night bombing before the battle began was made as ordered, and among the visible results were explosions and fires at Busigny station, and in the villages of Villers-Outreaux and Fresnoy-le-Grand. When the battle opened, at 5.50 a.m. on the 29th of September, there was mist and drizzle which, with the smoke from the bombardment, made air co-operation nearly impossible. This was particularly unfortunate because there were happenings which called urgently for elucidation.

The key of the enemy position was the angle of the Schelde canal at Bellenglise, where the assault was made by the 46th (North Midland) Division of the IX Corps. Equipped with life-belts, and carrying mats and rafts, the 137th Infantry Brigade of this division stormed the canal under cover of the mist and of smoke. Many of the men dropped down the sheer side of the canal, swam or waded across, and climbed the opposite side to attack the German trenches on the eastern bank: some crossed by foot-bridges which the enemy had not had time to destroy. The

[1] See p. 533.

other two brigades of the 46th Division then passed through and swung away to the right, taking the German defences in the rear, and capturing Lihaucourt and Magny-la-Fosse. About this time tanks which had crossed over the canal tunnel to the north joined in the attack, and the 32nd Division passed through the 46th to continue the advance. The 32nd met with increasing resistance, but after some intense fighting they captured the western end of the Le Tronquoy tunnel, where they were joined by the 1st Division which had attacked on the right of the 46th. Captures by the IX Corps on the 29th amounted to 4,600 prisoners and 70 guns, of which all the guns and 4,200 of the prisoners had been taken by the 46th Division in an action as brilliant as any of its kind in the war.

The 27th and 30th American Divisions, which attacked simultaneously with the IX Corps, broke through the Hindenburg Line between Bellicourt and Vendhuille, and then, passing rapidly forward to their first objective, soon lost touch with the 3rd and 5th Australian Divisions in their rear. Eager to exploit their success, and no doubt confused and deceived by the smoke and the mist which made it difficult to be sure that the numerous entrances to the canal tunnel had all been found and blocked, the Americans would seem to have pushed on without misgivings. Many of the enemy troops, who had stayed quiet in the honeycombed tunnel during the bombardment, came from their hiding-places and cut off those Americans who had passed on. When the smoke and the mist began to clear, some of the advanced elements, realizing for the first time the precariousness of their position, fought their way back again, but many of them, nearly all belonging to the 27th American Division, were isolated.

The situation on this part of the front long remained obscure. Owing to the uncertain whereabouts of the American troops it was impossible to order useful artillery fire to support the advance of the 3rd and 5th Australian Divisions, and the infantry and the machine-gunners had to rely on themselves. After heavy fighting, a line was eventually established east of Nauroy—east of Bellicourt—west of Bony-Knoll. The III Corps, which attacked in co-operation with the 27th American Division on its right, had to fight hard all day, but made some progress. On the Third Army front the attack met with strong resistance which slowed the rate of advance, while on the right of the battle front the French First Army captured Urvillers and Cerizy, but was held east of those villages.

In general the results of the fighting on the opening day had been disappointing. The main reasons were that the enemy defences were of an intricate and formidable kind, that in such tangled country unsuitable for effective tank action the mist and smoke hindered the attacking troops, and that many of the German soldiers, who had been told not to give way, stood their ground without thought of a to-morrow. Furthermore there were the consequences, to which reference has already been made, of the enthusiasm, not tempered by experience, of the American troops. Had it not been for the fine effort of the 46th Division, by which the German defence system had been breached, the attack might well have been written down as a failure.

A contributory cause of the unsatisfactory nature of the day's progress was almost certainly the curtailment of aircraft co-operation. The contact patrol observers, even though the aeroplanes were flown close to the ground, could report little of what was happening in the morning, and try as they might they could not obtain any adequate idea of the positions reached by the Americans. In the afternoon, when visibility improved slightly before heavy rains began again at 5 p.m., reports were made which threw some light upon the general situation, but much was still left in obscurity, more particularly because signals from the ground, in particular of flares which would have been of great use to the air observers, were few. The artillery observers had some success in the afternoon and sent down information about many favourable targets of guns, troops, and transport.

Attempts were made to drop phosphorous bombs to form smoke screens at the places and times specified in orders. On the whole, owing to the general unfavourable conditions, and to the confusion on the ground, and sometimes to technical deficiencies by which the bombs failed to release, the numbers dropped were insufficient to produce really effective screens.

An attack made against the enemy kite balloons about 10 a.m. on the 29th of September by No. 84 Squadron led to much fighting. The attack was made by one Flight of S.E.5a's with two Flights above to provide protection, and as soon as the lower Flight pilots dived against the balloons ten Fokker biplanes dropped down after them. The two protecting Flights engaged the Fokkers to such effect that the attack on the German balloons was successful and five of them were sent blazing to earth: one Fokker was also destroyed in flames and one S.E.5a was shot down within the enemy lines. While this fight was in progress there was a clash a little to the south between twenty-nine British fighters and twenty Germans in which five enemy and two British were shot down. Apart from this intensive period of fighting, the German air service was not unduly active during the day, although there was some bombing of the British back areas in the morning.

The day bomber squadrons of the head-quarters IX Brigade attacked the German aerodromes in the morning of the 29th as ordered. No. 27 (D.H.9) Squadron bombed Busigny with an escort of Bristol fighters of No. 62 Squadron which sent down three of six intervening Fokkers in flames: one bomber was shot down and the observer in another was wounded. No. 98 (D.H.9) Squadron attacked the enemy aerodrome at Montigny with an escort of S.E. 5a's, of No. 1 Squadron: there was much spasmodic fighting over the target in which an S.E.5a was shot down. On the Fourth Army front the day bomber squadron of the V Brigade, No. 205 (D.H.9a), attacked the villages of Brancourt and Beaurevoir, and that of the III Brigade, No. 57 (D.H.4), on the Third Army front, bombed Esnes and Walincourt.

In rainstorms during the night of the 29th/30th of September, when air bombing was impossible, the IX Corps captured Le Tronquoy and the whole of the canal tunnel defences. The weather was overcast on Monday the 30th, with occasional rain, when the IX Corps and the Australian Corps successfully continued the operations. The 1st Division attacked south of the canal and made contact with the 32nd Division at the Le Tronquoy tunnel defences, while, to the north, the 5th and 3rd Australian Divisions made progress on Bony Spur and east of Nauroy. Farther north the III Corps overcame a stubborn opposition, with the result that the enemy evacuated Vendhuille and withdrew across the canal. Air co-operation during the day was limited by the bad weather conditions, and attempts which were made to find the American troops suspected to be still holding out within the enemy lines, and to drop food upon them by parachute, were unsuccessful.

On Tuesday the 1st of October the military pressure was intensified and, with the return of fine weather, the squadrons of the Royal Air Force were active all day. The four head-quarters day bomber squadrons, with fighting escorts, were concentrated against the important junction at Aulnoye where the railway line from Mézières and Hirson linked with the main line to Maubeuge, Namur, and Germany. The attacks chiefly demonstrated, once again, that inferior equipment is wasteful of effort. Twenty D.H.9's and two D.H.4's, representing two of the bomber squadrons, set out at 6.15 a.m. with their escort, but seven of the D.H.9 pilots were compelled to turn back with engine trouble. Eventually twenty-six 112-lb. bombs were dropped on the Aulnoye sidings from 11,000 feet and four appeared to hit. In the second attempt twenty-nine D.H.9's from the other two head-quarters day bomber squadrons left at 8 a.m. and were joined by fifteen S.E.5a fighters. Before the lines were crossed fifteen of the bombers turned back with engine trouble, and another because the pilot was ill: two of those which had engine trouble crashed, one of them being blown up by its bombs. As soon as the remaining thirteen bombers crossed the lines they were assailed by a large German fighting formation, and after dropping their bombs on the enemy trenches they retreated under the protection of the S.E.5a fighters. Thus, in the two morning attempts, no more than eleven D.H.9 pilots bombed their allotted objective. Of the thirty-eight which did not do so, twenty-one turned back because of failing engines, two on account of sickness, and one because of damage by anti-aircraft gun fire; the remainder dropped their bombs haphazardly near the trenches owing to the presence of German fighting aircraft. Attempted attacks made by two of the squadrons in the afternoon were more successful. Of twenty-one D.H.9's which set out, with thirteen S.E.5a's as escorts, three turned back with engine trouble, but the others bombed the Aulnoye objective and exploded an ammunition train in the sidings. The attacks on the junction were continued during the night by Handley Pages of No. 207 Squadron, one of which dropped a bomb of 1,650-lb. weight, but the visibility was poor and the results of this bombing, as of many other attacks on the enemy lines of communication, were not observed. An exception was the setting fire to trains at Bertry and Beaurevoir by bombers of No. 102 Squadron of the III Brigade.

The Battle in Flanders

[Maps, pp. 550, and at end]

In accordance with the general Allied plan of campaign the Flanders offensive, directed by His Majesty the King of the Belgians, had begun at the end of September. The front of attack extended from Dixmude to St. Eloi, and the forces involved were the Belgian Army, some French divisions, and the British Second Army under General Sir Herbert Plumer. The general direction of the advance was to be towards Ghent, and it was hoped that with the help of surprise full advantage could be taken of the weakening of the German forces on this front, and the Allies enabled to clear the enemy from the Belgian coast.

As the Belgians were short of aircraft, and because Sir Douglas Haig was unable to spare any Royal Air Force units working with the British armies, the Vice-Admiral, Dover Patrol, was called upon for help and he readily responded. He placed the Fifth Group (Brigadier-General

C. L. Lambe) at the disposal of the Belgian Army for the Flanders operations. The units concerned were:

Eighty-second Wing: Squadrons, 38 (F.E.2b), 214 (Handley Page), and 218 (D.H.9).

Sixty-first Wing: Squadrons, 202 (D.H.4), 204, 210, and 213, all Sopwith 'Camel', and 217 (D.H.4).

The other Royal Air Force units involved in the Flanders battle were those with the II Brigade (Brigadier-General T. I. Webb-Bowen) attached to Sir Herbert Plumer's Second Army. They were:

Second (Corps) Wing: Squadrons, 4, 7, and 53 (R.E.8's) 10 and 82 (Armstrong-Whitworths).

Eleventh (Army) Wing: Squadrons, 29, 41, and 74 (S.E.5a's), 70 (Sopwith 'Camel'), 79 (Sopwith 'Dolphin'), 48 (Bristol Fighter), 206 (D.H.9), and 149 (F.E.2b).

Sixty-fifth (Army) Wing: Squadrons, 65 (Sopwith 'Camel'), 108 and 211 (D.H.9).

The French General Degoutte, whose services had been placed by Marshal Foch at the disposal of the King of the Belgians as chief of staff, issued on the 25th of September his plans for the employment of the Allied air services. The main bombing was to be done by the British squadrons with the object of interrupting the enemy's rail and road communications, the dividing line between the Fifth Group and the II Brigade being Zarren–Cortemarck–Lichtervelde.

The distant offensive patrols were to be supplied by the British fighters, the Fifth Group taking an area from the sea to a line north of Houthulst forest, and the II Brigade from that point to Perenchies. The French and Belgian fighters were given an inner patrol line mainly in protection of the squadrons co-operating with the Belgian and French divisions.

As secrecy was essential there was no abnormal air activity before the attack was launched at 5.30 a.m. on the 28th of September. The success was immediate along the whole front of attack, and the Germans were driven headlong from their positions. By the end of the day the British divisions had passed beyond the limits of the 1917 battles and had captured Kortewilde, Zandvoorde, Kruiseik, and Becelaere: on the left of the British the Belgian troops had cleared the enemy from the Houthulst forest. The weather was poor, and the pilots and observers whose duty was direct co-operation with the advancing troops had to take the utmost risks in order to keep touch with the battle. A feature of the co-operation on the British front was the employment of the wireless telephone, by which Nos. 7, 10, and 53 Squadrons were able to make some useful reports by word of mouth of enemy movements.

The main targets of the Fifth Group bombers were the railways at Thourout, Cortemarck, and Lichtervelde, and in the attacks three trains were set on fire and three ammunition dumps exploded. The chief objectives for the II Brigade bombers were the railways at Menin, Wervicq, and Roulers.

The most intensive of the day's attacks, however, were those made from a low height, without thought for the risks involved, by bombers and fighters against troops and transport, and they caused confusion and panic among the retreating Germans. The losses in these low attacks were somewhat heavy, sixteen aeroplanes failing to return on the II Brigade front, and eleven to Fifth Group aerodromes: a violent rainstorm which blew up in the morning was partly responsible for these losses.

There was no respite for the bombers throughout the night of the 28th/29th of September. Seventeen tons of bombs were dropped by the Fifth Group night-flying pilots on the Ostend–Bruges–Thourout railways, on Melle sidings, and on the junction at Thielt, and seven tons by the II Brigade night bombers on the junctions at Menin, Roulers, and Courtrai. The head-quarters IX Brigade also helped. Handley Pages of No. 58 head-quarters squadron were diverted to attacks on Ingelmunster junction at which they aimed nine tons of bombs: many of the crews made three trips.

The days which followed were wet, but although military movements were thereby made difficult because of the scarcity of good roads, the British and Belgian forces pressed the defeated enemy, and by the evening of the 1st of October the left bank of the Lys had been cleared by the British from Comines southwards, while the Belgians had reached the general line Moorslede–Staden–Dixmude. There ensued supply difficulties, and it became necessary to pause in order to organize the lines of communication, part of which ran through country which had been devastated by years of struggle: it was not until the 14th of October that the battle could be resumed.

The work of the air squadrons, after the opening day of the battle, was curtailed by the bad weather. During a temporary improvement on the 1st of October, however, the air offensive was prosecuted with full force, and reinforcements of enemy fighters could do little to hamper the British low-flying attacks on the retreating German troops, and upon the railway communications. During the day's flying operations about twenty-four tons of bombs were dropped by the British squadrons, and ten enemy aeroplanes were destroyed.

At 6 p.m. on the 1st of October messages were received from forward Belgian and French divisions to the effect that their food reserves had been exhausted, and that the bringing forward of supplies would certainly be delayed owing to the damaged state of the roads. Belgian aviation head-quarters was accordingly ordered to attempt the delivery of 15,000 rations by air on the 2nd of October, and No. 218 (D.H.9) Squadron from the Fifth Group and No. 82 (Armstrong-Whitworth) Squadron from the II Brigade were placed at the disposal of the Belgian air force to help in the work. During the night the rations were transported to the various aerodromes. Five to ten rations were packed in small sacks of earth which were carried in the cockpits of the aeroplanes and thrown overboard at specified places from a height of about 300 feet. The sacks burst on landing and the earth damped the force of the impact so that the rations suffered little or no damage. The total of Allied aeroplanes engaged numbered eighty, and the whole 15,000 rations, weighing about thirteen tons in all, had been dropped, without mishap, in four hours, that is to say by 11 a.m. on the 2nd of October.

The weather was bad on the 3rd of October, but there was an improvement in the evening, and the night bombers aimed more than twenty tons of bombs at the enemy railway communications. Throughout the 4th, and during the succeeding night, the bombing of the enemy communications and columns continued, a notable result on the 4th being great destruction at Lichtervelde railway sidings.

The Second Battle of Le Cateau
[Map, p. 437]

Along 250 miles of the Western front the final battles of the war were approaching a climax. The action directed by the King of the Belgians had reached a stage when Lille was threatened from the north, Cambrai had been outflanked, St. Quentin had fallen, the greater part of the Hindenburg Line had been taken, and the French and American troops to the south had made important progress. The German armies had suffered a series of defeats during which, between the middle of July and the end of September, they had lost nearly 4,000 guns, 25,000 machine-guns, and more than a quarter of a million of prisoners. The disheartened and depleted enemy forces were in the last of their organized defensive positions, and they knew that the next Allied effort was likely to eject them into open country with their faces set for home. On the main British front, while movements were being made preliminary to the final effort, the air bombing continued to be directed chiefly against railway junctions on the lines of communication, the most important target being Aulnoye junction on which more than twenty-five tons of bombs were dropped between the 1st and 5th of October.

The next great action on the main British front began in the early morning of Tuesday, the 8th of October. Along seventeen miles from south of Cambrai to Sequehart, and along four miles of French front on the British right, the line sprang into action and, although the German troops fought with the courage of despair, their resistance was vain. What had been left of the Hindenburg defence system was captured and the Germans moved back in some confusion.

The weather during the night before the action was wet, and only No. 101 (F.E.2b) Squadron could bomb objectives on the British front. With daybreak, however, the weather improved, and all except the head-quarters high-flying squadrons were able to play a part. A feature of the day's battle was the touch maintained with the advancing troops from zero hour until fading light, about 5.30 p.m., by the pilots and observers of the corps squadrons. Messages picturing the tactical progress of the fighting were received from the air in the Central Information Bureau with great regularity. An important part of the work of co-operation was the laying of smoke screens by aircraft to cover attacks on specific objectives, mainly villages, on the outskirts of which German machine-gun defences had been concentrated. As an example, No. 35 (Armstrong Whitworth) Squadron, which was working with the XIII Corps on the left flank of the British Fourth Army, maintained a smoke screen, between 6 a.m. and 8 a.m., west of Serain. During this time relays of aeroplanes dropped bombs of the 40-lb. phosphorous type at intervals of time not exceeding twenty minutes, and it was reported that the bombing was effective in screening the high ground, with its observation points, in front of the attacking troops of the British XIII Corps.[1]

About noon on the 8th of October a message from an observer of No. 35 Squadron was received in the Central Information Bureau telling of German columns converging upon Clery. A Sopwith 'Camel' Squadron, No. 208, which had been allotted for attacks upon such targets, was sent out in the afternoon and the pilots bombed and shot at the enemy columns. The corps squadron aeroplanes also took a hand in this work, but there was no attempt to make a concentration of aeroplanes against the reported columns.

The single-seater fighter squadrons with the Fourth Army had been ordered to make offensive patrols to protect the co-operating British aeroplanes. 'It is *essential*', the orders stated, 'that Corps machines are not interfered

---

[1] One 40-lb. phosphorous bomb was said to have produced a screen lasting some twenty minutes over about 220 yards of front.

'with during the operation.' The arrangements allowed for a relay of patrols on the 8th, at two or three squadron strength, over the Fourth Army front from 5.30 a.m. onwards. Although these strong patrols saw large enemy fighting formations from time to time during the day there were few close encounters. The length of the Fourth Army front was no more than eight miles, and the V Brigade disposed of nine fighter squadrons, yet the German pilots were still able to interfere with the work of the British co-operating aeroplanes. The elusiveness of the German fighters was aided by cloud masses at about 2,000 feet, and in their game of hide and seek they were also helped by the slight superiority of climb and speed which the *B.M.W.* engine gave to the Fokkers in which it was fitted.

On the Third and First Army fronts the fighter squadrons were mainly employed on low-flying attacks. Opposite the Third Army plentiful targets were found up to a distance of twelve miles east of the line of battle, and the low bombing caused much confusion among the enemy columns. On the First Army front, in connexion with the operations conducted by the Canadians in the Cambrai area, the low-flying pilots paid special attention to enemy movements on the roads radiating east and north-east from Cambrai, and also to railway traffic in the same area.

Owing to the low clouds, the head-quarters fighting and bombing squadrons did not fly on the 8th of October. The day bomber squadrons with the three armies in the battle area, however, were able to attack targets, mostly fortified villages, opposite their respective fronts.

During the night of the 8th/9th of October, when the Canadians forced their way into Cambrai, the bombers of the head-quarters IX Brigade attacked railway communications, mainly the junctions at Aulnoye and Valenciennes. On the latter junction ten tons of bombs were dropped by the Handley Pages of No. 58 Squadron, and many hits were reported, including one by a 1,650 lb. bomb. The night-bombing squadrons with the Third and First Armies attacked enemy railway communications opposite their fronts: an ammunition train near Avesnes-le-Sec was exploded by a bomb. One of the night-bombing objectives on the First Army front was Denain station, where British kite balloon observers had reported great activity in the afternoon of the 8th. German night bombers were also operating, particularly in the Fourth Army forward area.

On the 9th of October the advance was resumed, cavalry assisting, along the whole front, and by nightfall Cambrai was three miles inside the British area. The air operations were mainly of the low-flying kind. As a result of morning air reports which told of crowded columns moving towards Le Cateau, every available aeroplane of the V Brigade was diverted in the afternoon of the 9th to attack them. As an example, the Sopwith 'Camel' pilots of No. 208 Squadron dropped one hundred and sixty 25-lb. bombs and fired about 9,000 rounds of ammunition into the retreating enemy.

The objectives allotted to the head-quarters day bombers on the 9th were the railway junctions at Aulnoye and Mons, but the squadrons which set out for Aulnoye were bothered by the low clouds and attacked Valenciennes junction instead. On the Army fronts the day bombers continued to attack railway and tactical objectives.

Wet weather on the evening of the 9th, which continued during the morning of the 10th, kept the aeroplanes on the ground, but when the conditions improved in the afternoon there were some low-flying attacks. The harassed German troops found a temporary line on the 10th along the river Selle, and in face of their resistance attempts made by the cavalry to force a crossing of the river were unsuccessful.

For the next few days, while the Allied movements were continuing, the weather was unfavourable for flying. By the advance made between the 8th and the 10th of October possession had been gained of the double line of railway from St. Quentin through Busigny to Cambrai. While the repair of this important section of communications was being made, there were local operations as a result of which, by the 13th, the river Selle had been attained at all points south of Haspres and a number of bridge-heads had been established. On the same day, to the north, the outskirts of Douai had been reached, and, to the south, Laon had fallen to the French.

Flanders

[Map, at end]

The resumption of the offensive in Flanders began in improved weather at 5.45 a.m. on the 14th of October. The attack was delivered along the whole front from Dixmude to Comines on the river Lys, and was immediately successful. Roulers was surrounded on the same day, as was Thourout on the 15th, and by the 17th the Germans had evacuated Ostend. Three days later the northern flank of the Allied armies rested on the Dutch frontier, and the Germans had no other concern than to extricate their troops as best they could from the Belgian pocket. The Allied advance through Belgium had carried the armies far to the east of the enemy defences about Lille, while progress on the Le Cateau front had turned the Lille defences from the south. The result was that the enemy forces between the Sensée and the Lys were compelled to withdraw, and Lille fell on the 18th. Thereafter the Allied troops pressed forward steadily and by the evening of the 22nd had reached the general line of the Schelde along the whole front from Valenciennes to near Avelghem, south-east of Courtrai.

The 14th of October, the day the Flanders offensive was resumed, was sufficiently fine to enable the Royal Air Force to support the attack with its full resources. The air work was almost entirely offensive. The exceptions were spotting flights which were made in co-operation with a bombardment in the coastal area by monitors and by Royal Marine Artillery siege guns, and reconnaissance and artillery work by the corps squadrons on the Second Army front. The bomber and fighter squadrons flew from aerodrome to target, and then back again to replenish their fuel and to reload with ammunition. All day the destruction went on. Among the bombers was the American No. 7 Naval Squadron of the northern bombing group making its first raid. More than two thousand bombs of a total weight of about forty tons were dropped by the British squadrons on the Flanders front. Troops in retreat and confused columns of transport were attacked from low heights again and again, and the railway junctions, notably those at Thielt, Deynze, Lichtervelde, Courtrai, Mouscron, Audenarde, and Melle, were also bombed. The important Melle sidings, south-east of Ghent, where activity was seen to be intense in the afternoon of the 14th, were again attacked after dark by No. 214 (Handley Page) Squadron; among the bombs dropped was one of 1,650-lb. weight. The visibility was clear and the night-flying crews saw the ground panorama in unusual detail. An ammunition train in the Melle sidings exploded and carried destruction over a wide area. Another notable raid on the night of the 14th/15th of October was made by the Handley Pages of No. 58 head-quarters Squadron, which dropped about six tons of bombs on the junctions at Audenarde (one of 1,650-lb. weight) and Tournai.

On the 15th and 16th, when many targets must have been exposed to air attack, there was mist and rain, and little useful flying was possible. On the 17th, when visibility improved, there were air reconnaissances from low heights, some of them made by the fighter pilots at the request of the chief of staff to the King of the Belgians, to determine how far the enemy had evacuated the coastal towns, and whether the coastal defence batteries were still active. At 9.20 a.m. a pilot of No. 204 Squadron, seeing no movement on the aerodrome at Ghistelles, landed and was told by excited Belgian peasants that the Germans had just left. Another pilot, of No. 210 Squadron, who landed his Sopwith 'Camel' in the market square at Ostend received a few parting shots from the last members of the German garrison to leave the town. The retreating enemy troops on the 17th had to suffer heavy bombing, but respite was at hand. For about ten days, while the Germans were going back as fast as they could, rain and mist made relentless air attacks impossible. The air superiority of the Allies was overwhelming, the targets which streamed towards the bottle neck into Germany were innumerable, the retreating troops were depressed in body and mind, the setting indeed was such as to ensure the most awesome effects for the rigorous employment of air power, but the quality of mercy rained from the clouds.[1]

The Selle River
[Maps, pp. 437, 550, and at end]

Meanwhile, major operations had been resumed on the Le Cateau front on the 17th of October, when the Fourth Army attacked in conjunction with the French First Army on its right. The Germans were holding the wooded country east of Bohain, as well as the line of the Selle river, in strength, and for two days they defended well, but by the evening of the 19th of October the enemy troops had been driven across the Sambre-et-Oise canal almost everywhere south of Catillon. Next day, the 20th, the Third Army, assisted by the right wing of the First, came fully into action against the line of the Selle north of Le Cateau and, in face of strong resistance, forced the passage of the river, took Solesmes, and sent patrols forward to the river Harpies. Meanwhile the troops of the First Army had captured Denain. The operations were made in bad weather and little flying was possible. On the 18th of October there were a number of low-flying attacks, and during the night of the 18th/19th Handley Page bombers of Nos. 58 and 207 Squadrons dropped about four tons of bombs on Namur railway station, on the Namur–Mons railway line, and on Charleroi.

The capture of the Selle positions was followed on the 23rd of October by a larger operation which had for objective the Sambre-et-Oise canal from the junction with the French, and thence by way of the western edge

[1] His Majesty the King of the Belgians, in a letter which he addressed to Earl Curzon of Kedleston on the 20th of October 1918, said: 'I feel it is 'for me a duty to proclaim the splendid work of the Dunkirk British Avia-'tion under the orders of General Lambe. The share of those airmen in 'the great British-Belgian victory of the 28th–30th September was *very* 'important. One could never render a sufficient tribute of gratitude and 'admiration to those gallant aviators, who, notwithstanding the worst 'atmospheric conditions possible, accomplished with complete efficiency 'all the fighting, reconnaissance, and bombing missions asked for. No 'aviation service in the world could have done what they succeeded to do.'

of the Mormal forest to the neighbourhood of Valenciennes. The diary of the Fourth Army states: 'A few 'minutes before zero the enemy put down a heavy counter-'preparation in the vicinity of Bazuel, and in the area east 'of Le Cateau, using a large quantity of gas shell. This 'considerably interfered with the advance of the infantry, 'and, in addition, put about fourteen guns out of action. 'This counter-preparation was undoubtedly the result of 'insufficient counter-battery work. During the few days 'prior to the 23rd of October the weather was unsuitable 'for flying and observation was difficult, consequently few 'hostile batteries were located, and counter-battery work 'was restricted.'

In spite of the enemy resistance the Fourth and Third Armies advanced about six miles in two days. When the attack was begun on the 23rd the weather though misty was fine, and there was an outburst of air activity with more combats than for many weeks. No. 20 (Bristol Fighter) Squadron, after attacking Aulnoye junction with 112-lb. bombs, met a Fokker formation, and in the dog fight which ensued five of the enemy aeroplanes were destroyed: all the Bristol Fighters returned. The railway junction at Hirson was bombed on the 23rd by Nos. 98 and 107 Squadrons.

On the 24th the German air activity slackened, and although the British squadrons made many attacks on enemy columns few results were observed because of mist. On this day the junction at Aulnoye came under fire from British 6-in. guns, and air reconnaissances and photographs obtained on the 24th and following day revealed that the bombardment was effective. On the 25th and 26th the British corps aeroplanes were active, but few enemy aircraft were seen.

On the morning of the 27th of October Major William George Barker, who was on a 'refresher' course from England and was attached to No. 201 Squadron, was flying a Sopwith 'Snipe' when he destroyed four enemy aeroplanes in the neighbourhood of the Mormal forest. The combat report, written for Major Barker by the commanding officer of the squadron, reads: '8.25 a.m. Observed enemy

'two-seater at 21,000 feet N.E. of Forêt de Mormal.
'Enemy aircraft climbed east and Major Barker following
'fired a short burst from underneath at point-blank range.
'Enemy aircraft broke up in the air and one of the occupants
'jumped with a parachute. He then observed a Fokker
'biplane 1,000 feet below stalling and shooting at him, one
'of the bullets wounding him in the right thigh. He fell
'into a spin from which he pulled out in the middle of a
'formation of about 15 Fokkers, two of which he attacked
'indecisively, both enemy aircraft spinning down. He
'turned, and getting on the tail of a third which was attack-
'ing him, shot it down in flames from within 10 yards range.
'At this moment he was again wounded in the left thigh
'by others of the formation who were diving at him. He
'fainted and fell out of control again. On recovering he
'pulled his machine out and was immediately attacked by
'another large formation of 12 to 15 enemy aircraft. He
'got on the tail of one and from a range of less than 5
'yards shot it down in flames. At this moment he received
'a third wound from the remainder of the formation who
'were attacking him, the bullet shattering his left elbow.
'The enemy machine which wounded him closed to within
'10 yards. He again fainted and fell out of control to
'12,000 feet, and recovering was at once attacked by
'another large formation of enemy aircraft. He then
'noticed heavy smoke coming from his machine and, under
'the impression he was on fire, tried to ram a Fokker just
'ahead of him. He opened fire on it from 2 to 3 yards
'range and enemy aircraft fell in flames. He then dived to
'within a few thousand feet of the ground and began to
'fly towards our lines, but found his retreat cut off by
'another formation of 8 enemy aircraft who attacked him.
'He fired a few bursts at some of them and shaking them
'off dived down and returned to our lines a few feet above
'the ground, finally crashing close to one of our balloons...'
Major Barker, a Canadian, who was officially credited with
a total of 50 enemy aircraft destroyed, was awarded the
Victoria Cross.[1]

[1] Wing Commander W. G. Barker was killed on the 12th of March 1930 at Ottawa, Canada, as a result of a flying accident.

Another officer whose award of a Victoria Cross was announced in the same *Gazette* was Captain Andrew Weatherby Beauchamp-Proctor, born in South Africa, whose daring in the final months of the war was a matter for common talk on the Western front. As a pilot of No. 84 (S.E.5a) Squadron he was particularly successful against enemy kite balloons, sixteen of which he destroyed. He was brilliant in his low-flying attacks on enemy columns, and he was also officially credited with twenty-two enemy aeroplanes destroyed.[1]

In the last days of October, when there was a temporary lull in the advance on the ground, the corps squadrons were mainly concerned to co-operate with the British artillery in their bombardment of the enemy back areas and lines of communication. The weather had improved and the German pilots came out in force. Mindful of the vulnerable bombing targets which the German retreat had opened to air attack, the German command concentrated its air fighting strength in a desperate attempt to prevent the British day bombers from reaching the more obvious objectives. The enemy fighters flew in large formations, sometimes fifty strong, and there were many bitter engagements which culminated on the 30th of October in the most intense day of air fighting which the war had provided. The aim of the enemy air service was to keep open the bottle-neck of railway communications through Namur and Liége in order to facilitate the withdrawal of the German armies from Belgium and northern France. The German pilots, at great sacrifice, served their comrades on the ground well, and they had success when their opposition was directed against the D.H.9 day bomber, which had not the performance to fight a way through.

The main bombing targets allotted to the head-quarters day bombers were the railway junctions at La Louvière, Charleroi, and Namur, and also Mariembourg, north-east of Hirson. The head-quarters Handley Page night bombers were given the railway junctions at Namur, Louvain, and Termonde, while the F.E.2b's had Charleroi station for

[1] Flight Lieutenant Beauchamp-Proctor was killed in a flying accident at Upavon, Wiltshire, on the 21st of June 1921.

objective. If the weather was unsuitable for distant bombing the night bombers were to attack Mons and Maubeuge railway stations as alternative targets. The day bomber squadrons were Nos. 27, 49, and 107, all equipped with D.H.9 aeroplanes fitted with the 200 horse-power B.H.P. engine, and No. 205[1] Squadron which had the D.H.9a fitted with the 400 horse-power Liberty engine. The head-quarters night bomber squadrons were Nos. 58, 207, and 214 Handley Page squadrons, and No. 83 F.E.2b Squadron.

The relative performances of the D.H.9 (B.H.P.) and D.H.9a (Liberty) aeroplanes were:

	Speed in m.p.h. and rate of climb in min. to				Service ceiling
	10,000 ft.		15,000 ft.		
D.H.9	114	15·3	106	30·1	18,000 ft.
D.H.9a	120	11·8	114	22·8	19,000 ft.

The figures as tabulated must, however, be qualified. They are for aeroplanes in which the engines were running as desired, but whereas the Liberty engine usually ran well the B.H.P., because it was underpowered for the work it was required to do, could not be made to develop its full power consistently under the exacting conditions of active service. The table, therefore, may be looked upon as generally correct for the D.H.9a, but so far as it concerns the D.H.9 rather as an ideal which was not usually attained on service.

The difference in performance between the two types had an effect upon the employment of the fighter squadrons of the head-quarters Brigade. No. 205 (D.H.9a) Squadron was given Namur as objective, but no provision was made in the operation orders for fighting protection. The three D.H.9 squadrons, between them, had one two-seater and three single-seater fighter squadrons allotted for protective duties. In other words the D.H.9's were escorted both ways to the limit of the range of the fighters. What

[1] No. 205 Squadron began to re-equip with the D.H.9a at the end of August 1918, and was completely re-equipped by the end of September.

happened in the three days from the 28th to the 30th of October may be seen from the following summary table for the IX Brigade day bombers:

Squadron	28th Oct. (a) Objective.	29th Oct. (b) Where bombs were dropped.	30th Oct.
205 (D.H.9a)	(a) and (b) Namur.	(a) and (b) Namur.	(a) and (b) Namur.
27 (D.H.9)	(a) Manage. (b) Mons area.	Nil.	(a) La Louvière. (b) St. Ghislain and Quievrechain.
49 (D.H.9)	(a) La Louvière. (b) St. Ghislain.	Nil.	(a) Manage. (b) St. Denis, Élouges, Estreux.
107 (D.H.9)	(a) Mariembourg. (b) Hirson, &c.	(a) Mariembourg. (b) Anor, &c.	(a) and (b) Mariembourg.

The D.H.9a's flew at 17,000 feet and had little attention from enemy aircraft. The D.H.9's flew at about 13,000 feet, which was nearer their effective service formation-ceiling than that given in the table of performances on p. 545, and at this height they were subject to the full attention of enemy fighters. On the 28th Nos. 27 and 49 Squadrons, which were flying in company with No. 32 Squadron acting as escort as far as Mons, were attacked over Mons by about thirty Fokker biplanes. The bombs were dropped at once and a fight ensued in which a D.H.9 was shot down, two German aeroplanes were destroyed, and a D.H.9 pilot was wounded, but returned safely. On the same day, when No. 107 Squadron attempted to bomb Mariembourg, protected by No. 43 Squadron out (No. 1 Squadron was to meet the bombers for homeward escort), the objective could not be reached because the bombing formation was depleted through engine trouble, and the bombs were therefore dropped on the railway at Hirson. There was much fighting on the homeward journey, but the escorting S.E.5a's of No. 1 Squadron accompanied the bombers safely to the lines.

On the 29th, when Nos. 27 and 49 Squadrons were busy moving to more forward aerodromes, the bombers of No. 107 Squadron were barred from reaching their objective by enemy fighters which assailed them over Anor. An observer of the squadron was brought back dead, and an escorting aeroplane of No. 1 Squadron fell within the enemy lines: two enemy fighters were shot down.

On the 30th, when the D.H.9a's flew to Namur, as they had done on the two previous days, without impediment, the remaining head-quarters bombers were attacking various places, harassed by enemy fighters. No. 107 Squadron, escorted by S.E.5a's of No. 1 Squadron and by Sopwith 'Snipes' of No. 43 Squadron, alone bombed its allotted objective at Mariembourg after abortive attempts on the two previous days. The other two squadrons, and their escorts, were attacked by about thirty enemy fighters, and the bombs were dropped haphazardly. One bomber and four single-seater fighters were shot down, one bomber pilot and his observer crashed in the British lines and were killed, and two pilots returned wounded.

In the three days' bombing noted above, therefore, the D.H.9a's bombed the most distant of the objectives allotted without incident and without casualties. The three D.H.9 Squadrons, with fighter squadrons in support, did not bomb their allotted targets except on the 30th, when No. 107 Squadron reached Mariembourg, and in the attempted attacks casualties were suffered, and much energy employed. In summing up it is probably fair to say that to a great extent the energy expended by the D.H.9 squadrons was wasted. Bombs dropped at haphazard, when definite targets are being sought at a vital time, cannot be reckoned of much military account.

The air operations of the final phase of the war on the Western front have a twofold interest for the student. Owing to the configuration of the Holland–Belgian frontiers, the German forces, as they withdrew, were compressed more and more into the neck of communications about Liége. Should every available Allied bomber, including those of the Independent Force, have been concentrated against one or two selected vital objectives with the aim of cutting those communications? The actual day-bombing attempts which were made confirm yet again that the employment of inferior technical equipment makes the ability to fulfil an allotted task dependent too much upon chance and upon the will of an enemy.

The day bomber squadrons with the Brigades attached to the armies played a part in the attempts to cut the railway communications. The targets allotted were selected junctions along the lateral railways between Ghent and Avesnes, south of Maubeuge. The II Brigade in the north was given the junctions at Melle (south of Ghent), Audenarde, Sottegem, and Grammont; the X Brigade had the line between Tournai and Ath, but mainly the latter centre; the I Brigade, Mons; the III Brigade, Maubeuge; and the V Brigade Avesnes. For the most part, the bombers were able to fulfil their missions, although they were sometimes prevented from doing so by enemy fighters.

The most determined of the enemy defensive efforts was made on the 30th of October. On this day sixty-seven German aeroplanes were destroyed on the British front, and forty-one British aeroplanes were struck off the strength of the Royal Air Force squadrons as a result of enemy action.[1] The casualties to British personnel were 3 killed, 8 wounded, and 26 missing. The day bomber squadron, No. 98 (D.H.9), of the I Brigade, which set out, escorted by Sopwith 'Dolphins' of No. 19 Squadron, to bomb Mons on the 30th, was attacked by a large enemy formation, mainly composed of Fokker biplanes. The Germans fought all the way back to the lines, and ten of them were destroyed, four in flames. Of the British formation, five of the Dolphins and four of the D.H.9's fell in the enemy lines, a pilot and an observer came back wounded, and two D.H.9's crashed on landing. On the same day No. 88 (Bristol Fighter) Squadron of the X Brigade, while on offensive patrol twelve strong over Tournai, was first attacked by nine Fokkers which dived through the British formation. As the fight progressed

[1] His Majesty King George V sent the following telegram to the Secretary of State for the Royal Air Force: 'I offer you and the Royal Air Force my warmest congratulations on the successful results of air fighting on October 30th, and on beating all previous records. Such achievements testify to the spirit which animates all ranks in their determination to maintain our mastery in the air and cannot fail materially to assist the steady advance of my Armies in the field.'

about eight more German pilots joined in. The combats, fought out at close quarters, were of a confused kind, and when the engagement ended five German aeroplanes had gone down in flames and four more to crash, at a cost of one Bristol Fighter which fell in the British lines with its pilot and observer wounded.

On the morning of the 30th pilots of the Australian Squadrons in the X Brigade had reported great activity, with large numbers of aeroplanes, on the German aerodrome at Rebaix, north of Ath. All squadrons of the Eightieth Wing were thereupon ordered to make a low-bombing attack on the aerodrome. This took place at 2.30 p.m. and the aeroplanes engaged totalled sixty-two. The raid was led by the Wing Commander, Lieutenant-Colonel L. A. Strange, who reported as follows: 'Four 230-lb. 'bombs, six 112-lb. bombs, and 115 25-lb. bombs were 'dropped from under 1,000 feet. 5,400 rounds were fired at 'ground targets. Machines of No. 4 A.F.C. Squadron and 'No. 88 Squadron ably carried out escort for bombing 'machines. Machines of No. 103, No. 54, and No. 2 A.F.C. 'Squadrons carried out the bombing, as a result of which 'three hangars were completely destroyed and one par-'tially. Many bombs were observed bursting all round the 'remaining hangars, and it is almost certain that every 'machine on the aerodromes must have been destroyed. 'Two machines on the ground were totally wrecked. On 'the return journey the Scouts "contour chased"[1] along 'the roads causing great havoc to motor transport, horse 'transport, and troops, especially in the villages Ligne 'and Leuze. A staff car was shot up, ran into a ditch 'and overturned. Enemy aircraft were generally active 'throughout the attack, and as a result of numerous 'combats from varying heights—2,000 feet and upwards '—nine enemy aircraft were destroyed, four driven down 'out of control, and two driven down.'[2] Two British

---

[1] 'Contour-chasing' was a term applied to very low flying.

[2] Lieutenant-Colonel L. A. Strange tells of this attack, and of similar ones which he led about this time, in *Recollections of an Airman*. Other notable raids by the Eightieth Wing were on the German aerodrome at Haubourdin on the 16th of August, and on Lomme aerodrome on the 17th of August.

D.H.9's and one Sopwith 'Snipe' failed to return from the raid.

During the next few days, which were dull with some rain, air activity slackened considerably, but the bombing of enemy communications and low-flying attacks on the retreating columns continued. On the 1st of November the railway station at Brussels was attacked by D.H.9a's. Other targets were Maubeuge (instead of Charleroi which could not be reached because the leader of the bombing formation had to turn back with engine trouble), and Maubeuge again (instead of Mariembourg owing to bad weather conditions). The bombing by the squadrons with the Brigades attached to the Armies was little interfered with by the weather on the 1st of November, but on the 2nd and 3rd mist and rain made high bombing impossible. On these days, however, the fighter squadrons, in addition to their usual attacks from a low height on ground targets, bombed railway stations.

On the 4th of November, after an early mist cleared, activity in the air blazed up again, and although the end was so near the German air service fought with fine determination. On this day Sir Douglas Haig delivered a decisive blow on the fronts of the British Fourth, Third, and First Armies along thirty miles from Oisy on the Sambre to Valenciennes. The battle opened at dawn and there was success everywhere which broke, finally, the German resistance. During the ensuing night the enemy armies fell back all along the line.

In this final phase the squadrons of the Royal Air Force harassed the enemy columns with bomb and machine-gun, but the unfavourable weather conditions saved the Germans from a slaughter which the Allied air services had the means to inflict. One episode will be given to illustrate these last days of the air war. At 3.15 p.m. on the 9th of November the Eightieth Wing set out on one of its low-bombing expeditions. The way was led by the D.H.9's of No. 103 Squadron, closely followed by the Sopwith 'Camels' of No. 54 Squadron and by the S.E.5a's of No. 2 A.F.C. Squadron, all carrying bombs. The escorting squadrons were No. 88 (Bristol Fighters) and No. 4 A.F.C.

(Sopwith 'Snipes'). As the combined formation passed over Ath many good targets were visible on the Ath–Enghien road, but the leader, Major R. S. Maxwell, in a Sopwith 'Camel' of No. 54 Squadron, 'continued on to 'Enghien. There, there was great congestion of troops and 'transport of all descriptions on the roads, trains on the 'railways and in the station, also two aerodromes with 'machines on the ground. On one aerodrome a hangar 'was completely destroyed and one machine completely 'wrecked, and bombs seen bursting among other machines 'which must have been badly damaged. On another aero-'drome, one hangar and a machine on the aerodrome were 'destroyed in flames, and direct hits obtained on machines 'and hangars. Three large bombs and many 25-lb. bombs 'were seen to burst on troops and transport on the main 'Ath–Enghien road between Bassilly and Enghien, which 'was particularly congested, others on the roads north and 'south of main road, where there were many targets 'of troops, mechanical transport, and heavy transport. 'Lorries were seen to collide, one being set on fire, many 'others being destroyed by direct hits and others ditched. 'Horse transport was seen stampeding in all directions, 'and in numerous cases troops endeavouring to get into 'houses for cover were shot at and many casualties caused. 'In the station and junction at Enghien, no less than twenty 'direct hits were observed on trains. One train was set on 'fire from end to end, and was still burning furiously when 'the raid left, sheds and buildings in the station catching 'fire from it. A direct hit was obtained between some 'mechanical transport and a train where troops were en-'training at a siding just east of Bassilly and a 230-lb. 'bomb scored a direct hit on trains in Bassilly. Escorting 'machines of No. 88 Squadron meeting with no opposi-'tion came down and joined in the destruction being 'caused on the ground. The ground targets were so 'obvious and numerous that every pilot and observer 'kept firing until stoppages or lack of ammunition com-'pelled him to cease. The damage done and confusion 'caused was almost indescribable and impossible to give 'in detail. It must have been very great, every one 'agreeing that such an opportunity had never before been 'met with.'

There is one aspect of the air war on the Western front which demands summary consideration, namely the policy of continuous offensive as pursued by the British squadrons. It has been argued that the policy was ill conceived, or else that if it was sound in principle it was not applied with military wisdom. It has also been said that the air offensive was responsible for severe casualties, which led to the sending of reinforcements to France before they were adequately trained, with the result that they were offered as somewhat easy targets, so that the circle of heavy casualties and ill-trained reinforcements became a vicious one.

It is not difficult, with the whole panorama of the war unrolled, to parade wisdom, but judgement cannot be passed upon the merits or demerits of the air offensive policy unless the circumstances of the time are carefully weighed. The policy must be coupled with the name of Major-General H. M. Trenchard. He saw with clear vision that the aeroplane is essentially an offensive weapon, and although it was in the squadrons that the offensive spirit was cherished, it was the dominant and inspiring personality of Major-General Trenchard which fired and coloured that spirit.

In the early weeks of the war the Royal Flying Corps, splendidly trained for reconnaissance, made a valuable contribution to the British military effort. Those who flew, and those whose part was to keep the aeroplanes serviceable, were conscious that they were giving real help to the army. When, however, the race to the sea had ended and the opposing armies went to earth there was a time when the Royal Flying Corps could do little. While the British army, in the battles of Ypres in October and November 1914, was being battered by overwhelming numbers, the squadrons fretted because of their comparative inactivity. The time was one of crisis, as the flying officers well knew. They saw the thin line of British infantry, utterly weary, locked in struggle night and day without respite, while they themselves were often kept idle on the ground because the weather was judged unsuitable for flying, or else, when they flew, were without the means to strike at the enemy. There was a feeling, not always concealed, among those who so magnificently defended the Channel ports in the Flanders mud, that the Royal Flying Corps could hardly lay claim to be a fighting service.

These feelings helped to shape the air offensive policy. It was impossible, with the type of officer which the air service attracted, to imagine that any comfort might be drawn from the doctrine that they also serve who only stand and wait. Between the man in the trenches and the man in the aeroplane there was kinship of spirit. The flying officers knew that the soldier was on the stretch for twenty-four hours in the day, whereas they had their time of relaxation. Whatever could be done to assist the infantry must be done, and there was, in consequence, a restless searching, from beginning to end of the war, after ways and means to add to the effectiveness of the help given to the infantry. The question of risks was entirely secondary, as it would be again in comparable circumstances. The British army from 1914 to 1918 fought a long series of battles, mostly offensive. It would not be in place here to argue whether the almost continuous fighting was necessary. All that need be noted is the fact and it was inevitable that the intensity of the effort in the air should be comparable with the fighting on the ground. The co-operating two-seater aeroplanes needed elbow room, or freedom for action, in the air above the German defence systems, and it was natural that the fighter pilots should expect to patrol beyond the two-seaters, still farther over enemy territory, in order to ensure the necessary freedom. That the offensive patrol system did, in fact, keep the air free to a remarkable extent for the British army co-operation aeroplanes, and so enable the pilots and observers to fulfil the tasks upon which the army staffs set such value, has been made apparent throughout this history. That fact alone may be said to provide adequate justification.

The critic may argue, however, that the German air service did what was required in the way of co-operation, no less than the British, and without recourse to a costly system of offensive patrols. The answer to this contention is a twofold one. In the first place, it must be remembered that the German armies in 1914 swept forward into Belgium and a part of France, and that when at last they stood upon a line it was mostly one of their own choosing. Wherever they could they stayed on the hills and ridges, upon the commanding heights, and the result was that for long periods, over a great part of the Western front, the Germans had the use of observation posts on the ground which gave a wide field of view. They were thus able, with the aid of telescopes and field-glasses, to compile military information at their leisure in some safety. There was one way only in which the Allies might counterbalance this very important geographical disadvantage, and that was by an adequate employment of aircraft for observation, together with the establishment of a local air superiority in order to make this observation possible. In the second place, leaving out of account the advantages which the Germans enjoyed because of their better ground observation, the amount of work which was done by the German air service in co-operation with the German armies was very much less than that done for the British armies by the British squadrons. This was mainly because the British army waged a series of offensive battles, whereas the German army for the greater part of the war defended strongly fortified positions. As has been said, whether or not the British offensives were justified, in scale and number, is not a matter for the air historian. All that he is concerned to note is that British military policy resulted in continuously expanding demands for aircraft co-operation.

It may be that after what has thus far been written, the critic of the air offensive policy will not be unduly disputatious. By all means, he may say, employ a screen of fighters to ensure an area of comparative freedom for the co-operating aeroplanes: such a barrier, for example, as was arranged during the highly successful battle of Messines on the 7th of June 1917. But what justification, he may ask, can be adduced for the employment of fighters on monotonous patrol of a defined line while bombers, or formations engaged on long-distance photography or reconnaissance, were being compelled to fight their way through unprotected: surely it would have been wiser to use the fighters for direct protection. In fact, such protection was often provided, more particularly when it seemed that strong opposition would be encountered. Alternatively, or by way of supplement, the timing of the offensive patrols was closely co-ordinated with the passage of the bombing or similar formations. What sometimes happened was that the patrols became closely engaged with enemy fighters, with the result that the bomber or reconnaissance aircraft, which had to continue on their way, received no help if and when they themselves were assailed later. The argument against the provision of general protection is unanswerable. As much as anything it was a matter of arithmetic. If an adequate escort was to be provided for every aeroplane which crossed the lines to do a job of work, it would have been necessary to expand the number of fighters many times, or else to cut down the amount of work attempted. Aeroplanes, no more than policemen, cannot be distributed in protection of each possible victim of a marauder.

There were instances on the Western front, as was inevitable, when the air staff work was faulty, or when the judgement, upon which some particular arrangement was based, may be questioned. It may be said perhaps with truth that the offensive patrols were too much a matter of routine, that their direction and co-ordination were not always sufficiently characterized by an alert imagination. We are not here concerned with the details, however, but with the general principle, and there can be no doubt that the doctrine of the offensive was and is sound. A fleet, while awaiting a favourable time for attack, may seek temporary refuge within suitable harbours from a stronger fleet, as an army may shelter behind entrenchments or other obstacles. An air force has no such opportunity for passive defence except withdrawal, if such be possible, from the theatre of operations. The conflict must go on. As in a game of football, the side which gives way will quickly find the opposing side pressing. What was notable in the war was that any relaxation of the British air offensive found the German air service gaining distance in the air.

The idea that the air can be controlled by a defensive policy was dissipated above the struggling armies at Verdun in 1916. So long as the French air service acted on the offensive, so long were the French pilots and observers able to fulfil their missions. When, however, the French allowed themselves, for a time, to be thrown back on the defensive in the air, they were not only unable to do useful work themselves, but they could also not prevent the German airmen from doing very much what they wished to do. When the French returned to the air offensive, they quickly recovered the advantages they had temporarily lost. The experiences at Verdun have already been reviewed at length,[1] but the testimony of General von Hoeppner, the commander of the German air service, may be repeated: 'In the battles of attrition before Verdun, the aeroplane 'barrage came to be regarded as the universal panacea 'against the enemy air forces. This notion spread over the 'whole Western front and had the most disastrous in-'fluence upon the methods of use of the airmen. The quite 'intelligible wish of the infantry and artillery to be rid of 'enemy aircraft could, it was thought, only be met by 'keeping German aeroplanes constantly flying up and down 'the lines. It is not possible to keep down the enemy by 'this means . . . this kind of aerial line patrol merely meant 'an unlimited waste of strength to the detriment of our 'own reconnaissance work. . . .'

Finally, when the use, admittedly worthy, which the Germans were able to make of their air squadrons is generally reviewed, the question of equipment must be taken into full account. Except for one comparatively brief period the technical qualities of the best of the German aeroplanes were as good as, or superior to, those of the Allies. A main reason for this, unexpected as it may appear at first reading, was the pre-war development of the Zeppelin airship. Because she fostered the airship,

[1] Vol. II, pp. 164-8.

Germany found herself developing also engines of comparatively high power. The result was that German aircraft designers began the war with what was to prove an advantage. When high-powered engines were demanded for aeroplanes, Germany possessed the experience and could make the necessary adaptations with no great difficulty. In the one period when the German aeroplanes were technically inferior to the British, that is in 1916 when the F.E.2b, de Havilland 2, and Nieuport Scouts, came along to oust the Fokker monoplane, the German air service was ineffective. The morale of the service was shattered and was a subject for bitter denunciation by other branches of the German army. The defensive spoiling achievements of such units as the Richthofen *Jagdstaffel* cannot be divorced from the quality of their equipment.

At those times when the best of the British aeroplanes were inferior in performance to the fighters of the German air service, notably in the spring of 1917, the British air offensive went on, although the cost increased. The British squadrons maintained their morale, and their efforts in adversity stimulated the admiration of the other branches of the army which they flew to help. Had they attempted less, they would have suffered less. So much may be conceded. But it has never been the British way for one service to hold anything back when another service was giving all. Nor will it be.

The tale is told. It may not, however, be out of place to take this last opportunity to suggest that all that has been written, whether of operations over the land to help the armies, or over the seas by way of an extension of naval activities, or of attacks independent of naval and military operations against enemy industrial or similar targets, has a unity, the unity of the element which sustained the aircraft.

As the author of this history takes leave of his readers he is conscious that much has been left unsaid. Many gallant deeds, on the ground as in the air, have gone unrecorded. It must be appropriate that the last word should be with the flying personnel. They had their time in the air tense with exhilaration and danger, but when they turned their backs upon the battle-field the war was left behind. They flew home to well-cooked meals, to a modest luxury, and to comparative peace. There were many hours to be passed upon the ground, and although a part of them might sometimes be needed for the recuperation of body and nerve, there were inevitably long spells of leisure which, dubiously employed, would make poor preparation for duties in the air demanding a clear eye, unerring judgement, rapidity of action, and a cold and calculating courage. Much has been written, when the writing of such books was in fashion, to show that the tedium of leisure was too lightly overcome. It would be idle to suggest that young men of high spirits could sustain their hours of ease with monkish contemplation. Although, however, there was gaiety on the ground, it was not of a kind to affect seriousness of purpose in the air. Some words of Sir Walter Raleigh, who began this history, may fittingly be taken to bring it to a close: 'Critics who speak of what they have 'not felt and do not know have sometimes blamed the air 'service because, being young, it has not the decorum of 'age. The Latin poet said that it is decorous to die for 'one's country; in that decorum the service is perfectly 'instructed.'

INDEX

Abbreviations

Br. = British	L. Cr. = Light Cruiser
Fr. = French	Pte. = Private
Ger. = German	S/m. = Submarine

Officers and men who are mentioned more than once in the events described are here given their highest rank.

A.B.C. Motors, Limited, 43n.
Abu el Lasan, bombed, 184
Abu Suwana, 185
Adastral House, Air Ministry H.Q., 24n.
Addison, Rt. Hon. C., Minister of Munitions, 65; 68n.
Aerial Operations Committee, 17
Aerodromes, bombing of, 158–63, 394–6, 549
Aerodromes and Landing-grounds, see 'Palestine, Air Operations in'; 'Mesopotamia and Persia'; 'Italian front'; 'Macedonia'; 'Mediterranean 1918'; 'Naval air developments and operations, 1918'
Aeroplanes:
Disposition of, on charge of R.A.F., 31/10/18, App. xli
types:
British and French: Blackburn 'Kangaroo,' 340, 345; Bristol Fighter, 37, 57, 178; D.H.4, 38, 52, 123, 165–7, 169, 449, 454; D.H.6, 331–2, 334–6, 345, 350; D.H.9, 42n., 53, 128, 142, 166, 169–70, 449, 454, 544–6; D.H.9a 146, 545–6; F.E.2b, 123, 142, 158, 164, 345; Handley Page, 121, 123, 142, 156, 166–8, 209–10, 229; Handley Page (Super) 173–4; Martinsyde, 179, F.4, 445n.; R.E.8, 37; S.E.5, 37, 178; Sopwith 'Camel', 149, 353, 371–3; Sopwith 'Snipe', 149; Vickers 'Vimy', 166n.; see also App. xxvii
German: Albatros, 29; Brandenburger, 359; Fokker D.VII, 445, 537; Halberstadt, 29
Affule, El, bombed 178; 221–2, 235–6
Agents, landing of (Macedonia), 305–7
Aintree, National Aircraft Factory, 54, 56–7

Air Board, 5–9; Second, meetings of, 22n., 33, 37, 43, 48, 166–7, 169
Air Council, 13; formation of, 22–4; 26; composition of at end of war, 27; 170–2
Aircraft carriers, see *Ark Royal, City of Oxford, Engadine, Empress, Furious, Manxman, Peony, Riviera*
Aircraft Manufacturing Company, 38
Aircraft Production Department, *Lecture Branch*, 88; see also 'Supply and Man Power—problems of'
Air Force Act, 22n.
Air Force Bill (29th Nov. 1917), 22
Air Ministry: Gen. Smuts recommends formation of, 11–13, App. ii; Sir D. Haig's views, 13–15; Adm. M. Kerr's views, 18; Air Policy Committee formed, 19; Mr. Bonar Law's Statement (16/10/17) 19, 20; Bill to constitute, approved (6/11/17) 20–1; President of Air Board (Lord Cowdray) resigns, 21; the first Air Council (3/1/18), 22–3; accommodation for, 24; composition of Air Council at end of war, 27; see also 'Royal Air Force'
Air Organization Committee, 13
Air Policy Committee, 19, 90, 103, 172
Air Raids on Great Britain, summary statistics of, 1914–18, App. xliv
Airships:
British: Naval, built 1914–18, App. xxxiv; *Rigid,* C.23A, 349; R.29, 347–8; *Non-rigid,* s.s. T.1, 338n.; s.s. 'Twin', 338; ss. Z.1, 348
German: destruction of, *L. 53,* 373; *L. 54,* 367; *L. 60,* 367; *L. 62,* 355–7
Aisne, battle of, 1918, 397–400
Albert, capture of, 472
Aldeburgh, 335n.
Aleppo, bombed, 237–8

INDEX

Alexandria, 315–17, 325
Allen, Capt. J. R., 386
Allenby, Gen. Sir E. H. H., 175, 177, 180–1, 183, 191–5, 199–200, 205–6, 210–11, 229, 231, 235–7, 257–8, 262–3
Amberkoj, 302, 309–10, 328
America, *see* 'United States'
American Aircraft Construction Board, 80
American Army, *see* 'Army, American'
Amiens, battle of:
   Preparations, 417–18; scheme of employment of R.A.F., 433–6; British, French, and German air strength, 434–6; order of battle, App. xxiv; offensive begins (8/8/18), 437; use of smoke screens, 440; *air attacks on Somme bridges*, 441–2, 446–52, commentary, 454–62; German air reinforcements, 442–4; the Fokker D.VII, 445; R.A.F. casualties (8/8/18), 445–6; concentration of R.A.F. (10/8/18), 453; reliability of the D.H.4, 454; *lessons of the battle*, Gen. Rawlinson's appreciation of work of R.A.F., 463–4; memo. by G.O.C. V Brigade, App. xxv; co-operation with Tank Corps, 464–5; the importance of contact patrol work, 466–7
   Bombing attacks (*British*), 437, 441–2, 446–54
   Contact patrol (*British*), 466–7
   Fighting in the air, 441–4, 446–54, 462, 466
   French Air Service, work of, 467–8
   Low-flying attacks (*British*), 437–41, 451
   Photography, air (*British*), 454
'Amman, bombed, 188
Ammunition, dropping of by air, 484, 503
Andrano, 327
Anor, bombed, 546
Answald, Ger. aircraft carrier, 358
Anti-Aircraft defences: Western front, scheme of, 428–9; deliveries of guns and ammunition (excluding Naval), 1916–18, App. xxxviii; number of guns on Western front, July and November, 1918, App. xxxix; in Great Britain, schedule of types of aircraft guns, height-finders, searchlights, sound-locators, and strength of personnel, 10th June 1918, App. xlv
Aqaba, 184, 204–5, 233*n*.
Arab co-operation with the British, *see* 'Palestine, air operations in, 1918'
Ark Royal, Br. aircraft carrier, 315, 323
Army:
   British:
     Length of front held by, various dates, 1917 and 1918, App. xlii
     First: 433, 470, 484–5, 488, 492–3, 495–6, 497, 499–500, 501, 504, 511–13, 516, 518, 541, 550
     Second: 409, 433, 473, 486, 510, 512, 531
     Third: 82, 434, 469–70, 472, 474, 476, 478, 481, 484–5, 492–3, 495, 497, 499, 501, 504–5, 511–13, 518, 523, 541–2, 550
     Fourth: 401, 413, 415–8, 433–4, 436, 438*n*., 454, 461, 463, 469–70, 474, 476, 478, 481, 484, 492, 500, 505, 511–13, 523, 537, 541–2, 550
     Fifth: 82, 433, 473, 484, 486, 512
   Corps:
     I, 245–6
     III, 451, 476, 523–4, 527, 530
     IV, 470, 483, 504, 513–14, 523
     V, 470, 476, 523–4
     VI, 470, 504, 514, 518
     IX, 397–9, 523–4, 527, 529–30
     XI, 275
     XII, 302–3, 308, 313
     XIII, 523, 536
     XIV, 274, 280, 289
     XVI, 296, 302–3, 313
     XVII, 492–3, 495–6, 497, 513–15
     XVIII, 513
     XX, 175–8, 182, 202–3, 206, 210, 220, 223
     XXI, 175–6, 182, 203, 206, 210, 217–18, 220, 235–7
     XXII, 413, 513–14
   Australian, 433*n*., 440, 476, 523–4, 530
   Camel Transport, 189
   Canadian, 433*n*., 440, 484–5, 492–3, 495–6, 499, 513–14
   Cavalry, 433*n*., 468, 484–5, 523

INDEX

Army: British—*continued*
  Desert Mounted, 201, 206, 217, 226, 235–7
  Tank, 433n., 464–5, 469, 471
  Divisions:
    Cavalry:
      2nd, 484; 4th, 222, 227–8, 235; 5th, 222, 235, 237
      Australian 190, 197, 235–6
      New Zealand, 190
    Infantry:
      1st, 527, 530; *1st (Canadian)*, 492, 497; *2nd (Australian)*, 481; *2nd (Canadian)*, 486, 488; *3rd (Australian)*, 472, 527, 530; *3rd (Canadian)*, 486, 488; *4th*, 484, 492; *4th (Australian)*, 440; *4th (Canadian)*, 492; *5th*, 280; *5th (Australian)* 438, 527, 530; *7th*, 289; *7th (Indian)*, 191–2, 200, 235; *8th*, 397, 399; *10th*, 202, 223–4; *11th*, 514; *12th*, 413; *13th*, 413; *15th*, 413; *18th*, 472; *19th*, 397, 399n.; *21st*, 397, 399; *22nd*, 295, 302, 304; *23rd*, 274, 276, 289; *25th*, 397, 399; *26th*, 295, 302; *27th*, 300; *28th*, 302; *32nd*, 527, 530; *34th*, 413; *41st*, 274, 276, 280; *47th (North Midland)*, 526–8; *48th*, 289; *50th*, 397, 399; *51st*, 413–14, 486, 488; *52nd*, 175, 192, 492; *53rd*, 223; *56th*, 514; *57th*, 492, 496–7, 519, 521–2; *60th*, 187, 190, 197–8; *62nd*, 413–14; *63rd (Naval)* 492, 496–7, 519–21; *74th*, 192; New Zealand, 477
  Brigades:
    Cavalry:
      1st (Aust.) Light Horse, 234
      11th, 228
      11th (Indian), 267
      13th, 218, 222
      Camel, 205
      New Zealand, 188
    Infantry:
      29th, 202; *137th*, 526; *158th*, 223; *179th*, 187–8; *181st*, 187.
      Tank: *3rd*, 484, 523; *4th*, 523; *5th*, 523
  Regiments:
    Cavalry:
      Auckland Mounted Rifles, 187

Australian Light Horse, 1st, 187, 189
Australian Light Horse, 3rd, 222
Australian Light Horse, 5th, 233
Dragoon Guards, 5th, 438
Hodson's Horse, 218
Hussars, 14th, 249
Jodhpore Lancers, 201
Middlesex Yeomanry, 228
  Infantry:
    Gurkhas, 1/7th, 267
    London, 2/18th, 186
    London, 2/19th, 186–7
    London, 2/20th, 180
    Sikhs, 53rd, 201
    South Wales Borderers, 7th, 295
American:
  First, 508
  Corps:
    II, 523–4
  Divisions:
    27th, 527–8; *30th*, 527
Austrian:
  Fifth, 289
  Sixth, 289
Bulgarian:
  First, 309–10
  Eleventh, 310
French:
  First, 413, 418, 435–6, 451, 455, 467–8, 505, 523, 528, 541
  Third, 435n.
  Fourth, 399n.
  Sixth, 397–9, 400
  Tenth, 473
German:
  Second, 436, 441
  Sixth, 436
  Seventh, 436, 456
  Ninth, 456
  Eighteenth, 436
Greek:
  Divisions:
    Crete, 302
    Seres, 302
Italian:
  Third, 286
  Fourth, 287, 289
  Sixth, 289
  Eighth, 289
  Tenth, 289, 291
  Twelfth, 289

Army: Italian—*continued*
    Corps:
        XI, 289
        XII, 289
        XVI, 326
    Serbian:
        First, 301
        Second, 301
    Turkish:
        Fourth, 223, 228, 231, 235, 238
        Fifth, 181
        Seventh, 214–15, 220, 222–3, 228, 238
        Eighth, 211, 214–15, 222–3, 238
    Corps:
        III, 182
        XIII, 244
        XVIII, 245
        XX, 182
        Asia, 227
    Divisions:
        3rd (Cav.), 199
        24th, 196–7, 199
    Brigades:
        Caucasus Cav. 195, 199
Arnaville, bombed, 121
Ars, bombed, 149
Ashington, 330
Asquith, Rt. Hon. H. H., 32*n*., 62; 65
Athus, 124
Aubigny-au-Bac, bombed, 471–2
Audenarde, bombed, 540
Audun-le-Roman, bombed, 149
Aulnoye, bombed, 530–1, 535, 537, 542
Austin Company, 33
Austrian Army, *see* 'Army, Austrian'
Auxi-le-Chateau, aerodrome, 400, 432
Awoingt, bombed, 523
Azraq, 213

Babannit, 238
Bacon, V.-Adm. Sir R. H. S., 383
Baghdad, 247–8
Bailey, Capt. G. B., 497, 521
Bainville-sur-Madon, 124
Baird, Maj. J. L. 13*n*., Parliamentary Under Secretary of State for R.A.F., 23, 27
Baker, Lt. L. W., 203
Baku, 253–7
Balata, 220
Balfour, Rt. Hon. A. J., 58–9, 85

Balloons:
    British: Palestine operations, 202–4
    Bases:
        No. 1, 314; *No. 2*, 315; *No. 3*, 315; *No. 4*, 315; *No. 5*, 315; *No. 6*, 314
    Wings: 1st, 504; *4th*, 275
    Companies: 20th, 280; *21st*, 176, 202–3, 209; *22nd*, 302; *23rd*, 247, 263
    Sections:
        3, 289*n*.; *7*, 289*n*., 290; *26*, 302–3; *27*, 302–3; *33*, 289; *49*, 176, 202–3, 209; *50*, 176, 202–3, 209; *51*, 247; *52*, 241, 247; *54*, 203; *57*, 202–3, 209
    German: Balloon barrages, Allied aeroplanes destroyed by, 156–7
Bannu, 269
Bapaume, battle of:
    Sir D. Haig's plans, 469; air concentration, 469–70; preliminary operations at Albert (21st/22nd Aug. 1918), 471–3; Main attack begins (23/8/18), 472–4; Sir D. Haig's telegram defining change of offensive tactics, 473–4; Wireless Central Information Bureau (C.I.B.), establishment of, 474–5; low-flying attacks on enemy anti-tank batteries, 477–8; capture of Bapaume, 481; the dropping of ammunition by parachutes, 484
    Bombing attacks (*British*), 471–2, 476, 478–81
    Contact patrol, 482–3
    Fighting in the air, 472, 479–81, 484
    Low-flying attacks (*British*), 471, 474–9, 482–3
    Wireless telegraphy (*British*), 474–5, 482–3
Baquba, 245, 247
Baring, Maj. the Hon. M., 115
Barker, Capt. A. T., 361*n*.
Barker, Miss L. C., 71
Barker, Maj. W. G., 284; awarded V.C., 542–3
Barnes, G. N., 67
Barracca, Maj., 286
Bates, Maj. F. A., 294*n*., 302
Bazuel, Ger. aerodrome, bombed, 509
Beatty, Adm. Sir David, 329–30, 369

INDEX

Beauchamp-Proctor, Capt. A. W., awarded V.C., 544
Beaurevoir, bombed, 531
Belgian Air Service, co-operation with, 534; strength of aircraft, May/June, 1918, App. xl
Belgians, H.M. King of, 510, 531–2, 535, 540, 541*n*.
Belgium, German retirement from, 544–51; Allied bombing attacks on communications during, 544–51; concentration of German fighting squadrons in defence against, 544; weakness of D.H.9 as a day bomber, 544–7; low-bombing attacks on German aerodromes, 549–50
Bell, Lt. E., 180
Below, Gen. Otto von, 273
Beni Sakr tribe, 195, 199
Bentley, Lt. W. O., 34
Berehaven, 338
Bergues, 88
Bertangles, aerodrome, bombed, 161, 480
Bertry, Ger. aerodome, bombed, 521, 531
Bévillers, Ger. aerodrome, bombed, 521
Bewsher, Capt. P., 386
Bicharakoff, Lt.-Col., 248–9, 252–3
Birdwood, Gen, Sir W. R., 512
Bir Salem, 209
Bizerta, 314, 317
Blacklock, 2nd A/M. W. M., 378
Blarges, No. 12 Ordnance Depot, bombed, 423–4
Boddam-Whetham, Commr. E. K., 369*n*.
Bohemia Limited, 55
Boisdinghem aerodrome, 480
Bombing:
  Concentrated bombing schemes, 407–11, Memoranda by Inter-Allied Transportation Council, 407–8, views of Gen. Plumer, 408–9; memo. by Maj.-Gen. J. M. Salmond, 409; organization of, 409–10, App. xxi; results and reports on, 410–11; summary of methods of bombing, App. xxiii; statistics, Mar.–Oct. 1918, 491; weakness of D.H.9 as a day bomber, 544–7, relative performance of, in comparison with D.H.9a, 545
  Attacks:
  (British) *Independent Force*: 120–1, 126–35, 138–41, 143–52, Aerodrome bombing, 158–64, App. xiii; *Palestine Operations*, 176–8, 182, 184–8, 193, 199–200, 204, 213–16, 218–20, 222, 224–6, 231–4, 236–8; *Mesopotamia, Persia, and India*, 241–2, 246; *Italian front*, 277, 279, 288, 291–2; *Macedonia*, 294–5, 297, 300, 305, 312; *Mediterranean*, 318, 320–1, 324–8; Naval air operations, Home Waters, 1918, 386–90, 393–6; *Champagne, offensives in*, 402–3; against German lines of communications, 410–11; *Hamel, attack on*, 417; *Amiens, battle of*, 437, 441–2, 446–54; *Bapaume, battle of*, 471–2, 476, 478–81, 508–9; *Scarpe, battle of*, 486–91; *Drocourt-Quéant Switch*, 495, 501; *Havrincourt and Epéhy, battle of*, 504–5; *St. Mihiel, battle of*, 508–9; *Hindenburg line, breaking of*, 519–23, 526, 529–31, 535–8; *Flanders, battles in*, 533–5, 539–40, 544–51; (French) 119–21; (German), against Independent Force, 126–7; main attacks on British aerodromes and depots (1917–18), 161–2; *Palestine operations*, 189, 199, 204–5, 213–14, 230; *Mesopotamia*, 246; *Italian Front*, 277–9; *Mediterranean*, 324–5; *Naval air operations* (1918) 370, 376; *Champagne, offensives in*, 400; against Allied lines of communications, 419–31; *Bapaume, battle of*, 479–80; activity on British front in France, May–Oct. 1918, App. xliii
Bonn, bombed, 146, 151; 147
Borkum, Ger. Naval Air Base, 353, 358–9, 360, 375
Boroevitch, Gen. von, 285
Borton, Brig.-Gen. A. E., 209–10, 229–30
Boulay, Ger. aerodrome, bombed, 146, 148, 159
Boulogne, bombed, 479–80

Bous, Mannesmann works at, bombed, loss of output, 153
Bouvincourt, Ger. aerodrome, bombed, 459
Bowman, Capt. C., 447
Boyd, Lt. J., 305
Boyd, Capt. K. G., 346
Boyd, Maj. O. T., 247
'Boyd Cable', see 'Ewart, Col. E. A.'
Bradley, Maj. C. R. S., 269
Bradley, Lt.-Col. R. A., 247
Brancker, Maj.-Gen. W. S., 15–16; Controller-General of Equipment, 22; Master-General of Personnel, 27; 43, 48, 74*n*., 79
Brasier Company, 36
Bray Dunes, aerodrome bombed, 161
Brébières, bombed, 488
Brest, American seaplane base, 338
Brigades (R.F.C. and R.A.F.): I, 435, 449–51, 470, 479, 485–6, 489, 492–5, 498–9, 512–13, 516, 548; II, 480, 486, 493, 501, 512–13, 532–3, 548; III, 400, 435, 449, 469–70, 474, 476, 478, 482*n*., 491, 493, 498–9, 506, 512–13, 519, 548; V, 434, 436, 439*n*., 451, 453, 463, 469, 474–6, 478, 482*n*., 512–13, 524–5, 529, 537–8, 548; VII, 275, 280, 382, 385; VIII, 128, 135; IX, 401–4, 407, 409, 411–14, 433*n*., 434–5, 446, 449–50, 452–3, 470, 474, 476, 480, 485–6, 488–9, 493, 501, 508, 513, 518–19, 521, 526, 529, 533, 546; X, 435, 469, 486, 494, 512, 548–9; *Palestine*, 202, 209–10, 224; *Training (Egypt)*, 202, 208
Briggs, Lt.-Gen. Sir C. J., 296, 302
Brindisi, K/B base at, 314–15, 317*n*., 319
British Aviation Mission to U.S.A., 79
British Cellulose and Chemical Manufacturing Company, 96
British War Mission to U.S.A., 50*n*.
Broumousky, Capt., 286
Brown, Capt. A. R., 224
Brown, Lt. J. N., 490
Bruges, 382, 384, 389; bombed, 393, 395, 533
Brussels station, bombed, 550
Buchanan, Lt. W. J., 305–7
Buhl, Ger. aerodrome, bombed, 148, 159
Buk bridge, bombed, 324

Bulfin, Lt.-Gen. Sir E. S., 206
Bulgaria, see 'Macedonia'
Bulgarian Army, see 'Army, Bulgarian'
Burbach, bombed, 120, 126, 146–7, 154
Burnett, Lt.-Col. C. S., 209
Busigny, bombed, 519, 521, 526, 529
Byng, Gen. the Hon. Sir J. H. P., 512

Cairo, 325
Calais, No. 2 Base, M.T. Depot, bombed, 298, 429–31, 462
Cambrai, bombed, 453, 472, 476, 479, 489–90, 493, 501; 537 (re-occupied)
Cameron, Lt.-Col. D. C., 234
Campagne, ammunition dump, bombed, 425
Campbell, Maj.-Gen. Sir F., 269
Campoformido, bombed, 288
Canal du Nord, battle of, 518–23
Candas, 274–5
Cantin, bombed, 489, 491
Capel, airship stn., 348
Carbery, Capt. D. H. N., 482, 522
Carr, Lt. J. B., 190
Casarsa, bombed, 279
Casualties, total of, all causes, to Air Service personnel 1914–18, App. xxxvi; comparison by months, July 1916–July 1918 (Western front), App. xxxvii
Cattaro, 319; bombed, 321
Cavalletto, M., 289*n*.
Cavan, Lt.-Gen. the Earl of, 280 289
Cavers, Lt. J. P., 300
Cayley, Maj.-Gen. Sir W. de S., 243, 245–6
Caza Piazza, 281, 289*n*.
Cecil, Lord Hugh, 13*n*.
Cellonite Company, 96
Central Information Bureau, 474–5, 487, 503, 517, 525, 536
Cerniste, bombed, 305
Cestovo, bombed, 305
Chacksfield, Lt. J. C., 261
Chailly-en-Brie, aerodrome, 412
Châlons-sur-Marne, 134
Chamberlain, Rt. Hon. Austen, Chairman of the Man-Power Distribution Board, 63
Chamberlain, Rt. Hon. Neville, Director-General of National Service, 65, 82

INDEX

Chambley, Ger. aerodrome, bombed, 121
Champagne, offensives in, 27th May–2nd Aug. 1918:
   Aisne, battle of, German offensive (May 1918), work of No. 52 Squadron, 397–400; *the battle of the Matz,* Gen. Foch requests British air assistance, 401; IX Brigade R.A.F. moves south, 401; concentration of French squadrons, 402; German attack launched (9/6/18), 403; French counter-attack, 404–5; Gen. Foch memo. on disposition of German forces, 405–6; return of IX Brigade, R.A.F. to British area, 407; *Marne, Second battle of,* IX Brigade, R.A.F. co-operation, 412–15
   Bombing attacks (*British*), 402–3
   Fighting in the air, 399, 403, 414, 417
   French Air Service, co-operation with, 401–4, 412–14, 435
   Low-flying attacks (*British*), 400, 403–4, 414, 417
   Photography, air (*British*), 410
   Reconnaissance, air (*British*), 397–9, 404
Chanak, bombed, 324
Charleroi, bombed, 541
Charlton, Brig.-Gen. L. E. O., 436, 475, 512, 525
Chase, Pte. W. F., 361n.
Chaulnes, bombed, 402, 459
Chauncey, A., 74n.
Chauvel, Lt.-Gen. Sir H. G., 199, 206, 226, 227
Chaytor, Maj.-Gen. Sir E. W. C., 206, 210, 227–8, 230–4
Chepeldze, bombed, 294
Chetwode, Lt.-Gen. Sir P. W., 206, 223
Churchill, Rt. Hon. Winston S., Minister of Munitions, 17n., 53n., 68n., 82–4
Cinarli, bombed, 305
City of Oxford, Br. aircraft carrier, 315
Clark, Lt. J. W. G., 521
Clemenceau, M. Georges, 105, 108–11, 297
Clements, Lt. J. B. V., 482, 522

Clement-Talbot Company, 36, 49, 51, 55–6
Coalition Ministry, formation of, 65
Coastal motor-boat operations, 367–75
Cobbe, Lt.-Gen. Sir A. S., 263, 265
Coblenz, bombed, 129, 140, 143, 150
Cologne, 124, 139–40, 147; bombed, 129, 132, 143, 144–6
Committee of Imperial Defence, 58–9
Communications, lines of: *Allied,* German attacks on, 419–31; *German,* Allied attacks on, summary of results of, 157–8, 407–11, 476, 521, 535, 537, 544–51
Conflans, 124
Conrick, Lt. F. C., 224
Constantinople, bombed, 324
Contact Patrol (British): *Amiens, battle of,* 466–7; *Bapaume, battle of,* 482–3; *Scarpe, battle of,* 487, 489; *The Drocourt-Quéant Switch,* 497–8, 501–3; *Havrincourt and Epéhy, battle of,* 506; *Hindenburg line, breaking of,* 519–22, 528, 536
Corfu, 315, 317n., 319
Cortemarck, bombed, 533
Cottle, Capt. J., 287
Coudekerque, aerodrome, bombed, 161, 394; 384n.
Courcelles, bombed, 148–9
Courtrai, bombed, 533, 540
Cowdray, Rt. Hon. Lord, President of the Air Board, 6–9, 13n., 17n., 18–19; resignation of 21; 34, 45, 48, 166, 167n.
Cox, Sir Percy Z., 262
Cramaille aerodrome, bombed, 400
Cramlington, 330–1
Crawford, Lady Gertrude, 73
Crete, 323
Crossley Motors Ltd., 55
Culley, Lt. S. D., 371–3
Cunard Steam Ship Company, Ltd., 54
Curacoa, Br. L. Cr., 358
Curzon, Lord, 5, 30–1, 32

Damascus, 235–7; bombed, 236
Darley, Capt. C. H., 393
Darmstadt, bombed, 143–5
Dawes, Lt.-Col. G. W. P., 297
Dawnay, Lt.-Col. A. G. C., 193
Dawson, Lt. S., 365n.

566 INDEX

Debeney, Gen., 435, 467
de Castelnau, Gen., 115
Degoutte, Gen., 532
de Havilland, G., 169
Deiran, 176
Demir Hisar, bombed, 294
Demir Kapija, bombed, 303
Dempsey, Capt. J. A. D., 180
Denain, bombed, 501, 538
de Pass, Lt. R. D., 300
Depots, Ammunition, German bombing of, 423–5; No. 2 Base, M.T. Depot, Calais bombed, 298, 429–31, 462
Der'a, bombed, 213, 232
Derby, Earl of, 4–5, 23; Secretary of State for War, 17n., 19; Director of Recruiting, 62
Derby, National Shell Factory, 51
'Derby Scheme', 62
Deynze, bombed, 540
Diaz, Gen., 288–9
Dickey, Capt. R. F. L., 361n.
Dickson, Capt. W. F., 365n.
Dillingen, bombed, 128
Dixon, Charles, 89
Doig, 1st Air Mechanic, 180
Dosson, 290
Douai, bombed, 479, 491, 501
Douglas-Pennant, Hon. Violet, 73
Dover, 385–6
Drama aerodrome, bombed, 294, 313, 324
Dreyfus, Dr., 96
Drocourt–Quéant Switch, 492–503: plans, 492–5; the attack begins, 495; German retirement to Canal du Nord, 499–500; economy in use of fighter squadrons, R.A.F. orders, 500–1; work of the R.A.F. Corps Squadrons reviewed, 501–3; dropping ammunition by parachutes, 503
Bombing attacks (*British*), 495, 501
Contact patrol, 497–8, 501–3
Fighting in the air, 496, 498–9, 501
Low-flying attacks (*British*), 496, 500
Photography, air (*British*), 503
Wireless telegraphy (*British*), 501–3
Drummond, Capt. R. M., 183
Drury, Capt. P. D., 180

Duckham, Sir Arthur, Director-General of Aircraft Production, Ministry of Munitions, 27; 57
Dudley National Projectile Factory, 51
Dungeness, s.s., 345
Dunkirk, 384–6
'Dunsterforce', 248–57
Dunsterville, Maj.-Gen. L. C., 247, 249–50, 253, 257
Durazzo, bombed, 321, 327–8
Düren, bombed, 143–4, 145
Düsseldorf, 118
Duval, Gen., 105–6, 115

Earl of Peterboro', Br. Mon., 326
East Fortune, 347, 365
Eaton, Ensign J. A., U.S.N.F.C., 361n., 362
Egna, bombed, 288
Ehrang, 148; bombed, 152
Ellington, Maj.-Gen. E. L., Controller-General of Equipment, 27
Elouges, bombed, 546
Empress, Br. aircraft carrier, 315, 318
Engadine, Br. aircraft carrier, 314
Engines, aero:
  Disposition of, on charge of R.A.F., 31/10/18., App. xli
  types:
   A.B.C., *Dragonfly*, 43–4; A.R.I., 34; Bentley Rotary, 34, 42–4, 51; B.H.P., 32–4, 37–8, 42, 51, 142, 143n., 169, 545; B.M.W., 445, 537; Clerget, 34, 42; Curtiss, O.X.5, 331; Fiat, 42, 123n.; Hispano-Suiza, 29n., 31–7, 42, 51; Le Rhône, 34; Liberty, 51–3, 98, 146n., 169, 545; R.A.F., 34, 45, 51n., 331n.; Renault, 45, 51n.; Rolls-Royce, 34, 45–6, 48–51, 55, 98, 123n., 169, 339, 454; Sunbeam, 32–5, 37, 42, 51, 53; Wolseley, 36n.
Ennemain, Ger. aerodrome, 456, 458
Enzeli, 251, 253, 256
Epinoy, Ger. aerodrome, 486
Equancourt, bombed, 452–3
Ermerchicourt, Ger. aerodrome, bombed, 486, 505, 521
Essad Bey, Col. 195–6
Essen, 150n.
Estourmel, Ger. aerodrome, bombed, 504–5

INDEX

Estreux, bombed, 546
Etaples, railway bridge and hospitals, bombed, 419-21
Étreux, Ger. aerodrome, bombed, 480, 493, 509
Everidge, Maj. J., 247
Ewart, Col. E. A., 87-9

Factories, National: Aintree, Aircraft, 56-7; Derby, Shell, 51; Dudley, Projectile, 51; Finchley, Balloon, 56; Greet, Radiator, 55-6; Hayes, Aircraft, 56; Heaton Chapel, Aircraft, 55-6; Kensington, Aircraft, 56; Richmond, Aircraft, 54; Sudbury, Radiator, 55-6; Waddon, Aircraft, 54, 56
Falkenhayn, Gen. von, 181, 185
Falls, Capt. C., 227n., 297n., 304n., 327n.
Feisal, Emir, 183, 185, 193, 204n., 206, 212
Felixstowe, 352, 361n., 362-3, 369, 376-8
Fellowes, Lt.-Col. P. F. M., 393-4
Ferrero, Gen., 326-7
Fienvillers, 275
Fieri, bombed, 326
Fighting in the air:
  Economy in use of fighter squadrons, R.A.F. orders, September 1918, 500-1; policy regarding employment of fighter squadrons, Brig.-Gen. Longcroft's instructions re, 22nd September, 1918, 506-7; concentration of German fighting squadrons in Belgium, 544; discussions of British policy on Western front, 552-8; see also App. XX
  Independent Force Operations, 129-32, 139, 141, 143, 146-9; *Palestine air operations*, 178, 183, 204, 207-8, 210, 213-14, 229-30, 237-8; *Mesopotamia*, 241; *Italian Front*, 276, 281-2, 287-8, 291; *Macedonia*, 300-1, 305; *Mediterranean*, 321, 326; *Naval air operations, Home Waters*, 1918, 353, 359-64, 369, 377-9, 396; *Champagne, offensives in*, 399, 403, 414, 417; *Amiens, battle of*, 441-4, 446-54, 462, 466; *Bapaume, battle of*, 472, 479-81, 484; *Scarpe, battle of*, 487-91; *Drocourt-Quéant Switch*, 496, 498-9, 501; *Havrincourt and Epéhy, battle of*, 505-6; *Hindenburg Line, breaking of*, 521, 529-30; *Flanders, battles in*, 546-50
Finchley, National Balloon Factory, 56
Finlay, Lt. G., 224
Fismes, aerodrome, 397, 399
Flanders, battles in (28th Sept.–11th Nov. 1918):
  General Allied plans, 531; plan for employment of Allied air services, 531-2; the attack at Ypres (28th Sept.–2nd Oct.), 532-3; food dropping by aeroplanes, 534; resumption of offensive (14th Oct.), battle of Courtrai, 539-40; Germans evacuate Belgian coast, 540; work of 5th Group, tribute by H.M. King of Belgians, 541n.; see also Belgium
  American Air Service, co-operation with, 539
  Belgian Air Service, co-operation with, 534
  Bombing attacks (*British*), 533-5, 539-40, 554-5
  Fighting in the air, 546-50
  Low-flying attacks (*British*), 533-4, 540, 549-51
Flavelle, Lt. G. A., 433n.
Flavy-le-Martel, bombed, 403
Fleet, see 'Naval air operations (Home Waters), 1918'
Flights, 'C' (142 Sqdn.), 210; 'X' 184, 193, 204-5, 212-13, 233n.; 'Z' 280-1
Flying-boats, see 'Seaplanes'
Foch, Marshal F., 104, 107-13, 115-16, 148-9, 151, 164, 174, 392-3, 397, 400-1, 405-6, 412-15, 417-18, 424, 438, 455, 469, 508, 510, 532
Food, dropping of, by air to forward troops, 534
Foreste, Ger. aerodrome, 456
Franchet d'Espérey, Gen., 296-7, 299, 308, 311-12, 327
Frankfurt, 124; bombed, 143, 145-6, 148
Franklin, H. H., Manufacturing Company, 50n.
Freiburg in Breisgau, bombed, 121, 130

568 INDEX

French Air Service: Independent Force Operations, 124–5, 134; *Macedonia*, 305; *Matz, battle of*, 1918, 401–4; *Marne, second battle of*, 412–14; *Amiens, battle of*, 435, 467–8; strength of aircraft, all fronts, May/June, 1918, App. xl
French Army, *see* 'Army, French'
French, Field-Marshal Sir John, 61
Frescaty, Ger. aerodrome, bombed, 148–9, 151, 159–60
Fresnoy-les-Roye, bombed, 403
Froville, Chateau de, 128
Fuller, Brevet-Col. J. F. C., 471, 477*n*.
Furious, Br. aircraft carrier, 351*n*., 363–5
Furness-Williams, Capt. F. H., 183*n*.
Furse, Dame Katherine, 72–3
Fuweile, El, bombed, 184

Galata, bombed, 324–5
Galatea, Br. L. Cr., 364
Gallipoli, bombed, 324
Galvayne, Lt. U. F. A., 363
Gamble, C. F. Snowden, *The Story of a North Sea Air Station*, 361*n*.
Gardner, Maj. G. D., 294*n*.
Geddes, Sir Eric, First Lord of the Admiralty, 17*n*., 19
Genoa, 317
George, Rt. Hon. D. Lloyd, Minister of Munitions, 60–3; Prime Minister, 7, 10, 18, 21, 65, 75, 82, 109, 274
George, Gertrude A., 74*n*.
German Air Service:
Palestine, air operations in, 208; *Italian front*, 273; use of parachutes, 282; *Naval air operations, Home Waters*, 1918, 358–64, 376–80; *attacks on Allied lines of communications*, 419–31; *Amiens, battle of*, 436, 442–3; Fokker DVII, 445; 456, 458, 462; *Bapaume, battle of*, 479–80, 484; policy of air fighting discussed, 556–7; casualties, 1914–18, App. xxxvi
Seaplane Units:
'*Flanders I*', 376–80
Squadrons:
No. 4 (Bombing), 279
German Army, *see* 'Army, German'
Ghedi, 275

Ghistelles, Ger. aerodrome, 540
Gibraltar, 315–17
Giralda, s.s., 346
Gordon, Wing Capt. R., 315
Gorgop, 300
Göring, *Hauptmann*, H., 442*n*., 443–4
Goss Printing Company, 54
Gough-Calthorpe, V.-Adm. the Hon. Sir S. A., C.-in-C. Med., 314, 318
Gouraud, Gen., 510
Graham, Maj. R., 390
Grant, Corpl. F., 360*n*.
Gray, Lt. W. E., 395
Greek Air Service, co-operate in Mediterranean operations 1918, 323
Greek Army, *see* 'Army, Greek'
Greet, National Radiator Factory, 55–6
Grey, C. G., 45*n*.
Grossa, 276, 281, 289
Grosskreutz, Maj., 102*n*., 118*n*., 119*n*., 120, 153*n*.
Groups, R.A.F.: Adriatic, 314; Aegean, 315, 323–5; Egypt, 315, 325; Gibraltar, 315; Malta, 314; Portsmouth, 332; South Western, 332; *5th*, 384–5, 391, 513, 531–3; *27th*, 173
Groves, Capt. R. M., R.N., 330–1
Gueira, El, 204, 233*n*.
Guillaumat, Gen., 295–6
Gulemenli, 302
Gumuljina, 313
Guns, *see* 'Anti-aircraft defences'
Gwynne-Vaughan, Mrs. H. C. I., 72*n*., 73–4

Hagendingen, bombed, 141, 154
Haggerston, Maj. T., 362
Haidar Pasha, bombed, 324
Haifa, 235–7
Haig, Field-Marshal Sir Douglas, 2–4, 13–16, 23, 29, 66, 77, 90–1, 114, 121–2, 125, 164–5, 168–71, 382–3, 391–3, 405, 412–13, 415, 417–18, 434, 455, 469, 473, 485, 502, 508, 531, 550
Haig, Lt. F. W., 198
Hajdarli, 302
Halahan, Lt.-Col. F. C., 385
Ham, bombed, 402
Hama, 238*n*.
Hamadan, 247, 257
Hamel, attack on, (4/7/18), 415–17

INDEX 569

Hanmer, Capt. H. I., 190, 228
Hargreaves, Lt. W. H., 203
Harland & Wolff, 174
Harmsworth, Capt, the Hon. H. A. V. St. G., 27*n*.
Harvey, Sir H. Paul, 13*n*.
Harwich, 376
Harwich Force, 353–5, 358, 367, 371–2, 374–6
Haslam, Lt. J. A. G., 466
Haubourdin, Ger. aerodrome, bombed, 549*n*.
Haussimont, aerodrome, 413
Havrincourt and Epéhy, battle of, 504–6; preparatory actions, 504–5, main attack, 505–6
  Bombing attacks (*British*), 504–5
  Contact patrol, 506
  Fighting in the air, 505–6
  Low-flying attacks (*British*), 505
  Wireless telegraphy (*British*), 506
Hawkcraig Experimental Station, 341
Hayes, National Aircraft Factory, 56
Haynecourt, Ger. aerodrome, 486
Heath, Lt. G., 364
Heaton Chapel (Manchester) National Aircraft Factory, 55–6
Hejaz railway, attacks on, 177–80, 193–4
Heligoland, 358–9
Heligoland Bight, mine-fields in the, 350–5
Henderson, Arthur, 60
Henderson, Lt.-Gen. Sir David, 9, 13, 15, 29*n*., 91*n*., 167; Vice-President of the Air Council, 22, 25, resigns, 27
Herbert, Brig.-Gen. P. L. W., 208
Hindenburg Line, breaking of:
  General Allied situation, Sept. 1918, 510; strategic plan of Marshal Foch; role of British forces, 510; description of Hindenburg Line, 511–12; Sir Douglas Haig's policy, 512; plans for preliminary operations, 512–13; R.A.F. on Western front, 513; *Canal du Nord*, battle of, preparations and air plans, 513–14; scheme of R.A.F. co-operation, 514–18; the battle, 518–23; *Capture of the Hindenburg Line*, air co-operation, 524–6; the attack, 523–4, 526–31; capture completed, 535; Cambrai captured, 537; German retirement to the river Selle, 538; *see also*, 'Scarpe', 'Drocourt–Quéant Switch', and 'Havrincourt and Epéhy', battles of
  Bombing attacks (*British*), 519–23, 526, 529–31, 535–8
  Contact patrol, 519–22, 528, 536
  Fighting in the air, 521, 529–30
  Low-flying attacks (*British*), 520–3, 536–8
  Photography, air (*British*), 522–3
Hirson, bombed, 542, 546
Hirtzel, Maj. C. H. A., 302
Hodge, Rt. Hon. John, Minister of Labour, 65
Hodges, Maj. S. G., 302
Hodson, Capt. J., 361*n*., 362
Hoffman, Lt. von, 286
Hogg, Brig.-Gen. R. E. T., 513
Holland, Hannen and Cubitt, Ltd., 54
Homs, bombed, 237
Honeysuckle, Br. sloop, 319
Horne, Gen. Sir H. S., 484, 512
Hudova aerodrome, bombed, 294–5, 303; 307
Hunter, Sir J., 16; Administrator of Works and Buildings, 23, 27
Hyderabad, the Nizam of, 146*n*.
Hydrophones, experiments, 341–2

Imbros, 315, 323; bombed, 324–5
Independent Bombing Force: Policy, 101–17; legal aspect of bombing, 101–3; organization of a strategic bombing force, 104; Inter-Allied Aviation Committee, Supreme War Council, discussions, 104–7, Gen. Duval's views, 105–6; proposals for Inter-Allied Bombing Force, 107; *Joint Note, No. 35*, 107–8, Apps. ix and x; Marshal Foch's memo. (14/9/18), 109–10, 113, App. viii; Inter-Allied Independent Air Force, constitution of, 111–12, Maj.-Gen. Trenchard to command, under supreme command of Marshal Foch, 110–12; the French view, 114–16; programmes for expansion of, 110–13; organization of No. 27 Group, 173–4; the Handley Page (V. 1500), 173–4; *see also* Apps. v, vi, and xi

Independent Force, operations of the: *The Luxeuil Bombing Wing*: co-operation with the French Air Service, 118–19; causes amalgamation of German Home Defence units, the Kaiser's Order in Council, 119–20; reprisals for sinking hospital ship *Asturias*, 121; disbanded, 121–2, Sir D. Haig's views, 122; *Forty-First Wing*, formation, 122–4; Admiralty contribution, 123; plans for employment of, in co-operation with the French, 124–5; *Eighth Brigade*, formed, 128; co-operation with French Eastern Group of Armies, 134; *Independent Force*, formation of, 135; Gen. Trenchard's policy, 135–8; a successful raid on Thionville, 140–1; the D.H.9, 142; increase in strength, 142; seven Handley Pages lost, 147; co-operation with the French and American armies, 148–9, 151; the arrival of the 85th and 88th Wings, 150; general observations on effect of bombing, 152–6; effect of attacks on Volklingen Steel Works, 153–4 and App. xiv; the German balloon barrage, 156–7; summary of results of bombing against rail communications, 157–8; the effect of aerodrome bombing, 158–64; expansion programmes, 164–74; the relative value of day and night bombing, 166–8; D.H.4's or D.H.9's? 169–70; the 'Rothermere' programme, 170–1; List of attacks by British aircraft, showing casualties, App. xiii

Fighting in the air, 129–32, 139, 141, 143, 146–9

Photography, 129, 131

Statistics, 123, 152, 163*n.*, Apps. xii, xiii, and xv

India, War operations in, 268–72

Ingelmunster, bombed, 533

Inter-Allied Aviation Committee, 106–7

Inter-Allied Bombing Force, 107–8, 111–12, 164

Ismail Hakki Bey, Gen., 268

Istrana, 276, 281; bombed, 277, 279

Italian Air Service, *Mediterranean Operations, 1918*, 321, 326; strength of aircraft on all fronts, May–June 1918, App. xl; *Bomber Group, No. 18*, 112*n.*

Italian Army, *see* 'Army, Italian'

Italian Front:
Allied help to Italy, the battle of Caporetto, 273; work of German Air Service, 273–4; R.F.C. and R.A.F. co-operation, 274–6, 283–7, 291–2; Rapallo conference, 274; air situation on arrival of British, 276–8; Allied air superiority in January 1918, 279; reduction in strength and redistribution of British forces (March 1918), 280–1; Austrian offensive (15/6/18), 283–5; the Italian counter-attack, 285; Austrian retreat, 285, part played by R.A.F., 285–6; Italian offensive (2/7/18), 286–7; further reduction in strength of British forces (Sept. 1918), 288; *the battle of Vittorio Veneto*, preparations for, 289–90; organization of R.A.F., 289*n.*–90; the battle begins, 291, Armistice, 291–2

Aerodromes and Landing-grounds: (*Allied*), *see* Caza Piazza, Grossa, Istrana, Limbraga, Malcontenta, Milan, Sarcedo, S. Luca, Verona, Villaverla; (*enemy*), *see* Casarsa, Pergine, San Felice

Bombing attacks: (*British*), 277, 279, 288, 291–2; (*enemy*), 277–9, 282

Fighting in the air, 273, 276, 281–2, 287–8, 291

Low-flying attacks: (*British*), 282–7, 291–2; (*enemy*), 283, 291

Photography, air, 273, 276–7, 290

Reconnaissance, air (*British*), 276–7, 280–3, 287, 292; (*German*), 273

Jackson, Capt. W. D., 365–6

Jangalis, 249–51

Jenin, bombed, 178, 219; 213, 215, 219*n.*, 222

Jericho, 186, 194*n.*

Jerrard, Lt. A., awarded V.C., 281

Jerusalem, 194*n.*, 201

Jisr ed Damiye, bombed, 186, 188

INDEX

Johnson, Air Mechanic, 355n.
Johnson, Claud, 45–7, 49, 51, 86–7
Joint War Air Committee, Est. of, 4; 6
Jonkoping, s.s. (Swedish), 350
Joubert de la Ferté, Lt.-Col. P. B., 280
Joyce, Lt.-Col. P. C., 184
Julis, 176, 178
Junction Station, 176, 186, 194n., 202, 209, 236
Junor, Lt. H. R., 213–14

Kaiserslautern, bombed, 126, 131, 146, 150
Kakara, bombed, 294
Kalafrana, 314
Karlsruhe, bombed, 119, 128, 135, 139, 143, 146
Kassandra, 315, 324
Kazvin, 248, 252–3, 256
Keating, Lt. J. A., U.S.A., 447
Kensington, National Aircraft Factory, 56
Kerr, Adm. Mark E. F., 18; Deputy Chief of the Air Staff, 22
Keyes, V.-Adm. Sir Roger, 383–4, 388, 391–2, 394
Kifri, 247, 257, 263
Killingholme, 355, 357–8
King, Eng. W. H., 348n.
Kirech, 302
Kirkuk 245; bombed, 246
Kitchener, Lord, Secretary of State for War, 58–9, 85
Klemp D., *Archivrat*, 138n.
Kosturino defile, bombed, 308, 311–12
Kryesna pass, bombed, 310–12
Kuchi bridge, bombed, 326
Kuchik Khan, 249–51
Kuleli Burgas, bombed, 324

Labour, industrial unrest, 60, 64, 66; App. xxxi and xxxiii; *see also* 'Supply and Man Power, problems of'
La Ferté, aerodrome, 400
Lahana, 302
Lahore, 271
La Louvière, bombed, 546
Lamb, Lt. R., Royal Scots Fus., 305
Lambe, Brig.-Gen. C. L., 385, 532
Lanchester Company, 33n.
Lancing, National Timber Drying Kilns, 55–6

Law, Rt. Hon. A. Bonar, 5, 19, 103
Lawrence, 2nd Lt. H., 490
Lawrence, Col. T. E., 183–4, 212–13, 229
Lawson, Capt. W. B., 145
Learned, Ensign N. J., 348
Le Bourget, aerodrome, 413
Le Cateau, bombed, 491, 508
Leckie, Capt. R., 360–2
Le Fevre, 2nd Lt. F. E., 156
Le Hameau, aerodrome, 485, 487, 516
Leigh-Mallory, Maj. T. L., 464
Lemnos (Talikna), 323
Lewin, Brig.-Gen. A. C., 263, 265
Lichtervelde, bombed, 533, 535, 540
Limbraga, 281, 290
List, 358–9
Livunovo, bombed, 294, 310
Locust, Br. destroyer, 345
Loewenhardt, *Leutnant*, 443
Lomme, Ger. aerodrome, bombed, 549n.
Londonderry, the Marchioness of, 71
Longcroft, Brig.-Gen. C. A. H., 470, 506, 512
Longmore, Wing Capt. A. M., 314
Longuyon, 124
Lough Swilly, 338
Low-flying attacks by aeroplanes:
  British: enemy defensive measures against, July 1918, App. xxii; *Palestine air operations*, 176–8, 182, 187, 200, 218–21, 224–7, 231–3; *Mesopotamia, Persia, and India*, 240, 242–3, 250–1, 255, 257, 261, 265–6, 269–72; *Italian front*, 282–7, 291–2; *Macedonia*, 300, 303, 305, 308–11; *Mediterranean*, 326, 328; *Champagne, offensives in*, 400, 403–4, 414, 417; *Amiens, battle of*, 437–41, 451; *Bapaume, battle of*, 471, 474–9, 482–3; *Scarpe, battle of*, 485–91; *Drocourt–Quéant Switch*, 496, 500; *Havrincourt and Epéby, battle of*, 405; *Hindenburg Line, breaking of*, 520–3, 536–8; *Flanders, battle in*, 533–4, 540, 549–51
  enemy: *Italian front*, 283, 291
Ludlow-Hewitt, Brig.-Gen. E. R., 512
Luxeuil (Bombing Wing), 118, 121, 126

Ma'an, 183; bombed, 184, 204
Macedonia, final air operations, 1918:
Strength of R.A.F., 293–4; British attack (May 1918), 295; Greek Army co-operates, 295; change in French high command, 296; change in command of Sixteenth Wing R.A.F., 296; preparations for final offensive, 297–8; German bombing on depots in France (May 1918), influence of, on supplies to British Salonika Army, 298–9; plans for the offensive, 299–301; the Franco-Serbian offensive, 301–2; British attack opens, 302; R.A.F. order of battle (18/9/18), 302; battle orders for R.A.F., 303; the landing of Agents, 305–7; the Bulgarians retreat; 307; effect of low bombing, 310–12; hostilities cease (30/9/18), 311
Aerodromes and Landing-grounds: (*Allied*), see Amberkoj, Gorgop, Gumuljina Hajdarli, Kirech, Lahana, Marian, Mudros, Philippopolis, Snevche, Stavros, Stojakovo, Thasos, Yanesh; (*enemy*), Drama, Hudova, Livunovo
Bombing attacks (*British*), 294–5, 297, 300, 305
Fighting in the air, 300–1, 305
French Air Service, co-operation, 305
Low-flying attacks by aeroplanes (*British*) 300, 303, 305, 308–11
Naval air co-operation, 294–5, 309–10, 328
Photography, air, 297, 301
Reconnaissances, air (*British*), 296, 301, 303–4, 307–11, 313
Wireless Telegraphy (*British*), 304–5
McAnally, H. W. W., Assistant Secretary Air Council, 23
McBain, Maj. W. R. B., 302
McCudden, Maj. J. T. B., awarded V.C., 432
Mackay, Capt. D. R. G., 151
Mackay, Lt. G. C., 390
Mackay, Lt. M. C., 254–5
Maclaren, Maj. A. S. C., 210
McLean, Capt. J. Y., 302
Macmillan, N., 74*n*.
Mafraq, bombed, 232

Mahan, Capt. A. T., 94
Mainz, bombed, 129, 146; 141
Malcontenta, 287
Malta, 314, 316–17
Manage, bombed, 546
Mangin, Gen., 414
Mannheim, 124; bombed, 127–8, 131, 134, 139–40, 143, 145–6, 150, 154–6
Mannock, Maj. E., awarded V.C., 432–3
Man-Power, see 'Supply and Man Power, problems of'
Man-Power Committee (August 1917), 67, 74–6
Man-Power Distribution Board, 63–4, 65
Manston, 379
Mantua, 275
Manxman, Br. aircraft carrier, 314
Marcoing, bombed, 472
Marian, 294, 302
Mariembourg, bombed, 546–7
Marinopolje, bombed, 294
Marne, Second battle of, 412–15
Marquion, bombed, 471, 488, 495
Marquise Depot, bombed, 161–2
Marshall, Lt.-Gen. Sir W. R., 239–40, 244, 246–7, 254, 262, 268
Martin, Percy, Controller of Petrol Engine supply, 31; 34, 48
Matz, battle of, 400–7
Maubeuge, bombed, 550
Mawdsley, Lt. S. G., 348
Maxwell, Maj. R. S., 551
Mayen Company, 32*n*., 37
Mazze, M., 289*n*.
Mediterranean, operations in the, 1918: R.A.F. reorganization scheme and duties (1/4/18), 314–16; *Kite balloons with convoys*, 316–18, 322; *U.39* bombed in Straits of Gibraltar, 318; *the Otranto barrage*, 318–19, R.A.F. co-operation, 319–23, strength of Barrage Force (September 1918), 322*n*.; *the Aegean Group*, organization of, 323, duties, 323–4; *the Egypt Group*, organization and duties, 325–6; *Albanian operations*, co-operation with Italian Army, 326–8
Aerodromes and bases (*British*), see Alexandria, Andrano, Bizerta, Brindisi, Corfu, Crete, Genoa,

INDEX 573

Mediterranean—*continued*
    Gibraltar, Imbros, Kalafrana, Kassandra, Lemnos, Malta, Milo, Mityleve, Mudros, Otranto, Port Said, Santa Maria di Leuca, Skyros, Stavros, Syra, Suda Bay, Taranto, Thasos; (*enemy*), *see* Drama, Fieri, Galata, Nagara, Tirana
    Bombing attacks (*British*), 318, 320–1, 324–8; (*enemy*), 324–5
    Fighting in the air, 321, 326
    Greek Air Service, co-operation, 323
    Italian Air Service, co-operation, 321, 326
    Low-flying attacks (*British*), 326, 328
    Photography, air, 327
    Reconnaissance, air (*British*), 320
    Wireless telegraphy (*British*), 320
Melbourne, Australian L.Cr., 361
Melle, bombed, 533, 540
Menin, bombed, 533
Mesopotamia and Persia, air operations in, 1918:
    Mesopotamia, situation in spring of 1918, 239–40; enemy propaganda among native tribes, 240, 244; operations in Tuz Khurmatli–Qara Tepe Area, 241–6; disposition of Thirty-First Wing R.A.F. (May 1918), 247: *Persia and the Caspian Sea*, Operations of the 'Dunsterforce', 248–51; the Christians of Urmia, 251–2; the Caspian operations, 252–7, report of R.A.F. detachment on evacuation of Baku, 254–6, the 'Norper Force' operations, 257–61, the adventure of Lt. T. L. Williams, 258–61; *the autumn campaign in Mesopotamia*, general situation, 262–3, R.A.F. work during the summer months, 263–5, the final offensive, 265–8; defeat of the Turks at Sharqat, 267; occupation of Mosul, 268
    Aerodromes and Landing-grounds: (*British*), *see* Baghdad, Baquba, Enzeli, Hamadan, Kazvin, Kifri, Mianeh, Mirjana, Ramadi, Samarra, Tikrit, Tuz Khurmatli, Zenjan

    Bombing attacks:
      (*British*), 241–2, 246
      (*German*), 246, 250–1, 254
    Fighting in the air, 241
    Low-flying attacks by aeroplanes: (*British*), 240, 242–3, 250–1, 255, 257, 261, 265–6
    Photography, air, 248, 263
    Reconnaissances, air: (*British*), 240–6, 250, 254–8, 263–7
    Statistics, 268
Meteren, 417
Metz-Sablon, 124; bombed, 128, 131, 133, 139, 148–9, 151–2
Metz-Woippy, 124
Mézières, bombed, 149, 151
Mianeh, 252
Milan, 275
Miletkovo, bombed, 301, 305
Mills, Lt.-Col. R. P., 274
Milne, Gen. Sir G. F., 293–9, 308–9, 312, 328
Milner, Rt. Hon. Lord, 19, 67
Milo, 317
Mirjana, 241, 247, 263
Mitchell, Shaw & Company, 54
Mitylene, 323
Moberly, Brig.-Gen. F. J., 239*n*
Moislains, Ger. aerodrome, bombed, 459, 472
Moll, *Kapitänleutnant*, 351*n*., 358*n*.
Money, Pte. J. N., 360*n*.
Mons, bombed, 538, 541
Montagu, Rt. Hon. E. S., Minister of Munitions, 65
Mont d'Origny, Ger. aerodrome, 480–1, 493
Montgomery, Gen. Sir A., 438
Montichiari, 275
Montigny, Ger. aerodrome, bombed, 529
Montoy, Ger. aerodrome, 148
Morgan, Lt. A. E., 261
Morhange (Morchingen), Ger. aerodrome, bombed, 120, 152, 159–60
Motor Radiator Manufacturing Company, 55
Moulin-les-Metz, bombed, 121
Mouscron, bombed, 540
Mudauwara, bombed, 185, 204
Mudros, 309–10, 315, 323
Mullion, 338*n*., 343, 349
Mulock, Lt.-Col. R. H., 173

Munday, Capt. A. H., 355–7
Munitions Council (Aug. 1917), 68
Munitions, Ministry of, Controller of Aeronautical Supplies, 15; 29; Aeronautical Department formed, 31; 53–5, 57, 60–1, 64, 68–9, 82–4
Munitions of War Acts, 1915–17, 61
Mustard, Lt. E. A., 229

Nagara, bombed, 324
Namur, bombed, 541, 546–7
Nancy, 123, 135*n*., 165
Napier Company, 33*n*.
National Factories, *see* 'Factories'
Naval Air Developments and Operations, 1918:
Home waters, measures taken against enemy submarines, use of aeroplanes for patrol of inshore waters, 329–30, Capt. R. M. Groves' scheme, 330–1, the D.H.6, 331–4, the housing of personnel, 332–3; Admiralty policy and scheme for employment of aircraft, 334–5; Admiralty air requirements for, 336–40, engine output the limiting factor, 338–9, the Large America flying-boat, 338–40, programme and strength of aircraft at Armistice, 340, the Blackburn Kangaroo, 340; *Hydrophone experiments*, 341–3; *Anti-submarine aircraft patrols*, statistics for 1917–18, 343–5, Apps. xvii, xviii; *U-boats destroyed*, 345–8; Convoys, aircraft escort, 348–50, kite balloons for convoys, 350; *Mine fields in the Heligoland Bight*, 350–5, towed lighters for flying-boats, 352–3, air reconnaissances of the Heligoland Bight, 353–5, 357–8; *destruction of Zeppelin 'L.62'*, 355–7; rescue of American airmen, 358; German seaplane bases, 358, German aircraft carriers, 358, German air strength and equipment, 359, operations in North Sea, 359–64; British air attack on Tondern Airship base, 365–7, the destruction of Zeppelins *'L.54'* and *'L.60'*, 367; *Coastal motor-boat operations*, 367–75; flying off lighters, trials, 370–1, destruction of Zeppelin *'L.53'*, 372–4, engagement between aircraft and motor-boats, 374–5; the German Seaplane unit *'Flanders I'*, superiority of, 376–80; *The Belgian Coast and Flanders*, reorganization of the Dover–Dunkirk command, 380–2, 384, German offensive March and April 1918, effect on, 383, air strength at Dunkirk, 382–7, U.S. Northern Bombing Group, 383–4, plans for raids on German U-boat bases, 383–4, formation of 5th Group, R.A.F., 385, plans for Naval operations against Zeebrugge Canal and Ostend harbour, 385–7, operations 387–91, request for air reinforcements, 391, the formation of Eighty-Second Wing, 392, low-bombing attacks on Zeebrugge lock gates, 393–5, the bombing of Varssenaere aerodrome, 395–6
Aerodromes, stations, and bases (*British*), *see* Ashington, Berehaven, Brest, Capel, Coudekerque, Cramlington, Dover, Dunkirk, East Fortune, Felixstowe, Harwich, Killingholme, Lough Swilly, Manston, Mullion, Queenstown, Redcar, Seaton Carew, Teteghem, Waterford, Westgate, Yarmouth; (*enemy*), *see* Borkum, Heligoland, List, Nordeney, Nordholz, Tondern, Varssenaere, Wilhelmshaven, Zeebrugge
American Air Service, co-operation, 384, 395
Bombing attacks (*British*), 386–90, 393–6; (*enemy*), 370, 376, 394
Fighting in the air, 353, 359–64, 369, 377–9, 396
Photography, air, 385, 388–9
Reconnaissance, air (*British*), 353–5, 357, 359, 363, 367, 385, 389–90
Wireless Telegraphy, 354–5, 370, 373, 375–6
Naval, and Naval Air co-operation, *Palestine Air Operations*, 176; *Macedonia*, 294–5, 309–10, 328
Nazareth, 207, 211
Nesle, bombed, 403
Neumann, G. P., 274*n*., 277*n*.

INDEX 575

Newall, Lt.-Col. C. L. N., 123, 128, 135
Newbolt, Sir Henry, *Naval operations*, 319*n*., 322*n*., 329*n*.
Night-fighting, formation of No. 151 Sqdn., 428–9; 472, 480, 506
Nordeney, 358–9, 375
Nordholz, 355
Norman, Sir Henry, 27
'Norper force', 257–61
Northcliffe, Lord, 21, 50, 98
Nowshera, 268
Nunan, Lt. S. A., 224
Nursing Service, R.A.F., 74

Ochey, aerodrome, 120, 123*n*., 124–5; bombed, 126–7
Offenburg, bombed, 139
Offoy, Ger. aerodrome, bombed, 472
Oliver, Wing Commr. D. A., 314
Ophelia, Br. destroyer, 348
Oppau, 124; bombed, 134, 146, 154
Orneaux, aerodrome, 412
Ostend, 384, 388–90; bombed, 393, 533
Otranto, 314–15, 319, 326; Barrage, 318–23
Ouse, Br. destroyer, 346–7

Padua, 274; bombed, 279
Paine, Maj.-Gen. Sir G. M., 13*n*., 15–16; Master-General of Personnel, 22; Inspector-General of the R.A.F., 27; 121
Palestine, air operations in, 1918:
  Disposition of Palestine Brigade R.A.F., 176; *The Jordan Valley*, 177–83; the attacks on the *Hejaz railway*, 177–80, 193–4; Gen. Liman Von Sanders assumes command of Turkish armies, 181–2; *Co-operation with the Arabs*, the Arab Campaign, 183–5, ('X' Flight), 184–5, 204–5, 212–14; 228–30, 235, 237–8; *the 'Amman raid*, 185–91; effect of German offensive in France on policy in Eastern theatres, Gen. Smuts' visit, 191–2; *the Es Salt attacks*, 194–200; minor operations, 200–2; *the final offensive*, Gen. Allenby's plans, 205–7, the offensive opens, 207, German aircraft, 208, 215, order of battle, Palestine Brigade, 209, Air Staff plans, 210–11, Bombing of the Turkish Central Telephone exchange at El Affule, 214–15, smoke screens, 217, march of the Desert Mounted Corps to El Affule and Nazareth, 217, 222, Turkish retreat begins, 218–19, the effect of low-flying attacks, 218–29, the Turkish Eighth Army débâcle, 220–2, the '21st September, 1918', 224–8, the Turkish Seventh Army defeated, 228; *Chaytor's Force*, its responsibilities, 230–1, operations against Turkish Fourth Army, 231–5; the advance on, and fall of Damascus, 235, the advance on Aleppo, 237, Aleppo entered, 238, the Armistice, 238; *see also* App. xvi
  Aerodromes and Landing-grounds: (*British*), see Abu Suwana, Affule El, 'Aqaba, Azraq, Damascus, Deiran, Der'a, El Gueira, Haifa Hama, Homs, Jenin, Jericho, Jerusalem, Julis, Junction Station, Ma'an, Quneitra, Quntilla, Ramle Er, Riyaq, Sarona, Suez, Tahonie; (*German*), see Affule El, Aleppo, Babannit, Balata, Damascus, Der'a, Haifa, Jenin, Ma'an, Qatrani, Ramle Er, Riyaq
  Artillery co-operation, 176, 178
  Bombing attacks (*British*), 176–8, 182, 184–8, 193, 199–200, 204, 213–16, 218–20, 222, 224–6, 231–4, 236–8; (*German*), 189, 199, 204–5, 213–14, 230
  Fighting in the air, 178, 183, 204, 207–8, 210, 213–14, 229–30, 237–8
  German Air Service, 208, 215
  Low-flying attacks (*British*), 176–8, 182, 187, 200, 218–21, 224–7, 231–3
  Naval, and Naval air co-operation, 176
  Photography, air, 177–8, 193, 201–2, 204–5, 214, 216, 218
  Reconnaissance, air (*British*), 176–9, 181–2, 184–90, 193–202, 204–5, 208–10, 212–13, 215–16, 218–20, 222, 224, 226, 228, 231, 233, 236–7
Palluel, bombed, 495

576 INDEX

Panderma, bombed, 324
Parks and Depots, R.F.C. and R.A.F. 'X' Aircraft Park (Egypt), 202, 209; 'Z' Aircraft Park (Italy), 275–6; Aircraft Park (Baghdad), 247; Stores Depot (Egypt), 202
Paton, D., W/T. Operator, 348n.
Pattinson, Sqdn. Ldr. L. A., 128n., 147
Pattinson, Capt. T. C., 355–7
Pennington, Lt. K. M., 252, 261
Penstemon, Br. sloop, 317–18
Peony, Br. aircraft carrier, 315
Pergine, 287; bombed, 288
Péronne, bombed, 452–4
Pershing, Gen. J. J., C.-in-C. American Forces in France, 52, 77, 79, 384, 510
Persia, air operations in, 248–61
Pétain, Gen., 435, 508
Peters, Lt. G. C., 230
Pettingen, 124
Pezarches, aerodrome, 412
Phaeton, Br. L. Cr., 364
Philippopolis, 313
Phillimore, Rear-Adm. R. F., 351n.
Photography, air: *Independent Force*, 129, 131; *Palestine air operations*, 177–8, 193, 201–2, 204, 205, 214, 216, 218; *Mesopotamia, Persia, and India*, 248, 263; 270; *Italian front*, 276–7, 290; *Macedonia*, 297, 301; *Mediterranean*, 327; *Naval air operations, Home Waters, 1918*, 385, 388, 389; *Champagne, offensives in*, 410; *Amiens, battle of*, 454; *Drocourt-Quéant Switch*, 503; *Hindenburg line, breaking of*, 222–3
Picard, Commandant L., 402
Pierce Arrow Company, 50
Pitcher, Brig.-Gen. D. Le G., 512
Plumer, Gen. Sir H. C. O., 274, 280, 408, 512, 531–2
Pont-à-Vendin, bombed, 491
Pope, Lt. R. A. B., 497
Pope, Lt. R. P. P., 254–5
Porte, Commr. J. C., 352
Port Said, 315–17, 325
Primrose, Lt.-Col. W. H., 217
Princess Mary's R.A.F. Nursing Service, 74
Pritchard, Sergt. H., 394
Prölss, *Kapitänleutnant*, 373
Propaganda, value of in Aircraft Production, 85–9; *see also* Col. E. A. Ewart
Purvis, Lt. M. C., 145, 387

Qantara, 202, 209
Qatrani, bombed, 186
Queen Mary's Army Auxiliary Corps, 72
Queenstown, 338
Quievrechain, bombed, 546
Quneitra, 236
Quntilla, 184

Railways, *see* 'Communications'
Ramadi, 247, 363
Ramle, Er, 201–2, 209, 221–2, 230
Rapallo, conference at, 274–5
Rawlinson, Gen. Sir H. S., 415–17, 463, 512
Reading, Lord, 50n.
Rebaix, Ger. aerodrome, bombed, 549
Reconnaissances, air:
  Maj.-Gen. J. M. Salmond's instructions *re* (11/6/18), 405
  (*British*), *Palestine*, 176–9, 181–2, 184–90, 193–202, 204–5, 208–10, 212–13, 215–16, 218–20, 222, 224, 226, 228, 231, 233, 236–7; *Mesopotamia, Persia, and India*, 240–6, 250, 254–8, 263–7, 269–71; *Italian Front*, 276–7, 280–3, 287, 292; *Macedonia*, 296, 301, 303–4, 307–11, 313; *Mediterranean*, 320; *Naval air operations, Home Waters, 1918*, 353–5, 357, 359, 363, 367, 385, 389–90; *Champagne, offensives in*, 397–9, 404
Redcar, 350
Redoubt, Br. destroyer, 371
Reinhard, *Hauptmann*, 442
Rhône Usines du, 97
Ribot, M., French Premier, 78
Richmond (London), National Aircraft Factory, 54
Rieux, bombed, 523
Risalpur, 268–9, 271
Riviera, Br. aircraft carrier, 314
Riyaq, 236
Robertson, Lt.-Col. E. D. M., 377
Robertson, Gen. Sir W. R., 2, 10
Robinson, Maj. F. L., 247
Robinson, W. A., Secretary to Air Council, 23, 27

INDEX

Roe, Ensign J. J., U.S.N.F.C., 360*n*.
Roisel, bombed, 471
Rolls-Royce Company, 45–6, 48–51, 86
Rombach, bombed, 144
Ross, Wing Commr. R. P., 314
Rotherham, 64
Rothermere, Lord, President of the Air Board, 22; first Secretary of State for Air, 22, 26; resignation of, 27, 103
Roulers, bombed, 533
Royal Aircraft Factory, 96
Royal Air Force:
War Cabinet discussions relating to creation of, 4–5; 'Surplus Aircraft Fleet', 6, 9; War Cabinet Committee formed, 7; General Smuts' views (28/7/17), 8–11; Sir D. Henderson's memo. (19/7/17), 9–10, App. i; General Smuts' report (17/8/17) recommends formation of Air Ministry, 11–13, App. ii; War Cabinet accepts report, 13; Air Organization Committee, formation of, 13; Sir D. Haig's comments on Gen. Smuts' report, 13–15, App. iii; Gen. Smuts' views on possibilities of bombing offensives, 15–16; Appointment of Sir J. Hunter to supervise construction of new aerodromes, 16; 'Aerial Operations Committee', 17–18; Adm. Mark Kerr's memo. on delay in forming Air Ministry, 18–19; 'Air Policy Committee', 19; Mr. Bonar Law reviews situation (16/10/17), 19–20; bill to constitute Air Ministry approved (6/11/17), 20–1; Lord Cowdray (President of Air Board) resigns, 21; Air Force Bill receives Royal assent (29/11/17), 22; Air Council, composition of (3/1/18), 22–3; Maj.-Gen. Trenchard appointed Chief of Air Staff, 22–4; H.M. the King approves title, 24*n*.; Titles for commissioned ranks, 25–6; Maj.-Gen. Trenchard resigns, 26; other resignations, 27; Memo. on responsibility and conduct of Air Ministry, App. vii; composition of Air Council at end of War, 27; strength of at Armistice, 90, App. xxvi; Policy of air fighting on Western front discussed, 552–7; location of units Western front, 11/11/18, App. xxx; strength of aircraft, all fronts, May–June 1918, App. xl; strength of personnel August 1914 and Nov. 1918, App. xxxv; strength in personnel in various theatres of War, 31/10/18, App. xlvi; *see also* 'Supply and Man Power, problems of'
Royal Air Force Nursing Service, 74
Royal Flying Corps: Government decision to double strength of (2/7/17), 2, Sir D. Haig's views, 2–4
Royalist, Br. L. Cr., 364
Royal Naval Air Service: decision to increase strength of (2/7/17), 2; Sir Douglas Haig's views, 2–4; Amalgamation with R.F.C., 24–5
Rozoy-en-Brie, aerodrome, 412
Rumilly, bombed, 521
Ryan, J. D., Under Secretary for Aviation, U.S.A., 53*n*.

Saarbrücken, bombed, 129, 131, 139, 141, 148
Saigneville, No. 20 Ordnance Depot, bombed, 423–4
St. Christ, Ger. aerodrome, 458; bombed, 459
St. Denis, bombed, 546
St. Ghislain, bombed, 546
St. Maur, Ger. aerodrome, bombed, 509
St. Mihiel, battle of, French-American attack, R.A.F. co-operation, night-bombing, 508–9
St. Pol Depot, bombed, 161–2
Salmond, Maj.-Gen. J. M., Director General of Military Aeronautics, 77, 169; G.O.C. R.A.F., France, 142*n*., 387, 405, 407, 409, 411, 433, 441, 463, 508
Salmond, Maj.-Gen. W. G. H., 210, 229
Salonika, 302, 310
Samarra, 245, 247, 263
Samson, Col. C. R., 370–1
Sanders, Gen. L. von, 181–2, 190, 194–6, 207–8, 211, 215, 218–19, 222, 231

S. Luca, 290
S. Pelagio, 276
San Felice, bombed, 277
Santa Elena, Ger. aircraft carrier, 358
Santa Maria di Leuca, 315, 320
Sarcedo, 281, 289*n*.
Saris, 176
Sarona, 176, 209, 222, 236
Savory, Sqdn. Commr. K. S., 123*n*.
Scaife, 2nd Lt. T. E. G., 497*n*.
Scarpe, battle of, 484–91:
  Plans for 484–5, organization of low-flying attacks, 485–6, the attack, 486–91
  Bombing attacks (*British*), 486–91
  Contact patrol, 487, 489
  Fighting in the air, 487–91
  Low-flying attacks (*British*), 485–91
  Wireless telegraphy (*British*), 487
Seaplanes:
  British:
    Disposition of, on charge of R.A.F., 31/10/18, App. xli
    Types: Short, 378–9; *Large America*, 336*n*., 337–40, 342, 353–4, 357, 377; *see also* App. xxvii
  German:
    Second Seaplane Division, importance of, 358
    Types: Brandenburg, 359; Dornier, 359; Friedrichshafener, 359; Gotha, 359
Seaton Carew, 330–1, 345–6
Selle, battle of the (17th–25th Oct. 1918), 541–2:
  Bombing attacks (*British*), 541–2
  Fighting in the air, 542
  Low-flying attacks (*British*), 541–2
  Photography, air, 542
Serbian Army, *see* 'Army, Serbian'
Sharqat, 267
Sharwood, Lt. A. C., 361
Sheffield, 64
Shekleton, Lt.-Col. A., 197
Shunet Nimrin, bombed, 187, 189
Siddeley Deasy Company, 34, 38, 51*n*.
Siddons, Capt. V. D., 183*n*.
Silly, Capt. B. J., 144
Simon, M. St. L., vol. v. *For* Lt.-Col. *read* Col.
Simpson, 2nd Lt. E. A., 447
Simpson, Joseph, 88
Sims, V.-Adm. W. S., U.S.N, 384*n*.

Sinjabis, the, 240
Sir Thomas Picton, Br. Mon., 326
Sitapur, 268
Skyros, 323
Slessor, Wing Commr. J. C., 461
Smart, Capt. B. A., 365*n*., 366–7
Smith, Lt. H. J., 346
Smith, Capt. Ross M., 214, 229–30, 237
Smoke screens, used in Palestine campaign, 217; on Italian Front, 283; Naval air operations (Home Waters), 1918, 373, 385, 388–90; Amiens, battle of, 440; Hindenburg Line, breaking of, 528–9, 536
Smuts, Lt.-Gen. the Hon. J. C., 7–11, 13, 15–19, 24, 39–42, 67, 74, 90, 191
Smythies, Maj. B. E., 485, 487, 516, 520
Snapdragon, Br. sloop, 317
Snevche, 303
Somain, bombed, 476, 479, 489–90
Somme bridges, bombing of, 441–2, 446–52, a commentary, 454–62
Sopwith Aviation Company, 54
Spondon, 96
Springs, Lt. E. W. (U.S.), 499
Squadrons (R.F.C. and R.A.F.):
  Bombing, increase of, 2, 3; list of on Western front 1914–18, App. xxviii
  Australian Flying Corps:
    No. *1* (see No. 67); No. *2*, 401, 549–50; No. *3*, 416, 433*n*., 440, 524; No. *4*, 549–50; No. 67, 176–8, 182, 198, 202, 207, 209, 216, 219, 224–5, 231–3, 236–8
  R.F.C. and R.A.F.:
    No. *1*, 441, 469*n*., 470, 476, 482, 491, 529, 546–7; No. *3*, 469*n*., 470, 476, 517; No. *4*, 532; No. *5*, 433*n*., 440, 485, 487, 489, 493, 496, 498–9, 514; No. *6*, 433*n*., 469, 485, 493, 496, 524; No. *7*, 532–3; No. *8*, 416, 433*n*., 464–6, 469, 471, 484–5, 493, 496, 516, 524; No. *9*, 416, 433*n*., 440, 524; No. *10*, 532–3; No. *11*, 449, 470, 518; No. *12*, 514; No. *13*, 493, 497, 514–16, 519, 521–2; No. *14*, 176–8, 183–4, 168, 188, 190, 194, 199, 201–2, 209–10, 214, 225, 236; No. *15*, 524; No. *17*, 293–5, 302–3, 305, 309–10, 313;

INDEX

Squadrons—*continued*
No. *18*, 462, 485–6, 489, 494, 517n., 520, 523; No. *19*, 450, 517, 548; No. *20*, 506, 542; No. *22*, 268, 450, 462, 485–6, 487, 489, 494, 498, 505, 517; No. *24*, 439; No. *25*, 407, 518; No. *27*, 401, 412, 442, 446, 449–50, 452, 459, 472, 476, 480, 491, 529, 545–6; No. *28*, 274–6, 278n., 279–80, 282, 287–90, 292; No. *29*, 409, 532; No. *30*, 241, 244, 247, 257, 263; No. *31*, 268–71; No. *32*, 401, 412, 450, 452, 480–1, 501, 546; No. *34*, 274–7, 279–81, 287, 289–92; No. *35*, 433n., 524, 536; No. *36* (H.D.), 330; No. *38*, 391, 532; No. *40*, 432, 450, 485–6, 487–8, 489, 494, 498n., 516, 523; No. *41*, 532; No. *42*, 275–7, 280; No. *43*, 401, 412, 441, 447, 480–1, 490, 546–7; No. *45*, 149–50, 274–5, 281–3, 287–8; No. *47*, 293–5, 302–3, 305, 309–10, 312–13; No. *48*, 480, 532; No. *49*, 401, 403, 409, 412, 441, 446–7, 449–50, 452, 476, 480, 523, 545–6; No. *52*, 397–400, 485, 487, 489, 493, 496, 514; No. *53*, 532–3; No. *54*, 412, 441, 448, 469n., 470, 476, 482, 485, 487, 494, 496, 516, 522, 549–51; No. *55*; 123, 126, 127n., 128–32, 134–5, 139–40, 143–5, 147, 151–2; No. *56*, 453, 469n., 470, 504, 517; No. *57*, 449, 459, 470, 491, 518, 523, 529; No. *58*, 409, 476, 479, 488, 509, 518, 526, 533, 537, 540–1, 545; No. *59*, 477, 482, 514, 522; No. *60*, 432, 469n., 470, 517; No. *62*, 407, 449, 452, 472, 480, 490, 501, 529; No. *63*, 241, 244–5, 247, 263, 265–6; No. *64*, 450, 485, 487, 494, 498, 505, 516, 523; No. *65*, 532; No. *66*, 274–6, 279, 281–2, 284, 288–9, 292; No. *70*, 501, 532; No. *72*, 240–2, 244, 247–8, 251–3, 257–8, 263, 265–6; No. *73*, 401, 412, 442, 446, 450, 465n., 469, 471, 476, 482, 484–5, 488–9, 493, 524; No. *74*, 432, 532; No. *79*, 532; No. *80*, 401, 412; No. *82*, 413–14, 532, 534; No. *83*, 409, 476, 479, 508–9, 518–19, 545; No. *84*, 480, 506, 529, 544; No. *85*, 432; No. *87*, 469n., 470, 517; No. *88*, 548–9, 550–1; No. *97*, 142, 150–1; No. *98*, 391–2, 409, 412, 441, 447, 449, 459, 480–1, 490–1, 529, 542, 548; No. *99*, 128, 135, 139–41, 147; No. *100*, 123, 126–8, 133–5, 141–2, 147, 156, 164; No. *101*, 416–17, 476, 478, 505, 526, 536; No. *102*, 470, 476, 478–9, 493, 505, 531; No. *103*, 401, 403, 409, 520, 549–50; No. *104*, 128, 135, 138–9, 146–7, 151; No. *107*, 409, 412, 441, 448–9, 476, 480–1, 490, 542, 545–7; No. *108*, 532; No. *110*, 142, 146–8, 150; No. *111*, 176, 183, 202, 209, 215, 225, 232; No. *113*, 176, 182, 188, 192, 200, 202, 209–10, 217–18, 224–5, 232, 235–6; No. *114*, 271; No. *115*, 142, 146; No. *139* (formation), 280n., 287–92; No. *142*, 178, 182, 200–2, 209–10, 214, 216, 225, 228, 231; No. *144*, 202, 209, 213–14, 225, 232–3, 236; No. *145*, 202, 209, 215, 221, 225; No. *148*, 479, 485, 488, 492, 495; No. *149*, 532; No. *150*, 293–5, 302–3, 309, 313; No. *151* (formation), 428–9; 472, 480, 506; No. *166*, 173; No. *201*, 382–3, 437–8, 469n., 471, 516, 542; No. *202*, 382, 384–5, 532; No. *203*, 382, 478, 516, 522; No. *204*, 382, 384, 395, 532, 540; No. *205*, 417, 441, 448, 451, 453–4, 459, 529, 545–6; No. *206*, 382, 532; No. *207*, 382, 384–5, 387, 409–10, 433n., 451, 472, 476, 479, 488, 495, 508–9, 518, 521, 531, 541, 545; No. *208*, 382, 485, 487, 494, 536, 538; No. *209*, 382, 439, 485, 487, 494, 505, 516, 522–3; No. *210*, 121, 382–3, 395, 532, 540; No. *211*, 382, 384, 391, 395, 532; No. *213*, 382, 384, 388, 390, 395, 532; No. *214*, 382, 384–5, 387–95, 532, 540, 545; No. *215*, 142, 145, 147, 151, 155, 382, 384, 386–7; No. *216*, see No. *16*, R.N.A.S.; No. *217*, 346, 382, 384, 532; No. *218*, 395–6, 532, 534; No. *220*, 315; No. *221*, 315; No. *222*, 315; No. *223*, 315; No. *224*, 315, 327; No. *225*, 315; No. *226*, 315, 328; No. *227*, 315

Squadrons—*continued*
  R.N.A.S.:
    No. *16* (formerly 'A' later No. *216*),
      123, 128, 132–5, 139, 145–7, 151,
      387; List of on Western front,
      1914–18, App. xxix
American, see 'U.S.A. Air Service'
Stafford, 2nd Lt. E. R., 221
Statistics: *Supply and Man-Power*, 28–31, 33–4, 39*n*., 42, 51, 56, 77–8, 85, 90–3; Apps. xxxi, xxxiii; *Independent Force*, 152–3, 163*n*., Apps. xii, xiii, xiv, xv; *Palestine*, 234, 238; *Mesopotamia*, 268; *Naval Air Operations, Home Waters, 1918*, 343, 349, Apps. xvii, xviii; *Western Front*, Allied and German air strength, 435–6, Apps. xxvi, xl, xlvi; *R.F.C., R.N.A.S. and R.A.F.*, strength, 1914 and 1918, App. xxxv, casualties, 1914–18, App. xxxvi, July 1916–July 1918, App. xxxvii; *Aircraft and Engines*, Apps. xxvii, xxxi, xxxii, xl, xli; *Anti-Aircraft*, Apps. xxxviii, xxxix, xlv; *Air Raids on Gt. Britain*, 1914–18, App. xliv; *Bombing on Western front*, 491, App. xliii
Stavros, 294, 315, 323
Stearns, F. B., and Company, 50*n*.
Stent, Capt. F. W., 183
Stojakovo, 310
Storr, Maj. C. L., 13*n*., 17*n*.
Strange, Lt.-Col. L. A., 549
Stubbington, Sergt. H. R., 355*n*.
Sturdee, Adm. F. C. D., 379
Stuttgart, 124; bombed, 129, 146; 139–40
Stuttgart, Ger. aircraft carrier, 358
Submarines:
  British: C.25 damaged by German aircraft, 380
  German, see Mediterranean, 1918, Naval air developments and operations (Home Waters), 1918, and U boats, also Apps. xvii and xviii
Suda Bay (Crete), 315, 323
Sudbury, National Radiator Factory, 55–6
Suez, 233*n*.
Sunbeam Company, 33*n*.
Supply and Man Power, problems of: air programmes, Sir D. Haig's demands, 28–30; engine requirements, 30–2; Aeronautical Dept. Min. of Munitions formed, 31; the Hispano-Suiza engine, 29, 31, 32, 35–7; standardization of engines, 32–4, position in March 1917, 34; the Sunbeam-Arab, 34–5; the B.H.P. engine, 37–9; War Cabinet discussions on supply problems, 39–42, Gen. Smuts' memo. (18/9/17), 39–41; the War Priorities Committee, 42; the Bentley Rotary and Dragonfly engines, 43–4; the Rolls-Royce engine, 45–51; Mr. Claud Johnson's views and proposals, 46–9; the manufacture of Rolls-Royce parts in America, 50; the Liberty engine, 51–3; *National Aircraft Factories*, 53–7, expenditure on, 54–5, the cost and output, 56–7; *Man-Power*, 57–70, position at end of 1914, 58, Mr. Balfour's proposals (Jan. 1915), 58–9, Lord Kitchener's views, 59–60, industrial unrest, 60, 64, 66; the Ministry of Munitions, creation of, 60–1; the 'Derby' scheme, 62; Trade Union views on 'dilution', 62–3; the Man-Power Distribution Board, 63–4; Man-Power Committee, 67; munitions, programme for 1918, 68; R.F.C. man-power requirements, 69–70; *Women, employment of in the Air Services*, 70–4; the R.A.F. Nursing Service, 74; Prime Minister's Man-Power Committee, 75–6; American mechanics, 77–8; *America and the air war*, their programme and progress, 75*n*., 78–81; the timber question, 80–1; effect on production of the German 1918 offensive, 82; the engine position, 83–4; Ministry of Munitions training schemes, 84; labour employed in aircraft industry (1916–18), 85; Propaganda, 85–9; Air expansion programme (1918), 89–90, position at the Armistice, 90; aircraft wastage, importance of reserves, 91–4; the position summarized, 95–100; failure of supply programmes, Independent Force, 164–73; supply of aircraft for Naval air operations, 330–4, 335–40; App. iv

INDEX 581

Supply and Man Power—*continued*
Statistics, 28–31, 33–4, 39n., 42, 51–3, 56, 63, 77–8, 84–5, 90–3, App. xxxi and xxxiii
Supreme War Council, 104–8, 111
Sweetser, Capt. A., 78n., 80n.
Swindon, National Timber-Drying Kilns, 55–6
Sydney, Australian L. Cr., 361
Sykes, Maj.-Gen. F. H., appointed Chief of the Air Staff, 27, 106
Symonds, Lt. T. S., 497
Syra, 315, 323

Taft-Pierce Manufacturing Company, 50n.
Tahonie, bombed, 204–5
Tank, 270
Tantonville, aerodrome, 132
Taranto, 314–16, 319
Taylor, 2nd Lt. L. G., 156
Taylor, Col. M. G., 419n.
Technical superiority of the Fokker, D.VII, 445, 537; D.H.9a over the D.H.9, 545–6
Tennant, Rt. Hon. H. J. (Under-Secretary of State for War), 5
Teteghem, aerodrome, bombed, 161, 394
Thasos, 294–5, 315, 323
Thielt, bombed, 533, 540
Thionville, 124; bombed, 129, 134, 140, 148–9, 151
Thomas, Holt, 18
Thomson, 2nd Lt. F. E., 228
Thomson, Lt.-Gen. Sir W. M., 257–8
Thourout, bombed, 395, 533
Thyne, Capt. T. K., 365n.
Tikrit, 265
Timber-drying kilns, National, 56
Times, The, 60
Tirana, bombed, 326
Todd, Lt.-Col. G. E., 297, 302
Tondern, bombed, 365–7
Tournai, bombed, 540
Traill, Lt. J. H., 230
Transjordan, operations in, 185–90
Trècon, aerodrome, 400
Trenchard, Maj.-Gen. Sir H. M., 19; Chief of the Air Staff, 22–4, resignation, 26; 40, 104–8, 110–13, 115–16, 123; in command of Independent Force, 135, 136n., 137–8, 142, 149, 163–4, 167–9, 172–4, 552
Treves, bombed, 148
Treviso, bombed, 279
Tul Karm, bombed, 214–15
Turkish Army, *see* 'Army, Turkish'
Tuz Khurmatli, 244–5
Tyrwhitt, Rear-Adm. R. Y., 352, 355, 358, 370, 372–4, 376

U.39, Ger. S/M., 318
UB.12, Ger. S/M, presumed destruction of, 346
UB.83, Ger. S/M, presumed destruction of, 348
UB.103, Ger. S/M, destruction of, 348
UB.115, Ger. S/M, presumed destruction of, 348
UC.70, Ger. S/M, destruction of, 346–7
Ulleswater, Br. destroyer, 367–8, 369–70
United States of America, supply questions, Rolls-Royce engine parts ordered, 50; the Liberty engine, 51–3; air war programmes, 78–81; the timber question, 80–1
Air Service: co-operation in Belgian and Flanders operations, 384, 395, 539; Northern Bombing Group, formation of, 383–4; *see also* App. xix; strength, May/June 18, App. xl
Squadrons: No. 7 (Naval), 539; *No. 17*, 395, 469–70, 476, 484, 506, 517; *No. 148*, 469–70, 498, 506, 517

Valenciennes, bombed, 476, 479, 489–91, 501, 537–8
Valentine, Br. destroyer, 364
Varssenaere, Ger. aerodrome, bombed, 395–6
Vaughan, Lt. A. D., 497
Venice, bombed, 279
Venizelos, M., 295
Verney, Capt. R. H., 33
Verona, 275–6
Vickers Company, 44, 46
Victoria Cross: award of, to Maj. W. G. Barker, 542–3; Capt. A. W. Beauchamp-Proctor, 544; Lt. A.

INDEX

Victoria Cross—*continued*
Jerrard, 281; Maj. J. T. B. Mc-
Cudden, 432; Maj. E. Mannock,
432–3; Capt. F. M. F. West,
465–6
Vignacourt, aerodrome, 429
Villalta, 276, 280
Villa Margherita, 290
Villaverla, 281, 289*n*.
Villeseneux, 134
Villorba, 290
Vindictive, Br. L. Cr., 388–91
Violent, Br. destroyer, 367
Vittorio Veneto, battle of, 288–92
Voisin, Gen., 467*n*.
Volklingen, bombed, 126, 153–4,
Appendix xiv
Volpersweiler, Ger. aerodrome, bombed,
159–60
Voluntary Aid Detachment, 72
Vyvyan, Capt. V., R.N., 167

Waddon, National Aircraft Factory,
54, 56
Walmsley, Capt. J. B., 300
War Cabinet, meetings and decisions in
connexion with creation of R.A.F.,
2–4, 7–8, 10–11, 13–21, 26
Waring, Lt. E. F., 346
War Priorities Committee, 17, 42,
74–6
Wasnes au Bac, bombed, 520
Waterford, 338
Watson, Mrs. Chalmers, 72*n*.
Weather: effect of on the work of aircraft: *the Independent Force operations*, 120, 126, 129–30, 131, 134,
139, 143, 145, 146, 149, 150, 152;
Palestine, Air Operations in, 176–7,
179, 182, 186, 187, 188, 189, 190,
198, 200, 206, 216, 224; *Mesopotamia,
Persia, and India*, 240–2, 244–5, 247–
8, 255, 262, 269; *Italian front*, 281,
283, 285, 288, 290; *Macedonia*, 308,
310, 311; *Naval Operations, Home
Waters, 1918*, 368–76, 378, 386–90,
393; *Aisne, battle of*, 397; 410–11;
Amiens, battle of, 437, 460; *Bapaume,
battle of*, 471, 478, 480–3, 495, 504;
Scarpe, battle of, 486, 488–91; *Drocourt–Quéant Switch*, 495; *Havrincourt
and Epéhy, battle of*, 504; *Hindenburg
Line, breaking of*, 519, 521, 526, 528–

31, 536–8; *Flanders, battle in*, 533–5,
539–40, 544, 550
Webb-Bowen, Brig.-Gen. T. I., 275,
280, 512, 532
Weir, Rt. Hon. Lord, of Eastwood,
Controller of Aeronautical Supplies,
Ministry of Munitions, 15; Director-
General of Aircraft Production, 22;
appointed Secretary of State, R.A.F.,
27, 103; 31, 35, 37, 42*n*., 43, 48,
81, 84, 92, 104, 109–10, 166, 169,
172
Wervicq, bombed, 533
West, Capt. F. M. F., awarded V.C.,
465–6
Westgate, 379
Wiesbaden, bombed, 150–1
Wilhelmshaven, 358
Williams, Capt. F., 132, 135
Williams, Lt. N. E., 365–6
Williams, Lt.-Col. R., 179, 209
Williams, Lt. T. L., 258–61
Willys Overland Company, 33
Wilson, Gen. Sir. H., 107, 109
Wilson, Lt.-Gen. Sir H. F. M., 302
Wings:
  R.F.C. and R.A.F.:
  Second, 532; *Fifth*, 176, 200–2, 209;
  Ninth, 402, 407, 449*n*.; *Tenth*,
  485; *Eleventh*, 532; *Fourteenth*,
  275, 280, 282, 289–90; *Fifteenth*,
  434; *Sixteenth*, 297, 302, 310–11;
  Twenty-second, 434, 464, 525;
  Thirty-first, 247; *Fortieth*, 176,
  178, 197, 199–200, 202, 209, 236;
  Forty-first, 122–35; *Fifty-first*,
  274–5, 280, 402, 449*n*.; *Fifty-
  fourth*, 407*n*.; *Sixty-first*, 382, 394,
  532; *Sixty-second*, 323; *Sixty-
  third*, 323; *Sixty-fourth*, 325, 382;
  Sixty-fifth, 382, 532; *Sixty-sixth*,
  314, 327; *Sixty-seventh*, 314, 327;
  Eightieth, 549–50; *Eighty-first*,
  407; *Eighty-second*, 392, 532;
  Eighty-third, 135; *Eighty-fifth*,
  150; *Eighty-sixth*, 173; *Eighty-
  seventh*, 173; *Eighty-eighth*, 150
  R.N.A.S.
  No. 3, 118, 121–2, 126
Wireless Telegraphy:
  British: Macedonia, 304–5; Mediterranean, 320; Naval air operations (*Home Waters*), *1918*, 354–5,

INDEX

Wireless Telegraphy—*continued*
    370, 373, 375–6; *Bapaume, battle of,* 474–5, 482–3; *Scarpe, battle of,* 487; *Drocourt-Quéant Switch,* 501–3; *Havrincourt and Epéhy, battle of,* 506
    Turkish: Palestine operations, 215
Wireless telephony, experiments during battle of Amiens, 464–5
Wolseley Company, 34–6
Women, employment of, in air services, 70–4
Women's Army Auxiliary Corps, 72–3
Women's Legion, 71, 73
Women's Royal Air Force, 73
Women's Royal Naval Service, 73

Yanesh, 302, 305–6, 310
Yarmouth, 353–4, 357, 359, 361*n.*, 369, 372, 374, 376–7
Yenikoi, 302
Yeulett, Lt. W. A., 365*n.*, 366
Young, Capt. C. L., 361*n.*
Ytres, bombed, 491
Yuille, Capt. A. B., 428

Zeebrugge, 348, 376–7, 379, 382, 384; bombed 386; Naval operations against, 387–91; low bombing attacks on lock gates, 393–5
Zenjan, 257, 263
Zeppelin airships, *see* 'Airships, German'
Zweibrücken, bombed, 131

Printed in Great Britain
by Amazon.co.uk, Ltd.,
Marston Gate.